MODERN NIGERIA

Recent Titles in Understanding Modern Nations

Modern France
Michael F. Leruth

Modern Philippines
Patricio N. Abinales

Modern Germany
Wendell G. Johnson and Katharina Barbe

MODERN NIGERIA

*Alex Egodotaye Asakitikpi and
Aretha Oluwakemi Asakitikpi*

BLOOMSBURY ACADEMIC
NEW YORK • LONDON • OXFORD • NEW DELHI • SYDNEY

BLOOMSBURY ACADEMIC
Bloomsbury Publishing Inc
1385 Broadway, New York, NY 10018, USA
50 Bedford Square, London, WC1B 3DP, UK
29 Earlsfort Terrace, Dublin 2, Ireland

BLOOMSBURY, BLOOMSBURY ACADEMIC and the Diana logo are trademarks of
Bloomsbury Publishing Plc

First published in the United States of America 2024

Copyright © Alex Egodotaye Asakitikpi and Aretha Oluwakemi Asakitikpi, 2025

For legal purposes the Acknowledgments on p. xvi constitute an extension of this copyright page.

Cover images © Trentinness/Dreamstime; World History Archive/Alamy; Sergii Koval/Alamy; Michael Tubi/Alamy

All rights reserved. No part of this publication may be reproduced or transmitted in any form or by any means, electronic or mechanical, including photocopying, recording, or any information storage or retrieval system, without prior permission in writing from the publishers.

Bloomsbury Publishing Inc does not have any control over, or responsibility for, any third-party websites referred to or in this book. All internet addresses given in this book were correct at the time of going to press. The author and publisher regret any inconvenience caused if addresses have changed or sites have ceased to exist, but can accept no responsibility for any such changes.

Library of Congress Cataloging-in-Publication Data

Names: Asakitikpi, Alex Egodotaye, author. | Asakitikpi, Aretha Oluwakemi, author.
Title: Modern Nigeria / Alex Egodotaye Asakitikpi and Aretha Oluwakemi Asakitikpi.
Other titles: Understanding modern nations.
Description: New York: Bloomsbury Academic, 2025. | Series: Understanding modern nations | Includes bibliographical references and index.
Identifiers: LCCN 2023027168 (print) | LCCN 2023027169 (ebook) | ISBN 9781440865565 (hardback) | ISBN 9798765112052 (pb) | ISBN 9781440865572 (ebook) | ISBN 9798216172093 (epub)
Subjects: LCSH: Nigeria–Civilization. | Nigeria–Social life and customs. | Nigeria–Encyclopedias.
Classification: LCC DT515.22 A83 2025 (print) | LCC DT515.22 (ebook) | DDC 966.9–dc23/eng/20230606
LC record available at https://lccn.loc.gov/2023027168
LC ebook record available at https://lccn.loc.gov/2023027169

ISBN: HB: 978-1-4408-6556-5
PB: 979-8-7651-1205-2
ePDF: 978-1-4408-6557-2
eBook: 979-8-2161-7209-3

Series: Understanding Modern Nations

Typeset by Deanta Global Publishing Services, Chennai, India

To find out more about our authors and books visit www.bloomsbury.com and sign up for our newsletters.

This book is dedicated to our children, David and Ann, as well as to all Nigerian youths who are looking forward to the Nigeria of their dreams.

CONTENTS

SERIES FOREWORD	xiv
ACKNOWLEDGMENTS	xvi
PREFACE	xvii

Introduction		1
1	Geography	7
	Overview	7
	Benue River	9
	Climate	10
	Desertification	12
	Fauna	13
	Flora	14
	Jos Plateau	15
	Major Cities	16
	Natural Resources	18
	Niger Delta	19
	Niger River	20
	Population	21
	Rainforest	23
	Savannah	24
	Transportation and Waterways	25
	Urbanization and Its Impact	26
2	History	29
	Overview	29
	Timeline	49
	Agitation for Independence	58

	Awolowo, Obafemi	59
	Azikiwe, Nnamdi	60
	Balewa, Abubakar Tafawa	61
	Benin Empire	62
	Colonial Nigeria	63
	European Explorers and Christianity	65
	Ife Kingdom	66
	Islam and Trade	67
	Kingdom of Zaria	68
	Macaulay, Herbert	69
	Nigerian Civil War (1967–70)	70
	Nri Civilization	71
	Oyo Empire	73
	Sokoto Caliphate	74
3	Government and Politics	77
	Overview	77
	Administrative Division and Structure	79
	All Progressives Congress	80
	Buhari, Muhammadu	81
	Constitutional Development	83
	Correctional Institutions	84
	Corruption	85
	Criminal Law	86
	Democratic Rule	87
	Early Political Parties	88
	Human Rights	90
	Independent National Electoral Commission	91
	Jonathan, Goodluck	92
	Law Enforcement	94
	Legislature	95
	Military Rule	96
	People's Democratic Party	97
	Political Parties and Their Formations	98
	State and Local Governments	99
	Supreme Court	101
4	Economy	103
	Overview	103
	Agriculture Sector	107
	Domestic and International Trade	108

	Exports	109
	Financial Institutions	111
	Foreign Investment	112
	Forex and Currency Exchange	113
	Imports	115
	International Trade Policy	116
	Manufacturing Sector	117
	Mining Sector	118
	Nigerian Stock Exchange	120
	Oil and Gas Sector	121
	Poverty	122
	Private Sector	124
	Reserves and Foreign Debt	125
	Trade Partners	126
	Trade Unions and the Labor Movement	127
5	Religion and Thought	129
	Overview	129
	Adeboye, Enoch	132
	Aladura Church	133
	Catholicism	134
	Celestial Church of Christ	135
	Christ Apostolic Church	136
	Inter-religious Conflicts	138
	Islamic Movement	139
	Oyedepo, David	140
	Pentecostalism	141
	Reformed Ogboni Fraternity	142
	Synagogue Church of All Nations	143
	Traditional Religions	144
6	Social Classes and Ethnicity	147
	Overview	147
	Hausa/Fulani	150
	Ibibio People	151
	Igbo	152
	Ijaw People	153
	Kanuri People	154
	Middle Class	155
	Minority Ethnic Groups	156
	Nupe People	158

	Rural Population	159
	Tiv People	160
	Urban Poor	161
	Yoruba	162
7	**Gender, Marriage, and Sexuality**	**165**
	Overview	165
	Court Marriages	167
	Domestic Violence	168
	Dowry and Bride-Wealth	169
	Family Planning Law	170
	Family Roles	171
	Gay and Lesbian Individuals	172
	Gender Relations	173
	Human Trafficking	174
	Kinship and In-Laws	175
	Marriage Law	176
	Sex Trade	177
	Traditional Weddings	178
	Western Weddings	179
8	**Education**	**181**
	Overview	181
	Indigenous Education System	184
	Islamic Education	185
	National Entrance Examinations	186
	Nomadic Schools	188
	Pre-Tertiary Education	189
	Private Universities	190
	Public Universities	191
	Tertiary Education	192
	West African Examination Council	194
9	**Language**	**197**
	Overview	197
	English Language	200
	Foreign Languages	201
	Hausa Language	202
	Igbo Language	203
	Local Dialects	204
	Pidgin English	205
	Yoruba Language	206

10	Etiquette	209
	Overview	209
	Business Entertainment	212
	Courtesy and Respect	213
	Entertainment and Gift-Giving	214
	Food and Table Manners	215
	Greetings	216
	Housewarming	217
	Naming Ceremonies	218
11	Literature and Drama	221
	Overview	221
	Achebe, Chinua	224
	Adichie, Chimamanda Ngozi	225
	Atta, Sefi	226
	Clark, John Pepper	227
	Hafsat, Abdulwaheed Ahmed	229
	Fiction and Nonfiction Literary Works	230
	Indigenous Drama	231
	Ogunde, Hubert	232
	Okri, Ben	233
	Saro-Wiwa, Ken	234
	Soyinka, Wole	236
	Tales by Moonlight	237
	Tutuola, Amos	238
	Traditional Performances	239
12	Art and Architecture	241
	Overview	241
	Bead Art	244
	Benin Artwork	245
	Brazilian Architecture	246
	Bronze Casting	247
	Embroidery	248
	Ife Artwork	250
	Igbo Artwork	250
	Indigenous Architecture	252
	Iron Smelting	253
	Onobrakpeya, Bruce	254
	Painting	255
	Palace Decoration	256

Sculpture	257
Terracotta	259
Textiles	260
Wood Carving	261

13 Music and Dance — 263
Overview	263
Ade, King Sunny	267
Afrobeat	268
Contemporary Nigerian Dance	269
Folk Songs	270
Fuji Music	272
Gospel Music	273
Hip Hop Music	274
Kuti, Fela	275
Nigerian Music Producers	277
Regional Music	278
Traditional Dance	279
Traditional Musical Instruments	280
Uwaifo, Victor	281

14 Food — 283
Overview	283
Alcoholic Beverages	286
Eastern Cuisine	287
Holiday Feasts	288
Local Drinks	289
Middle Belt Cuisine	291
Northern Cuisine	292
Palm Wine	293
Snacks	294
Southern Cuisine	295
Southwestern Cuisine	296

15 Leisure and Sports — 297
Overview	297
Athletics	301
Basketball	303
Boxing	304
Cinemas	306
Dating	307
Domestic Travel	308

Football (Soccer)	309
Horse Riding	311
Shopping	312
Table Tennis	313
Weightlifting	315
Wrestling	316
16 Media and Popular Culture	319
Overview	319
Digital Social Media	322
Magazines	323
Media, Privately Owned	324
Movie Industry	325
Music Industry	327
National Broadcasting Commission	329
National Film and Video Censors Board	330
Newspapers	331
Piracy	332
Radio Broadcasting, Publicly Owned	333
Television Broadcasting, Publicly Owned	334
Appendix A: A Day in the Life	337
Appendix B: Glossary of Key Terms	341
Appendix C: Facts and Figures	344
Appendix D: Holidays	350
Bibliography	354
Index	370

SERIES FOREWORD

We live in an evolving world, a world that is becoming increasingly globalized by the minute. Cultures collide and blend, leading to new customs and practices that exist alongside long-standing traditions. Advancing technologies connect lives across the globe, affecting those from densely populated urban areas to those who dwell in the most remote locations in the world. Governments are changing, leading to war and violence but also to new opportunities for those who have been oppressed. The *Understanding Modern Nations* series seeks to answer questions about cultures, societies, and customs in various countries around the world.

Understanding Modern Nations is geared toward readers wanting to expand their knowledge of the world, ideal for high school students researching specific countries, undergraduates preparing for studies abroad, and general readers interested in learning more about the world around them. Each volume in the series focuses on a single country, with coverage on Africa, the Americas, Asia and the Pacific, and Europe.

Each country volume contains sixteen chapters focusing on various aspects of culture and society in each country. The chapters begin with an Overview, which is followed by short entries on key topics, concepts, ideas, and biographies pertaining to the chapter's theme. In a way, these volumes serve as "thematic encyclopedias," with entries organized for the reader's benefit. Following a general Preface and Introduction, each volume contains chapters on the following themes:

- Geography
- History
- Government and Politics
- Economy
- Religion and Thought
- Social Classes and Ethnicity
- Gender, Marriage, and Sexuality

- Education
- Language
- Etiquette
- Literature and Drama
- Art and Architecture
- Music and Dance
- Food
- Leisure and Sports
- Media and Popular Culture.

Each entry concludes with a list of cross-references and Further Readings, pointing readers to additional print and electronic resources that might prove useful.

Following the chapters are appendices, including "A Day in the Life" feature, which depicts "typical" days in the lives of people living in that country, from students to farmers to factory workers to stay-at-home and working mothers. A Glossary, Facts and Figures section, and Holidays chart round out the appendices. Volumes include a Selected Bibliography as well as sidebars that are scattered throughout the text.

The volumes in the *Understanding Modern Nations* series are not intended to be comprehensive compendiums about every nation of the world, but instead are meant to serve as introductory texts for readers, examining key topics from major countries studied in the high-school curriculum as well as important transitioning countries that make headlines daily. It is our hope that readers will gain an understanding and appreciation for cultures and histories outside of their own.

ACKNOWLEDGMENTS

We wish to express our gratitude to the numerous people and colleagues who contributed in many ways in making this book a reality. First, we thank our children, David and Ann, not only for their patience during the course of writing the book but also for their enthusiasm regarding matters concerning their motherland. Although in the diaspora, they are passionate about the political and economic development of Nigeria, which was a constant motivation for us. We also want to express our gratitude to our colleagues and friends, too numerous to mention individually, with whom we have engaged both formally and informally during our various conversations around matters that pertain to Nigeria. Finally, our gratitude goes to Kaitlin Ciarmiello and Maxine Taylor, the former and current senior acquisitions editors at ABC-CLIO, respectively, as well as other staff members whose patient guidance and invaluable support have made this book see the light of day.

PREFACE

Attempting to write about modern Nigeria is as daunting as it is exciting. Although titled *Modern Nigeria*, it is imperative that we go back in time to capture the remarkable antiquity of the indigenous groups, kingdoms, and empires that make up the country today. Its vast geographical space, diverse cultural groups, and complex history means that no one single book can claim to do sufficient justice to such a project, however tenaciously the authors may have tried. Nonetheless, it is an exhilarating exercise to be conscious of some of the critical moments in Nigeria's history and capture some of its unfolding moments. No time in the country's history has been as momentous as the beginning of the third decade of the twenty-first century. Of critical importance is the security issue that is perpetrated not only by the Boko Haram and ISWAP religious fundamentalists, but also by Fulani herdsmen and the secessionist groups in the southeastern and southwestern parts of the country. The kidnapping and killing of Nigerians depict a period of grave concern reminiscent probably only of the Trans-Atlantic slave era—that dark history of West Africa from the seventeenth to the nineteenth century when slave raiders and traders unleashed terror and fear in many communities to satisfy the Europeans' demand for slaves. What has made the current situation so deplorable is the fact that it is happening in the twenty-first century that boasts of sophisticated technological gadgets, which can be deployed to locate and frustrate those involved in the dastardly act. The inability to bring the crisis under control speaks to the ineptitude of the Buhari and Tinubu administrations in tackling the problem that has brought unprecedented economic hardship and fear to Nigerians. However, it is not only the terror at home that has been responsible for Nigeria's current woes. The COVID-19 pandemic, starting from March 2020 until the end of 2021, and the Ukraine–Russia war, which started in February 2022 and still ongoing, are part of the crises that have compounded the economic woes in modern Nigeria. Despite these tragedies, however, Nigerians have displayed remarkable resilience and are preparing for the daunting task of taking their country back and charting a new pathway toward sustainable development as they wait anxiously for the courts determination on the 2023 presidential election petitions. As historians, it is our desire to provide a synopsis of some sort to high school students, university undergraduates, and lay-people alike who would want to have a compendium that will provide useful information about the country.

The book is organized in a logical sequence starting with the geography of Nigeria including its size, neighbors, and the geomorphology of the land among other geographical information. This is followed by the country's history starting from ancient times to the present. Other entries include the economy and politics of the country. On the economy, we have tried to focus on the country's economic type and level of development. Although we are aware of the dynamic nature of Nigeria's economy, we have attempted to provide basic useful financial information, its gross domestic product (GDP), and other common economic indicators, some of which might be dated by the time the book finally makes it to the shelves. The same applies to the political terrain of the country especially because the 2023 presidential election has not been legally concluded as the nation awaits the judgement of the Presidential Election Tribunal. To provide the most current information on these entries we have relied on the sidebars to provide up-to-date information at the time of going to press. However, we have also provided both historical and contemporary information regarding the country's system of government, its political life, and history. We are also aware of the diverse ethnic groups in the country and the complex social classes that define the social organization of the society, so what we have done is to provide some basic information about the distribution of wealth and the profile of specific ethnic groups including the three major ones. The diversity in ethnic groups is also reflected in the people's marriage ceremonies and gender roles. Even though there is a common thread in legal marriages especially among the dominant Christian and Muslim populations, we are conscious of the varied traditional forms which are influenced by different cultural factors, and these are noted in the entries.

Education is an important aspect of life of the average Nigerian. The education entry is rather complex not only because of the various regulatory bodies at the state and federal level, but also because of the huge disparity between the North and South of the country in terms of educational attainment. What we have attempted to do is to provide key information that is uniform across the country and how the various education boards are structured. To understand Nigeria and its people we found it expedient to also include music and dance, art and architecture, food, leisure and sport, media and popular culture, as well as the social and cultural etiquettes of various ethnic groups to provide useful information to non-Nigerians who may want to visit the country or to Nigerians who have not been privileged to visit other parts of the country.

In preparing this book, we have relied heavily on academic materials including books, journals, and other online sources, which have been listed in the bibliography. As much as possible we have sought to present issues using Nigerian voices, scholarships, and discourses; while refraining from being judgmental or analytical in the materials used. In doing so, we have tried to present a balanced view of the subject, and where there are dissenting views among scholars or leading figures in the field, we have noted this and provided relevant materials (further reading) that interested readers may want to pursue further. As academics ourselves, with teaching experience at the university level for over twenty years, we find these materials useful in providing extensive information, debates, and tentative or critical conclusions that will stimulate readers in making their own reasoned contribution to the body of literature on any field of interest that has been presented in this book. While the preparation and writing of this book has been most demanding because of our personal teaching, research, and administrative commitments at our institutions, the completion of the work is most rewarding at two levels. First, it is a great privilege to be invited by ABC-CLIO publishers to consider getting involved in this project and to see it to its completion. Second, it is a great privilege to make our modest contribution in the ever-dynamic process of modern Nigeria, the most populous black country in the world with all its potentials, challenges, and contradictions. It is our hope that those who will read this book, or sections of it, will find it as rewarding as we have in its preparation.

Introduction

Nigeria, the most populous nation in Africa, is a country of great diversity, rich in culture, and a long history extending back to prehistoric times. It is situated in West Africa and shares borders with the Republic of Chad, the Republic of Cameroon, the Republic of the Niger, and the Republic of Benin. Nigeria has a total land area of 910,768 square kilometers, a total water area of 13,000 square kilometers, a total coastline of 853 kilometers, and a territorial sea area of 12 nautical miles. The country is positioned slightly below the equator which makes it sunny for most of the year. In some northern sections, such as Maiduguri in the Northeast, the temperatures can be as high as 40 degrees Celsius; while in the Jos Plateau area, temperatures can be as low as 5 degrees Celsius. Nigeria has two major seasons, namely the dry (Harmattan) season, which spans between October and March, and the wet (Rainy) season, which occurs between April and September. Nigeria is home to a diverse number of fauna and flora, many of which can be found in rural areas and nature reserves. Major urban cities include Lagos, Abuja, Port Harcourt, Aba, and Kano, and they are characterized with commercial activities, higher levels of infrastructural development, diversity in ethnic representation, and high population density.

In ancient times, the area now known as Nigeria, witnessed the rise of various indigenous empires. These include the Benin Empire which was a dominant state in the South-South region, the Nri Empire in the Southeast, the Oyo Empire in the Southwest, the Sokoto Caliphate in the Northeast, and Kanem-Borno Empire in the Northwest. However, when the Europeans arrived in the sixteenth century, they brought with them their desire to exploit the abundant resources of the region, particularly in coastal areas like Bonny, Calabar, Warri, and Lagos. Trade in slaves, ivory, and other commodities blossomed, while the ancient empires disintegrated. The trade in slaves was a dark period which led to the British installing their control under the guise of establishing peace and order. This control was solidified with the amalgamation of the northern and southern protectorates into one colony known as Nigeria in 1914 and governed through a system of indirect rule. The colonial period brought many changes to Nigeria including Western education, Christianity, and other elements of Western culture. The economic structure of the country also changed, as Nigerians became increasingly involved in the export of cash crops such as cocoa, rubber, and palm oil. Modern Nigeria gained independence from British colonial rule in 1960 with three dominant ethnic groups namely the Hausa/Fulani, Yoruba, and Igbo. Other ethnic groups include the Kanuri, Tiv, Ibibio, Nupe, Ijaw (Ijo), and Urhobo. Together, they represent over 500 indigenous languages spoken across the country.

The colonial period imposed diverse policies, particularly in the northern and southern regions. These policies resulted in divisions which reflected in the political and administrative units that were inherited after political independence. Unfortunately, the policy of divide and rule continued into the post-independence period leading to a series of military coups d'état and a brutal civil war known as the Nigerian Civil War (or the Biafran War), which lasted between 1967 and 1970. Following the civil war, Nigeria emerged as a united country under the leadership of General Yakubu Gowon. The government then proceeded to implement policies aimed at achieving national unity and economic development. One of these policies was the creation of six states in 1967, which have since increased to thirty-six under the current federal system of government. Since 1966, after the first military coup, most of independent Nigeria has been marked with military regimes and a series of autocratic decrees.

Democratic Nigeria has been in existence since 1999. However, modern democratic Nigeria has faced many challenges since independence, including insecurity, instability, corruption, and economic inequality. Insecurity has affected economic activities, particularly in the northern part of the country, where the insurgency of Boko Haram and the Islamic State of West African Province (ISWAP) has led to the displacement of millions of people and the destruction of infrastructure. Insecurity has also discouraged foreign investment and negatively affected Nigeria's image in the international community. Insurgencies have been a recurring social problem since the 1980s when the *Maitatsine* riots broke out in Kano and Kaduna states in the Northwest. Since then, the country has witnessed a series of agitations from the Niger Delta Avengers in the South-South to the Indigenous People of Biafra (IPOB) in the Southeast, to the self-styled Yoruba nation activist, Sunday Igboho, in the Southwest, to the Fulani herdsmen and Boko Haram terrorist group in the North. At various times these groups have threatened the peace and development of the country with the deaths of thousands of Nigerians in the process. Unfortunately, successive governments have not succeeded in solving the intractable problem of agitations for secession and self-determination by various ethnic groups in the country. On the other hand, corruption has further fueled the social crisis in the country. Nigeria has been ranked among the most corrupt nations in the world by Transparency International. Corruption has affected every aspect of the economy, including government spending, public procurement, and the allocation of resources. Corruption has also undermined the rule of law and weakened institutions, which has discouraged foreign investment.

Notwithstanding the challenges enumerated above, Nigeria has made some progress, particularly with its democratic governance since 1999. The Fourth Republic, established in 1999, has seen Nigeria emerge as a regional power and a leader in African Affairs, especially when the country overtook South Africa to become the largest economy in Africa after the economy was rebased and worth over 519 billion dollars in 2014. Nigeria has witnessed a smooth transition of political power from one administration to the other. The 2015 handing over of power by Goodluck Jonathan, an incumbent president, to Muhammadu Buhari of the opposition All Progressives Congress was the hallmark of political maturity in the country to date. Unfortunately, the 2023 presidential election has proved to be problematic as both internal and international observers have questioned the process that produced Mr. Bola Tinubu of the ruling All Progressives Congress as the winner of that election. The various petitions filed by four opposition parties are indicative of the problems that are associated with the elections, which have caused some political actors and national statesmen such as former president Olusegun Obasanjo to state that the conduct of the 2023 general election has reversed the gains of the democratic process in the country back to the pre-2015 era. The complexity of the Nigerian electoral process, characterized by a combination of manual ballot boxes, automated machines such as the bimodal voter accreditation system (BVAS), the problem of capacity and logistics, and the moral character of the staff of the Independent National Electoral Commission (INEC), has proved to be the most challenging in conducting free, fair, and credible elections in the country.

In terms of economic development, the country is rich in natural resources such as oil and gas, solid minerals, and agriculture. Nigeria's economy is heavily reliant on oil and gas, which accounts for over 90 percent of its export earnings and about 60 percent of government revenue. The country is the largest oil producer in Africa and the twelfth largest in the world. However, the oil sector has been plagued with several challenges including oil theft, pipeline vandalism, and low oil prices, which have affected Nigeria's revenue and foreign exchange earnings. Apart from oil and gas, Nigeria's agriculture sector is another important contributor to the economy. The sector employs over 70 percent of the population and accounts for about 25 percent of GDP. Nigeria is one of the largest producers of several agricultural products such as cassava, yam, cocoa, and palm oil. However, the sector faces several challenges, including poor infrastructure, low productivity, and inadequate funding. Nigeria's solid minerals sector has also been identified as a potential source of revenue for the country. The country is endowed with several mineral resources such as tin, limestone, coal, and gold. However, the sector is underdeveloped due to a lack of investment, poor infrastructure, and weak regulatory framework. One of the major challenges facing Nigeria's economy is corruption.

The huge abundance of natural resources and the paradoxical poverty that is pervasive in the country has led to the theorizing that, rather than a blessing, the natural resources may be regarded as a curse due to the inability of successive governments, both military and civilian, to harness the natural resources in order to develop the country and its people. The country's heavy reliance on oil has been the bane of successive governments as the volatility of global oil prices affects budgeting and infrastructural development. Furthermore, the decline in economic growth following the drop in oil prices since 2014 has significantly stagnated growth leading to calls from experts for economic diversification away from oil. The Buhari-led government (2015–2023) responded positively to these calls by encouraging an agricultural business economy to meet domestic food security and generate export earnings. Unfortunately, this agricultural policy was not successful partly because of the astronomical rise in the cost of farm inputs due to high exchange rates, corrupt practices, the hijacking of the process by "political farmers," and the increasing insecurity in the country.

Despite these economic challenges, the private sector has proved to be a strong force in the sustenance of Nigeria's economy. The private sector, which includes high capital businesses such as the Dangote group of companies, the privately owned Innoson Motors, dozens of private media houses, music and movie production companies, estate development agencies, schools, universities, churches, and retail sales of imported goods, all contribute significantly to sustaining the Nigerian economy. Small-scale businesses including tailoring, hairdressing, carpentry, catering, telecommunication, and foodstuff market sales have also enabled entrepreneurial activities to reduce unemployment. The private sector is also very vibrant in providing much-needed services such as healthcare, banking, transportation, logistics, critical skills development training, to mention a few. The resilience of the average Nigerian is demonstrated in their ability to see opportunities even in the face of adversity. It is partly for this reason that Nigerians are regarded as among the happiest people on earth given the harsh conditions in which they live and the limited opportunities that are offered to them by their government. The unreliable supply of electricity, for example, which would have discouraged small businesses such as tailoring, barber shops, or welding have seen the ingenuity of the small-scale entrepreneur circumventing these challenges to still make a living out of the situation. The film industry, commonly referred to as Nollywood, is a classic case of how indigenous ideas, creativity, and doggedness can blossom even in the face of great adversity and limited infrastructure. Today, the Nollywood film industry is the second largest in the world, second only to India's Bollywood. Nigerians have also displayed similar resilience and productivity in the music industry, fashion industry, real estate, and education. Nigerians are very fashionable, and they take their appearance very seriously, and are very trendy. Their social life is colorful with an array of both traditional attires and foreign designer clothing. Nigerians are known for their boisterous life, effervescence, and friendliness. Foreigners who come to the country are generously welcomed and feel at home at once. Nigerians' hospitality to foreigners is self-contradictory, as they restrain themselves from displaying the same ebullience to themselves. This inconsistency has been attributed to the divisive politics that have divided the people along ethnic and religious lines. Some political observers have consistently maintained that until these divisions are reduced by the same politicians who have created them, the country will continue to falter along those lines and the country will not fully harness its true potential.

Education is big business in Nigeria, primarily because the citizens have a great thirst for knowledge, and because the government has failed to invest in the expansion of schools to cater to the teeming population that is eager to acquire Western-style education. The meager budgetary allocation to the education sector and poor remuneration of teachers have led to the near collapse of government schools, giving rise to the provision of private education from kindergarten to institutions of higher learning. While parents sacrifice a great deal to educate their children, the sad reality is that most graduates end up not being employed or are underemployed leading to frustration and the need to travel out of the country for greener pastures. It is no wonder that Nigerians can be found in almost all countries of the world; not because they want to do so, but because they can hardly actualize their dreams in the country of their birth. The flip side is that, once settled in a country with a functional system, Nigerians excel in any field of endeavor including academia, business, politics, film, music, and the media more broadly. But those who, for whatever reason, stay behind in the country also make the best of a bad situation. Nigerians do not allow the reality of poverty, poor infrastructure, or the harsh economic condition to define them. Nigerians are vivacious in nature, and they turn their bad circumstances, created by poor political leadership, into a world of fun and excitement. Through drama, theater, and stand-up comedy, they craft their skills by using the challenges they face as materials for their performances. The antagonism of the government, notwithstanding, dramatists and comedians use their performances as a soothing balm that helps them and their audience to cope with their harsh condition. The same is also true with sports, especially football, which tends to unite the country during major competitions that involve the Nigerian national team. For this reason, some individuals and civil societies have made calls to the government to use sports as an effective tool in not only promoting healthy competition but also as a platform to unite the country further.

Modern Nigeria is a complex entity in which understanding it will mean tracing its existence from its prehistory to its colonial and post-colonial periods. Within these periods are changes that its culturally diverse people have undergone, its transforming political process, as well as its natural geographical and variegated contours. These factors have not only shaped the country's social, cultural, economic, and political landscapes, but they have also shaped the realities that characterize Nigeria such as the current cases of kidnapping, terrorism, ethnocentrism, religious intolerance, and poverty. However, despite these negative and despairing outlooks are the virtues of resilience, doggedness, unity, progress, and development which Nigeria's millennials and Generation Z have attempted to embrace as their way of making a difference. Their efforts to "take back our country" during the 2023 general election reflect what modern Nigeria aspires to become irrespective of ethnicity, religion, gender, or social class. If these efforts of the youth come to fruition, with the swearing-in of credible political leaders, Nigeria will surely begin to take its place in the comity of nations and truly become the giant of the continent of Africa.

CHAPTER 1

Geography

OVERVIEW

The Federal Republic of Nigeria is in West Africa and lies between latitude 4 degrees and 14 degrees and longitude 3 degrees and 14 degrees, positioning it slightly below the equator. The country is bordered by the Republic of Benin to the southwest with a boundary line of 773 kilometers; Cameroon to the southeast with a boundary line of 1,690 kilometers; and the Republics of Niger and Chad to the north with a boundary stretch of 1,497 kilometers and 87 kilometers, respectively. The southern limit of the country does not share boundaries with any country but tapers into the Atlantic Ocean. With a total land area of 923,768 square kilometers, Nigeria is the fourth largest country in West Africa (next to Niger, Mali, and Mauritania) and the fourteenth on the African continent. To put it in perspective, Nigeria is almost three times the size of Ivory Coast, the fifth largest country in West Africa, and more than five times the size of Togo and Benin Republic combined. Nigeria has a total land area of 910,768 square kilometers, a total water area of 13,000 square kilometers, a total coastline of 853 kilometers, and a territorial sea area of 12 nautical miles. The temperature of the country is influenced by its position in relation to the equator, which makes the sunshine high in the sky at midday throughout the year. However, due to the size of the country and its proximity to the Atlantic Ocean in the South, there is a considerable variation in the average number of hours of sunshine. While the coastal region in the Niger Delta enjoys about 1,500 hours of sunshine per annum, the northern section has an average of over 3,000 hours. The temperatures in the Niger Delta are stable averaging between 25 degrees Celsius and 27 degrees Celsius all year round. In the northern part of the country, on the other hand, temperatures fluctuate from as low as 5 degrees Celsius around the Jos Plateau in the middle belt to highs of 40 degrees in Maiduguri in the Northeast. Unlike South Africa and Europe with four seasons, Nigeria has only two seasons: the dry season and the wet season. The dry season is usually witnessed from October to March while the wet season (or Rainy Season) is between April and September, but this range varies considerably. Its border with the Atlantic Ocean in its southernmost part makes the Niger Delta the wettest region in the country with an average rainfall of over 3,000 mm per annum. This amount of rainfall decreases steadily northward with less than 250 mm of rainfall annually at the northernmost fringes of the country.

The availability of sunshine and the rainfall pattern witnessed in the country have considerable influence on the vegetation types and the types of crops the people cultivate as well as the predominant occupation of the people. For example, ethnic groups in the Niger Delta region, because of the presence of rivers and creeks, are mostly fishermen who sometimes, especially among the Ijo (Ijaw) cultural group, build their houses on stilts on the rivers. On the other hand, the Yoruba ethnic group that occupies the southwestern part of the country cultivates yam, corn, and cocoa; and the Tiv and Idoma who occupy the middle belt are great cultivators of yams, beans, and other food crops, while those in the North are famous for the production of cereals and groundnuts.

Nigeria may be divided into two relief regions, namely, the upland and lowland areas. The upland areas may be further divided into seven relief regions namely, the High Plains of Hausaland, the Jos Plateau, the Biu Plateau, the Western Uplands, the Mandara Mountains, the Eastern Highlands, and the Oban Hills. On the other hand, the lowlands may also be subdivided into seven regions: the Sokoto Plains, the Chad Plains, the Niger-Benue Trough, the Coastal Plains of Southwest Nigeria, the Coastal Plains of Southeast Nigeria, the Lowlands of Southeast Nigeria, and the Niger-Delta. The formation and relief of the country are greatly influenced by River Niger and River Benue, which divide the country into three large sections due to their meeting at the Lokoja Confluence thereby forming a Y-shape. The first section, called the Western Relief Block, lies between the Middle Niger, the Lower Niger, and the Atlantic Ocean. The second section, called the Eastern Relief Block, lies between the Benue River, the Lower Niger, and the Atlantic Ocean. The third section, which lies on the upper section of the confluence of the two rivers, is the Northern Relief Block, and constitutes the largest of the three Blocks. It is characterized by a gentle rise in sea level with a low elevation of less than 150 meters above sea level (ASL) around the Niger-Benue Trough, increasing in height to a level of 600 meters ASL and peaking at 1,200 meters ASL at the Jos Plateau in the High Plains of Hausa land. However, the relief drops at the Sokoto Valley in the Northwest and around the Lake Chad region in the Northeast, both at a low elevation of less than 300 meters ASL. The Western Relief Block rises gently from the Atlantic Ocean in the Niger Delta with a general elevation less than 150 meters ASL to reach the high plains and hills that reach over 300 meters ASL and peaking at over 1,000 meters in the Idanre Hills in Ondo State. The Eastern Relief Block, with an elevation of over 300 meters ASL comprises three upland areas that are defined by extensive low-lying plains. Of the three upland areas are the Uguemi Hills and Udi-Nsukka Plateau in Enugu State, extending to Kogi, Anambra, Imo, and Abia States. This relief tapers down to the Lower Benue to the North and to the Cross River Valley in the East with a general elevation of less than 150 meters ASL. The second of the upland areas that make up the Eastern Relief Block, and the smallest of the three uplands, is the Oban Hills located around northern Calabar in Cross River State. The upland rises over 300 meters ASL and is separated from the largest of the uplands by the Cross River Valley. The third and largest of the high plains that make up the Eastern Relief Block rises from the Benue Valley to form a belt of high plateau and hills in Taraba State in the Northeast of the country. Also found in this block are the Chappal Waddi Hills in Taraba state. At a height of 2,419 meters, the Chappal Waddi is the highest point in Nigeria. Together with the famous Mambilla Plateau with an average elevation of 1,600 meters (5,249 ft.) above sea level, they constitute the largest uplands of the Eastern Relief Block. Other high elevations that are in this Block are the Shebshi Mountains and Alantika Mountains located in Adamawa state. The highlands and lowlands provide the drainage system of the country with the Niger-Benue basin, the Lake Chad basin, and the Gulf of Guinea basin as the country's major drainage areas.

There are three soil types in Nigeria distributed along the vegetation zones. In the Niger Delta region, the soil is rich in humus, and it is generally fertile for the cultivation of tubers such as cassava, yam, and cocoyam, as well as a variety of vegetables. The second soil type is the most common and it is found in most parts of the southwestern and southeastern parts of the country as well as in the middle belt up to the North of the country. This soil type is characterized by reddish laterite soil and is less fertile than the other soil types. However, with the effective use of irrigation and the adoption of mixed-cropping methods this soil type still provides great agricultural yields. Some of the major food crops this soil type sustains include yam, sorghum, millet, guinea corn, and cash crops such as cashew and citrus fruits. The third soil type is found mainly in Kano and Sokoto states in the Northwest of the country. It is made up of mixed soils containing locally derived granites and loess, making the soil fertile for crop cultivation. Some of the best-known crops produced in this region include groundnut and other legumes such as beans and *acha*.

The natural landscape of Nigeria makes it a haven for tourism. Some of the great land formations such as the Mambilla Plateau and the Mandara Mountains constitute some of the most iconic scenery in Nigeria even though they have not yet been fully harnessed by the government or private tourism investors. Some of the more developed sites for tourism in Nigeria include the Olumo Rock in Abeokuta, Ogun State, the Obudu Cattle Ranch in Cross Rivers State, and the Badagry and Eko beaches in Lagos among other places. The Ikogosi Warm Spring and the Erin-Ijesha Waterfalls are also potential sites for tourism in the country.

Further Reading

Robson, L. (2005). *Nigeria*. London: Evans Brothers Ltd.

BENUE RIVER

River Benue (or the Benue River) is the fifth longest river in Africa and the second largest in Nigeria next only to the Niger River. In total, the Benue River is 673 miles (1,083 kilometers) in length. It has its source in the high plains of the Adamawa Plateau in northern Cameroon at a height of 4,400 ft. (1,340 meters). The river descends rapidly more than 2,000 ft. (600 meters) from its source over several falls and rapids in its first 240 kilometers (150 miles). The river is dammed at the Garoua and Lagdo reservoirs (in Cameroon) and, thereafter, it flows uninterrupted throughout its course. It enters Nigeria from the Mandara Mountains in Borno State and meanders through the towns of Jimeta in Adamawa state and Ibi in Taraba state before serving as a tributary to the Niger River. However, the Benue River has its own tributaries, and the most important ones include the Faro River, and the Mayo Kebbi, which, during the flood seasons between the months of September and October, connect with the Logone River to form part of the Lake Chad system. Other tributaries of the river include the Taraba River and River Katsina Ala in Taraba and Benue states, respectively. Between Yola in Gongola state in Nigeria's Northeast and in Makurdi in the middle belt, the Benue River is joined by the Gongola River, which is its primary tributary, and then flows East and South for about 300 miles (480 kilometers). Before intensive farming in the Lokoja region (due to a smaller population to feed at the confluence), the Benue River and the Niger River discharged a greater volume of water than they do in the present day with the former discharging much more volume than the latter. The construction of irrigation systems along the Lokoja region has reduced the discharge considerably with a current estimated discharge of 1,700 cubic meters per second (60,000 cubic ft. per second) for the Benue River and 12,500 cubic metres per second (44,000 ft. per second) for the Niger. Important settlements that are established along the banks of the Benue River include Numan and Jimeta, both in Adamawa state. Numan is a thriving town of over 100,000 people. It is also a port on the Benue River, located about 30 miles (50 kilometers) from Yola opposite the mouth of the Gongola River. The town is home to the Bwatiye (Bachama) people who have been occupying the area since the nineteenth century, first at Lamurde and then the town of Numan in the early twentieth century. The town is a commercial center for the distribution of groundnuts and cotton. Other goods that are distributed in the town include fish, goat, cattle, sheep, millet, cowpeas, and sorghum. Like Numan, Jimeta is a town on the South bank of the Benue River and serves as a port for Yola. During the rainy season merchants trade in groundnuts and cotton from Cameroon into Nigeria and in return carry hides and skins from the hinterland of Yola to Cameroon.

See Also: Agriculture Sector (Chapter 4); Niger River (Chapter 1); Transportation and Waterways (Chapter 1).

Further Reading

Grove, A. T. (1957). *The Benue Valley*. Ministry of Natural Resources, Northern Nigeria.

CLIMATE

Nigeria's location on the western coast of the continent gives it a tropical climate. However, the size of the country and its geographical position in relation to the equator also provides two major seasons, the dry and wet seasons. The dry season is usually experienced between October and March and the rainy (wet) season between April and

The Impact of Climate Change

Nigeria is one of several countries in the world that is significantly affected by the severe impacts of global warming due to the emission of ozone-depleting chemicals. Between June and November 2022, Nigeria recorded some of its deadliest floods with over 200 flash floods, hundreds of casualties and an estimated 1.5 million displaced people, and over 500,000 hectares of farmland destroyed, especially in the South and North-central regions of the country. Climate change has also had devastating effects in Nigeria, especially in increased temperature resulting in desertification and drought in most Northern states of the country. These devastations have renewed calls by climate activists, environmentalists, and civil societies for the Nigerian government to act more decisively in eliminating gas flaring and reduce greenhouse gas emissions. The government has promised to continue with its efforts to achieve a net zero carbon emission by 2060.

September. But there is a variation in the seasons between the southern part of the country and the northern part. While the rainy season starts earlier and ends later in the South with an average rainfall of nine to ten months, in the northernmost parts of the country the rainy season lasts for only between two to four months, which threatens livelihoods through droughts. The seasons are greatly influenced by the Southwest Trade Winds that blow air from across the Atlantic Ocean to the North of the country leading to rainfall. Sometimes, especially along the coastline, the rainfall leads to a rise in sea levels and produces destructive waves that cause erosion in those areas. These erosions are more prominent in Lagos along the Bar Beach and Badagry Beach. It is, however, far more destructive in the Niger Delta especially in Brass and Forcados, where the erosion rate has been estimated to be between 16 to 20 meters per annum. The Northeast Trade Winds, on the other hand, blow hot air across the Sahara Desert through northern Nigeria to the South. The hot dry air that blows from the North makes the region dry and in the months of December, January, and February, the hazy dusty wind (called the Harmattan) makes breathing difficult and produces misty weather conditions that are hazardous to the aviation industry leading to air crashes.

Four major climate types are distinguishable in Nigeria. These are the tropical monsoon climate found in the southernmost part of the country; the tropical savannah climate which dominates the western part of the country; the Sahel climate that characterizes the northern part of the country; and the Alpine climate which is dominant in the highland regions of the country. The Monsoon climate is characterized by heavy rainfall that lasts for several days and for the most part of the year. The rainfall in this area (that is the southernmost part of the country) averages 2,500 mm per annum and leads to seasonal flooding with occasional loss of life and destruction of property. In the coastal plains of Southeastern Nigeria, and especially in the Niger Delta region with a flat topography, vast areas are either waterlogged or completely submerged under water for several months. Other places that also witness flooding during the rainy season include Lagos, Ibadan, and Aba. However, the flooding can be minimized in these cities if the proper drainage system is maintained.

The tropical savannah climate stretches from Ondo in the Southwest to Calabar in the Southeast and has a total rainfall of 1,750 mm to 2,000 mm per annum. The Sahel climate covers over three-quarters of the country with an average rainfall of less than 1,000 mm, while the Alpine climate is restricted to the hilly regions of central Nigeria.

Due to human activities in the country, the climate is undergoing significant change with marked seasonal differences. The northern part of the country is currently experiencing extreme dry conditions with an increase in droughts and desertification in most parts of the region including Kano, Sokoto, Borno, and Yobe states forcing the Fulani cattle herders to migrate southward in search of pasture for their cattle leading to frequent clashes between them and local farmers. In the southern part of the country, there is also an increase in flooding.

See Also: Desertification (Chapter 1); Rainforest (Chapter 1); Savannah (Chapter 1).

Further Reading

William, C. J. R and D. R. Kniveton, eds. (2011). *African Climate and Climate Change: Physical, Social and Political Perspectives*. New York: Springer.

Williams, M. (2014). *Climate Change in Deserts: Past, Present and Future*. Cambridge: Cambridge University Press.

World Bank. "Nigeria." *Climate Change Knowledge Portal*. https://climateknowledgeportal.worldbank.org/country/nigeria/vulnerability

DESERTIFICATION

Desertification, the process of desert encroachment in a particular region, has become a perennial problem in Nigeria, especially in the northern parts of the country. States such as Borno, Gombe, and Jigawa in the Northeast, and Sokoto, Katsina, and Kano in the Southwest have been severely affected. In most parts of northern Nigeria, desertification has increased in intensity caused mostly by leaching of farmlands and the process of indiscriminate tree felling for domestic use. The most important factor for desertification in the North, however, is the Northeast Trade Wind that blows across the Sahara Desert southward through the Republic of Niger and across the northern parts of Nigeria extending to the middle belt including Kwara State in the South. Many factors are responsible for desert encroachment in the country. Some of the factors responsible for desertification in this region include overgrazing and deforestation. Other factors include the felling of trees for domestic use such as cooking and house building. The high demand for wood products for the manufacture of household materials such as tables, chairs, canoes, has significantly increased the demand for the felling of trees. The bad habit of not replacing trees with the planting of new ones is regarded as one of the most important threats to land in Nigeria. Besides human induced factors, climate change is another factor for the increase in desertification in Nigeria. Estimates have suggested that desert encroachment in the northern part of Nigeria is moving at about 2 kilometers per annum with the forecast that by 2050 most parts of northern Nigeria (especially Sokoto, Kano, Adamawa, Gongola, and

Taraba) will be severely threatened. The overgrazing of shrubs and vegetation by cattle and other domestic animals are a major source of desertification in Nigeria and the continuous shortage of fodder for cattle has become a major source of conflict between the nomadic cattle herders and the farmers that till the land for the cultivation of both food and cash crops. This situation has not only caused fracas in the middle belt such as Benue State, but it has also created tension among nomadic cattle herders and farmers in the southern part of the country. As desertification becomes intense in the northern part of the country, cattle herders in those areas are forced to migrate to the South where they can provide fodder for their cattle to maintain their livelihood. This tense situation has led the federal government to intensify efforts to curb desertification in the country by encouraging the planting of trees and providing cheap kerosene for cooking by subsidizing the product for poor households in the country. Recently, the federal government has also proposed to have "colonies" for the grazing of cattle in the country even though this suggestion has not been accepted by the majority of the southern state governors.

See Also: Climate (Chapter 1).

Further Reading

Audu, A. I. and L. A. Adie (2018). "Desertification in Northern Nigeria: Causes and Consequences." *The Environmental Studies*, 1(2): 20–37.
Mortimore, M. (1989). *Adapting to Drought: Farmers, Famines and Desertification in West Africa*. Cambridge: Cambridge University Press.
Olagunju, T. E. (2015). "Drought, Desertification and the Nigerian Environment: A Review." *Journal of Ecology and the Natural Environment*, 7(7): 196–209.

FAUNA

Nigeria's diversity in biomes and ecosystems provides a rich habitat for a variety of animal species from the largest primates to antelopes and to small rodents and reptiles. The tropical rainforest in the Niger Delta is a natural home to the forest elephants, gorillas, and chimpanzees. The deforestation of the region, however, endangers most of these large animals and they are on the verge of becoming extinct. Although the government, as well as non-governmental organizations such as the World Wildlife Fund (WWF), are making concerted efforts to protect these animals, such efforts do not match the aggressive destruction of the natural forest either due to urbanization with the need for arable land or for the construction of roads and other amenities in the area. These large animals are now confined to the nation's game reserves such as the Cross River National Park in Cross Rivers State, the Kainji Lake National Park in Kwara State, the Gashaka-Gumti National Park in Taraba State, and the Yankari National Park in Bauchi State. Other types of animals found in this region that are less endangered, due to their body size and their ability to procreate much faster than the larger animals, include a wide variety of monkeys, the commonest being the bushbabies, famous for their night cries. There are also a variety of reptiles including different species of snakes and lizards. Some of the most poisonous snakes in Nigeria such as the python and cobra are found in most parts of the country. Some of the animals that provide meat protein for those who live in the tropical forest include antelopes, porcupines, squirrels, bush rats, and other small animals referred to by the people as "bushmeat." Freshly killed bushmeat is highly priced because of its freshness and natural taste. Moving northward, the savannah is home to lions and other large animals such as giraffes, gazelles, wildebeest, and many more.

Besides animals there are also a variety of birds, from the kites, grey parrots, and guinea fowl to rare eagles in the mountainous regions of the country such as those found in the Mambilla Plateau in the Northeast and the forest regions of the Niger Delta. Most Nigerian cultural groups regard the eagle as a mystical bird. Among the Urhobo of Delta State, for example, having the feather of an eagle in one's bowler hat is a symbol of great prestige and spiritual power. The eagle is also represented in the Nigerian Coat of Arms as a symbol of the country's strength and influence. Vultures are common in the northern part of the country, while the white egrets that are more common also in the North migrate with the cattle of the nomadic Fulani to the South as they serve as parasites and feed off the ticks on the cattle. Also common are a wide variety of butterflies. Nigeria is regarded as one of the countries with the most diverse species of butterflies, especially in the Calabar region in Cross River State and the Ota region in Ogun State, respectively.

See Also: Flora (Chapter 1); Rainforest (Chapter 1); Savannah (Chapter 1); Urbanization and its impact (Chapter 1).

Further Reading

Ajayi, S. S. and K. R. N. Milligan (1975). *The Wildlife of Nigeria: A Guide to Yankari and Borgu Game Reserves*. Ibadan: Ibadan University Press.

AZ Animal. "Nigeria." https://a-z-animals.com/animals/location/africa/nigeria/

Egborge, A. B. M. (1993). *Biodiversity of Aquatic Fauna of Nigeria*. Lagos: Natural Resources Conservation Council.

FLORA

Nigeria's climate and its soil types accommodate a variety of plant species consisting of the evergreen forest of the Niger Delta to the deciduous trees of the savannah in the middle belt to the cacti of the northernmost part of the country. The saltwater swamp of the Niger Delta consists primarily of mangrove and raffia palms and these trees are used by the locals to build houses and extract roughages for various household products such as ropes, fire tinder, and the sap of the raffia palms to produce the popular local gin (*ogogoro*). Also found along the coastal swamp are the West African mangrove species, namely the tall red mangrove, the dwarf red mangrove, the black mangrove, and the white mangrove. Other trees found in the mangrove swamps include the nipa palms, the chandelier trees, varieties of bamboo trees, and the *Gnetum africanus*, a species of the evergreen climbing shrubs. Toward the North of the Niger Delta are rainforests made up of different species of trees, while the savannah region of the country is home to a greater variety of trees, grasses, and shrubs. Some of the most dominant ones are the Corkscrew Eucalyptus, the Senegal Gum Acacia, the Umbrella Acacia, and the *Khaya Senegalensis*. Most of the plants found in all regions of the country have cultural, medicinal, and spiritual significance. Palm trees, for example, are used not only for its palm fruits and wine, but they are also used as a demarcation plant to determine communal boundaries. Various shrubs, barks of trees, and roots have been harnessed for various medicinal purposes, especially the *Dogo Yaro* tree (Neem tree) that has been used for centuries to treat malaria and the paw-paw tree for the treatment of yellow fever and jaundice. Large trees such as the baobab, *Obeche*, *Iroko*, and other similar trees have been used for centuries by various ethnic groups as sites for rituals and other spiritual performances where it is believed some of the gods and spirits reside. In worshipping these spiritual entities, the people were also engaged in the conservation of nature thereby protecting the natural environment. However, with the introduction of Christianity and Islam, as well as the introduction of Western drugs, these cultural practices are dying out and, in the process, the natural environment is threatened by modern demands including the harnessing of the forest plants for furniture, the building of houses, and other necessities of modern life. As the population increases there is a greater demand for land resulting in the clearing of large expanses for settlement purposes as well as for farmland to increase food production, especially in the densely populated region of the Southeast. The increase in foreign demand for cash crops such as cocoa, palm oil, and kola nuts also means that a large expanse of natural vegetation is cleared for plantations, this is more evident in the southwestern States of Ondo, Ogun, and Ekiti, and Edo State in the Niger Delta.

See Also: Fauna (Chapter 1); Rainforest (Chapter 1); Savannah (Chapter 1); Urbanization and its Impact (Chapter 1).

Further Reading

Naturalist. "Flora in Nigeria." https://www.inaturalist.org/projects/flora-of-nigeria
Steentoft, M. (1988). *Flowering Plants in West Africa*. Cambridge: Cambridge University Press.

JOS PLATEAU

The Jos Plateau is the largest high plain in Nigeria with a total land area of 8,600 square kilometersand bounded by a 300- 600-meter beast ledge. It is in Plateau State in North-central Nigeria, and the state derives its name from the highland, which peaks at 1,829 meters (6,000 ft.) in the Shiroro Hills. On the east of the plateau is the adjoining highland known as the Bauchi Plateau. The Jos Plateau was formed by eroded gneiss that accumulated because of extinct volcanic cones that created massive granite intrusions. The plain is dated to the late Precambrian and Ordovician periods while the volcanic activities occurred during Jurassic and Pliocene times. Due to its high elevation, the Jos Plateau has a semi-temperate climate with temperatures ranging from 5 degrees Celsius during the months of December and January to 24 degrees Celsius during the hot months. Due to its varied landscape and altitude, the Jos Plateau has abundant rainfall ranging from 1,300 mm (51 inches) per annum in Jos to over 1,500 mm (59 inches) in the surrounding plains. The Jos Plateau is the source of several rivers including the Kaduna and Karemi rivers which flow into the Niger River; and the rivers Dep and Wase, which flow into the Benue River. The steepness of the plateau produces several waterfalls with the most popular being the Gurara Falls. Artefacts such as hand axes, bruins, and points indicate that the Jos Plateau is one of the oldest archaeological sites in Nigeria. The region has been inhabited continually since the Acheulean period of the Late Stone Age, peaking in prehistoric times around the fourth century BCE with the Nok civilization. The Nok figurines discovered in this region indicate that the people had complex social and economic organization and advanced knowledge of the use of furnaces. In contemporary times the region is characterized by diverse cultures of over fifty distinct ethnic groups making the region one of the most diversified in the country. The largest and most well-known of these groups include the Angas and Birom. Intensive farming over the millennia and commercial mining that started in the twentieth century have led to the displacement of the original forests in the region to what is now savannah grassland with an abundance of the cactus family. The main crops that are cultivated in this region include grains such as sorghum, millet, and *acha* (a local grain type sometimes referred to as "hungry rice"). Other crops that are cultivated in commercial quantities include potatoes, yams, and green vegetables. The region also sustains many goats, sheep, and cattle, which has made it home to some Fulani cattle herders. The Jos Plateau is, however, known for its large deposits of tin, iron, and columbite. Tin has been exploited and mined for centuries but only became commercially exploited from the early nineteenth century by the British colonial government. Other minerals found around the plateau include kaolin, uranium, lead, and tantalite. These minerals have not yet been fully exploited in commercial quantities.

See Also: Agriculture Sector (Chapter 4); Mining Sector (Chapter 4); Natural Resources (Chapter 1); Savannah (Chapter 1).

Further Reading

One Earth. "Jos Plateau Forest-Grassland." https://www.oneearth.org/ecoregions/jos-plateau-forest-grassland/

Onuh, Gideon. (2016). *The Blessed Plateau: A Journey Through Central Nigeria*. CreateSpace Independent Publishing Platform (Self publication).

MAJOR CITIES

The city of Aba is the capital of Abia State located in the southeastern part of Nigeria. Informally referred to as the Taiwan of Nigeria because of its boisterous commercial activities and the economic hub of the Southeast, Aba is about 7,000 square kilometers in area and has a total population of approximately three million inhabitants. Its population is predominantly made up of the Igbo ethnic group who are mainly traders. The city of Aba is the home to major industries in the Southeast that produce automobiles, textiles, glass, computers, machines, and other goods and services.

Lagos State is the commercial hub of Nigeria and the former political and administrative capital of the country. Lagos is located at the tip of southwestern Nigeria, and it is the only megacity in the country with a total population of approximately twenty million inhabitants. The city has encroached into its neighboring states of Ogun and Oyo with its inhabitants commuting daily from both states to the city of Lagos to work or for business. Lagos, locally known as Eko, is a beehive of commercial, economic, and political activities. As the former capital of Nigeria, most of the social life still revolves around politics, economics, and social life. The Eko for show syndrome is one of the most enduring urban lifestyles in the country with the hustle and bustle of daily life as well as its nightlife.

Abuja is Nigeria's political and administrative capital, which took over from Lagos on December 12, 1991, after the botched Gideon Okar coup in that year. Abuja is one of the fastest-growing cities in the world with an estimated 34 percent growth rate annually. The metropolitan area of Abuja is estimated to be over six million persons making it the second most populous metro in the country after Lagos. Because of its centrality in Nigeria, it serves as a melting pot of cultures and ethnicities and home to a growing number of immigrants, especially from the neighboring West African region. Since assuming the official position as Nigeria's capital, the city has been undergoing a rapid pace of physical development. Thus, one of the driving economic forces of the city is real estate, which provides substantial revenue for the city as well as employment for the growing population. The city is serviced by a well-developed transport system that combines a road network and an airport that has both international and domestic terminals. The highways also connect the city to neighboring states such as Niger, Nasarawa, Plateau, Benue, and Kogi. Abuja city is under the administration of the Abuja Municipal Area Council while the Federal Capital Territory Administration is responsible for the Federal Capital Territory. The FCT is headed by a Minister who appoints members to the Abuja Metropolitan Management Council. The core of the city is the Central Business District, which houses the administrative offices of the executive, legislative, and judicial arms of the federal government. Most multinational corporations also have their offices in this district. Other important sites in this district include Eagle Square where presidential inauguration ceremonies take place, the Ministry of Defence Headquarters, and the Nigerian cultural center complex. Another important district is Asokoro District, which is home to Aso Rock, the seat of the Federal Government. The district is also home to federal cabinet ministers and the diplomatic community. Maitama District is a high-brow commercial area. Abuja is dotted with parks which residents use as relaxation spots. There are also informal spaces (known also as bush bars) where local foods, snacks, and drinks are sold.

Port Harcourt is the capital of Rivers state and its largest city. It is in the Niger Delta region, and home to the Ikwerre and Okrika people among other groups. Before becoming an important port for the British colonial administration, the area was an important commercial center for the sale of marine products and farm crops among the locals within the region. The discovery of coal in Enugu in the Southeast by the British in the early twentieth century, led to the construction, in 1912, of a rail line connecting Enugu with the coastal city of Port Harcourt for the export of coal to Britain. The city would assume a much more buoyant status after crude oil was discovered in commercial quantity in 1956 leading to the rapid development of the city to accommodate the influx of migrants from within and outside the country. Today, the population of the city is estimated to be over two million making it one of the most densely populated cities in the country.

Popular residential areas in the city include the government residential area (popularly called GRA), D-Line, Elelenwo, Rumuola, Rumuokoro, and Woji among other places. The best-known industrial area is in Trans Amadi. Port Harcourt is regarded as the oil capital of the country, and it is home to multinational oil companies including Royal Dutch Shell and Chevron as well as two Nigerian refineries. However, the oil exploration in the region has caused great environmental concerns including oil spillage, water and soil pollution, and the endangerment of aquatic lives. Apart from the environmental issues Port Harcourt is a boisterous city and a beehive of social activities. Nightlife is usually vibrant with numerous night clubs, cinemas, restaurants, and brothels, which service the large population.

Kano city is an ancient commercial city dating back to the fifteenth century as the commercial hub for the sale of hides and skins, dye, and cash crops such as groundnut. Today, the ancient city is inhabited by the local Hausa population while the modern city (Sabon Gari) is home to non-locals, mostly internal migrants from other states, especially from the southern part of the country. Kano city has an estimated population of over four million inhabitants making it the second largest city in Nigeria by population next to Lagos. Sabon Gari is occupied predominantly by ethnic groups such as the Igbo, Yoruba, and Edo from the southern part of the country as well as foreign nationals mainly those from Niger, Chad, Mali, India, Lebanon, and Pakistan. The city is well planned with a good road network and drainage system. The city's industrial estates are in Sharada.

See Also: Middle Class (Chapter 6); Poverty (Chapter 4); Urban Poor (Chapter 6); Urbanization and its Impact (Chapter 1).

Further Reading

Mabogunje, A. L. (1990). *Cities for all the Challenges for Nigeria*. Abuja: Federal Ministry of Works and Housing.

Statista. Largest cities in Nigeria in 2022. https://www.statista.com/statistics/1121444/largest-cities-in-nigeria/

NATURAL RESOURCES

Nigeria has abundant natural resources both renewable and non-renewable. By far the most common and abundant natural resources even though often overlooked are solar, water, and wind of which Nigeria has a quantum supply although their potentials have not yet been fully harnessed for development purposes. While water sources have been exploited by local peoples from time immemorial for agricultural activities and for local consumption, the resource has also been harnessed to power the country's hydroelectric dams for the supply of electricity. The major hydroelectric dams are in Niger state (the Shiroro and Kainji dams) and Kwara State (the Jebba dam). Next to the renewable resources are the non-renewable resources that have been intensely exploited over the past one hundred years. They include coal, tin, columbite, iron, and a host of others. Coal is found in large deposits in Enugu and its environs, the Benin-Ondo axis, and the Lafia-Obi region in the Southwest with a total estimated deposit of 123 million metric tonnes. Coal was first mined in large quantities by the British colonial government in 1915 and was exported to Britain for its industrial growth. By the late 1950s, coal began to lose its place in production with the discovery of oil in 1956 and the industrial shift to more reliance on crude oil products. From the late 1950s onward, the most intensely exploited natural resource in Nigeria has been crude oil. Nigeria is the tenth country in the world with the largest crude oil deposit estimated to be over 37 billion barrels. However, with the rate of exploitation, it is estimated that Nigeria's crude may become exhausted by 2075, while natural gas will still be sustainable until 2150. Nigeria's oil and gas represent the main source of revenue for the country accounting for 80 percent of its total national revenue and contributing about 10 percent to its gross domestic product (GDP). Nigeria has a total natural gas deposit of 600 trillion cubic feet, placing the country as the third worldwide with this natural resource. Both crude oil and natural gas are primarily deposited in the Niger Delta states of Edo, Delta, Cross Rivers, Ebonyi, Ondo, Bayelsa, and Abia, which make up the oil-producing states in the country. Some deposits have, however, been reported in some northern states such as Gombe, Gongola, and Bauchi states. In February 2019, President Buhari flagged off the spud-in ceremony at the Kolmani River II Well, and on November 22, 2022, he witnessed the validation phase of the first integrated Oil Development Project in the northern part of the country. Nigeria is also rich in mineral deposits including gold, turquoise, aluminium, and bitumen. Bitumen, exploited for road construction, is found in large quantities in central Nigeria with an estimated deposit of about forty-two billion tonnes. Importantly, too, are the deposits of iron ore and tin which have been exploited for centuries by local people, especially in the Jos region of central Nigeria where archaeological findings suggest that the local people that were responsible for the Nok civilization had a great knowledge of the minerals and had extracted them for various uses including the production of iron tools for farming and weapons for hunting and protection. For development purposes, limestone, which occurs in various parts of the country, including Igbeti and Ibadan, is exploited to produce cement and for use in the steel industry located in Delta State (Delta steel complex) and in Kwara State (Ajaokuta steel rolling mill).

See Also: Exports (Chapter 4); Mining Sector (Chapter 4); Oil and Gas Sector (Chapter 4).

Further Reading

Embassy of Nigeria in the Netherlands Website. (2022). "Nigerian States and their Natural Resources." https://nigerianembassythehague.nl/about-nigeria/natural-resources/

Headquarters Abuja. "Nigeria Natural Resources." https://foreignaffairs.gov.ng/nigeria/natural-resources/

NIGER DELTA

Nigeria's Niger Delta is one of the largest deltas in the world with an area of about 70,000 square kilometers. It is found in the southernmost part of the country made up of nine states namely, Abia, Akwa Ibom, Bayelsa, Cross River, Delta, Edo, Imo, Ondo, and Rivers. All these states are officially recognized as oil producing except Cross River state. The

Niger Delta region covers an approximate land area of 70,000 square kilometers (27,000 square miles) constituting about 8 percent of the total mass of the country. The region may be divided into three broad areas, namely, the Western Niger Delta, the Central Niger Delta, and the Eastern Niger Delta. The Western Niger Delta, which is made up of diverse cultural and ethnic groups, comprises Delta, Edo, and Ondo states. The major ethnic groups of this region are the Ijaws (Ijo, Izon), Isoko, Itsekiri, and the Urhobo, all in Delta State, while the Afenmai, Auchi, Bini, Esan, and Igarra occupy most parts of Edo State, and in Ondo State the primary people that occupy the southernmost part of the state are the Ilaje and Ijaw ethnic groups. The Central Niger Delta is the largest of the three and like the Western Niger Delta, is home to diverse cultural and ethnic groups. Among them are the Abua, Brass, Ikwerre, Kalabari, Okrika, Ogoni, and the Ekpeye and Ndoki tribes of Rivers State. Other tribal groups that make up this region are the various Igbo groups that make up Abia and Imo states. The third region, the Eastern Niger Delta is the smallest region, and it is made up of Cross River and Akwa Ibom states that are populated by the Ugep, Afang, Ibibio, and Efik ethnic groups. All the inhabitants of the Niger Delta are traditionally farmers and fishermen, but these sources of livelihood have been strained due to oil exploration and extraction resulting in oil spillages that cause great damage to farmlands and water bodies and all the land and marine lives. The Niger Delta is rich in crude oil with an estimated deposit of thirty-seven billion barrels locked up in the region. This natural resource makes Nigeria the leading oil producer on the African continent and the eighth largest producer in the world with a daily extraction of two million barrels. Crude oil was first discovered in Oloibiri, a quiet town in Rivers State in 1956. Two years later the first shipment of crude oil out of the country was celebrated by the Royal Dutch Shell Company. Since then, and especially from the 1970s after the Nigerian civil war, oil has become the main source of revenue to the Nigerian government contributing about 10 percent to the national GDP. The sharing of the revenue derived from the sale of crude and the lack of development of communities in the region has become a major source of conflict between local communities and the federal government as well as with the multinational oil companies that operate in the region.

See Also: Natural Resources (Chapter 1); Niger River (Chapter 1); Oil and Gas Sector (Chapter 4).

Further Reading

Alagoa, A. J. (1972). *A History of the Niger Delta: An Historical Interpretation of Ijo Oral Tradition*. Port Harcourt: Onyoma Research Publications.
Ekeh, P. P. (2007). *History of the Urhobo People of Niger Delta*. Buffalo: Urhobo Historical Society.
Niger Delta Swamp Forest. https://www.oneearth.org/ecoregions/niger-delta-swamp-forests/

NIGER RIVER

River Niger (or The Niger River) is the third longest river in Africa next only to the Congo and Nile rivers. It is the main river in West Africa with a total length of 4,180 kilometers (2,600 miles) and a drainage basin area of 2,117,700 square kilometers. The source of the

River Niger is in the Guinea Highlands on the East of the Fouta Djallon in Southeastern Guinea. From there it runs through the Republics of Mali, Niger, Benin, and Nigeria where it tapers into an extensive maze of delta and empties itself into the Gulf of Guinea in the Atlantic Ocean. Flowing from Jebba town in Kwara State, the Niger enters its lower course as it is joined by the Kaduna River, its important tributary at that section. The Kaduna River is important to the Niger River because at that point the Kaduna River provides about one-quarter of the River Niger's annual discharge just below the Niger-Kaduna confluence. At Lokoja in Kogi State, the Niger turns southward, and it is joined by its main tributary, the Benue River, which joins the Niger River and forms a Y-shape with the tail extending toward the southernmost part of the country's Niger Delta. At the Niger-Benue confluence, the Niger River is about a kilometer wide and the Benue slightly wider. Together, they form a lake-like stretch of water about 3 kilometers wide characterized by isolated islands and sandbanks. From Lokoja the river flows steadily southward to Idah in Benue state and then to Onitsha in Abia State. Onitsha serves as the river's largest settlement in Nigeria and the third largest riverine town after Bamako in Mali and Niamey in Niger Republic. At Aboh in Delta State the river starts to splinter into many branches before reaching the Gulf of Guinea and empties itself into the Atlantic Ocean. Navigation along the river is seasonal due to fluctuations that are determined by the dry and rainy seasons. The Niger River begins its annual flood between September and May with a peak in November each year. This seasonal flood makes the bank of the river, as well as its deltas, very fertile for agriculture and fishing. This partly explains why those who settle at the banks of the river such as the Nupe, Igbos, and Ijaws, are great farmers and fishermen. The Niger River is a major resource for the country especially in the production of hydropower. Jebba town is home to one of Nigeria's three major dams that provides electricity to the national grid. The dam generates 578.4 megawatts of electricity to the nation. The river also provides seafood such as fish, shrimps, crabs, and other such foods which serve as a major source of protein to the people that settle along the river's bank, and by extension to Nigerians in general. The river also provides jobs to those who occupy its bank such as fishing, canoe production, net production, and mending, as well as commercial trading along the bank of the river.

See Also: Benue River (Chapter 1); Niger Delta (Chapter 1); Transportation and Waterways (Chapter 1).

Further Reading

Gibbal, J. (1993). *Genii of the River Niger*. Chicago: University of Chicago Press.

POPULATION

Nigeria's population has grown exponentially from 17 million in 1921 to over 200 million in 2022. The exact figure of the country's population is a matter of great debate and conjecture as most of the country's censuses have been fraught with malpractices, inflation of ethnic groups' numbers for economic and political reasons while the total number of immigrants, especially from its neighboring countries has not been well documented due to the country's accommodation of people's free movements in the West African sub-region in line with its policy on the free movement of people across borders. However, estimates by the World Bank, the United Nations, World barometer, and the federal government itself place the country's population between 200 million and 220 million. Undoubtedly, the country is the most populous in Africa and the sixth largest in the world. It is further estimated that one in every four Black persons in the world is a Nigerian. With a fertility rate at 5.417 per woman and a population growth rate at 2.6 percent, Nigeria will become the third largest country in the world next only to India and China by 2050, especially if we also consider the fact that the female population is roughly half of the total population with a reproductive population (that is, women who are in the fifteen to forty-nine years' age bracket) of 43 percent.

In terms of distribution, the country has a youthful population with children below fifteen years of age constituting about 46 percent while those who are sixty-five years and older make up just 3 percent of the total population and those who are between fifteen and sixty-four years make up 51 percent of the total population. One key implication for this age distribution is the high dependency ratio of the population to the workforce. Theoretically, one Nigerian worker is responsible for the upkeep of one Nigerian dependant. In practice, however, because of high unemployment (estimated at 40 percent), low access to education and the acquisition of skills, and low earnings of the working class, economic growth is hampered and the quality of life of the average Nigerian is severely compromised. It is not surprising, therefore, that Nigeria's life expectancy is low at fifty-six years, with women having a slightly higher life expectancy rate at fifty-seven years than their male counterpart at fifty-five years. Infant mortality (i.e., the number of deaths among children below twelve months) is fifty-four per one thousand births; child mortality (death among children between one and five years) is ninety per one thousand; and maternal mortality (that is the death rate of mothers who give birth) is 576 per 100,000. Nigeria has a population density of 221 people per square kilometer (571 people per square mile), but this is not evenly distributed across the country. For example, while the five eastern states and Lagos state are the most densely populated with an average population density of 286 people per square kilometer, the northern states are more sparsely populated with an average population density of 206 people per square kilometer, while most states in the middle belt and those in the Niger Delta are moderately populated with an average density of 216 people per square kilometer.

Approximately, 49 percent of the population live in rural areas while the remaining live in urban and semi-urban areas. The most populous city in Nigeria is Lagos with an estimated population of twenty million people as estimated by the state government although the controversial census figure gives a total population of the state as slightly less than ten million. Kano State, which is in the northern part of the country, is the second largest with an estimated population of seven million. Nigeria's annual population growth rate is estimated to be 2.5 percent.

See Also: Major Cities (Chapter 1); Urbanization and Its Impact (Chapter 1).

Further Reading

Adamu, S. O. (2000). *Population Census in Nigeria*. Ibadan: SAAL Publications.
National Population Commission. https://nationalpopulation.gov.ng/

RAINFOREST

The rainforest is one of Nigeria's two main vegetation types and it can be divided into three vegetation zones, namely, the mangrove forest, the freshwater swamp forest, and the tropical rainforest. The mangrove forest is found along the coast of the Niger Delta and covers a flat zone of about 40 kilometers. The mean annual rainfall that sustains the mangrove forest is very high, peaking at about 3,000 mm. The region is characterized by a maze of lagoons and a network of creeks which overflow their banks during the rainy season. During this period of overflow, the area is waterlogged, and the swamp waters flow as high tides, causing the sea water to flow onto the land, sometimes causing damage to farmland and property. The salty water that flows onto the land provides a harsh condition for all types of plants to grow in the area. Thus, the dominant vegetation type found in this region are the rich variety of mangrove trees. Among these varieties is the red mangrove that is famously used for pit props, while other species are used for building stilt houses and for the building of boats and canoes for fishing and transportation along the Delta creeks. These trees reach a height of between 10 meters and 15 meters and grow very close together forming a dense mass with their roots penetrating the swampy soil. Besides the mangrove trees are also found coconut trees that grow along the coastal beaches especially in Badagry in Lagos state. The freshwater swamp forest is like the mangrove forest but with a marked difference in environmental condition that restricts the tide from reaching the area. This condition provides a freshwater swamp and therefore freshwater plants dominate. The commonest vegetation type in this area is the raffia palm, valued for its sap that is tapped to produce palm wine (or *Oguro* in the local parlance). Other benefits of the raffia palm are its use for house building and in the production of handwoven cloth forms among pre-colonial Ijaw societies. The tropical rainforest is the most extensive of the forest vegetation extending across the country from the Benin area in the Midwest to the Oban Hills in Cross River State. This region, which is characterized by high rainfall of about 2,000 mm per annum and high temperature, provides the perfect conditions to sustain a dense vegetation that is dominated by a variety of tree species. This vegetation type is characterized by tree crowns that have distinctive layers (or storeys). The top storey of the tropical rainforest is made up of large trees that are over 30 meters tall with some of the trees reaching a height of up to 60 meters. Their crowns form a dense canopy that covers the floor of the forest. The trees that make up these top storeys are of great value to the people and country. Some of them include the mahogany tree, the iroko, obeche, sapele wood, and many others whose products are used for timber, furniture, and ship building. Next to the top storey, are the middle storey trees found in the tropical forest zone. The middle storey is made up of trees that grow up to 24 meters with their branches intertwining. Their crowns also form a dense canopy providing shade at the floor of the forest. There are different species of trees in this vegetation zone, and they are of economic value to those who live in the area. Due to the continuous rainfall in this area, coupled with the great variety of trees found in this region, the forest is usually evergreen as different species shed their leaves at different times of the season. At a height of about 5 meters to 12 meters the ground storey is made up of shrubs, herbs, and a variety of grasses, which form a dense tangle at the feet of the giant trees that make up this vegetation zone. The limits of sunlight at the floor of the forest influence the shrubs and grasses to grow in dense masses wherever sunlight is available. This condition also sustains parasitic plants that attach themselves to other plants and derive their nutrients from them. Other plants are the climbers, which have their roots but use other trees as support and climb their way up using the trunks and branches of other trees. Other species of trees that make up the tropical rainforest are the saprophytes and epiphytes. The former is sustained by dead plants at the foot of the forest while the latter have their roots exposed but somehow attach themselves to other trees and climb their way up with the support of other plants. Population growth, urbanization, and human activities in this vegetation zone have threatened the survival of the tropical rainforest in Nigeria. Today, the tropical forest is restricted to remote areas in the Southwest in the Idanre Hills in Ondo state, the Osun Valley in Osun State, along the Benin River in Edo State, and stretching to the Obudu Plateau in Cross Rivers State. Some of the human activities that cause the tropical rainforest to shrink include the increasing demand for land for crop cultivation, the establishment and expansion of export cash crops such as cocoa in the Southwest and palm oil and rubber in the Midwest and delta region, the expansion of settlements leading to road construction among other developments in this region.

See Also: Savannah (Chapter 1); Urbanization and its Impact (Chapter 1).

Further Reading

Environmental Issues in Nigeria. https://rainforests.mongabay.com/20nigeria.htm

SAVANNAH

The savannah is one of Nigeria's two main vegetation types. It covers over two-thirds of the country from the Southwest to the northernmost parts of the country. The savannah is characterized by grasses with intermittent scattered trees, otherwise referred to as parkland and sometimes the trees grow close together otherwise referred to as woodland. There are three main types of savannah vegetation namely, the Guinea savannah, Sudan savannah, and Sahel savannah. The first is the commonest in the country extending from Enugu in the East to Benue state in the middle belt and extending to Zaria in the North. It is found in areas where the mean annual rainfall is between 1,000 mm and 1,500 mm. The vegetation type is characterized by tall grasses and trees which vary in terms of their density. However, because the trees do not receive an abundance of rainfall throughout the year the trees shed their leaves during the dry season which lasts for between four and six months. During this period, the vegetation experiences extensive wildfires. In wetter areas where this vegetation type is found, especially along the river valleys, the vegetation is dense, and some forest vegetation (known as gallery forest) is maintained due to the moist conditions that are prevalent in the area. The major food crops produced in this vegetation zone include tubers such as yam and cassava; grains, such as rice and guinea corn. On the other hand, the Sudan savannah covers an area with an annual rainfall of between 650 mm and 1,000 mm and a dry season that extends between six and eight months. This vegetation type stretches from Sokoto and Kano in the Northwest of the country to

Borno State in the Northeast. The Sudan savannah is characterized by short grasses that are between 1.5 meters and 2 meters high with scattered trees that are much shorter than those found in the Guinea savannah. Some of the trees found in this area include acacia, baobab, and the doum palms. These trees play important social and cultural roles in the lives of people who live in these areas. They are used for medicinal and other cultural activities, but due to population growth in this area and the cultivation of a wide expanse of land by farmers, the natural vegetation of the Sudan savannah has been significantly altered and replaced with farmland and fallow land. The major crops that are produced in this vegetation zone include groundnuts, wheat, and millet. These crops are grown mostly in Kano, Sokoto, Yobe, and Borno States. The Sahel savannah is found in the uppermost part of Borno State in the northeastern part of the country where mean annual rainfall is less than 650 mm and a much longer period of dry season, usually longer than eight months. The vegetation mostly comprises short grasses with intermittent scattered trees of the acacia family. However, there are pockets of tall trees around the Lake Chad region due to the seasonal flooding of the lake that provides sufficient nutrients to support the trees. The area also supports a sizable number of cattle, sheep, and goats.

See Also: Desertification (Chapter 1); Rainforest (Chapter 1).

Further Reading

Bailey Rigina. (2022, March 28). "Savanna Biome: Climate, Locations and Wildlife." *Treehugger.* https://www.treehugger.com/land-biomes-savannas-373494

Norman, D. (1982). *Farming Systems in the Nigerian Savanna*. New York: Routledge.

TRANSPORTATION AND WATERWAYS

Nigeria has different transport systems including roads, rail, air, and waterways. The most used among citizens is road transportation. Nigeria has over 113,000 kilometers of surfaced roads with the longest stretching from Iddo in Lagos State to Maiduguri in Gongola State. The roads are divided into three categories namely, federal roads, state roads, and local government roads. The first are those that connect one state to another and are usually dualized. The state roads are made of a network of interconnecting roads to major cities and towns across each state, while local government roads are small roads that connect communities in the state and these roads may not be tarred. However, a significant portion of the roads, especially in the southeastern and south-south parts of the country are poorly maintained due to their neglect by successive governments. The road conditions have worsened especially in the eastern part of the country where gully erosion has rendered some sections impassable and, in some instances, the roads have been cut into two depriving motorists from having a smooth ride from one part of the region to the other. The difficult terrain in the Niger Delta region and the poor conditions of the roads have also been the major cause of vehicular accidents not only in the eastern part of the country but the country in general. However, the Federal Roads Maintenance Agency (FERMA) initiated a project in 2004 with a goal to patch 32,000 kilometers of federal roads across the country and the agency has, so far, repaired about 130 major roads out of the targeted 500 roads. The railroads in Nigeria were developed by the British colonial government for the primary purpose of transporting raw materials and finished goods from the hinterland to the ports from where they were shipped to Britain. For this reason, the railway system cuts across the country from Lagos to Kano. The major export product from the North to the Lagos port was tin. From Port Harcourt is a major railroad to Maiduguri with hides as the major export commodity that was transported from the North. In all, Nigeria has approximately 4,000 kilometers of narrow-gauge track. Currently, Nigeria has enlisted the support of Chinese firms to expand the rail network and modernize it by building new standard-gauge rail to link Lagos and Kano states, as well as from Abuja to Kaduna, and Lagos to Ibadan. The federal government has developed a 20-year strategic plan that will lead to the construction of 8,000 kilometers of standard rail lines that will link the northern part of the country to the southern part. Nigeria has eighteen airports both international and local. The three major internal airports are the Murtala Muhammed International Airport in Lagos in the South, the Nnamdi Azikiwe International Airport in Abuja, the Federal Capital Territory, and the Mallam Aminu International Airport in Kano, in the North. Other domestic airports serve the purpose of providing fast but expensive transportation for businessmen and women as well other private citizens who can afford the high fares. Nigeria's inland waterways are approximately 8,600 kilometers with the Niger and Benue rivers being the most important. The riverine areas of the Niger Delta, including those of Ondo and Lagos states, provide transportation to local dwellers and a source of fishing to several inhabitants along the coast. Among these groups are the Ilaje and the Urhobos in Ondo State, and the Ijaw in the Niger Delta. Other uses of the rivers include hydroelectric power generation, irrigation, and domestic supply. The Nigerian Ports Authority (NPA) is the official organ of the government that manages the ports. The port at Lagos is the busiest in the country handling over two-thirds of the country's non-oil trade in its twin facilities at Apapa and Tin Can Island. The second busiest seaport is the Delta Port Complex with facilities in Burutu and Port Harcourt. This port is the main petroleum outlet in the country.

See Also: Benue River (Chapter 1); Major Cities (Chapter 1); Niger River (Chapter 1).

Further Reading

Emmanuel, O. A., P. I. Ifabiyi, and A. U. Chijioke (2018). "Opportunities and Challenges of Inland Waterways Transport in the Southwest Coastal Belt of Nigeria." *Bhúmi, The Planning Research Journal*, 6(1): 10–17.
National Inland Waterways Authority. (2023). https://niwa.gov.ng/

URBANIZATION AND ITS IMPACT

Urbanization, the process of a settlement area becoming densely populated and having specialization in economic and social activities, predates colonial rule and the coming of the first Europeans to modern Nigeria in the fifteenth century. Some of the well-known pre-colonial urban centers were established as early as the fourth century CE. These settlements include the Nok civilization in modern-day central Nigeria, the Benin Empire established by the Bini ethnic group in modern-day Edo State, the Igbo-Ukwu civilization of southeastern Nigeria, the Old Ife kingdom in southwestern Nigeria, and the Kanem-Bornu Empire in the North among other notable empires and kingdoms. These kingdoms were ruled by heads of state variously known as Oba, Obi, Alaafin, Ubandoma, and Emirs. During this pre-colonial period, women also ruled as paramount kings among their people, one of the most popularly known being Queen Amina of Zaria, who was the paramount ruler and Commander-in-Chief of the army. The establishment of colonial rule and the introduction of Western political and economic practices partly led to the demise of these traditional urban centers, which gave rise to post-colonial cities and towns that are today scattered all over the country. The development and proliferation of modern urban centers in Nigeria was facilitated by the building and distribution of modern road and rail networks that connected the North to the South and from the Niger Delta to the Southeast and to the Northeast. This transportation network was established to transport cash crops such as cocoa and minerals such as tin. These economic activities led to the concentration of workers and other allied persons at strategic foci along the railway stations. Thus, among the earliest towns that were established were those along the railway lines such as Enugu, Kafanchan, Makurdi, and Nguru. Second, administrative towns were established due to colonial offices that were set up in some areas. Some of the earliest colonial administrative towns include Enugu, Ibadan, Calabar, Kaduna, and Lagos. The production and exportation of natural resources like coal and tin also led to the growth of new towns such as Aba, Bukuru, and Jos. As new towns and cities were being formed, due to economic activities introduced by the colonial government, pre-colonial towns were declining because of the pull factors of the new emerging cities that attracted populations in the old towns to migrate to the new emerging towns. Some such towns included Benin City, Ede, Ile-Ife, Oyo, Katsina, Yola, and Maiduguri, among others. However, settlements that effectively combined the key functions of political administration, commercial activities, education services, and residential housing became the major cities in modern Nigeria. These major cities include Lagos, Abuja, Port Harcourt, Kano, Enugu, and Ibadan, among others. By the early twenty-first century, Lagos has earned the status of a mega city with a population of over twenty million and its complex beehive of social, cultural, political, and economic activities that dominate other cities in the country. Although Nigeria has witnessed an upsurge of urbanization, only about 52 percent of Nigerians live in urban centers, with the majority still living in rural areas. The concentration of people in major urban centers such as Lagos, Port Harcourt, Aba, and Kano also means that infrastructures in these areas are overstretched while overcrowding creates endemic social problems such as sanitation issues and crime.

See Also: Major Cities (Chapter 1); Middle Class (Chapter 4); Transportation and Waterways (Chapter 1); Urban Poor (Chapter 4).

Further Reading

Mabogunje, A. (1968). *Urbanization in Nigeria*. London: University of London Press.
Urbanet. (2018). "Urbanisation in Nigeria – Infographics." https://www.urbanet.info/urbanization-in-nigeria-infographics/

CHAPTER 2

History

OVERVIEW

The piecing together of modern Nigeria is based on archaeological excavations and studies which shed light on human occupation, movements, and material cultures. Archaeological professor, Thurstan Shaw, believes that human occupation in what is known today as modern Nigeria, goes back to 100,000 years ago during the Late Stone Age. This period, however, witnessed a lot of migration with settlements springing up in hilly locations, rocky shelters, and more open spaces like lowlands near major water bodies. It is believed that these movements were mainly from northern to southern areas of now modern-day Nigeria caused by the drying up of the Sahara region which caused drastic ecological changes. These constant group movements also contributed to the development of many of the language groups and cultural traits we have today.

These bands of migrating peoples seemed to have more control over their environment than their ancestors some 5,000 years before and thus it was not surprising to see a shift from hunting gathering to more settled societies. Within these settlements, the people grew their own food, reared animals, and produced agricultural and hunting tools as well as weapons for defense. In the rainforest and savannah regions, yam and palm oil were the major crops grown; while in the northern or Sahel region, cereals such as African Rice, sorghum, and millet were the major agricultural staple. In terms of animal rearing, it is believed that animals like goats, sheep, and cattle were reared while horse domestication was prevalent in the northern region of the country.

The northern region of Nigeria was believed to have been made up of sparsely populated societies. However, the people were able to develop technologies to travel the major river body which today is known as Komadugu Gana. Evidence of this technology comes in the form of an 8,000-year-old dugout canoe discovered in 1987 a few kilometers from the village of Funa close the Komadugu Gana river, which flows in present-day Yobe State.

The Need for More Research and Education

The prehistory of Nigeria has been well documented in some instances, but it still faces enormous challenges in terms of research work to uncover most parts of the varied cultural history of the peoples that make up the country. The need for the government to support prehistoric studies has been echoed by archaeologists, anthropologists, linguists, and scholars of African studies, but these calls have not received the attention they deserve. The same is true of Nigeria's colonial history and the post-colonial era, especially with regard to the multiple factors that led to the civil war and the lessons to be gained from it to further peace and unity in the country. The exclusion of Nigerian history in the syllabus of high schools has stripped citizens of their knowledge of the past and limits their ability to forge common national values that everyone will subscribe to and acknowledge—that they are Nigerians before any other ethnic or religious identity.

The canoe which was named "Dufuna canoe" is, so far, the oldest boat in Africa, and the second oldest worldwide. The area eventually became well developed in terms of economies founded on agriculture and pastoralism. It was from these settlements that the Kanem-Bornu Empire emerged.

In central Nigeria, evidence abounds which indicates an early invention of iron technology established as early as 700 BCE, making these areas the earliest dates for iron smelting and iron production in Africa. Peoples of the region were able to locally source, mine, and refine copper, lead, tin, and zinc. A major location where evidence of iron smelting furnaces was found was in a town known as Taruga on the Jos Plateau in North-central Nigeria. There, the artifacts which today are classified as the "Nok Culture" were discovered. The Nok culture is characterized by life-size terracotta figures that include human heads, human figures, and animals. The Nok people are thought to have begun smelting iron by 600 to 500 BCE and possibly some centuries earlier. The Nok people were agriculturalists who produced iron and stone tools to cultivate agricultural crops. Evidence of iron smelting in other areas of central Nigeria include Benue, Bauchi, and Niger (excavations at Kainji Dam revealed ironworking that dates to the second century BCE).

Evidence of iron smelting technology was also discovered in the southeastern region of Nigeria. There, one of the earliest copper working and bronze casting sites was discovered at Igbo-Ukwu a town southeast of present-day Onitsha. This site dates to the ninth century CE with artifacts made from copper alloy using a technique known as *cire-perdue* (the lost-wax method). The artifacts are believed to be associated with the *Eze-Nri* political institution common among the present-day Igbo people. Based on the artifacts, it is believed that the people of the area were great craftsmen, had specialized symbols of wealth, and yielded much political power.

Similarly, in the southwestern region was evidence of bronze sculpture production at Ife and Benin going as far back as the early fourteenth century CE. The artifacts also confirm the rise and flourishing of complex and technologically advanced societies representing present-day Yoruba and Benin Kingdoms. These kingdoms represented pre-colonial urbanization which included the development of political systems, economic sustainability strategies, housing structures, trade relations, food, art, and knowledge production. Major kingdoms of note in modern Nigeria's pre-colonial history include the Hausa, Kanem-Bornu, Borgu, Nupe, Tiv, Yoruba, Benin, Igbo, Calabar, and Ijaw.

British Occupation of the Niger Area

One of the earliest European accounts of present-day Nigeria was in 1472 when Portuguese explorers headed by Ruy de Sequeira arrived in Benin during the reign of Oba Ewuare. However, it was not until 1486, based on an invitation by the reigning Oba Ozolua, that a team of explorers headed by Joao Aveiro could make the journey from the coast to the Benin Empire. Joao Aveiro was able to convince the Benin king to allow Portuguese Christian missionaries to begin a church mission in his kingdom. The trade relations between Benin and Portugal were so good that, in 1514, Oba Esigie sent an ambassador to Portugal and the following year Portugal sent Christian missionaries to strengthen the drive of developing churches and schools. Through these efforts the king's son and other high chiefs were not only baptized but also taught how to read and write Portuguese. Some scholars even suggest that in 1600, the Itsekiri people, neighbors of the Benin people, also sent their people to Portugal to be educated. Scholars opine that the major objective of West African kings and chiefs for sending their sons to Europe was to better understand the "White" man's technology, science, philosophy, and culture to enhance their understanding of the European merchants they traded with. Through these trading relations, crops currently regarded as a staple in many West African dishes were introduced. These include crops such as maize, cassava, tomatoes, cocoyam, and rice which the Portuguese brought from the Americas in exchange for Benin brass and copper art, gold, ivory, and pepper. Soon the West African peoples of the shores would begin to exchange slaves for these crops, firearms, and luxury goods (e.g., cloth, household utensils, etc.) manufactured in Europe.

However, scholars believe that as early as 1441, Portuguese traders had been kidnapping natives along the Senegambia coasts and exporting them to Europe as domestic slaves. Later, the discovery of the West Indies and the development of sugar, tobacco, and cotton plantations in the Americas made the slave trade a very lucrative business first for Portugal but later to the Spanish, French, Dutch, and the British. Slaves became of high demand as cheap labor to work on these plantations.

Between 1450 and 1807 the Trans-Atlantic Slave Trade thrived making Europe and its investors very wealthy indeed. This slave trade, however, was the fourth and shortest in duration of three previous African slave trades namely: Trans-Saharan—from the Sahara Desert to Northern Africa; Red Sea—from surrounding areas of the Red Sea to the Middle East and India; and Indian Ocean—from Eastern Africa to the Middle East, India, or plantation islands located in the Indian Ocean. The Trans-Atlantic Slave Trade which lasted between the fifteenth and eighteenth centuries resulted in the deportation and enslavement of more than twelve million Africans. Many community leaders of pre-colonial Nigeria exchanged slaves mainly to gain access to European weapons which they used to raid other communities and defend themselves from similar raids.

Seeing the potential profit that could be made from the slave trade, King Charles II of England issued the Royal Charter of January 10, 1663. The charter granted the Company of the Royal Adventurers of England Trading, exclusive monopoly to the trade goods produced in Britain for slaves and to search for gold on the West African coast in the interest of Britain. In 1672, King Charles and his brother James, Duke of York, established their own slaving company which they called the Royal African Company leading to the decline of the Royal Adventurers.

By 1807, Britain no longer viewed the slave trade as profitable and wished to divert to the purchase of palm oil. In addition, the rise of slave revolts, the American Civil War, calls for the end of slavery, and the growing industrial revolution made Britain consider diverting their economic activities to other areas. The British Parliament thus voted for the abolition of the slave trade. To initiate this, the 1841 Niger Expedition was organized as a journey supported by the British Crown and its government as well as members of British missionary societies. Their aim—to persuade African slave traders to stop the trade and embrace commercial farming for export to Britain. Among the expedition crew were officials empowered to make anti-slavery trade treaties with the natives in the interest of the British Crown. Also, among the crew was Ajayi Crowther (a freed slave) who represented the Church Missionary Society (CMS) and served as an interpreter. However, the expedition was deemed a failure because many of the European crew members died of fever while the main objective was not achieved. Many natives at the seaports were reluctant to stop the slave trade and replace it with agricultural commercial activities because they felt the slave trade was more profitable. In addition, the natives were afraid that stopping the trade would leave them defenseless and open to attack from neighbors who still practiced the trade through other European slave dealers. At the end, the surviving members of the expedition recommended that the only way Britain could stop the slave trade in West Africa was through naval and military force.

With the aid of freed slaves from Sierra Leone and Brazil, church missionaries began penetrating the hinterland. In 1846, The CMS established a mission in Abeokuta through the assistance of Ajayi Crowther, while the Presbyterian Church established a site in Calabar. Politically, the British government set about getting community leaders at the shores to sign treaties of protection. Through these treaties, the British assured the rulers that they would protect them against possible neighboring invasions from slave raiders and thus bring peace to these areas.

In 1849, John Beecroft was appointed by the British as the first Consul at the Bight of Biafra and Benin. Beecroft represented the British interest, and his main job was to ensure that the traditional rulers signed these treaties of protection. In addition to giving protection to indigenous communities through British military might, these treaties also gave the British access to the hinterland of the Niger-Benue and Delta areas and allowed European trading companies to operate in these territories. Through Beecroft, trade between British merchants and African traders was regulated thus making this the first direct political influence of the British in what would later become Nigeria.

In 1850 and 1856, The Court of Equity was established in Bonny and Calabar, respectively, with the aim of settling disputes between British cargo owners and local traders of the Delta region. The British made John Beecroft the chairman of these courts. However, the courts were always in favor of the British firms and cargo owners with little powers given to the local traders and their rulers. This meant that the locals could not make decisions as to the sales and profits of their goods. Through these courts, the British controlled not only the waterways through which goods were traded in the Niger Delta regions but also the political affairs of the people by exiling rulers who refused to cooperate and installing ones who did. Between the 1860s and 1870s the British were in political and economic control of the Niger-Benue and Delta areas. In 1891, the British established the Oil Rivers Protectorate with its headquarters in Calabar and, by 1893, the region formally became known as the Niger Coast Protectorate.

The British invasion met with resistance from major indigenous traders of the Delta region. Prominent were Jaja of Opobo and Nana Olomu of Itsekiri. In 1869, Jubo Jubogha (renamed Jaja by the British) established a settlement to be known as Opobo which, in 1873, was formally recognized in Europe. As the self-declared king of Opobo, Jaja took advantage of French and German interests in the Niger oil trade. From Opobo, he was able to gain a monopoly of the palm oil trade, often making the independent British intermediaries redundant by shipping the oil straight to Liverpool. This however caused his fall-out with British businesspeople whose profit had been significantly slashed. Jaja taxed British businesspeople who wanted to trade in oil until 1887 when he was arrested. Jaja was exiled and transported to various countries until he ended up in the West Indies where he was celebrated as a gallant hero, a symbol of African bravery and freedom. In 1889, Jaja was granted permission to return home, but he never reached Opobo as it is believed that he was poisoned by the British en route. He was buried in Tenerife in the Canary Islands, but his body was later returned to Opobo and is now in a sacred shrine behind the palace of the *Amanyanabo* of Opobo.

Likewise, Nana Olomu was a wealthy Itsekiri trader who through his wealth was able to build a formidable military army. Like Jaja, he took control of the palm oil trade and developed a capital at Ebrohimi. His control over the trade was so strong that, in between 1886 and 1887, he was able to freeze the price of palm oil by 40 percent until European merchants agreed to trade within the terms of local producers and suppliers. He was able to continually outwit the British merchants at their own game by ensuring that all treaties were void of clauses that allowed British traders free access to trade within his kingdom. Eventually, the British traders felt the need to curb Nana's powers and a request for an expedition was sent to England. Nana was accused of engaging in the slave trade, human sacrifice, and turning the Urhobo people against the British. In 1894, Ebrohimi was attacked by British forces, however, Nana was able to repel the British who suffered immense casualties. Eventually Ebrohimi fell due to betrayals by local rivals who helped the British with logistics and intelligence reports. Nana was eventually captured and exiled to Ghana.

In 1879, George Taubman Goldie formed the United Africa Company (which in 1881 became the National African Company) through an amalgamation of smaller British firms which operated in the Niger Delta region. Two years later, he renamed his company the National African Company and bought off French companies operating in the region thereby making Britain the major European force. Goldie drew up more than 400 political treaties with the rulers of the lower Niger and some Hausa Emirs assuring them of British protection in exchange for their allegiance. Goldie's role in securing modern-day Nigeria for Britain was especially important in the wake of the 1885 Berlin Act which saw Europe's scramble for Africa. In 1886, Goldie obtained a Royal Charter for the National Africa Company and renamed it the Royal Niger Company. Goldie's company became a major force in the Delta region subduing the local rulers under its authority and forming a governance which enforced British law and order. Goldie's enterprise was significant in aiding Britain's ability to secure not only the South-south region of Nigeria, but also the southeastern and Niger-Benue region.

In the southeastern region, the British met with stiff resistance from the fierce Arochukwu tribe who for centuries had dominated the slave trade in the region. Scholars believe that they had orchestrated the sale of over four million Igbo men and women through raids and kidnappings. It is believed that they were highly feared not only because of their war tactics but also because of strong spiritual powers which they used to maintain their position and monopoly as slave raiders for centuries. The Arochukwu people were not ready to give up their main source of wealth and thus put up stiff resistance against British calls to end the slave trade. In 1902, the British military with support from the Royal Niger Company captured Arochukwu and destroyed their spiritual shrines. Their priests were executed, signalling an end to Arochukwu's reign of terror. This enabled the British and Goldie the opportunity to secure the region. After this success, the British went on to execute several other punitive attacks in Southeast Nigeria resulting in resistance such as the Ekumeku Movement of the Anioma people against Royal Niger Company and later colonial rule from 1883 to 1914.

Meanwhile, in present-day Lagos, its seaport was a thriving center for the slave trade due to the influence of King Kosoko. King Kosoko had come to power by overthrowing and exiling Prince Akitoye, the rightful king, to Badagry in 1845. With Akitoye exiled, Kosoko made Lagos the biggest slave port in the West African region, and this made him very popular among powerful slave trade merchants within Lagos as well as European slave dealers. After numerous warnings to desist from the act, the British attacked Lagos in June and November of 1851. However, Kosoko, through the leadership of his army head, General Oshodi Tapa, won the battles. The British reinforced and attacked a month later with more powerful weapons including cannon (which the Yorubas gave the name *Agidingbi* because of the loud noise they made). On December 26, 1851, after a five-day bloody battle, Lagos fell. Kosoko fled Lagos which originally boasted around 22,000 inhabitants but was now left with around 5,000 inhabitants consisting mainly of the elderly and children. On January 1, 1852, Akitoye was reinstated upon which he signed a treaty with the British which banned all slaving activities in Lagos. In 1861, Consul John Beecroft, the British representative signed a treaty with Akitoye's son, Dosumu. This treaty annexed the Lagos seaport to the British and prevented the sale of slaves from the hinterland to the Lagos seaport. With this treaty, Lagos became a British Colony.

The British then turned their attention to the Ekiti *Parapo* War which had been raging for over fifteen years between Ibadan forces and the allied forces of Ekiti, Ijesa, Egba, Ijebu, and Ife. These wars were an aftermath of the fall of the Oyo Empire thirty years earlier in 1833. The Yoruba warring chiefs welcomed the British as peacemakers in ending the war by signing treaties in 1886. Part of these treaties included conditions that all signatories must direct future disputes to the British governor resident in Lagos. When, in 1891, the

Ijebu ruler refused to obey this order, the British forcibly occupied the area after four days of fighting. With this defeat, the other Yoruba leaders signed away their sovereignty in 1893 and came under the Protectorate of Lagos. This became the first hinterland occupation of the British which, before then, had been limited to the coastal shores.

By 1897, Benin represented the last major stronghold in southern Nigeria to fall under British rule. That year, the British military forces invaded Benin, burned it down, killed several of its inhabitants, and looted the palace of its treasures. The reigning king at the time, Oba Ovonramwen, was captured and exiled to Calabar where he eventually died in 1914.

In northern Nigeria, two major empires dominated the region, namely the Sokoto and the Bornu empires. However, the powers of the Sokoto Caliphate, created after the Usman Dan Fodio's Jihad, had started to wane. In 1885, the Sultan of the Sokoto Caliphate signed a treaty with the National African Company, thus giving the company political and commercial domination over the Sokoto territory which spanned the banks of the Benue River and the Middle Niger River areas. Britain was also able to secure a section of the Borgu Empire which had been a source of tension between France and Britain. However, the Emir of Nupe remained resilient and their slave raids became a major issue for the Royal Niger Company in their ambition to establish peace in order to obtain a commercial foothold in the region. It was believed that the Emir had an army of about 30,000 which was formidable against the 1,000-standing army of the Royal Niger Company. It took the intervention of the British military special unit known as the West African Frontier Force to crush the Nupe forces in 1897. At the fall of Lokoja, the Nupe Emir fled and the heir to the throne accepted the terms of the Company. From there, the Emir of Ilorin was also subdued and signed treaties with the Company.

In December of 1889, Colonel Lugard took over the administration of the Royal Niger Company as the final stage of revoking the Royal Niger Charter. On January 1, 1900, the British flag was hoisted in Lokoja signalling British government control over the northern region with Colonel Lugard as its new High Commissioner. The new commissioner took over the political expansion of British interests while the Royal Niger Company focused on matters relating to the company's trade and economic advancements.

Under the leadership of Fredrick Lugard, the British took over the issue of the Emirs of Yola and Bauchi. Even though the emirs were under the authority of the Sokoto territory, they refused to adhere to the treaty and continued with their slave raids. It was not until 1901 that the British could take control of these areas. The British then turned their attention to the Emirs of Bida and Kontagora. Their slave raiding operations, as well as attacks and excessive tolls on caravans that passed through their territories, continued despite warnings from the British of dire consequences. By 1902, both Emirs had fled and were declared deposed. They were subsequently replaced with Emirs handpicked by the new British commissioner with a signed agreement to obey the laws of the Protectorate and agree that all minerals in the area belonged to the British Crown. In 1903, the British had to crush new resistance from the Sultan of Sokoto and Emirs in Kano and Zaria after which, British-appointed Emirs were installed.

The domination of the Bornu region was more complicated due to German and French interests in the area. Although British representatives had signed treaties with Bornu rulers first in 1824 and again in 1855, these treaties were vague and thus not binding. By 1890, when the Protectorate of Northern Nigeria was being created, and Bornu was included based on international agreements, Britain had neither occupied nor secured a treaty with the Bornu rulers. In 1897, after a series of expeditions carried out by the French in Bornu areas close to the British borders, the British felt the need to make their territorial ownership known by occupying Bornu. Unfortunately, Britain could not fulfill this ambition due to limited military forces at the time. However, when the French-ousted ruler appealed to the British for protection against the French army, it set off a series of activities which led to tensions between France, Germany, and Britain for the Bornu area. In addition to these tensions, were collaborative resistance from ousted Fulani Emirs and leaders from the now disintegrating Kanem-Bornu Empire. It was not until 1903 that the British were able to quell all northern resistance and claim occupancy of northern Nigeria under the leadership of Colonel Lugard.

With the successful occupation of northern Nigeria, the now Lord Lugard appointed former military officers within the West African Frontier Force to serve as Residents. He considered such personnel as valuable in the consolidation of Britain's colonial hold of the provinces. He argued that as soldiers they had been exposed to, and thus gained knowledge of, the people and the country during their various military expeditions. The Residents were given political powers over their assigned provinces, while the Emirs and native chiefs were to report to them. The appointed Residents depended on these traditional rulers to advise them on matters relating to indigenous cultures and customs. Lugard ensured that the political system of Fulani rule was retained as he supported the British belief that the Fulani ethnic group was more intelligent than the other "pagan" groups in the region; and thus, Fulani rule would be better for ensuring good governance, justice, law, and order in the area. This enabled the British to govern the region indirectly.

Although Britain had been able to politically subdue the indigenous peoples that made up the now Northern and Southern Protectorates, administration was still cumbersome and expensive. With the recommendation of the Selborne Committee Report of 1899, that the protectorate of Northern and Southern Nigeria along with Lagos be combined into a multinational state, the creation of Nigeria as one colony under British rule was initiated through two major amalgamations. In 1906, the once autonomous Colony of Lagos (with its headquarters in Lagos City) and the Protectorate of Southern Nigeria (with headquarters in Calabar) were unified and renamed the Colony and Protectorate of Southern Nigeria. At this time, the Protectorate of Northern Nigeria (with its headquarters in Kano) and Southern Protectorates were independent of each other. The second amalgamation took place in 1914 as the unification of the Southern and Northern Protectorates with Lord Frederick Lugard as its first appointed governor-general. This amalgamation formed present-day Nigeria under an Indirect Rule System. In 1940, during the Second World War, Nigeria was divided into four administrative sections namely the Colony of Lagos, the northern, eastern, and western provinces.

In terms of commerce, the British colonial government introduced Shillings and Pence as the legal tender for British West Africa (Nigeria, Ghana, Sierra Leone, and the Gambia) in 1880. This made trading within the British colonized areas easier and secure from other European countries operating in West Africa. In 1912, the West African Currency Board (WACB) was established which issued the first set of banknotes for the West African region.

Colonial Nigeria

Colonial rule in Nigeria as with many other colonies sited in Africa was designed to improve the economies of the mother country. Agriculture was a major channel through which Nigeria sustained the industrialized economy of the British state. Through agriculture, Nigeria supplied Britain with raw materials in the form of cash crops (cocoa, cotton, groundnut, palm oil, etc.). The cash crops were exported and later imported back to the colonies as finished consumable products. To ensure the smooth transportation of goods, the British built railway networks. The first being in 1898 from Lagos to Ibadan, while the Baro to Kano line was built in 1907. Soon the railway networks had extended to Minna, Kaduna, Port Harcourt, and Maiduguri.

British middlemen dominated the trade of the mass-produced cash crops leaving local farmers and traders with minimal power and control over pricing and sales. The British colonial administration also dominated other areas such as taxes and levies, education, health, service delivery, etc. To consolidate their rule, the British colonial government developed four major constitutions between 1922 and 1954 and these are as follows: the Clifford Constitution (1922), The Richards Constitution (1946), The Macpherson Constitution (1951), and the Lyttleton Constitution of 1954.

The British colonial rule was dominated by British-appointed officials which caused a lot of agitation within the country. Among the educated elites was a growing resentment against the British rule which was seen as denying indigenes access to power while exploiting them economically. This resulted in the formation of political parties, the first of which was on June 24, 1923, when Herbert Macaulay established Nigeria's first political party, the Nigerian National Democratic Party (NNDP). However, its operations were limited to Lagos.

The global depression of the late 1920s and early 1930s resulted in higher taxes to which there were several protests in colonized Nigeria. A good example was the Igbo market women's revolt which occurred between November and December 1929. Thousands of Igbo market women came out in a massive protest against the colonial imposed taxes (taxing women in the Igbo culture was culturally not accepted). The protest spread through many of the colonial divisions in southeastern Nigeria without much violence. However, at Aba, it is recorded that more than 100 women were killed by soldiers and the police deployed to the scene. At the end of the two months' rebellion, the British were forced to drop the tax plan and curb the excessive powers of their appointed warrant chiefs.

Economically, Nigerian merchants were prospering despite the financial limitations placed on indigenous operations. In 1929, the first indigenous bank in Nigeria was established by Winifred Tete-Ansah a Ghanaian nationalist with financial support from other West Africans at the time. The bank, which was called Industrial and Commercial Bank, unfortunately, went into liquidation after a year and some months in operation. This was mostly due to the hostile conditions indigenous traders had to endure operating under the British-controlled economic system. Winifred Tete-Ansah through the help of old and new supporters tried again under the new name Mercantile Bank in 1931. Mercantile Bank placed more emphasis on meeting the financial needs of the western region of Nigeria and became the bankers of the Nigeria Cocoa Marketing Board. The bank was thus able to stay in operation for six years with branches in Lagos and Aba. Mercantile Bank was followed by National Bank of Nigeria in 1933 which eventually became one of the largest indigenous banks in Nigeria staying in operation until 1992 when it was liquidated.

In the 1930s a new political movement was established through the Lagos Youth Movement which was formed by Lagos youths in 1934. On November 2, 1935, the name was changed to Nigerian Youth Movement (NYM) to reflect the desire of its party members to make the party a national one. The party had branches all over Nigeria and through it, the seed for independent indigenous rule was sown. However, it was highly criticized for mainly representing Christian and southern Yoruba views.

The seed of indigenous rule blossomed between the 1940s and 1950s in the form of political elites who led national political parties. In the northern section of the country, the Bauchi Improvement Union was formed in 1943 by Mallam Sa'adu Zungur as one of the earliest political movements in northern Nigeria. In 1944, the National Council of Nigeria and the Cameroons led by Nnamdi Azikiwe was established. It is regarded as the first national party in Nigeria due to its ability to mobilize its members from all over the country. For example, in 1948, Mallam Sa'ad Zungar was appointed the party's Secretary in a bid to ensure national representation. In the western region, the *Egbe Omo Oduduwa* was inaugurated in 1945 as a pan-Yoruba cultural society. In 1948 its members declared it as a non-political organization for men and women of Yoruba nationality. This helped to attract a large membership of the NYM to it. In March 1950, the association became the political party known as Action Group led by Obafemi Awolowo. In 1951, the party became recognized as the western region's political party and included membership from minority ethnic groups like the Benin, Urhobo, and Itsekiri.

The 1940s also witnessed the establishment of indigenous banks. One of them was the Agbonmagbe Bank Limited set up on May 2, 1945, by Chief Mathew Adekoya Okupe, his wife Mrs. Regina Adekoya Okupe, and Mr A. Alade. The bank originally started as a certified cooperative bank until 1945 when it obtained its license. The bank had branches in Lagos (Ebute-Metta, Ifo, and Mushin), Ogun State (Ago-Iwoye and Sagamu, and Ijebu-Igbo), and Kaduna State (Zaria). When the bank faced liquidation, it was taken over by the western Nigeria Marketing Board and renamed Wema Bank in 1969. This makes Wema Bank the oldest indigenous operating bank in Nigeria.

The 1940s, however, witnessed an increase in the cost of living in Nigeria. This high cost of living resulted in Nigeria's first nationwide worker's strike which lasted for forty-four days. The strike was led by Michael Imoudu, a member of the NCNC Executive Council.

The late 1940s was an era of political awakening in northern Nigeria. On December 6, 1946, the Northern Elements Progressive Association (NEPA) was formed in Kano as the first political party in northern Nigeria. The party's leader was Habib Raji Abdallah who in 1947 was made the president of the Zikist Movement. The party witnessed a lot of colonial disapproval due to this association and its radical stance. The party was eventually disbanded in 1949 only to metamorphose as the Northern Elements Progressive Union (NEPU) on August 8, 1950. Prominent members including Bello Ijumu, Habib Raji Abdallah, Abubakar Zukogi, Abdurrahman Bida, and Sa'ad Zungar were identified as leftist fundamentalists who fought for the poor and oppressed (the *Talakawa*). In doing so, the founding principles of the party went against colonialism and the traditional northern oligarchy.

In September 1948, Mallam Rafih (a civil servant of the Nigerian Railways) formed the *Jam'iya Mutanen Arewa Ayau* (the Association of Northern People Today). In October of the same year, R. A. B Dikko (first trained medical officer from Northern Nigeria) and Mallam Abubakar (editor of the northern-based newspaper *Gaskiya Ta Fi Kwabo*) formed the *Jam 'iyyar Jama 'ar Arewa* (Northern Nigerian Congress). The founding members of these two associations had their base as members of Katsina College Old Boys Association. In late October of 1948 both associations merged to form *Jam'yyar Mutanen Arewa* (The Northern People's Congress). In 1951, *Jam'iyyar Mutanen Arewa* became the Northern People's Congress. On October 1, 1951, the NPC was declared a political party with Shetima Ajima as its President, Abubakar Tafawa Balewa its vice-president and Aminu Kano its secretary, while Ahmadu Bello though not holding any apparent position was a powerful member.

In 1951, there was an initial collaboration between the two northern political parties. However, due to NEPU's radical stance, members of the NPC (who were mainly colonial government employees and thus more conservative in nature) in fear of losing support from the colonial government and the northern elites, had to disassociate themselves from the party. The NPC eventually contested against NEPU to win the political seats for the northern region. The NPC eventually became the ruling party in Nigeria's First Republic.

In 1957, the eastern and western regions declared self-rule with the northern region following in 1959. As a way of allaying the fears of the minorities, the "Bill of Rights" which spoke to the concept of basic human rights and freedom was incorporated into the new constitution to protect the rights of minority ethnic groups.

As the regions prepared for independence, other major events occurred in Nigeria during the late 1950s. In 1956, crude oil in commercial quantity was discovered in Oloibiri (present-day Bayelsa State) by Shell BP. The first oil field began production in 1958.

In March 1958, the Central Bank of Nigeria was established under the Central Bank Act of 1958. On July 1, 1959, the Central Bank of Nigeria began issuing the national currency and the notes and coins produced by the West African Currency Board were withdrawn.

In 1959, Nigerians went to the polls under the supervision of the British administration to vote in their preferred leaders for the soon-to-be independent Nigeria. During this first election, the NPC and NCNC formed a coalition and AG was the opposition party. The result was the emergence of Tafawa Balewa (under the NPC) as Nigeria's Prime Minister and Nnamdi Azikwe (under NCNC) as the governor-general (although this position was largely ceremonial). The coalition was dominated by the NPC which technically meant that the leadership of the country was under the control of the prime minister and the Northern premier. They made it clear that their aim was largely to ensure that the northern region catches up with the southern regions. They believed that the northern region had been underdeveloped and thus made little to no progress under colonial rule unlike the southern regions which were made up of more educated and qualified citizens. To achieve this, citizens from the northern region were favoured in terms of appointments and promotions at the detriment of more qualified citizens from southern regions. In the southwestern region, Awolowo retained the AG party head while Ladoke Akintola was made the premier of the western region succeeding Awolowo.

Post-Colonial Independent Nigeria

On October 1, 1960, Nigeria gained its independence from colonial rule and was formally incorporated into the Commonwealth. However, Nigeria's First Republic witnessed a lot of turmoil. In the southwestern region, there were agitations from sections within the Action Group who wanted more recognition at the federal level believing that being an opposition was side-lining them from gaining benefits at the national level. The leader of this agitation was Ladoke Akintola, the premier of the western region. His agitations were encouraged by the Prime Minister for the North in a bid to gain the support of the western region. Akintola eventually formed his own party— the NNDP. The northern region also witnessed a series of protests especially from the northern opposition party, the United Middle Belt Congress (UMBC) which represented the interests of the Tiv ethnic group. The Tiv who formed the majority population of the middle belt wanted a Middle Belt State to be carved out of the northern region; a request that the NPC (the ruling party) refused. The Tiv riots were thus against the intolerant rule of the NPC, accusing the party of making it impossible for their opposing voices to be heard. The Tiv riots were often violent and destructive, spanning a period of five years (1960–65).

In 1962, Nigeria formally became a federation and on July 1, 1962, the words "Federation of Nigeria" which was the term printed on Nigerian bank notes at independence was replaced with "Federal Republic of Nigeria" to reflect this new status. The year 1962 also witnessed Nigeria's first National Census after independence. The National Census was an important event as it determined the number of seats which would be allocated to each region at the Federal Assembly. The 1953 census conducted under British rule indicated that the northern region had the highest population. Realizing the importance of the population numbers assigned to the regions, the southern regions were alleged to have manipulated their figures in the 1962 census as a tactic to gain more seats at the national assembly. It was alleged that the southwestern region inflated their numbers by 70 percent compared to the 30 percent increase from the northern region. Realizing this, the northern ruling party cancelled the results and another more "credible" one was conducted in November of the following year; this time manipulated by the NPC indicating an increase of the northern population by eight million.

The alleged manipulations of the southwestern region did not go unnoticed and on October 1, the Prime Minister in his nationwide broadcast announced that investigations were underway to uncover plots by some politicians to overthrow the government. To prevent this, a ban on public meetings in the western region was enforced. In November of 1962, Obafemi Awolowo and twenty-six others, mainly from the Action Group party (including Anthony Enahoro and Lateef Jakande) were arrested on charges of treason and corruption. With this arrest, Akintola became the major political leader in the Southwest, but this was met with great disapproval from supporters of Awolowo. As an ally of the Prime Minister, Akintola enjoyed federal privileges, and this sparked bloody clashes between the supporters of the opposing parties. By 1963, the clashes had become even more intense and bloody. Rather than declare a state of emergency to douse the tension, the NPC opted to carve Benin and Delta provinces out of the western region to form the Midwest region in August of 1963. Dennis Osadebay was made the first premier of the region. However, the crisis in the western region persisted to which the prime minister indicated no further federal intervention would be made.

On October 1, 1963, Nigeria became a Republic and Nnamdi Azikiwe became Nigeria's first president while Tafawa Balewa retained the status of the more powerful prime minister. This paved the way for the first elections conducted for and by Nigerians held between December 1964 and March 1965. The NPC and NNDP formed the alliance party called the Nigerian National Alliance (NNA); while NCNC and AG formed the alliance party called the United Progressive Grand Alliance (UPGA). As a protest against what they believed would be an unfair election, UPGA members boycotted the national elections. This allowed Tafawa Balewa to be sworn in for a second term as Nigeria's prime minister in January 1965.

Despite the political skirmishes, 1965 witnessed several laudable achievements. In August 1965, the 26-story building named *Ile Awon Agbe* (which in Yoruba means 'House of Farmers') was commissioned in Ibadan which at that time was under western region control. The building was later renamed Cocoa House because it was funded and built on the proceeds of the region's cocoa exportation. The building stands on 1.7 hectares of land with a height measuring about 105 meters making it the first skyscraper in sub-Saharan Africa. Unfortunately, on January 9, 1985, the entire building was razed to the ground by fire sparked by an electrical fault. The building was subsequently renovated and reopened for commercial use in August 1992. The building is owned by Odua Investment Company and managed by Wemabod Estates.

In December 1965, the first Niger Bridge was completed and commissioned by prime minister Alhaji Tafawa Balewa. The bridge crosses the River Niger and links Asaba in Delta state with Onitsha in Anambra State. In 1967, to stop federal forces from entering Onitsha, the Biafran forces blew it up. After the war, the bridge was repaired in 1970 courtesy of a grant from West Germany. However, in 1987, fears of the poor state of the bridge and the possible catastrophe that could occur if not attended to, initiated the need to build a second Niger Bridge. However, this would not be realized until 2012, under Goodluck Jonathan's administration, when the contract for the final planning and design of the Second Niger Bridge would be approved.

Nigeria's Military Eras

On January 15, 1966, Nigeria witnessed its first military coup spearheaded by senior military officers of the Nigerian Military Force. These include Major Kaduna Nzeogwu who was the Chief Instructor at the Nigerian Defence Academy (Kaduna), Major Timothy Onwuatuewgu, Major Emmanuel Ifeajuna, Major Adewale Ademoyega, and Chris Anuforo. The coup plotters claimed that the level of corruption was high while the ordinary citizens were left in poverty. The coup plotters attacked in Kaduna, Lagos, and Ibadan. At the end of that fateful Saturday, major political figures were murdered including Nigeria's first prime minister—Abubakar Tafawa Balewa—Ahmadu Bello (the then premier of the Northern Region), as well as major military officers like Samuel Ademulegun, Ralph Shodeinde, Chief Samuel Akintola, Festus Okotie-Eboh, and Brig. Zakariya Maimalari. In some cases, as with Sir Ahmadu Bello and Brig. Samuel Ademulegun their wives were killed along with them. On that fateful day, the president at the time, Nnamdi Azikiwe, was out of the country.

Major Nzeogwu was eventually captured and imprisoned by the Nigerian army led by Major General Umunnakwe Aguiyi Ironsi making the coup a partially successful one. Based on the prevailing circumstances, the then Acting President Nwafor Orizu made a nationwide broadcast announcing the voluntary handing over of power to the Nigerian military headed by Major General Aguiyi Ironsi. Major General Aguiyi Ironsi on January 17, 1966, became the first Nigerian military head of state marking the end of Nigeria's First Republic.

On assuming power, Ironsi was faced with agitations from the Niger Delta region in February of 1966 headed by Isaac Adaka Boro. Isaac Boro together with fellow Ijaw men formed the Niger Delta Volunteer Force and declared the secession of the Niger Delta Republic on February 23, 1966. The secession was in protest of the oppression, neglect, and underdevelopment of the Niger Delta region where the wealth of the new Nigeria stemmed from. Together with his troupe, the Isaac Boro–led force fought the Nigerian federal army in a twelve-day battle. The secessionists were eventually defeated, and its leaders sentenced to death for treason (this sentence was however reversed on the eve of the Nigerian Civil War which saw Isaac Boro fighting and dying on the side of the Nigerian forces against the Biafran forces).

Crushing the Niger Delta secession was just the beginning of Major General Aguiyi-Ironsi's leadership problems. The fact that Ironsi did not execute the now-imprisoned coup plotters, and his formulation of a unified civil service, made the core elites of the northern region believe that he was in support of the aborted coup. On July 17 and 18, 1966, a countercoup was carried out, this time headed by northern military officers prominent of which was Brig. Gen Murtala Ramat Mohammed. In the countercoup Aguiyi-Ironsi was assassinated along with senior army officials from southeastern Nigeria. Aguiyi-Ironsi had only spent 194 days in power. To prevent the North from carrying out their threats of secession, the emerging leadership was handed over not to Murtala Ramat Mohammed, but to Lt.-Col. Yakubu Gowon on July 29, 1966, who at that time was the most senior army officer from the northern region. Between July and October of 1966, Northerners turned against Igbo residents in the area, killing thousands of Igbo civilians. The massacre of the Igbos was so great that many had to flee the North leaving behind their businesses, properties and for some their children from marriages with Northerners. The indifference to the massive killings by the Gowon-led government enraged the Igbo people. They felt even more slighted when the Gowon-led government on May 5, 1967, replaced Nigeria's four regions with twelve states. Although Gowon's government indicated that this decision was to give minority ethnic groups in the southeastern region a voice; the Igbo people who were the dominant ethnic group saw this as a move to reduce their voice in the eastern region. In response, the then military head of the now defunct southeastern region, Colonel Ojukwu, declared the eastern region an independent country which he called the Republic of Biafra on May 30, 1967. The proposed Republic was carved out of the southeastern region and included the crude oil–rich regions of Nigeria. To prevent the now impending possibility of a civil war, peace talks were initiated and held in Aburi Ghana. Unfortunately, on getting back to Nigeria, there were accusations and counter-accusations from both sides of not keeping to the Aburi agreements. The result was the bloody Civil War which spanned from July 1967 to January 1970. Most of the minority groups represented in the now disintegrated southeastern region fought on the side of the Nigerian federal government afraid of being under an Igbo-dominated rule. This decision led to the deaths of thousands of minority group members in the hands of the Biafran army.

Indeed, the war claimed the lives of millions of promising Nigerian youths, one of such was Emmanuel Ifeajuna. In 1954 during the British Empire and Commonwealth Games held in Vancouver Canada, Emmanuel Ifeajuna came to the spotlight as the first Black athlete to win a gold medal and set a new Commonwealth record during the Men's High Jump event. He remained Nigeria's only Commonwealth Gold Medallist until 1966. He was believed to have taken an active part in the failed 1966 coup; accused of shooting and killing Prime Minister Tafewa Balewa. After the failed coup, Emmanuel Ifeajuna escaped to Ghana and later joined the Biafran forces during the Civil War. Ifeajuna and three other men were however executed in 1967 by the Ojukwu-led secession army due to their negotiation with the Nigerian government of an early ceasefire. Such an act was considered by Ojukwu and the Biafran people as the ultimate act of betrayal. However, a few days after this execution, Nigerian Military forces captured Enugu, initiating a genocide of great magnitude for the Biafran people; and thus, bringing to reality to what Ifeajuna and his colleagues had tried to prevent. The genocide ended the civil war with the Biafran forces accepting defeat.

After the war, and under Nigeria's first military regime headed by Gowon, Nigeria joined the Organization of Petroleum Exporting Countries (OPEC) in 1971. The rise in the price of crude oil during this period brought in much revenue for Nigeria, making the exploration of crude oil Nigeria's main source of income till today. In 1972, the Indigenisation Decree was promulgated but took effect on March 31, 1974. With the Indigenisation Decree, ownership of major business organizations was transferred from foreign ownership to majority Nigerian ownership. On January 1, 1973, Nigeria's money system changed to a decimal currency following the recommendations of the Decimal Currency Committee, set up in 1962. The new currency unit was called "Naira" and was equivalent to ten Shillings; while the minor unit was the "Kobo," a hundred of which made one Naira. It is believed that the federal commissioner for finance between 1967 and 1971, Chief Obafemi Awolowo, was the brain behind the formulation of the currency names. Naira was derived from the word "Nigeria" while "Kobo" was derived from a corruption of the word copper, the metal from which the coins were made.

The Gowon-led regime also initiated several projects ranging from the development of federal university sites, roads, federal establishments, etc. Socially, on May 22, 1973, the National Youth Service Corp was established as a reconciliatory, reconstruction and rebuilding strategy after the Nigerian Civil War. The Corp service is a one-year compulsory program for Nigerian graduates under the age of thirty. On the completion of their tertiary education, graduates are posted to states outside their geopolitical region and states of origin. At the end of the service year, a certificate of completion is awarded which serves as a prerequisite for government employment and appointments.

Lt.-Col. Yakubu Gowon's regime was overturned in July 1975 through a coup headed by Brig. Gen. Murtala Ramat Mohammed. Murtala Mohammed was very active during the civil war as a brave soldier contributing immensely to the victory of the Nigerian forces. Now, as head of state, Murtala Mohammed put into motion policies to counter corruption and inflation in the country. He also initiated the movement of the federal capital from Lagos (which he said was overcrowded) to Abuja and created more states. However, Murtala Mohammed spent only 200 days in office before he was assassinated (along with his aide and driver) on February 13, 1976, in an abortive coup led by Lt.-Col. Buka Suka Dimka. Dimka hailed from present-day Plateau State and was trained in Australia. He was an active player in the 1967 counter coup and again supported Murtala in the 1975 coup. Some historians believe that his motive for assassinating Murtala was hinged on an unfulfilled promise by Murtala to create a Midwest State of which Dimka would be made the governor. On resuming power, Murtala did not do this, and this made Dimka very angry. Dimka, however, publicly identified deficiency, corruption, unlawful arrests, and detention of persons without trial, and so on, as his motivation. The coup, however, was thwarted by Colonel Ibrahim Babangida. Dimka along with his coup plotters were eventually tried by a military tribunal, charged under a new decree hurriedly formulated to try coup plotters for treason with a maximum sentence of public execution. This process was adopted from Ujukwu's 1967 trial in Enugu of Ifeajuna and his collaborators who were charged with treason and eventually executed. Thus, the execution of Dimka and his fellow coup plotters in May of 1976 was the first of its kind in modern Nigeria.

Following the aborted coup, Nigeria's Supreme Military Council appointed Lt.-Gen. Olusegun Obasanjo as the new head of state. To facilitate the transition from military to democratic rule, the drafting of a new constitution was initiated. The new constitution changed Nigeria's system of governance from the British Parliamentary system to the United States presidential system. The new constitution initiated by General Obasanjo required that cabinet positions reflect the federal character with each state in the federation producing at least one cabinet member. The new constitution was published in September 1978 which officially meant that political parties could be formed and contest for elections. Olusegun Obasanjo handed over power on October 1, 1979, making him the first military government to hand over power to a civilian democratically elected government.

Under Obasanjo's leadership, the Nigerian National Petroleum Company was established as a merger of the Nigerian National Oil Corporation and the Federal Ministry of Petroleum on April 1, 1977. Through the NNPC, the federal government of Nigeria coordinated the activities of international oil exploration companies.

On February 11, 1977, the N20 banknote was issued as the highest denomination at the time. On the note was the face of the late head of state, General Murtala Ramat Muhammed who was assassinated the year before. On October 1, 1978, General Murtala was declared a national hero. On July 2, 1979, the N1, N5, N10 were introduced reflecting other prominent heroes like Tafawa Balewa and Herbert Macaulay.

The Second World Black and African Festival of Arts and Culture (FESTAC '77) was held in Nigeria between January and February 1977. The event attracted participants from fifty-six African nations and included dance, music, art exhibitions, drama, etc. The festival locations in Lagos included the National Theatre (which was completed in preparation for the event), the National Stadium, and Tafawa Balewa Square; while other venues were located in Kaduna where the Durbar events happened.

After thirteen years of military rule, Shehu Shagari was sworn in on September 13, 1979 as Nigeria's first executive president and head of state, thus signalling the beginning of Nigeria's Second Republic. However, Shagari's government was riddled with corruption and nepotism. It was thus not a surprise that on December 31, 1983, the government was overthrown by the military government headed by Major General Muhammadu Buhari with General Babatunde Idiagbon as the chief of staff and second in command. The new regime reeled out their various policies including the War Against Indiscipline (WAI), currency change and currency exchange rate policy, the import substitution and industrialization policy, the go back to the land program, and the war against illicit drug trafficking. The aim of these policies was to encourage a culture of discipline and organization within the Nigerian citizenry, the growth of local manufacturing industries, agriculture, and the national economy; however, it had a zero tolerance of disobedience to its laws.

Buhari's led regime was accused of being very brutal, infringing on the human rights of Nigerians. This caused a lot of apprehension until on August 27, 1985, when Buhari's regime was overthrown in a bloodless coup headed by General Ibrahim Babangida. In 1986, Babangida launched the Structural Adjustment Program as part of the requirements for taking an IMF loan. In 1987, the Mass Mobilisation for Self-Reliance, Social Justice, and Economic Recovery (MAMSER) was launched as a way of improving Nigeria's economy. Babangida's regime was the second longest military rule in Nigeria, and it turned out to be the most corrupt of all the military regimes Nigeria had ever witnessed. It goes down in history as being the government which institutionalized corruption and its practices. In 1992, after much pressure, Babangida initiated the conduction of elections to set Nigeria back on course for democracy. However, on June 12, 1993, Babangida annulled the presidential elections, the results of which indicated that Moshood Abiola, the party candidate for the Social Democratic Party (SDP) was the winner. The annulment resulted in nationwide protests and rather than hand over the country's governance to SDP, Babangida handed over to an interim government headed by Ernest Shonekan. Shonekan spent only three months as an interim head before the government was once again taken over by the military in November 1993 this time headed by General Sani Abacha.

On seizing power, General Sani Abacha dissolved the interim government thus making null and void the elections earlier held. The acclaimed winner of the elections, Chief MKO Abiola went on exile and returned in June 1994. In a press briefing, Abiola declared himself the president of Nigeria and demanded the military government of Abacha to immediately vacate the position. In response, Abacha ordered Abiola's arrest on charges of treason. Despite national and international outcries, Abiola remained in custody until his sudden death on July 7, 1998.

Abacha's military regime will also be remembered for the arrest in 1994 of Ken Saro-wiwa and eight members of the Movement for the Survival of the Ogoni People (MOSOP) for inciting the murder of four chiefs. Despite overwhelming evidence of their innocence, the nine men were found guilty and sentenced to death. Their sentencing caused national and international outcry and even appeals from the Pope to spare the lives of the men. However, on November 11, 1995, the men were executed. It soon became obvious to Nigerians that Abacha (due to the way by which he seized power), was suspicious of everyone and everything and would not hesitate to crush any signs of opposition or disloyalty. In March 1995 he ordered the arrest of General Obasanjo along with other ex-military officers like General Shehu Musa Yar'Adua (who eventually died in detention) on accusations of treason and attempting a coup to overthrow his government. In 1997, Abacha again ordered the arrest and trial of his Chief of Army Staff, Oladipo Diya along with five other military officers also on accusations of attempting a coup against his government. The six men were sentenced to death and were to be executed in April 1998. However, much to the relief of the men, their families and Nigeria as a whole, Sani Abacha died in office on June 8, 1998.

At the sudden death of Abacha, General Abdulsalami Abubakar took over power. On resuming power, Abdulsalami Abubakar promised Nigerians that he would ensure a return to civilian rule. He released those imprisoned by Abacha including General Olusegun Obasanjo and Lieutenant General Diya. To facilitate his promise to Nigerians, General Abdulsalami established the Independent National Electoral Commission (INEC) to oversee the elections into various public positions in local governments, the state assemblies, governors, and finally the office of a democratically elected president. And, to the joy of Nigerians, in May 1999, Olusegun Obasanjo was elected as the president of Nigeria and Commander-in-Chief of the Armed Forces. This marked the end of military rule in Nigeria till date.

Nigeria's Return to Democracy

Olusegun Obasanjo was sworn into power on May 29, 1999, under the political party of the People's Democratic Party (PDP). Obasanjo served two terms (eight years) during which some milestone achievements were recorded including the introduction of higher Naira denomination notes (N100, N200, N500, and N1000), the establishment of GSM, the Niger Delta Development Commission from the oil revenue and the Universal Basic Education Program aimed at enhancing the literary level of Nigerians. Obasanjo's resolve to curb corruption in the country resulted in the establishment of the Independent Corrupt Practices Commission (a body established to investigate reports of corruption) in 2000; as well as the Economic and Financial Crimes Commission (a law enforcement agency set up to investigate financial crimes) established in 2003. In 2004, Obasanjo launched the National Economic Empowerment and Development Strategy (NEEDS). During his tenure, he was able to use the increase in oil revenue to see the growth of the Nigerian economy to 6 percent from 3 percent, an increase in the country's foreign reserves from $22 billion in 1999 to $43 billion in 2007. He was also able to secure a debt cancellation from the Paris Club. However, his attempt at a third term and his high-handedness made him very unpopular especially during his second term in office.

On October 27, 1999, the Sharia law was reintroduced in Zamfara State. By 2001, eleven other northern states (Bauchi, Borno, Gombe, Jigawa, Kaduna, Kano, Katsina, Kebbi, Niger, Sokoto, and Yobe) also adopted the Sharia law for both civil and criminal matters. This raised fears among Christians who called northern Nigeria their home and waves of inter-religious violence erupted leaving many dead and properties destroyed.

On April 21, 2007, Umaru Musa Yar'Adua emerged as the winner of the Nigerian presidential elections and was sworn in on May 29, 2007. Unfortunately, Umaru Musa

Yar'Adua did not complete his tenure. On November 23, 2009, he was flown out of the country for the treatment of an unknown ailment. This left a power vacuum until February 10, 2010, when the Federal Executive Council of Nigeria in response to a Supreme Court of Nigeria ruling using the "Doctrine of Necessity" transferred power to Goodluck Jonathan, the then vice president. This action made Goodluck Jonathan the Acting President of Nigeria. Consequently, President Yar'Adua's death was announced on May 5, 2010. On May 6, Goodluck Jonathan was sworn in as the president and Commander-In-Chief of the Armed Forces. On May 18, Namidi Sambo replaced Goodluck Jonathan as the vice president. The duo ultimately contested for the position of President and Vice-President and were sworn in on May 29, 2011.

Goodluck Jonathan as the fourteenth head of state of Nigeria, continued with the seven-point agenda of late Umaru Musa Yar'Adua. Under his leadership, roads and rails were constructed, along with other laudable infrastructural projects. In December 2014, a commemorative N100 Naira note was released to commemorate Nigeria's one-hundredth anniversary. However, despite the able declarations of Goodluck Jonathan, his tenure was riddled with corruption, and he was accused of being too weak to stop it. Insecurity took a violent turn with the Boko Haram insurgency gaining a strong foothold in northeastern Nigeria. By May of 2013, a state of emergency was declared in three of the states namely Yobe, Borno, and Adamawa. Although troops were sent to the region to restore peace, in April 2014, more than 200 girls were abducted from their boarding schools in the middle of the night in northeastern town of Chibok. This resulted in national and international outrage with the hashtag #bringbackourgirls.

Muhammadu Buhari won the 2015 presidential elections. With the poll victory of Muhammadu Buhari, the ruling party shifted from PDP to APC (All Progressives Congress) thus ending the sixteen-year rule of the former. This poll victory will go down in history as the first time an incumbent president will be defeated by the opposition party in a general election. In addition, it will also go down in history that Goodluck Jonathan was the first Nigerian president to accept his defeat at the polls, and appealing to agitating factions of his party to accept the results and congratulate his opponent.

Muhammadu Buhari served two terms (eight years). Unfortunately, his tenure was marked with heightened inflation, insecurity, and corruption. Critics of his administration noted nepotism which favoured only the Fulani ethnic group in northern Nigeria. Although his emphasis on building local infrastructure and agriculture was laudable, the high rate of kidnappings and killings made the positive strides seem negative. His government met international condemnation when on October 20, 2020, innocent Nigerian youths holding the Nigerian flag were massacred at the Lekki Toll Gate when protesting the spike in police brutality (#endsars). Again, on March 28, 2022, sixty-two passengers traveling on the Abuja-Kaduna train were kidnapped while six were reportedly killed when the rail was bombed by terrorists. The Buhari-led government was accused of being indifferent forcing family members of the kidnapped victims to negotiate ransoms to free their loved ones. Between March and October of 2022, the hostages were released in small batches with the largest and final release being twenty-three victims on October 5, 2022. This, and many other attacks and kidnappings by train and road made mobility very unsafe; and in pre and tertiary educational institutions made school attendance fearful.

Despite these negatives, Buhari's led government had many positives. In September 2018, construction of the second Niger Bridge began under Muhammadu Buhari's government, funded through the Presidential Infrastructure Development Fund created by the presidency. In December 2022, the bridge was officially opened thus making trade and accessibility in the southeastern region easier. On October 25, 2021, President Muhammadu Buhari launched the e-Naira which is a digital currency produced by the Central Bank of Nigeria. In July of 2022, the NNPC ceased to be a government-owned corporation and became a profit company with the sole license to operate in Nigeria's petroleum industry. On October 26, 2022, the federal government announced the redesigning of high denominations (200, 500, and 1,000) of the Naira notes as a way of reducing money laundering and corruption.

Further Reading

Africa Facts Zone. (2021, August 16). https://twitter.com/AfricaFactsZone/status/1427388579752419328

Amoah, F. E. K. (1992). "Oral Tradition and Ethnicity in the Creation of New States in Nigeria: The Case of Akwa Ibom." *Research Review (NS)*, 8(1&2): 76–89.

Ariye, E. C. (2013). "The Ijo (Ijaw) People of Delta State: Their Early History and Aspects of Social and Cultural Practices." *Historical Research Letter*, 8: 25–31.

Babagana, A. (2017). *Kanuri Complete*. ResearchGate Online Publication. https://www.researchgate.net/profile/Babagana-Abubakar-2

Balabkins, N. (1980). "Indigenisation – The Nigerian Experience." *Africa Insight*, 10(1): 21–6.

Blogger. (2013). "Ijaw People: Nigeria's Aboriginal Water People of Niger Delta." https://kwekudee-tripdownmemorylane.blogspot.com/2013/02/ijaw-people-nigerias-aboriginal-water.html

Cyffer, N. (n.d.). "Kanuri and Its Neighbours: When Saharan and Chadic Languages Meet." A Research on Linguistic Contact and Conceptualization in the Wider Lake Chad Area *The Project: Linguistic Innovation and Conceptual Change in West Africa*, funded by the Australian Science Fund (FWF), Project number P 15764.

Encyclopedia.com. (2019). *Ibibio*. https://www.encyclopedia.com/humanities/encyclopedias-almanacs-transcripts-and-maps/ibibio

Falola, T. and H. Mathew. (2008). *A History of Nigeria*. New York: Cambridge University Press.

Falola, T. and A. Genova. (2009). "Historical Dictionary of Nigeria." In *Historical Dictionaries of Africa, No. 111*. Maryland: The Rowman & Littlefield Publishing Group Inc.

HiztoryBox. (2020, August 13). "Joao Alfonso D'Alveiro Visits to Benin Kingdom." https://www.hiztorybox.com.ng/joao-alfonso-dalveiro-visits-to-benin-kingdom/#:~:text=He%20was%20a%20national%20Executive,government%20of%20General%20Sani%20Abacha.&text=He%20was%20appointed%20State%20Commissioner,the%20Federal%20republic%20of%20Nigeria (accessed February 4, 2023).

Naankiel, P. (2015). "A Brief History of the Pre-colonial Economy of the Jukun." *Sokoto Journal of History*, 4: 150–60.

Nathan Nunn. (2017). "Understanding the Long-Run Effects of Africa's Slave Trades." *Voxeu*. https://cepr.org/voxeu/columns/understanding-long-run-effects-africas-slave-trades#:~:text=Between%201400%20and%201900%2C%20the,colonies%20in%20the%20New%20World.

National African Language Resource Center (NALRC). (n.d.). *Language & Culture: Studying Ijaw in the United States*. www.nalrc.indiana.edu

Nigeria Nostalgia Project. (2016, January 25). https://nigerianostalgia.tumblr.com/post/138068975920/the-portuguese-were-the-first-european-travelers

Ogundiran, A., ed. (2005). *Precolonial Nigeria: Essays in Honor of Toyin Falola*. Trenton: Africa World Press, Inc.
Okey, I. (2007). "History of Pre-colonial Southern Nigeria." In S. A. Idahosa (ed.), *Nigerian Peoples and Culture*, 41–62. Benin: Benson Idahosa University.
Rotimi, K. (2008). "Jaja and Nana in the Niger Delta region of Nigeria: Proto-Nationalists or Emergent Capitalists." *The Journal of Pan African Studies*, 2(7): 48–58.
Sidi, T. S. (2012). "A History of the Nupe, C1068-1810 A.D." PhD Thesis submitted to the school of Postgraduate Studies Ahmadu Bello University, Zaria.
Terlumun, U. (2015). "Migrant Groups and Inter-Group Relations in Tiv Society of Central Nigeria: Pre to Post-colonial Era." *International Journal of Arts and Humanities (IJAH) Bahir Dar-Ethiopia*, 4(1): 88–97. doi: https://dx.doi.org/10.4314/ijah.v4i1.6
Uwagbale Edward-Ekpu. (2021). "How the Language of the Edo People of Nigeria made Its Way into Portuguese Creole." *Quartz*, July 23, 2021. https://qz.com/the-ftc-is-preparing-an-investigation-into-amazon-1850072340
Weor, J. (2005). "The Narratives of Origin and Migration of the Tiv People (of Nigeria) as an Indigenous Interpretation of the Book of Exodus." *Scriptura*, 90: 885–91.
Yahya, M. (2003). "The Nupe People of Nigeria." *Studies of Tribes Tribals*, 1(2): 96–110.
Ziri. (2019). "Brief History of the Benin Empire: The First Schools and Churches." *Opera News*. https://ng.opera.news/ng/en/religion/9f830d38781a007eca619a81bfa9d804

TIMELINE

1300–1600: Trans-Saharan Trade thrives. Goods are transported across the Sahara Desert from northern states in Nigeria to Europe and the Middle East. Through these trade routes, Islam as a religion, knowledge and way of life was also transported into northern Nigeria while goods like leather, cloth, spices, and forged metal items were traded. Also traded were slaves from ethnic groups further south of Nigeria who were sold as domestic help, farm and construction labor in the Middle East and Europe.

1450–1807: What starts as a friendly relation with the Benin people at the shores of the Atlantic with Portuguese traders, explorers and missionaries turned into the Trans-Atlantic Slave Trade. Through this slave trade, millions of Nigerians are sold to the Americas. A large part of the slaves were prisoners of war captured during the Usman Dan Fodio's Islamic Jihad which created the Sokoto Caliphate, kidnappings, and raids of villages in the southern part of Nigeria. Slaves were exchanged for agricultural food items, guns, cloth, domestic utensils, and tools manufactured in Europe. In 1807 the British Parliament vote for the abolition of the slave trade.

1841: The Niger Expedition is organized as a journey supported by the British Crown and its government as well as members of British missionary societies aimed at persuading African slave traders to stop the trade and embrace commercial farming for export to Britain.

1846: The Church Missionary Society (CMS) establishes a mission in Abeokuta while the Presbyterian Church of Scotland is also established in Calabar. Through the head of the Presbyterian Church the first printing press in Nigeria is established in 1846.

1849–1856: John Beecroft is appointed by the British as the first Consul for the Bight of Biafra and Benin. This is followed with the establishment of Courts of Equity established in Bonny and Calabar.

1851–1862: The British embarked on a battle for Lagos which at the time was a thriving slave port. On August 6, 1862 Lagos is occupied and made a British Colony.

1864: Ajayi Crowther is ordained as the first African Bishop by the Anglican Church.

1869–1873: Jubo Jubogha later (renamed Jaja by the British) established a settlement to be known as Opobo and declared himself the king. In 1873, Opobo was formally recognized by Europe as a major player in the palm oil trade.

1879–1881: In 1879, George Taubman Goldie formed the United Africa Company. In 1881 through the amalgamation of smaller British firms which operated in the Niger Delta region the company was renamed the National African Company.

1891–1893: The British established the Oil Rivers Protectorate in 1891 which spanned from the Niger Delta coastal region of Calabar to the Western Delta region. In 1893, the region was formerly known as the Niger Coast Protectorate.

1897: On the January 8, 1897, the name "Nigeria" appeared for the first time in *The Times* in an article written by Miss Flora Shaw who was the paper's feature writer covering issues on Britain's colonies. She later became the wife of Nigeria's first governor-general, Lord Lugard.

1900: On the January 1, 1990, the territories of the Royal Niger Company were formerly taken over by the British Imperial government. The areas today known as Nigeria was divided into two administrations under Northern Nigeria and Southern Nigeria.

1901: Under the Slavery Proclamation, anyone born after April 1, 1901, is declared a free born.

1906: On May 1, 1906, Lagos Colony was incorporated into the Colony and Protectorate of Southern Nigeria. This amalgamation created an administrative unit made of the Eastern Province with headquarters in Calabar, Central Province with headquarters in Warri and the Western Province with headquarters in Lagos. Each headquarter was headed by a commissioner.

1912: The Southern Nigeria Civil Service Union was formed. It was later renamed the Nigerian Civil Servant's Union.

1912: The West African Currency Board (WACB) issues the first set of banknotes for the West African region.

1914: The amalgamation of the three protectorates namely the Lagos Colony with Lagos City as its base, the Southern Protectorate with Calabar as its base, and the Northern Protectorate with Kano as its base. Thieamalgamation of the Southern and Northern protectorates formed the present-day Nigeria of which and Frederick Lugard was appointed the first governor.

1921–1922: Formal teaching in what was to be called the Katsina Training College was officially opened as the first of its kind in northern Nigeria in 1922. Prominent northern elites and political leaders went through this college. The college was eventually moved to Kaduna and then Zaria where it was renamed Barewa College.

1922: Part of former German Colony Kamerun is added to British colonial Nigeria.

1923: The Clifford Constitution was established, and this allowed indigenous representation in Nigeria's governance.

1923: On June 24, 1923, Herbert Macaulay established Nigeria's first political party, the Nigerian National Democratic Party (NNDP). Egerton Shyngle was elected as its president and T. H. Jackson its secretary. Its operation was however limited to Lagos.

1925: West African Students' Union (WASU) was founded.

1929: The Aba Women's Riot took place. It was an all-women's riot which forced the British colonial government to bow to the women's demands of removing the female tax as well as warrant chiefs who had been disrespectful to women.

1929: The first indigenous bank in Nigeria called Industrial and Commercial Bank was established.

1931: The Nigerian Union of Teachers (NUT) is established.

1934–1936: Lagos Youth Movement was formed by youths in Lagos. On November 2, 1935, the name was changed to the Nigerian Youth Movement to reflect the desire of its party members to make the party a national one.

1943: The Bauchi Improvement Union was formed by Mallam Sa'adu Zungur as one of the earliest political movements in northern Nigeria.

1944: The National Council of Nigeria and the Cameroons (NCNC) led by Nnamdi Azikiwe is regarded as the first national party in Nigeria due to its ability to mobilize its members from all over Nigeria.

1945–1951: *Egbe Omo Oduduwa* was inaugurated as a pan Yoruba cultural society. In 1948 its members declared it as a non-political organization for men and women of Yoruba nationality. In March 1950, the association became the political party known as Action Group led by Obafemi Awolowo. In 1951, the party became recognized as the western region's political party and included membership from minority ethnic groups like the Benin, Urhobo and Itsekiri.

1945: Workers strike over the increase in the cost of living. The strike which lasted for forty-four days was Nigeria's first nationwide strike. The strike was led by Michael Imoudu, a member of the NCNC Executive Council.

1946–1954: Three major constitutions were established by the British colonial government namely: The Richards Constitution, MacPherson Constitution (1950), and the Lyttleton Constitution (1954).

1946–1950: On December 6, 1946 the Northern Elements Progressive Association (NEPA) was formed in Kano as the first political party in northern Nigeria. The party witnessed a lot of colonial disapproval due to its radical stance. The party was eventually disbanded in 1949 only to metamorphose into the Northern Elements Progressive Union (NEPU) on August 8, 1950.

1948–1951: Dr. Dikko, M. Yahaya Gusau, Amino Kano and Abubakar Imam form the Jam'iyyar Mutanen Arewa. In 1951 the association became the political party named the Northern People's Congress (NPC).

1948: University College Ibadan is established as the first university college in Nigeria.

1952: The British colonial government implemented the ordinance to regulate the banking system in colonial Nigeria.

1953: Kyari Magumeri was promoted to the rank of a Captain in the British Army based on his gallantry during the First and Second World Wars. This promotion made him the first Nigerian in this rank.

1956: Anthony Enahoro of the Action Group (western region) moved the motion for the attainment of self-governance in Nigeria. The following year, the eastern and western regions declared self-rule. As a way of allaying the fears of the minorities, the "Bill of Rights" which incorporated the concept of basic human rights and freedom into the new constitution to protect minorities was passed.

1956: Petroleum was discovered in the Niger Delta region of Nigeria.

1959: Northern Region declared self-rule.

July 1, 1959, the Central Bank of Nigeria (CBN) replaced the WACB legal tender.

1959: Nigerians go to the polls under the supervision of the British administration to vote in their preferred leaders for the soon-to-be-independent Nigeria. During this first election, the NPC and NCNC formed a coalition and AG was the opposition party. The result was the emergence of Tafawa Balewa (under the NPC) as Nigeria's prime minister and Nnamdi Azikiwe (under the NCNC) as the governor-general (although this position was largely ceremonial) while the Action Group party was the opposition party led by Obafemi Awolowo.

1959: On October 31, 1959, the western region sent out the first television signals not only in Nigeria but in the whole of Africa. The station was established by an act of the Region's House of parliament. The major reason why the station was set up was to act as an additional means of improving the region's school systems which was handicapped by a shortage of qualified teachers.

1960: October 1, 1960, Nigeria gained its independence from colonial rule ushering in the First Republic. At independence, Nigeria adopted the British Westminster structure of governance. Under this structure, Tafawa Balewa is the prime minister while Nnamdi Azikiwe is the president. At the regional level, the northern region is headed by Ahmadu Bello the Sardauna of Sokoto, the eastern region is headed by Michael Okpara while the western region is headed by Ladoke Akintola. In the same year, Nigeria was formally incorporated into the Commonwealth.

1962: The first census under the independent Nigeria was conducted in May 1962 of which the results were rejected (fresh census exercise was repeated in 1963). On July 1, 1962, the words "Federation of Nigeria" printed on Nigerian bank notes were replaced with "Federal Republic of Nigeria."

1962: A State of Emergency is declared in the western region due to internal party conflicts between loyalists of Obafemi Awolowo and Ladoke Akintola. Senator M.A. Majekodunmi, the then federal minister of health is appointed as the Administrator of the region. Obafemi Awolowo and twenty-six other members of the Action Group party were charged for treason in November of 1962. By September 1963 they were found guilty and sentenced to ten years in jail. Akintola went on to form his own party which he called the United Progressive Party.

1963: The mid-western region is carved out of the western region and Dennis Osadebay was made the head. In the same year, Nigeria is formally declared a Republic.

1964–1965: The first elections conducted for and by Nigerians were held between December 1964 and March 1965. This allowed Tafawa Balewa to be sworn in for a second term as Nigeria's prime minister in January 1965.

1965: August 1965, the 26-story building named *Ile Awon Agbe* (which in Yoruba means "House of Farmers") was commissioned in Ibadan by the then western region. The building which was later renamed Cocoa House (since it was funded and built on the proceeds of the region's cocoa exportation) goes down in history as being the first skyscraper in sub-Saharan Africa.

1966: Flora Nkiru Nwapa published the novel "Efuru." *Efuru* became the first English novel to be written and published by an African woman. In 1970 Flora founded the Tana Press making her one of Africa's pioneer female publishers. Today is known as the mother of modern African literature.

1966: On January 15, 1966, Nigeria witnessed its first military coup spearheaded by senior military officers of the Nigerian military Force.

1966: Coup plotters are captured and imprisoned by the Nigerian army led by Major General Umunnakwe Aguiyi Ironsi making the coup a partially successful one. Major General Aguiyi Ironsi took overpower on January 17, 1966 as the first Nigerian military head of state. This marked the end of Nigeria's First Republic.

1966–1967: Major General Aguiyi-Ironsi spent 194 days in power and on July 17 and 18, 1966, ushered in another coup this time headed by Northern military heads. The countercoup witnessed the assassination of Aguiyi-Ironsi and the systematic elimination of army officials from southeastern Nigeria. The emerging leadership was handed over to Lt.-Col. Yakubu Gowon on July 29, 1967, who at that time was the most senior army officer from the Northern Region.

1967–1970: On May 5, 1967, Nigeria's three regions were replaced with twelve states. On May 30, 1967, Ojukwu declared independence from Nigeria and the formation of the Republic of Biafra. The result was the bloody Civil War which spanned from July 1967 to January 1970.

1971: Nigeria joins the Organization of Petroleum Exporting Countries (OPEC). The rise in the price of crude oil brings in much revenue for Nigeria, making the exportation of crude oil Nigeria's main source of income till today.

1973: On January 1, 1973, the Nigerian Naira was changed from metric to decimal. The major unit was the Naira while the minor unit was the Kobo. Obafemi Awolowo who was Nigeria's previous federal commissioner of finance gave the new currency the name "Naira" which was derived from the words Nigeria and "Kobo" derived from a corruption of the word copper from which the coins were made. Prior to this, the West African Currency Board (WACB) issued bank notes and coins as legal tenders in Nigeria, Ghana, Sierra Leone, and the Gambia.

1973: The National Youth Service Corp was established.

1975–1976: Lt.-Col. Yakubu Gowon's regime was overturned in July 1975 through a coup headed by Brig. Gen. Murtala Ramat Mohammed. Murtala Mohammed was assassinated on February 13, 1976, in an abortive coup.

1976–1978: The leadership of the country was passed on to Murtala Mohammed's deputy, Lt.-Gen. Olusegun Obasanjo. A new constitution was drafted which adopted the American presidential system. The new constitution was published in September 1978 which officially meant that political parties could be formed and contest for elections.

1977: On February 11, 1977, the N20 banknote was issued as the highest denomination at the time. On the note was the face of the late head of state, General Murtala Ramat Muhammed who was assassinated the year before. On October 1, 1978, General Murtala was declared a national hero.

1979: Shehu Shagari is sworn in on September 30, 1979, signaling the beginning of Nigeria's Second Republic.

1983–1985: Shehu Shagari's government is overthrown by the military government headed by Major General Muhammadu Buhari with General Babatunde Idiagbon as the chief of staff and second in command. The new regime introduced War Against Indiscipline (WAI), currency change and currency exchange rate policy, the import substitution and industrialization policy, the go back to the land program, and the war against illicit drug trafficking.

1985–1993: On August 27, 1985, Buhari's regime is overthrown in a bloodless coup headed by General Ibrahim Babangida. In 1986, Babangida launched the Structural Adjustment Program as part of the requirements for taking an IMF loan. Babangida's regime was the second longest military rule in Nigeria.

1993: On June 12, 1993, Babangida's regime annulled the presidential elections, the results of which indicated that Moshood Abiola the party candidate for the Social Democratic Party (SDP) was the winner. The annulment resulted in nationwide protests and Babangida handed over to an interim government headed by Ernest Shonekan. Shonekan spent three months as an interim head before the government was once again taken over by the military in November 1993 this time headed by General Sani Abacha.

1994–1999: Moshood Abiola was arrested for treason and subsequently died in custody on July 7, 1998. In 1995, former military leader Olusegun Obasanjo, along with other ex-military men such General Oladipo Diya, General Shehu Musa Yar'Adua (who eventually died in detention), was also jailed for treason on accusations of attempting a coup to overthrow the Sani Abacha regime. In the same year, Ken Saro-Wiwa and other Ogoni activists were imprisoned and eventually executed by hanging by the Abacha Regime.

1998–1999: Sani Abacha died in office on June 8, 1998, and was preceded by General Abdulsalami Abubakar. On resuming power, Abdulsalami Abubakar established the Independent National Electoral Commission (INEC) to oversee the elections into various public positions in local governments, the state assemblies, and governors, and finally the office of a democratically elected president. In May 1999, Olusegun Obasanjo was elected as the president of Nigeria. This marked the end of military rule in Nigeria till date.

1999– Reintroduction of Sharia law in twelve northern states sparking protests by northern-based Christians.

1999–2007: Olusegun Obasanjo is sworn into power on May 29, 1999, under the political party of the People's Democratic Party (PDP). Obasanjo served two terms (eight years) In 2006, a national census was conducted. Obasanjo was also able to secure debt relief from the London and Paris Club.

2004–2006: The rise of the Niger Delta Militants with violent clashes in the region.

2007–2010: On April 21, 2007, Umaru Musa Yar'Adua emerged as the winner of the Nigerian presidential elections under the People's Democratic Party and was sworn in on May 29, 2007. On November 23, he was flown out of the country for the treatment of a then-unknown ailment. This left a power vacuum until February 10, 2010, when the Federal Executive Council of Nigeria in response to a Supreme Court of Nigeria ruling was forced to transfer presidential power to Goodluck Jonathan, the then vice president using the "Doctrine of Necessity." This action made Goodluck Jonathan the Acting President of Nigeria. Consequently, President Yar'Adua died on May 5, 2010, at the Aso Rock Presidential Villa and was buried the next day according to Islamic rites in his hometown in Katsina. On May 6, Goodluck Jonathan was sworn in as the substantive president of Nigeria and on May 18.

2011–2014: Goodluck Jonathan wins the presidential elections. His tenure is rocked with Boko Haram insurgencies and attacks which began in the early 2010 in the northern section of Nigeria. By 2013 a state of emergency had been declared in the North. The highlight being the kidnapping and abduction of more than 200 girls in the northern town of Chibok. By 2014 Boko Haram had captured several towns along the Lake Chad region despite the intervention of federal troops.

2015–2023: Muhammadu Buhari is sworn on the platform of the All Progressives Congress. On October 25, 2021, President Muhammadu Buhari launched the e-Naira which is a digital currency produced by the Central Bank of Nigeria. On November 22, 2022, the first oil drilling project was launched in the Kolmani River Field in Bauchi, northern Nigeria.

Further Reading

Akinwale, E. A. (2014). "A Historical and Comparative Analysis of Colonial and Post-colonial Bureaucracy in Nigeria." *Journal of Public Administration and Governance*, 4(2): 1–11. doi: 10.5296/ jpag.v4i2.5602.

BBC News. (2019). "Nigeria Profile – Timeline." https://www.bbc.com/news/world-africa-13951696

Britannica, T. Editors of Encyclopaedia. (2022, March 1). "Olusegun Obasanjo." *Encyclopedia Britannica*. https://www.britannica.com/biography/Olusegun-Obasanjo

Britannica, T. Editors of Encyclopaedia. (2022, September 16). "Sani Abacha." *Encyclopedia Britannica*. https://www.britannica.com/biography/Sani-Abacha

Central Bank of Nigeria. (October 2022). "History of Nigerian Currency." https://www.cbn.gov.ng/Currency/historycur.asp#:~:text=In%201991%2C%20the%2050K%20and,2001%20and%20October%202005%20respectively

Chidume, C. G. and U. U. Nmaju. (2019). "The Aro Hegemony: Dissecting the Myth and Reality." *Journal of Tourism and Heritage Studies*, 8(1): 76–87. doi: https://doi.org/10.33281/JTHS20129.2019.1.6

Duke, J. (2010). "The Impact of Colonialism on the Development of Management in Nigeria." *International Journal of Business Management*, 5(8): 65–75.

Edo, S. and A. Ikelegbe. (2014). "The Nigerian Economy: Reforms, Emerging Trends and Prospects." *Centre for Population and Environmental Development (CPED) Monograph Series* No. 8.

Enyioko, N. (2021). "Aba Women's Riots (November to December, 1929)." *SSRN Electronic Journal*, 1–11. doi: 10.2139/ssrn.3818954

Ezeibe, C. (2009). "Relevance and Limitations of Yar'adua's 7 Point Agenda." *African Renaissance*, 6(3&4): 33–41. https://www.researchgate.net/publication/281625097_Relevance_and_Limitations_of_President_Yar'adua's_7_Point_Agenda

Ikpe, U. (2000). "Patrimonialism and Military Regimes in Nigeria." *African Journal of Political Science*, 5(1): 146–62.

Momoh, M. (2022, November 24). "Nigeria Discovers, Launches First Crude Oil Field in North in 62 Years." *The East African*. https://www.theeastafrican.co.ke/tea/rest-of-africa/nigeria-discovers-crude-oil-field-in-north-4032002

Muhammad, M. (2014). "Military and Politics." In A. Bako, M. Muhammad, Y. Isma'ila, and M. A. Rufai (eds.), *Issues on Nigerian Peoples and Culture*, 1–14. Wudil: Kano University of Science and Technology.

Nunn, N. (2008). "The Long-Term Effects of Africa's Slave Trades." *Quarterly Journal of Economics*, 123(1): 139–76.

Ogundele, S. (2010). "Understanding Nigeria within the Context of the Atlantic World." *The African Diaspora Archaeology Network*. http://www.diaspora.uiuc.edu/news0910/news0910.html

Ojo, E. O. (2010). "Government by Incompatibles: A Case Study of the 1960–1964 Nigerian Federal Government." *African Journal of Political Science and International Relations*, 4(9): 340–9.

Omede, A. (2012). "The Nigerian Military: Analysing Fifty Years of Defence and Internal Military and Fifty Years of Internal Operations in Nigeria (1960–2010)." *Journal of Social Science*, 33(3): 293–303.

Oxford Department of International Development. (n.d.). "Sharia Implementation in Northern Nigeria after 15 Years." https://www.qeh.ox.ac.uk/content/sharia-implementation-northern-nigeria-after-15-years (accessed February 4, 2023).

Remitly. (n.d.). "Everything You Need to Know about Nigerian Currency." https://blog.remitly.com/currencies/facts-you-probably-didnt-know-nigerian-naira/ (accessed February 5, 2023).

The Guardian. (n.d.). "Emmanuel Ifeajuna: Commonwealth Games Gold to Facing a Firing Squad." *The Guardian*. https://www.theguardian.com/sport/2014/jul/13/commonwealth-games-emmanuel-ifeajuna-nigeria

This Day. (2022). "Gearing up to Relieve FESTAC'77@45." https://www.thisdaylive.com/index.php/2022/07/12/gearing-up-to-relieve-festac-77-45/ (accessed February 5, 2023).

Udo, R. K., A. Kirk-Greene, M. Hamilton, A. Ajayi, and T. Falola. (2022, December 4). "Nigeria." *Encyclopedia Britannica*. https://www.britannica.com/place/Nigeria

AGITATION FOR INDEPENDENCE

Agitation for independence in the pre-Nigerian nation-state began with resistance from indigenous rulers who fought to maintain autonomy over their land, economy (especially over trade routes) and people. In some cases, their resistance resulted in wars with the British as was the case with the Aniocha war (1883–1914), the Ijebu war (1892), the Benin Expedition (1897), and the Aro-Anglo war (1901–02). There were also missionary-educated elites who between 1860 and 1880 began to question the motives of missionary activities in Africa. They questioned the missionary's concept of Christianity especially as it related to justice, political power, rule of law, and their apparent racist worldview of White superiority over Africans and their ways of life.

Some of these educated elites were not only intellectuals but also successful businessmen and women who had taken up financial opportunities that opened trade with European companies operating in Africa. This included freed slaves from Brazil and migrants from Sierra Leone and Liberia. Despite their educational training, they were nevertheless conscious of their Black race and strongly defended Black dignity and unity. By 1880, some of them began to express their disapproval through newspapers indigenously established. The first of these indigenously established papers was the *Lagos Times and Gold Coast Advertiser* founded by Richard Beale Olamilege Blaize (a Sierra Leonean). The paper came out fortnightly but had a wide circulation (London, Accra, Togo, Freetown, and old Dahomey). One of the paper's aims was to make it a point of duty to publicly point out the gray areas of British colonial rule. Journalism thus laid the foundation for giving West Africans a voice to protest colonial rule and the stranglehold they felt Europe had on the African economy.

Nigeria became a colony in 1914 but this did not reduce the agitations. Some internal factors that sparked off protests include the colonial structure which did not consider the indigenes as eligible for top civil service positions, the imposition of taxes, land expropriation under the guise of achieving government projects with little to no compensation, and the country's state of economic depression. External factors included agitations from Nigerian students abroad for the independence of African colonies under European rule. Added to this were embittered returnee soldiers of the Second World War who came home with a different perspective of their British leaders.

After the Second World War, political parties were formed. The Nigerian National Democratic Party formed on June 24, 1923, by Herbert Macaulay is a prominent example. The party was especially bold in challenging colonial rule and its practices. This was followed by the formation of other political parties that had more of a regional outlook. Thus, in 1951, Obafemi Awolowo formed the Action Party which represented the western region, dominated by the Yoruba people; the eastern region dominated by Igbo people threw their weight behind the National Council of Nigeria and the Cameroons founded by Herbert Macaulay and Nnamdi Azikiwe, and the North had the Northern People's Congress with Tafawa Balewa as its leader.

See Also: Azikiwe, Nnamdi (Chapter 2); Awolowo, Obafemi (Chapter 2); Balewa, Abubakar Tafawa (Chapter 2); Colonial Nigeria (Chapter 2); Macaulay, Herbert (Chapter 2).

Further Reading

Auwalu, M. (2015). "Federalism and National Integration: The Myth of the Agitations for Confederation of Ethnic Nationalities in Nigeria." *Online Journal of African Affairs*, 4(1): 13.

Ibhawoh, B. (1989). "Nigeria." In H. Guntram and K. David (eds.), *Nationalism: A Global Historical Overview*, Volume 3, 1945 to 1989. Santa Barbara: ABC-CLIO.

Ogunbanjo, B. (2001). "Political Parties and Federalism in Nigeria: Understanding the Evolution of the Dialectical Relationship." *The Constitutional Development* (Centre for Constitutionalism and Demilitarisation, Nigeria), 2(2): 12–35. https://hdl.handle.net/10520/AJA15955753_296.

Ubaku, C., A. Emeh, and A. Nkiru. (2014). "Impact of Nationalist Movement on the Actualization of Nigerian Independence, 1914–1960." *International Journal of History and Philosophical Research*, 2(1): 54–67.

AWOLOWO, OBAFEMI

Obafemi Jeremiah Oyeniyi Awolowo was born March 1909 in Ikenne Ogun State. He was the first Premier of Western Nigeria between 1954 and 1960.

Obafemi Awolowo attended the Baptist Boys High School after which he started his career as a teacher. In 1927 he qualified as a shorthand typist and served as a clerk at the Wesley College Ibadan after which he became a correspondent for the *Nigerian Times*. He furthered his education through a correspondence course with the University of London and earned the Bachelor of Commerce. He continued by enrolling to study Law at the University of London in 1944 and was called to Bar by the Honorable Society of the Inner Temple in 1946.

Awolowo embarked on several business ventures but the major one that connected him to politics was the *Nigerian Tribune,* a newspaper he founded in 1949. The major aim of the newspaper was to serve as a mouthpiece for the *Egbe Omo Oduduwa*, a Yoruba sociocultural group which later became the political opposition party (Action Group) during Nigeria's First Republic. During the Colonial Era, the newspaper maintained an anti-colonial stance but served the interests of the Yoruba people at independence.

On the platform of the Action Group party, Awolowo became the first premier of the western region in 1954. Awolowo believed in "welfare politics" and the belief that education was an important part of fostering national development. As the premier, he introduced free primary education and health care for children in the western region. Through an act of the western region's House of Parliament, the first television service in Africa was established in 1959. It was prompted by Awolowo's desire to improve the region's school system which at that time was handicapped by a shortage of qualified teachers. These lofty projects were sustained by the cocoa business which boomed in the region.

Unfortunately, power struggles within the Action Party led to violence in the western region. Chief Akintola, the party's deputy leader ultimately broke away to form the National Democratic Party which governed the region until 1966. Awolowo along with some other Action Party faithful were arrested in 1963 and charged for conspiring with the Ghanaian authorities to overthrow the Nigerian government. Awolowo was sentenced to ten years imprisonment but only spent three when he was released after a Coup that suspended the Nigerian federal constitution.

During the Nigerian Civil War (1967–70), Awolowo served as the Commissioner of Finance and as vice-chairman of the Federal Executive Council. He resigned this position in 1971 as a protest the military's continuous rule. When the military conducted elections to facilitate the democratic handing over to the Third Republic, he contested for but lost the presidential seat under the Unity Party of Nigeria. He ran again for the presidential seat in 1983 and upon this second defeat resigned from active politics. He died four years later in 1987.

Awolowo was the author of many books which today shapes the school of thought known as "Awoism."

See Also: Agitation for Independence (Chapter 2); Azikiwe, Nnamdi (Chapter 2); Balewa, Abubakar Tafawa (Chapter 2); Colonial Nigeria (Chapter 2); Macaulay, Herbert (Chapter 2).

Further Reading

Ajayi, A. (2010). "The Development of Free Primary Education Scheme in Western Nigeria, 1952–1966: An Analysis." *OGIRISI a New Journal of Africana Studies*, 5(1). doi: https://doi.org/10.4314/og.v5i1.52320

Britannica, T. Editors of Encyclopaedia. (2022, May 5). "Obafemi Awolowo." *Encyclopaedia Britannica*. https://www.britannica.com/biography/Obafemi-Awolowo

Falola, T. (2012). *Power Politics or Welfare Politics? Chief Obafemi Awolowo in the History of African Nationalist Political Thought*. Austin: University of Texas.

AZIKIWE, NNAMDI

Benjamin Nnamdi Azikiwe was born November 1904 in Zungeru, Niger State and was the first president of Nigeria (1963–66).

Azikiwe spent his first eight years of life in the northeastern region of Nigeria where he learned the Hausa language and culture. In 1912, his father sent him to Onitsha, his hometown to expose him to the Igbo language and people. At Onitsha, Azikiwe attended missionary schools, but his stay was cut short when in 1914, he was bitten by a dog. This prompted his father to send him to Lagos to heal and resume his schooling. In Lagos, he learned the Yoruba language before returning to Onitsha in 1918 when his father was transferred to Kaduna. He left Onitsha in 1920 when his father was again transferred to Calabar where he continued his secondary education, but later returned to Lagos where he eventually finished. It is believed that his secondary school education exposed him to Pan-Africanism and its ideologies.

After his secondary school education, Azikiwe was employed in 1921 as a clerk with the Treasury Department; an experience which exposed him to the racial biases of the colonial government. He left the job for the USA when he gained admission to Storer College in 1925. He furthered his education at Lincoln University where he was awarded a BA (Honors) Political Science in 1930 and an MA in Religion and Philosophy in 1932. He earned another MSc in Anthropology from the University of Pennsylvania in 1933.

Azikiwe returned to Africa and began working for the Ghanaian newspaper *African Morning Post* as its editor in 1934. On this platform he wrote against colonial restrictions and discriminations against Africans. In 1936, he was tried for sedition, but his conviction was overturned on appeal. He returned to Nigeria in 1937 to set up his own chains of newspapers which included the *West African Pilot, Southern Nigerian Defender, Eastern Guardian,* and *The Comet.* Through these channels, Azikiwe confronted and criticized the colonial government putting immense pressure on them to grant Nigeria and indeed other African colonies freedom.

Azikiwe's chains of newspapers also served as platforms to initiate his political ambitions and promote the cause of the National Council of Nigeria and the Cameroons (NCNC), a political party he co-founded in 1944. NCNC became prominent in the eastern region and in 1951 became the opposition party upon which he became the premier of the eastern region. In 1960, Azikiwe became the governor-general and in 1963 Nigeria's first president. The military coup of 1966 ended his tenure and when the Nigerian Civil War (1967–70) broke out he was a major defender of the Biafran cause. The devastating effect of the war on the Igbo people prompted him to appeal to the Biafran military leader to end the war and accept the "one Nigeria" call.

Under the Nigerian People's Party, Azikiwe contested for the presidency in 1979 and again in 1983 but both attempts were unsuccessful. He eventually resigned from active politics and died in May 1996.

See Also: Awolowo, Obafemi (Chapter 2); Balewa, Abubakar Tafawa (Chapter 2); Constitutional Development (Chapter 3); Democratic Rule (Chapter 3); Macaulay Herbert (Chapter 2).

Further Reading

Britannica, T. Editors of Encyclopaedia. (2022, November 12). "Nnamdi Azikiwe." *Encyclopedia Britannica.* https://www.britannica.com/biography/Nnamdi-Azikiwe

Flint, J. (1999). "'Managing Nationalism': The Colonial Office and Nnamdi Azikwe, 1932–43." *The Journal of Imperial and Commonwealth History,* 27(2): 143–58. doi: https://doi.org/10.1080/03086539908583061

BALEWA, ABUBAKAR TAFAWA

Abubakar Tafawa Balewa was born December 1912 in Bauchi State. He was the first prime minister of Nigeria between October 1, 1960, and January 15, 1966.

Tafawa Balewa started his education at a Koranic school but was later transferred a Western-based school at the current Tafawa Balewa Elementary School in Bauchi. Between 1928 and 1933 he trained at Barewa College (now Katsina Teacher Training College) where he completed his formal education. After his educational training, he was employed at Bauchi Middle School and in 1941 he was made the headmaster of the school. In 1944 he and other teachers from northern Nigeria were selected to study at the University of London's Institute of Education between 1945 and 1946 where he received a Teacher's Certificate in History. On his return, he became an Inspector of Schools under the colonial government. In 1952, he was made the minister of works and later the minister of transport.

Tafawa Balewa's political career started in 1946 when he was elected to the northern House of Assembly and in 1947, he became a member of the Legislative Council where he was known to be very vocal in the defense of the rights of the northern people of Nigeria. His activities resulted in his election in 1948 as the vice president of the Northern Teacher's Association (the first trade union in northern Nigeria). He believed that the structural regional division of Nigeria at the time was not in favor of the northern people; and he was especially worried about the slow adoption to "civilization" in the northern region. For him, as long as the Native Administration did not ascribe more roles and responsibilities to the educated members of the northern region, he did not believe Nigeria was ready to be an independent nation.

He was a foundational and active contributor to the establishment of the Northern People's Congress which originally started as a cultural organization in 1949 but became the winning political party in 1957 resulting in Tafawa Balewa becoming the prime minister of Nigeria. As the prime minister of Nigeria, he formed a coalition government aimed at uniting the three regions that formed Nigeria at the time with the NPC (representing the northern region), the National Council of Nigeria and the Cameroons (NCNC) representing the eastern region and the Action Group representing the western region.

Though internal political wrangling threatened the stability of his government and eventually led to his violent assassination in January 1966; Tafawa Balewa is remembered for the important roles he played in the sustainability of peace and unity in Africa. He was at the forefront in the formation of the Organization of African Unity, spearheaded negotiations for peace during the Congo crisis and was a vocal protester against the massacre of South African students at Sharpeville. His official visit in 1961 to the United States based on the personal invitation of President John F. Kennedy led to both leaders declaring their "opposition to racial discrimination under any name or in any guise."

See Also: Awolowo, Obafemi (Chapter 2); Azikiwe, Nnamdi (Chapter 2); Democratic Rule (Chapter 3); Legislature (Chapter 3).

Further Reading

Blackpast. (2022). "Sir Abubakar Tafawa Balewa (1912–1966)." https://www.blackpast.org/global-african-history/balewa-sir-abubakar-tafawa-1912-1966/

Britannica, The Editors of Encyclopaedia. (2022, January 01). "Sir Abubakar Tafawa Balewa." *Encyclopedia Britannica*. https://www.britannica.com/biography/Abubakar-Tafawa-Balewa (accessed December 14, 2022).

BENIN EMPIRE

The Benin kingdom was founded on a patriarchal age-grade system that evolved within a cluster of thirty-one independent villages. Each village was headed by *Odionwere* (the eldest male) who was supported by four elders ranked in order of seniority. Together they formed the *Edionwere*, an administrative council that oversaw the activities of their village. The *Edionwere* was obliged to involve the *Edion* age grade which consisted of the oldest patriarchal male of each family unit most of whom were above fifty years. The *Edion* age grade was followed by the *Ighele* age group which consisted of men thirty to fifty years. The *Ighele* carried out the decisions of the *Edionwere* while also serving as the work and military force of the community.

Conflicts frequently arose within the *Edionwere* until Igodo the spokesman for the *Odionwere* of Ugbeku village took over. Igodo was an eloquent speaker and leader, believed to have acquired powers from the sky. He adopted the title *Ogiso* meaning 'king with authority from the sky' giving him authority above the *Edionwere*. Through this authority, he united the clustered independent villages under one monarchy called the *Ogiso* Dynasty (traced to 500 CE). He named the territory *Igodomigodo* meaning 'the town of Igodo' and made Ugbeku its capital. As king, Igodo Ogiso ruled with the support of the *Edionwere* which served as the custodians of tradition and history. By 1200 CE the *Ogiso* dynasty had collapsed to be replaced with the *Eweka* Dynasty which reigned until 1897 when Benin came under British colonial rule. Under the *Eweka* Dynasty the kingdom was called *Ubini*, meaning "a land of inexhaustible resources."

The *Eweka* Dynasty was riddled with internal political instability due to disputes between the Oba (king) and the *Edionnisen* (the patriarchal council of elders inherited from the *Ogisi* Dynasty). To increase the authority of the monarch, the first Oba, Eweka I, replaced the *Edionnisen* with the *Uzama*, a six-man political institution of elders. This constituted king makers had limited effect, however, as the *Uzama* remained powerful due to their traditional roles of regulating and influencing succession to the throne supported by their hereditary positions. Another major restructuring was done by Oba Ewuare (1440–72), who established the *Eghaevbo n'Ore* (Town Chiefs) and the *Eghaevbo n'Ogbe* (Palace Chiefs) as additional non-hereditary political groups. Ewuare also incorporated the crown prince into the *Uzama*, thus, converting it into the *Uzama n'Ihinron*, a seven-membership group. Ewuare went on to divide the city into Ogbe (where he and his palace officials lived) and Orenokhua (an area outside the city walls where the *Uzama n'Ihinron* lived). With this geopolitical restructuring the Oba ascribed supreme control to himself (although still obliged to consult with the *Uzama*). Oba Esigie (1504–50) further established the *Iyoba*, a fourth political group headed by the Queen mother.

Benin reigned as a wealthy and powerful military kingdom that was economically sustained through trade and the internal production of agriculture, metals, and crafts. It was one of the few pre-colonial civilizations that was not dependent on European trade due to her control and domination of local trade routes.

See Also: Benin Artwork (Chapter 12); European Explorers and Christianity (Chapter 2).

Further Reading

Ekeh, P. (2000). "Contesting the History of Benin Kingdom." *Research in African Literature*, 31(3): 147–70. doi: https://doi.org/10.1353/ral.2000.0081

Osadolor, O. (2001). "The Military System of the Benin Kingdom c1440-1897." Thesis submitted to the Department of Philosophy and History in partial fulfilment of the requirements for the award of Doctor of Philosophy, University of Hamburg, Germany.

COLONIAL NIGERIA

On August 6, 1861, Lagos became Britain's first crown property in Nigeria following the signing of a treaty between the king of Lagos and Consul John Beecroft (the British representative). At that time Beecroft was also in charge of the Bights of Benin and Biafra having signed similar treaties with various chiefs from Niger Delta regions as well as Fulani Sultans in the northern region. Unfortunately, Beecroft's administration was not very successful due to scarce manpower. To tackle this problem, the Selborne Committee was formed and in 1899, it was decided that the area be divided into three provinces namely the Northern (comprising current northern and middle-belt Nigerian states) and Southern Protectorates (comprising current eastern and western Nigerian states) and the Colony of Lagos. In 1906, Lagos was merged with the Southern Protectorate.

In 1914, the amalgamation of Northern and Southern Protectorates under one colonial administration formally established the colonial state of Nigeria. Lord Lugard who served as Nigeria's first governor initiated the Native Authority system (Indirect Rule) whereby the politico-religious authority of traditional rulers was retained. The rulers were mandated to ensure the British colonial objectives of replacing the slave trade with what the British called "legitimate commerce" was achieved. This included the production and exportation to Britain of palm oil, timber, cotton, and other cash crops. This method was effective in the Fulani Caliphate states as well as the Yoruba states but not so in the eastern sections because many of the ethnic groups that made up this section did not have sovereign political leaders.

In 1922, The Clifford Constitution was established to rectify the inadequacies of the Lugard system especially in terms of administrative powers and indigenous representation. Unfortunately, Clifford's introduction of taxes witnessed revolts during his tenure including the famous Abba Women's war.

In 1935, Sir Bernard Bourdillon took over and in 1939 he divided the South into eastern and western provinces to allow for better and more effective administration. He set up regional councils which acted in an advisory capacity. His system of governance accommodated suggestions and advice from the growing nationalist representatives, and this made him well liked especially by the Nigerian Youth Movement.

Bourdillon was succeeded by Sir Arthur Richards in 1945. Richards initiated a constitution which combined representatives of the Native Authorities and the regional councils together under one legislative body operating from Lagos. The Richards' Constitution was criticized especially by the NCNC for its lack of clarity especially as it related to the power of the traditional chiefs within the regions. The constitution was ultimately rejected by Nigerian leaders. Sir Richards himself was criticized for not consulting with the Nigerian populace and this was partly the cause of the country-wide strike of 1945.

In 1947, Richards was replaced with Sir John Macpherson who was more willing to accommodate suggestions and recommendations from provincial and regional representatives. In 1951, a Constitutional Conference of southern and northern delegates was held in Ibadan. The Macpherson Constitution was established in 1951 which aimed to capture the rights of the Nigerian people and the regions. Unfortunately, the constitution did not work as a single unit mainly because the representatives of the three regions could not come to an agreement in relation to the pattern of governance the new Nigeria should follow. In 1953, the regional representatives met again for a three-week conference held in London to discuss the territorial divisions and political organization of the federal and regional governments as well as the status of Lagos.

In 1957 an Independence Conference was held in London, and it was during this conference that all three regional representatives agreed for the initiation of an independent Nigeria in the year 1960.

See Also: Agitation for Independence (Chapter 2); Macaulay, Herbert (Chapter 2).

Further Reading

Utuk, E. I. (1975). "Britain's Colonial Administrations and Developments, 1861–1960: An Analysis of Britain's Colonial Administrations and Developments in Nigeria." Dissertations and Theses. Paper 2525.

EUROPEAN EXPLORERS AND CHRISTIANITY

Christianity was first introduced to Nigeria in the fifteenth century through the Portuguese leader, Henry the Navigator, whose ships were accompanied by Roman Catholic priests who attempted to spread the gospel in Benin and Warri. However, the priests made little impacts on the indigenous leaders who were more interested in the luxury goods and guns they traded for captured slaves.

Between the 1830s and 1840s slave trade saw a drastic declined due to Britain's drive to replace it with a more "legitimate trade" in agriculture and other raw materials from Africa. This resulted in the seizure of slave ships bound for the Americas and Brazil which were diverted to Sierra Leone (many of whom later migrated to present-day Nigerian states of Ogun and Lagos); while freed slaves from America were shipped to Liberia, and many from Brazil taken to various West African seaports. As freed slaves, they embraced the doctrines of various Christian Missionary Societies (CMS) which also introduced Western education and technical skills. This exposure empowered the freed slaves and encouraged them to tap into the British legitimate trade thus transforming many into wealthy traders.

Due to their Western education, technical skills, and direct access to British/European political and religious influences, the freed slaves had an edge over their indigenous brothers and sisters. This made traditional rulers welcome them as important human capital for rebuilding an alternative political and economic structure to replace that built on the slave trade. The British also identified the freed slaves as important resources in their ambition to legitimize colonization. Various Christian Missionary Societies (CMSs) like the Methodist, Baptist, and Presbyterian; and the Roman Catholic Church (this was especially the case for Brazilian freed slaves) likewise encouraged the freed slaves to collaborate with them in preaching the gospel and gaining converts. Through this effort, churches were planted, schools built, and religious institutions established. These projects were usually headed by European representatives of the religious body and supported by a converted freed slave. Due to the high rate of death by heat-stroke or malaria, a number of the European missionaries could only spend a few years at a time in Africa leaving a lot of the physical driving force in the hands of the converts with strict supervision from the mother church in Europe.

Christian institutions developed in Nigeria were determined to abolish traditional cultural practices and the worship of traditional gods; all of which were declared acts of sin and darkness. They preached that there was a direct relationship between accepting Christianity and spiritual, economic, social, and political development. Through their efforts, the first printing press in Nigeria was established by the Presbyterian Mission in 1846 at Calabar; and in 1859, Reverend Henry Townsend of the Anglican mission inaugurated the first newspaper in Nigeria, *Iwe Irohin Yoruba fun awon Egba ati Yoruba*.

There were cases when the missionary church got involved with local politics. A good example occurred when the Egbas requested for the Anglican missionary to support their fight to ward off Dahomey military threats.

See Also: Catholicism (Chapter 5); Inter-Religious Conflicts (Chapter 5); Islam and Trade (Chapter 2); Pentecostalism (Chapter 5).

Further Reading

Strickland, M. (1999). "The History of Christianity in Nigeria: A Case Study with Special Emphasis on Southern Baptist Mission Work." A senior thesis in General Studies submitted to the General Studies Council in the College of Arts and Sciences at Texas Tech University.

IFE KINGDOM

Scholars of Yoruba history and culture literally translate the word "Ile-Ife" to mean "a wide and original home." Ile-Ife is believed to be the ancestral home of the Yoruba people, representing the oldest surviving dynasty in Yorubaland. Based on archaeological and anthropological evidence, Ife is believed to be the outcome of the amalgamation of thirteen to sixteen communities which occurred between the ninth and eleventh century. Oral accounts suggest that these dispersed but autonomous villages recognized Obatala as their leader; an authority that was challenged with the coming of Oduduwa who promoted a more centralized political system. Some oral accounts suggest that Obatala was Oduduwa's older brother while others believe that Oduduwa was a migrant from Mecca. Scholars of Ife history believe that the ensuing conflict may have lasted from the beginning of the ninth century until the beginning of the eleventh century. It took the intervention of *Ifa* (*Orunmila* the god of wisdom) for peace to prevail.

By the twelfth century, Ife was a thriving urban settlement which was encircled by two major city walls. Within the city walls were residential and religious structures as well as road pavement networks made from broken potsherds. Archaeological evidence discovered at *Ita Yemoo* represents a site where remains of a potsherd pavement which covered a surface area of more than an acre in size are preserved. The introduction of potsherd pavements was believed to have been introduced by Luwo Gbagida a female *Ooni* (monarch) who reigned in Ife in the tenth century. According to oral tradition, she was a monarch who did not like her clothes and shoes to be soiled and thus instructed her subjects to construct the pavements which also encouraged a culture of cleanliness.

The people of ancient Ile-Ife were heterogeneous groups that claimed their descent through a common ancestor and were governed by a political system headed by an *Ooni*. The *Ooni* ruled with the support of a team of chiefs and religious personnel who in turn were guided by gods, deities, rituals, and festivals. Today the *Ooni* of Ife is still considered a powerful leader and likened to a god by the Yoruba people. Scholars have likened the *Ooni* and his palace as the hub of a wheel from which everything radiates. This can be represented in two major ways. First, is the physical design of Ife where the *Ooni*'s palace is at the center in front of which is a major market known as *Oja'ba* (literally meaning the king's market). All major roads in the city of Ife radiate from the *Ooni*'s palace and lead to neighboring towns. Second, the *Ooni*'s presence and personality serves as the center of all traditional rituals and festivals, activities that represent the very existence of Ile-Ife itself and these ritual festivals attract several people within and outside Nigeria.

The history of the Ife Empire speaks of a powerful and complex social, cultural, and political system that has lasted for more than 2,000 years.

See Also: Ife Artwork (Chapter 12); Oyo Empire (Chapter 2); Yoruba (Chapter 6).

Further Reading

Osasona, C., L. Ogunshakin, and D. Jiboye. (2009). "Ile-Ife: A Cultural Phenomenon in the Throes of Transformation." In C. Osasona, L. Ogunshakin, and D. Jiboye (eds.) *African Perspectives: The African Inner City*, i–xi, Ibadan: Shaneson Ltd.

ISLAM AND TRADE

The history of Islam and trade revolve around the peoples that make up the northern section Nigeria. These include the Kanuri people of Kanem-Bornu (the oldest ethnic group in modern Nigeria to have embraced Islam) and the *Hausa-bakwai* Empires. Islam was first introduced to West Africa through Islamic traders, missionaries, and scholars from the Mediterranean and in extension the Middle East through Sudan and Mali into the Kanem-Borno Empire. A few trade routes were established, the major one being the Trans-Saharan route. Thus, in the process of these interactions, Islam as a way of life was introduced. In Kanem-Bornu, the introduction of Islam was a peaceful one with Islamic merchants even settling down and marrying from the empire.

In the case of the *Hausa-akwai* Empires, Islam was not fully accepted until the Fulani Jihad took place in 1804 and later in 1808 before the conversion could manifest in its entirety. The Holy War was spearheaded by Usman Dan Fodio, who was from the Fulani ethnic tribe. The Fulani people were believed to have migrated into northern Nigeria in small pockets and established themselves into the Hausa society. It is believed that the Fulani as well as other commoners were treated as second class citizens with limited to no rights. Usman was appalled by the high level of corruption, oppression, and low morality the Hausa rulers and elites displayed against both the common man and their slaves. He was also opposed to the traditional forms of worship and rituals the Hausa people conducted. Through preaching and teachings, he was able to gather a followership of believers to fight for a social change through an adherence to Islamic tenets. The Holy War which was later to be known as the Fulani Jihad took place in 1804 and later in 1808. It resulted in the establishment of the Sokoto Caliphate and the forceful spread of Islam to Nupe, Jukun, and parts of Yorubaland.

At the death of Usman Danfodio's brother and son, who headed the western and eastern sections of the new emirate, anarchy set in. The rulers that followed were not as enthusiastic as the founding fathers and revolt after revolt against the authority of the Sokoto headship was recorded between 1837 and 1851. This made resistance to British rule very weak and the concept of indirect rule easier to achieve.

Islam brought a number of changes to the Nigerian socioeconomic as well as religio-political landscape. Because the religion spread through trade routes of the Trans-Saharan trade, there was an influx of goods coming into and out of northern Nigeria. This also encouraged and improved diplomatic relations with empires northern Nigeria traded with. Islamic education naturally flourished resulting in the formation of Islamic educational centers especially in Kanem-Borno. In Hausa states such as Kano and Zaria, chronicles of events within the empire were recorded and today are valuable records for piecing together events of the time. The accounts speak of the sociopolitical situation of Kano and its neighboring states from the fourteenth century.

See Also: Explorers and Christianity (Chapter 2); Islamic Education (Chapter 8); Islamic Movement (Chapter 5).

Further Reading

Abbass, I. (2010). "The State and Rural Zaria from Affluence to Poverty: Historical Bank." *International Journal of Economic Development Research and Investment*, 1(2&3): 83–100.
Omotosho, S. (2011). *ISL 372: Islam in Nigeria*. Lagos: National Open University of Nigeria.

KINGDOM OF ZARIA

Zaria was established as one of the seven original Hausa empires that shared a common ancestry traced to *Bayajidda*. The people of Zaria were known as *Zazzagawa* or *Zage* and were mainly traders, farmers, hunters, and iron smelters. Their state was originally known as *Garin Dan Zau,* and its first king was *Gunguma* (grandson of *Bayajidda*). This name was later changed to *Zazzau* (named after a sword). *Zazzau* was a sword which symbolized political as well as spiritual power and authority. Historians have put the date of this name change to around 1536. Historians believe that *Gunguma* represented the original political state during the dynasty reign of *Bayajidda;* and *Zazzau* after. Historians believe the change of name was a result of heavy attacks the town faced in the thirteenth century which prompted the emergence of defense tactics and a change in the political system; including the kingship structure now headed by the *Sarki*. Evidence obtained through the *Zaria Chronicles*, suggests that the empire was ruled through a long line of rulers. The acceptance of Islam by the ruling elites in Zaria (1450–56) further changed the political, social, and economic structure of the kingdom.

The empire of *Zazzau* was characterized by wars of territorial expansion as well as attacks from neighboring Hausa empires between the sixteenth and eighteenth century. To protect its core borders, *Bakwa Turunku* the ruling monarch at the time decided to rebuild the old and more spacious town of *Birnin Zaria* (renamed after his daughter) as the empire's city capital. To do this, the town had to be fortified by *ganuwa* (a complex town wall formation) with nine gates; a construction, records indicate, took five years to complete. It was soon after this period that Queen Amina, the daughter of *Sarkin Zak-zak* reigned. She was known for her fierceness; and records indicate that she conquered and subdued surrounding kingdoms including Bauchi, Nupe, and Jukun (AKA *Kwararrafa*). During her 35-year reign, her kingdom spread and was economically enriched through trade and tributes paid by surrounding empires such as Katsina and Kano. The level of economic prosperity of the empire attracted a lot of migrants, traders, craftsmen, scholars, and refugees.

After the death of Queen Amina, the empire fell under the Jukun Kingdom and later, Songhai Empire. Between 1805 and 1808, it was invaded by the Fulani Jihadists. By 1900, *Zazzau* was taken over by the British. By 1904, roads, rail lines, and telephone networks were constructed thus connecting Zaria to Kano and Bauchi. This encouraged European military forces, colonial officials, as well as manufacturing companies to move to Zaria. By 1911, the British Cotton Growing Association built a cotton processing plant in the city, and in 1918 the Nigerian Tobacco Company also set up a factory. Thus, under British rule, Zaria became an important center for infrastructural development in northern Nigeria. Today, Zaria, is still one of the major cities in Kaduna, northern Nigeria and is the location of Ahmadu Bello University as well as the Nigerian College of Aviation Technology.

See Also: Hausa Language (Chapter 8); Hausa/Fulani (Chapter 6); Sokoto Caliphate (Chapter 2).

Further Reading

Abbass, I. (2010). "The State and Rural Zaria from Affluence to Poverty: Historical Bank." *International Journal of Economic Development Research and Investment*, 1(2&3): 83–100.
Britannica, T. Editors of Encyclopaedia. (2011). "Zaria." *Encyclopedia Britannica*, June 17. https://www.britannica.com/place/Zaria-Nigeria.
Usman, S. (2007). "A History of Birnin Zaria from 1350–1902." Master Thesis submitted to Ahmadu Bello University, Zaria.

MACAULAY, HERBERT

Olayinka Herbert Samuel Heelas Badmus Macaulay was born on November 14, 1864, in Lagos. His parents were ex-slaves who were freed and resettled in present-day Sierra Leone. His father was Thomas Babington Macaulay while his mother was the daughter of Bishop Samuel Ajayi Crowther. Both parents eventually came to Nigeria, their traditional home to settle. Herbert Macaulay's father is credited for being the founder of CMS Grammar School, the first secondary school in Nigeria, which Herbert Macaulay attended (1877–80). Before then, he had attended missionary primary schools in Lagos.

After his secondary school education, Macaulay took up a clerical job with the Department of Public Works, Lagos. In 1890, he was sponsored by the colonial government to further his education in Plymouth, England, and he earned a degree from the Royal Institute of British Architects, London, and certificates in music from Trinity College and Music International College both in London.

Macaulay returned to Lagos in 1893 and continued with the Colonial Civil Service as a surveyor. He resigned from this position in 1898 amidst a lot of allegations which he levelled against the government and which the government also had against him. He accused the government of racial discrimination and of using double standards in their rule over the Lagos Colony, while his office of employment accused him of corrupt practices for private gains. After his resignation, he practiced as a private surveyor for the Lagos socialites but by 1900, he began to venture into politics and became more vocal against colonial rule and practices. He co-founded the *Nigerian Daily News*, a newspaper that served as a platform for him to publicly oppose the colonial government on issues ranging from finances, levies, taxes, and land appropriation. He also legally served as a defender of Lagos elites against colonial injustice such as in famous Apapa and Aleko cases.

Through his writings, Macaulay became very popular. In June 1923, he founded the Nigerian National Democratic Party, and this became Nigeria's first political party. His party contested for and won three electoral seats in the 1923, 1928, and 1933 elections. Through the party, he fought for self-governance for Lagos, education, Africanisation of the civil service, and the non-discrimination of private economic enterprises.

Though Macaulay was barred from taking on any public office due to two legal convictions against him (the first was for fraud for which he served two years in prison and the second for sedition for which he spent six months in prison); he nevertheless had sufficient influence over the country's affairs, and this earned him the title "Father of Nationalism."

In 1944, Macaulay teamed up with Nnamdi Azikiwe to form the more national political party, the National Council of Nigeria and the Cameroons (NCNC). He made Azikiwe the president of the party. The party had a national outlook with the aim of bringing Nigerians together to demand for independence. Unfortunately, Macaulay never saw this dream become a reality as he died in May 1946.

See Also: Agitation for Independence (Chapter 2); Azikwe, Nnamdi (Chapter 2); Colonial Nigeria (Chapter 2).

Further Reading

Zaccheus Onumba Dibiaezue Memorial Libraries. (2022). "Herbert Macaulay." https://zodml.org/discover-nigeria/people/historicalpeople/herbert-macaulay

NIGERIAN CIVIL WAR (1967–70)

The Nigerian civil war officially broke out on the July 6, 1967, following the counter coup of 1966. The genesis of the war can be traced to anti-Igbo sentiments developed in the northern region after the murder of top northern political leaders a year before. This ushered in the short-lived military term of Gen Aguiyi-Ironsi. For the northern region, Aguiyi-Ironsi's leadership represented the Igbo people's determination to dominate Nigeria's political sphere. In July 1966 Aguiyi-Ironsi was assassinated in a counter coup led by top military officers from northern Nigeria. July 1966, Lt.-Col. Yakubu Gowon (from the northern region) took over. The 1966 genocide killings of Igbos in the northern region caused many to flee to the eastern region. For the Igbo people, Gowon's government, and its call for Igbo killings to stop did little to protect and address the lawless violence against their relatives in northern Nigeria.

It was within this context that the Igbo people of Nigeria's eastern region began discussions to secede under the leadership of Lt.-Col. Ojukwu. In January 1967, the Nigerian Supreme Military Council arranged a meeting of military rulers and representative officers of each region for discussions in Aburi, Ghana, under the auspices of General Ankrah (who at that time was the head of Ghana's military government). Unfortunately, the result was all but positive and despite the intervention efforts of personalities like the late Emperor Selassie and Dr Martin Luther King to resolve the now apparent face-off between the federal government of Nigeria and the Igbo leaders headed by Lt.-Col. Ojukwu neither side were ready to back down.

On May 27, 1967, the federal government under a decree, replaced the three-region format with twelve states. The aim being to empower minority ethnic groups especially those which formed the former eastern region. In response, Ojukwu declared the now former eastern region an independent and sovereign nation under the name "Biafra" on May 30, 1967. The result was the Nigerian civil war which started with the first bullet shot by the federal government on the early morning of July 6, 1967. At the start of the war, the federal government assumed that the standoff would not last longer than 48 hours. They were very wrong. The Biafran troops were war ready, having acquired weapons from France, Spain, and Portugal; and recruiting their army personnel from the University of Nsukka and the general Igbo populace.

The ensuing battle raged until December 1969 when the people of Biafra were faced with hunger due to a blockade of food into the region by the federal government. Added to this was the resistance of minority ethnic groups from the Niger Delta region against the Biafran rule. It was these factors that defeated Biafra and not necessarily the Nigerian military troops. Eventually, on January 12, 1970, Lt.-Col. Effiong had no choice but to announce the surrender of Biafra. The reign of authority had been handed over to him by Ojukwu who fled to Abidjan on January 10, 1970 "in the interest of peace."

See Also: Military Rule (Chapter 3).

Further Reading

Kirk-Greene, A. H. M. (1975). "The Genesis of the Nigerian Civil War and the Theory of Fear." *Research Report No. 7*. Uppsala: The Scandinavian Institute of African Studies.

Lasse, H. and A. D. Moses. (2014). "The Nigeria–Biafra War: Postcolonial Conflict and the Question of Genocide." *Journal of Genocide Research*, 16(2–3): 169–203. doi: 10.1080/14623528.2014.936700

Omaka, A. (2014). "The Forgotten Victims: Ethnic Minorities in the Nigeria-Biafra War, 1967–1970." *Journal of Retracing Africa*, 1(1): 25–40.

NRI CIVILIZATION

The Nri civilization represents the oldest kingship system in Igboland and is believed to have reached its peak between 1250 and 1670 CE. It was founded by the Umueri people which is made up of four autonomous clans namely: Enugwu-Ukwu, Nawfia, Agu-Ukwu, and Enugwu-Agidi. These four clans were bound together by a common patriarchal ancestor known as Eri. According to oral history, Eri is believed to have descended from the sky and settled around the Anambra River valley. Sent by the Supreme God, Chukwu, to establish the Nri civilization, he was both a religious and political leader. Eri is said to have introduced *eke, oye, afor* and n*kwo* as names of the four days that make up the Igbo week, while a month had seven weeks and a year thirteen months. This calendar system was central to trade as it was used in the calculation of Igbo market days.

Through Eri's influence the *Eze Nri* (literally meaning "King of Nri"), a political system that dates to the end of the ninth century was established. He developed a system regulated by a series of religious and cultural practices as well as ritual cleansings and taboos all of which bound the Umueri clans together and guided their thoughts and behaviors. This ideology of unity through the guidance of ancestral standards and principles is conceptualized in the Igbo worldview referred to as *Omenani*; which captures unified moral definitions of right and wrong, cultural norms of appropriate behavior, artistic values, and aesthetic displays.

The political structure that governed the Nri civilization has been likened to a democratic system due to the equivalence of general assemblies that were often convened, and all adult members including women and representatives of age grades were obliged to attend. During such meetings major controversial issues that concerned the state were discussed and opinions as to the appropriate actions that should be taken decided. Decisions taken were then communicated to the *Eze Nrin* who on his part ruled with the support of two groups of state councils namely the *Nzemabua* and *Ndi Nze*. Both groups were made up of men who had proved through their achievements worthy to be awarded an *Ozo* title (founded on a hierarchical format from major to minor titles based on age and achievement) and the supporting *Ofo* (a wooden stick) as a symbol of authority. The council members represented the various categories of *Ozo* titles and the lineage members that made up the kingdom. The *Ndi Eze* attended to matters relating to the *Ozo* title, while *Nzemabua*, the most powerful traditional group in the Nri civilization, deliberated with the *Eze Nri* on matters that affected the internal and external affairs of the state. Other groups that helped to maintain law and order include the *Dibia,* a fraternity of traditional healers and diviners; and the *Agbala Nri* oracle cult believed to have mystical powers and insight.

The Nri civilization was very advanced, and its people have been identified as the producers of the ancient Igbo-Ukwu art culture.

See Also: Igbo (Chapter 6); Igbo Artwork (Chapter 12); Kingdom of Zaria (Chapter 2).

Further Reading

Keazor, E. (2018). "Igbo Historiography Milestones: Triumphs and Challenges." Being a paper delivered at the Igbo Conference at the School of Oriental and African Studies, London.

Obiozor, W. (2014, December 27). "The Umunri-Enugwu Ukwu Ancestral Connection: A Historical Perspective." Presentation at the UmuNri Colloquium – Enegwu-Ukwu Diaspora Mass Return, Awka, Anambra State Nigeria.

OYO EMPIRE

The Old Oyo Empire was in the savannah region of ancient Yorubaland. Old Oyo is different from the current "New Oyo"; the later growing from *Ago-Oja,* a location originally used as a hunting/farming camp following the fall of Old Oyo and the abandonment of its capital by the *Alaafin* (king) and entourage. The presence of the *Alaafin* at *Ago-Oja* is believed to have attracted people from nearby locations to also settle, resulting in the quick growth of the camp into the thriving city known today as New Oyo. As with Old Oyo, New Oyo grew with the *Alaafin's* palace and an associated marketplace serving as the core. The Alaafin's palace represented political and spiritual stability while the market represented a flourishing economy.

Archaeological evidence suggests that Old Oyo spread over a geographical space of more than 5,000 hectares which was fortified with five layers of walls. The inner wall enclosed the palace, residential structures, and the major market. The inner wall was followed by two main outer walls which served as major defense structures, and each was surrounded with a ditch that was as wide as five meters to strengthen the fortification. The fourth and fifth walls did not have ditches and archaeologists believe the land within these walls may have been used as farmland.

The political system that governed the Old Oyo Empire was headed by Alaafin and his council of seven patriarch heads known as the *Oyomesi* who served as kingmakers and advisers. Collectively, the *Oyomesi* were more powerful than the *Alaafin* especially as their positions were hereditary and not appointed; meaning they occupied their positions for life. Members of the *Oyomesi* include *Bashorun* (spiritual leader and guardian of the *Oyomesi*); *Agbakin* (high priest responsible for conducting the worship of *Oranmiyan* founder of Old Oyo and lastborn of *Oduduwa*), *Alapinni* (head of the *Egungun,* an ancestral cult represented by masquerades), *Laguna* (position similar to a Minister of Foreign Affairs), *Samu* (position similar to a Special Adviser to critical matters), *Akinniku* (adviser on military issues), and *Asipa* (the most junior member of the council who ran their errands). After the *Oyomesi* Council were captains of military nobility known as *Eso*. *Eso* was made up of ten men within seven groups with each group headed by an *Oyomesi* council member. Despite the supervision from council members, the *Eso* as an entity was headed by Are *Onakakanfo* who served as the Commander-in-Chief of the Oyo army and reported directly to the *Alaafin*. Unlike the *Alaafin* and *Oyomesi*, the *Eso* and the *Are Onakakanfo's* positions were not hereditary.

Old Oyo economically thrived due to the trade of agricultural and animal products as well as internally produced commodities like pottery, jewelry, cloth, and iron tools. Unfortunately, the complex political checks and balances of the empire resulted in internal conflicts which weakened its overall administration. By the 1830s, Old Oyo had collapsed from Fulani jihadist attacks on its northern borders. Today, the people of New Oyo still celebrate the rich culture, religion, and philosophy of their ancestors.

See Also: Benin Empire (Chapter 2); Ife Kingdom (Chapter 2); Yoruba (Chapter 6).

Further Reading

Biobaku, S. (n.d.). "The Pattern of Yoruba History." *Africa South*, 2(2): 63–7.

Britannica, T. Editors of Encyclopaedia. (2021, September 19). "Oyo Empire." *Encyclopedia Britannica*. https://www.britannica.com/place/Oyo-empire

Ogundiran, A. (2012). "The Formation of an Oyo Imperial Colony during the Atlantic Age." In C. Monroe and A. Ogundiran (eds.), *Power and Landscape in Atlantic West Africa: Archaeological Perspectives*, 222–52. doi: https://dx.doi.org/10.1017/CBO9780511921032

SOKOTO CALIPHATE

Sokoto Caliphate was originally part of the seven Hausa states which trace their ancestry to *Bayajidda*, a patriarchal hero. According to Hausa oral history, *Bayajidda* came from Baghdad (Middle East) as a refugee. He eventually arrived at Daura and helped the local people kill a snake which prevented them from accessing their drinking well. In exchange for his bravery, the monarch of the time, Queen Daurama married him. Together they bore a son, Bawo who also had six sons: Rano, Kano, Biram, Gobir, Katsina, and Zaria. Together, they formed the *Hausa-Bokwoi* (Hausa seven) or the Habe Kingdom (pre-Islamic name for the Hausa Kingdom) with Daura serving as the central mother state.

Sokoto Caliphate was established by Usman Danfodiyo (a Fulani) whose ancestors were Muslim scholars that migrated from Futa Toro. Usman was born in 1754 at Gobir and raised under strict Muslim tenets. He specialized in health, astronomy, arithmetic, Arabic as well as reading the Quran. He eventually became a teacher, writer, and preacher of the Islamic precepts. As he grew up, he became increasingly concerned about non-Islamic practices of the Hausa leaders, their form of oppressive rule, and the heavy taxes they imposed. Usman began a social reform through educational enlightenment and preaching. This strategy attracted the followership and support of intellectuals, students, and members of mass society (including women, the poor, and underprivileged). He called for the purification of the soul based on Islamic tenets, defending the poor against the oppressive rich and powerful, stopping corrupt practices and shunning material and earthly wealth. By late 1770, he had a great following, and this was seen as a threat to the rulers of Gobir prompting an attempt on his life. Usman fled from Gobir to Gudu (this incident is likened to the flight of Prophet Mohammad (SAW) who fled Medina to Mecca). This flight made him realize that force was the only way to bring about the needed social change. A Jihad was thus planned and carried out in June 1804, in a battle against the Gobir forces in Takbin Kwotto. Even though the Gobir forces were better armed, Usman's army won the day. With this victory, Usman's army went on to successfully take over other Hausa states as well as Nupe, Jukun, and part of Yoruba land.

The Jihad of 1804 led to the establishment of the Sokoto Caliphate. In 1812, Usman divided the Caliphate into the eastern section which consisted of Sokoto, Gobir, Katsina, Kano, Daura, Zaria, Keffi, Nassarawa, Katagun, Bauchi, and Adamawa with the capital in Sokoto; and western section which comprised of Kebbi (Gwandu), Yauri, Nupe, Borgu, and Ilorin with its capital at Gwandu. He appointed his son, Mohammed Bello to head the eastern section and his younger brother Abdullahi Fodiyo to head the western section. At the death of Usman in 1817, his son took over as the Caliph. Successive Caliphs were constantly at war defending the empire against raids, revolts, and attacks against their strict Muslim doctrines and power. The Sokoto Caliphate eventually came under British control in 1903.

Being a scholar himself and the author of more than a hundred books written in Arabic, Fulfulde, and Hausa; Usman encouraged education within the Caliphate. His daughter, Nana Asma'u, was a major flagbearer of this educational campaign. She composed poems and songs, (which according to sources are still sung today) to educate rural women about Islam and their responsibilities as a wife to her family.

See Also: Hausa/Fulani (Chapter 6); Kingdom of Zaria (Chapter 2).

Further Reading

Adeleke, A. (2005). "Islam and Hausa Culture." *Lagos Historical Review*, 5: 99–110.

Bergstrom, K. (2002). "Legacies of Colonialism and Islam for Hausa Women: An Historical Analysis, 1804–1960." *Working Paper #276, Women & International Development*. Michigan State University.

Munir, A. and G. Odeh. (2014). "The Establishment of the Nigerian Sokoto Caliphate: An Inquest into the Background History of the 1804 Jihad in Hausa Land, 210 Years After." *Al-Qalam*, 19(2): 61–71.

Nwabara, S. (1963). "The Fulani Conquest and Rule of the Hausa Kingdom of Northern Nigeria (1804–1900)." *Journal de la Société des Africanistes*, 33(2): 231–42. doi: https://doi.org/10.3406/jafr.1963.1370

CHAPTER 3

Government and Politics

OVERVIEW

After its independence in 1960, Nigeria inherited from Britain, its colonial master, a federal form of the Westminster system, which is made up of an executive branch of government that is responsible to the legislature. Alhaji Sir Abubakar Tafawa Balewa was the prime minister and head of government while Queen Elizabeth II of England was the ceremonial head of state. Three years after independence Nigeria became a republic. Although the country still retained the Westminster system, it replaced the Queen as head of state with a ceremonial president, a position Dr. Nnamdi Azikiwe occupied until 1966 when the first republic was sacked by the Nigerian military junta. The country, during the first republic, was administratively divided into regions headed by premiers. The premier of the northern region was Ahmadu Ibrahim Bello who led the region from 1959 to 1966; the western region was first headed by Obafemi Jeremiah Awolowo from 1959 to 1960, and then by Samuel Ladoke Akintola, from 1960 to 1966. Michael Iheonukara Okpara was the premier of the eastern region between 1960 and 1966; while Chief Dennis Chukude Osadebay was the premier of the mid-western region from 1964 to 1966. Politics was mainly along regional and ethnic lines with the Northern People's Congress (NPC) led by the Sardauna of Sokoto, controlling the dominantly Hausa/Fulani northern region. The Action Group (AG) led by Chief Awolowo had its strong hold in the predominantly Yoruba western region, while Dr Nnamdi Azikiwe's National Council of Nigeria and the Cameroons (NCNC) dominated the eastern region although with some influence in the western region. In the First Republic, the NPC controlled the federal parliament and formed a coalition government with the NCNC while the AG was the official opposition party. Besides, these three major political parties, however, were other "smaller" parties that were also founded by ethnic groups such as the Igala Union party to represent mainly the Igala ethnic group; the Midwest Democratic Front representing the ethnic minority groups of Benin, Urhobo,

Ijaw, and Itsekiri nations. Others include the grassroots party represented by the Zamfara Commoners Party and the United Middle Belt Congress, among other similar parties.

The First Republic was abruptly terminated in the 1966 coup that led to the assassination of prominent political figures including the prime minister, Tafawa Balewa, the finance minister, Festus Okotie-Eboh, and the premiers of northern and western regions, Sir Ahmadu Bello and Samuel Akintola, respectively. The countercoup of July 1966 which led to the Nigerian Civil War between 1967 and 1970 heralded the involvement of the military in Nigeria's politics. After the end of the First Republic in 1966, Nigeria witnessed an uninterrupted military rule for thirteen years until the Second Republic was inaugurated in 1979 with the adoption of the presidential system of government. The presidential system, which was designed along the United States presidential system, is composed of three arms of government, the Executive, the Legislature, and the Judiciary. The amendment and adoption of the 1979 Constitution provides for the separation of powers among the three branches of government. The executive arm of government is made up of the President, the vice president, and the Federal Cabinet of appointed ministers. The president also doubles as the Commander-in-Chief of the Armed Forces and assumes executive powers that the prime minister had in the Westminster system of the First Republic. The Legislative arm of government is made up of the Senate (Upper House) and House of Representatives (Lower House). The Legislative branch of government commands legislative power in the country and it is responsible for passing laws in the country and holds the executive branch accountable. While the Legislature creates laws, its powers and procedures are guided and limited by the constitution. Also, for any law passed by the legislature to be official, the executive arm of government through the president must ascend to it. The president also has the constitutional right to veto or refuse ascent to any law passed by the legislature. The Judiciary, as the third arm of government, comprises the Supreme Court and the lower courts of the land. The cardinal functions of the Judiciary are to interpret the constitution and uphold justice in the land, preserve the rule of law, and hear cases and apply the law. Together the three arms of government provide leadership and governance in the country. While the arms of government are expected to be independent and serve as checks to one another, in practice this cardinal characteristic has been compromised by politicians as they pledge allegiance to the president either because they belong to the same political party or for some other gratifications that may be associated with the allegiance. The politicization of the appointment of judges has also compromised the independence of the judiciary, which has become a concern in the country.

The December 1983 coup that terminated the Second Republic also led to the suspension of the constitution and successive military regimes that will span another sixteen years of military dictatorship that was ruled by decrees. In 1999 the Abdulsalami military administration conducted a successful general election, which Olusegun Obasanjo and his People's Democratic Party won. That same year, the military handed over power to a civilian government. After completing his two-term as president, Obasanjo was accused of plotting to extend his presidency for a third term, but this move was aborted when in May 2006 the Senate rejected a constitutional amendment to permit a third term by the incumbent president. Subsequently, in April 2007 a presidential election was conducted, and Musa Yar'Adua of the PDP was victorious and was sworn in as president and commander of the Armed Forces on May 29. Since 1999, Nigeria has enjoyed uninterrupted civilian regimes, which has helped to deepen democratic rule in the country. Although the Buhari civilian administration has failed to curb insecurity in the country characterized by kidnappings, Nigerians are still optimistic that the February 25 presidential election would be held successfully, and a new government will be sworn in on May 29, 2023.

Although most Nigerians are optimistic about the deepening of democratic values in the country, others are still concerned about the structure of the country starting with the constitution. Critics of the constitution have complained of too much power at the center at the expense of the states, which restricts the practice of true federalism. Another concern that has been raised is the seeming contradiction of the constitution that recognizes Nigeria as a secular state but makes provision for some states to apply the Sharia or Islamic law. Another concern is the structure of the composition of the House of Representatives, which is determined by various factors including population size of states and the number of their local government areas. These issues, including fiscal federalism and revenue allocation, state policing, devolution of power, resource control, among others, have led to calls for restructuring in the country.

Further Reading

Adejumobi, S., ed. (2010). *Governance and Politics in Post-Military Nigeria: Changes and Challenges*. New York: Palgrave Macmillan.

Dudley, B. (1982). *An Introduction to Nigerian Government and Politics*. Bloomington: Indiana University Press.

Nigeria – Government. https://photius.com/countries/nigeria/government/index.html

Nigeria High Commission. http://www.nigeriahc.org.uk/government-politics

Olayiwola, P. H., J. I. Ugwuanyi, A. B. M. Akuche, and C. C. Mba (2022). "Federalism and the Politics of Restructuring in Nigeria." *African Renaissance*, 19(3): 225–49.

ADMINISTRATIVE DIVISION AND STRUCTURE

Nigeria practices a federal system of government with the country headed by an elected president. The president is the executive head of state and Commander-in-Chief of the armed forces. Besides the executive arm of government is the legislative arm of the federal government made up of the National Assembly. The National Assembly is a bicameral chamber with the senate constituting the Upper House and the House of Representatives constituting the Lower House. The Senate is presided over by the Senate president while the Lower House is headed by the Speaker of the House of Representatives. The Senate is composed of 109 members, comprising three elected members from each Senatorial District of the thirty-six states and one from the Federal Territory. On the other hand, the Lower House is made up of 360 members drawn also from the thirty-six states of the federation. Members of the Federal House of Assembly are elected from their constituencies and serve a four-year term. Unlike the president of the country with a constitutional maximum two four-year terms in office, members of the House of Assembly may be elected repeatedly to the House. One of its key statutory functions is that the National Assembly acts as a check to the federal executive arm of government. Other oversight functions of the National Assembly include the screening and confirmation of ministerial, judicial, and diplomatic positions as well as the constitutional power to impeach federal judges and other high officials such as the president and Auditor-General of the federation. The third arm of the federal government is the judiciary, which is made up of the Supreme Court, the Court of Appeals and the High Courts and other trial courts, collectively referred to as the National Judicial Council. The Supreme Court is the highest court in the land presided over by the Chief Justice of the Federation.

Nigeria is divided into thirty-six states and one federal territory. Each of the states is headed by an elected executive governor who is responsible for the running of the state together with the state cabinet. The state cabinet is made of commissioners who are appointed by the governor and approved by the State House of Assembly. The State House of Assembly is made up of elected members from all the local governments of the state. The state governor and the cabinet are responsible for the development of the state based on the federal allocation of funds from the federal government and other internally generated revenue from the state. By far, Lagos state is the wealthiest of the states. It has a private wealth of $97 billion and ranks as the fourth wealthiest city in Africa.

The Local Government Areas (LGAs) constitute the third tier of government. There are 774 LGAs. Kano state has the highest number of LGAs with forty-four and the least is Bayelsa State with nine, while the Federal Capital Territory has six. The LGAs are made of the Local Government chairman, and together with the councillors, they constitute the governing body. They are responsible for the development of the country at the grassroots by providing and maintaining health posts and dispensaries, engaging in vital registrations including birth, death, and marriage. They are also responsible for the authorization and maintenance of various types of burial grounds, the maintenance of sanitation, and the collection of taxes and levies at the grassroots. The LGAs are further divided into wards for easy administration. Together, the federal, state, and local government constitutes the political administration of the country.

See Also: Constitutional Development (Chapter 3); Corruption (Chapter 3); Legislature (Chapter 3); State and Local Governments (Chapter 3).

Further Reading

Fashagbe, J. Y., R. Ajayi, and C. Nwankwo, eds. (2019). *The Nigerian National Assembly*. New York: Springer.
National Assembly of the Federal Republic of Nigeria. (2023). https://nass.gov.ng/

ALL PROGRESSIVES CONGRESS

The All Progressives Congress (APC) was Nigeria's ruling party when it came into power on May 29, 2015 after defeating the then-incumbent People's Democratic Party (PDP) at the presidential election of that year. The APC is a product of an alliance between the Congress for Progressive Change (CPC), the Action Congress of Nigeria (ACN), and the

All Nigeria People's Party (ANPP). The CPC, which was headed by Muhammadu Buhari had its influence in the northwestern part of the country while the ACN, headed by Bola Tinubu, had its stronghold in the southwestern states, and the ANPP, a splinter of the All Progressives Grand Alliance (APGA), has a strong influence in the Southeast. The formation of the APC as a political party was, therefore, a tactical and strategic political move that was necessary to defeat the PDP as the dominant party, which before 2015, had ruled the country since the return to a democratic rule in 1999. The merger of the three major opposition parties to form the APC also saw the emergence of Bola Tinubu as its national chairman and Muhammadu Buhari as its flag bearer at the 2015 general election after defeating Rabiu Kwankwaso and Atiku Abubakar in the party's primaries. The party's national colors are green, white, blue, and red and uses the broom as its national symbol. At the 2015 general election the APC polled a total number of 15,424,921(53.96 percent) against PDP's 12,853,162 (44.96 percent) and won twenty-one states against PDP's fifteen states plus the Federal Capital Territory. At the National Assembly, the APC won a total of 60 seats against PDP's 49 seats at the Upper Chamber and 225 seats against PDP's 125 in the House of Representatives, making it the dominant party controlling both the Executive and Legislative arms of government. After serving as the country's ruling party between 2015 and 2019, the APC contested the 2019 general election and emerged victorious by defeating its closest rival the PDP by 55.6 percent of the votes against the latter's 41.2 percent and still controls both the Upper House and Lower House of the National Assembly. The current national chairperson of the party is Abdullahi Adamu, and Iyiola Omisore as its national secretary. The APC campaigned against insecurity and corruption as well as providing basic social amenities to the citizens with a strong political philosophy that many consider to be central left, which favors a controlled-market economy policy as against a neoliberal economic policy. Thus, the APC-led government has strong regulatory powers over the economy and other social activities. As part of its policy, the APC is a strong advocate for state's rights and supports the establishment of state power generation and state police. However, its president is less favorable to a true federalism and advocates for the concentration of power at the center.

See Also: People's Democratic Party (Chapter 3); Political Parties and Their Formations (Chapter 3).

Further Reading

All Progressive Congress (APC). (2023). https://officialapc.ng/
Yahaya, J. U. (2018). *The History of Merging Parties: Formation of APC in Nigerian Politics.* London: Scholars' Press.

BUHARI, MUHAMMADU

Muhammadu Buhari is a retired major general in the Nigerian army and was a former head of state of Nigeria from December 31, 1983 to August 27, 1985. Buhari was born on December 17, 1942, in Daura, in modern-day Katsina State to Hardo and Zulaihat Adamu, a humble Fulani family. After the death of his father in 1946, young Buhari was raised by his mother. In 1962 he attended the Nigerian Military Training College and the officer cadet training at the Mons Cadet School, Aldershot, England. In 1963, Buhari was commissioned a second lieutenant in the Nigerian army and served in Abeokuta as the Platoon Commander of the Second Infantry Battalion. In July 1966, he was among a group of young Nigerian army officers led by lieutenant general Murtala Muhammed that organized a "countercoup" against the military junta headed by General Aguiyi-Ironsi. The countercoup led to the Nigerian Civil War, which broke out in July 1966. At the start of the war, Buhari was assigned to the First Division of the Nigerian army in Makurdi, and thereafter occupied various positions until the end of the war in 1970. As Acting Director of Transport and Supply in the Nigerian army, Lieutenant Colonel Buhari was part of a military group that overthrew the Gowon-led military government in July 1975. He was rewarded by the new head of state, Murtala Muhammed, by becoming the governor of northeastern state from August 1, 1975 to February 3, 1976 and governor of Borno State from February 3, 1976 to March 15, 1976. General Olusegun Obasanjo as head of state in 1976 appointed Buhari as the Federal Commissioner for Petroleum and Natural Resources and in 1977 Buhari became the first chairperson of the newly established Nigerian National Petroleum Corporation. The return to democratic rule in 1979 was cut short when Buhari and his army officers overthrew the Shagari-led civilian administration on December 31, 1983. As military head of state, Buhari was known for his discipline and anti-corruption stance. His regime was also infamous for the draconian decrees that infringed on human rights notable among which were Decree Number 2 and Decree Number 4 of 1984. After he was overthrown in 1985 by General Ibrahim Babangida, Buhari served a three-year detention in Benin City until he was released in December 1988 after the death of his mother. Buhari retired from the army and became a farmer in his hometown. On the return of democracy in 1999, Buhari became interested in politics and contested the 2003 presidential election as the flagbearer of the All Nigeria People's Party and lost to Olusegun Obasanjo of the People's Democratic Party. In 2007, Buhari contested the presidential election again and lost to Musa Yar'adua. In 2011, Buhari contested for the highest position in the land on the platform of the Congress for Progressive Change but lost to Goodluck Jonathan. On his fourth attempt, under the banner of the All Progressives Party, Buhari emerged as the winner of the presidential election in 2015 defeating the incumbent president. He was sworn in on May 29, 2015, as Nigeria's fifteenth president. Buhari contested again for a second term in office in 2019 and defeated his closest rival at the polls, Abubakar Atiku, to secure another four-year term in office.

See Also: All Progressives Congress (Chapter 3); Corruption (Chapter 3); Military Rule (Chapter 3).

Further Reading

Kamoru, I. (2020). *The Secret of Muhammadu Buhari of Nigeria: Amazing Adventure and Historical Facts of President Muhammadu Buhari of Nigeria*. London: Scholars' Press.

Lawal, J. A. (2017). *Buhari: The Making of a President*. Ibadan: Safari Books.

Usman, A. K. (2002). *Muhammadu Buhari: The Spirit of a Man: An Epic on Former Head of State of Nigeria, Muhammadu Buhari (rtd)*. Zaria: Amana Publishers Limited.

CONSTITUTIONAL DEVELOPMENT

Constitutional development in Nigeria effectively started in 1914 after the amalgamation of the Northern Protectorate and Southern Protectorate by Sir Frederick Lugard. The amalgamation stirred agitations among the small, educated elite in Nigeria for increased political reforms that would give locals more rights to participate in their political affairs. The appointment of Sir Hugh Clifford in 1922 in replacement of Lord Lugard led to the establishment of the first constitution in Nigeria named after Sir Clifford. The 1922 Clifford Constitution was developed based on the merger of the Colony of Lagos Legislative Council with the National Council. The constitution provided for the first time, the elective principle that saw the election of ten Nigerians to fill some Council positions out of the total forty-six Council positions. The Legislative Council made laws in response to local exigencies, but this power was subject to the veto powers of the governor. Despite this positive development the franchise of locals was limited as the Executive Council was still dominated by British nationals, with vested powers to formulate policies under the authority of the colonial power. This limitation, among others, led to the increased agitation for self-governance and an increase in nationalist consciousness. The Richard's Constitution of 1946 was a significant development because it gave Nigerians, for the first time, a majority both in the regional and national legislative assemblies. It also brought the North under the same administrative control with the South with the main objectives of promoting unity in the country and to encourage greater local participation of Nigerians in their internal affairs. For effective administration, the country was divided into three regions, namely, the East, North, and West, each with its legislative council. The North was made up of a House of Assembly and a House of Chiefs, which was made up of first-class emirs. In the West and East both regions were made up of a unicameral legislature. Each of the House of Assembly comprised fourteen official members and fifteen unofficial members. Key functions of the House of Assembly included deliberations on the annual budgets of the regions, and to serve as an electoral college for the Central Legislature. Following Richard's Constitution was the MacPherson Constitution named after its author Sir John MacPherson who became the governor of the country in 1948. In drafting the constitution, Sir MacPherson avoided the errors of the past by involving the educated elites in drafting the constitution and giving the people a voice on how they should be governed. After due consultations with the people, the main provisions of the MacPherson Constitution included the introduction of a federal system with powers divided between the central and regional legislatures, flexibility of electoral laws at the central and regional levels, retention of the three regional structures but with the northern and western regions having a bicameral legislature while the eastern region with a single chamber legislature. One of the shortcomings of the MacPherson Constitution was its inherent contradictions to the principles and norms of federalism, which led to a series of constitutional conferences that produced the Lyttleton's Constitution in 1954 and six years later to the Independence Constitution in 1960. The Lyttleton's Constitution, named after Oliver Lyttleton, the secretary of state for the colonies, was significant in one important way as it introduced the office of the speaker both in the central and regional legislature to replace the governor-general and regional governors, respectively. It also provided for the position of the prime minister at the center and the office of the premier in the regions, which the country adopted upon gaining its political independence on October 1, 1960.

See Also: Administrative Division and Structure (Chapter 3); Democratic Rule (Chapter 3); Early Political Parties (Chapter 3); State and Local Governments (Chapter 3).

Further Reading

Aghalino, S. O. (2006). "Dynamics of Constitutional Development in Nigeria, 1914–1999." *Indian Journal of Politics*, 40(2): 49–62.

Olamide, O. (n.d.). "History of Nigerian Constitutional Development." *Nigerian Constitutional Law*. https://djetlawyer.com/history-nigerian-constitutional-development/

Udoma, U. (2021). *History and the Law of the Constitution of Nigeria*. New York: Bowker Publisher.

CORRECTIONAL INSTITUTIONS

The modern Correctional Institutions in Nigeria started in 1861. That was when conceptually, Western-style prisons were created in Nigeria. After Lagos was announced as a colony in 1861, the institution of formal machinery of governance began. At this level, the preoccupation of the colonial authorities included the protection of trade, the assurance of the income of British traders and the activities of the missionaries. Consequently, in 1861, the governor of the Lagos colony created a police force of approximately twenty-five constables. This was followed in 1863 by the institution in Lagos of four courts: a police court to resolve petty disputes, a court to adjudicate the additional serious cases, a slave court to try cases arising from the efforts to get rid of the trade in slaves, and a poster court to resolve disputes among merchants and traders. The functioning of the courts and the police in this colonial setting essentially meant that jail was required as a logical end of the system. And it was shortly afterwards in 1872, that the Broad Street jail was established as the last link within the criminal justice system, with an initial inmate capacity of 300. The status quo remained until in 1934 when some efforts were made to modernize the jail service following the appointment of Colonel V. L. Mabb was appointed Director of Prisons by the then governor, Sir Donald Cameron. Though a military man, Mabb understood what prisons ought to be and centered his attention on the formation of a unified jail structure for the country with the establishment of the Prisons Warders Welfare Board. Besides the expansion of prisons throughout the country, there were no major transformations within the service until the 1970s. In 1972, the prison service witnessed some reorganization with the establishment of its modest three Directorates. In 1980 these directorates were increased to six, and to eight Directorates in 1993 with the introduction of employees' coaching and Non-Custodial Directorates. In 1986 there was a reorganization of the Prisons with the creation of the Customs, Immigrations and Prisons Board, which centralized the administrations of those paramilitary services within the Board. Currently, the Service boasts more trained men and women than at any other time in its history. Among the officers are medical and environmental health officers, sociologists/psychologists, lawyers, general directors, and engineers, among others. In its efforts to accommodate international best practices, the Service pursued a logical conclusion in the passage of the Nigerian Correctional Service Act of 2019.

See Also: Criminal Law (Chapter 3); Human Rights (Chapter 3); Law Enforcement (Chapter 3).

Further Reading

Agomoh, U., A. Adeyemi, and V. Ogbebor. (2001). *Nigerian Prison Service and Penal Reform in Nigeria*. Lagos: PRAWA.

Saleh-Hanna, V. (2008). *Colonial System of Control: Criminal Justice in Nigeria*. Ottawa: University of Ottawa Press.

CORRUPTION

The history of state corruption dates to pre-independent Nigeria when the British colonial government was accused of manipulating the 1959 elections. However, that accusation cannot be compared to what followed independence. Since 1960, both individual political actors and state institutions have been embroiled in various corruption scandals. Various surveys conducted both by local and international institutions (such as the Institute for Development Research of Ahmadu Bello University, Zaria, and Transparency International, respectively) have found an entrenched state corruption in state organs of governance and parastatals, chief among which include the Nigerian police force, political parties, the National Electric Power Authority, the Nigerian National Petroleum Corporation, the Nigerian Customs, all public utility boards, and the federal and state ministries. The gross looting of state treasury has been more noticeable, however, during military regimes especially during the mid-1980s to the inception of the Fourth Republic in 1999. The flagrant disregard for the rule of law and the lack of accountability by government officials made governance a personal rather than a public service, which fuelled and sustained corrupt practices by leaders. The General Olusegun Obasanjo military regime from 1976 to 1979 was associated with scandals ranging from the siphoning of state funds through the award of major contracts including the building of refineries, the construction of roads, and the hosting of the Nigerian festival (FESTAC) in 1977. Also important was the Operation Feed the Nation program and the Land Use Decree of 1978, which benefited a few at the expense of the majority in the country. The General Ibrahim Babangida military administration (1985–93), however, institutionalized, and legalized corruption in Nigeria. Material gifts including cars, monies, and political appointments were traded for favors and to buy loyalty of critics including labor leaders, union activists, and political commentators. The Gulf War windfall estimated to be over US$12.4 billion was never accounted for nor were the contracts for the building of roads, bridges, and development projects ever completed. At this time, oil blocs were unilaterally assigned to cronies of the military junta while import licenses were given to the highest bidder. The General Sani Abacha military administration that followed from 1993 to 1998 consolidated the massive looting of the treasury by state officials. It was only after the sudden death of the head of state in 1998 that the massive looting of the treasury could be ascertained. However, it was not only the military era that recorded massive looting of the treasury. The civilian regimes of Chief Olusegun Obasanjo (1999–2007); Goodluck Jonathan (2011–15); and the Buhari administration (2015–date) have all recorded corrupt practices at various levels, especially in the oil and gas sector, the aviation industry, the finance and banking sector, the defense and health ministries. Corrupt practices also filter down to the state and local government levels with massive looting of the treasury and the siphoning of monies meant for capital projects. The establishment of the Independent Corrupt Practices and Other Related Offences Commission (ICPC) and Economic and Financial Crimes Commission (EFCC) to curb corruption in the public sector has led to the arrest and prosecution of some political actors at the federal level as well as some former state governors and local government councillors. However, these efforts have not significantly reduced state corruption in the country.

See Also: Administrative Division and Structure (Chapter 3); Constitutional Development (Chapter 3); Democratic Rule (Chapter 3); Military Rule (Chapter 3).

Further Reading

Mustapha, M. (2010). "Corruption in Nigeria: Conceptual and Empirical Notes." *Information, Society, and Justice,* 3(2): 165–75.
Olaleye-Oruene, T. (1998). "Corruption in Nigeria: A Cultural Phenomenon." *Journal of Financial Crime,* 5(3): 232–40.
Osoba, S. O. (2007). "Corruption in Nigeria: Historical Perspectives." *Review of African Political Economy,* 23(69): 371–86.
United Nations Office on Drugs and Crime. (2019). *Corruption in Nigeria: Patterns and Trends.* Vienna: UNODC.

CRIMINAL LAW

In 1904, after consolidating their hold over northern Nigeria, the British colonial government introduced the Criminal Code. In 1914, the Northern and Southern Protectorates were merged. This resulted in a situation in which three criminal justice systems were in operation throughout the country: the English criminal law in Lagos, the Criminal Code in the North, and the indigenous criminal law customs in the South. To incorporate all three, the British government in 1916 created the provisions of the Criminal Code applicable to the entire country. This caused tons of conflict particularly between the Criminal Code and the sharia law in the northern part of the country. Among the key areas of dispute was that the Islamic law allowed the infliction of penalization unrecognized by the Criminal Code. Islamic law additionally did not recognize provocation to mitigate a sentence of death to homicide. To resolve this conflict, Section 4 of the Criminal Code was amended. The section ab-initio stated that "No person shall be prone to be tried or reproved in any court in the country, except a native court, for any offence except below the specific provision of the code or another ordinance or some law or some order-in-council created by his majesty for Nigeria." The change removed the phrase "other than a native tribunal" from Section 4 of the Criminal Code. This change was interpreted in several quarters to mean the abrogation of the powers of the native courts. However, the criminal jurisdiction of the native courts was saved by the provisions of Section 10 of the Native Court Ordinance of 1933. This development caused more conflict within the northern region. To resolve the discontent, a committee was set up in 1958 to deal with the difficulty. The committee proposed the complete recognition of both the English criminal law, and the Islamic law, or a Hybrid of both. After heated debates and substantial consultations, a hybrid became the excellent choice and became implemented in the northern part of the country shortly afterward. The Penal Code became additionally modeled after the Indian Penal Code of 1860. The Administration of Criminal Justice Act (ACJA) was signed into law in 2015 in a bid to revolutionize the management of criminal justice in Nigeria. It repealed the Criminal Procedure Act (CPA) and Criminal Procedure Code (CPC) of southern and northern Nigeria, respectively. The reasons for the Act are to ensure that the administration of criminal justice in Nigeria promotes efficient control of criminal justice institutions, rapid dispensation of justice, safety of society from crime, and safety of the rights and interests of suspects, defendants, and victims. Another key function of the Act is to enhance the rapid management of criminal justice. According to Hon. Justice Walter Onnoghen, the Chief Justice of Nigeria in 2017, delay in the management of justice is a primary challenge in the Nigerian Judiciary. Delay has through the years been a primary obstacle to the rapid dispensation of criminal justice in Nigeria. The Act became consequently enacted to deal with this problem, among others.

See Also: Correctional Institutions (Chapter 3); Human Rights (Chapter 3); Law Enforcement (Chapter 3); Supreme Court (Chapter 3).

Further Reading

Olong, A. (2011). *The Administration of Criminal Justice in Nigeria: A Case for Reform*. Moldova: LAP LAMBERT Academic Publishing.

Ushie, E. M. and F. N. Akwaji. (2021). *Corruption and the Criminal Justice System*. London: Routledge.

Yakubu, J. A. and A. T. Oyewo (2000). *Criminal Law and Procedure in Nigeria*. Lagos: Malthouse Press.

DEMOCRATIC RULE

Since independence on October 1, 1960, Nigeria has had a protracted democratic rule. For the sixty-three years of its existence as an independent nation it has been ruled by the military for thirty-three years and by civilians for thirty years. The First Republic was between 1960 and 1966 when the military overthrew the Tafawa Balewa-led civilian government. The military ruled from 1966 till 1979 when the Obasanjo military administration handed over power to Shehu Shagari who led the Second Republic until December 1983 when the military sacked his government and held on to power until 1999 after the abortive Third Republic that would have been headed by Chief Moshood Abiola, the presumptuous winner of the 1993 presidential election, but was aborted by the Babangida military administration in that same year. It took another six years of military rule before power was handed over to a civilian regime when the Fourth Republic was inaugurated and headed by Olusegun Obasanjo, a retired military general. From 1999 to date has been the longest period of uninterrupted democratic rule Nigeria has witnessed and has remained stable. At independence, the constitution favored a parliamentary system of government and Dr. Nnamdi Azikiwe became the country's Governor-General, representing the Queen of England as the ceremonial head of government, while Sir Abubakar Tafawa Balewa became the country's prime minister, who exercised executive powers and was responsible for the running of the government. At the regional level, the premier of the northern region was the Sardauna of Sokoto, while Obafemi Awolowo became the premier of the western region and Chief Michael Okpara the premier of the eastern region. The first democratic rule shared powers between the federal government and the regional governments and recognized the exclusive power of the federal government in matters that concerned defense, currency, citizenship, and external affairs while the regions had concurrent constitutional powers in matters pertaining to the judiciary, education, health, and tax. When Nigeria became a republic in 1963, it scrapped the office of the Governor-General and established a parliamentary system of government that became independent of the British Crown effectively ending the constitutional recognition of the Queen of England as the head of the Nigerian government. The Second Republic witnessed the flurry of political activities in Nigeria after the creation of nineteen states to replace the regional governments. The 1979 elections were contested by seven political parties with the National Party of Nigeria (NPN) emerging as the ruling party headed by Alhaji Shehu Shagari and the Unity Party of Nigeria (UPN), led by Chief Obafemi Awolowo as the official opposition party. From 1999 to date the Independent Electoral Commission has registered over ninety political parties with eighty-four contesting the 2019 general elections that saw the return of Muhammadu Buhari for another four-year term as the executive president of the country. Uninterrupted democratic rule in Nigeria has witnessed a progressive recognition and upholding of key human rights that are enshrined in the constitution including the rights to freedom of speech and association, which were denied Nigerian citizens during military regimes in the country.

See Also: Administrative Division and Structure (Chapter 3); Azikiwe, Nnamdi (Chapter 2); Balewa, Abubakar Tafawa (Chapter 2); Constitutional Development (Chapter 3); Independent National Electoral Commission (Chapter 3); Jonathan, Goodluck (Chapter 3); Political Parties and Their Formations (Chapter 3); Military Rule (Chapter 3).

Further Reading

Agbaje, A. A. B., L. Diamond, and E. Onwudiwe, eds. (2000). *Nigeria's Struggle for Democracy and Good Governance*. Ibadan: Ibadan University Press.

Edigheji, O. (2020). *Nigeria: Democracy without Development. How to Fix it*. Lagos: A'Lime Media Limited.

Omotoso, F. and M. Kehinde. (2016). *Democratic Governance and Political Participation in Nigeria, 1999–2014*. Cameroon: Spears Media Press.

EARLY POLITICAL PARTIES

The history of Nigerian political parties predates the country's independence in 1960. The formation of political parties in Nigeria was a direct response to colonial rule by the British government and the determination of professional groups such as the Nigerian Union of Teachers and the Nigerian Law Association, which were formed in the 1920s to serve as a voice for their members to propagate their desire for self-determination. Other non-political groups such as the Nigerian Produce Traders Association and the pan-ethnic group associations such as the Igbo Federal Union, the Borno Youth Movement and the Egbe Omo Oduduwa became the forerunners of Nigeria's political parties. Other groups such the West African Students Union, the Lagos Youth Movement and the Nigerian Youth Movement became the vanguard of the nationalist movement. The earliest registered political party in Nigeria was the Nigerian National Democratic Party, which came into existence in 1922 as a brainchild of Herbert Macaulay who is today generally referred to as the father of Nigerian nationalism. Although the NNDP dominated the political landscape only in Lagos, it provided the pathway for the formation of other political parties in the country. Thus, by 1944 a truly national political party, the NCNC, was formed with Mr. Herbert Macaulay as its national president and Dr. Nnamdi Azikiwe as its general secretary. The formation of the NCNC accelerated the formation of other political parties in Nigeria. The MacPherson Constitution of 1951, which increased the membership of the central and regional assemblies and the advocacy for a quasi-federalism led to the formations of other political parties. Notable among them were the AG headed by Chief Obafemi Awolowo, the NPC led by Sir Ahmadu Bello, and the NCNC led by Dr. Nnamdi Azikiwe. The formation of these political parties also brought about the emergence of political leaders in the three regions, namely, Obafemi Awolowo becoming the premier of western region; Ahmadu Bello as the premier of northern region; and Nnamdi Azikiwe as the premier of eastern Nigeria when it became a federating unit in 1954. After the first military interference in politics between 1966 and 1979, more political parties were registered in anticipation of the Second Republic. In addition to the established political parties, new parties that were formed during this period included the Greater Nigerian Peoples Party (GNPP), the NPN, the People's Redemption Party (PRP), and the UPN. The return of military rule in January 1984 witnessed the abrogation of all political parties in Nigeria until 1992 when only two parties were permitted to contest the abortive Third Republic. The two parties were the National Republic Convention (NRC) and the Social Democratic Party (SDP). However, with the commencement of the Fourth Republic starting from 1999, Nigeria has recorded over eighty official political parties but with less than 10 percent of that number being active in the political landscape. The independent national electoral commission officially registered eighteen political parties to contest the 2023 presidential election with the three dominant parties being the APC, the People's Democratic Party (PDP), and the Labour Party (LP).

See Also: Administrative Division and Structure (Chapter 3); Constitutional Development (Chapter 3); Legislature (Chapter 3); Political Parties and Their Formations (Chapter 3).

Further Reading

Aregbesola, B. S. (2014). *Nigerian Political Parties and Politicians: Winding Road from Country to Nation*. Scotts Valley, CA: CreateSpace Independent Publishing.

Sklar, R. L. (1962). *Nigerian Political Parties: The Social Basis and Structure of a Party System in Emergent Africa, Volume 2*. Princeton: Princeton University Microfilms.

Sklar, R. L. (2016). *Nigerian Political Parties: Power in an Emerging African Nation*. Princeton: Princeton University Press.

HUMAN RIGHTS

Constitutionally, the Nigerian government recognizes the rights of its citizens including the right to life, freedom of association and movement, freedom of worship, freedom from discrimination on religious, gender, or tribal grounds, freedom to privacy and freedom of expression, among others. These rights were enshrined in the 1960 constitution and have been upheld by subsequent constitutional amendments. As a member state of both the African Union and the United Nations, Nigeria has human rights obligations at the regional and international levels. However, human rights abuses have been recorded in Nigeria especially during the military era. The suspension of the constitution by all the military junta was a flagrant denial of the constitutional rights of the citizens and an open expression of the disregard of the military to uphold the dignity of Nigerian citizens. Decree 2 of 1984, which empowers the military government to arrest and detain anyone without any charge; and Decree 4 of 1984 that made it a criminal offense for any media house to publish any material that is considered by the military government to tarnish its image or considered as embarrassing to the government represented how intolerant military regimes were of criticism from the public. During the military regimes it was commonplace for citizens, especially those who were critical of the government, to be arrested and tortured without following any due process. In some cases, such people disappeared or were brutally assassinated by the state. In instances where media houses were regarded as "anti-government" due to their editorials that were critical of government activities, they were censored and in the 1990s especially during the military regimes of Babangida and Abacha over eight newspaper houses were forcefully closed. The summary execution of Ken Saro-Wiwa and his colleagues (the Ogoni nine) by the Abacha government in 1995 for their campaign against human rights and the environmental degradation of the Niger Delta became the hallmark of government brutality against its people. While there is much improvement of upholding human rights in Nigeria by civilian regimes, there are still disturbing cases of human rights abuses by politicians who display their political might by using the police to intimidate and arrest their political opponents or other perceived enemies. The most notorious human rights crime committed by successive civilian regimes is the manipulation of the electoral process especially with regards to election rigging and other electoral malpractices that disenfranchise citizens or intimidation by political thuggery. However, by far, the most notorious human rights crime that successive Nigerian governments have committed against its people is corruption, expressed by the stealing of public funds that deny citizens of basic social amenities such as quality education, healthcare services, the supply of pipe-borne water, and the provision of a good road network. This denial of basic common decency is what drives thousands of Nigerians out of the country to seek better living conditions. While various human rights bodies and organizations have been formed in Nigeria to promote the rule of law and the enforcement of human rights in the country, some of these abuses still go on unabated. The massacre of Nigerian youths at the Lagos state toll plaza in October 2020 in protest police brutality (#Endsars) is a reminder of human rights abuse during a civilian regime.

See Also: Correctional Institutions (Chapter 3); Criminal Law (Chapter 3); Human Trafficking (Chapter 7); Law Enforcement (Chapter 3); Supreme Court (Chapter 3).

Validity of the February 2023 Elections
The Nigerian presidential and National Assembly elections were held on February 25, 2023 with eighteen political parties contesting for the president, senatorial seats, and House of Representatives positions. The Independent National Electoral Commission (INEC), chaired by Professor Mahmood Yakubu, declared the ruling party's All Progressives Congress flagbearer, Bola Ahmed Tinubu, winner of the presidential election. Atiku Abubakar of the PDP came second and the Labour Party flagbearer, Peter Obi, third. However, local, and international observers have expressed concerns about the conduct of the elections primarily because of the violence, voter intimidation, and vote buying that characterized the election as well as the inability of INEC to follow its internal process to upload polling unit results to its portal on the election day as promised by its chairman. These observations have prompted at least four opposition parties (PDP, Labour Party, All People's Movement, Action Alliance), in separate petitions, to challenge the credibility of the process and the legitimacy of declaring Bola Tinubu the winner of the election. On September 6, 2023, the Presidential Election Tribunal dismissed all the petitions filed by the opposition parties and upheld the decision of INEC. While the APC supporters have hailed the judgement, supporters of the four opposition parties have questioned the neutrality of the tribunal in its judgement. At least the PDP and the LP have vowed to appeal to the Supreme Court as the final arbiter on the 2023 presidetial election.

Further Reading

Aka, P. (2016). *Human Rights in Nigeria's External Relations: Building the Record of a Moral Superpower*. Maryland: Rowman and Littlefield.
Amnesty International. (n.d.). "Nigeria." https://www.amnesty.org/en/location/africa/west-and-central-africa/nigeria/report-nigeria/

INDEPENDENT NATIONAL ELECTORAL COMMISSION

The INEC was established in 1998 as the statutory organ of government charged with the responsibility of conducting credible, free, and fair elections in Nigeria. Although a parastatal of government it is expected by law to be autonomous and neutral in its dealings with electoral matters. Its overall vision is to be one of the best electoral management bodies in the world that meets the aspiration of Nigerians. The chair of the commission is appointed by the president of the country subject to the approval of the Nigerian Senate. At its inauguration in 1998 by General Abdusalami Abubakar in anticipation of the elections to usher in the Fourth Republic, Justice Ephraim Akpata became its first chairperson. The 1999 elections were conducted and presided over by Ephraim Akpata, which saw Olusegun Obasanjo emerging as the winner of that election. The sudden death of Justice Akpata in January 2000 created a vacuum in the INEC leadership. President Obasanjo subsequently appointed Abel Guobadia who became the substantive Chief Electoral Officer after his approval by the Senate. Guobadia presided over the 2003 presidential and gubernatorial elections, which also saw Obasanjo emerging as the presidential winner for a four-year second term. After Guobadia's retirement in 2005, Professor Maurice Iwu became the INEC boss. Iwu conducted and presided over the 2007 general elections which saw Umaru Musa Yar'adua as the winner of the presidential election. After serving a five-year term, Iwu was replaced by Professor Attahiru Muhammadu Jega, who was appointed by President Jonathan in 2010. Under a tight schedule, Professor Jega conducted the 2011 general elections that proclaimed Goodluck Jonathan as the winner of the presidential election. Jega served as chair of INEC for a five-year term, which ended on June 30, 2015. He was replaced by Professor Mahmood Yakubu who was appointed to occupy the position by President Muhammadu Buhari on October 22, 2015. Although the conduct of elections by INEC has been fraught with irregularities and accusations and counter accusation by politicians and political commentators, Mahmood Yakubu as the chairman of INEC has proven resilient in ensuring a sustainable democratic transition in Nigeria since 1999. Before 1999 other election management bodies had served as forerunners to INEC, albeit with different names. The electoral body that ushered in the aborted Third Republic was known as the National Electoral Commission of Nigeria. NECON was headed by Professor Eme Awa from 1987 to 1989; Professor Henry Nwosu, from 1989 to 1993 Professor Okon Uya, from 1993–1994; and Chief Sumner Dagogo-Jack, from 1994 to 1998. The Federal Electoral Commission, headed by Chief Michael Ani, ushered in the Second Republic, and was inaugurated by General Olusegun Obasanjo in 1978. Chief Ani was later succeeded by Justice Victor Ovie Whiskey. The first electoral body (also known as the Nigerian Federal Electoral Commission) was headed by Chief Eyo Esua who supervised the 1964 general elections. Throughout its history, the Nigerian electoral body has faced major challenges chief among which is election rigging by politicians and the daunting task of ensuring that elections are credible, free, and fair. However, President Muhammadu Buhari has vowed to bequeath a credible election to Nigeria in the 2023 presidential election under the chairmanship of Professor Mahmood Yakubu.

See Also: Democratic Rule (Chapter 3); Legislature (Chapter 3); Political Parties and Their Formations (Chapter 3).

Further Reading

INEC Website. https://inecnigeria.org/2023-general-elections-updates/
Iyayi, F. (2007). *Elections, INEC, and the Problem of Election Mindsets in Nigeria*. Abuja: Electoral Institute, INEC.
Yagboyaju, D. A. and A. T. Simbine. (2020). "Politics, Political Parties and the Party Interest in Nigeria: Whose Interest?" *International Letters of Social and Humanistic Sciences*, 89: 33–50.

JONATHAN, GOODLUCK

Goodluck Ebele Jonathan was the twelfth vice president and the fourteenth president of Nigeria. He was born on November 20, 1957, in what is now Bayelsa State to a humble canoe-making family. He had his tertiary education at the University of Port Harcourt graduating with a PhD in zoology. He started his political career in 1998 and became the deputy governor of Bayelsa State on May 29, 1999, and on December 9, 2005, he was sworn-in as the state's governor after his boss, Diepreye Alamieyeseigha, was impeached from office. In 2008, he secured the ticket to be the running mate to Musa Yar'adua and was sworn in as Nigeria's twelfth Vice-President on May 29, 2008. After becoming vice president, Goodluck Jonathan was highly instrumental in negotiating with the major militant groups in the Niger Delta and he embarked on the presidential amnesty that was subsequently offered to all the militant youths in the region who surrendered their weapons and accepted the amnesty deal. The sudden death of President Umaru Musa Yar'adua on May 5, 2010 made Jonathan to become the substantive head of state after he was sworn in as president on May 6, 2010. He later nominated Namadi Sambo to become his vice president. After completing Ya'adua's tenure, Jonathan declared his interest to run for the presidency in his own right for the 2012 general election. He retained Namadi Sambo as his running mate and defeated his closest rival Muhammadu Buhari and was sworn in as the president to rule for four years. As president, Goodluck Jonathan identified corruption, electric power, and electoral reforms as his primary focus. On the country's economy, Goodluck Jonathan's administration was famous for the Transformation Agenda which was a five-year development plan designed to address issues of poverty, inequality, unemployment, and the diversification of the economy. Jonathan achieved marginal stability in the supply of electricity through the power sector reform, which was a contributing factor to the growth of the Nigerian GDP. The restructuring and rebasement of the Nigerian economy in 2014 made Nigeria to become the largest economy in Africa by overtaking South Africa. Jonathan's establishment of the economic management team, made up of technocrats from the public and private sector, strengthened the transformation agenda significantly. The major highlight of the Jonathan administration's domestic policy centered around the Boko Haram insurgency, which killed thousands of Nigerians mainly in the northeastern part of the country. The Jonathan administration responded by deploying a joint force of police, military, and state security agents to establish checkpoints around the country's borders to stop the flow of Boko Haram's resources. He also imposed curfews on the northeastern states that were affected by the attacks, but these measures were not sufficient as some Boko Haram sympathizers and financiers occupy senior positions in the military and police force who provided the terrorist group with intelligence. Politically, Goodluck Jonathan was tolerant, but this attribute was also one of his major weaknesses as he was unable to prosecute corrupt officials in his government. There were various cases of the diversion of funds meant for the development of the country by public officials who amassed wealth for themselves at the expense of the country. However, Goodluck Jonathan will be remembered for his patriotic spirit and magnanimity as the first sitting Nigerian president to concede to his opponent in a general election leading to a peaceful transfer of political power to a political opponent on May 29, 2015. In his concession speech, Jonathan is remembered for his now famous statement that the personal ambition of an individual is not worth the blood of a Nigerian.

See Also: Democratic Rule (Chapter 3); Independent Electoral Commission (Chapter 3); People's Democratic Party (Chapter 3).

Further Reading

Jonathan, G. E. (2018). *My Transition Hours*. Kindle.

Uzukwu, M. (2014). *Moving Forward: A Biography of Goodluck Ebele Jonathan*. Yenegoa: Feli Publisher.

LAW ENFORCEMENT

The Nigerian police force is an arm of government responsible for law enforcement and order in the country. The Nigeria Police Force was first established in 1820. In 1879 a 1,200-member armed paramilitary Hausa Constabulary was created while a comparable force, the Niger Coast Constabulary, was created in Calabar in 1894 under the officiated Niger Coast Protectorate. In 1896 the Lagos Police was created. In the North, the Royal Niger Company created the Royal Niger Company Constabulary in 1888 with headquarters at Lokoja. When the Protectorates of Northern and Southern Nigeria was proclaimed in 1914, a part of the Royal Niger Company Constabulary became the Northern Nigeria Police, and a part of the Niger Coast Constabulary became the Southern Nigeria Police. During the colonial period, most police officers related closely with the local governments (ethnic authorities). The NPF is headed by the Inspector-General of Police and performs traditional police responsibilities of maintaining law and order and is responsible for the country's internal safety generally, including the prisons, immigration, and customs services. The governing body of the Nigerian police is the Ministry of Police Affairs. Administratively, the Nigerian police force is divided into seven departments. These departments are administration, which coordinates all the departments and ensures policy and procedural processes; the Operations Department that is responsible for the planning, organization, and execution of security issues including communication network and crime control and prevention; Department of Logistics and Supply, responsible for the provision of uniforms, vehicles, and the maintenance of barracks, offices, and other buildings of the police; the Department of Investigation and Intelligence that oversees the investigations of narcotics and other criminal cases; the Department of Training and Command, which ensures the uniform and standard training requirements in all Police Colleges and Training Schools in the country; the "F" Department that is in charge of research, planning, and management of information; and the "G" Department that is saddled with the responsibility of information, communication, and technology policies for the Nigeria Police Force. On the other hand, the organizational structure of the Nigeria Police Force is designed along the six geopolitical zones of the country. The organizational structure includes the Police Headquarters in Abuja, the Zonal Headquarters, the State Commands Headquarters, the Divisional Police Headquarters, the Police Stations, the Police Post, and the Village Police Post.

Over the years, the image of the Nigeria Police has been tarnished due to its negative attitude to work, unethical behavior, and ominous disregard for essential human rights. The most notorious of its unethical behaviors are the mounting of roadblocks where motorists must give bribes to ply the roads and the extra-judicial killing of citizens. Surveys have consistently shown that about 70 percent of officers of the Nigerian police were not interested in the job at the time of recruitment; they simply joined because they wanted a job to earn a living or have legal access to power and ammunitions.

See Also: Correctional Institutions (Chapter 3); Criminal Law (Chapter 3); Human Rights (Chapter 3).

Further Reading

Chukwuma, U. M. (2018). *Professionalism, Reform, and The Nigerian Police Force*. Independent Publication.
Rotimi, K. (2002). *The Police in a Federal State. The Nigerian Experience*. Ibadan: College Press.
The Nigeria Police Force. https://www.npf.gov.ng/aboutus/Force_Structure.php

LEGISLATURE

Nigeria's federal legislative unit, the National Assembly, comprises the House of Representatives and the House of Senate. All members of the National Assembly are elected every four years. Though Nigeria commenced with a parliamentary system of government at independence in 1960, because of its British Colony, it later adopted the presidential system just like that of the United States in 1979. The motive of this alteration was to achieve greater and improved separation of powers among the three branches of government. Therefore, like its legislative mandate, the present-day Constitution offers the National Assembly extensive oversight powers. They consist of management of federal budget expenditures, the power to recommend, advise and consent on essential government appointments, the power of approval of agreements proposed through the government and the power to impeach the president and his deputy. Various elected and unelected officials are instrumental to the functioning of the National Assembly. Key members of the National Assembly leadership consist of the Majority Leader, the Minority Leader, the Chief Whip, and the Minority Whip. Among the unelected officials of the National Assembly are the Clerk and the Sergeant-at-Arms. Also essential to the efficient functioning of the National Assembly are the numerous committees that are set up to monitor governmental operations, to help focus public attention on major issues, conduct research, or revise bills, among other functions. While the Nigerian Constitution calls for each house of the National Assembly to create committees; a joint committee on finance and a public financial committee, it allows for the creation of many other committees as it deems fit. The National Assembly may also set up special committees such as standing committees, and ad hoc committees. The legislative procedure in Nigeria includes the houses of the National Assembly and the president. Typically, as soon as a bill (government, private, or member's bill) is brought to the National Assembly, it undergoes a rigorous procedure prior to its enactment into law, which incorporates three readings of the bill, scrutiny through the applicable committee in which amendments can be made, and presidential assent. The legislative branch, the National Assembly, which is stated to have been modeled after the United States Congress, is a bicameral body with a 360-member House of Representatives and a 109-member Senate. At the state level, power is vested in the state House of Assembly whose seats vary from twenty-four to forty members depending on the population of the state. The legislative power in Nigeria is shared through the National Assembly and the state legislatures. The Nigerian Constitution enumerates the legislative mandate of the National Assembly in the Second Schedule. The National Assembly can legislate on subjects enumerated in the Exclusive Legislative List in Part I of the Second Schedule to the exclusion of state legislatures, including on aviation, citizenship, marriage (besides the ones contracted in Islamic or customary law), and prisons. In addition, the National Assembly and state legislatures share the power to make legal guidelines on subjects concerning the Concurrent Legislative List. The legislative power of the National Assembly is exercised through bills adopted in each of the House of Representatives and the Senate. Similar model of a bill, which may also originate in both houses, should be adopted through each of the houses of the National Assembly. The legislative power of the National Assembly is checked by the veto power of the president, even though this power is not always absolute.

See Also: Administrative Division and Structure (Chapter 3); Constitutional Development (Chapter 3); Democratic Rule (Chapter 3); Supreme Court (Chapter 3).

Further Reading

Fagbadebo, O. and M. O. A. Alabi, eds. (2023). *The Legislature in Nigeria's Presidential Democracy of the Fourth Republic: Power, Process, and Development*. Cham, Switzerland: Springer.

Lafenwa, S. A. (2015). *The Legislature and Democratic Governance in Southwestern Nigeria*. LAP Lambert Academic Publishing.

Ojo, T. I. (1997). *Nigerian Legislature: Its Origin, Organization, Processes, Procedures, and Practices*. Zaria: Administrative Staff College of Nigeria.

Ubhenin, O. E. (2010). *The Nigerian Legislature: Cases and Concepts*. Moldova: LAP Lambert Academic Publishing.

MILITARY RULE

The military has ruled Nigeria for a considerable number of years since the country's independence in 1960. The first coup d'état was carried out on January 15, 1966, by Lieutenant Colonel Patrick Chukwuma Nzeogwu and his military boys, but this was short-lived as Johnson Thomas Umunnakwe Aguiyi-Ironsi, the then General Officer Commanding the Nigerian Army, seized power from the ensuing chaos that followed the Nzeogwu coup. But Nzeogwu's regime as Nigeria's first military head of state was short-lived as a second coup was organized six months later on July 29 of that year. The second coup was regarded as a counter coup organized mainly by military officers from the North against the perceived domination of military officers from the Southeast to control the country. The second coup saw the emergence of Yakubu Gowon as the new military head of state and chairman of the Supreme Military Council, the highest ruling organ of the junta. Gowon ruled the country from July 1967 to August 1975 when he was ousted by General Murtala Muhammed who ruled the country as head of state from August 1975 to February 1976 when he was killed in an aborted coup spearheaded by Buka Suka Dimka on February 13, 1976. The unsuccessful coup brought General Olusegun Obasanjo, Murtala second-in-command, as the new military head of state. Obasanjo ruled the country until 1979 when the government was handed over to a civilian regime headed by Alhaji Shehu Shagari. After securing a second term as president of the Second Republic, Shagari's administration was toppled by General Muhammadu Buhari on December 31, 1983. Buhari ruled as Nigeria's head of state for twenty months and a palace coup led by General Ibrahim Babangida brought an end to the fifth military rule in Nigeria. Babangida, who conferred on himself the title of military president also set up the Armed Forces Ruling Council as the highest organ of government during his regime. Babangida ruled between 1985 and 1993 until he was forced to step down and an interim civilian regime was sworn-in on August 26, 1993, headed by Ernest Shonekan. Less than three months later, General Sani Abacha sacked the interim government on November 17, 1993, and made himself the head of state and chairman of the Provisional Ruling Council of Nigeria. At his sudden death in 1998, General Abdusalami Abubakar became the head of state and conducted the election that ushered in the Fourth Republic in 1999. During the military regimes, the Nigerian constitution was suspended, and the country was ruled by decrees. It is during the military regimes that Nigeria's states were created by decrees. First in May 1967 when the regions were dissolved, and twelve states were created by the Gowon-led administration. Between 1976 and 1987 the states were further divided into nineteen states, and to thirty-six states by 1996. In total, the military has ruled the country for thirty-three years since independence. During the civilian regime of Obasanjo from 1999 to 2007, he vowed to stop military rule permanently in Nigeria by retiring some of the top military officers who had benefited from military rule either as military administrators or ministers. It is left to be seen if his strategy will stop military coups in Nigeria.

See Also: Buhari, Muhammadu (Chapter 3); Corruption (Chapter 3); Democratic Rule (Chapter 3); Nigerian Civil War (Chapter 2).

Further Reading

Akinnola, R. (2013). *Fellow Countrymen: The Story of Coup D'etats in Nigeria.* Abuja: Rich Konsult.

Fandom. (2023). "Military Coups in Nigeria." https://military-history.fandom.com/wiki/Military_coups_in_Nigeria

Nyangoro, J. E. (1993). "Military Coups d'etat in Nigeria Revisited: A Political and Economic Analysis." *American Review of Politics* 14: 129–47.

Smart, U. E. (1998). *The History of Coups in Nigeria.* Nigeria: Gaek Moke Limited.

PEOPLE'S DEMOCRATIC PARTY

The PDP began in 1997 under the leadership of Dr. Alex Ekwueme as a protest group against the dictatorship of the then military head of state, Sani Abacha. Ekwueme under the platform which he called the Institute of Civil Society with the aim of confronting the then military dictator who had indicated his plan to perpetuate himself as a civilian president. A declaration which saw other presidential aspirants from other political parties stepping down and accepting Sani Abacha as their preferred candidate. Ekwueme with his group later known as the G-18 wrote a letter to Abacha in February of 1998 advising him to resign and follow the laid down procedure for seeking presidential nomination from any of the existing political parties. This bold move attracted more members to the group and by March of the same year, they had become G-34. With the death of Abacha in June 1988, an 11-month transition program was initiated by the new head of state, General Abubakar. On August 18, 1998, more than twenty political associations under the leadership of the G-34 came together to form what will today be known as the PDP. Dr. Alex Ekwueme was made the chairman of the Steering Committee and Professor Jerry Gana the party secretary. It was under the PDP political party that Olusegun Obasanjo along with his running mate, Atiku Abubakar emerged as the president and vice president of the Federal Republic of Nigeria on May 29, 1999. Unfortunately, by 2005, the party had begun to crumble with major founding members leaving the party while others joined opposition parties. Notable was Atiku Abubakar who defected to become the flagbearer for an opposition party, the Action Congress while still serving as the vice president of Nigeria under PDP. However, despite these setbacks, the PDP won the presidential seat at the 2007 General Elections which made Mallam Umaru Musa Yar'Adua Nigeria's president. In that year, the party also won twenty-eight Governorship seats, 88 out of 109 Senate seats and 266 out of 360 Seats in the House of Representatives. The victory of Yar'Adua at the polls, his seven-point agenda of making Nigeria one of the twenty leading economies in the world by 2020 and his sincerity of purpose made PDP strong again. Thus, PDP was able to remain the ruling party in Nigeria from 1999 until the 2015 elections when the APC with its presidential candidate, Muhammadu Buhari, took over. Since this defeat, the PDP has been a major opposition to the ruling party. A number of factors can be said to have led to PDP's failure at the polls. Corruption was at the front burner, the high-handedness of its officials, and internal divisions within the party. These caused the Nigerian populace to question the party's philosophies and ability to lead.

See Also: All Progressives Congress (Chapter 3); Independent Electoral Commission (Chapter 3); Political Parties and Their Formations (Chapter 3).

Further Reading

Nwala, T. U. (1999). *Peoples Democratic Party (PDP) (of Nigeria): History and Challenges*. Abuja: PDP National Secretariat.
PDP Website. (2023). https://peoplesdemocraticparty.com.ng/

POLITICAL PARTIES AND THEIR FORMATIONS

Nigeria operates a multi-party-political system, and it is becoming more diverse in its political landscape especially in relation to political parties and their formations. In the 2019 general elections, for example, eighty officially registered parties from all the six geopolitical zones participated. Of these parties, however, only two, the All Progressives Congress party (the ruling party currently) and the PDP (the opposition party) are the most popular. They both have established structures and office secretariats in all the thirty-six states including the Federal Capital Territory. For this reason, no other party besides the two is represented in the Federal House of Assembly either in the Senate or the House of Representatives. Although some strides were made in the 2019 elections, there was no meaningful impact on the electoral seats. The third most important party by performance was the APGA, which won Imo state in the Southeast. However, internal wrangling has led to the systematic disintegration of the party in the state. Historically, the formation of political parties in Nigeria was along tribal lines especially the pre-independent political parties of Chief Obafemi Awolowo (Action Group) and the NPC led by Tafawa Balewa. Other similar tribal parties include the Zamfara Commoners Party, Igala Union, Igbirra Tribal Union, Kano People's Party, and the Midwest Democratic Front. Exception to these tribal parties was the NCNC party led by Dr. Nnamdi Azikiwe, which seemed more nationalistic in its spread than the other parties. However, the Second Republic witnessed an eclectic formation of political parties drawn from all ethnic groups in Nigeria. This evolution was necessitated by the fact that the country had been divided into nineteen states and for a political party to win a two-third majority as the constitution required, parties can only have a chance of winning elections by mobilizing electorates from the federation. Thus, even though still predominantly a northern party, the NPN had Dr. Alex Ekweme, an Igbo politician from the Southeast, as the running mate to the party's flag bearer, Alhaji Shehu Shagari who is from the North. The same calculation also applied to other political parties that contested the general elections of 1979. Formation of political parties in Nigeria is scarcely based on ideological persuasions rather it is based on the simple calculation to win elections both at the federal and state levels. It is for this reason that politicians are easily persuaded to abandon one party and join another. This phenomenon was apparent during the 2015 elections that saw the merger of three parties (Action Congress of Nigeria, Congress for Progressive Change, and All Nigeria People's Party) to form the All Progressives Congress that ousted the ruling PDP. One important development of the formation of political parties in Nigeria is the interest of religious leaders not only in politics but also in forming political parties, some of which include the FRESH party of Pastor Chris Okotie. Also, even though organized labor under the banner of Nigeria Labour Congress (NLC) formed a political party in 2002, the party has not been popular until in 2022 when it adopted Mr. Peter Obi as its presidential flag bearer, which has led to a somewhat political movement in Nigeria.

See Also: Constitutional Development (Chapter 3); Democratic Rule (Chapter 3); Early Political Parties (Chapter 3); Independent Electoral Commission (Chapter 3); Military Rule (Chapter 3).

Further Reading

Odigwe, D. A. (2015). "Nigeria Political Parties and Internal Democracy." *African Journal of Governance and Development*, 4(2): 65–78.

Ologbenla, D. K. (2007). "Political Parties and the Nigerian Political Process: 1999–2006 and Beyond." *LWATI: A Journal of Contemporary Research*, 4: 283–97.

The Independent National Electoral Commission. https://www.inecnigeria.org/

STATE AND LOCAL GOVERNMENTS

State creation in Nigeria began in 1967 under the military government of Yakubu Gowon. The aim at that time was to break down the three plus one region formation promulgated by the Richard's Constitution under the colonial government and give minority ethnic groups a voice. At that time, the three regions consisted of the northern (dominated by the Hausa-Fulani), western (dominated by the Yoruba), and eastern (dominated by the Igbo) while a fourth one (mid-western region made up of Benin and Delta peoples) was created by the indigenous government led by Tafawa Balewa. The minority agitations had prevailed during the colonial period due to their fears of being politically dominated by the three dominant ethnic groups, leading to agitations for separate regions. During the colonial period, agitations like the Calabar-Ogoja-River (COR) State Movement in the eastern region, The Benin and Delta Movements in the western region, and the Middle Belt Movement in the northern region made the colonial government made the colonial government to incorporate the protection of minority rights into the independent Nigeria's constitution. However, at the advent of the Nigerian Civil War in 1967, Yakubu Gowon's military-led government introduced the twelve state structure made up of North-Western State, North-Eastern State, Kano State, North Central State, Benue-Plateau State, and West Central State (carved from the northern region) (West Central State was however renamed Kwara State in 1968); Western State and Lagos State (carved from western region); Mid-Western State (the new region was transformed into a state); East Central State, Rivers State and South-Eastern State (carved out of the eastern region). More states were created when Yakubu Gowon's regime was toppled in 1976 by Murtala Mohammed. Between March and May of 1976 the following states were created: Anambra and Imo (created by splitting East Central into the two states), South-Eastern State was renamed Cross River State, Bauchi, Borno and Gongola States (created from the North-Eastern State), Niger and Sokoto States (created from part of North-Western State), North Central State was renamed Kaduna State, Ogun, Ondo and Oyo States (carved from Western State), Mid-Western State was renamed Bendel State, Benue and Plateau States (carved out of Benue-Plateau State), and The Federal Capital Territory, thus bringing the states to nineteen (plus Kano, Lagos and Kwara States). Between 1987 and 1991, the military government of Ibrahim Babangida first created Akwa Ibom (created from Cross River State) and Katsina State (created from Kaduna State). Then in 1991 the following states were added: Adamawa and Taraba (created from Gongola State), Jigawa (created from Kano State), Kebbi (created from Sokoto State), Yobe (created from Borno State), Kogi (created from Kwara State), Osun (created from Oyo State), Abia (created from Imo State), Anambra and Enugu States (Anambra was separated from its capital Enugu to form the two states), and Edo (renamed from Bendel State then divided into the two independent states of Edo and Delta). This brought the total number of states in Nigeria to thirty. In October of 1996 under the military regime of Sani Abacha, six more states were created namely: Bayelsa (created from Rivers State), Ebonyi (created from parts of Abia and Enugu States), Ekiti (created from Ondo State), Nasarawa (created from Plateau State), Gombe (created from Bauchi State), and Zamfara (created from Sokoto State). The states represent the second-tier of the three-tier government structure of Nigerian governance. Each state under the democratic dispensation is governed by an elected governor who serves as the executive along with the state judiciary and House of Assembly (a replica of the national level). The importance of this is reflected at the national level where the president must appoint at least one member from each of the thirty-six states. State representation must also be done at the National Assembly.

The third tier is the Local Government which is meant to serve the grassroots under the jurisdiction of the state's government. It is the duty of each state's executive administration to ensure that all LGAs under its jurisdiction is guided by appropriate laws, is run by a democratically elected council, and provides each council with the structure, composition, finance and functionality it needs to operate. Each LGA is made up of legislative and executive members. The legislature is made up of elected councillors mandated to make laws which will guide the governance and administration of their LGA; and the executive which consists of the chairman, secretary and supervisory councillors who together govern the area to ensure economic and social development and political stability. Altogether, Nigeria has 774 LGAs. The importance of local government representation is evident at the State House of Representatives where all the LGAs must be represented.

Although the three-tier structure of government was developed to ensure progress, unity and development in Nigeria, this has not been the case. Over the years, the motive for creating states has shifted from giving minority ethnic groups a voice and a platform to develop within Nigeria as a country, to sustaining selected ethnic dominance thereby giving their representatives access to national resources. For example, out of the thirty-six states plus the FCT, the Hausa-Fulani have fourteen, other ethnic minorities from the old northern region have five, the Yoruba have six, ethnic minorities of old western region have two, the Igbo have five while other ethnic minorities of the old eastern region have five. At the National Assembly as well as the State House of Assembly, this advantage has meant policies often favor some geopolitical zones over others, and more access to national resources for some areas than others.

Unfortunately, this access to power and resources at the national and state levels has not translated to progress at the local government level. Many have accused states governors of usurping the powers of the LGAs for their own selfish interests. The result is that many LGAs are grossly underfunded and thus lack the ability to empower their people or develop their areas.

See Also: Administrative Division and Structure (Chapter 3); Constitutional Development (Chapter 3); Corruption (Chapter 3); Democratic Rule (Chapter 3).

Further Reading

Adeyemi, O. O. (2013). "The Politics of States and Local Governments Creation in Nigeria: An Appraisal." *European Journal of Sustainable Development*, 2(3): 155–74.

Akpan, P. A. (1990). "Local Government Structure as a Spatial Framework for Rural Development in Nigeria." *Public Administration and Development*, 10(3): 263–75.

Ota, E. N., C. Ecoma, and C. G. Wambu (2020). "Creation of States in Nigeria, 1967–1996: Deconstructing the History and Politics." *American Research Journal of Humanities and Social Sciences*, 6(1): 1–8. doi: 10.21694/2378-7031.20005

Rulers. (2023). "Nigeria." https://rulers.org/nigastat.html

Salami, A. T. (2021). "Local Government and the Constitution: The Nigerian Experience." *Journal of Public Administration, Finance and Law*, 22: 359–68.

SUPREME COURT

There is only one Supreme Court of Nigeria (SCN) in the country, and it is the highest court in the land. It is in the Central District, Abuja, in what is known as the Three Arms Zone, so called because of the proximity of the offices of the Presidential Complex, the National Assembly, and the Supreme Court. The court is the supreme emblem of equal justice for all Nigerians, and one of its key functions is to interpret the Nigerian constitution in relation to all matters that pertain to the country. Thus, the Supreme Court, from its interpretation of the constitution, can declare if the Legislative or Executive arm of government acts illegally or in violation of the country's constitution. The coinage Supreme Court was first used in 1863 by the colonial administration through the enactment of the Supreme Court Ordinance No. II which established it as a colony with civil and criminal jurisdiction. In 1963, following the proclamation of the Federal

Republic of Nigeria and the constitution which came into operation on October 1, 1963, Section III of this constitution gave legal instrument that gave birth to the Supreme Court following the abolition of Section 120 which abrogated the appellate jurisdiction of the judicial committee of the Privy Council which was Nigeria's apex Court. This Act also gave it the status of the highest court in the judicial hierarchy while the Independence Constitution of 1960 vested in it the jurisdiction of the Federal Supreme Court. The 1979 Constitution in its Section 210 (1) gave it the name SCN. The court operates as the apex court on matters involving both federal and state laws. The Supreme Court adjudicates matters between the federal government and state government or between two state governments. It also has appellate jurisdiction to hear and determine appeal cases from the Court of Appeal. Thus, the Supreme Court is the final arbiter regarding disputes between the federal and state government or concerning appeals from other subsidiary courts in the land. The Supreme Court is composed of the Chief Justice of Nigeria and not more than twenty other Chief Justices appointed by the president after being recommended by the National Judicial Council and subject to the Senate's confirmation. Although at present the Supreme Court comprises the Chief Justice and twelve other Justices. They are required to retire after a mandatory service age of seventy. Before someone may be certified to be a justice of the Supreme Court they need to have been certified to practice as a legal practitioner for a duration of at least fifteen years. The current Chief Justice of Nigeria is the Honorable Mr. Justice Olukayode Ariwoola.

See Also: Administrative Division and Structure (Chapter 3); Criminal Law (Chapter 3); Legislature (Chapter 3).

Further Reading

Mwalimu, C. (2005). *The Nigerian Legal System*. New York: Peter Lang.
Supreme Court of Nigeria. https://supremecourt.gov.ng/supreme-court-rules

CHAPTER 4

Economy

OVERVIEW

According to the World Bank 2020 report on Nigeria's development update, the economy was still recovering from the 2016 recession when the Covid-19 pandemic emerged in early 2020. Nigeria faced a twin problem of the collapse of global oil prices in the 2014 and 2016 fiscal years, and the lower domestic oil production, which put the brakes on economic activity. Although Nigeria's oil sector accounts for less than 10 percent of gross domestic product (GDP), it accounts for about 90 percent of Nigeria's export and about 70 percent of the government's revenue, as well as provides over 90 percent of the country's foreign exchange earnings. On the other hand, agriculture contributes about 24 percent to the country's GDP. Although still largely informal, the agricultural sector is one of Nigeria's key economic sectors as it does not only contribute significantly to the GDP, but it also provides 40 percent employment to the citizens making it the largest economic sector by labor force. The sector accounts for about 70 percent of employment in the rural area where 50 percent of the citizens live. While the contribution of the agricultural sector is significant its output is relatively small compared to countries that engage in large-scale mechanized farming such as South Africa or Vietnam. Even though the Buhari administration (2015–2023) made agriculture one of its cardinal economic policies, the constant fracas between Fulani cattle herders and local farmers, as well as poor storage facilities failed to register any appreciable progress in this sector. However, the financial and insurance sector has made impressive progress in the country, and it is one of the fastest-growing sectors of the economy with an average of 8 percent year-on-year growth. Another fast-growing sector of the economy is transportation and storage with an average of about 12 percent, even though it witnessed a drop in 2022 compared to its performance in 2021 despite the challenges posed by the Covid-19 pandemic. The communication and information sector remains one of the strongest economic sectors in the country with a consistent year-on-year growth rate of about 10 percent. Despite some the challenges faced in this sector due to the strict regulations imposed by the Buhari administration, it has continued to thrive mainly because of the proliferation of new forms of communication and information dissemination such as the social media and online radio and television stations. The Ukraine war, the Covid-19 pandemic, and the presidential and general elections held in the first quarter of 2023 are all factors driving the relevance of the communication and information sector. International trade between Nigeria and other African countries has also witnessed marginal growth especially with Nigeria signing the African Continental Free Trade Agreement in 2019. Other sectors of the economy that have made some marginal growth include the construction industry, real estate, entertainment, and recreation.

Every sector of the economy has recorded differing levels of growth, thus, placing more stress on the already strained economy. Owing to the negative outcomes of the 2016 recession, the Nigerian government adopted the Economic Recovery and Growth Plan (ERGP), which is a Medium-Term Plan for 2017–20, with the purpose of restoring economic growth while leveraging the ingenuity and resilience of the Nigerian people— the nation's most priceless asset. The ERGP builds on existing sectoral strategies and plans, such as the National Industrial Revolution Plan, and the Nigeria Integrated Infrastructure Master Plan. The ERGP will strengthen the successful components of these previous strategies and plans while addressing challenges observed in their implementation. Among the top priorities of this plan include—stabilization of the macroeconomic environment with low inflation, stable exchange rates, and sustainable fiscal and external balances; using agriculture to achieve food security, create jobs, and save foreign exchange from food imports that can be produced locally; and ensuring energy sufficiency (through combined use of power and petroleum products).

In addition, the plan aspires to improve Nigeria's inadequate transportation infrastructure to support the economy and to reduce the major cost and constraint for businesses, as well as to drive industrialization focusing on Small and Medium Scale Enterprises. The National Industrial Revolution Plan was developed in 2014, by the Federal Ministry of Industry, Trade and Investment in order to create jobs, maintain trade balance, and boost competitive advantage and to increase and sustain the manufacturing sector's contribution to the GDP by over 10 percent in the near future. The project focuses on three sectors where the ministry sees potential comparative advantages: agriculture, solid minerals, as well as oil and gas.

To this end, to ease the process of doing business and to make the Nigerian business environment friendlier, the long-awaited Companies and Allied Matters Bill (CAMA) 2020 Act was signed into law, which had been in the pipeline for over thirty years. It has been lauded as a huge business reform because the new Act repealed and replaced the extant CAMA 1990 with key amendments that attempt to remove some bottlenecks from the old Act. Also, it is expected to improve Nigeria's ease of doing business among other countries, thus, making Nigeria competitive on the global business stage. Similarly, it is expected to increase private sector participation. Despite these efforts, the poverty level, partly fueled by high unemployment levels and corruption, continues to rise. The poverty headcount rate, for example, currently stands at 40.1 percent of the population, thus, making Nigeria one of the poorest nation-states in the world, while unemployment rate stands at 27.1 percent as at the first quarter of 2020.

Many factors have been identified as contributing factors to the rising poverty and unemployment rates, which range from government corruption, lack of economic infrastructure, poor access to education, and poor access to healthcare. This is underpinned by the near absence or weak state institutions that ought to efficiently and effectively supervise the various funds allocated for the purpose of building the necessary infrastructure to spur economic development and subsequently create jobs, thereby reducing poverty. Meanwhile, the government has turned to the once neglected agriculture sector as a means of resolving the growing poverty and unemployment problems. The country has an estimation of eighty-four million hectares of arable land and over 60 percent of it is largely uncultivated. The sector is made up of four sub-activities: crop production, livestock, forestry, and fishing. Thus, various agricultural policies and initiatives underpinned by the adoption of the *Agriculture Promotion Policy 2016–2020 Document*, have been implemented from 2016 to date.

Nigeria is currently repositioning herself to harness the largely untapped natural resources—in particular, the mining sector, which is estimated to generate about $500 million annually in revenue to the government. Nigeria is endowed with vast reserves of solid minerals, including, but not limited to, precious and base minerals, industrial minerals, energy minerals, and metals scattered in more than 500 locations and remained untapped. Historically, the country was a major exporter of tin, columbite and coal in the 1960s to early 1970s. But the sector witnessed decline in economic activity owing to the discovery of crude oil and its neglect has given rise to illegal mining and smuggling of precious metals out of the country. Hence, to benefit from the revenue, the government of Nigeria in 2016 adopted the Roadmap for the Growth and Development of the Nigerian Mining Industry, as well as the Presidential Artisanal Gold Mining Development Initiative (PAGMI), which was launched in 2019, to resolve all militating factors impeding the growth and full liberalization of the sector. More so, the manufacturing sector has also received some boost through various government initiatives. In the same vein, the financial institutions are stepping up, although not enough, to improve credit availability to the private sector to boost growth. For instance, the total net domestic credit in the Nigerian economy currently stands at N35.51 trillion (equivalent to over $80 billion) of which credit to the private sector constitutes 74 percent, while credit to the government constitutes 26 percent. The central bank of Nigeria as of July 2020, rolled out an intervention fund of N220 billion (equivalent of over $700 million) to support SMEs.

While the Nigerian Stock Exchange has made steady progress in improving transparency in its operation, calls have been made for the exchange to contribute more to the development of the country, especially in the areas of much-needed infrastructure development. On the international trade front of Nigeria's economy, the government has undertaken various reforms to ease the business climate and make the country more attractive to foreign investments. For instance, with the new trade policy, as well as the new CAMA 2020 Act, it is expected that major concerns of domestic traders and foreign investors, ranging from business ownership, business registration processes and strenuous registration requirements, as well as multiple taxation will be addressed. It is also expected to boost export and import, which has consistently been on the decline owing to the ongoing pandemic and the global oil price shock. Statistically, exports are expected to fall by US$40.3 billion, 9 percent of GDP owing to the current halt on international trade. On the other hand, imports are expected to fall by US$50.5 billion, 12 percent of GDP, due to sluggish demand and disruptions in global supply chains, as well as the halt on international trade. Aside from the impact of Covid-19, the chronic problem of port congestion has over the years undermined Nigeria's international economic potential. Among the chief factors are the delays at Nigeria's ports caused by inefficient border administration, which seems to stem from general mismanagement, undeveloped transport infrastructure and corruption. Another is the acquisition of import and export licenses, which has become prone to bribery and corruption, as containers lie waiting to be approved for export or for clearing. Therefore, these militating factors contribute to chronic congestion of ports, in particular, the Apapa and Tin Can ports in Lagos being the busiest, thus, creating a higher financial cost and time to clear goods from Nigeria's major ports. This makes doing business in Nigeria very difficult, as a result, most Greenfield investments, which are foreign direct investments, are redirected to neighboring countries with better and efficient ports.

The Covid-19 pandemic and its unexpected impact on global trade, as well as the fluctuating global oil price, has also negatively impacted Nigeria's external reserve causing an increase in the country's foreign debt. This is because the government increased its borrowing, as there is a need to offset the revenue shortfall resulting from export and international trade decline. Although Nigeria's debt profile is below international benchmark, the National Bureau of Statistics and the Debt Management Office reported that on March 31, 2020, the total debt portfolio of Nigeria stood at N28.63 trillion, representing about 28.1 percent to GDP ratio. Overall, most of this debt is owed to the domestic market, while foreign component of the debt is relatively low. Likewise, the low oil prices and the hard lockdown of Nigeria's economy have also reduced the amount of forex in circulation and weakened the Nigerian Naira, which places further strain on the already fledgling manufacturing sector and other sectors that require forex for survival. Over and above, the Nigerian labor union, through its labor movement, has been in the forefront of ensuring that government trade policies, as well as the private sector employment of the country's labor force are done on fair and transparent grounds. In other words, the welfare and plight of Nigerian workers must be at the center stage of doing business in Nigeria.

Further Reading

Africa Development Bank. (2023). https://www.afdb.org/en/countries-west-africa-nigeria/nigeria-economic-outlook

Dozie, P. (1999). *Perspectives on Nigeria's Economic Development (Volume I)*. Ibadan: Safari Books.

Dozie, P. (2012). *Perspectives on Nigeria's Economic Development (Volume II)*. Ibadan: Safari Books.

Usman, Z. (2022). *Economic Diversification in Nigeria: The Politics of Building a Post-Oil Economy*. London: Zed Books.

AGRICULTURE SECTOR

The agricultural sector is an important one with the potential to generate employment, reduce poverty levels, drive food sufficiency, as well as contribute massively to the gross domestic product (GDP) of Nigeria. The country has an estimation of over eighty-four million hectares of arable land and over 60 percent of it is largely uncultivated. The sector is made up of four sub-activities: crop production, livestock, forestry, and fishing, with over 50 percent of agricultural activities taking place in the northern region of the country. Moreover, with the ongoing ISWAP and Boko Haram insurgency in the northern region, although difficult to estimate, Nigeria has recorded a decline in agricultural activities, thereby pushing the price of farm produce high. Prior to the discovery of oil in the mid-1950s, the agriculture sector accounted for about 70 percent of the nation's export and was famous for the export of groundnut and palm oil kernels. Major crops produced include beans, rice, sesame, cashew nuts, cassava, cocoa beans, groundnuts, gum arabic, kolanut, maize (corn), melon, millet, palm kernels, palm oil, plantains, rice, rubber, sorghum, soybeans, bananas, and yams.

As such, the sector accounted for about 50 percent of total employment until the mid-1990s, when the ratio to employment began to decline. However, with the discovery of oil, the sector was neglected and its potential largely untapped over the years, which has led to the dwindling performance of the sector both domestically and internationally. Nonetheless, with the dwindling fortune of the oil and gas sector, there has been a renewed effort through various policies and programs, to revive the agricultural sector. This is owing to the sector's resurgent importance to the economy. Using the International Labor Organization (ILO) modeled estimates; in 2019 the sector employed about 35.1 percent of Nigerians. Similarly, the sector's gross value addition to the economy currently stands at 21.9 percent and the sector grew by 2.20 percent in the first quarter of 2020. This collective value to the nation's economy propelled the government to formulate and adopt policies and programs that will spur the rejuvenation of the sector and place it on a sustainable path.

Fundamental to the advancement of these policies and programs is the *Agriculture Promotion Policy 2016–2020 Document*—a policy that aspires to meet domestic food security goals, generate exports, and support sustainable income and job growth, as well as to provide a disciplined approach to building an agribusiness ecosystem. The implementation of the policy is supervised by the Federal Ministry of Agricultural and Rural Development (FMARD), which has also developed programs in collaboration with domestic and international partners, to accelerate the policy goals. Among the programs is APPEALS 9 Agro-Processing, Agricultural Productivity Enhancement and Livelihood Improvement Support, which is a World Bank–assisted program that aims to enhance agricultural productivity of small- and medium-scale farmers and improve value addition along priority value chains in the participating states. Another is the Livelihood Improvement Family Enterprise (LIFE), which aspires to improve the livelihood of women and youth by promoting on-farm and off-farm business activities. Also is the Zero Reject Project, targeted to ensure quality control and standardization of farm produce for quality consumption and export. Furthermore, the Central Bank of Nigeria–funded microfinance bank, Nigeria Incentive-Based Risk Sharing in Agricultural Lending (NIRSAL), and its Anchor Borrower's Scheme, provides credit guaranteed loans to MSMEs farmers, as well as creates a link between produce processing companies and farmers, respectively. As a result, produce such as rice, being Nigeria's main staple, has soared from 3.7 million metric tonnes in 2017 to eight million metric tonnes in 2020, with the nation aiming at eighteen million tonnes by 2023. It is currently Africa's largest rice producer and the world's largest cassava producer.

See Also: Exports (Chapter 4); Manufacturing Sector (Chapter 4); Mining Sector (Chapter 4); Oil and Gas Sector (Chapter 4); Private Sector (Chapter 4).

Further Reading

Food and Agriculture Organization of the United Nations (FAO). (2022). "Nigeria at a Glance." http://www.fao.org/nigeria/fao-in-nigeria/nigeria-at-a-glance/en/

Mbah, E. N. and E. M. Igbokwe. (2014). "A Review of Agricultural Transformation Agenda in Nigeria: The Case of Public and Private Sector Participation." *Research Journal of Agriculture and Environmental Management*, 3(5): 238–45. https://www.researchgate.net/publication/267507156_

The Federal Ministry of Agriculture and Rural Development (FMARD). (2020). https://fmard.gov.ng/

DOMESTIC AND INTERNATIONAL TRADE

Tangible data on Nigeria's domestic trade is insufficient; this is because domestic trade activities are largely informal in nature. Thus, the informal economy represents 41 percent of GDP and employs about 53 percent of Nigeria's active labor force. However, the trading of food items—such as livestock and agricultural produce—dominates domestic trading. These items are notably sourced from the northern part of the country where about one million households keep livestock, grow farm produce, and sizable numbers are employed in livestock slaughtering, butchering, and trading, as well as the production of cotton and textile materials. Furthermore, in the southern part of the country, but not limited to other parts of the country, the most traded are motor spare parts and second-hand clothing among others. The domestic market is dominated by small and medium businesses and petty traders. Moreover, the construction, transportation and financial activities are equally important and contribute to domestic trade. But the growth of domestic trading has been hampered by various challenges ranging from lack of infrastructure, power supply, and tough business climate.

On the other hand, international trade serves as a crucial sector toward the Nigerian GDP and governmental revenue. However, international trade—consisting of imports and exports—are constrained by several trade barriers. According to the World Economic Forum report, the most commonly mentioned are lack of transport infrastructure, and inefficiency and opacity in border administration. Delays at Nigeria's ports are caused by inefficient border administration, which seem to stem from general mismanagement, undeveloped transport infrastructure, and corruption. Business operators constantly complain about dealing with too many government agencies, arbitrary fees requested by some government officials, illegal clearing agents at the ports, and poor infrastructure.

This militating factor contributes to the chronic congestion of ports, in particular, the Apapa and Tin Can ports in Lagos being the busiest.

For example, the moving of goods from the ports can take up the entire day rather than forty-five to sixty minutes, which poses a major challenge for importers and exporters of time-sensitive or temperature-controlled products. Another is the acquisition of import and export licenses, which has become prone to bribery and corruption, because agencies ask for documentation which is not always communicated in advance and for fees beyond the statutory rates. This has negatively impacted on the cost and time of import and export. According to the World Bank report of doing business, the cost of export and import in Nigeria costs about $219 and $181 per container, respectively, while in other countries it averaged about $130 and $125, respectively. Likewise, it takes about twenty-three and thirty-four days to export and import goods in Nigeria, respectively, but in other countries, it takes around sixteen days to export and seventeen days to import. Finally, is the issue of maritime piracy, which continues to undermine Nigeria's trade potential, because over 80 percent of shipments to Nigeria are done via the sea.

Due to trade occurring almost exclusively via sea or air, Nigeria's ports, and airports thus act as the gateway for goods entering and leaving Africa's largest economy. By share of trade, Apapa Port is the busiest of Nigeria's ports, exporting 87.64 percent of all trade exports and receiving 48.86 percent of all imports to the country in the first quarter of 2020. The port is in Lagos and was first constructed in 1913 and expanded in 1922 to improve the western African nations' trade potential. Apapa is followed by Port Harcourt, sending 8.7 percent of exports and receiving 7 percent of imports, then followed by Tin Can Island located in Lagos which in turn services 2.3 percent of exports and receives 17.6 percent of all imports. Other notable ports that facilitate trade are Calabar Port and Warri Port. Nigeria's most operated airports facilitating trade are Muhammed Murtala airport in Lagos, Abuja airport in the capital, Port Harcourt airport and Kano airport.

See Also: Exports (Chapter 4); Financial Institutions (Chapter 4); Foreign Investment (Chapter 4); Forex and Currency Exchange (Chapter 4); Imports (Chapter 4); International Trade Policy (Chapter 4); Nigerian Stock Exchange (Chapter 4); Reserves and Foreign Debt (Chapter 4); Trade Partners (Chapter 4).

Further Reading

Anowor, O. F. and H. U. Agbarakwe. (2015). "Foreign Trade and Nigeria Economy." *Developing Country Studies*, 5(6): 77–83.

Observatory of Economic Complexity. (n.d.). *Nigeria Trade | Data*. OEC. https://oec.world/en/profile/country/nga/#tariffs

World Integrated Trade Solution. (2020). "Nigeria Trade Statistics." https://wits.worldbank.org/CountryProfile/en/NGA

EXPORTS

Nigeria is predominantly an oil-exporting nation, with its exported goods commonly being divided into two categories: crude oil and non-crude oil exports. In the first quarter of

2020, crude oil exports (including liquefied natural gas) represented 85.03 percent of all total exports, with non-crude oil, representing the remaining 14.97 percent. However, compared to 2018, a remarkable percentage decrease was observed in the oil industry, where in 2018 it made up just over 91 percent of total exports. The reduction can be due to the severe fluctuation in oil prices that occurred in February and March, as happened in 2016. Throughout the 2013–18 period, oil saw a decline in export value by an estimated 43.3 percent, which resulted in a loss of over US$32 billion. However, it should be noted that the 2018 value was a recovery from the more significant lower amount in 2016 of US$27 billion.

As oil dominates exports, comprising over 80 percent, export destinations also reflect the current demand for Nigeria's oil, but as noted, Nigeria has other (even if relatively small) products that are sought after globally. In the first quarter of 2020, for example, 8.90 percent of exports consisted of vessels and other floating structures. Furthermore, Nigeria has a growing agricultural industry, led primarily by sesame seeds, natural cocoa butter, cashew nuts, and raw cocoa beans. Agricultural exports predominately head to Europe and Asia and accounted for 3.09 percent of total exports. Nigeria also has recently seen an uptick in the export of precious metals, which through the 2013–18 period has increased in value from US$24 million in 2013 to US$577 million in 2018, representing a 2,280 percent rise. It is expected that the exportation of precious metals and agricultural products will only increase in the coming decade, furthering the much-needed diversification in the Nigerian export sector.

In 2019 Nigeria exported the value of US$49.89 billion in goods, largely to Europe—38.43 percent and Asia 31.28 percent, with the lion's share of 15.61 percent of exports headed to India—mostly oil. Nigeria's largest European markets were Spain at 9.87 percent, and the Netherlands at 9.72 percent—these markets were also dominated by the demand for oil. Moving beyond Europe and Asia and closer to home, other significant markets for Nigerian exports are South Africa with a share of 7.82 percent and Cameroon with 7.39 percent—in total African destinations comprised 23.96 percent of total exports. Beyond the exports of goods, Nigeria also has a large and growing array of services that are being exported. In 2015, Nigeria exported the value of US$2.74 billion in services to overseas markets. These consisted of sea transport services at 64.5 percent of the total, government services at 18 percent, and financial services at 9.4 percent of all services exported. It is estimated that service exports will reach the value of over $7 billion by the end of 2022. Exports are expected to fall by US$40.3 billion, 9 percent of GDP owing to halts on international trade during the Covid-19 pandemic.

See Also: Domestic and International Trade (Chapter 4); Imports (Chapter 4); International Trade Policy (Chapter 4); Natural Resources (Chapter 1); Oil and Gas Sector (Chapter 4); Trade Partners (Chapter 4).

Further Reading

National Bureau of Statistics. (2020). *Foreign Trade in Goods Statistics*. Abuja: National Bureau of Statistics.
Nigerian Custom Headquarters. (2013). *Nigeria's Import, Export and Transit Process Manual*. Ibadan: Safari Books Limited.

The Future of the Nigerian Economy
Despite Nigeria's high inflation rate at 21 percent, unemployment rate at 33 percent, and intermittent power supply, Nigeria's economic growth for 2023 is projected at 3 percent. However, the uncertainty that surrounds the peaceful transition of the Buhari government to the Tinubu administration is a major concern among economic analysts. In addition to the restiveness that the February 25 presidential elections have generated, the Central Bank of Nigeria's redesign of the higher denominations of 200-, 500-, and 1,000-Naira notes, which has led to a financial squeeze due to low liquidity circulation, may have adverse effect on business and further reduce the 3 percent projected growth for 2023. Accessing the new Naira notes from banks and ATMs and withdrawal limits is a major issue that the Tinubu-led government, starting from May 29, 2023, must address decisively to ensure any meaningful economic growth. The volatile nature of the Nigerian economy has also led to the Nigerian Economic Summit Group to project that the country's unemployment may hit 37 percent by the end of 2023.

Nigerian Export Promotion Council. (2018). https://nepc.gov.ng/
World Integrated Trade Solution. (2018). *Nigeria (NGA) Exports, Imports, and Trade Partners.* WITS. https://wits.worldbank.org/countrysnapshot/en/NGA

FINANCIAL INSTITUTIONS

The Nigerian financial institution consists of two sub-sectors: the banking and non-banking; that is, the financial and insurance sub-sectors, respectively. The banking and non-banking sectors account for 87.02 percent and 12.98 percent of the sector, respectively. The financial institutions' dates as far back as the colonial era and commercial banks have been the oldest with the establishment of the Bank of British West Africa in 1899, now known as First Bank of Nigeria (FBN). Its initial purpose was to meet the commercial needs of the colonial government. But over the years, the sector has been saturated by indigenous banks and is increasingly playing a vital financial intermediary role in Nigeria's financial system. This is done by engaging in mobilizing funds from the surplus sector of the economy and lends such funds to the deficit sector. In this way, it intermediates between the people with surplus funds and those in deficit.

The financial institutions as a corporate entity that deals in financial claims is controlled by the government through various regulatory bodies such as the Central Bank of Nigeria (CBN) being the country's apex bank, the Nigeria Deposit Insurance Corporation (NDIC), National Insurance Commission (NAICOM), and the Securities and Exchange Commission (SEC). The annual contribution of the sector to the economy ranged between 8 to 10 percent and as at Q1 of 2020, growth in this sector in real terms stood at 20.79 percent, which is 0.61 percent higher from the last quarter of 2019. The financial institutions are, thus, among the fastest-growing sectors in the Nigerian economy. Meanwhile, compared to its financial capacity, the financial institutions have been playing less of a role in the development of Nigeria in the areas of infrastructural development. Some economists have argued that banks are reluctant and restrained to invest in infrastructural development, as well as give out enough loans, due to government's public-private partnership policy inconsistency and excessive exposure to intensified risks.

In Nigeria, non-performing loans (NPL) represent one of the most serious liquidity challenges facing the Nigerian financial institutions. Bank loans are regarded as risk assets because the monies advanced as loans by the banks belong to depositors. NPL arises in the event of massive defaults by borrowers, which makes it difficult for depositors' monies to be available on demand. As of 2019, NPLs stood at N1.44 trillion (equivalent to about $3.5 billion) and due to the growing concern, the government has given more powers to the Asset Management Corporation of Nigeria (AMCON) to enforce debt recovery from defaulters. In addition, in 2020 the CBN issued new guidelines on global standing instruction (GSI)—effective from August 1, 2020, which gives banks the power to debit loan and accrued interest due from bank accounts of loan defaulters. The insurance companies are faced with structural issues, such as weak regulatory framework, lack of skilled personnel, inadequate access to information technology, as well as Nigerian market doubts about insurance companies. Over and above, credit provided by the institutions to the private sector stands at 22.1 percent to the GDP.

See Also: Forex and Currency Exchange (Chapter 4); Foreign Investment (Chapter 4); Nigerian Stock Exchange (Chapter 4); Reserves and Foreign Debt (Chapter 4).

Further Reading

Ighoroje, J. E. and H. Egedi. (2015). "An Evaluation of the Roles of Financial Institutions in the Development of Nigeria Economy." *G.J.I.S.S.*, 4(4): 1–4. https://www.longdom.org/articles/an-evaluation-of-the-roles-of-financial-institutions-in-the-development-of-nigeria-economy.pdf

Nairametrics. (2019, October 01). "Evolution of Nigerian Banks in 59-Years." https://nairametrics.com/2019/10/01/evolution-of-nigerian-banks-in-59-years/

Nairametrics. (2020, May 26). "Financial Institutions Still the Fastest Growing Sector in Nigeria." https://nairametrics.com/2020/05/26/financial-institutions-still-the-fastest-growing-sector-in-nigeria/

FOREIGN INVESTMENT

Foreign investment remains an important financial tool in the development of Nigeria's infrastructure and wider economy. Through the efforts of the Nigerian Investment Promotion Commission (NIPC), foreign investment has increased year-on-year. But in 2019, it was reported that the total inflow of foreign investment equated to just over US$3.3 billion, increasing total foreign stock in Nigeria to the amount of US$98.6 billion. This represented a decrease by over $3 billion from 2018—mostly due to a fall in oil prices. This is because the oil and gas sector attract most of the foreign investment, while others include the energy, real estate, and agriculture sector among others. Meanwhile, the United States and United Kingdom are the most significant sources of foreign investment in Nigeria. Several French corporations are also prominent in the oil, processing, and construction industries.

Similarly, portfolio investments, through purchase of government-issued bonds, are also a source of foreign investment in Nigeria. But, as at the end of April 2020, Foreign Direct Investment (FDI) received was estimated at $18.5 million, down from $110.9 million received earlier in January 2020. FPI, on the other hand, recorded a 3,297 percent decline from $2.30 billion in January to $67.9 million inflow in April 2020. This has been attributed to the ongoing pandemic. However, as at the end of 2019 fiscal year, the country moved up fifteen places, on the World Bank's Ease of Doing Business Index, in which Nigeria ranked 131 in the ease to do business rating. In fact, Nigeria has consequently been in the top ten most improved nations in the list for both 2019 and 2020, with its most significant improvements being reduction in registration times for new businesses and reduction in construction permit fees.

Nigeria has also improved with the enforcement of contracts and the registration of property, nonetheless, the judiciary system is still constrained by several unresolved cases causing a backlog in the system. Moreover, factors militating against Nigeria's slow improvement lie with the country's poor electricity supply and transport infrastructure resulting in high operating cost within the nation. This has resulted in Nigeria losing Greenfield investments to neighboring countries, such as Togo and the Republic of Benin. Others are weak investment regulatory framework, weak and multiple taxation system, as well as strenuous business registration process. Furthermore, the overreliance on the oil industry leads to vulnerability to market shifts that can cause concern for international investors. There is also the concern of security, especially in the Northeast of the country, where extremist and insurgent operations have caused jeopardy in assets and business operations. Finally, with the signing of the CAMA 2020 Act into law, it is expected that some of the structural problems, in terms of easing the business registration process will be resolved, thus, will increase foreign investments from mere 0.4 growth registered in March 2020 to a higher growth to the GDP.

See Also: Financial Institutions (Chapter 4); Forex and Currency Exchange (Chapter 4); Nigerian Stock Exchange (Chapter 4); Poverty (Chapter 4).

Further Reading

National Bureau of Statistics. (2022). "Gross Domestic Product (GDP)." https://nigerianstat.gov.ng/
Nordea. (2020, July). *Foreign Direct Investment (FDI) in Nigeria—Investing—Nordea Trade Portal.* Nordea Trade. https://www.nordeatrade.com/en/explore-new-market/nigeria/investment

FOREX AND CURRENCY EXCHANGE

During colonial rule and the years following independence in 1960, currency exchange in Nigeria was almost exclusively handled by overseas commercial banks. Furthermore, as the Nigerian Pound at this point was still pegged to the British Pound Sterling, convertibility was not a major issue. And thus, having a dedicated currency exchange system was not a priority issue for the newly independent nation of Nigeria. On January 1, 1973, the Nigerian Naira replaced the British Pound and was adopted as the country's legal tender and its legal trading currency. By the end of the 1970s two Naira was equivalent to one

Pound and 55k was equal to $1. However, in the 1980s this started to change, slightly due to Nigeria drifting further away from the United Kingdom, but more so because of the significant increase that the export sector was experiencing with the fast-growing oil industry. To assist in this development and to ease the process of exportation, the Nigerian government introduced a more centralized control structure for currency exchange. In 1986 this was realized with the creation of the Second-tier Foreign Exchange Market (SFEM). This entity was created to better align the Naira's exchange rate to global market forces, allowing for greater ease in international trade. Three years later in 1989, another major step occurred with the introduction of the Bureaux de Change, this was implemented to assist in the facilitation of privately conducted foreign exchange. Further liberalization followed in 1995, with the creation of the Autonomous Foreign Exchange Market (AFEM), which allowed for better exchanges at market-determined rates through selected dealers by the Central Bank of Nigeria. This process toward liberalization was furthered with the introduction of the Inter-bank Foreign Exchange Market (IFEM). In short, Nigerian foreign exchange in the past forty years has been impacted by three prime factors: first, by the changing nature of international trade, second by diverging institutional changes in the economy, and third by the structural shifts in production.

The Nigerian forex market is one of the most volatile in the world, because of the weak nature of the Naira in the international market. Unfortunately, the strength of the Naira against most foreign currencies is tied to the global price of oil. Hence, with the continued fluctuation and declining oil price, the Naira also continues to weaken in value. In 2015 the exchange rate was US$1 to N199, and by December 2022, the Naira was devalued to around N750 to the dollar. The Tinubu's administration, starting from May 29, 2023, allowed the Naira to "float," which devalued the currency further to its lowest rate at 900 Naira to US$1. Despite this devaluation, is also the issue of availability, accessibility of forex and multiple exchange rates. Nonetheless, the CBN is working to unify the exchange rate and make forex readily available, similarly, the Chinese Yuan and Naira currency swap agreement is expected to support the Naira international trading value. The Currency Swap Agreement is designed to aid trade transactions between China and Nigeria and remove the need to first source for the "greenback" (US Dollars) before payments for transactions involving the two countries can be made. Finally, over the years, foreign remittance from Nigerians in diaspora has steadily become the backbone of the country's foreign exchange inflows. In 2018, for example, foreign remittances to Nigeria equaled US$25 billion, representing 6.1 percent of GDP. This also represents 14 percent year-on-year growth from the $22 billion receipt in 2017. The 2018 figure translates to 83 percent of the Federal Government budget in 2018 and eleven times higher than the FDI flows in the same period, and it is expected to grow further in the coming years. But it has been predicted that the ongoing pandemic might reduce inflow.

See Also: Financial Institutions (Chapter 4); Foreign investment (Chapter 4); Nigerian Stock Exchange (Chapter 4); Reserves and Foreign Debt (Chapter 4).

Further Reading

CBN. (2020, August 18). *Central Bank of Nigeria | Exchange Rate*. Central Bank of Nigeria. https://www.cbn.gov.ng/rates/ExchRateByCurrency.asp

Central Bank of Nigeria. (n.d.). "Foreign Exchange Market in Nigeria." https://www.cbn.gov.ng/IntOps/FXMarket.asp

Nairametrics. (2020, August 09). "Exchange Rate Unification: CBN Devalues Official Rate to N380/$1." https://nairametrics.com/2020/08/09/exchange-rate-unification-cbn-devalues-official-rate-to-n380-1/

IMPORTS

Nigeria has been a high importer of food items, and it is well known for having the penchant for importation of goods and services, ranging from luxury goods, to vehicles, refined petroleum products and even agricultural produce, which can be produced locally. In fact, records from 2000 to 2015, for example, show that the top imports were food items such as, wheat, rice, sugar, milk, frozen meat, and canned food. Also, petroleum products, such as motor spirit and used motor vehicles topped the list as well. But in August of 2019, Nigeria abruptly shut its borders with Benin Republic to stop the illegal importation of food items such as, rice, palm oil, frozen poultry products, used vehicles and several other products under partial or outright ban in Nigeria. Also, such importations undermine the economy and efforts to revive domestic agriculture. Moreover, the closure resulted in an increase in the production of domestic agriculture produce, in turn, causing an increase in the price of food items because domestic production is not sufficient to service domestic demand.

Notwithstanding, in 2019, Nigeria imported just over US$44 billion worth of goods from trade partners, and unlike exports, Nigeria's imports are not solely dominated by the oil industry. In the first quarter of 2020, imported goods to Nigeria consisted of manufactured goods with a share of 63.04 percent of imports, petroleum products at 22.19 percent, raw material goods at 7.28 percent, and agricultural goods at 6.19 percent of all imports. Notably, the products that are imported are predominately from secondary and tertiary products, consisting of various chemical products, machinery, refined petroleum and gas, solid mineral, food and live animals, crude inedible materials, beverages and tobacco, manufactured goods, textiles, plastics and rubbers and miscellaneous manufactured articles among others being imported. As of the first quarter of 2020, Nigeria's largest import partner by a large margin is China, which supplies around 26.28 percent of all imports, these being predominantly machines, textiles, and various metals. Whereas, twenty years ago, China was Nigeria's eighth trading partner globally, and currently, China is Nigeria's largest trading partner when it comes to imports.

Furthermore, refined petroleum, which serves as one of the largest of Nigeria's imports, originates chiefly from the Benelux regions, specifically, the Netherlands, which accounts for about 11.14 percent and Belgium, which accounts for about 6.11 percent of petroleum imports. Meanwhile, agricultural products, such as durum wheat, seeds and frozen meat are imported mostly from the United States and Eastern Europe, with significant contributions from Canada and Argentina, which represents about 6.19 percent of the total imports. With the increase in demand for tertiary products for growth of Nigeria's industrialization, the importation of services is becoming more of a significant and important factor in Nigerian market demands. In 2015 Nigeria imported US$15.6 billion worth of services. These consisted of 27.5 percent being sea transport services, 22.5 percent toward air transport services, 12.8 percent to business, professional and technical services, and 8.6 percent in governmental services. It is estimated that this total will only become more significant, reaching US$50 billion by the end of 2023. However, imports are expected to fall by US$50.5 billion, which is 12 percent of GDP, due to sluggish demand and disruptions in global supply chains, as well as the halt on international trade during the peak of the Covid-19 epidemic.

See Also: Domestic and International Trade (Chapter 4); Exports (Chapter 4); International Trade Policy (Chapter 4); Trade Partners (Chapter 4).

Further Reading

Export Genius. (2022). "Nigeria Import Data." https://www.exportgenius.in/export-import-trade-data/nigeria-import.php

Nigerian Custom Headquarters. (2013). *Nigeria's Import, Export and Transit Process Manual*. Safari Books Limited.

World Integrated Trade Solution. (2018). *Nigeria (NGA) Exports, Imports, and Trade Partners*. WITS. https://wits.worldbank.org/countrysnapshot/en/NGA

INTERNATIONAL TRADE POLICY

As of the first quarter of 2020, data from the National Bureau of Statistics, reports that foreign trade contributed a total of 15.09 percent to Nigeria's nominal GDP down from 16.95 percent contribution in the same quarter of the previous year, as well as the preceding quarter's 15.66 percent. Nigeria's trade (both exports and imports) is heavily dominated by the oil industry, a condition that has led to detrimental consequences when the value of oil fluctuates heavily, as witnessed in recent times. These detrimental consequences occurred in 2016 when Nigeria plummeted into its first trade deficit or negative trade balance and recession in decades, due to a shock in the global oil prices. It is in the context of such a reality that the continued diversification and liberalization of Nigeria's trade operations have become a priority for government agencies. One such agency is the Nigerian Office for Trade Negotiations (NOTN) founded in early 2017, in reaction to the 2016 recession that was largely caused by a slump in oil prices. The NOTN operates in conjunction with the Nigerian Investment Promotion Commission (NIPC), to foster trade deals that will simultaneously create value chains that link both internationally and regionally, and to grow the Nigerian domestic market. In this sense, the NOTN aims its trade policy at maximizing economic potential while also rebalancing economic anomalies in the domestic market.

As such, in response to a recent decline in trade-to-GDP shares and adapting to the issues and realities ushered in by the 2020 pandemic, the NOTN has provided a new trade policy roadmap that will dictate its policies in the years and perhaps decades to come. The roadmap reveals policy measures created to address current pandemic-related issues and provide frameworks in which to utilise opportunities created by the pandemic. According to the NOTN, the new trade policy is a shift from the old trade regime because it contains proactive strategies and responsive policy measures to address current and future challenges. It also aspires to recover economic losses, sustainably grow the economy, and sustain the economy through a broad multi-sectoral and coordinated response by Nigeria domestically, regionally, and internationally. Most importantly, it is revealed that the new trade policy aims at achieving a trade share that contributes at least 50 percent to the GDP and increases employment share in trade-related industries to 28 percent by the year 2023. In addition, the new trade policy framework seeks to make Nigeria one of the fifteen largest economies in the world by 2025.

The roadmap also aims to promote "rapid development" of Nigeria's digital economy; formalization of Nigeria's large informal economy; and further develop MSMEs and integrate the business into global value chains (GVCs). This is achievable by exploiting newly created opportunities in new trade agreements that will facilitate growth in key areas toward diversification, which include but not limited to manufacturing, health, processed and semi-processed exports, services, innovation, research and development, science and technology, E-Commerce, teleworking, telemedicine among other service-related exports. As a member of the African Union (AU) and a signatory to the African Continental Free Trade Agreement, which aspires to create a single trading bloc, Nigeria hopes to leverage her position as the continent's largest economy and population to advance industrialization to boost exportation of Nigerian-made goods. This is because the manufacturing and agriculture sectors have been viewed as crucial to the diversification of the Nigerian economy.

See Also: Domestic and International Trade (Chapter 4); Exports (Chapter 4); Imports (Chapter 4); Trading Partners (Chapter 4).

Further Reading

Briggs, I. N. (2007). *Nigeria: Mainstreaming Trade Policy into National Development Strategies.* Addis Ababa: Africa Trade Policy Center.

Itugbu, S. (2017). *Foreign Policy and Leadership in Nigeria: Obasanjo and the Challenge of African Diplomacy.* London: I.B. Tauris Publisher.

World Trade Organization. (1998). "Nigeria 1998." https://www.wto.org/english/tratop_e/tpr_e/tp075_e.htm

MANUFACTURING SECTOR

The Nigerian manufacturing sector is comprised of thirteen activities: oil refining; cement; food, beverages, and tobacco; textile, apparel and footwear; wood and wood products; pulp paper and paper products; chemical and pharmaceutical products; non-metallic products, plastic, and rubber products; electrical and electronic, base metal, and iron and steel; motor vehicles and assembly; and other manufacturing. Historically, the development of the manufacturing sector has been marred with a series of policy inconsistencies and distractions attributable to the discovery of oil. For instance, from a modest 4.8 percent in 1960, the contribution of manufacturing to the nation's GDP increased to 7.2 percent in 1970 and to 7.4 percent in 1975. However, in 1980, it declined to 5.4 percent but then surged to a record high of 10.7 percent in 1985 to the GDP. By 1990, manufacturing contributed 8.1 percent to the GDP but then dropped to 7.9 percent in 1992, 6.7 percent in 1995 and fell further to 6.3 percent in 1997. As of 2001, it dropped further to 3.4

percent from 6.2 percent in 2000. But it increased to 4.16 percent in 2011 which is less than what it was in 1960. The top manufacturing cities are Aba, Kano, Lagos and Awka, while the top indigenous manufacturers include the Dangote group and Innoson Motors.

In the first quarter of 2020, the manufacturing sector contributed about 9.65 percent to the GDP, which is lower than the 9.79 percent recorded in the first quarter of 2019 but higher than the 8.74 percent recorded in the fourth quarter of 2019. Similarly, the sector experienced a slow real GDP growth of 0.43 percent in the first quarter of 2020, owing to the 8-week lockdown, because of the Covid-19 pandemic. Furthermore, year-on-year, the sector contributes over $30 billion to the economy, also using the modeled ILO estimate, the sector employs about 12.23 percent of Nigeria's labor force. This is up from about 10.2 percent in 2010. Submissions have been made by economists and industrialists—such as the Manufacturers Association of Nigeria (MAN), that the contributions from the manufacturing sector to the country's Gross Domestic Product (GDP) are still poor, considering its huge untapped potential. Among the many militating factors impeding the sector's development include lack of funds, poor and deteriorating infrastructural services, mostly power supply.

Other militating factors include high and unplanned inventories including dumping of all manner of finished goods from other countries, has led to the lack of competitiveness of "made in Nigeria" goods; multiple taxation by all levels of government; availability, accessibility of forex and multiple exchange rates and weak regulatory framework. With the African Continental Free Trade Agreement coming on stream, the Nigerian government with interest to tap into the market has highlighted some key initiatives underpinned by the Economic and Sustainability Plan, to boost the sector. These include providing incentives to support industrial hubs, review of local fiscal and regulatory incentives to support the development of industrial cities, parks, and clusters, as well as to rationalize tariffs and waivers on the equipment and machinery imports required for the sector. In addition, the CBN is working to unify the exchange rate and make forex readily available to the sector. Importantly, the recently passed CAMA law (discussed in the previous sections) is an attempt to address most of the identified challenges to the sector.

See Also: Agriculture Sector (Chapter 4); Domestic and International Trade (Chapter 4); Mining (Chapter 4); Oil and Gas Sector (Chapter 4); Private Sector (Chapter 4).

Further Reading

A Brief Overview of the Nigerian Manufacturing Industry. (2019). https://thechrisogunbanjofoundation.org/a-brief-overview-of-the-nigerian-manufacturing-industry/

Nairametrics. (2020, August 04). "Manufacturing Sector in Nigeria and the Reality of a 'New Normal.'" https://nairametrics.com/2020/08/04/manufacturing-sector-in-nigeria-and-the-reality-of-a-new-normal/

MINING SECTOR

Nigeria is endowed with vast reserves of solid minerals, including, but not limited to, precious and base minerals, industrial minerals, energy minerals and metals scattered in more than 500 locations. The largely untapped deposits of forty-four minerals include bitumen (found in the Southwest region), limestone (found in the Southwest and North-central regions), gold (found in the Southwest, Northwest, and central regions), iron ore (found in the Northeast, North-central, and the Southeast regions). Also, barites are found in the North-central region; coal in the North-central and Southeast regions; lead-zinc in the Southwest and Northeast regions of Nigeria. However, the mining sector contributes only about 0.3 percent to the economy. This contribution is a reversal from the historically higher percentages of about 4 percent to 5 percent to GDP in the 1960s to 1970s. Historically, the country was a major exporter of tin, columbite and coal in the 1960s to the early 1970s.

Activities in this sector began to nose-dive considerably by the mid-1970s due to several political and economic factors, especially the significant focus on crude oil production as a major source of foreign exchange for the country. Over the years, efforts have been made by successive governments to revive the sector, to raise its contribution to the GDP and generate more jobs. The decades of reform saw key changes including the passage of Nigerian Minerals and Mining Act of 2007—being the principal legislation that regulates the sector; the Nigerian Mineral and Metals Policy 2008; the creation of a modern Mining Cadastre system; the refinement of the tax code; and the expansion in airborne mapping of the country to sharpen knowledge of the mineral endowments. However, the sector largely remains underdeveloped, thus, leaving the deposit sites prone to illegal mining and banditry as being witnessed in the northwestern state of Zamfara, where gold is illegally mined and routinely smuggled to Niger and Togo. In fact, the government estimates that the nation lost a total of $3 billion from 2012 to 2018 owing to illegal mining.

Nonetheless, with the advent of the oil price crash and its subsequent negative impact on Nigeria's revenue, the government looks to generate extra revenue from mining through royalties and taxes. To actualize this, in 2016, the government published its *Roadmap for the Growth and Development of the Nigerian Mining Industry*, and one of the targets of the roadmap is the growth of the sectors' total contribution (direct and indirect) to Nigeria's GDP to about 10 percent, create about 250,000 jobs, as well as generate an annual revenue of about $500 million to government by 2026. Two gold refineries were licensed in early 2020 to produce and sell to the Central Bank of Nigeria to hold for reserve and to export. In July 2020, the first gold bar was produced and bought by the CBN for about $600,000. Similarly, the Presidential Artisanal Gold Mining Development Initiative (PAGMI), launched in 2019, aims to foster the formalization and integration of artisanal gold mining activities into Nigeria's legal, economic, and institutional framework. The roadmap and the initiative, hopes to address the key challenges facing the sector, ranging from limited geoscience data and information, infrastructural development, security issues, project funding, illegal mining and community challenges, and lack of robust fiscal framework.

See Also: Agriculture Sector (Chapter 4); Manufacturing Sector (Chapter 4); Natural Resources (Chapter 1); Oil and Gas Sector (Chapter 4); Private Sector (Chapter 4).

Further Reading

CNBC Africa. (2020, July 16). "Nigeria Hopes Gold Mining Reforms can bring in $500 mln a Year." https://www.cnbcafrica.com/mining/2020/07/16/nigeria-hopes-gold-mining-reforms-can-bring-in-500-mln-a-year/

KMPG. (2017). "Nigerian Mining Sector Brief." https://assets.kpmg/content/dam/kpmg/ng/pdf/advisory/ng-Nigerian-Mining-Sector.pdf

Reuters. (2020, February 05). "UPDATE 2-Nigeria Sets Ambitious Target for Mining Sector Growth." https://af.reuters.com/article/metalsNews/idAFL8N2A53IU

The Ministry of Mines and Steel Development. (2020). "President Reiterates Commitment to Combat Illegal Mining Activities, Expresses Concern over Loss of $3b to Smuggling of Gold." https://www.minesandsteel.gov.ng/2020/07/16/president-reiterates-commitment-to-combat-illegal-mining-activities-expresses-concern-over-loss-of-3b-to-smuggling-of-gold/

NIGERIAN STOCK EXCHANGE

The Nigerian Stock Exchange (NSE) services the largest economy in Africa and is championing the development of Africa's financial markets. The NSE, a registered company limited by guarantee, was founded in 1960 as the Lagos Stock Exchange but in 1977 changed its name to the Nigerian Stock Exchange. It is licensed under the Investments and Securities Act (ISA) and is regulated by the Securities and Exchange Commission (SEC) of Nigeria. The NSE is one of the most developed stock exchanges in Africa and offers a range of instruments for investors in the equities, bonds, and derivatives market. Currently, it is the fifth largest stock exchange in Africa, with a market capitalization of $44 billion dollars, which translates to about 8.83 percent to the GDP. As of the end 2019 fiscal year, it had 161 listed companies on the stock exchange. The Exchange offers listing and trading services, licensing services, market data solutions, ancillary technology services and more. The Nigerian Stock Exchange is committed to adopting the highest levels of international standards. To support this commitment, the NSE belongs to several international and regional organizations that promote the development and integration of global best practices across its operations. It is a member of the International Organization of Securities Commissions (IOSCO), the World Federation of Exchanges (WFE), Sustainable Stock Exchanges (SSE) Initiative, the SIIA's Financial Information Services Division (FISD) and the Intermarket Surveillance Group (ISG). The Exchange is a founding member and executive committee member of the African Securities Exchanges Association (ASEA). In addition, it continues to provide issuers and investors with a responsive, fair, and efficient securities market, using cutting-edge technology, and providing local and foreign investors access to the Nigerian securities market in an environment of strong regulatory framework and reliable trading and settlement systems.

The NSE continues to evolve to meet the needs of its valued customers and to achieve the highest level of competitiveness. In 2013, for example, it launched its next-generation trading platform, X-Gen, intended to enable electronic trading for the retail and institutional segments and in 2017 it launched X-academy, an innovative online learning platform that offers users ease of access to highly structured and comprehensible self-paced capital market and soft skills learning content, at their convenience. It remains an open, professional, and vibrant exchange, connecting Nigeria, Africa, and the world. Economic and financial analysts widely agree that the reforms on the Nigerian capital market since the global financial crisis have been helpful in raising the level of transparency and investors' confidence. This has equally primed the market to play a more significant role in the economy than ever before. To achieve this goal, the NSE serves as a vehicle for wealth generation and distribution; a platform for mobilizing savings for investments; enhancing public-private partnership initiatives and permits efficiency and effectiveness in capital flows. In addition, it facilitates financial literacy to empower people; supports raising of capital for business growth and dynamism; promotes corporate governance and social responsibility; and provides government financing for developmental projects.

See Also: Financial Institutions (Chapter 4); Forex and Currency Exchange (Chapter 4); Foreign Investment (Chapter 4).

Further Reading

Areago, R. B. (1990). *Nigerian Stock Exchange: Genesis, Organization, and Operations*. Ibadan: Heinemann Education Books (Nigeria) Limited.

Arinze, P. (2012). *Understanding the Nigeria Stock Exchange*. Moldova: LAP LAMBART Academic Publishing.

Oji, H. (2020, January 06). "Repositioning NSE for Contribution to 2020 Growth Plans." *The Guardian*. https://guardian.ng/business-services/repositioning-nse-for-contribution-to-2020-growth-plans/

The Nigerian Stock Exchange. (2019). "NSE Launches X-Academy e-learning to Provide Quality and Affordable Learning Experience." http://www.nse.com.ng/mediacenter/pressreleases/Pages/nse-launches-x-academy-e-learning-to-provide-quality-and-affordable-learning-experience.aspx

OIL AND GAS SECTOR

Nigeria is the largest producer of oil and gas in Africa and among the top twenty in the world, with a daily capacity of more than 2.5 million barrels per day. Meanwhile, its proven oil reserves stand at thirty-seven billion barrels, making it the tenth most rich oil nation on earth. Crude oil was discovered in 1956, at Oloibiri, Bayelsa State in the Niger Delta region and the first oil field began production in 1958. The crude from this region comes in two types: "light" and "sweet," as the oil is largely free of sulfur. It is also the largest producer of sweet oil within the Organization of Petroleum Exporting Countries (OPEC). Nigeria has a total of 159 oil fields and 1,481 wells in operation, mainly small and scattered in different states, mostly in the southern part of the country. Importantly, oil and gas accounts for more than 90 percent of Nigeria's export and about 70 percent of the government's revenue, as well as provides over 90 percent of the country's foreign exchange earnings.

The major players in the sector include Shell, Exxon Mobil, Total, Chevron, and the Nigerian National Petroleum Corporation. Its main oil and gas export partners ranked according to top destinations are India, Spain, United States, France, South Africa, United Kingdom, Netherlands, and Germany. As at the first quarter (Q1) of 2020, the sector grew at an annual growth rate of 11.30 percent, as well as contributed 9.50 percent to the aggregate real GDP in the same quarter. Nonetheless, the development of the sector and production capacity has been strained over the years, owing to a plethora of problems affecting the industry. The first problem is the obsolete laws and the country's weak capacity and political unwillingness to enforce regulations. The content of the 1969 Petroleum Act, for example, which governs the activities of the industry, is laden with red-tape and over-regulation of the sector among others. In addition, weak regulatory capacity has resulted in various oil spills and gas-flaring (with an estimated loss of $18 million daily) causing environmental degradation and air pollution to the host communities. Another is pipeline vandalism which is rampant and costs the country millions of dollars in losses annually.

Finally, is the problem of corruption and lack of government funding for the maintenance of key facilities. For instance, almost all of the oil extracted is refined overseas, because the existing three major refineries: Warri refinery, Port Harcourt refinery, and Kaduna refinery (controlled by the government through the Nigerian National Petroleum Corporation) are operating at below production capacity due to years of neglect, embezzlement of funds, and the lack of government funding for maintenance. Nevertheless, to address these problems, the Petroleum Industry Bill (PIB) was passed on July 1, 2021, to provide a legal framework through which the activities and operations in the Nigerian Upstream, Midstream, and Downstream sectors can be governed, regulated, and taxed for the development of the host communities as well as the Nigerian nation as a whole. Last, the near completion of the privately owned Dangote Refinery in Lagos, with production capacity of 650,000 barrels per day, is expected to cover the shortfall of refined products and reduce cost to Nigerians in the long term.

See Also: Agriculture Sector (Chapter 4); Domestic and International Trade (Chapter 4); Exports (Chapter 4); Manufacturing Sector (Chapter 4); Mining Sector (Chapter 4); Natural Resources (Chapter 1); Niger Delta (Chapter 1); Private Sector (Chapter 4).

Further Reading

Bloomberg. (2020, June 05). "INSIGHT: Nigerian Petroleum Industry Fiscal Bill—Encouraging Investment?" https://news.bloombergtax.com/daily-tax-report-international/insight-nigerian-petroleum-industry-fiscal-bill-encouraging-investment
Ekhator, Eghosa Osa. (2016). "Public Regulation of the Oil and Gas Industry in Nigeria: An Evaluation." *Annual Survey of International & Comparative Law* (Article 6), 21(1): 43–9. http://digitalcommons.law.ggu.edu/annlsurvey/vol21/iss1/6
IEA. (2020). "Atlas of Energy." http://energyatlas.iea.org/#!/tellmap/-1920537974/0
Oyedele, Taiwo. (2021, July). "The Petroleum Industry Bill (PIB): Top 20 Changes you Should Know." *PricewaterhouseCoopers Nigeria*. https://www.pwc.com/ng/en/assets/pdf/pib-top-20-changes-you-should-know.pdf
The Department of Petroleum Resources. (2020). "Petroleum Refineries and Petrochemicals." https://www.dpr.gov.ng/downstream/refinery/

POVERTY

The average household size in Nigeria is 5.0 and the poverty headcount rate currently stands at 40.1 percent of the population, thus, making Nigeria one of the poorest nation-states in the world. The poverty headcount ratio defines the proportion of the population that is living in the households where the value of per capita total consumption expenditure is below or equal to the poverty line. This means that four out of ten Nigerians live in extreme poverty, in other words, they live below the international poverty threshold of $1.90 per day. The rural areas account for more than 50 percent of the poverty headcount, while the urban areas account for the rest. On one hand, nationally, the poverty gap stands at 12.9 percent of the population. Poverty gap measures the depth of poverty, in other words, it measures the extent to which a person falls below the poverty line as a percentage of the poverty line. Meanwhile, Nigeria's Gini coefficient stands at 0.35.1, which means that income inequality is relatively high.

Theoretically, the Gini Coefficient is a statistical measure of economic inequality in a country. The index ranges from near 0, which indicates perfect equality and 100 (or the value of 1), which means perfect inequality. Meanwhile, the country ranks low on the Human Development Index (HDI), with a value of 0.534 and life expectancy and unemployment level currently stand at fifty-four years and 27.1 percent, respectively. Generally, the poverty rate is mostly concentrated in the northern region of the country, with an average of 50 percent in each state, while the lesser poverty rate is in the southern region, with an average of 20 percent in each state. According to UNICEF, Nigeria has the second-highest burden of malnourished children in the world, with a national prevalence rate of 32 percent of children under five; this is even though food accounts for 50 percent of household expenditure in the country. Meanwhile, there have been various poverty eradication programs adopted by different administrations, with the latest being the National Social Intervention Programmes (NSIP).

NSIP is overseen by the Ministry of Humanitarian Affairs, Disaster Management and Social Development, which was introduced in 2016 and anchors other programs such as the N-Power, Conditional Cash Transfer (CCT), Government Enterprise and Empowerment Programme (GEEP) and the Home-Grown School Feeding Programme (HGSF). These programs focus on ensuring a more equitable distribution of resources to vulnerable populations, including children, youth, and women. Since 2016, the programs combined claimed to have supported more than four million beneficiaries country wide. However, like previous programs, the NSIP has not been very successful because of varying underlying structural constraints that still exist. For instance, the government's inability or unwillingness to invest in the rural economy and infrastructure will continue to impede any social intervention programs. In essence, the incessant government corruption and the lack of economic infrastructure to support economic growth at every level are essential to pull people out of poverty. In addition, poor access to education and healthcare are equally contributing factors, because a population that is not educated lacks the skills to pull themselves from the cycle of poverty. Also, a population without access to proper healthcare services will likely be economically unproductive. But foundational to the contributing factors of poverty is the lack of or the weak state of the social, economic, and political institutions. The absence or the weak nature of these institutions has made various programs unsustainable, as well as prone to looting and diversion of funds meant to address poverty eradication across the country.

See Also: Trade Unions and the Labor Movement (Chapter 4); Rural Populations (Chapter 6); Urban Poor (Chapter 6).

Further Reading

Ajakaiye, D. O. I. and A. Olomola. (2003). *Poverty in Nigeria: A Multi-dimensional Perspective*. Ibadan: Nigerian Institute of Social and Economic Research Publication.

Duze, M. C., H. Mohammed, and I. A. Kiyawa. (2008). *Poverty in Nigeria: Causes, Manifestations and Alleviation Strategies*. Abuja: Adonis and Abbey publishers Limited.

National Bureau of Statistics. (2023). https://nigerianstat.gov.ng/

Vanguard Nigeria. (2020, August 16). "Interrogating Strategies to Poverty Reduction." https://www.vanguardngr.com/2020/08/interrogating-strategies-to-poverty-reduction/

PRIVATE SECTOR

Nigeria has a vibrant private sector due to the creativity, resourcefulness, and doggedness of the citizens. Despite the poor economic condition that challenges the setting up of businesses in the country, Nigerians have devised various ways to set up small- to medium-scale businesses to circumvent some of the most challenging issues in the country such as epileptic power supply, weak institutional policies and capacity, and corruption at various institutional level. Some of the most important private sector units include the textile industry, food, pharmaceutical, music, and education, among others. However, some of these firms are not wholly owned by Nigerians. A significant number of private organizations are owned by other African entrepreneurs or non-African foreign businesses due to the large market Nigeria represents. Capacity utilization of indigenously owned firms hover around 55 percent and 66 percent for very large firms with employment capacity of over five hundred staff. This has been explained to be due largely to the mean age range of old equipment. The unfavorable exchange rate of the Naira to the Dollar (approximately N500 to US$1) and the high cost of tariff for the importation of machines and spare parts contribute to the average capacity utilization of indigenous firms. Value added per worker in the private sector as a measure of productivity is primarily determined by the size of the firms with the smallest (micro) firms having less value added per worker than bigger firms. Nevertheless, the private sector contributes significantly to employment in the country and in the expansion of the market value of the economy. Between 2015 and 2023, there is an estimated employment loss of 15 percent in the private sector, mainly among the big companies. Unfortunately, there has not been any substantial growth in most sections of the private sector in the past ten years leading to a sluggish growth in the economy and a weak economic forecast for the country for 2023. Most economic reports have indicated that there has been a slight decline of access to capital for expansion, especially among small- and medium-scale businesses. The volatile international economic environment due to the Ukraine–Russia war, the political instability in the country because of the challenge of the February 25, 2023, presidential election by contested political parties, and the redesign of the higher denomination of the Naira which has led to cash crunch in the country are all predictive factors that will further undermine the private sector in the country. Although the average Nigerian is resilient and savvy in business matters, the huge challenges faced by citizens in the country may create a despondent spirit among young entrepreneurs who are beginning to immigrate to other countries where infrastructure are in place and the political and economic conditions are stable and hospitable for businesses to thrive. It is to be seen how the political scenario in Nigeria will play out as the Presidential Election Petition Tribunal handles the cases before it and how the judgment will affect not only the private sector but Nigeria's economy.

See Also: Agriculture Sector (Chapter 4); Manufacturing Sector (Chapter 4); Mining Sector (Chapter 4); Oil and Gas Sector (Chapter 4).

Further Reading

Momoh, M. A. (2019). "Private Participation in Infrastructure: The Nigerian Experience." *International Journal of Economics and Finance*, 11(9): 55–66. https://www.researchgate.net/publication/335252934_Private_Participation_in_Infrastructure_The_Nigerian_Experience

Nairametrics. (2020, January 08). "Banks' Loan to Private Sector Increases by N3.47 Trillion in 2019." https://nairametrics.com/2020/01/08/banks-loan-to-private-sector-increases-by-n3-47-trillion-in-2019/

The World Bank. (2023). "Domestic Credit to Private Sector (0 percent of GDP) – Nigeria." https://data.worldbank.org/indicator/FS.AST.PRVT.GD.ZS?locations=NG

RESERVES AND FOREIGN DEBT

The National Bureau of Statistics and the Debt Management Office reported that on, March 31, 2020, the total debt portfolio of Nigeria stood at N28.63 trillion, representing about 28.1 percent to the GDP. With N18.64 trillion hailing from domestic sources, the remaining N9.99 trillion was sourced from foreign creditors. In total, the debt portfolio equates to US$79.3 billion. Nigeria's domestic debt stood as of March 31, 2020, at US$51.6 billion, or 65.11 percent of total debt. The largest of these being obtained from Federal Government Bonds (FGN Bonds), which accounted for 72.65 percent of domestic debt, and 50.77 percent of the overall total debt portfolio. Other contributions of domestic debt arose from Nigerian Treasury Bills and Promissory Notes, which account for 18.24 percent and 6.59 percent, respectively, of the domestic debt portfolio. In 2006, Nigerian officials were successful in negotiating a debt repayment plan with the Paris Club—a group of creditor nations. At the end of the negotiations, Nigeria's then foreign debt of US$20 billion was reduced to around US$3.5 billion.

At the time, this was received with great applause, as funds that were previously allocated to the repayment of the debt and the paying of its interest, were now free to be reallocated to provide better infrastructure and other governmental services to the country. Nevertheless, since 2006 debt has been steadily rising, especially between the 2015–20 periods, where outstanding foreign debt escalated from US$9.7 billion to US$27 billion. Governmental actors state that this significant increase was required to offset the loss in oil revenue, caused specifically by the 2016 fall in oil prices. Nigeria's foreign debt as of March 31, 2020, stood at US$27.6 billion, or as 34.89 percent of the total debt portfolio. This consisted of multilateral agreements, which comprise 45.75 percent of foreign debt. This source of debt was negotiated with either the World Bank Group or the African Development Bank Group.

The largest of these was with the IDA, which credited US$9.6 billion to Nigeria; this is 35 percent of all foreign debt. Regarding bilateral negotiations, these totaled 13.89 percent of foreign debt, with the lion's share being provided by China, which totals US$3.1 billion. The remaining 40.37 percent of foreign debt takes the form of commercial bonds such as Eurobonds and Diaspora Bonds, these in combination supplied US$10.8 billion of Nigeria's foreign debt. As released on August 13, 2020, the Nigerian Reserves were estimated to be valued at US$ 35.6 billion, (down from $36.57bn on June 1 to $35.89bn on July 28) with US$35 billion of this amount being in liquid stocks. The fluctuation is caused by the rise and fall of oil prices. Nigeria's reserves are held by the Central Bank of Nigeria and are utilized in the making of payments and to meet debt obligations. They comprise a blend of foreign currencies, deposits, bonds, and governmental securities. Foreign reserves are important in their role at supporting the local currency values and in controlling inflation. Foreign reserves also act as a guarantee in financing the import of goods and services.

See Also: Domestic and International Trade (Chapter 4); Financial Institutions (Chapter 4); Foreign Investment (Chapter 4); Trade Partners (Chapter 4).

Further Reading

Central Bank of Nigeria. (n.d.). "Movement in Reserves." https://www.cbn.gov.ng/intops/reserve.asp

National Bureau of Statistics. (2020). *Foreign Trade in Goods Statistics*. National Bureau of Statistics.

National Bureau of Statistics. (2021). *Nigerian Domestic and Foreign Debt (Q1 2020)*. National Bureau of Statistics.

TRADE PARTNERS

Nigeria traded worldwide with about 100 countries, but the composition of trade by country had changed over the years. During the colonial era, for example, Britain was Nigeria's dominant trading partner. As late as 1955, for example, 70 percent of Nigeria's exports were to Britain and 47 percent of its imports were from Britain, with finished or manufactured goods, as well as luxury goods being the most imported. In turn, Nigeria exported mostly raw materials, solid minerals, and petroleum products to the British market. Similarly, over the years, there has been a decline in trading between Nigeria and the United States, one-time Nigeria's main trade partner after Britain. This is mainly because the United States reduced its import of Nigeria's oil (which constitutes Nigeria's largest export to the United States), owing to their increase in domestic production of petroleum products. Although Nigeria still imports United States made goods, such as wheat, vehicles, machinery, kerosene, lubricating oils, jet fuel, civilian aircraft, and plastics, there is a decrease in the volume of goods as Nigeria steadily shifts toward the East for its imports. At the end of 2019 fiscal year and the first quarter of 2020, it was reported that the major exporting partners for Nigeria was led by India, which is the destination of 15.61 percent of all exports, this was followed by Spain being the destination of 9.87 percent, the Netherlands with 9.72 percent, South Africa with a share of 7.82 percent and followed closely by Cameroon being the destination of a further 7.39 percent of total exports. The above are the top five export partners of Nigeria, but other important partners are Italy with 3.98 percent, France with 3.91 percent, the United Kingdom with 3.62 percent, Portugal with 3.08 percent, and Indonesia with 2.82 percent. Hence, the above ten nations represent 67.83 percent of all Nigerian export destinations.

Regarding imported goods, at end of the 2019 fiscal year and the first quarter of 2020, Nigeria's imports were dominated by China, which is the origin of 26.28 percent of total Nigeria imports, other import partners are the Netherlands with a share of 11.14 percent, the United States with 10.45 percent, India with 7.92 percent, and followed by Belgium which is the origin of a further 6.11 percent of imports. Other significant partners that are the source of imports are Germany at 3.04 percent, the United Arab Emirates at 2.86 percent, and Italy with 2.74 percent, the United Kingdom with 2.11 percent, and France with 1.83 percent of all imports to Nigeria. The above ten trade partners represent the origin of 74.47 percent of all Nigeria's imports. Overall, considering imports and exports, the five most impactful trade partners toward the Nigerian economy are Spain, India, the Netherlands, South Africa, and China. Perhaps, as Asian products have increased in demand in Nigeria, traditional chief import markets such as the United States and the United Kingdom have decreased, with the former shrinking by 54.6 percent and the latter by 30 percent in the 2013–18 periods. Thus, traditional trade partners have been eclipsed by other markets in both Europe with the Benelux region and Spain, and its Asian counterparts, which are dominated by China, India, and increasingly South Korea.

See Also: Domestic and International Trade (Chapter 4); Exports (Chapter 4); Foreign Investment (Chapter 4); Imports (Chapter 4); International Trade Policy (Chapter 4); Reserves and Foreign Debt (Chapter 4).

Further Reading

National Bureau of Statistics. (2020). *Foreign Trade in Goods Statistics*. National Bureau of Statistics.
OEC. (2020). "Nigeria." https://oec.world/en/profile/country/nga
Workman, D. (2022). "Nigeria's Top Trading Partners." https://www.worldstopexports.com/nigerias-top-trading-partners/

TRADE UNIONS AND THE LABOR MOVEMENT

Trade unionism is now a universal phenomenon operating in almost every organization—public and private industry, institution, profession, and trade. It is considered a product of the industrial revolution, which was designed as an instrument mainly to put up a united and collective fight against exploitation of workers by employees in factories. In Nigeria, workers have various unions which serve as the mouthpiece of members within the profession, but they fall under the larger coalition of two unions—the Nigerian Labor Congress (NLC) and the Trade Union Congress (TUC). Like other trade unions across the world, unions in Nigeria were created to protect and advance workers' rights by negotiating with company managements, when necessary, in securing reasonable wage and salaries, favorable conditions of services commensurate with the nature of work, facilities of housing, medical care, education, travel and recreation among others.

The trade union and labor movements in Nigeria date to 1912 when the workers in the Southern Nigerian Civil Service under the then colonial administration organized themselves into workers representatives. Then, in 1914, it metamorphosed into the Nigeria Civil Service Union (NCSU). Other unions which emerged during this period were the Nigeria Native Staff Union (NNSU), Nigerian Union of Railwaymen, Nigerian Mechanics Union, and the Nigerian Union of Teachers (NUT). In February 1978, the Nigeria Labor Congress was formed and inaugurated, which was made up of some of the previously mentioned unions. Currently, it is the largest union by membership and affiliation in Nigeria, which caters for mostly junior servants and workers—with about four million members and twenty-six affiliations, while TUC which caters for senior servants and workers accounts for less members and affiliations. Other existing unions—affiliated to either NLC or TUC include the Petroleum and Natural Gas Senior Staff Association of Nigeria, National Union of Petroleum and Natural Gas Workers, and Nigeria Medical Association.

Also, are the Academic Staff Union of Universities, Nigeria Union of Teachers, Non-Academic Staff Union of Universities, Academic Staff Union of Polytechnics, and the National Association of Medical Doctors. The Nigerian Labour Act of 1971 is the primary legislation which deals with the relationship between employers and employees. Unfortunately, the Act appears to cover only clerical or junior-staff types of roles and not "persons exercising administrative, executive, technical or professional functions as public officers or otherwise," among other extant clauses that need to be revised to reflect current working conditions in Nigeria. Moreover, there have been calls for the review of the Act, but these have not been successful. Nigerian unions are not affiliated to political parties but are active players in the political space.

The NLC, for example, was dissolved twice due to conflicts with military regimes. First was in 1988, under President Ibrahim Babangida because they opposed the Structural Adjustment Programme and the second was in 1994, under the regime of Sani Abacha, owing to their agitation for the restoration of democracy and respect for human rights in the country. Largely, the unions remain influential and powerful in that they can hold the government to ransom, either by crippling the economy or paralyzing service delivery in strategic areas. Due to their activities, the national minimum monthly wage was increased from N18, 000.00 (equivalent of $47) to N30, 000.00 (equivalent of $78) in 2019, after years of debate with the government.

See Also: Manufacturing Sector (Chapter 4); Mining Sector (Chapter 4); Oil and Gas Sector (Chapter 4); Poverty (Chapter 4); Private Sector (Chapter 4).

Further Reading

Adewunmi, F. (1997). *Trade Unionism in Nigeria: Challenges for the 21st Century*. Lagos: Friedrich Ebert Foundation.

Ananaba, W. (1970). *The Trade Union Movement in Nigeria*. New York: Africana Publishing Corporation.

KPMG. (2019). "The Labour Act for Review." https://home.kpmg/ng/en/home/insights/2019/11/the-labour-act-for-review-.html

Premium Times. (2017, September 30). "Nigeria's 10 Most Powerful Trade Unions." https://www.premiumtimesng.com/news/headlines/244650-nigerias-10-powerful-trade-unions.html

CHAPTER 5

Religion and Thought

OVERVIEW

Nigeria is a religious country with diverse religions and religious groups. Religion plays a central role in the lives of Nigerians and most of them believe that religion and personal responsibilities are important for maintaining good social relationships and personal prosperity. In other words, they do not believe that human agency alone is enough to guarantee success and so a great deal of reliance on prayers, fellowships, and religious rituals are important ingredients in securing both social and economic success. Religion, the belief in the existence of a higher power and its influence on the lives of mortals, is used to explain social, economic, and health conditions, as well as personal failures and successes in Nigeria. Religion serves an important role in offsetting the stresses and anxieties that otherwise would have led to depression and other mental health problems, particularly in the face of poverty, political uncertainty, and other forms of deprivation and oppression the country has witnessed since its independence in 1960. Beliefs that one's problems will be resolved by God are widespread and commonplace in all parts of the country irrespective of whether they are Christians, Muslims, or adherents to indigenous religions.

Religion has had a strong influence over the lives of Nigerians long before the introduction of foreign religions such as Christianity and Islam. The earliest religions in Nigeria are those associated with different ethnic groups such as the Yorubas, Igbos, Ijaws, Hausas, Efik, Nupe, Edo, Urhobos, Calabar, and other ethnic groups that today constitute modern Nigeria. All cultural groups acknowledge the existence of God as the Almighty Creator of heaven and earth and they have various names for God such as Eledumare among the Yoruba, Chukwu among the Igbo, Ubangiji among the Hausa, Osanobua among the Bini, Oghene among the Urhobo, and Abasi among the Efik. Most cultural groups also believe in the existence and influence of other lesser deities who are connected to the almighty God but through whom they may offer their prayers to receive intervention in their earthly pursuit. There are also community and personal gods that guide individual families in taking decisions on behalf of the members. When the society is in distress, for example during times of drought, poor harvest, and unexplained diseases, the gods are consulted for the cause of the social problem and solutions are proffered through the priests and priestesses who serve as intermediaries between the society and the deities. When individuals want to embark on an important venture such as trade, marriage, or politics, the gods are consulted, and the necessary prayers and sacrifices are offered for the protection of the individuals and for success in the venture.

Throughout its subsequent history in Nigeria, religion has continued to play a central role in the lives of the peoples that make up the country and how their spiritual devotion influences their existence and social relations. The fabric of Nigerian society, its values, and social regulations are closely associated with the religious beliefs and thoughts of those who practice both endogenous and introduced religions. For this reason, from a Western perspective, Nigerians may be regarded as highly religious and superstitious in their thought pattern and ways of life. In their everyday conversations, it is not uncommon for people to invoke the name of some deity as an assurance of their honesty or commitment to a course. Similarly, they sometimes call on their gods for protection against any evil calamity. For example, the typical Christian would say "by the grace of God, I will do so and so" or "God helping me, I will succeed in this or that enterprise." Among the Muslims, it is common to hear them say *"in sha Allah"* (translated to mean God permitting) in their conversations, acknowledging that power does not rest with them but with God. Among the traditional religious adherents, they invoke the gods they serve to assure someone of their sincerity in matters that pertain to honesty, loyalty, or to give assurance. For example, to prove their innocence they may declare that *Sango* (the Yoruba god of thunder) should strike them dead if they are the culprit of an accusation. It is not uncommon also for the average Nigerian, especially those from the South, to engage in some religious rituals and activities before embarking on any enterprise.

In pre-colonial Nigeria, the ethnic groups that made up the country were usually united by their religious groups and served as a unifier against other ethnic groups or those who do not belong to the same religion. The introduction of foreign religions predates modern Nigeria. Christianity was introduced into the country from the fifteenth century through the creeks of the Niger delta by the Portuguese missionaries. Some of the missionaries later moved to the Southwest starting from Lagos to evangelize the people, build hospitals, and establish schools. In the northern part of the country, the Evangelical Church of West Africa (ECWA) was established in 1954 by Christian mission organization, Serving in Mission (SIM) in the middle belt of the country. The Catholic Church took a firm foothold in the eastern part of the country and today the Igbos who dominate this region are predominantly Catholics. The Efik and Ibibio in the South-South are mostly Lutherans, while the Yorubas are Anglicans. Although Christianity became widespread in the South, it did not wipe out indigenous religions and their traditional practices. Indeed, soon after the establishment of Christianity, the converts became dissatisfied with the practicality of the religion, as they observed that the God of the bible did not act fast enough in solving their problems nor strong enough to deal with the powers of witches and wizards that were believed to be widespread in the regions. This dissatisfaction led to some converts establishing a syncretic version of their newfound faith or establishing a new form of religion that has the bible as its base but a touch of indigenous practices. The former, for example, include denominations such as Christ Apostolic Church, Cherubim and Seraphim Church, and the so-called African Churches that infused traditional practices with Christianity such as the permission for members to be polygamous with mainstream Christian beliefs and practices. Those who were completely dissatisfied with the new religion also founded new churches such as the Olumba Olumba movement in the South-South, and the Aladura and celestial churches in the Southwest. Much later, starting from the 1970s, the new Pentecostal movement began to gain ground in the South starting with the establishment of the Church of God Mission by the late Bishop Benson Idahosa, first in Benin City, and later to other parts of the country. The Pentecostal movement, known for its prosperity message and charismatic leaders became the new religion in southern Nigeria and soon proliferated to other parts of the country with a huge followership in foreign countries especially in the United States, the United Kingdom, and Europe generally. By the end of the twentieth century the Pentecostal movement had become the dominant religious group in the South with an estimated followership of seventy million. Not to be left out in this new movement, the Catholic Church also joined in the Pentecostal frenzy by formally recognizing the Catholic Charismatic movement within the church, which was made popular by its youth. Unlike the mother church, the catholic charismatic movement holds night vigils and engages in evangelism.

In the northern part of the country, Islam was first introduced to the indigenous people long before the establishment of Nigeria as a nation-state. The trans-Sahara trade between the locals and the Berbers of North Africa was the conduit for the spread of Islam into the northern part of what would become Nigeria. By 1802 Uthman dan Fodio had carried out Jihads (holy wars for the propagation of Islam) to the major towns and cities in the region and by 1807 had consolidated the Sokoto Caliphate and subsumed the smaller ethnic groups under its Islamic rule. By the end of the first decade of the nineteenth century, Islam had become the dominant religion in the northern part of the country. While in the middle belt the local ethnic groups converted to Islam, the majority were converted to Christianity through the Evangelical Church of West Africa or stuck to their traditional religious practices. Despite the evangelization in Nigeria, the indigenous religious practices did not become extinct. Indeed, most converts to the new religions of Christianity and Islam were also involved in traditional religious practices behind the scenes especially when calamity strikes such as diseases and plagues as well as poor harvests. Although the association with traditional religions has become unpopular in the country especially among the educated, various forms of traditional practices are still common. In some instances, some traditional religions such as the *Ogboni* have been reformed and it is a popular fraternity among the elites and politicians. In the Niger delta region, various forms of traditional religions still exist. For example, among the Urhobo people are the *Igbe* and *Olokun* religious groups that worship marine deities. Among the Ibibio and Efik of Cross River and Akwa Ibom, the religious practice of ancestor worship still exists. Although it has greatly waned, the New Yam festival in the Southeast of the country is still practiced in honor of *Ani*—the goddess of the Earth. In all these practices, what is significant and a common thread among the various religious beliefs and practices is the acknowledgment of the supernatural world and its relevance to mortals, and Nigerians are heavily influenced by this belief in the supernatural.

Further Reading

Sasu, D. D. (2022, December 12). "Distribution of Religions in Nigeria 2018." *Statista.* https://www.statista.com/statistics/1203455/distribution-of-religions-in-nigeria/

Vaughn, O. (2016). *Religion and the Making of Nigeria*. Durham: Duke University Press.

ADEBOYE, ENOCH

Pastor Enoch Adejare Adeboye is the General Overseer of the Redeemed Christian Church of God, headquartered at kilometer 46, along the Lagos-Ibadan expressway in Southwest Nigeria. Adeboye is not the founder of the church but was appointed to lead the church in 1981 after the founder and first Overseer, Pa Josiah Olufemi Akindayomi got a revelation that the young university mathematics lecturer was to succeed him. Pastor Enoch Adeboye was born on March 2, 1942, in his hometown of Ifewara in Osun State. Born into a humble family with little means the young Enoch was however determined to succeed in his academic pursuit. He started his journey by enrolling at the Ilesa Grammar School in 1952 after which he gained admission into the University of Ife (now Obafemi Awolowo University), in the old Oyo State and bagged a bachelor's degree in mathematics in 1967. Thereafter, he proceeded to the University of Lagos where he obtained his master's degree in hydrodynamics in 1969 and a doctoral degree from the same university in applied mathematics in 1975. His Christian journey began in 1971 after his daughter was "miraculously" healed of an unnamed illness at the small RCCG church in Lagos. In that same year the university lecturer became "born again"—the acceptance of Jesus Christ as his personal Lord and Savior and the renouncing of all other gods and divinity. His subsequent devotion to the church led to his ordination as a pastor in 1977 and later became the interpreter to the pastor of the church Rev. Akindayomi, a position he held before he was appointed the General Overseer of the church after the death of the founder.

Pastor Adeboye's leadership position in the church forced him to resign as an academic staff of the University of Lagos and he has since then devoted his life to the leadership and growth of the church. He infused new dimensions of worship into the church by introducing the use of local drums to accompany the singing of hymns while the choir was encouraged to clap their hands and dance in praise and worship. His vision to spread the gospel through the church to every corner of Nigeria and beyond marked a significant turning point in the history of the church making it one of the largest Christian churches in the world in the twenty-first century. In 1991 he moved the headquarters of the church from Ebute-Metta in Lagos to its permanent site along the Lagos-Ibadan expressway. He also introduced the Open Heaven program and under his leadership the church has grown to become one of the largest churches in the world with an approximate membership of twenty-five million who regularly worship in the 40,000 parishes in 186 nations worldwide. He is credited with having organized one of the largest single gatherings of people in the world when he officiated in the 1998 Holy Ghost Congress at the Lekki Beach in Lagos with an estimated seven million worshippers in attendance. The Holy Ghost Congress is now a yearly event at the headquarters of the church at the Lagos-Ibadan Expressway where over ten million worshippers attend physically or connect through various social media outlets. Pastor Adeboye is well regarded both in the religious and political circles in Nigeria and overseas. Among some of his numerous awards are the Commander of the Order of the Niger (CON) and Order of the Federal Republic of Nigeria (OFRN). In 2009 he was named by the Newsweek magazine as one the fifty most influential people in the world. He is married to Pastor Foluke Adenike Adeboye, and they have three children together. He is highly respected for his humility both as a pastor and as a leader. He refused to be called by any other appellation such as Bishop, His Excellency, but he is affectionately called Daddy by his church members and other pastors in other denominations.

See Also: Aladura Church (Chapter 5); Oyedepo, David (Chapter 5); Pentecostalism (Chapter 5); Synagogue Church of All Nations (Chapter 5).

Further Reading

Bible-David, R. (2009). *Enoch Adeboye Father of Nations*. California: Biblos Publisher.
The Redeemed Christian Church of God. (2023). https://www.rccg.org/

ALADURA CHURCH

Aladura is a Yoruba word which means "prayer warriors" or "praying people." In Nigeria, the Aladura Church is known officially as The Church of the Lord (Aladura) Worldwide (TCLAW), an African Indigenous Church (AIC) founded by Primate Josiah Olunowo Ositelu. Pa Ositelu was formerly a member of the Christian Missionary Society (CMS) of the Anglican Church where he served as a catechist and pupil teacher while preparing for admission into St. Andrew's College (Oyo) to become a professional teacher. His ambition to be a teacher was eventually abandoned when he recounted a troubling vision he had to his spiritual father, Prophet Somoye, who advised him to undergo fasting and prayer to better understand his spiritual calling. On completing this spiritual exercise, Ositelu developed a form of Christianity that involved healing using holy names and water, faith, prayer and night vigils. Unfortunately, his version of Christianity was not acceptable by the Anglican Church where he served and when he refused to abandon his practice, he was dismissed in 1927. Ositelu then embarked on a two-year discipleship under Prophet Somoye to further develop his spiritual gifts after which he began his prophetic preaching and evangelical career. Ositelu's popularity grew, and he was known to demonstrate God's powers through miraculous healings and victory over satanic powers. He had his first open air revival in 1929 during which there were many testimonies with indigenous religious priests relinquishing their traditional symbols of power and renouncing their previous religious beliefs and converting to Ositelu's version of Christianity.

TCLAW was inaugurated in July 1930 with only ten people but by 1945, the church had expanded to other parts of southwestern Nigeria and later to Sierra Leone and Liberia: and by 1961 to London. Today the church also has branches in Ghana, Togo, and Ivory Coast. The church believes strongly in the use of prayer and fasting for healing, as well as the use of the Book of Psalms, holy words, and night vigils for spiritual battles. Spiritual battles are also fought with the use of holy words created by the church ministers as led by the Holy Spirit based on the Biblical verse of Ezekiel 33:7. Church ministers carry staff of office as part of their spiritual regalia which also serves as a symbol of power and authority. With the staff and rosaries, TCLAW ministers consecrate fruits, water, and individuals. They also practice the spiritual exercise of physically rolling from one end of the 'mercy' ground to the other based on the prescriptions of the officiating minister. Due to their belief that the church is holy, members are required to take off their shoes. TCLAW still maintains several Anglican Church practices such as the use of hymns, harvest, Lent and the celebration of Palm Sunday and Easter. The church also has an annual spiritual festival called Tabieorar or Taborar which takes place in August, the end of the church's spiritual calendar. The festival is thus a time of joy when individual vows are made and predictions as they concern members, the church and the nation are delivered by TCLAW ministers.

See Also: Celestial Church of Christ (Chapter 5); Pentecostalism (Chapter 5), Reformed Ogboni Fraternity (Chapter 5); Traditional Religions (Chapter 5).

Further Reading

Peel, J. D. Y. (1997). *Aladura: A Religious Movement Among the Yoruba*. Lit Verlag Publisher.
The Church of the Lord. (2007). *The Church of the Lord (Aladura) Worldwide (TCLAW) Organisation*. https://www.aladura.net/

CATHOLICISM

Catholicism is one of the oldest Christian denominations in Nigeria and one of the largest with an estimated membership of fifty-two million. The eastern part of the country is the home of Catholicism in Nigeria with the Igbo ethnic group constituting over 70 percent of the total population of Catholics in the country. The Catholic Church of Nigeria is affiliated to the Roman Catholic Church worldwide and recognizes the Pope as its spiritual leader. The Catholic Bishop Conference of Nigeria is presided over by the Archbishop of Owerri, Most Reverend Lucius Ugorji, who took over from Augustine Obiora Akubeze, the Archbishop of Benin City, in March 2022. The hierarchy of the Catholic Church in Nigeria is made up of the Archbishopric, the Bishopric, and the forty-four suffragan dioceses that are scattered all over the country. There are two Cardinal Archbishops, one in Abuja, and the other in Lagos, while Mary, Queen of Nigeria and Saint Patrick of Ireland are recognized as the official patrons of Nigeria. The Catholic Church is one of the churches responsible for the introduction of Western education in Nigeria. However, most of its schools have been taken over by the Nigerian government and structured along other government schools with a uniform curriculum. With the granting of licenses to non-governmental organizations to operate private universities in Nigeria, the Catholic Church has also become active in tertiary education in Nigeria with seven universities that are affiliated to the church. These universities are situated not only in the eastern part of the country, but they are also established in Lagos and Ogun states as well as in the Federal Capital Territory, Abuja. The Catholic Church has grown significantly in Nigeria since the 1900s. Although there was a poor presence of Catholics in the North especially after the Nigerian civil war in 1970, the second wave of migration of the Igbo people to the North from the late 1970s witnessed the reestablishment and growth of Catholicism in the North especially in Kano and Plateau states where a sizeable number of Igbos reside. In 1998 the Catholic Church of Nigeria hosted Pope John Paul II who officiated the ceremony that led to the beatification of the Blessed Cyprian Michael Iwene Tansi. The ceremony was held at Oba, the Onitsha Archdiocese, a local parish that was established by the Apostle of Eastern Nigeria, Bishop Joseph Shanahan.

The training of Catholic priests is a cardinal focus of the church and for this reason there are several seminaries that meet this need in the country. There are about twenty Major Seminaries and over twenty-five Minor Seminaries scattered all over the country. There are also about twenty Catholic Missionary Societies in the country. From the late 1980s, the Catholic Church has witnessed an upsurge of Pentecostal tradition especially among its youths and young adults in institutions of higher learning. The Charismatic Movement tends to incorporate some aspects of Pentecostalism such as the conduction of night vigils, praying in tongues, and the use of drums in their praise and worship.

See Also: European Explorers and Christianity (Chapter 2); Pentecostalism (Chapter 5); Traditional Religions (Chapter 5).

Further Reading

Makozi, A. O. and G. J. A. Ojo. (1982). *The History of the Catholic Church in Nigeria*. Ibadan: Macmillan Nigeria.
Nigeria Catholic Network. (2022). https://www.nigeriacatholicnetwork.com/

CELESTIAL CHURCH OF CHRIST

The Celestial Church of Christ (CCC) is a syncretic church that combines mainstream Christianity with traditional beliefs and practices. The church was founded in September 1947 in Port Novo in the Republic of Benin by Pa Samuel Bilewa Joseph Oshoffa. Oshoffa was born in 1909 in Dahomey (modern Benin Republic) and trained as a carpenter. He was born into a Protestant family but in May 1947, he received a heavenly vision and experienced a spiritual calling after he was divinely empowered to heal the sick and raise the dead. This experience led him to establish the CCC in September 1947. With a small followership, the church began to grow. Its leaders were known mainly by their ability to see vision and prophecy. They were also known for their distinctive prayer style which combined the use of candles and spirit possession. By the 1960s, the church had become one of the dominant Christian groups in Benin Republic and became officially recognized by the federal government of that country in 1965. By the following decade, the founder of the church received a divine command to expand his church to other parts of the world.

In 1976, Prophet Oshoffa moved to Lagos in Nigeria where he established a branch of the church. Within five years the church gained so much popularity among Nigerians that the headquarters of the church were established in Lagos and became one of the dominant African-initiated churches in the country. Over the years the Celestial Church has expanded to other countries in Europe, North America, and other parts of the world. The church is known for its unique practices which include its prayer style, the adornment of white garments by its members, and the non-use of foot wears by members. Prayers are not only conducted in the church premises, but they may be held in open grounds that have been consecrated or by the bank of a river. Celestial members are found by the beach with their candles to pray for the sick and ward off any evil spell that might be tormenting members. Before embarking on a cleansing ritual, the prophets and prophetesses (*woli*) receive divine revelation of the source of an ailment through spirit possession and vision. Once the course of the ailment is ascertained, the prescribed rituals will then be performed. For effective exorcism, members engage in fasting and abstinence from sexual intercourse while women under menstruation are not allowed to participate in the rituals. The use of white garments by members is influenced by the vision given to the founder who was instructed to raise men and women that will represent the angelic group on earth that will serve God. The white garment, thus, signifies purity and holiness toward God. Members of the church are forbidden from smoking cigarettes, consuming alcohol, and eating pork. Participation in idol worship, the use of black magic, and fetish cultic activities are also prohibited. In Nigeria, membership cuts across all social classes but the church is most popular in the Southwest of the country.

See Also: Aladura Church (Chapter 5); Pentecostalism (Chapter 5); Reformed Ogboni Fraternity (Chapter 5); Traditional Religions (Chapter 5).

Further Reading

Celestial Church of Christ. (2023). https://celestialchurch.com/
Gold-Idowu, B. (2021). *Research on the Celestial Church of Christ*. Kindle Edition.

CHRIST APOSTOLIC CHURCH

Christ Apostolic Church (CAC) originated from the *Aladura* movement in Ijebu Ode (current Ogun State) in 1918. Sexton Ali of the St Saviour's Anglican Church was inspired by a spiritual dream which emphasized the power of prayers. He related the dream to four elders of the church and together, they formed a prayer band and embarked on various prayer sessions and evangelical activities emphasizing faith-based healing. In the same year, there was an outbreak of influenza, and many patients turned to the prayer band for healing. By 1919, the prayer band had become a movement with a strong leaning on faith and a rejection of Western and traditional forms of medicine. Unfortunately, the doctrines of the prayer band conflicted with the Anglican Church leading to the leaders either being dismissed or voluntarily leaving the Anglican faith. The movement which was referred to as the *Egbe Aladura* (Yoruba expression meaning the prayer group), eventually became more formal and named themselves the Prayer Band. Over the years, the name changed

Ongoing Religious Violence
Sadly, religious intolerance and attacks have not abated in Nigeria despite calls for peace and unity in the country. Jihadist groups such as Boko Haram and ISIS, have continually attacked both churches and mosques in northern Nigeria. Incursion into the southern part of the country is becoming a matter of concern, with the June 5, 2022, massacre, for example, where forty worshippers were killed in a church in Owo, Ondo state. These killings have generated fear among citizens and restricted travel within the country. To stem the religious conflicts and killings international organizations championed by the United States Embassy in Lagos have been mediating with various groups including the federal government, various religious groups including the Christian Association of Nigeria (CAN), the Society for the Support of Islam, the Islamic Society of Removal of Innovation and Reestablishment of the Sunna (JIBWIS), the Nigeria Inter-Religious Council, and other similar bodies. Only time will tell if these efforts will yield positive results.

---

from Precious Stone, Diamond Society, and later to Faith Tabernacle. It was not until 1924 that the name Christ Apostolic Church would be formally registered.

The man who is believed to have unified the prayer bands into CAC is Joseph Ayodele Babalola who was born into an Anglican family. His original intention was not to be a spiritual leader but rather a civil servant with the Public Works Department. His spiritual journey started while at work when he heard a voice instructing him to go into the world and preach the gospel. He went into a seven-day fasting and praying exercise after which he received a prayer bell which he used to exorcize evil spirits and a bottle of "life-giving water" which he used to heal diseases. He became a great prophet, evangelist, and healer: delivering people from evil spirits and organizing prayer meetings to teach members about the power and efficacy of prayers. His activities, however, did not only attract the wrath of the missionaries but also the colonial government, which issued a warrant for his arrest. He was eventually arrested in Benin City in 1932 and jailed for six months. Despite this sentencing, his fame grew, and thousands followed him and his teachings.

Babalola was later invited in July 1930 to preach at the Faith Tabernacle annual conference during which he was alleged to have raised a dead child to life. This sparked a revival which lasted for sixty days and thousands of people from different religious backgrounds including Muslims and traditional worshippers as well as Christians of different denominations attended. The great revival unified the various prayer bands with new members joining from within and outside Nigeria. This encouraged leaders of Faith Tabernacle to seek associations with international churches. Unfortunately, by 1941 due to disagreements in terms of doctrines, there was a split with a faction breaking away under the name Apostolic Church while the larger faction, led by Babalola, maintained Christ Apostolic Church from which several branches were established.

Today, the church has spread worldwide and encouraged Christian based education by establishing schools including the Joseph Ayo Babalola University which was established in 2004 in Ikeji-Arakeji (Osun state) by the Christ Apostolic Church Worldwide.

See Also: Aladura Church (Chapter 5); Celestial Church of Christ (Chapter 5); Pentecostalism (Chapter 5), Traditional Religions (Chapter 5).

Further Reading

Alokan, A. (1991). *The Christ Apostolic Church: C.A.C. 1928–1988*. Lagos: Ibukunola Printers Nigeria Limited.

Christ Apostolic Church Worldwide. (2016). https://www.cac-worldwide.org/

INTER-RELIGIOUS CONFLICTS

Inter-religious conflicts in Nigeria are usually between Christians and Muslims and date back to the colonial era. Squabbles between these religious groups were recorded in the northern part of the country in the late 1940s and 1950s but they were insignificant to what was to follow from the 1970s and 1980s. A major inter-religious conflict first broke out in 1976 at the Ahmadu Bello University, Zaria, when students of both religions clashed leading to the death of dozens of students. After the quelling of the violence by the military government, an Islamic movement sprang up led by Mohammed Marwa in Kano State. To nip the movement in the bud, the leader of the group was arrested and later died in detention. The violence that followed the death of Mohammed Marwa (also known as *Maitatsine*, a Hausa word meaning he that curses) in 1980 marked the beginning of the upsurge of inter-religious conflict in Kano. The followers of Marwa, referred to as *Ya Tatsine* (Hausa word meaning those who curse/use obscenities) caused major riots in Kano city as well as in Sabon Gari, the designated area for Christian settlers from the southern part of the country. This conflict dominated the religious landscape of Kano, Kaduna, and Katsina states throughout that decade. One of such hotspots was the College of Education, Kafanchan in southern Kaduna where the violence that started at the university in Zaria had led to a sharp division between the Christian and Muslim groups resulting in clashes between the Fellowship of Christian Students (FCS) and the Muslim Students' Society (MSS) that were characterized by hate speeches, intolerance, and violent demonstrations between the groups that led to the loss of lives and properties. By the early 1990s hostilities between Christians and Muslims were becoming more widespread in the country. The Muslims began to claim ownership of the North with disregard for the Christian minority. The crusade of the German evangelist Reinhard Bonnke, in 1991 in Kano state, led to another spate of riots and a call for the complete ban of Christian activities in the state, especially open-door crusades and evangelism. By the first decade of the twenty-first century, the clamor for the imposition of Sharia law began to gain currency. By the mid-2000s, starting with Zamfara State in the Northeast, nine states in the predominantly Muslim North had succeeded in instituting Sharia as the main framework for all civil and criminal laws despite the federal constitutional position of the country as a secular state. This imposition of Sharia in some states in the North has further created tension not only in the affected states but throughout the northern region of the country. By the second decade of the twenty-first century, Boko Haram (Hausa phrase, meaning Western culture is taboo) had established itself as the dominant Islamic fundamentalist group in the North, especially in the northeastern section. In 2013, a Christian secondary school in Chibok town in Borno was vandalized and burned down on the night of April 15, 2014, and 207 of its girls were adopted by Boko Haram leading to a global outcry with the hashtag #bringbackourgirls for the release of the kidnapped Christian girls. While inter-religious conflict is rampant in the Muslim-dominated North of the country, the South has witnessed relative calm with very little cases of hostility between the Christian majority and Muslim minority.

See Also: Catholicism (Chapter 5); European Explorers and Christianity (Chapter 2); Pentecostalism (Chapter 5), Islamic Movement (Chapter 5); Traditional Religions (Chapter 5).

Further Reading

Falola, T. (2000). *Violence in Nigeria: The Crisis of Religious Politics and Secular Ideologies*. New York: University of Rochester Press.

ISLAMIC MOVEMENT

Islam is one of the two dominant religions in Nigeria, with most Muslims living in the northern and southwestern parts of the country. Estimates of the Muslim population range from 48 percent to 51 percent of the total population of the country's 200 million. Nigeria is, thus, home to the largest Muslim population in Africa south of the Sahara. The introduction of Islam to Nigeria predates modern Nigeria and goes as far back as the eleventh century when traders from North Africa engaged in commercial activities with the people of Kano, Zaria, and what is today northern Nigeria. By the early 1800s Shehu Uthman dan Fodio had established the Sokoto Caliphate that imposed an Islamic rule on the vast territory of northern Nigeria as well as part of the middle belt to the southernmost part of Kwara State. The political structure of the Caliphate provided a perfect system that eventually served the purpose of the British colonial government, which established a successful indirect rule in the northern part of the country. Most of the Nigerian Muslims are Sunnis, which belong to the Maliki school of jurisprudence and majority of the Sunnis belong to Sufi Brotherhoods including the Qadiriyyah and the Tijaniyyah movements. However, a smaller portion of the Muslim faithful belong to the Shafi Madhhab movement. A significant number also belongs to the Ahmadiyya movement. The Ahmadiyya movement is an old group dating back to 1916 when it was established in Sokoto State and gradually spread to other parts of the North including parts of the Southwest. Currently, they make up about 5 percent of the total Muslim population in Nigeria. It is one of the most established Islamic movements in the country with a regular newspaper, *The Truth*, which is published weekly. The Shia Islamic movement is a relatively new movement dating back to the 1980s. Its founder in Nigeria, Ibrahim Zakzaky, is a prominent and influential cleric whose efforts at evangelism have grown the population of Shia Muslims to about four million. The Maitatsine movement, which started in Kano in the early 1980s by Mohammed Marwa became one of the most radicalized Islamic movements in the northern part of the country. The movement seems to have been successfully curtailed by the successive regimes in Kano

State. The most militant Islamic movement in the twenty-first century is Boko Haram, which associates Western culture and artifacts as evil and a taboo. The overall goal of the movement, therefore, is to impose strict Sharia laws based on the Islamic code of conduct on the country. If this goal is not achieved, the movement will agitate to carve out an independent state or "caliphate" from the northeastern part of Nigeria and parts of Chad and Cameroon, to practice an "unadulterated" form of Islam. The movement has been widely condemned by the Nigerian Federal Government and by the international community with the United States labeling it as a terrorist group. So far, the coalition efforts of the Nigerian and Cameroonian governments to root out the Islamic movement have not been successful.

See Also: Islamic Education (Chapter 8); Inter-Religious Conflicts (Chapter 5).

Further Reading

Nigerian Supreme Council for Islamic Affairs (NSCIA). (2023). https://www.nscia.com.ng/

Thurston, A. (2016). *Salafism in Nigeria: Islam, Preaching, and Politics*. Cambridge: Cambridge University Press.

OYEDEPO, DAVID

Bishop David Olaniyi Oyedepo is the founder and presiding pastor of The Winners Church (aka David Oyedepo Ministries). The church is headquartered in Ota, Ogun State, Nigeria. David Oyedepo was born on September 27, 1954, in Osogbo, Oyo State. He hails from Omuaran in Kwara State. He was raised by his maternal grandmother in Osogbo where he attended his elementary education. He later proceeded to Kwara Polytechnic (now Kwara State University) where he studied architecture. He worked briefly at the Ministry of Housing in Ilorin before resigning to pursue a career in the ministry. He later proceeded to Honolulu University, Hawaii, where he received a doctoral degree in human development in 1982. On his return from the United States, he married his wife, Florence Abiola Akano (later Mrs. Faith Oyedepo). They both have four children. Bishop Oyedepo is regarded as one of the leading Pentecostal pastors in Nigeria with an estimated church membership of over eight million. He organizes the yearly Shiloh program, which is held at the church headquarters and attracts people from within and outside the country. The Winners Auditorium in Ota is reputed to be one of the largest in the world with a sitting capacity of 50,000 worshippers. Bishop Oyedepo is also regarded as one of the wealthiest pastors in the country with a total worth of $150 million. He has four private jets and several properties around the world including South Africa, the United Kingdom, and the United States where he has some of his church branches. He is the Chancellor of Covenant University, Ota, Ogun State, and Landmark University, Omuaran, in Kwara State. Both universities were founded by him under the umbrella of his church. The Winners' church has also established both primary and secondary schools mostly in the southern part of the country and the Federal Capital Territory, Abuja. Bishop Oyedepo has expressed his concern with politics in Nigeria and its political leaders. He openly encourages his church members to pray for the nation.

See Also: Adeboye, Enoch (Chapter 5); Pentecostalism (Chapter 5); Synagogue Church of All Nations (Chapter 5).

Further Reading

Covenant University. (2023). "The Chancellor." https://www.covenantuniversity.edu.ng/about-us/overview/the-chancellor

Living Faith Church Worldwide International. (2023). https://faithtabernacle.org.ng/

PENTECOSTALISM

Pentecostal churches in Nigeria have their origin in African Initiated Churches (AICs) and the introduction of international Pentecostal churches such as the Assemblies of God in 1939 and Foursquare Gospel Church in 1954. In the 1960s and 1970s there was a wave of spiritual revivals among Christian university students, most of whom were influenced by AICs and an exposure to American televangelism and their preachers. Many founders of Pentecostal churches traveled to the US to attend Christian crusades and gain spiritual training from their schools and ministries.

The main emphasis of most Nigerian Pentecostal churches is the encouragement of a spiritual relationship with Jesus Christ as Lord and savior through a process of being "born again"; baptism in the Holy Spirit (the manifestation of which is speaking in tongues); prayer as a key element in obtaining power to defeat evil spirits; spiritual discipline through regular fasting and a daily reading of the Bible for guidance; and regular payment of tithes and offerings for the development and growth of the Lord's kingdom on earth. Some Pentecostal churches also believe in spiritual rituals such as washing the feet, hands, and head; anointing services with oil and water, the use of symbolic items such as handkerchiefs, bottles of oil and water to heal, night vigils, and the attendance of annual prayer crusades.

Under the Christian Association of Nigeria, the Pentecostal Fellowship of Nigeria (PFN) was established. PFN serves as an umbrella body which coordinates the activities of Pentecostal, Evangelical, and Charismatic Ministries, Churches, and Associations in Nigeria. Over the years, PFN has served as a major voice in Nigerian politics. In 1986, during the military era of General Ibrahim Babangida, the PFN youth wing staged a protest against Nigeria being made a member of the Organization of Islamic Conference based on the fear of a northern Nigeria agenda to convert Nigeria into an Islamized state, which is against the secular status of Nigeria as enshrined in the Constitution. Based on this, prominent PFN leaders like Benson Idahosa called for a Christian political reform in Nigeria. In 1988, leaders of the PFN backed Christian candidates for the 1993 elections and when MKO Abiola rose as a presidential candidate, he was also supported. The annulment of the 1993 elections was very disappointing. Thus, when Olusegun Obasanjo contested for the presidential seat in 1999, he was seen as an answer to Idahosa's call because Obasanjo was a practicing Christian of the Baptist Church. Obasanjo's eventual election as Nigeria's president as well as the selection of Assemblies of God church member, Anyim Pius Anyim, as the secretary to the federal government of Nigeria, also in 1999, was regarded as a great victory for PFN members all over the country.

Today, Nigerian Pentecostal churches are known for their prosperity messages, pioneered by Bishop Benson Idahosa, the founder of the Church of God Mission International. Prior to this, the emphasis of Pentecostal churches was the belief in ascetic life and the shunning of worldly wealth and material possession as Jesus did.

See also: Adeboye, Enoch (Chapter 5); Catholicism (Chapter 5); European Explorers and Christianity (Chapter 2); Inter-Religious Conflicts (Chapter 5); Oyedepo, David (Chapter 5); Synagogue Church of All Nations (Chapter 5).

Further Reading

Marshall, R. (2009). *Spiritualities: The Pentecostal Revolution in Nigeria*. Chicago: The University of Chicago Press.
Pentecostal Fellowship of Nigeria. (2023). https://pfnlagosstate.org/

REFORMED OGBONI FRATERNITY

foundation is not clear as some authorities put it in 1918 while others say it is 1914. However, what is agreed on is that it was founded by a Christian, Deacon Jacobson Ogunbiyi. The original aim of its establishment was to bring together believers of the Christian faith with the objective of promoting good values, discipline, and justice in the society, but this was later expanded to accommodate different religious faiths. The members are bound together with the philosophy of "Ogbonism" which involves the fear of God, and the golden rule of do unto others as you would others do unto you.

The ROF is an offshoot of the Ogboni Fraternity (or Ogboni cult) making outsiders assume the tenets and ideologies of the former apply to the latter. Members of the ROF have on several occasions tried to convince the public that the secrecy and rituals that surround the Ogboni Fraternity do not apply to the ROF. The Ogboni Fraternity originated from the Yoruba people and today has members within Nigeria as well as in Togo and the Republic of Benin. The Ogboni Fraternity is a cultural and religious group whose activities are believed to improve its members' economic status by spiritually creating national and international opportunities for them. The Ogboni Fraternity originated from the Aborigine Ogboni which dates to 4500 BCE with the coming of Oduduwa to Ile-Ife. It was a secret society which served as a link between the people and the gods as well as a check on ruling monarchs to discourage the abuse and misuse of power. The members were few and worshiped the Earth Goddess. Being a member meant going through secret initiations and rituals; the process of which could not be divulged to anyone outside the Ogboni cult. Though the Aboriginal Ogboni was highly revered and was regarded as the highest court in Yoruba land it, nevertheless, could not withstand the colonial government and the new political, judicial, and religious system it promoted. To survive and sustain its relevance, the Aboriginal Ogboni metamorphosed into the Ogboni Fraternity. Though the Ogboni Fraternity did not have as much power and political influence as the aboriginal version, it still maintained a brotherhood bound by secrecy like its predecessor.

On the contrary, the ROF is not considered to be a secret society nor do members have affiliations with political parties or traditional authorities. Rather, ROF serves as a network for its members who share economic, political, and social bonds based on godly precepts. It encourages its members to be law-abiding, serve charitable causes, and support all humankind irrespective of color, race, or belief. The ROF encourages men from twenty-one years to be members and this can be extended to their wives who must be thirty years of age and above. Women without male member referral must be forty years to be accepted. The ROF has about 940 conclaves in Nigeria as well as in Cameroon, Belgium, Italy, and England.

See Also: Aladura Church (Chapter 5); Celestial Church of Christ (Chapter 5); Traditional Religions (Chapter 5).

Further Reading

Akintola, A. (1992). *The Reformed Ogboni Fraternity: Its Origin and Interpretation of its Doctrines and Symbolism*. Ogbomosho: Ogunniyi Printing Works.

Canada: Immigration and Refugee Board of Canada. (2012, April 13). "Nigeria: The Reformed Ogboni Fraternity (ROF), Including the Nature of its Belief System and Its Purpose; Whether Membership is Compulsory, Especially for Children of Members, and Consequences for Refusing to Join the ROF; Whether Positions within the ROF Are Inherited." *NGA104054.E.* https://www.refworld.org/docid/50aa3c6c2.html

SYNAGOGUE CHURCH OF ALL NATIONS

The Synagogue Church of All Nations (SCOAN) is one of the dominant Christian churches in Nigeria, founded by Pastor Temitope Balogun Joshua. The church is headquartered in Ikotun in Lagos State with a worldwide membership of over six million. The church has only one branch located in Ghana, but it reaches millions of its members through its social media platforms and its official television, Emmanuel TV. The official YouTube of the church has over one million subscribers and over 400 million views, while it has over three million followers on Facebook. The church is popular for its miraculous healing including blindness, lameness, and other disabilities, but unlike other major Pentecostal television channels, Emmanuel TV does not dwell on "prosperity preaching" nor does it engage in fundraising on air. The church is also known for its "Anointing Water," which is sanctified by T. B. Joshua and given to the sick for their healing. A local politician in Sierra Leone claimed in 2015 that the church's Anointing Water helped reduce the spread of the deadly Ebola virus that ravaged that country between 2014 and 2015. Various celebrities within and outside Nigeria, including the popular Nollywood actor Jim Iyke, and the Kenyan Olympic gold medalist, Mercy Cherono, have claimed that the church, through its senior pastor, delivered them from demonic and spiritual oppression. Such deliverances and healings have made the church a popular religious destination among religious tourists.

Notable visitors who have visited the church include the late Winnie Mandela, and the late Zulu king, Goodwill Zwelithini kaBhekuzulu. Others are the President of Tanzania, John Kagufuli and the late Ghanaian President, John Evans Atta Mills as well as the football legend and current President of Liberia, George Weah. The church, through its senior pastor, T. B. Joshua, has brokered peace among political leaders on the African continent. Prominent among which was Joshua's mediation in the aftermath of Tanzania's election in 2015 in which he convened a reconciliatory meeting between the president, John Magufuli (a SCOAN member) and the opposition leader, Edward Lowassa.

The Synagogue, Church of all Nations, engages in philanthropic activities both in Nigeria and outside the country. The church is one of the few ones with a presence in the northeastern part of the country, which has been ravaged by the militant Boko Haram religious group. The church provides shelter and food for displaced persons in the region. It also regularly distributes food and money to the handicapped in other northern states including Abuja, the federal capital. The church also helps orphans, widows, and the elderly. Outside Nigeria, the church has made huge donations to countries such as Ghana, Ecuador, the Philippines, India, and Haiti toward those that were affected by natural disasters. Other donations were for the building of schools, the award of scholarships to indigent students, and toward supporting refugees. It is estimated that the church has given out over $20 million in aid and for this reason, pastor T. B. Joshua was awarded a national honor by the federal government of Nigeria in 2008, and a letter of appreciation was sent to him by the United Nations in 2014. Pastor T. B. Joshua died suddenly on June 5, 2021.

See Also: Adeboye, Enoch (Chapter 5); Aladura Church (Chapter 5); Oyedepo, David (Chapter 5); Pentecostalism (Chapter 5).

Further Reading

Official website of the Synagogue Church of All Nation (SCOAN). (2022). https://www.scoan.org/about/the-scoan/

Tonga, G. and F. Tonga. (2021). *T. B. Joshua: Servant of God*. Coventry: En Gedi Publishing Limited.

TRADITIONAL RELIGIONS

If modern estimates, derived from various surveys, are to be taken as an absolute guide, there would appear to be almost no adherents to traditional religions in Nigeria. According to some surveys, such as those of the United Nations and the Pew Forum, there are about 51 percent Christians and 47.8 percent Muslims in Nigeria and the remaining 1.1 percent as adherents to other religious groups including indigenous religions. While these figures might lead to the assumption that indigenous religions have no place in Nigeria and among its peoples, much depends on our understanding of the Nigerian society in modern times. The foreign religions of Christianity and Islam, in their dominant position in the country, makes traditional religion unpopular and provides a platform to stigmatize those who adhere to traditional religions. For this reason, the survey figures may not entirely provide the true picture of religious practices in Nigeria. It is not uncommon for a Nigerian who professes to be a Christian or a Muslim to participate in traditional religious festivals and engage in rituals that are strictly associated with traditional religions and beliefs. The resilience of traditional religions in Nigeria can best be understood by the share number of traditional practices that are still pervasive in all corners of the country, but this is much more so in the southern part of the country where a few people still practice the religion of their ancestors. The worshippers of the Osun goddess who congregate annually to celebrate her protection and blessings have made the state government declare a state holiday in honor of the goddess and allow devotees who are state workers to celebrate the event without any hindrance. The official recognition of the Osun festival is a testament to the relevance of the deity to the people of the state. Among the Urhobo of Delta State, the worship of various marine deities and ancestor veneration is still common. Notable indigenous religions common to them are the *Igbe* movement and the *Olokun* religious group. Among the Igbo of eastern Nigeria, the worship of *Ani*, though becoming less popular, is still venerated especially in their celebration of the New Yam festival. Among the Efik, Ibibio, and Affang of the Calabar region, ancestral cults, and the worship of a variety of deities is manifested in the people's colorful masks and masquerades that are displayed during their festivals. In urban cities such as Lagos, the *Eyo* festival still attracts a large followership, and it has somewhat become the cultural face of Lagos State. Thus, even though majority of Nigerians claim to be Christians or Muslims, many of them still retain in their daily lives' elements of traditional religious beliefs: they participate by acknowledging and sacrificing to their ancestors, participate in traditional religious festivals, and resort to the protective power of charms and amulets prepared by traditional religious priests. The same is also true in the northern part and the middle belt of the country where there is a fusion of traditional religious practices and the dominant Islamic rites and rituals.

See Also: Aladura Church (Chapter 5); Celestial Church of Christ (Chapter 5); Reformed Ogboni Fraternity (Chapter 5).

Further Reading

Idowu, E. B. (1994). *Olodumare: God in Yoruba Belief*. Lagos: Wazobia.

McKinnon, A. (2021). "Christians, Muslims and Traditional Worshippers in Nigeria: Estimating the Relative Proportions from Eleven Nationally Representative." *Social Surveys. Review of Religious Research*, 63: 303–15.

CHAPTER 6

Social Classes and Ethnicity

OVERVIEW

Nigeria is a country with diverse ethnic groups totaling over 250 with distinct cultures and languages. Prior to the colonization of the country by the British Empire between 1897 and 1960, the various ethnic groups interacted with each other through trade, marriage, and warfare. Thus, social relations had been intense among the ethnic groups for centuries. The era that predates colonial rule also witnessed various degrees of development in agriculture, sculpture, poetry, music, medicine, and many other specialized fields. This degree of specialization also meant a social hierarchy in the societies even if it was not as marked and divided as it is in the modern era. Three major criteria defined social class in traditional societies namely, the ability to feed every member of the household, the ability to provide shelter and security, and being worthy of receiving a chieftaincy title or other formal social, political, religious, or cultural recognition. All these criteria were hinged on the virtues of hard work, honesty, and altruism. The specialization of people also meant that they must work hard to support themselves and their large households. The larger the household and the ability to successfully feed all members was the hallmark of economic achievement and social responsibility by household heads. Failure to support members adequately attracted shame and disgrace. Although the household, usually headed by a man, was made up of large family members consisting of the biological children of the polygamous man, the intention was not just to bring children into the world but to also demonstrate that he could provide for them until they set up their own families. However, hard work alone was not enough to attract respect and social class. The ability of elders in the society to be fair in their judgment in adjudicating cases and display wisdom in public gatherings were essential to place one in the highest rung of the social ladder. The common saying among Nigerian traditional societies that a good name is better than riches epitomizes the place of integrity and honesty in local traditional societies. While a person

Ethnicity and the 2023 Elections
The presidential elections of February 25, 2023, and the states governorship and houses of assembly elections of March 18, 2023, respectively, unfortunately, have further exacerbated the ethnic divide in Nigeria. Ethnicity has always played an important part of Nigeria's politics, but never in the history of elections has ethnicity been so decisively used by political parties to curry for votes. The ethnic card was used extensively in Lagos, Rivers, and Kano states toward achieving political goals. But it has created tension with some Nigerians of different ethnic group being told to vote for certain political parties or leave the state to their home state. This development has been condemned by various civil society groups and religious bodies, but sadly, not by the federal government. In all the ethnic tensions created by the general elections, President Buhari did not make any national broadcast to calm the country. Some senior citizens in the country have cautioned that if the situation is not well handled by the incoming government from May 29, 2023, the situation may escalate and further create divisions that could plunge the country into more social, economic, and cultural problems.

---

who displayed hard work and honesty is accorded respect in the society, those who, in addition showed emotion and passion toward the welfare of others by supporting them in material, physical, political, and even religious ways, were held in the highest regard. It was judged as immoral for someone to relish in other people's calamity and misfortune. Anyone who did not show empathy was regarded as antisocial and summarily tagged a witch. Such labeling acted as a deterrent and a strong sanction against those who were not altruistic in their daily interactions.

The interaction of traditional societies with Europeans, starting from the late fifteenth century, and the subsequent colonization and amalgamation of the various societies that make up modern Nigeria brought significant change in the definition of social class. Members of traditional societies who were regarded as prosperous and accorded the highest respect in the land but did not embrace the early Europeans and their cultural artifacts including their religion, education, and political system, soon found their downward spiral both in political terms and in their socioeconomic status. The earliest members who decided to attend the introduced schools and embraced Christianity (in southern and central Nigeria) became the new elites of the emerging nation-state. It needs to be stated, however, that the practice was somewhat different in the northern part of the country where Islam had been introduced to the local people since the thirteenth century. Furthermore, the introduced religion of Islam became fully established and had a strong hold on the local people after the jihadist movement waged by Uthman dan Fodio starting from the early nineteenth century. The establishment of the Caliphate also meant that those who did not wholly embrace the new religion were excluded from accessing political power and denied the social status they would have once enjoyed.

The prestige that was associated with Christianity and the ability to speak fluent English in the South, and in the North, Islam, and Arabic, became the defining criteria for social standing in colonial Nigeria. In addition, were the extraneous factors of working for the colonial government and the ability to acquire certain gadgets such as transistor radio, bicycle, fan, or being tagged a government official. It needs to be noted that the reluctance of the vast majority to embrace Western education (for example in the North) or the lack of opportunity to access this new form of education (in the Niger Delta and the Middle Belt) also meant that only the few that did (especially in the Southwest and Southeast) became constitutive of the emerging elitist group in the country. This small group also became the nationalists who fought for the independence of the country.

The first military coup in 1966 ushered in a radical definition of social class at least in the political space. No longer was access to political power defined by education and a nationalist credential, but by one's position in the army even if the top brass received only minimal formal education. The civil war of 1967 to 1970 also redefined access to political power by ethnicity as the Igbos of the Southeast who attempted but lost the bid to secede meant that they lost out in the new political dispensation with the North benefiting substantially in the post-civil war political order. Hence, the military rules from 1967 to 1999 were headed by officers from the North except by a twist of fate that produced in 1976, Olusegun Obasanjo, a military general from the Southwest, assuming the head of the military government after the assassination of General Murtala Muhammed who became head of state in a bloodless coup in 1975. This meant that most of the military brass was made up of Nigerians from the North who, with some selected cronies from the South, became the new political elite in the country. This new political elite that emerged during the military era amassed stupendous wealth accumulation which significantly polarized the middle class and the upper class. This group, with the northern oligarchs who represent the northern Caliphate became the power brokers in the country. The return to democratic rule in 1999 opened the political space for more southern Nigerians to access political power. As politics and access to economic resources are mutually reinforcing in Nigeria, the new elite group that emerged (both in the North and in the South) subsequently witnessed the consolidation of wealth accumulation by politicians and "businesspeople" with much of the population deprived of basic social amenities.

The new arrangement to the accumulation of capital, wealth, and private access to resources changed the dynamics of social class significantly in modern Nigeria. Those who have access to financial resources and other means of production including political power, ownership of media industry, and to a lesser extent access to quality education became the new social elites. Political elites in modern Nigeria derive their resources through birthright (based on the political position of parents or other family members), the ability to negotiate one's way through the labyrinths of political maneuverings, through political godfathers, or through political thuggery.

Besides politics and business, social class is also defined by educational attainment and professional careers. Broadly, those who have professional careers such as medical doctors, lawyers, accountants, bankers, engineers, are well respected in the society primarily because they earn much more than the average worker. University professors are also respected not so much for their earnings but because they are regarded as the eggheads of the society with great intellectual depth and insight. However, other means of defining social status have emerged especially from the 1970s. One of such is the ability to display great wealth even if the source of the wealth cannot be satisfactorily explained. The display of wealth in public arenas through lavish spending (or the "spraying of money" in local slang) during social engagements (such as weddings, birthday parties, or funerals) or by driving expensive cars and living in exclusive houses, have redefined social status in modern Nigeria. The virtues of honesty, altruism, and hard work that once defined social status in the society have been forgotten as the desired qualities in defining social status in modern Nigeria.

Broadly categorized, Nigeria is made up of an upper class, consisting of politicians, captains of industry, media moguls, religious leaders, and other amorphously defined "businessmen and businesswomen." The last group consists of those who front for politicians to launder public money or who use their political connection to access economic resources such as oil wells and oil blocks, or bogus government contracts. The upper class is made up of about 1 percent of the country's population and members of the class cut across all ethnic groups in the country with the majority drawn from the three major ethnic groups of Hausa/Fulani, Igbo, and Yoruba. Next to the upper class is the middle class, made up of professionals such as medical doctors, engineers, accountants, university professors and other professionals who have no connections to the political class. They are well respected in the society, but they do not have the social capital the upper class has and so do not display any form of significant wealth even though they have prestige in the society. This class is made up of approximately 15 percent of the population. The last group, the lower class, is made of the vast majority of the population who make up more than 75 percent of the total Nigerian population. This group is made up of Nigerians who have no basic education with the majority from the northern part of the country. In the South of the country the lack of decent employment also puts those who are educated with at least a higher institution degree under this category. On the average, members of the lower class spend less than US$2 a day while over 50 percent of them (mostly in the northern part of the country) live in abject poverty with little or no access to modern healthcare services, nutritious food, pipe-borne water, and electricity. By ethnicity, the majority of those in the North are in this class partly because of their poor access to education and a patronage structure that sustains a culture of giving handouts to people without necessarily empowering them.

Further Reading

Abah, O. S., ed. (2005). *The Geographies of Citizenship in Nigeria*. Zaria: Tamaza Publisher.
Akpan, W. (2007, September 25). "Ethnic Diversity and Conflict in Nigeria: Lessons from the Niger Delta Crisis." *Accord*. https://www.accord.org.za/ajcr-issues/ethnic-diversity-and-conflict-in-nigeria/
Falola, T. (2021). *Understanding Modern Nigeria: Ethnicity, Democracy, and Development*. Cambridge: Cambridge University Press.

HAUSA/FULANI

The Hausa/Fulani ethnic group is made up of two distinct ethnic groups: The Hausa and the Fulani. It is only in Nigeria that these two ethnic groups are so combined based on religious, political, and economic ties they have shared over the years. Combined, they are the largest ethnic group in Nigeria with an estimated population of sixty million constituting about 30 percent of the country's total population. They are predominantly found in the northern part of the country and majority of them practice the Sunni Islamic faith although with an increase in Shiite and Ahmadiyya adherents. Their major language is Hausa but with a sizable number speaking Fulfulde, the indigenous language of the Fulani. Traditionally, the Hausa-Fulani organize themselves in a strict political hierarchy with the Emirs (rulers) at the top of the political leadership who rule based on Islamic law (shari'a) and ensure that law and order are maintained throughout their jurisdictions. The Emir is assisted by his council of advisers including the Waziri (who serves as Prime Minister), the Madaki (Commander of the Army), Galadima (Head Administrator of the Palace), Hakimi (Head Tax Collector), Sarkin Fada (Head of the Palace), Sarkin Pawa (Official Butcher Head) Sarkin Ruwa (Head of Water Bodies), Maaji (Royal Treasurer), and the Alkalis (royal interpreters of the Sharia law). This organized system of political order also confers political power, authority and prestige among members creating a sort of elite class. By extension, those who hold these positions and those close to them also become part of the upper class in northern Nigeria. Besides politics, the Hausa/Fulani are enterprising farmers, craftsmen, traders, and businesspeople. They are known for farming their products such as groundnut, onions, tomatoes, beans, millet, maize, and vegetables. Through trade some have become extremely wealthy and command respect in Nigeria and abroad. Aliko Dangote, who is from the North and started as a trader is now the richest man in Africa and among the fifty richest people in the world. Similarly, traders and businesspeople, though not as successful as Dangote, are all part of the upper class in Nigeria. Those who engage in small-scale businesses such as leather works, weaving, silver, and gold smithing, as well as in the production of tourist items belong to the middle class. Although those who make the middle class cannot easily be ascertained, the majority of those in the North belong to the lower class, characterized by the Almajiri (street urchins) who live on the generosity of those in the privileged classes.

See Also: Hausa Language (Chapter 9); Igbo (Chapter 6); Kingdom of Zaria (Chapter 2); Minority Ethnic Groups (Chapter 6); Sokoto Caliphate (Chapter 2); Yoruba (Chapter 6).

Further Reading

Arewa24. (2020). https://arewa24.com/en/
Hill, P. (1972). *Rural Hausa: A Village and a Setting*. Cambridge: Cambridge University Press.
Imoagene, O. (1990). *The Hausa and Fulani of Northern Nigeria*. New-Era Publishers.
Salamone, F. (2009). *The Hausa of Nigeria*. Maryland: Rowman and Littlefield Publisher.

IBIBIO PEOPLE

The Ibibio people are the fourth largest ethnic group in Nigeria, and they are mainly found in the present-day state of Akwa Ibom and in smaller numbers in Cross River and in the eastern part of Abia State. Outside Nigeria, the Ibibio can also be found in southwestern Cameroon and Ghana. Ibibio subgroups include the Annang, Efik, Eket, Oron, and Ibeno. The Ibibio people are believed to be the oldest inhabitants of the southeastern region of Nigeria. The name represents both the people and their language, both of which are believed to be the core from which other ethnic groups may have developed. Some scholars speculate that the core Ibibio people came from the *Afaha* descent whose original home is *Usak Edet* in present-day Cameroon. Historians believe that the migration process took two directions. The first was through the land, from which they came into present-day Nigeria, and settled down at Ibom with the Arochukwu people between 1300 and 1400 CE. Historical accounts indicate that there was a major clash or series of clashes between the Igbo and Ibibio people due to power scuttles over resources and trade routes in the sixteenth century. The Igbo people are believed to have teamed up with the Efik people who at that time had superior fire power and spiritual charms. This caused a branch of the Abak, Uyo and Ikot Ekpene subgroups of the Ibibio people to leave the area they had occupied for several decades to look for new lands. The second group of Ibibio migrants from *Usak Edet* migrated by sea and these represent the Oron, Eket and Andoni people. The Ibibio people are patriarchal, headed by a politico-religious head known as *Ikpaisong* who ruled with the support of the *Mbong Ekpuk* (a committee of male family heads). Together, they formed the *Obong Ikpaisong* (the traditional Council), and their decisions were enforced through the *Ekpo/Ekpe* or *Obon* society. The Ibibios were great traders, fishermen and wood carvers.

See Also: Minority Ethnic Groups (Chapter 6); Nri Civilization (Chapter 2).

Further Reading

Amoah, F. E. K. (1992). "Oral Tradition and Ethnicity in the Creation of New States in Nigeria: The Case of Akwa Ibom." *Research Review (NS)*, 8(1&2): 76–89.

Sheshi, S. T. (n.d.). "A History of Nupe, C. 1068–1810 A.D." Being a thesis submitted to the School of Postgraduate Studies, Ahmadu Bello University, Zaria, in partial fulfilment of the requirements for the award o of Doctor of Philosophy (PhD) in History.

IGBO

The Igbos are the third largest ethnic group in Nigeria. They occupy the southeastern part of the country. The Igbos are the most widespread in the country with some of them to be found in other parts of the country such as in the South-south region of Rivers and Bayelsa States. They also occupy parts of Delta and Lagos states and are also to be found in most parts of northern Nigeria. They are estimated to have a population of over twenty-four million constituting about 18 percent of Nigeria's total population. They speak the Igbo language with varying dialects. Igbo is a tonal language belonging to the Sudanic linguistic group of the Niger-Congo language family. They claim to be an autochthonous ethnic group and trace their ancestral home to Nri Town in the Awka District of modern-day Anambra state. The Igbos are known chiefly in the field of education, farming, and trading. The main crops they produce are yam, cassava, and a variety of vegetables. Yam is their chief crop, exclusively associated with men. The New Yam festival, which is celebrated at the beginning of the harvest period, is a common feature among them. They have also been involved in the production of palm oil and fruits, especially cashew. They uphold a moral philosophy of general reciprocity and demonstrate a melioristic position in the face of adversity. Their political system before the introduction of Western democracy was gerontocracy based on the agnate (*umunna*) group system and the age-grade system where social and political functions are distributed along age brackets. The *umunna* is organized at three levels namely, the family level, which is the primary level, followed by the village (*ebo*) level, and finally the town level, which comprises a conglomerate of villages. The transition from one age grade to another is usually between three to six years' interval depending on the community. Except for some few Igbo communities that practice some form of social discrimination that defines some members as born free and others as untouchables (*osu*), the Igbo nation is primarily egalitarian. Such political structure makes the Igbos very individualistic in their social and economic relations, which also provides room for fierce competition among them. Thus, social prestige and influence was not derived from political position but rather on economic and social capital. This partly explains why their presence is not pronounced in Nigeria's political landscape. Rather, they tend to dominate in the field of trade and commerce. For this reason, a sizable number of them belong to the country's middle class in terms of standard of living and in some instances, they also belong to the upper class. They are very industrious and successful in their business enterprise and equally lavish in their spending especially during festive periods such as funerals, Christmas, and Easter when they normally travel home to the Southeast to celebrate with relatives. They also participate in the local festivals characterized by masquerades, locally referred to as *Mmanwu*, which is used to celebrate the New Yam festival.

See Also: Hausa/Fulani (Chapter 6); Igbo Artwork (Chapter 12); Igbo Language (Chapter 9); Minority Ethnic Groups (Chapter 6); Nri Civilization (Chatper 2); Yoruba (Chapter 6).

Further Reading

Isichei, E. (1975). *A History of the Igbo People*. London: Palgrave Macmillan.
Uchendu, V. (1987). *The Igbo of Southeast Nigeria*. New York: Van Nostrand Reinhold Company.
Widjaja, M. (2020). "The Guide on Igbo Culture and Language." IgboGuide.org. https://www.igboguide.org/

IJAW PEOPLE

The Ijaw people (also known as Ijo or Izon) are made up of forty to fifty affiliated clans or *Ibe* and are the major ethnic group which dominates the southern region of Nigeria. Historical accounts indicate that the Ijaw people may have a common ancestry with the Yoruba people of ancient Ife. The founding father is identified as Prince Ujo who led a migration out of ancient Ife to Benin City. From Benin, the prince moved on to the Niger Delta region where he settled. In this new area, he found groups of people known as the *Oru* with whom he merged and built communities. This new fusion is the foundation of the Ijaw people, and this is believed to have occurred between 500 BCE and 1000 CE. The people practice a relatively decentralized political system with each *Ibe* united through this common patriarchal ancestor. The Ijaw people are bound together by a common belief in masked spirits and mermaids from which elaborate festivals and ceremonies are conducted in worship and reverence for protection and enrichment. Water bodies are a significant part of the Ijaw make-up as it not only shapes their primary occupation of fishing but also their religion and culture. They supported their primary occupation of fishing with the farming of agricultural crops like rice, plantain, cassava, banana, cocoyam, palm oil/kernels, as well as timber. They traded products like salt, fresh fish, smoked or dried fish for essential tools and other materials. The Ijaw people were one of the first ethnic groups in Nigeria to encounter European traders and explorers and were later very active in the slave-trader era. The Ijaw people were a greatly feared group as they raided communities on the waters and the land to capture slaves and trade them for weapons and luxurious items such as cloth, beads, and mirrors. Besides their notorious activities in the slave trade industry, they were also known for their production and trade in palm oil which was exported to Europe. The Ijaw people were proud and fierce warriors that dominated major water bodies and protected their trade routes with fleets of canoes. With these traits they were able to ward off rival groups from their territories. These traits were also identified as major factors behind the twelve-day resistance of the Niger Delta Volunteer Force headed by Isaac Boro in his bid to liberate the Ijaw people. In recognition of this fear, every year on May 16, the present-day Bayelsa Government celebrate the bravery of Isaac Boro and what he stood for in relation to Ijaw history.

Today, the Ijaw people can be found settled around major water bodies in present-day states of Ondo, Delta, Edo, Bayelsa and Rivers in Nigeria as well as Sierra Leone and Gabon.

See Also: Benin Empire (Chapter 2); Minority Ethnic Groups (Chapter 6); Southern Cuisine (Chapter 14).

Further Reading

Blogger. (2013, February 8). "Ijaw People: Nigeria's Aboriginal Water People of Niger Delta." https://kwekudee-tripdownmemorylane.blogspot.com/2013/02/ijaw-people-nigerias-aboriginal-water.html

HistoryVille. (2022, March 7). "Isaac Adaka Boro (1938–1968): Nigeria's First Secessionist." https://www.thehistoryville.com/isaac-adaka-boro/

KANURI PEOPLE

The Kanuri people were the major ethnic group which dominated the Northeast region of Nigeria, and they trace their origin to the great Kanem-Bornu Empire. The Kanuri people are believed to have occupied the Lake Chad region as far back as the seventh century under the *Duguwa* aristocracy. In around 850 CE, a man called Sayf bin Yazan (some scholars refer to this personality as Saif Ibn Dhi Yazan) was believed to have migrated from Yemen to the Lake Chad area. He united the people of Kanuri with his people and this unification formed the Kanem-Bornu Empire. He ruled this empire under the *Sefawa* Dynasty for about 800 years. Scholars believe that the Kanuri people had a well-established system that was based on a nomadic culture. With the establishment of the *Sefawa* Dynasty, the Kanuri people became more sedentary as traders, fishermen, farmers, hunters, cloth dyers and weavers, blacksmiths, and horse riders. By the fourteenth century, the capital which had been established in Kanem was captured. By the sixteenth century, another capital was established in Borno, and the empire became known as Kanem-Borno.

Scholars theorize that Islam was first introduced to Kanem-Bornu through Berber and Arab Muslim traders, missionaries, and scholars; and to the ruling dynasty in 1086 CE when a *Sefawa* king called Humai bn Selemma (some scholars refer to him as Umme Jilm) converted to Islam. Islam played a major role in the development of the empire. The people were highly educated, producing great Islamic scholars and poets; and by the thirteenth century the empire had become a major center for Islamic knowledge. It was known for its administrative and military skills; attributes that saw its great expansion and the development of diplomatic relations with North African countries such as Egypt and Tunisia as well as some southern European countries such as Turkey, Rome, Greece, and Spain.

Unfortunately, the rising domination of the Sokoto Caliphate, the decline of the Trans-Saharan trade and the scramble for Africa under British, French, and German rule resulted in the steady decline of the empire. Today, the largest population of the Kanuri people can be found in the Northeast section of Nigeria; while pockets can be found in northern Cameroon, western Chad, southeast Niger, and smaller representations in Gabon, Sudan, and Libya. They all still recognize the Sheu (Sheikh) of Bornu who reigns from his palace in present-day Maiduguri (northeastern Nigeria) as their traditional head.

See Also: Minority Ethnic Groups (Chapter 6); Sokoto Caliphate (Chapter 2).

Further Reading

Hiribarren, V. (2016). "Kanem-Bornu." In J. M. MacKenzie (ed.), *Encyclopedia of Empire*, 1–6. John Wiley & Sons Ltd. doi: https://doi.org/10.1002/9781118455074.wbeoe014

Kamta, F. N., H. Azadi, and J. Scheffran. (2020). "The Root Causes of the Crisis in Northeast Nigeria: Historical, Socioeconomic and Environmental Dimensions." *Mediterranean Journal of Social Sciences*, 11(3): 95–104. doi: https://doi.org/10.36941/mjss-2020-0033

MIDDLE CLASS

Nigeria's middle class has grown substantially since independence. It is estimated that over sixty million Nigerians (35 percent of the total population) are in this economic class. The bulk of the middle class is made up of civil servants and small and medium-scale businessmen and women who cut across all ethnic groups and constitute about three-quarters of the labor force in the country. The middle class in Nigeria can further be subdivided into three, namely, the upper middle class, the middle middle class, and the lower middle class. The upper middle class is made up of professionals such as engineers, doctors, professors, lawyers, accountants, and other similar professions. Others in this category are successful businessmen and women who have no direct contact with politicians and therefore work very hard to make an honest business. This class has an average household monthly income of US$3,000 with access to good health care services (usually government specialist and teaching hospitals and private healthcare services) and quality education (mostly private education service) for their children. They own their houses and live in relative comfort, and they can, from time to time, afford to go on vacation with their families both within and outside the country. Those that belong to the middle middle class have less earning power with an average household monthly income of US$2,000. They also can afford to access private healthcare services and have their children in private schools though with lower quality compared to the previous group. Members that occupy the third category, the lower middle class, live a somewhat marginal lifestyle with an average household monthly income of less than US$1,000. Although some patronize private schools and put their children in private schools with lower standards than the previous group, majority of them, nevertheless, patronize government public hospitals and public schools. The middle class is the backbone of Nigeria's economic growth, through micro, small and medium enterprises, the middle class supports the government in creating jobs for citizens and empowering citizens in their purchasing power thereby boosting the economy. With the employment of about sixty million Nigerians, the middle class contributes over 48 percent to the country's gross domestic product (GDP). However, the widening income inequality in the middle class in Nigeria is diminishing, leading to an estimated thirteen million children out of school as those in the lower middle class increasingly struggle to sustain members of their households. As the economy struggles under the weight of fluctuating crude oil prices, the volatility of the Naira, and the corrupt practices in the country leading to decaying infrastructure, the future seems to be bleak for the expansion of the middle class. It will take the government's determination, and the doggedness and ingenuity of the middle class to strengthen further the gains that have been recorded. It remains to be seen how the middle class in Nigeria will respond to the enormous challenges it faces under the government's tight fiscal policy.

See Also: Major Cities (Chapter 1); Rural Population (Chapter 6); Urban Poor (Chapter 6); Urbanization and its Impact (Chapter 1).

Further Reading

Campbell, J. (2019, June 21). "Nigeria's 'Emerging Middle Class' Is Leaving." Council on Foreign Relations. https://www.cfr.org/blog/nigerias-emerging-middle-class-leaving
Corral, P., V. Molini, and G. Oseni. (2015). *No Condition is Permanent: Middle Class in Nigeria in the Last Decade*. Washington, DC: World Bank Group: Policy Research Working Paper 7214.
Robertson, C., N. Ndebele, and Y. Mhango. (2011). *A Survey of the Nigerian Middle Class*. Johannesburg: Renaissance Capital.

MINORITY ETHNIC GROUPS

One major feature of the Nigerian state is its diversity in terms of ethnic groupings. There is no precise figure regarding the number of ethnic groups in the country, but various authorities have estimated the number to be between 250 and 750 depending on the criteria used in their identification and classification. While most of these ethnic groups may have some affinity with the dominant cultural groups of Hausa/Fulani, Igbo, and Yoruba, many others have distinct traits and attributes that give them a sense of unique identity. Some of these traits include their language, dress code, architecture, worldview, and cuisine. By far, the most diverse region in the country is the Middle Belt with an estimated over

100 linguistic and ethnic groups. The largest of these groups are the Tiv, who inhabit most parts of Benue state. They are known for the cultivation of yam, maize, and as fishers. They are closely associated with the food basket of the country based on their successful farming of fish and plant products. They are famous for their unique cultural black-and-white handwoven textiles and their exotic and elegant dance. Next to the Tiv are the Idoma and Nupe people who inhabit most part of the country's North-central and speak the Idomoid and Nupoid languages, respectively, which have linguistic affinity with both the dominant Yoruba and Igbo languages of Southwest and Southeast Nigeria, respectively. Like the Tiv, they also grow yam, cassava, maize, and raise goats, sheep, and chickens. They are also famous for their craftsmanship in weaving, embroidery, bead making, and metal work. Other ethnic groups in this region include the Ebira, Gbagyi, Jukun, and Bachama, among others. On the eastern flank of the middle belt are the Angas, Berom, Shendam, Gemai, Jawara, and Tarak, among other ethnic groups. They occupy mostly the states of Plateau and Nasarawa where they also collectively constitute the majority. They are predominantly Christians making Christianity the dominant religion in the region. Islam and the various indigenous religions constitute the minority religion. Toward the South of the country, especially in the Niger Delta region are a diverse cultural group. Edo State, in the midwest, is home to the Bini (Edo), the Ishan, Etsako, to the South of the state. The Bini are famous for their wood carving, sculpture, iron smelting and casting. The face of Nigeria's FESTAC 77 was an adaptation of Bini art that represents the artistic genius of the people who share some historical, political, and cultural affinity with their Yoruba neighbors. The Benin kingdom is one of the oldest consistent traditions in Nigeria spanning over one thousand years. The present Oba (king), HRH Erediawa II is the thirteenth from inception. At the peak of the Benin kingdom in the sixteenth and seventeenth centuries, its political power and influence extended to modern-day Lagos State, which was an extension of the Benin Empire. In fact, the original name of Lagos, Eko, is a Bini word for that territory. To the North of Edo State are the Affemai and Igarra who share some cultural, religious, and linguistic affinity with the Igala and Nupe people. In Delta State, the dominant ethnic groups are the Urhobo, Itsekiri, and Ijaw people who occupy the city of Warri. Among the Urhobo, there are other sub-cultural groups such as the Isoko, Uvwie, Okpe, and Ugwhevwien. They can be found in towns such as Okpara, Effurun, Ughelli, Abraka, Eku, Sapele, and Aladja. The Urhobo are known to produce cash crops such as palm produce and rubber. They also produce cassava for domestic use and for export. The Ijaw also inhabit Brass, Burutu, Forcados, and other riverine areas in the Niger Delta. In size, the Ijaw is the largest minority group in the country with an estimate of over four million occupying parts of Delta, Rivers, and Ondo states. They are known for their fishing prowess and their characteristic stilt houses that are built on water bodies. Their distinctive language, which belongs to the Niger-Congo language family. To the South-south of the country are to be found the Kalabari, Efik, Ogoja, Calabar, Anang, and Ibibio cultural groups. They are mostly found in Rivers, Akwa Ibom, Cross Rivers, and Bayelsa States. The Calabar region is known for its colorful masquerades as well as their rich cuisine. The Efik and Ibiobio, the two ethnic groups that dominate Akwa Ibom state are closely related historically, linguistically, and culturally. In the Northeast of the country, the major ethnic groups are the Kanuri and Fulani. Others are Hausa, Bade, and Karekare.

The Kanuri have a long and prosperous past epitomized by the Kanem-Borno Empire, which flourished between the ninth and nineteenth centuries. Modern Kanuri people are known for their fish farming. Also, in the Northeast are the Banso (Panso), Batta, Baya, Bilei, Botlere,Daka, Palli, Ga'anda, Gira, Gombi, Gude, Gwa (Gurawa), Holma, Ichen, Jibu, Jirai, Kaka, Kambu, Kanakuru (Dera)Kilba, Lakka, Lala, Mambilla, Margi, Mbula, Muchaila, Pire, Shuwa, Teme, Tur, Ubbo, Verre, and Waja ethnic groups in Adamawa state. In Taraba state, also in the Northeast, among other ethnic groups are the Yott, Vommi, Tikar, Tigon, Shomo, Sate, Sakbe, Poll, Pkanzom, Panyam, Nyandang, Nyam, Ndoro, Munga (Lelau), Mumuye, Mbum, Lamja, Lama, Kwanchi, Kutin, Kuteb, Kunini, Kugama, Koma, Kenton, Karimjo, Kaba (Kabawa), Jonjo (Jenjo), Jero, Jahuna (Jahunawa), Gwom, Gonia, Gornun (Gmun), Gengle, Diba, Chukkol, and the Chamba. In Borno State, are the Chibok ethnic group that became famous because of the kidnapping of 276 secondary school girls by the Islamic fundamentalist group, Boko Haram. Other ethnic groups in the state include the Buduma, Chinine, Dghwede, Gamergu-Mulgwa, Gavako, Gwoza (Waha), Kanembu, Mandara (Wandala), and the Mobber people. In Yobe state, also in the Northeast, are the Shuwa, Ngizim, Manga (Mangawa), and the Bade people. These various groups that make up the Nigerian state have co-existed since pre-colonial times and they have continued to maintain their cooperation despite some recent challenges such as the religious crisis that are prevalent in some states such as Plateau and Kaduna as well as the Boko Haram and ISWAP (Islamic State of West Africa Province) insurgency.

See Also: Ibibio People (Chapter 2); Ijaw People (Chapter 6); Kanuri People (Chapter 6); Local Dialects (Chapter 9); Nupe People (Chapter 6); Tiv People (Chapter 6).

Further Reading

Egwemi, V., T. Wuam, and C. Orngu, eds. (2014). *Federalism, Politics, and Minorities in Nigeria.* Makurdi: Bahiti and Dalila Publisher.
World Directory of Minorities and Indigenous Peoples. (n.d.). "Nigeria." https://minorityrights.org/country/nigeria/

NUPE PEOPLE

Nupe is known both as the language spoken as well as the group of people that speak it most of whom are currently located in the states of Niger, Kwara, Kogi, Nasarawa, and Abuja. Traditionally, the people were farmers, hunters, and fishermen due to the presence of the Rivers Niger and Kaduna which flowed through the ancient Nupe kingdom. The rivers not only served as a source of livelihood, but also as a means of transportation, communication, transfer of knowledge, networks, and the building of relationships. The presence of the two rivers also encouraged trade as major market centers were established. At strategic locations along these rivers, taxes and tributes were collected for the passage and protection of goods and other cargo to the Nupe kingdom. Their trade history with Hausa kingdoms to the North and the Yoruba kingdoms to the South goes as far back as the fifteenth century. In fact, some scholars of history even claim that the traditional masquerade of *Egungun* was introduced to Yorubaland through this relationship. According to Nupe oral tradition, the Nupe kingdom was founded by a man known as Tsoede (also known as *Edegi*). Tsoede was born as the son of an Igala king and a Nupe mother. As a royal prince in the Igala court of his father, Tsoede was exposed to both worlds of his parents. When he came of age, he decided to go to Nupe, his mother's homeland. There he met what scholars refer to as the Bini Confederacy which was made up of semi-independent city-states governed by subgroups that had developed twelve semi-independent but complex sociopolitical societies. Historians believe that between the fifteenth and sixteenth century CE, Tsoede was able to unite these states into one powerful and independent kingdom. Under his rule, he extended the Nupe kingdom, making good use of their traditional science of metallurgy to produce iron weapons of war. Historical accounts suggest that Tsoede met his death during one of such expansion expeditions. Nevertheless, the dynasty he established thrived until the coming of the Islamic Jihadists and later the British colonial rule. Nupe land had an abundance of iron ore which resulted in the establishment of guilds that not only produced weapons, but also tools as well as art works. Besides iron works, the Nupe people were also known for their production of glass, beads, pottery, leather, handwoven and dyed cloth which were highly priced outside the kingdom. The Nupe people are known for their mystical powers and rituals. Evidence of this is captured in the personality of Sango, a Yoruba deity, and past Alaafin of Oyo. Sango's father was *Oranmiyan* (son to Oduduwa) while his mother was the daughter of the reigning Nupe king of the time.

See Also: Kingdom of Zaria (Chapter 2); Minority Ethnic Groups (Chapter 6); Sokoto Caliphate (Chapter 2).

Further Reading

Naankiel, P. W. (2015). "A Brief History of the Pre-colonial Economy of the Jukun." *Sokoto Journal of History*, 4: 150–60.

Yahaya, M. K. (2003). "The Nupe People of Nigeria." *Studies Tribes Tribals*, 1(2): 95–110.

RURAL POPULATION

Nigeria's rural population is estimated to be 49 percent of the total population. This population contributes to the country's economic and social growth. These citizens are responsible for the production of most agricultural produce in the country and serve as the bastion on which the country thrives. In the northern part of the country, rural folks are responsible for the production of tomatoes, onions, groundnut, vegetables as well as in the supply of cow, goat, and sheep meat. Some of the most intricate embroideries also come from the North. In the middle belt rural folks cultivate the land and produce such diverse crops as yam, rice, millet, sorghum, and soya beans. In the Southwest, cash crops such as cocoa are the prerogative of rural folks. In the Southeast yams, taro, and cassava are produced in large quantities by the rural population. In the South-south rural folks supply the country with fish, periwinkle, shrimps, and other sea foods. They are responsible for the production of some cash crops such as rubber, palm kernels, and palm oil. The rural folks are also the custodians of indigenous knowledge and practices. For instance, they still practice traditional healings, which most of the population rely on as their form of health care service. Current interest in African medicine is encouraging studies into the working models of these ancient practices that the people still depend on for their survival. Some rural dwellers still practice their traditional religions and adhere strictly to the norms and values prescribed by their ancestors and deities. It is not uncommon for educated urban citizens calling on Nigerians to revert to virtues that still characterize rural life. Virtues such as honesty, empathy, and altruism, which are scarce commodities in urban Nigeria but are still upheld in rural communities, have become the reference point for political leadership and economic relations in the country. While rural dwellers still have a lot to offer in terms of food sustenance and values, they are often neglected by federal and state governments. Most of the rural population do not have access to basic social infrastructure such as roads to transport their crops, electricity to preserve their produce, and access to capital to expand their enterprise. This neglect of rural areas makes those living in rural areas vulnerable to exploitation by intermediaries who buy agricultural products at a very low price and sell them at exorbitant prices in the cities. The exploitation and neglect of rural people deprive them of making a decent living, thereby contributing to their poor standard of living and low quality of life despite their enormous contribution to the nation. For this reason, young people in rural communities are migrating to the cities in search of better opportunities thereby contributing to the increase in population density in the cities and putting a strain city infrastructure. With this rate of rural-urban migration it is projected that by 2050 three-quarters of the country's population will be urban dwellers leaving only the elderly and children in rural areas.

See Also: Middle Class (Chapter 6); Poverty (Chapter 4); Urban Poor (Chapter 6).

Further Reading

Hill, P. (1972). *Rural Hausa: A Village and a Setting*. Cambridge: Cambridge University Press.
Trading Economics. (n.d.). "Nigeria – Rural Population." https://tradingeconomics.com/nigeria/rural-population-percent-of-total-population-wb-data.html

TIV PEOPLE

The Tiv people are the major ethnic group which dominates the middle-belt region of Nigeria. They can be found in present-day Benue, Taraba, and Nasarawa States in Nigeria. They trace their ancestry to their founding father, a man called Tiv. They are believed to have migrated from the Swem Mountain (some scholars believe this is located somewhere in the Bamenda Plateau in present-day Cameroon while others identify it as either the Obudu or Sonkwalla hills in Nigeria's Cross River State) to the Benue River Valley in Nigeria between c.1500 and 1600. The migration was a slow one due to conflicts overfishing rights in some areas but more so in the vicinity of powerful kingdoms such as the Jukun and Hausa who were notorious for their slave raids. This forced the Tiv people to move westward toward the Benue River. Eventually, they learned to live with their enemies, intermarried and settled down. This marked a major transition in the history of the Tiv people as they stopped the culture of migrating hunter-gatherers and developed a more sedentary society built on farming. Their chosen occupation of farming meant land was their life and they were ready to fight for, secure and defend their land and its resources. It was based on this philosophy that the Tiv people built a relationship of conflict and mutual understanding with their neighbors. As farmers, the Tiv exchanged their farmed products for items such as spices, horses, and farming tools. By the middle of the middle of the eighteenth century, the strength of their domineering neighbors had waned, and this empowered the Tiv people who started to expand and even become a major threat to their former enemies.

See Also: Benue River (Chapter 1); Minority Ethnic Groups (Chapter 6).

Further Reading

Woer, J. (2005). "The Narratives of Origin and Migration of the Tiv People (Of Nigeria) as an Indigenous Interpretative Resource for the Interpretation of the Book of Exodus." *Scriptura*, 90: 885–91.
Wuam, T. (2013). "Tiv Origins of Nationhood and Migration into the Benue Valley, c. 1500–1900." *Journal of Tourism and Heritage Studies*, 2(2): 36–42.

URBAN POOR

Nigeria is estimated to have about 51 percent of its population (approximately 100 million people) residing in urban centers, which are spaces for intense economic, political, and social activities. Since independence in 1960, urban centers have enjoyed the focus of government in terms of infrastructural development and the provision of social amenities such as hospitals, universities, and electricity. The neglect of rural communities has led to the mass movement of teenagers and young adults to the cities to enjoy the bright side of city life. However, poor planning by the government in projecting population growth and providing matching social amenities, have created enormous social problems in Nigeria's urban centers such as Lagos, Port Harcourt, Kano, Ibadan, Onitsha, and Aba. Poor town planning and ineffective bylaws, coupled with corruption of government officials, rural migrants to cities have witnessed the indiscriminate building of shacks resulting in the development of slums. As slums develop without any social amenities from the government, most urbanites who dwell in these areas usually live marginal lives with compromised quality of life. Coupled with high unemployment due to low skills and poor education, an army of urban poor has been created. The urban poor are characterized by very low income, no access to political power, poor access to education and healthcare services, as well as a very low standard of living. So far, Nigeria has no comprehensive policy to improve the plight of the urban poor, which means that their population will continue to increase with a concomitant poor standard of living. The urban poor desire to make a living but scarce resources hinder them from making a decent living, and so resort to other means of survival including begging, prostitution, the sale of drugs, and other vices that have become commonplace in urban centers. This is not to say that all vices are traced to the urban poor, indeed, those who live in plush houses and engage in business are sometimes also involved in shady deals. However, the urban poor are so conspicuous in their daily struggle for survival that they epitomize all that is bad and filthy in the cities. The urban poor form a reservoir of desperate masses who are ready to engage in the most menial of jobs to keep them and their families alive. As they engage in menial jobs with low pay, they have difficulty keeping their children in school and, in no time at all, the young girls become pregnant and, in trying to provide for their young, they accept menial jobs with low pay, and thus the cycle continues. Ironically, they are the ones with the highest number of children as less than 10 percent of them practice family planning and still find solace in large numbers of children even if they can barely scrape a living. Due to their poverty, it is among the urban poor that the country records the highest incidence of diarrhoeal diseases, and high maternal and child mortality simply because of the unhygienic space that make up their dwelling places as well as the lack of access to quality health service. Despite the deplorable condition of the urban poor, they are the epitome of resilience, and, in many ways, they contribute to the vibrancy and growth of the city. Although the slums in which they live are usually adjacent to high-brow communities, they render their services to the rich and powerful in the cities. Most of the domestic workers that serve the upper class and middle class are recruited from the slums. The industrious young adults engage in car wash and barbering services. Some of the women have informal businesses such as the sale of vegetables and fruits, while some are popular for their roadside food otherwise referred to as "buka" by urbanites.

See Also: Major Cities (Chapter 1); Middle Class (Chapter 6); Poverty (Chapter 4); Rural Population (Chapter 6); Urbanization and its Impact (Chapter 1).

Further Reading

Bassey, B. (2021, September 14). "Understanding Dynamics of Urban Poverty in Nigeria: What Role for Urban Governance?" *Urbanet*. https://www.urbanet.info/urban-poverty-in-nigeria/
Makinwa, P. K. and A. O. Ozo. (1987). *The Urban Poor in Nigeria*. Evans Brothers.
Nwaka, G. (2012). "The Urban Poor, the Informal Sector and Environmental Health Policy in Nigeria." In H. Hahn and K. Kastner (eds.), *Urban Life-Worlds in Motion: African Perspectives*, 29–40. New Rockford: Transcript Publishing. doi: https://doi.org/10.1515/transcript.9783839420225.29

YORUBA

The Yoruba are one of the three major ethnic groups in Nigeria with an estimated population of forty-four million constituting about 24 percent of the total population of the country. They are predominantly found in the Southwest of the country, but they also have their kin in central Nigeria, especially in Kogi and Kwara states. They speak the Yoruba language, a highly tonal language, and a derivative of one of the Niger-Congo languages. The Yoruba trace their collective history to Oduduwa who is commonly regarded as the eponymous ancestor of the Yoruba nation. It is believed that he found his kingdom in Ile-Ife, which is today regarded as the spiritual home of the Yoruba group. While Ile-Ife is regarded as their spiritual home, the old Oyo Empire was regarded as their political headquarters. The Oyo Empire, which flourished between the tenth and eighteenth centuries, represented an advanced ethnic group with a well-defined political system, an organized social, economic, and religious structure as well as art and craft that still define the people in modern-day Nigeria. Their culture and tradition are still rooted in their traditional religious and spiritual concepts, cosmology, and practices, even though most of the Yorubas have embraced Islam and Christianity. Some religious movements such as the Celestial Church of Christ and the Cherubim and Seraphim group, both of which command a large Yoruba following are testaments of the successful blend of both indigenous and foreign religions, which also manifests in most parts of Yoruba life. While they may be well exposed to Western civilization, they still hold on to certain cultural practices. For example, the Yoruba may dress in fancy Western-styled clothes for their professional and everyday use, they nevertheless, will adorn themselves in traditional attires during important occasions such as weddings, birthdays, and housewarmings. The same applies to religious festivals. In Yorubaland, various religious festivals are held and celebrated in honor of the local deities. The most popular among these festivals are the Osun-Osogbo festival, held in honor of the Osun River goddess in Osun state. Others include Adamu Orisha (more popularly known as the Eyo Olokun festival) held in Lagos to celebrate the sea goddess Olokun. The Yoruba embraced Western education earlier than most ethnic groups in the country and so are today well educated and are exposed to Western cultures and societies. For this reason, they are well-placed in the social structure of Nigeria's social class contributing significantly to the country's upper class and middle class. They are found in such fields as medicine, law, engineering, and the financial sector. They travel widely for education, business, and recreation. Together with the Hausa/Fulani and Igbo ethnic groups, they constitute the main ethnic groups that have ruled the country since independence in 1960. Like other ethnic groups in the country, the Yoruba have a variety of rich cuisine some of which have become standards in the country's traditional food. Some of their traditional food include *amala* and *abula* soup, *moin-moin* and *eko*, *iyan* and *ewedu* soup as well as snacks such as *akara* and *wara*, among others.

See Also: Hausa/Fulani (Chapter 6); Ife Kingdom (Chapter 2); Igbo (Chapter 6); Minority Ethnic Groups (Chapter 6); Yoruba Language (Chapter 9).

Further Reading

Akintoye, S. A. (2021). *A History of the Yoruba People*. Dakar: Amalion.
Arifalo, S. O. (2001). *The Egbe Omo Oduduwa: A Study in Ethnic and Cultural Nationalism (1945–1965)*. Stebak Books.
Ogundiran, A. (2020). *The Yoruba: A New History*. Bloomington: Indiana University Press.

CHAPTER 7

Gender, Marriage, and Sexuality

OVERVIEW

The marriage system in Nigeria is often described as a union of two families rather than two individuals. Traditionally young couples were dependent on the elders of their families to choose their future partners. The selection was often based on some factors ranging from the family background regarding health (such as mental health and infectious diseases), historical accounts, place and circumstance of birth, and possible feuds. There are also cases where the union is determined by senior members of the family who wish to strengthen further their relationships through the union of their children. Thus, marriage was not based on individual choices but on family or societal considerations which were deemed to be in the interest of the whole rather than of the unit. This philosophy is based on the principle that marriage forms the bedrock of the family, and the family, in turn, is the foundation for the sustenance of society and its culture.

Within the family, gender roles are taught and enforced. Traditionally, most Nigerian ethnic groups are farmers. This primary occupation is supported by livestock raising, hunting, and other professions such as cloth and raffia weaving, iron smelting, jewellery making, pottery production, food manufacturing to mention a few. Within these occupations, gender roles are assigned, and often these roles are complementary. For example, in the cloth weaving industry, the women spin and dye the thread while the men weave the fabrics on narrow looms. The woven cloth forms are then marketed by both men and women to be used at various occasions. Likewise in the food production sector crops such as yams are grown by men but processed into powder (*Elubo*) by the Yoruba women as a staple meal (*Amala*). Thus, the gender roles practiced by many Nigerian cultures are traditionally based on a more parallel and interwoven concept when compared to the gender philosophy introduced by both the Islamic and Christian religions and later the Colonial Administration which governed Nigeria between 1914 and 1960.

Sexuality in traditional Nigerian culture is often based on initiation rites. For many ethnic groups in Nigeria, initiation rites mark a transition from childhood to adulthood. For some cultures, this transition means that the individual can be considered as an adult. With adulthood comes responsibilities which include getting married and starting a family which would contribute to the development of the society. Initiation takes place within age grades. Age grade refers to people born around the same period. Their time of birth unites them throughout their lifetime, and thus they get initiated together to bond them further.

In some Nigerian cultures, being initiated means that the initiate can become sexually active because he or she is no longer a child. While in some other cultures, it means that the individual must confine their sexual exploits to a socially recognized partner. In such a context, having several partners is a sign of childishness, and this is only tolerated if the individual is not initiated. Once initiated sexual exploits are curtailed and the initiated must take on the responsibility of building a home.

In many parts of Nigeria, as in Africa in general, pregnancy is considered a thing of joy and to protect both mother and child; it is often a taboo for the mother to have sexual intercourse for a considerable part of, if not throughout, the pregnancy period. It is believed that sexual intercourse during pregnancy could harm the child and cause the mother's milk to dry up.

Contemporary practices regarding gender, marriage and sexuality are based on varying factors, some of which include religious influences (the introduction of first Islamic religious practices and later Christianity), contact with foreign cultures (first from European explorers to colonial and post-colonial influences), introduction to other forms of education (especially those introduced by Islamic leaders and later missionary bodies) and Western-inspired urbanization.

Gender in Nigeria is primarily defined biologically and categorized into male and female. The female gender is appreciated for her ability to reproduce and increase the population of the society. Based on this a woman that is pregnant is given support by members of the community. This support is provided to her both by men and women. A woman that is taking care of a baby will find that members of the society will go to considerable lengths to support her and ensure that she can take care of the child and herself. Thus, women who have children have a higher status than women who have not been able to give birth. Mothers in the society are placed higher on the social ladder than those who do not have children. This social status ultimately influences her relations with other members of the society. This is also the case with men, who for different reasons, have not been able to impregnate a woman. Such men do not command much respect in the society compared to men who have children. This factor is what encourages many men to have more than one wife or relationship. The hope that the relationship will result in children is a major motivating factor. Men and women who have reached a certain biological age but who for one reason or the other are not married do not enjoy certain privileges and respect like those who are married.

Further Reading

Nwadiokwu, C. N., E. S. Nwadiokwu, E. N. Favour, and M. E. Okwuazun. (2016). "Rites of Passage African Traditional Religion." *International Journal of Education and Research*, 4(9): 41–50.

COURT MARRIAGES

Court marriages are officiated by registrars appointed by the Federal Government of Nigeria, and they must be conducted within a designated district that has been so licensed. A person intending to marry must obtain the form of notice provided by the registry for a specified fee. If the person is limited in their ability to read and understand the English language, then someone who can translate the content will be employed to render such services. Once the content of the form has been read and understood, the applicant signs the form. If the applicant cannot sign, due to a handicap or limitation in education he/she places a mark or a cross on the form of notice in the presence of someone who can read and interpret the form. The signed form, once submitted, is entered into the Marriage Notice Book. The document is made available for members of the public to view and make any objections known. A maximum of three months or twenty-one days will be given for public notice and if within this time frame objections are made or the couple does not appear, the application is either suspended or cancelled.

The couple on the appointed day will be given explanations concerning the laws that will bind them together as a couple. Thus, the registrar will ascertain that one of the parties has been resident within the district in which the marriage will be undertaken at least fifteen days preceding the appointed day. Second, that each of the parties is twenty-one years or older. Third, that there are no legal hindrances to the intended marriage. Finally, neither of the parties is married by a customary court to any other person. If any of the party is below twenty-one years of age, written consent from the father or mother must be provided. In the case where both are no longer alive, a representative of the parent must give the stated document. During the explanation, the intended couple will also be told about the prohibited degrees of penalties that may be incurred if any of them wilfully fails to make such information known. The punishment for such an offense is two years in jail.

At the end of the explanations, the couple will take their vows and sign to indicate they have understood, and they consent to the explanations. They must be accompanied by witnesses who will also sign to indicate that the activity was done lawfully. The registrar conducting the marriage must also sign as a representative of the Nigerian government. With the signing done, the registrar will issue a certificate of marriage as proof of the activity that transpired. The issuance of the document will be registered, and a duplicate version produced. The registrar will file the duplicate copy, and the original copy will be given to the couple as a marriage certificate. This may be followed by a reception, or a more religious wedding done a few days later either in a mosque or church.

See Also: Marriage Law (Chapter 7); Traditional Weddings (Chapter 7); Western Weddings (Chapter 7).

Further Reading

Nigeria Marriage Act. (1990). "Chapter 218." *Laws of the Federation of Nigeria*. Nigerian Constitution.

DOMESTIC VIOLENCE

Domestic violence is considered an act of physical, sexual, emotional, and psychological abuse against intimate partners or immediate family members. In Nigeria, victims of domestic violence are often women and girls because many of the ethnic groups that make up Nigeria, justify and support domestic violence perpetrated by men as a cultural norm which confers the husband/father with the power to discipline and enforce order within his household. Such cultural powers are further supported by religious doctrines which preach that women should be submissive and obedient to their husbands and fathers. However, women have also been known to display acts of domestic violence against their children, stepchildren (including children from extended families living with them) and domestic helps whom they claim need to be disciplined against immorality and laziness. Forms of domestic violence most prevalent in Nigeria include kicking, slapping, beating, raping, and even murder.

Reasons most identified for triggering domestic violence, especially against women, include a woman refusing to have sex with her male partner, suspicion of infidelity, accusations of disrespect or disobedience, neglecting home and children, fear of career growth, and infertility. Female perpetrators have been known to use reasons like suspicion of witchcraft, accusations of flirtatious activities, the victim symbolizes a relationship/person she despises. Cases of women being violent against their men also occur when the woman suspects infidelity, is starved of funds, or feels neglected/frustrated with the relationship. Unfortunately, many of these cases go unreported because the victim does not know their rights, is afraid or dependent on their assailant, afraid of social and family reproach/backlash, does not want to break up the home, or feels the need to protect the children.

Advocates against domestic violence in Nigeria have noted that the laws of the land are ambiguous and not strong enough to stop the now-rising incidents of domestic violence. Although Nigeria is a signatory to several treaties which aim to address the rights of women and girls, there are no laws which specifically criminalizes domestic violence. Under Nigeria's penal code, a husband can correct his wife if he does not inflict grievous hurt. Persons who inflict grievous bodily harm if convicted may serve up to seven years of imprisonment. Nigeria's criminal code as applied in the southern part of the country states that the person who unlawfully and indecently assaults a woman or girl is guilty of a misdemeanor and is liable to two years imprisonment. In Nigerian northern states where the Sharia Law is observed, a husband has the right to beat his wife but may only use a small implement and should not make a physical mark on her body.

Unfortunately, customary laws based on patriarchal traditions counter these codes. In addition, when domestic violence cases are formally reported, Nigerian law enforcement bodies have been accused of taking sides with the perpetrators and doing little to nothing to protect the victims. Except in cases of murder, the perpetrator of the domestic violence often gets away with the crime.

See Also: Gender Relations (Chapter 7); Human Trafficking (Chapter 7); Kinship and In-laws (Chapter 7).

Further Reading

Canada: Immigration and Refugee Board of Canada. (2007, August 10). "Nigeria: Domestic Violence; Recourse and Protection Available to Victims of Domestic Violence (2005–2007)." https://www.refworld.org/docid/46fa536f17.html

Eboka, T. (2017). "Understanding the Practice of Girl Marriage in Northern Nigeria from the Perspective of Key Decision Makers." PhD Thesis. https://www.academia.edu/43235783/PhD_Thesis_Understanding_the_practice_of_girl_marriage_in_Northern_Nigeria_from_the_perspectives_of_key_decision_makers

DOWRY AND BRIDE-WEALTH

In many Nigerian cultures, bride-wealth is referred to as "bride-price," and it is often used interchangeably with a dowry. Dowry for cultures outside Nigeria applies to the property or items a bride brings into her marital home. Though this is a commonly accepted practice in Nigeria (especially in the northern part of the country), it is not well recognized mainly because it is more of an internal arrangement between a daughter and her mother. The bride-price, on the other hand, involves negotiation between the groom's family and that of the bride. Most of the time, the bride and groom are not part of the negotiation.

Under the Nigerian Customary Marriage Law, the term "dowry" refers to the total of all the necessary sums of fees paid by a prospective husband to his intended in-law. This payment may be in stages or a lump sum and may be for selected members of the bride's family. This payment seals the marriage, and in some cases, no discussions can be done until the full payment is made. Nevertheless, within this context, it is likened to the bride-price and not dowry as other cultures see it. In traditional Nigerian societies, the bride-price took the form of manual labor on the part of the intended groom to his in-laws. This was supported by small amounts of cash and alcoholic drinks. In Nigeria, there is no blanket amount demanded for bride-price because it differs from one locality to another. It also depends on the negotiations that are carried out by the representatives of both families.

The amount of bride-price that can be demanded was curbed in the eastern part of Nigeria by The Limitation of Dowry Law of 1956. This law regulates the quantum of bride-price in Anambra, Imo, Cross River, and Rivers states. It is an offense to pay or receive any amount more than the maximum prescribed by this law. The offense is punishable on conviction to six months imprisonment. This law nevertheless does not insist that the full bride-price is paid before marriage. Part payment is acceptable before a valid marriage can take place. The bride-price should be paid to the father of the bride. In the absence of the father, payment will be made to the male head of the family; and if this is not possible, the payment is made to the guardian of the bride. Cultural groups that do not practice the patrilineal system such as the Ijaw in the Niger Delta, the bride-price goes to the girl's maternal uncles.

Some families, especially those in urban areas and who have high educational qualifications grant a waiver of bride-price with the explanation that they are not "selling" their daughter. In some other sections as among the Kagoro of Kaduna State, bride-price is not vital for a valid marriage.

See Also: Marriage Law (Chapter 7); Traditional Weddings (Chapter 7).

Further Reading

Marriage Act of Nigeria. (1914). Nigerian Constitution.
OnlineNigeria.com. (2022). "Bride Price Payment in Nigeria." https://www.onlinenigeria.com/marriages-in-nigeria/Bride-Price/.

FAMILY PLANNING LAW

Since the late 1980s various governments of Nigeria have developed and implemented diverse plans and policies in relation to family planning. A foundational policy of note is the National Population Policy for Development (1988) which remained the major family planning policy until issues like HIV/AIDS, gender inequality, and poverty made a review necessary. Other major initiatives were the National Reproductive Health Policy (2001) and National Strategic Framework and Plan for Reproductive Health (2002–2006).

Through these programs, the Nigerian government aimed at reducing the high maternal and child morbidity by encouraging Nigerian families to discard traditional family planning methods and adopt the ideology of planning and spacing their children. The government also needed to address issues of unwanted pregnancies, abortion rates, modern contraceptive knowledge/awareness, ensuring the availability of modern contraceptives and providing counseling to guide users in their selection.

Through the Federal Ministry of Health, the free commodity policy was adopted in 2011 which made modern family planning contraceptives available and free of charge to all women. To regulate the family planning roll-out, The Reproductive Health Service Policy was initiated. This policy states that information shall be provided freely to couples and individuals who seek counseling regarding the number and spacing of their children, ensure they have access to affordable contraceptive services, and assist couples who suffer from infertility issues. Although this policy covers adolescent and unmarried individuals who are sexually active and seek contraceptive counseling; such categories of people are not allowed access to more effective controlled methods such as IUDs or injectable contraceptives but are restricted to less effective contraceptives such as condoms.

The contraceptive services made available through Family Planning Clinics include behavioral change communication, counseling, the administering of contraceptives for the prevention of pregnancies, delays in childbearing, spacing of births, and prevention of STIs, HIV, and AIDS; the management of side-effects and complications because of the contraceptives administered; as well as referrals. Modern forms of contraceptives made available include temporary (short and long term) as well as permanent methods. The Family Planning Clinics also give initial counseling and referrals to patients diagnosed with reproductive cancers (e.g., breast, cervical, ovarian, prostate, etc.).

In 2012, the Nigerian government joined other nations at the London Summit on Family Planning to develop the Nigeria Family Planning Blueprint (Scale-Up Plan) with a mandate to achieve a 36 percent increase from 15 percent in Nigeria's Contraceptive Prevalent Rate (CPR) by 2018. In July 2017, the 2012 commitment was reviewed to 27 percent Modern Contraceptive Prevalent Rate (MCPR) among Nigerian women by 2020.

In 2019, the National Health Promotion Policy was finalized, and part of the goal was to train personnel in the administration and counseling of family planning issues. The laws that cover family planning administration do not recognize junior community health extension workers, community pharmacist, community midwives, and Proprietary Patent Medicine Vendors (PPMVs). These categories of people cannot administer injectable contraceptives as they are not regarded as trained enough in the administering and disposal of hormonal contraceptives. They can only refer clients to government-approved family planning centers.

See Also: Family Roles (Chapter 7); Marriage Law (Chapter 7).

Further Reading

Federal Ministry of Health. (2020, June). *Nigeria National Family Planning Blueprint (2020–2024)*. Abuja, Nigeria.

Federal Ministry of Health, Nigeria. (2005). *National Family Planning/Reproductive Health Policy Guidelines and Standards of Practice*.

Odimegwu, C. O. (1999). "Family Planning Attitudes and Use in Nigeria: A Factor Analysis." *International Family Planning Perspectives*, 25(2): 86–91.

FAMILY ROLES

In many Nigerian communities, the major definer for role association is age and gender. Age is a biological factor that gives prominence to individuals with relative age differences. Traditionally, this worked within age sets where those from a specific age grade must give respect to those in the age set above them. In contemporary urban Nigerian societies, this has been transformed to years of experience in a particular profession or career, professional qualifications as well as biological age. Such people are often ascribed more responsibility and thus enjoy more opportunities to have access to economic and political power than others. Such privileges are also given based on the assumption that older individuals will be fair and unbiased in their judgment. They are also expected to behave in a mature manner befitting their age because they are expected to have more wisdom than the younger people or people who do not have as much knowledge and experience in their profession. Thus, they are conferred with financial, social, and spiritual responsibilities.

Within the family, the father of the home is ascribed the highest honor mainly because of his age. Most marriages consist of couples where the husband is older than the wife. Sometimes the age difference is up to ten years or more. Based on this age gap, the wife is under obligation to respect and honor her husband. Second, the husband is assigned the role of taking final decisions on behalf of the family. Choices such as place of abode, children and family welfare, social relations, and even relations within the family are chaired by the husband. These cultural expectations put pressure on men to earn more than their wives. Many households consist of men that work in the formal sector and

Attitudes toward the LGBTQI Community

Nigeria is not only conservative in matters regarding gender, marriage, and sexuality, but its deep religious values along the Christian and Islamic faiths shape how the government and citizens respond to issues of sexual orientation and gender identity. The LGBTQI community is not recognized in Nigeria, and it is a crime for anyone to display these forms of sexual orientation or gender identity in any part of the country. The Same-Sex Marriage Prohibition Act of 2013 criminalizes all forms of same-sex relationship and offenders may face up to fourteen years in prison if convicted. However, before this Act was passed, the criminalization of same-sex relationships had been enshrined in the Sharia laws in most parts of northern Nigeria as far back as the early 1900s. In the southern part of the country, though not codified, the practice was regarded as a taboo among the cultural groups that make up the region.

---

women who work in the informal sector. Thus, while men work for established corporate organizations, women are usually traders or small to medium-scale business owners, which makes the men more knowledgable about happenings in the formal sphere when compared to their female counterparts.

The role of the children in the society is one of obedience, submissiveness, and support to the adults in the home. The adults in the house are under obligation to train the children to become responsible adults. They represent the younger generation who must accept to be guided by older members of the society. They are taught to respect elders mainly because of their age, achievements, and experience which for them translate to wisdom, direction, and support. These are essential ingredients for the integration of youths in the society and for them to become functional members of the society.

See Also: Gender Relations (Chapter 7).

Further Reading

Olawoye, J., F. Omololu, Y. Aderinto, I. Adeyefa, D. Adeyemo, and B. Osotimehin. (2004). "Social Construction of Manhood in Nigeria: Implications for Male Responsibility in Reproductive Health." *African Population Studies*, 19(2). https://tspace.library.utoronto.ca/handle/1807/4108

GAY AND LESBIAN INDIVIDUALS

In Nigeria, the concept of minority sexualities where gays and lesbians are categorized is persistently denied and even considered as an offense in the northern part of Nigeria under the Sharia legal system. In many societies, homosexuality is tabooed for discussion and practice. Individuals that display such tendencies face discrimination in various aspects of life ranging from social, political, and cultural.

Religion is a major factor that serves as the basis for the hostility against sexual minorities and its practice. Being a highly religious country, this makes it difficult for such ideologies to gain ground in public and private spaces. The major religions in Nigeria namely Islam and Christianity are highly intolerant to public displays of sexuality. The religious leaders preach against premarital and adulterous sexual intercourse for heterosexual members of the society. This makes them even more intolerant to homosexuality which is regarded as immorality and a sin against the Divine. This has been backed by the introduction of the Same-Sex Marriage Prohibition Act in the National Assembly.

For decades, the harm done during the time of the missionaries concerning the rape of young boys by priests was a secret. This was until the Nigerian Nollywood film *October 1* made these acts public. In this movie, the story is told of the constant sexual molestation and rape of a young prince who, though intellectually gifted, turned out to be a monster who raped virgins in his village. This was done as a revenge against his people for allowing such an act to happen to him. He felt defenseless, dirty, and angry and he wanted his people to share in this pain by eliminating their symbol of pride—namely young female virgins.

Such narratives make the subject of sexual minorities an unfavorable subject which many are not ready to promote and encourage. Though traditional cultural practices exist in Nigeria where women are culturally allowed to marry other women, the aim of this union is not for the sake of sexual relations between the two women. Rather, the aim is for the wife to seek a male partner who is ready to forfeit the rights to his children to the female husband of his partner. The child thus serves as the foundation for a new lineage under the female husband who takes up the social responsibility of caring and training the children so produced, while also taking care of the material needs of the married wife.

See Also: Gender Relations (Chapter 7); Marriage Law (Chapter 7).

Further Reading

Increse. (2009). *Report of Survey on Sexual Diversity and Human Rights in Nigeria.* https://www.sxpolitics.org/wp-content/uploads/2009/10/report-on-sexual-diversity-and-human-rights-in-nigeria-1.pdf

GENDER RELATIONS

Many Nigerian ethnic groups are patriarchal in nature, and thus a lot of power, authority and responsibility is ascribed to the men of the society. Such male authority is very predominant in the "nuclear" form of the traditional household which was traditionally an economic entity headed by a male figure. As an economic entity, activities which attracted more income were often reserved for the male head of the family. For example, among the Igbo people of southeastern Nigeria, Yam which was not only the principal crop of the people, but also had spiritual connotations, was the preserve of men. Lesser crops such as cassava, cocoyam, and vegetables were reserved for women. Likewise, among the Yoruba people of southwestern Nigeria, the production of narrow strips of cloth which was used as money, body adornment, royalty and trade outside the Yoruba culture was produced by the men; while broader strips which served functional values such as domestic and cultural values were regarded as a female occupation.

However, the sale and use of many of the items produced by the men were the responsibility of women. Through guilds, associations, and trade groups, women built capital independence by transforming the raw products of their men into economic, social, and domestic uses. Thus, though gendered occupations were prevalent, this did not mean that gendered relations were unequal to the extent of marginalization.

Some scholars have noted however the drastic changes to gender relations brought by foreign religious philosophies as promoted by Islam and later Christianity. These religious doctrines emphasized a dominant patriarchal structure which empowered the male gender far more than the traditional structures allowed. This empowerment was further strengthened with missionary schooling and colonial workforce structures which recognized the male members of traditional households as the source through which the new economic structure should be built upon.

The governments of post-colonial Nigeria unfortunately have not been able to restructure gender relations to enable women access to political, educational, economic, and social resources to empower them. Contemporary research on the gender relations in Nigeria (especially in the southern regions) shows that many Nigerian women earn less than their men. In the northern region which witnesses an even higher inequality in terms of gender relations has resulted in girl brides. The gender inequality is driven by factors like lack of access to education and skill empowerment which drives poverty. Prominent women like Chimamanda Ngozi propose that a possible solution to the gender inequality in Nigeria is the promotion of feminism. However, other people have observed that such a call should be supported with the promotion of family-centered values that promote social equity, responsibility, and respect for both genders.

See Also: Domestic Violence (Chapter 7); Family Roles (Chapter 7).

Further Reading

Alapo, R. (2014). "Gender and Ethnicity in Nigeria: Post-Colonial Societal Constructs on Culture and Class." Presented at the New York African Studies Association (NYASA) Conference, SUNY Cortland, New York, April 3–5, 2014. Published by CUNY (City University of New York) Academic Works.

Okonkwo, A. (2009). "The Evolution of Gender in Igbo Nation and the Discourse of Cultural Imperialism." BA Thesis submitted to the School of Culture and Society, Department of International Migration and International Relations.

HUMAN TRAFFICKING

The United Nations has identified human trafficking as a crime with low risks and high profits. Trafficking in persons may be for the individual to be forced into hard labor with limited economic reward, sexual exploitation, or trafficking persons for the removal and sale of organs and body parts. In Nigeria, these are becoming critical social issues. Human trafficking is thus a process of people being recruited in their community and country of origin and transported to a destination where they are exploited for purposes of forced labor, prostitution, domestic servitude, and other forms of exploitation (Makisaka, 2009:1).

Nigeria has been identified as a country of origin, transit, and destination for human trafficking with some cases of internal trafficking. The destinations for trafficked victims include West African countries (such as Côte d'Ivoire, Mali, Benin, Equatorial Guinea, Cameroon, Gabon, and Guinea) and North African countries (Libya, Algeria, and Morocco) have been identified as popular destinations within Africa. Outside Africa are Middle Eastern countries (Saudi Arabia) and European countries (Italy, Belgium, Spain, the Netherlands, Germany, and the United Kingdom) have also been identified (Policy Paper Poverty Series, 2006).

In 2003, Nigeria passed a national law against trafficking entitled Trafficking in Persons (Prohibition) Law Enforcement and Administration Act; as well as the Child Rights Act both in 2003. Nigeria is one of the few African countries to pass such laws. These efforts were supported by economic empowerment and reintegration programs. Unfortunately, these efforts have not yielded the desired results as the issue of human trafficking in Nigeria persists.

Factors identified as encouraging the persistence of human trafficking in Nigeria include poverty, followed by the hope of Nigerians to travel abroad in search of better opportunities. Such people are vulnerable and fall victim to traffickers who take advantage of their low economic status and desperation. There are also cultural practices whereby parents send their children to relatives in the cities in the hope that such relatives will take care of their children and expose them to better opportunities. Such children end up being trafficked within Nigeria to other states to engage in domestic work, laborers on-farm plantations, or prostitution. This is particularly prevalent in big cities such as Lagos and Port Harcourt. Most of the Nigerian women trafficked to Europe are from Edo and Delta States. Those trafficked to Libya and the Middle East are from the northern parts of Nigeria, especially Kwara, Kano, Kaduna, Niger, Borno, Taraba, Nassarawa, Plateau, Kebbi, and Zamfara. (UNESCO Policy Paper Poverty Series, 2006). More recently, the South American country of Venezuela has become a destination point for the trafficking of Nigerians. Most often the Nigerian victims are women and children.

See Also: Human Rights (Chapter 3); Sex Trade (Chapter 7).

Further Reading

Makisaka, M. (2009). *Human Trafficking: A Brief Overview. Social Development Notes; No. 122*. World Bank, Washington, DC. © World Bank. https://openknowledge.worldbank.org/handle/10986/11103

UNESCO. (2006). "Human Trafficking in Nigeria: Root Causes and Recommendations." Policy Paper, 14.2 E.

KINSHIP AND IN-LAWS

Kinship consists of people related through descent or marriage. In Nigeria, there are different forms of descent systems the most common being patrilineal where people trace their descent through their father's lineage. This explains why children bear their father's name and claim their inheritance from their father's side. This form of descent is prevalent among the Yoruba and Igbos. However, there are other groups that trace their descent through their mother's line (matrilineal) or from both sides (double descent). In the matrilineal system, the wife's brother has a stronger claim to the children than the biological father does. This practice is predominant among the ethnic groups of Abia State in eastern Nigeria. While the Yakurr people of Cross River State, practice the double descent system where individuals trace their heritage from both the father's and mother's side. Immovable properties such as trees and farmland are inherited through the patrilineal descent, while movable properties such as livestock are inherited from the mother's side. There are also cases where a man may decide to choose his mother's side over that of his father's for personal reasons.

In-laws are formed from marriage. In many Nigerian cultures, marriage is not between two people but between two families. This means that both the husband and wife must respect their in-laws, the wife must respect the people from whom her husband came from; likewise, the husband must respect and honor the people from which his wife came from. Both treat their parents-in-law like their biological parents. Thus, during the traditional marriage, the son is told that he has been adopted as a son into his wife's home and the wife is told that she has been adopted as a daughter into the home of her husband's parents.

The extended family is also respected though this is usually dependent on the position among the siblings. The first male/female, for example, will command more respect from their in-law's family due to the cultural responsibility it is often associated with. The married partner is expected to support this cause as part of their responsibility. This is especially the case with taking care of younger siblings and the parents as they advance in age.

See Also: Dowry and Bride-Wealth (Chapter 7); Family Roles (Chapter 7).

Further Reading

Akanle, O. and O. Olutayo. (2011). "Kinship Construction Variability among Nigerian International Migrants: The Context of Contemporary Diaspora." *Human Affairs*, 21: 470–80. doi: https://doi.org/10.2478/s13374-011-0044-2

Aniche, A. (2017). "Dwindling Impacts of Kinship/Extended Family System among the Ndi Igbo of South Eastern Nigeria." *Online Journal of Arts, Management and Social Sciences (OJAMSS)*, 2(1): 247–52.

MARRIAGE LAW

The 1949 Marriage Act was the first marriage law enacted in Nigeria. This Act was replaced in 1970 and again in 1999. The 1970 and 1999 versions of the Marriage Act recognized three types of marriages namely: Statutory, Customary, and Islamic.

Statutory Marriage according to the 1999 Marriage Act is monogamous. For this marriage to be binding, the couple must be over twenty-one (anyone who marries a person below this age without an approved parental consent is liable to two years imprisonment), recite their vows before a licensed official, and conduct the ceremony within a government-approved venue. A Marriage Certificate must be presented to the couple to serve as a proof of the solemnization and a formal document representing their marital status. Various conditions can make marriage under this law invalid. Couples marrying under this law should not have been married before. An unmarried person who knowingly enters a marriage with someone who is already married is liable to five years imprisonment. Officials who issue certificates of marriage to persons knowing that the information provided is false is liable to five years imprisonment. Having contracted a marriage under this law, anyone who marries again without a legal divorce is liable for five years imprisonment. Persons who: prevent a marriage from taking place under the pretense that their consent is required, serve as witnesses knowing that they are not qualified to do so, or impersonate to marry another person are all liable to imprisonment for five years.

The customary (traditional) marriage considers the over 250 ethnic groups that make up the Nigerian citizenry. Laws which solemnize unions under this Act are guided by traditions and cultural practices with little intervention from federal and state laws. The decision to get married is between the members (or representatives) of the two families. Under this section, polygyny is recognized and accepted along with the payment of a bride-price.

Islamic marriages are based on the tenets of the Quran which allows a man to marry up to four wives. Under this Act, a father has the right to conclude a marriage on behalf of his children and request a bride-price. Advocates against child marriages in Nigeria believe that the ordinances of Islamic marriages have sustained the practice. Although Nigeria adopted the Africa Charter on the Rights and Welfare of the Child as a way of prohibiting the practice of girl marriages in Nigeria, the practice is still rampant especially in northern Nigeria. The 2003 Child Rights Act (CRA) stipulates that a marriage of couples below the age of eighteen years must be annulled and those that granted and consummated the marriage be liable at conviction to five years imprisonment, a fine of N500,000, or both. However, the military amendments to the 1970 Marriage Act indicate that the Nigerian government cannot interfere with Islamic and customary marriages of any state. Thus, while many state governments in Nigeria adopted the CRA as law, many northern states are yet to do so.

See Also: Court Marriages (Chapter 7); Family Planning Law (Chapter 7); Traditional Weddings (Chapter 7); Western Weddings (Chapter 7).

Further Reading

Eboka, T. (2017). "Understanding the Practice of Girl Marriage in Northern Nigeria from the Perspective of Key Decision Makers." https://www.academia.edu/43235783/PhD_Thesis_Understanding_the_practice_of_girl_marriage_in_Northern_Nigeria_from_the_perspectives_of_key_decision_makers

Nigeria Marriage Act. (1990). "Chapter 218." *Laws of the Federation of Nigeria*.

SEX TRADE

The sex trade is an offshoot of human trafficking which has been categorized as a form of modern slavery because the victims are taken using threat, force, abduction, and/or deception for exploitation (Nnadi, 2013). The sex trade is also known as sex trafficking as it is a crime against women by forcing them to engage in sexual activities under duress with limited financial and material compensation. Often the victims are bought and sold several times to work in brothels and to satisfy the sexual desires of men. There are also cases where the victim is held against her will and forced to work in brothels to pay off a debt. The sex trade, even though a crime against the human rights of the female victims, is nevertheless thriving today because the perpetrators are influential people in various countries. Added to this is the fact that many countries where this act is carried out do not have strict laws, and when such laws exist, they are not enforced. The result is that the perpetrators get away with the crime while the female victims, if they eventually escape from the grip of their captors, live with fear and the shame the experience involves.

In Nigeria, many women and young girls are trafficked for the sex trade to various parts of Europe. The women and girls are often promised good jobs, but because of their poor state, they cannot afford the airfare, visa fees, and other financial commitments that will enable them to take up these jobs. They thus agree (sometimes with the knowledge of their parents) to accept loan offers from the traffickers with an agreement to pay back from their salaries. On reaching Europe, their passports are seized, and they are forced to work in brothels and do other kinds of forced labor to pay back their "debt." The sex trade has become a profitable business for such organized syndicates, and through this trap, many innocent women and children have been trafficked off to serve as prostitutes and engage in pornography.

The Nigerian government has taken steps to stem the activities of the sex trade and human trafficking treating it as a priority criminal justice issue. In 2003 the Federal Government passed the Trafficking in Persons (Prohibition) Law (Enforcement) and Administration Act 2003 which established the National Agency for Prohibition of Trafficking in Persons and other Related Matters August 26, 2003 (NAPTIP Act) (Nnadi, 2013). The NAPTIP Act seeks not only to reduce the sex trade of Nigerian women and girls within and outside the country but also to protect them as victims. The punishment for an offender is up to fourteen years imprisonment without the option of a fine.

See Also: Human Trafficking (Chapter 7).

Further Reading

Nnadi, I. (2013). "Sex Trafficking and Women – The Nigerian Experience." *Journal of Politics and Law*, 6(3): 179–87. http://dx.doi.org/10.5539/jpl.v6n3p179

TRADITIONAL WEDDINGS

Nigerian traditional marriages symbolize the union of two families. The process is initiated through an introduction where representatives of both families meet to negotiate the wedding terms and date. These meetings build affinal relationships.

In southern Nigerian traditional marriages, a noticeable feature is *Aso-ebi* (clothes sewn from matching cloths to indicate unity, blood bond, or association) worn by family members and guests. Matching *Aso-ebi* are worn by the groom's family, bride's family, bride's and groom's friends, and co-workers. However, the outfits of the bride and groom are distinguished as theirs are more elaborate. The wedding is usually sited at the bride's compound and coordinated by a Master of Ceremony (MC) who is grounded in the marriage customs of the bride's ethnic group. Part of the common activities performed in such traditional weddings include the payment and acceptance of bride-price, presentation of gifts to the bride's immediate family members and the presentation of the bride.

In northern Nigeria, the adoption of Islam allows a man to marry more than one wife. Based on Islamic teachings, the bride-price is low as it is believed that blessings are attracted into the marriage this way. On the wedding day (known as *Fatihah*), the women prepare the new bride through an event known as *Kunshi* (like a bridal shower). The wedding reception (known as *Walimah*) brings the two families together in celebration after which the bride is taken to her husband's house with gifts, words of advice, and prayers from her family.

In Nigeria, levirate marriage practices still occur when a husband dies. The widowed wife is offered the opportunity to be "inherited" by a male member of her late husband. The aim of the levirate marriage is to ensure that the wife and children of the late husband remain in the family lineage and get continued support even though the husband is no more. This option is the prerogative of the widow, and no bride-price is exchanged.

A unique traditional marriage practice which is prevalent among some ethnic groups in southern Nigeria involves a female husband. A female husband is usually a mature woman who may or may not be married and wishes to create a new lineage for herself. The female husband marries a younger woman by paying her bride-price and selecting a suiter for her. Children born through the union, bear the name of the female husband whom they see as their father.

Among some ethnic groups in southern Nigeria, when a man dies without a son, his daughters may collectively pay the bride-price of a girl and select a male partner from their father's line to perpetuate his name. Similarly, a man who has no sons may request one of his daughters to stay within the lineage to bear sons in his name. In northern and southeastern Nigeria, some ethnic groups practice a form of marriage which involves booking a girl from the womb or betrothing their young children to seal business bonds or friendship.

See Also: Court Marriages (Chapter 7); Marriage Law (Chapter 7); Western Weddings (Chapter 7).

Further Reading

Oke, A. (2022, April). "Traditional Marriage Rites: How it's done in Hausa Tradition." *Pulse.ng*. https://www.pulse.ng/lifestyle/relationships-weddings/traditional-marriage-rites-how-its-done-in-hausa-land/1y3xsmy

Olomojobi, Y. (2016, September 24). "Marriage in Nigeria across Ages: Problems and Prospects." https://ssrn.com/abstract=2858618 or http://dx.doi.org/10.2139/ssrn.2858618

WESTERN WEDDINGS

The introduction of Western forms of marriage is also known as the white wedding. Its introduction can be traced to the colonial era which encouraged the Christian definition of marriage: one man one woman. Marriages conducted under this Act are recognized by the Nigerian legal court system. Part of the characteristics of Western forms of marriage in Nigeria are that: the couple must be old enough (above eighteen years of age), must be of opposite sexes, must be marrying voluntarily (not forced), must not be married to another person (under the same Act), and must understand that the union is for life. Unlike the marriages conducted under the customary laws, dissolving the marriage has nothing to do with bride-price or the family members. The marriage union only recognizes the couple getting married, and to some extent the witnesses to the consummation. Dissolving the marriage at the courts means going through the legal system. The courts, thus, decide payments, property division, and child custody.

Due to the association of the Marriage Act with Christianity, powers are given to heads of churches to conduct marriage ceremonies and present the couple with a marriage certificate. The churches within this right, will give certain conditions. These may include that the couple be members of the church, must conform to the statutes of the denomination, and meet all regulations as prescribed by the church elders/leaders.

However, it is customary for couples to first conduct a traditional/customary marriage before doing a Western marriage in church. This arrangement, however, sometimes causes clashes between the ethnic customs of the couple and the Christian dictates of the church. Some customary practices and customs are not acceptable by some denominations in Nigerian churches. For example, some customary laws accept that a bride be pregnant before getting married; but many churches in Nigeria (especially the Pentecostal denominations) find this unacceptable. In addition, the church expects that the couple should, prior to getting married, live apart. But some ethnic groups (especially those in the South-south regions of Nigeria) accept and even encourage cohabiting before marriage. A number of Nigerian Christians do not accept traditional acts of consummation such as the payment of bride-price, performance of libation to the ancestors, the serving of traditional alcohol (such as palm wine or gin). Such aspects of Nigerian customary marriage laws are against the doctrines of many Nigerian Christian denominations.

Sometimes, the diverse variations of Christian denominations in Nigeria may result in family members within and between the couple attending radically different churches. Although the church or white wedding should take place in the bride's family church, there are many instances where the bride insists on making her church the wedding venue and not that of her parents.

Although the Church can intervene concerning a marriage on the brink of divorce, however, they cannot make legal pronouncements. This can only be done by courts.

See Also: Court Marriages (Chapter 7); Marriage Law (Chapter 7); Traditional Weddings (Chapter 7).

Further Reading

Esiri, M. O. (2021). "Social Change and Marriage Structure in Nigeria." *International Research Journal of Management, IT and Social Sciences*, 8(3): 228–35. doi: https://doi.org/10.21744/irjmis.v8n3.1487

Olomojobi, Y. (2016, September 24). "Marriage in Nigeria across Ages: Problems and Prospects." https://ssrn.com/abstract=2858618 or doi: https://dx.doi.org/10.2139/ssrn.2858618

CHAPTER 8

Education

OVERVIEW

Formal education, as it is widely practiced today in Nigeria, is the legacy of Islamic influence, in the North, Christian missions in the South, and British colonial rule. As early as the eleventh century during the Kanem-Bornu Empire, Islamic education was established in today's northeastern parts of Nigeria. Islamic education was later expanded and enforced by Uthman dan Fodio in the nineteenth century in the northwestern region of today's Nigeria. The early Quranic schools, (a system still in operation in many parts of northern Nigeria) were the offshoot of Uthman dan Fodio's empire. They were structured to empower pupils to become versed in the Quran, *Ahadith* (sayings and practices of the Prophet), Arabic reading and writing; and to build in them character, knowledge, and divine service to God through Islam.

In the southern part of the country, Western education was embraced through the efforts of various missionary bodies. The first elementary school was established in Badagry, Lagos, by the Methodist Church Mission in 1843. This was followed by other missionaries such as the Anglican Church Missionary Society (CMS) which established CMS Grammar School in 1859 (the first secondary school in Nigeria) in Bariga, Lagos. However, the colonial government took over educational matters in 1872 by providing financial support to the established missionary schools and regulating and coordinating education in the country. Based on a protest by Lagos Muslims to the colonial government that their taxes were being used to fund missionary schools, a Muslim primary school was established in Lagos in 1899.

However, the colonial government did not encourage post-secondary education. The first set of Nigerian graduates obtained their degrees from Sierra Leone, the United Kingdom, United States, and other Western countries. They felt compelled to get university degrees outside Nigeria because they realized that to occupy high colonial positions and be relevant in the global economy, they needed a higher degree which at that time was not available in Nigeria. These graduates began to put pressure on the colonial government until Britain was forced to set up the first tertiary institution in Nigeria, namely Yaba Higher College (established in 1932 but commenced studies in 1934) in Lagos. This development, however, was not adequate especially because Nigerians had, for decades prior to this period, obtained degrees abroad to qualify as lawyers, doctors, and engineers. Again, Britain was forced to consider the demands of nationalist groups who not only demanded a university, but also an "africanized" one. Thus, in 1948, the colonial government established the University College Ibadan in affiliation to the University of London. However, this establishment was just on paper as the university was underfunded. The University College Ibadan was upgraded to a university status in 1962.

During the colonial era, the southern part of Nigeria was more Western education conscious than the northern part. With the advent of industrialization, technologies and scientific breakthroughs, many Muslim intellectuals in southwestern Nigeria realized that the Quranic schools as operated in the northern part of Nigeria could not offer them the skills needed to participate as nationalists and government administrators, nor build careers in elite professions like law, engineering, education, public administration, and medicine. To bridge this gap, the Ansar-ud-Deen Society, Anwarul Islam, and the Ahmadiyya movement were established. Based on this consciousness, Muslims in Lagos established their own school which they called Talimul Islam Ahmadiyya Primary School in 1922. This was followed by other Muslim societies that established schools which fused Islam with Western education. However, these versions of Islamic education were condemned by Quranic scholars in the north who argued that more emphasis was placed on professional skills rather than building moral characters founded on Islamic laws and ethics. Northern Nigerian Muslims were of the conviction that such an unbalanced form of Islamic education would result in a breakdown in not only Islamic ethics, but also in other aspects of the society including politics, the judiciary, and security. These contrasting views resulted in the lack of a unified and coordinated syllabus within and between Islamic schools located in the northern and southern parts of the country. To standardize and integrate Islamic educational curriculum with the Western form at the pre-tertiary level in northern Nigeria, Alhaji Sir Ahmadu Bello, the Sardauna of Sokoto, established the National Board of Arabic and Islamic Studies (NBAIS) in 1960. Through the board, a common examination and certificate called the Senior Certificate of Arabic and Islamic Studies was established to qualify northern Nigerian students for admission into higher institutions in Nigeria. In 2011, the board as a National Examination and Regulatory body was expanded to cover the whole country.

Today, through the Ministry of Education, education at all levels is regulated by the government even though ownership varies from government, individuals, and religious to secular organizations. The government (both at the federal and state levels) is bound under Section 2 of the Compulsory Free Universal Basic Education Act, to provide free, compulsory, and universal basic education for every Nigerian child of primary and junior secondary school age. The Act empowers the government to allocate 2 percent of Consolidated Revenue Fund (CRF) to be used to execute the delivery of basic education; while 70 percent of the total allocation is to be designated for the use of infrastructural development which revolves around the buildings to accommodate teachers and learners; 15 percent is to be used for instructional materials such as text books, writing materials, science based equipment, etc., while the remaining 15 percent is to be used for the remuneration of caregivers, teachers and the professional development of the teachers. The Act adds that the parents of the child should ensure that the child attends and completes primary and junior secondary school education which is considered basic education.

Nigeria operates the 6-3-3-4 system of education, a four-tier system of education starting with the kindergarten, primary, secondary, and tertiary levels. To ensure that every Nigerian child has access to basic education, the Nigerian government set up the Universal Basic Education Commission and the National Commission for Nomadic Education. In 1999, the UBE was relaunched and signed into law in 2001. This made it compulsory for each child to go through nine years of primary and secondary school basic education. However, implementation of the UBE scheme is not equally applied in all the states of the federation. Even though this basic education is meant to be non-discriminatory, free, and compulsory and a right to all Nigerian children as enshrined in the constitution, some children are left out due to various factors including financial, cultural, and religious.

Post-secondary or tertiary education is overseen by three major bodies namely the National Universities Commission, National Board for Technical Education, and the National Commission for Colleges of Education. Admission into these tertiary institutions requires credit passes in senior secondary exit examinations conducted by National Examinations Council (NECO) and the West African Examination Council (WAEC). The combination of a Senior Secondary School Certificate (SSCE) as well as the Unified Tertiary Matriculation Examination score (obtainable through a computer-based examination coordinated by the Joint Admissions and Matriculation Board) qualifies a candidate for admission into several Nigeria's tertiary institutions.

To address the issue of low literacy level in Nigeria, the federal government launched the adult literacy and special education program that targets special groups such as disabled, nomadic, and migrant children, as well as the girl-child. Although these efforts are commendable, Nigeria is still a country with one of the highest numbers of out-of-school children in the world. Educational institutions at all levels are characterized by poor teaching materials, limited qualified teachers, and dilapidated buildings.

Further Reading

Adeyemi, K. A. (2016). "The Trend of Arabic and Islamic Education in Nigeria: Progress and Prospects." *Open Journal of Modern Linguistics*, 6: 197–201. doi: https://dx.doi.org/10.4236/ojml.2016.63020

Fafunwa, B. (2018). *History of Education in Nigeria*. New York: Routledge.

Moja, T. (2000). "Nigeria Education Sector Analysis: An Analytical Synthesis of Performance and Main Issues." Report Produced for the World Bank.

NBAIS. (2022). https://nbais.com.ng/

Otomiewo, U. (2011). "The Provision of Basic Education in Nigeria. Challenges and Way Forward." Mini dissertation submitted in partial compliance with the Degree of LLM, Faculty of Law, Centre for Human Rights, University of Pretoria, South Africa.

INDIGENOUS EDUCATION SYSTEM

Before the introduction of formal colonial education in Nigeria, Quranic schools were established in the northern, predominantly Muslim, regions. These Quranic schools represented a formal educational system through which young boys were taught Arabic and themes of the Islamic tenets under the tutelage of a Quranic teacher (Mallam). Some forms of arithmetic and civic education were also incorporated into the curricula.

In Nigeria's pre-colonial southern societies, indigenous education was based on gender and age grades. A major characteristic of this form of indigenous education was the emphasis on communal learning, responsibility, and sustainability within the society. A child growing up in an economy dependent on farming is taught about various trees, plants, soils, and weather patterns, while children in an economy dependent on fishing are exposed to various types of fish, where to get materials to build boats, how to read the tides, etc. Children are taught within a communal setting, and this encourages teamwork. In addition, indigenous education included teachings about communal spiritual philosophies and their connections to the people, history, culture, and norms. Through these communal knowledge learners form an identity within the society.

Within economically specialized communities, there were fields of teachings which prepared the learner for careers in medicine, religion/spirituality, vocational trades such as blacksmithing, wood carving, cloth weaving/dying, leather work, trade in specific items such as food and animals. These specialized forms of education were in addition to the general knowledge given at the communal level and were controlled through an apprenticeship system.

Apprenticeship training was prevalent in most regions of pre-colonial Nigeria. Training began with the formal handing over of the child by the parent/guardians to the master followed by an induction ceremony to formalize the acceptance. Once accepted, the master systematically reveals the complexity of the knowledge and explains the philosophy behind the profession. Masters train their apprentices to be altruistic, respectful, and humble. The duration for apprenticeship varies depending on the profession, field of study, and the master. For example, it may take between three to six years to train as a goldsmith and five to ten years to train as a medical doctor. Among medical professionals, for example, the master trains the trainee not only in the field of the properties that constitute the herbal mixtures, but also how to administer the mixtures, and the taboos associated with the herbal mixture.

In the southern part of Nigeria, because specialized professions like medicine, smithing, and textile production are associated with deities and elemental beings, the trainees at the end of their program are initiated into their spiritual cults. Trainees swear to protect, support, and uphold the integrity of the profession and its cult. In the Muslim-dominated regions, apprentices are taught to combine their fields of specialization with Islamic verses, doctrines, and practices.

Once completed the successful student is inducted into the guild of the profession and assumes the position of an expert. It is only after the induction and graduation that graduates can practice, become a master, and train others.

See Also: Islamic Education (Chapter 8); Nomadic Schools (Chapter 8).

Further Reading

Fafunwa, B. (1974). *History of Education in Nigeria*. New York: Routledge.

ISLAMIC EDUCATION

Islamic education revolves around the Quran, the Arabic language, logic, arithmetic, and the teachings of the Prophet. It was introduced to northwestern Nigeria by traders and scholars from Mali in the fourteenth century. In the fifteenth century, Fulani scholars migrated to areas like Kano bringing with them books on Islamic theology. Kano and Katsina later became centers for Arabic and Islamic learning. By the beginning of the nineteenth century, Uthman dan Fodio had established the Sokoto Caliphate and a more formal and structured Islamic curriculum.

Today, formal Islamic education in Nigeria can be classified into *Torbiyyah* (development schools), Quranic science and memorization schools (*Madrasah li ulumul Quran wa tohfiz*), colleges (*Kulliyat*) and classical Islamic universities (*Jamiat al-Islamiyyah*). Typically, Islamic education is divided into two broad categories, namely the pre-tertiary and advanced education. By far, the most common of Islamic education is the pre-tertiary category, which starts with children as young as three years. This first stage of Islamic education is devoted to teaching pupils how to recite portions of the Quran. The teacher (Mallam) leads the pupils in the recital of short verses (*ayats*) in the Quran. The pupils repeat after the teacher in a sing-song choral recital. This kindergarten phase of learning Quranic verses by rote is the foundation of Islamic education.

The second stage of the Islamic education consists mostly of adolescents. At this stage, students are introduced to the Arabic alphabet, the consonants (*babbaku*), and the vowels (*wasulla/farfaru*). Proficiency in these key topics forms the basis for fluency in the Arabic language and in the interpretation of the Quran. At this stage, pupils are provided with their writing slate (*allo*), a stylus, and ink. The teacher recites a portion of the Quran, and the pupils are asked to write them down for inspection. The primary focus at this stage is the ability of pupils to read chapters (*surahs*) of the Quran fluently, know the consonants and vowels of Arabic, and to construct grammatically correct sentences in Arabic. In addition to this, practicals on Islamic rituals, ablution, and prayers are learned. It is usually at this stage that most students (especially girls) drop out.

The next stage is the adult stage which admits young adults to deepen their understanding of the Quran. One of the key requirements for admission into this level is a demonstration that the candidate has completed the reading of the entire Quran at least once. The curriculum at this level includes the tradition of the Prophet (referred to as *Hadith*), advanced Arabic, Islamic jurisprudence (*fiqh*), the interpretation of the Islamic law (*Ilmul usul*), poetry (*Ishiriniyat*), logic (*al-mantiq*), and algebra (*al-jabr-wal muqabala*). It is only after the mastery of these subjects that students may proceed to study a specialized field in the university.

In 1922, the Katsina Training College was officially opened as the first of its kind in northern Nigeria. The college was associated with the teaching profession which at that time was considered prestigious. Prominent northern elites and political leaders went through the college including Ahmadu Bello (the Sardauna of Sokoto and first premier of northern Nigeria), Abubakar Imam (the editor of *Gaskiya Ta fi Kwabor*), Abubakar Tafawa Belewa (first Prime Minister of Nigeria), Aminu Kano (a nationalist), Yakubu Gowon (former Military Head of State), Murtala Mohammed (former Military Head of State), Professor Iya Abubakar (former Vice-Chancellor of Ahmadu Bello University), and Shehu Shagari (first Civilian Executive President of Nigeria) to mention but a few. The college was eventually moved to Kaduna and then Zaria where it was renamed Barewa College.

See Also: Indigenous Education System (Chapter 8); Nomadic Schools (Chapter 8).

Further Reading

Abubakar, A. A. (2017). "The Present state of Muslim-Education in Northern Nigeria: Progression or Regression." *The International Journal of Academic Research in Business and Social Sciences*, 7(5): 437–44. doi: http://dx.doi.org/10.6007/IJARBSS/V7-15/2981

NATIONAL ENTRANCE EXAMINATIONS

There are several examination bodies operating in Nigeria which are certified, approved, and monitored by the Federal Government of Nigeria to award Ordinary as well as Advanced Level certificates. These include:

The National Examination Council (NECO). NECO conducts the National Common Entrance Examination (NCEE), the Basic Education Certificate Examination (BECE), and the Senior School Certificate Examinations (SSCE).

NCEE examinations are taken by pupils in the sixth year of their primary schooling. It serves as an exit examination for this level and a qualifying exam for admission into the Nigerian secondary school system. The students are assessed in Mathematics, Basic Science and Technology, English, National Values Education, Quantitative, Vocational, and Verbal Aptitude.

The BECE examination is a Junior Secondary Certificate Examination written in the third and exit year of junior secondary school. The exam qualifies a candidate for admission into Federal Unity Colleges, Armed Forces Secondary Schools and other secondary schools coordinated by the federal government. Each state and the FCT also conduct their own BECE versions for candidates seeking admission into state and private schools.

The SSCE examinations are conducted nationwide as a senior secondary school exit qualification. There are two categories of this exam namely: internal examinations for candidates within a Nigerian school system and external examinations for private candidates outside the Nigerian school system. Candidates sit for a minimum of eight subjects and a maximum of nine. English and Mathematics are compulsory while other registered subjects are based on the intended course of study. NECO examinations are Ordinary Level qualifying examinations.

The Joint Admissions and Matriculation Board is a Nigerian federal government body established to conduct and moderate entry-qualifying examinations into Nigerian tertiary institutions. The examination, known as the Unified Tertiary Matriculation Examination, is a computer-based multiple-choice examination conducted nationally in JAMB-approved centers. Four subjects (of which English is compulsory) are selected by the candidates based on the core subject areas required for admission into their chosen universities.

The National Business and Technical Examinations Board (NAPTEB) conducts Technical and Vocational Education and Training (TVET) examinations at the Ordinary (National Business Certificate—NBC and the National Technical Certificate—NTC) and Advanced Levels (Advanced National Business Certificate—ANBC, the Advanced National Certificate–ANTC and the Modular Trade Certificate—MTC) to qualify for admission into colleges of science and technology. Admission into NAPTEB is through the National Common Entrance Examinations.

The Interim Joint Matriculation Board is a Nigerian University Commission (NUC) certified nine-month Advanced Level program moderated by the Ahmadu Bello University Zaria. Candidates select three subjects related to their desired course to qualify for direct entry into their chosen tertiary institution.

The Joint Universities Preliminary Examination Board (JUPEB) is a national examination body that conducts examinations for candidates who have gone through a minimum of one year in a Nigerian university-approved foundation or diploma program and seeking direct entry into Nigerian and foreign-based partner universities. JUPEB is an Advanced Level degree awarding program which qualifies candidates for direct entry admission into tertiary institutions.

See Also: Pre-Tertiary Education (Chapter 8); Tertiary Education (Chapter 8); West African Examination Council (Chapter 8).

Further Reading

Favioye. (2020). "WAEC, NECO and NABTEB: What you need to know about Nigerian Senior School Certificate Exams (SSCE)." *Opera News*. https://ng.opera.news/ng/en/education/35850a25c17912cfc8743450d4e28ee7

Joint Universities Preliminary Examinations Board. (2022). https://jupeb.edu.ng/

NABTEB. (2021). https://nabteb.gov.ng/

National Examinations Council. (2017). http://www.mynecoexams.com/index.html

World Bank Group. (2015). "Governance and Finance Analysis of the Basic Education Sector in Nigeria." Report No. ACS14245.

The Great Educational Divide

Education remains a paradox in the country as Nigerians are regarded as one of the most educated people in the world and yet have the highest number of out-of-school children in the world. The great divide between southern and northern Nigeria in terms of access to education is starkest of any country in the world. Out of the estimated number of twenty million out-of-school children, more than 80 percent are in the North. The efforts of government to reduce this staggering number by setting up nomadic schools and encouraging parents to allow their girl-children to attend schools have not been successful. The practice of the *Almajiri* system, the kidnapping of the Chibok girls and the mayhem associated with the Boko Haram terrorist group in the past ten years have further exacerbated the problem with no strategic intervention from the northern governors to solve the problem in sight.

NOMADIC SCHOOLS

In Nigeria formal education is generally provided by the federal and state governments as well as the private sector. However, due to the economic lifestyle of some ethnic groups that forces them to move from place-to-place formal conventional education is not practicable. The prominent nomadic groups in Nigeria are found in the northern region namely the Fulani, Shuwa, Buduma, Kwayam, Badawi, and in the South, the Ijaw and Ilaje groups found mainly in Delta, Rivers, Cross River, Akwa Ibom, and Ondo states. The first five groups are cattle herders while the last two groups are fishers. Because their economic activities do not encourage a sedentary lifestyle, they must move from place to place in search of fodder for their cattle and for fishing activities as dictated by the seasonal migration of fish species.

For an inclusive education and to cater for their unique lifestyle, the Nigerian federal government recognized the need to provide special education to these nomads (numbering over nine million) by establishing the National Commission for Nomadic Education via Decree 41 of 1989. Nomadic education refers to the formal schooling that is provided for nomadic itinerant populations in Nigeria. Together with the state and local governments of the affected states, the Commission is responsible for the provision of comparable education to children of nomadic populations using creative ideas to reach them. Depending on the state and the form of economic activity associated with each group, the Commission sets up on-site schools, schools with alternative intake, shift system schools, and the Islamiyya schools.

During the 1995/1996 school session, the Commission established 890 nomadic schools in 296 local government areas across the country. At the commencement of the school year, 88,871 pupils were registered in all the schools with 62 percent boys and 38 percent girls and a total number of 2,561 teachers. By 1999, the total number of enrolled children of cattle herders had increased to an impressive 12,517, while among migrant fishermen, the total number stood at 40,826 with a total number of teachers at 847.

The curricula of nomadic schools are not different from those used in conventional schools, what is different is the mode of delivery, which is characterized by high mobility. Despite these impressive efforts by the government, nomadic schools still face challenges, just like the conventional schools. First, the enrolment of pupils is still very low compared to the 3.1 million school-age children that need to be educated. Second, some of the enrolled students do not complete their program, such an attrition rate is more common among female students who are sometimes encouraged to get married rather than complete their education. Third, is the ability of the government to attract and retain qualified teachers who are willing to sacrifice part of their time to teach these special groups of students. Experts in nomadic education have made different perceptive suggestions on how to improve the quality of the education provided as well as how to improve enrolment and reduce drop-out rates.

See Also: Indigenous Education System (Chapter 8).

Further Reading

National Commission for Nomadic Education. (2017). "NCNE Brochure." https://nbais.com.ng/

PRE-TERTIARY EDUCATION

Nigerian pre-tertiary education began through the efforts of missionaries. However, the regions soon took over beginning with Awolowo's Universal Primary Education (UPE) program in 1955, followed by the eastern region and Lagos in 1957. Today, through the Universal Basic Education program, federal and state-owned schools are highly subsidized.

Pre-tertiary education in Nigeria begins with pre-school/primary education which is made up of nursery and kindergarten classes. Children are usually between the ages of three and five. And are taught numbers, letters, colors, and writing through games, music, videos, and art. English is the primary language of instruction even though the National Policy on Education prescribes children at this stage to be taught in the language of their immediate environment or mother tongue. In Nigeria, most preschools are privately owned by religious bodies or individuals. Unfortunately, many are unregistered, and thus limited monitoring is done. Admission documents include birth certificates as well as immunization cards.

Primary education in Nigeria begins around the age of six. At this stage, the major focus is reading, writing, and Mathematics. Supporting subjects include Nigerian languages, French, English, Elementary Science, Environmental Education, Physical and Health Education, Religious Knowledge, Agriculture/Home Economics, Social Studies, Civil Education, Arts and Crafts. At the primary level, the class teacher is expected to teach all the subjects offered irrespective of his or her subject training. Most primary school teachers at this level have the Nigeria Certificate in Education (NCE) which is the minimum educational requirement. However, issues such as lack of appropriate resources for teaching and learning still plague this phase.

The secondary or the post-primary phase consists of three years at the junior secondary and three years at the senior secondary level. Pupils are usually between the ages of eleven and thirteen when they begin this phase. Nigeria's Universal Basic Education covers the first nine years of formal education (consisting of six years in primary and three years at junior secondary). Thus, students enrolled in public schools enjoy government subsidies unlike the private schools which can be quite pricey. At the junior secondary level, students are exposed to pre-vocational and academic subjects. They are expected to offer a minimum of ten and a maximum of thirteen subjects. Qualifying national and state examinations are done to enable students to move from the junior secondary to either senior secondary schools, vocational training centers, or an apprenticeship program. However, most parents opt for the senior secondary curriculum in the belief that it promises more career and financial prospects. This stereotype changed slightly when the federal government upgraded technical vocational colleges to Science Technical Colleges.

At the senior secondary level, the federal government-owned unity schools are the optimal in terms of funding and facilities. However, several Christian-, community-, and individual-based secondary schools are striving to meet their standards, although parents pay an extremely high price for it. At the senior secondary level, students take a combination of core academic, trade and vocational subjects. To exit the senior secondary and vocational centers, students must pass national qualifying examinations.

See Also: National Entrance Examinations (Chapter 8); Tertiary Education (Chapter 8).

Further Reading

Nwangwu, R., A. Fagbulu, F. Aderogba, O. Olapeju, R. Yusufu, and K. Kalu. (2005). *Nigeria Education Sector Diagnosis (A condensed version): A Framework for Re-engineering the Education Sector*, edited by P. A. I. Obanya. Education Sector Analysis Unit, Federal Ministry of Education.

PRIVATE UNIVERSITIES

Private universities in Nigeria are wholly owned by private individuals, organizations, or non-governmental bodies and do not receive any subvention or subsidies from either federal or state governments. Private universities are for-profit establishments have been established to fill the gap of Nigeria's growing population and their high demand for tertiary education. Private universities in Nigeria date back to 1999. Prior to this time, tertiary education was the exclusive prerogative and responsibility of the government.

In 1999, the federal government through the National Universities Commission (NUC) granted licenses to the first set of private universities namely, Igbinedion University, Babcock University, and Madonna University. These pioneering private universities paved the way for other private individuals and organizations to establish universities in the country. By the end of 2022, Nigeria would have 111 private universities, 76 private polytechnics, and 17 private colleges of health in operation making the ratio of public to private-owned tertiary institutions almost equal. The drive for private universities in Nigeria has been spurred by the great emphasis Nigerians place on paper qualifications and university education; as well as the challenges the Nigerian government is facing with dwindling income to fund university education.

However, the prohibitive cost of maintaining quality education by attracting and retaining qualified and competent academics as well as equipping libraries, laboratories, and buildings, has proved for some a heavy investment to sustain. Private universities are run as a business venture, which means they are usually not affordable for everyone who desires a university education. This can be a limiting factor as all private universities in Nigeria are highly dependent on student tuition and other supplementary fees. Unfortunately, funds acquired through these channels are often not enough to offer specialized courses such as medicine, agriculture, information communication and technology (ICT) while applied and pure research are almost non-existent in Nigerian private universities.

Although private university ownership has become very profitable some are not well managed and thus run the risk of losing their operational licenses. The Nigerian Universities Commission (NUC) has over the years either withdrawn or refused to accredit some private university's academic programs due to their inability to meet required standards in terms of operation and curriculum delivery. Unfortunately, due to a poor monitoring system, and a high demand for university education some of these unlicensed universities still operate at the detriment of students who find out after graduation that their certificate is not recognized by the government.

Despite these problems, private universities bridge a big gap. As long as public universities are underfunded leading to incessant strike actions by staff and students, private universities will continue to thrive. They also seem to have a better management structure which ensures that there are no disruptions in the school calendar. Private universities play an important role in supplying the much-needed manpower Nigeria needs and thus they will continue to appeal to prospective students. Based on these factors, it is anticipated that more universities will be established in the future.

See Also: Public Universities (Chapter 8); Tertiary Education (Chapter 8).

Further Reading

Ojo, J. (2022, August 03). "Unwise Proliferation of Tertiary Institutions in Nigeria." *Punch Nigeria Limited*. https://punchng.com/unwise-proliferation-of-tertiary-institutions-in-nigeria/

Okeke, C. (2022, May). "Private Universities Now 111, As FG Issues 12 New Licences." *Daily Trust*. https://dailytrust.com/private-universities-now-111-as-fg-issues-12-new-licences

Musa, A., D. Gregory, and I. Abdulani. (2022). "Higher Education in Nigeria: Private Universities' Challenges and Coping Strategies." *Asian Research Journal of Current Science*, 4(1): 279–86.

PUBLIC UNIVERSITIES

University education in Nigeria dates to colonial times when the British colonial government established the University College Ibadan in 1948, as a campus of University of London. At Nigeria's independence in 1960, the first indigenous university, University of Nigeria, Nsukka, was established. Two years later, three more universities were founded namely, Ahmadu Bello University, Zaria, University of Lagos, and University of Ife (now Obafemi Awolowo University) and the now-independent University of Ibadan.

By far, public universities are much bigger in size and offer more variety of courses than private universities. The availability of specialized fields such as botany, zoology, languages, petroleum engineering, geology, and archaeology among others has made public universities much more diverse in their delivery and in the production of knowledge and graduates to fill critical positions and fields toward national development. Admission into federal universities is based on merit and theoretically prospective students may be admitted into any of the federal universities irrespective of their ethnic group, religion, and state of origin. However, current practices do not suggest this.

The high demand for university education has witnessed the establishment of more universities. Until 1979, university education was the exclusive preserve of the federal government. However, the amendment of the constitution in 1979, which previously placed university education under the preserve of the federal government, opened opportunities for state governments to provide, fund, and manage university education within their respective states. The first state university, Rivers State University of Science and Technology, was promptly established in that same year. Subsequently, other state governments followed with the founding of Ogun State University (now Olabisi Onabanjo University) in 1982 and the Lagos State University in 1983. In all the universities in Nigeria, both federal and state universities (public universities) account for the bulk of Nigeria's labor force.

Starting from 1986 when the Federal Military Government accepted the International Monetary Fund (IMF) loan with its attached stringent conditions and accompanying Structural Adjustment Programme (SAP), the government has witnessed significant dwindling in terms of funding the maintenance, development, and sustenance of universities. Major results for this financial problem are incessant strike actions by university academic and administrative staff unions protesting the neglect of universities' infrastructure and the non-payment of staff allowances and in some cases (especially with state universities) salaries. The year 2022 witnessed a prolonged strike action by the Academic Staff Union of Universities (ASUU) which meant university students were at home most of the year. Little wonder why there was heavy criticism of the federal government when members of the Nigerian Senate and House of Assembly proposed over fifty new federal universities, colleges of education, agriculture, health, technology and forestry and polytechnics to be established. Critics associated these calls for proliferation as political campaigns and not for national development.

Unfortunately, the poor state of Nigeria's public universities has led to the mass exodus of highly qualified lecturers to universities abroad, leading to a gross shortage of lecturers in most of Nigeria's public universities.

See Also: Private Universities (Chapter 8); Tertiary Education (Chapter 8).

Further Reading

Aloy, E. and S. Sule (2012). "Sixty-Five Years of University Education in Nigeria: Some Key Cross Cutting Issues." In N. Popov, C. Wolhuter, B. Leutwyler, G. Hilton, J. Ogunleye, and P. A. Almeida (eds.), *Education Provision to Everyone: Comparing Perspectives from Around the World*, 257–64. Sofia, Bulgaria: Bulgarian Comparative Education Society.

Babatola, J. and M. Babatola. (2020). "Structural Analysis and Policy Framework of Nigeria's Tertiary Education (1947–2020)." https://www.researchgate.net/publication/339593611 _Structural_Analysis_and_Policy_Framework_of_Nigeria's_Tertiary_Education_1947-2020

Lukman, O. O. (2018). "Historical Analysis of the Management of Public Universities in Nigeria." *Research & Reviews: Journal of Social Sciences*, 4(2): 264–7.

Ojo, J. (2022, August 03). "Unwise Proliferation of Tertiary Institutions in Nigeria." *Punch Nigeria Limited*. https://punchng.com/unwise-proliferation-of-tertiary-institutions-in-nigeria/

The Guardian. (2022). "2022 UTME: 1.4m Candidates' so far sat for Examination, Results Out Soon – JAMB." *Guardian News*. https://guardian.ng/news/2022-utme-1-4m-candidates-so-far-sat-for-examination-results-out-soon-jamb/

TERTIARY EDUCATION

Tertiary or higher education in Nigeria is a post-secondary qualification offered by universities, open distance learning centers, polytechnics, monotechnics, colleges of health science and technology, innovation, vocational and specialized enterprise institutions, and colleges of education. Currently, Nigeria has: 49 federal, 59 state, and 111 private universities; seventeen open distance learning centers; forty federal, forty-nine state, and seventy-six privately owned polytechnics; thirty-six monotechnics, seventy federal and state-owned as well as seventeen private colleges of health science and technology; 173 privately owned innovation enterprise institutions; seventy-nine vocational enterprise institutions, fifty-three specialized enterprise institutions; 123 technical colleges; and 219 colleges of education.

The first higher institutions established in Nigeria were technical schools built on the British colonial administration's need to address the shortage of technical and vocational skills. Based on this, the Yaba, Kaduna, Ibadan, Auchi, and Enugu Technical Colleges were established between 1901 and 1938. Later, these technical colleges were upgraded to polytechnics with the first being Yaba College of Technology in 1963. After independence, more polytechnics were established to provide instructional training in applied technology, sciences, commerce, and management through a blend of theory and practice. Monotechnics unlike polytechnics are single subject higher institutions that offer specialized technical programs in disciplines such as surveying, petroleum, mining, agriculture, forestry, maritime, metallurgy, and leatherwork. Polytechnics and monotechnic operate a two-tier structure of a National Diploma (OND) and a Higher National Diploma (HND). Between the OND and HND is a one-year industrial experience which serves as a prerequisite for HND admission.

Polytechnics, monotechnics, colleges of health science and technology, specialized, innovation, and vocational enterprise institutions as well as technical colleges are all under the National Board for Technical Education. Nigerian Colleges of Health Technology were established to train Public Health Care workers to meet the healthcare needs of Nigerians (especially at the grassroots level). They run certificate, OND as well as HND programs in lab technology, health extension work, health education, environmental health technology, paramedic, dental surgery technician, public health nursing, radiography technician, and traditional medicine.

Also to be noted under the healthcare line is the career in nursing which is coordinated and regulated by the Nursing and Midwifery Council of Nigeria (NMCN). This body is also responsible for the professional examinations which certify individuals to operate as nurses in Nigeria. There are two major channels through which an individual can become a nurse in Nigeria. The first is through an admission into the School of Nursing. Admission is based on five SSCE credits (English Language, Physics, Biology, Chemistry, and Mathematics) obtained from WAEC or NECO. It is a hospital-based training which takes three years to complete. On completion, a Certificate in General Nursing (license to practice as a Registered Nurse—RN) is awarded. The second channel is through the university and a bachelor's degree in nursing science is earned (entrance is based on the five credits as well as UTME scores). A university degree in Nursing is a five-year course which also includes attempting and passing the professional exam to be certified as an RN in the fourth year; and as midwives (RM) and public health nurses (RPH) in the fifth year.

The National Commission for Colleges of Education (NCCE) is a federal government body established in 1989. NCCE formulates policies regarding teacher education; and regulates, standardizes, monitors, and accredits teacher training institutions in Nigeria. Through colleges of education, the Nigerian Certificate of Education (NCE) can be obtained. This certificate represents the standard quality of teacher education in Nigeria.

Vocational Enterprise Institutes (VEIs) and Innovation Enterprise Institutions (IEIs) are special vocational centers established to train and award the National Vocational Certificate (NVC) and the National Innovative Diploma (NID), respectively. They offer specialized courses in media, telecom, computer, electronic, mechatronic, and building technologies, as well as courses in Petroleum Geo-Sciences, Cosmetology, and Beauty Therapy.

At the university level, the National Commission for Universities (NUC) regulates the public/private universities as well as open distance learning centers (see public and private university entries). Post-university qualifications for graduates who have postgraduate work-based skills as professionals at the supervisory/managerial levels and wish to gain job-specific academic qualifications can be obtained through Specialised Enterprise Institutions.

Unfortunately, many of Nigeria's tertiary institutions are grossly underfunded, with poor quality staffing, outdated, and overstretched infrastructures leading to graduates with limited skills to drive Nigeria's developmental needs.

See Also: National Entrance Examinations (Chapter 8); Private Universities (Chapter 8); Public Universities (Chapter 8).

Further Reading

National Board for Technical Education. (2022). https://net.nbte.gov.ng/
National Commission for Colleges of Education. (2021). http://www.ncceonline.edu.ng/colleges.php
National Universities Commission. (2022). https://www.nuc.edu.ng/
Otache, I. (2019). "The Dilemma of Polytechnic Education in Nigeria: The Way Forward." Paper Presented at the 5th National Conference Organized by the Academic Staff Union of Polytechnics (ASUP), Federal Polytechnic Idah, Kogi State.
Oyeleye, A. (2019). "Expert Seeks Introduction of Accreditation for Specialised Learning Institutions." *The Chronicle of Education*. https://thechronicleofeducation.net/expert-seeks-introduction-of-accreditation-for-specialised-learning-institutions/
Potokri, O. (2014). "Evaluation of Availability of Financial Resources and Manpower Development in Selected Monotechnics in Nigeria." *Industry & Higher Education*, 28(5): 361–70. http://dx.doi.org/10.5367/ihe.2014.0219
Sagbara, G. (2019). "Awareness of Vocational Innovation Enterprise Institutions among Teachers and Students in Secondary Schools in Rivers State." *Rivers State University of Education (RSUJOE)*, 22(1&2): 124–31.

WEST AFRICAN EXAMINATION COUNCIL

The West African Examination Council (WAEC) is a regional examination body that is responsible for the conduction and certification of exit examinations of secondary schools' final year students. Its primary mandate is to organize, coordinate, and conduct senior secondary schools' examinations and the issuance of certificates to candidates who attempt the examination. The Council was established in 1952 during the British colonial government in parts of West Africa to determine the examination of secondary school graduates of Anglophone West Africa, namely, Ghana, Liberia, Nigeria, Sierra Leone, and the Gambia. The certificates awarded are recognized in this region as well as internationally for admission for further studies. On average, the body conducts examinations to over three million candidates yearly and issues certificates to them for the examination they have attempted. Four major examinations are conducted under the umbrella of WAEC, these are international examinations, national examinations, examinations conducted in collaboration with other examining bodies, and examinations conducted on behalf of other examining bodies. The international examinations are conducted for all high school students in the five participating countries who are in their final year. These examinations are called the West African Senior School Certificate Examination (WASSCE). There are three major examinations conducted, which are: WASSCE for private candidates, usually held annually between January and February; the WASSCE for in-school students, commonly held between March and June every year; and the WASSCE for private candidates who might have been short of the desired credits, the examination is held between October and November, annually. This examination is also known as the General Certificate Examination (GCE). The national examinations are conducted by the national coordinating body of WAEC. Some of these examinations include the Junior Secondary School Certificate conducted in the Gambia, Ghana, and Nigeria; the Junior and Senior High Certificate Examinations for Liberia; the National Primary School and Basic Education Certificate Examination of Sierra Leone; and the Basic Education Certificate Examinations for Ghana. In collaboration with other international examination bodies, the Council also conducts professional examinations for bodies such as the City and Guilds of London Institute as well as the Royal Society for Arts of Britain. In addition to these collaborations, the Council also, on behalf of the University of London conducts the General Certification Examination and the Scholastic Aptitude Tests, and the Graduate Record Examination Testing Service for various institutions in the United States of America. Finally, the Council also conducts the Joint Admissions and Matriculation examination overseas on behalf of the Joint Admissions and Matriculations Board. Although since its inception the body has had some few scandals regarding leaked papers, overall, the Council has made significant strides toward achieving its mandate. Over the years the Council has played strategic roles in the education sector both in Nigeria and the West African region more generally in ensuring that credible examinations are conducted for students and with the certificates it issues secondary school graduates have been admitted into various tertiary institutions both within the country and internationally.

See Also: National Examinations (Chapter 8); Pre-Tertiary Education (Chapter 8).

Further Reading

WAEC Nigeria. (2020). https://www.waecnigeria.org/
World Bank Report. (2015). "Governance and Finance Analysis of the Basic Education Sector in Nigeria." World Bank Report No. ACS14245.

CHAPTER 9

Language

OVERVIEW

Language as an arbitrary vocal symbol employed by humans to communicate their thoughts, emotions, and convey information is universal, and it is what differentiates humans from other animals in the animal kingdom. Language is believed to have been developed by *Homo sapiens* (anatomically modern humans) over 50,000 years ago in Africa and later spread to other parts of the world due to human migration. Language serves as a means of identity of a group of people and the vehicle through which culture is transmitted from one generation to the next. The diversity of cultural groups in Nigeria also means that the country is multilingual with an estimated number of over five hundred languages and over one thousand dialects. Thus, the three major African language families are represented in the country. For example, Hausa, along with its various dialects is a member of the Afro-Asiatic family, while the Igbo and Yoruba languages belong to the Niger-Congo family, and Kanuri and Kanembu languages, spoken in northeastern Nigeria, belong to the Nilo-Saharan language family. The three major languages that are widely spoken in Nigeria are Hausa (with an estimated twenty-four million native speakers), Igbo (with estimated eighteen million native speakers), and Yoruba (with an estimated twenty million native speakers). Although English is the official language, most Nigerian languages are widely spoken both in the country, most especially in rural areas where various cultural settings of most peoples are still preserved. In these rural areas, local languages are the standard mode of communication in cultural performances such as songs, drama, and rituals. In performing religious and spiritual activities, it is believed by most people that using one's mother tongue conveys their deepest essence of their spiritual involvement and it is more authentic and effective than the use of English or any other foreign languages. Among the Yoruba, for example, the *Babalawo* (chief priest) is expected to consult the Ifa oracle using the Yoruba language. Although in some instances, the *Babalawo* may employ some

The Role of Language during the February 2023 Elections

The use of local languages especially the three dominant ones of Hausa, Igbo, and Yoruba during the February 2025 elections created a theater of support, jest, and division. Bola Tinubu's "Emi lo kan" speech dominated most part of the electoral campaign both for his APC party and the rival PDP and LP parties. *Emi lo kan* (a Yoruba phrase meaning "it is my turn") was used to galvanize Tinubu's Southwest political base in support of his bid to become the President of the country. The phrase was later used by the opposition parties, especially the LP, whose supporters referred to themselves as OBIdient, as a jamboree using it in slogans and songs to mock the APC candidate. English, Hausa, and Yoruba languages were also used by politicians to heat up the polity by their unguarded statements and inflammatory utterances. Various security agencies in the country, especially the Department of State Service, have called out politicians to be mindful of how their words can heat up the polity and lead to a security crisis.

---

esoteric language in their communication with the oracle, such language is, nevertheless, derived from the proto-Yoruba language. The same is true of the Igbo priest (*Dibia*) who is expected to use their mother tongue in their consultation of the oracle. This situation is however different in the northern part of the country where Islam is the prevailing and most dominant religion. The Imam, Arabic, the language of the Holy Quran, as the standard medium of prayers, homily, and divination. Although among non-Muslims, the native Hausa language is used by the *Boka* (priest) in consultation with the supernatural.

Language has served as a veritable tool in forging common alliance among cultural groups and in advancing their political aspirations in Nigeria. The *Egbe Omo Oduduwa* (Society of the descendant of Oduduwa), a sociocultural club established in 1945 by Chief Obafemi Awolowo in the United Kingdom, not only served as a platform that united Yoruba students in the UK, but it also became a platform used by Awolowo to launch his political career, who later became one of the key nationalists in the struggle for independence. Chief Obafemi Awolowo later served as the first Premier of the western region and later the Minister of Finance, Budget, and National Planning. The current Arewa Consultative Forum (a political and cultural club of northern leaders) in the northern part of the country and the *Ohanaeze Ndigbo* (a sociocultural club of the Igbo people) in the eastern part of the country have become the mouthpiece for the respective groups on matters that affect them. At these forums, it is customary that speeches and all business of the clubs are conducted in the local language, and decisions taken are codified in the tradition of the people to ensure that only authorized persons have access to such information. While language may serve as a tool for unity and advancing the course of a people who share a common ancestry, it also serves as a tool for disunity, tension, and civil strife. Classical cases in Nigeria include the bitter rivalry between the Tiv and the Idoma in the Middle Belt, and that of the Ijaw, Itshekiri, and Urhobo in Warri, Delta State. Even among cultural homogenous groups, differences in dialects may create sharp divisions between groups leading to strife and the disruption of peace in the community, such as the fracas between Yoruba groups of Ife and Modakeke in Osun State, the Igbo groups of Aguleri and Umuleri in Anambra State.

Language in Nigeria, thus, serves as a double-edged sword. Unfortunately, politicians and traditional rulers, with their chiefs, have exploited the divisionary aspect of language in the country to achieve selfish ends. However, it is not only people in positions of authority who use language negatively. Local farmers and traders have been known to discriminate against non-native speakers. For example, farm products may be sold at a higher price to a non-native speaker of a local language than to a native speaker. Among the Hausa people, for example, they are known to be flattered when southerners speak the Hausa language, which helps to facilitate business in the North. In a sense, these preferences and flattery are universal, but they are somewhat unique in Nigeria as a delicate balance that forges smooth social interactions among multilingual groups, but it is at once a potential source of combustion waiting to be ignited to consume the people.

The majority of Nigeria's indigenous languages have no written form and are, therefore, endangered according to several language scholars. Except for the three major languages of Hausa, Igbo, and Yoruba and a host of some minority languages, most indigenous languages have no documented orthographies or have been linguistically analyzed. For these reasons, Nigerian linguists and anthropologists have been calling on the federal government to allocate funds to embark on such a project to halt the endangerment of indigenous languages in the country. Most of the languages that have a written history were mostly through the support of Christian missionaries whose mission was to evangelize the people by translating the Holy Bible into the local languages. On the other hand, the Hausa language has a long history of writing dating back to the seventeenth century with the use of *ajami*, the Arabic alphabet. However, the modern Hausa orthography, called *boko*, was developed in 1930 by the British colonial government based on the Latin alphabet, which is still in use today.

As a multilingual country, Nigerians, on average, are bilingual, being fluent in their mother tongue and English. Traders who travel to other parts of the country are usually trilingual by speaking their mother tongue, English and an indigenous language, usually the dominant language used in the place they reside outside their home state. It is not uncommon therefore that southeastern traders living in Lagos state speak Igbo, Yoruba, and English fluently. The same is also true of Yoruba settlers in the northern part of the country who speak their mother tongue, Hausa, and English. Despite the various indigenous languages spoken in the country, English is still the most widely spoken in the country as most business transactions, especially in the southern part of the country, are conducted in English. For this reason, those who do not have a good command of the language tend to be limited in their business dealings. Generally, businesspeople with limited knowledge of English tend to maintain small- or medium-scale businesses. In the same vein, people with limited knowledge of English are disadvantaged when it comes to a career in politics. Similarly, the predominant use of English in Nigeria disadvantages rural dwellers where indigenous languages are predominantly spoken. Due to the high premium placed on Western education in the country, Nigerians who cannot speak standard English are mostly disregarded in public spaces which jeopardizes their chances to advance their economic and political careers. More concerning is the rapid change of the mass media and how the effect of globalization will further marginalize people with limited knowledge of English. As Western cultures and values continue to penetrate Nigerian homes through radio, television, and the internet there is every likelihood that this development will accelerate the extinction of minority languages in Nigeria and impoverish those who do not have the opportunity to learn the English language.

Further Reading

Blench, R. (2014). *An Atlas of Nigerian Languages*. Oxford: Kay Williamson Educational Foundation.

ENGLISH LANGUAGE

The English language was introduced in Nigeria in the late sixteenth century by Christian missionaries and British merchants in order to convert the locals and for commerce, respectively. The abolition of the slave trade in 1807 and the resultant return of some of the slaves to Nigeria, somewhat popularized the English language in selected towns where the freed slaves served as interpreters to the missionaries and merchants. The colonization of the country by Britain in 1884 established English as the official language of administration. The establishment of schools by the missionaries and later by the colonial administration further consolidated the place of English in the country as local languages were prohibited from being spoken in the schools. However, the spread of the language was not uniform in the country with the southern part of the country embracing the use of the language more than its acceptance in the North due to the high conversion of southerners to Christianity and the poor inroad Christianity made in the North where Islam (and the Arabic language) had been firmly rooted long before the sixteenth century. The reluctance of the North to embrace Western education also witnessed adherence to the Quranic schools which contributed to the slow pace of English penetrating northern Nigeria. Prior to 1960 when the country gained its independence, English was limited in usage even in the southern part of the country. The adoption of the language as the country's lingua franca after independence meant that English became the official medium of instruction in schools and the language of administration and commerce. Today, English has displaced most local languages and has become the standard medium of communication among scholars, politicians, businesspeople, musicians, and other entertainers, although the Hausa language is still a dominant language spoken among the locals. In most homes in urban centers, English has become the first language of children who can barely communicate in their mother tongue. This development has led language scholars, especially scholars of indigenous languages, to raise concern about the possible extinction of most indigenous languages in the next five decades. Despite this concern, parents still express preference to the English language for their children rather than their mother tongue and will prefer to enroll their children in schools that encourage the speaking of only English in the classroom. Thus, English language has become a status marker as the ability to speak the language fluently is not only a symbol of being educated and "civilized," but it also confers on the speaker wisdom and intelligence. However, while this disparity may serve as a source of tension in the society some scholars have argued that English, as a lingua franca in Nigeria is an instrument of unification of the country's diverse groups as well as a tool for national development.

See Also: Colonial Nigeria under British Rule (Chapter 2); Foreign Languages (Chapter 9); Pidgin English (Chapter 9).

Further Reading

Danladi, S. S. (2013). "Language Policy: Nigeria and the Role of English Language in the 21st Century." *European Scientific Journal*, 9(17): 1–21.

Mishina, U. L. (2019). "The Role of English in Nigerian Development." *GNOSI: An International Journal of Human Theory and Praxis*, 2(2): 57–64.

Taiwo, R. (2009). "The Functions of English in Nigeria from the Earliest Times to the Present." *English Today*, 25(2): 3–10.

FOREIGN LANGUAGES

As a destination center for non-citizens, foreign languages are commonly spoken in Nigeria, although most Nigerians do not speak the languages. Except the English language that has become the official language in Nigeria along with the three major languages of Hausa, Ibo, and Yoruba, Nigerians hardly speak foreign languages. One exception is Arabic that penetrated the country in the eighteenth century with the invasion of Uthman Dan Fodio of the Hausa states and his introduction of Arabic for Islamic scholarship. Arabic is still widely used today not for everyday interactions, but mainly for religious activities. Even though the country is surrounded by Francophone countries, French as a foreign language is not spoken widely in the country, although Nigerians who live along the Seme border as well as petty traders who criss-cross the border between Nigeria and Benin Republic are fluent in the local French language. Besides French as a foreign language in Nigeria, the major foreign languages that are spoken include Mandarin, and those of India, Pakistan, Turkey, and other local non-Nigerian languages from neighboring countries such as Niger Republic and Chad. The foreign languages that are thus spoken in Nigeria are usually not spoken by Nigerians themselves, but by non-citizens who reside in the country. Among the Chinese, Indians, and Pakistanis who have settled in the country, for example, they usually occupy a contiguous geographical space where they use their language as a vehicle to maintain their cultural heritage and define their identity. However, in their day-to-day interactions with Nigerians, English is used as the medium of interaction and for business. Generally, Nigerians are not given to learning foreign languages, besides English, probably because of the numerous languages that are indigenous to them. On the average Nigerians speak three languages—English, their mother tongue, and another indigenous language. For example, it is not uncommon for the average Igbo person to speak fluent English, Igbo, and Yoruba languages. Similarly, it is fairly common to see a Yoruba person fluent in English, Yoruba, and Hausa languages. The same is also true of those who live in the Niger Delta. They do not only speak English and the Pidgin version, but they also speak one or two local languages. However, it must be emphasized, as noted earlier, that the dominance of English as the official medium of communication is a threat to the continued existence of most indigenous languages in the country. Although attempts have been made by the federal government for Nigerians to learn a second foreign language such as French, by including it in the language curriculum of secondary schools, these attempts have not been successful. The few Nigerians who have shown interest in the language only use it to secure a job either as interpreters or as language teachers in secondary schools and universities. Thus, foreign languages in Nigeria only serve as a vehicle to maintain non-citizens' identity and to serve as an instrumental means to be employed.

See Also: English Language (Chapter 9); Local Dialects (Chapter 9); Pidgin English (Chapter 9).

Further Reading

Kwaja, I. I., S. B. Gella, and A. A. Salmana. (2017). "The Arabic and French Languages: Their Relevance to National Integration and Development in Nigeria." *International Journal of Advanced Scientific Research*, 2(1): 1–9.

HAUSA LANGUAGE

The Hausa language is one of the most widely spoken languages in Nigeria with estimated speakers of the language in the country at over twenty million. The language is also widely spoken in the West Africa subregion and places elsewhere as far away as Sudan and Eritrea. The Hausa language belongs to the Afro-Asiatic language family of the Chadic branch and is classified under the West Chadic subgroup. As one of the three languages recognized by the Nigerian constitution, Hausa is used predominantly in the northern part of the country in government establishments, commerce, media, and everyday interactions. In schools, especially at the primary level, Hausa is used as the medium of instruction, and only gives way to English as the medium of instruction at institutions of higher learning. The language is sometimes used in the House of Assembly in some of the northern states as well as in government ministries and parastatals. In transacting business, the language is predominantly used, and it is a major disadvantage if businesspersons from other parts of the country who transact business in the North cannot speak the language. Thus, the ability to speak fluent Hausa is a major asset in facilitating business deals in northern Nigeria. The Hausa language is standardized. There are several Hausa newspapers, the oldest being the *Gaskiya Ta Fi Kwabo*, which was established in 1939, and served as an important source of information to the locals during the Second World War, and later as a strategic awareness platform during the nationalist struggle in Nigeria and is today being used to sensitize northerners about political issues in the country. There are also local radio stations that broadcast in Hausa for the dissemination of information within and outside the country. Foreign radio stations such as the British Broadcasting Corporation (BBC), Voice of America, and Deutsche Welle, broadcast in the Hausa language to millions of listeners in Nigeria and other parts of West Africa and elsewhere. There is also a growing body of literature in Hausa after the first novel, *Ruwan Bagaja*, written by Abubakar Imam, was published in 1933 by the Translation Bureau of Northern Nigeria. Since then, other novels, poetry, and dramas have been published in Hausa. There are also musicians who write, compose, and sing in Hausa including famous musicians such as Dan Maraya Jos, Ali Jita, and Namenj. The North also has its version of Nollywood films (sometimes called Kannywood films) that are performed in Hausa for the entertainment of Hausa speakers.

Some of these films include the popular *Kasarmu Ce* (This is our land), *Yar Nono* (The Milkmaid), and *Mara Murya* (Voiceless). The Hausa language is becoming increasingly popular in southern Nigeria primarily because of the continuous movement of the Hausa people to the South where they do not only trade but settle in cluster areas called Hausa Quarters. With such settlements the Hausa language is predicted to grow in popularity.

See Also: Hausa/Fulani (Chapter 6); Igbo Language (Chapter 9); Local Dialects (Chapter 9); Yoruba Language (Chapter 9).

Further Reading

Olderogge, D. A. (1960). *The Origin of the Hausa Language*. Philadelphia: University of Pennsylvania Press.

Phillips, J. E. (2004). "Hausa in the Twentieth Century: An Overview." *Language in Africa*, 15: 55–84.

IGBO LANGUAGE

The Igbo language is one of Nigeria's three major languages, spoken by over fifteen million people in Nigeria, mostly in the southeastern part of the country. However, the high mobility of the Igbo people across Nigeria because of trading and other economic activities, the language is spoken in almost all parts of the country with a large number in Lagos and Kano states, the largest commercial states in the Southwest and the North, respectively. It belongs to the Niger-Congo language family of the Benue-Congo group. Around the Niger-Benue confluence, the language is believed to have been developed by a group of people around the ninth century CE who later spread across a large area of modern southeastern Nigeria. Igbo is one of Nigeria's official languages, along with Hausa and Yoruba. It is spoken in the Abia, Anambra, Ebonyi, Enugu, and Imo as well as regions of the southern Delta including Delta and Rivers states. Igbo is the predominant language of business and commerce in the five southeastern states of Abia, Anambra, Ebonyi, Enugu, and Imo. In the southern Delta region, it is used in mainstream media communication, such as radio and television to cater for the Igbo-speaking people of that state. The Igbo language has about thirty dialects including some that are not mutually intelligible, which has hampered the development of a consistent spoken and written Igbo language. Thus, standard Igbo tends to use vocabulary as well as lexis from other languages and other Igbo dialects. Normal Igbo sound inventory consists of eight vowels, thirty consonants, and two tones, based widely on evaluation. Igbo has only two types of syllables: consonant + vowel (the most common type of syllable), nasal vowel, or syllabic. No consonant clusters and no syllable-final consonants are available. Samuel Ajayi Crowther, an ex-slave, teacher, linguist, and a Yoruba man from the Southwest produced the first Igbo novel, *Isoama-Ibo: A Primer*, in 1857. Today, in an extended edition of the Latin alphabet, Igbo is printed. The vast spectrum of spoken dialects has, however, made it very difficult to agree on a standard orthography for the language. Like most African languages, the Igbo language is peppered with idioms and proverbs, and according to one of the most iconic Nigerian novelists of the Igbo extraction, Chinua Achebe, in his book, *Things Fall Apart*, noted that proverbs, among the Igbos, are the palm oil with which words are eaten. A demonstration that the art of stringing words in Igbo is not only for communication, but a reflection of one's mastery of the language and one who epitomizes wisdom in the society. Igbo as a formal language is still being taught in Nigerian schools, and as a degree qualification in the university. The Igbo language has also been well represented in Nigeria's Nollywood film industry.

See Also: Hausa Language (Chapter 9); Igbo Language (Chapter 6); Local Dialects (Chapter 9); Yoruba Language (Chapter 9).

Further Reading

Nwadike, I. U. (2002). *Igbo Language in Education: An Historical Study*. Enugu: Pacific Publishers.
Ogbalu, F. C. (1973). *Igbo Language and Culture*. Oxford: Oxford University Press.

LOCAL DIALECTS

Dialects refers to the variety of languages being spoken by groups of people, which are peculiar to them in terms of grammar, pronunciation, and vocabulary. Thus, the Yoruba language consists of several dialects such as Egba, Igun, Ilaje, Awori,Ijebu, Ijesha, among others. On the other hand, the Igbo language also has various dialects including those of Anambra, Orlu, Nsukka, Awka, Umuahia, among others. While Nigeria has about five hundred languages, there are about two thousand dialects derived from these languages making Nigeria one of the most linguistically diversified countries in the world. The region with the most diversified dialects is the Middle Belt of the country, where archaeologists, anthropologists, and linguists believe most languages in the country would have emerged, fanning out to other parts of the country and beyond. Although people who speak a variant of a language are sometimes disregarded as belonging to a minority group or considered as inferior to those who speak the dominant language, the dialect of a language defines the identity of the people and gives them a sense of a close bond in which they share a common eponymous ancestor and can trace their common heritage back to the distant past. Unfortunately, linguists have expressed concerns that due to factors such as mixed linguistic ecology due to urbanization, Western education, and the need to belong to the larger ethnic group, most Nigerian dialects are on the verge of extinction. Some scholars have gone as far as to caution that if urgent steps are not taken by the government and the people themselves, half of all Nigerian dialects will become extinct by the end of the twenty-first century. Various scholars have argued that Nigeria cannot fully develop as a nation by relying only on a foreign language such as English. While the English language has its benefits due to its global usage, linguists and anthropologists have raised serious concerns about the state of Nigerian languages and dialects. To arrest this situation, scholars have called on the federal government to redefine its language policy and embark on a language planning toward national development. Section 55 of the 1999 Constitution, besides advocating for the use of English, Hausa, Igbo, and Yoruba in conducting official business in the House of Assembly, it is completely silent on other languages and their dialects. Even the three major languages are hardly used in the Federal National House of Assembly, except in some northern states where Hausa is used periodically. Although Nigerians are proud of their heritage and display a remarkable knowledge and understanding of their culture and history, the majority seem to fall short in the most important vehicle that is used to transmit their culture from one generation to the other. If this trend of speaking only the English language is not reversed, it is almost certain that the fears of various scholars regarding the extinction of most Nigerian dialects will become a reality.

See Also: English Language (Chapter 9); Hausa Language (Chapter 9); Igbo Language (Chapter 9); Pidgin English (Chapter 9); Yoruba Language (Chapter 9).

Further Reading

Blench, R. (2014). *An Atlas of Nigerian Languages*. Oxford: Kay Williamson Educational Foundation.

Crozier, D. H. and R. Blench. (1992). *An Index of Nigerian Languages*. Dallas: Summer Institute of Linguistics.

PIDGIN ENGLISH

Pidgin English was developed in Nigeria in the seventeenth century as a contingency language by locals in the Niger Delta region of modern Nigeria to facilitate communication and trade between the early missionaries and the local traders. In modern times Pidgin English has become widespread in most parts of the country, especially in the southern part, where it is used informally in everyday interaction. Although previously regarded as the language of the non-literate, today, it is spoken not only by rural people in the villages and semi-urban centers, but also by educated Nigerians including professors, medical doctors, lawyers, and clergymen and women. Some scholars have argued that as a domesticated language in the country, rather than English or any of the three major languages, Pidgin English should be adopted as the country's lingua franca. Pidgin English is an eclectic way of appropriating words from different languages to form an intelligible unique language that facilitates communication among people of different cultural backgrounds who speak mutually unintelligible languages. It is not surprising, therefore, that in areas such as the Niger Delta with diverse cultures and languages without a dominant language would develop the Pidgin English. In the major states of the Niger Delta, which include, Edo, Delta, Rivers, Cross River, Bayelsa, and Akwa Ibom, Pidgin English serves as the most dominant language spoken both by the old and the young as well as to non-indigenes who reside in those states. To standardize the language, some scholars have attempted to associate it with the basic characteristics regarding its grammar, form, syntax, and morphology. However, these efforts have not yielded the desired results, so Pidgin is still mostly regarded as an informal medium of communication in Nigeria. Despite this limitation, Pidgin English is used in formal platforms such as television, radio, campaigns, among others. For example, the Delta State Broadcasting Service, relays some of its news in Pidgin English as its radio station. The British Broadcasting Service also does the same. To raise awareness and positively change negative behaviors and attitudes, the federal government, through the National Orientation Agency, relies more on using

Pidgin English in relaying its message to Nigerians targeting the elderly and rural people. Campaigns against smoking, risky sexual behavior, and child immunization, have all been very successful throughout the years as the government uses both indigenous languages and Pidgin English to drive home its messages. Pidgin English is also used in plays, drama, and music, which tends to resonate with the people in general. Fela Anikulapo Kuti is the most popular musician who used Pidgin in his songs to critique social ills in the society including corruption, oppression, and brutality. Over the years other musicians have also been successful in deploying Pidgin English in their art.

See Also: English Language (Chapter 9); Hausa Language (Chapter 9); Igbo Language (Chapter 9); Local Dialects (Chapter 9); Yoruba Language (Chapter 9).

Further Reading

Agheyisi, R. N. (1988). "The Standardization of Nigerian Pidgin English." *English World-Wide*, 9(2): 227–41.

Faraclas, N. (1996). *Nigerian Pidgin*. London: Routledge.

YORUBA LANGUAGE

The Yoruba language is one of the three major languages in Nigeria with an estimated speakers of eighteen million who occupy the southwestern and North-central parts of the country. However, because of trade and other socioeconomic activities a sizable number of them live in other parts of the country. Because Lagos State is in the Southwest and occupied by many Yoruba groups as well as other cultural groups from other parts of the country, Yoruba is widely spoken in the state both by native speakers and non-native speakers who have acquired the language as their second language. Although widely spoken at functions and other platforms, English is still the major language of communication in formal establishments such as the state House of Assembly and in classrooms. Business transactions are predominantly facilitated in English. The Yoruba language belongs to the Niger-Congo family and is classified under the Volta-Niger branch, and like some of the languages under this branch, Yoruba is a highly tonal language with three level tones. Like most other Nigerian languages, Yoruba has its varieties or dialects, and these are formally classified according to their regions, that is, Southeast, Southwest, Central, Northeast, and Northwest. Dialects in the Southeast include Ilaje, Owo, Ijebu, and Remo, while in the Southwest some of the dialects Awori, Ife, Idasha, and Ipokia. The central Yoruba dialects include Akoko, Ekiti, Igbomina, Akure, and Ijesha. Other dialects of the Yoruba language are Ibadan, Egba, Oyo, Eko in the Northwest, and in the Northeast are dialects such as Ijumu, Yagba, and Abunu, among others. Yoruba is a standardized language with the seminal work of Bishop Samuel Ajayi Crowther, a freed slave of the Yoruba tribe, who translated the Holy Bible from English to Yoruba in 1884, which led to the adoption of the Oyo Yoruba as a standardized language with a formal orthography that is still in use. Yoruba language is thus well developed with a substantial body of literature including books, newspapers, and dictionaries. The first indigenous newspaper in Nigeria, and indeed in Africa, *Iwe Iroyin Fun Awon Ara Egba ati Yoruba* (Iwe Iroyin, for short) was established in 1859, and it represented the intellectual and literacy of the Yoruba people at that time. Subsequent development especially in the print and media industry has seen tremendous progress made in the Southwest especially with the establishment of the first television station, Western Nigerian Television on January 1, 1959, in the then western region. The Yoruba language still plays important roles today in Nigeria, and especially in the Southwest where dramas and plays are staged in theaters using the language. It is also used as a medium of instruction in primary schools in rural communities and as a degree qualification offered in the university. The language is rich in idioms, proverbs, and allegories, depicting the philosophy and spirituality of the people who own the language. With such development and usage, the Yoruba language, unlike Nigerian dialects, is expanding and still performs important religious, spiritual, and other cultural functions in the country.

See Also: Hausa Language (Chapter 9); Igbo Language (Chapter 9); Local Dialects (Chapter 9); Pidgin English (Chapter 9); Yoruba Language (Chapter 6).

Further Reading

Akintoye, S. A. (2021). *A History of the Yoruba People*. Dakar: Amalion Publishing.
Fafunwa, B. A. (1974). *History of Education in Nigeria*. London: Longman.
Lawore, O. (2004). *Cultural Ethos of the Yoruba*. Ibadan: Ibadan University Press.

CHAPTER 10

Etiquette

OVERVIEW

Standard social and cultural etiquettes are widespread and varied in Nigeria primarily because of the diverse cultural groups that make up the country. In some areas such as the northern part of the country where cultural practices are heavily fused with Islamic laws and code of conduct, there are strict etiquette rules that should be observed in contrast to the South, where etiquette rules are somewhat relaxed and need not be strictly adhered to by the people or visitors especially in routine everyday interaction. In general, however, people from different ethnic and cultural groups tend to be polite and respectful of other ethnic groups. One of the most important things that cuts across all cultural groups in Nigeria is the need to show respect to others especially the elderly, either male or female. Most cultures in Nigeria have high regard for their elders and people usually frown at any form of disregard or disrespect toward them. Respect for the elders is a sign of good manners and a demonstration of the respect of the total culture of the people as the elders are regarded as the embodiment and custodian of the culture of the people. The second thing to be aware of in almost all the cultural groups in the country is greeting and showing genuine interest in the general welfare of those we interact with in the community. Failure to greet or engaging in brisk greeting is usually regarded as being rude and uncaring. Thus, Nigerians engage in an elaborate and sometimes ritualistic form of greeting especially among the Yoruba in the Southwest and the Hausa of northern Nigeria. Various cultures have different ways of greeting. Among the Yorubas, for example, the common way to show deference to an elderly person is for the young man to prostrate or bow his head. It is routinely expected that the son-in-law prostrates when greeting his parents-in-law. However, this form of greeting may be substituted with a slight bow of the head if the young man and his in-laws live in the city. Young women, on the other hand, are to greet their parents-in-law and other elderly people by kneeling with both knees on the ground. But, like the young man, if the lady and parents live in the city, she may greet her in-laws by bending her knees as a sign of respect. In doing

The Influence of Foreign Cultures

Nigerians are generally predisposed to new ideas and ways of life, even at the detriment of their own culture. For this reason, some of the core cultural patterns are becoming relaxed. As Nigerians travel abroad, they come back home with borrowed cultures that they display with some air of superiority. It is also for this reason that most Nigerians who travel abroad tend to speak only the English language and display foreign cultural traits that clash with traditional ways. The result is an increasing acculturation of indigenous and foreign cultures, especially in most urban centers in the country. Although the elders continue to express concern about this trend it goes on unabated. While some scholars have considered the phenomenon as inevitable due to the dynamic nature of culture and the force of globalization, others have called for a determined efforts by the government and the people to preserve their cultural identities against the onslaught of Westernization.

---

so, the younger person is not expected to walk away while greeting. As a rule, it is regarded as rude for the young man or woman to stretch their hands for a handshake with an elderly person. The same is true in other tribes although with slight variation and expectation. For example, in the Niger Delta region as well as among the Igbos, an elderly person may shake the hands of a younger person, but this gesture must be initiated by the older person. Among the Igbos, a chief or a titled person (signified by the wearing of a red cap) is given a special greeting. The young woman must greet by kneeling or slightly bending her knees while the young man must initiate the greeting by drawing the attention of the older person. However, among the O'kun Yoruba of Kogi State greetings among peers or between the young and the elderly may be greatly prolonged. When people of the same age group meet along the road, it is customary for both parties to squat for a considerable period while greeting. Among the Hausa of the northern part of the country, men also greet by squatting and flexing the right hand while exchanging pleasantries by asking after one's health, family, work, and other niceties. It is considered rude to engage in direct eye contact with an older person or someone of a higher social status and for the younger person to first ask after the health of the older person. It is also considered offensive and forward for the younger person to ask the older one how they are doing. It is expected that the older person asks first after the younger person's health, that of their parents, and other niceties before the younger person may reciprocate.

With regards to appointments, Nigerians, generally, are relaxed with time and punctuality. When a meeting is fixed it is customary for the younger invitees or those who occupy a lower social status to get to the venue first and wait for the arrival of the older ones or the "big men and women." This trend is what is referred to as "Nigerian time." Even though most Nigerians, especially those with a Western orientation, tend to condemn the practice, it is, nevertheless, widespread, especially among politicians, but less so among business associates. Invitations to gatherings such as birthday parties, a lunch, or a book launch are usually not responded to by indicating whether the invitation will be honored or not. Invited guests will show up without any prior notification or may not honor the invitation at all but will only apologize for their inability to attend the function several days after the event.

Attendance of guests to functions is not very strict and for this reason, hosts of events, as a rule, must make provision both for the invited and uninvited guests. It is characteristic of Nigerians when invited to an event to also take along with them one or two other persons so that an event that is planned for fifty guests may end up with a hundred or even 150 guests. If guests at the event are not satisfactorily catered for, the event is considered unsuccessful. At formal occasions, Nigerians tend to put on stylish clothes. Nigerians are very trendy with their dressing, and they are fashionable with appreciation for both Western and local clothes and designs. As a rule, Nigerians prefer their traditional attires when attending a traditional marriage ceremony, while at religious weddings the guests may wear either Western clothes such as suits or traditional attire, but the latter is preferred and highly regarded. Nigerians are loud and boisterous in their greetings and in their general conversations in public places. Among peers, the use of slang words, profanity, especially among the lower class is not uncommon. When discussing, they use their hands a great deal and gesticulate for emphasis while they use other non-verbal cues for communication. Respect for "private space" is alien to the average Nigerian as conversations take the form of slapping one another on the back, holding of hands, and jabbing. While this form of interaction is normal among men, there is a restriction to this type of behavior between men and women, especially in the northern part of the country, where there are strict codes of conduct and restrictions between men and women. While it is permitted for men and women to shake hands in the South this form of greeting is not permitted in the North except among family members, but even such filial "intimacy" may not be displayed in public.

Unlike Western cultures, it is not a cultural or social practice for the man to open the door for a woman nor is it expected for the woman to enter a house before the man. In practice, the reverse is the case—men are expected to proceed into a house before a woman while the woman is to give deference to the man except if the woman is older than the man. While privacy may be maintained, the average Nigerian is not offended when asked of their health, children, and work. In fact, it is expected. When planning a visit, it is not necessary to inform your guest of your intention although one may do so for assurance that the person will be at home during the visit. Nigerians welcome their visitors at any time even without being informed beforehand except when the visitor is coming from another town, city, or state. As a rule, such visitors are expected to bring along some snacks for the children in the home. The standard expected gifts include bread, biscuits, or other local snacks. If the visitor is coming from a relatively far distance, say from the North to the South and will likely spend a considerable number of days or weeks with the hosts, the expected gifts include foodstuffs such as tubers of yams, smoked fish or meat, onions, or tomatoes. For this reason, it is not uncommon to see Nigerians with large and multiple boxes and food items when traveling between states.

Further Reading

Commisceo Global. (2022). "Nigeria – Culture, Etiquette and Business Practices." https://www.commisceo-global.com/resources/country-guides/nigeria-guide

Udosen, N. (2018). *Fundamental Etiquettes for Young Nigerians: A Guide to Good Manners and Responsible Citizenship*. Kaduna: Tanar Educational Consultancy.

BUSINESS ENTERTAINMENT

Business entertainment in Nigeria is usually formal but relaxed. Business associates will invite potential business partners to lunch or dinner to discuss matters relating to contracts, partnerships, or consultancy of various financial magnitude. Such business entertainment is not lavish to avoid sending the wrong message of advanced fee fraud or other bogus business practices designed to hoodwink business associates. As a rule, Nigerians are very wary of unusual flatteries and opulent spending to impress business associates. Extravagant and lavish entertainment is a signal to the average Nigerian businessperson to become suspicious and proceed with the business transaction more cautiously. To avoid such wrong signals, the entertainment is kept at an acceptable standard but with a touch of class and professionalism. Corporate gifts may sometimes be distributed to attendees while exchange of complimentary cards is expected. Business entertainment may take place in the premises of the organization, or it may take place in a neutral venue such as an event center, a hotel, or a resort. Attendance is strictly by invitation as unexpected guests will send the wrong signal to the host and make them uncomfortable. Dressing will normally be formal, but a three-piece suit will be regarded as too formal, and this may hinder the free flow of conversation. Formal, well-cut trousers and a shirt with a knotted tie is appropriate. Traditional kaftan or the traditional *agbada*, especially in the northern part of the country are equally acceptable. Ladies may wear a "respectable" dress that does not reveal too much flesh either at the upper part of the arm or the thighs. Dress that reveals the cleavage will also draw disapproval and may cause the host to be uncomfortable. The dress code is stricter in the northern part of the country where the majority are Muslims and some of the states enforce the sharia (the Islamic code of conduct). Ladies may not put on the hijab (veil), but they must be properly dressed by covering most parts of their body. This is standard practice even if the guest is not a Muslim. Violation of this dress code may lead to a disruption of the entertainment as other guests will be offended and broad derogatory remarks may be made by disapproving male guests and this action may escalate to direct verbal abuse and insults. The foods served at business entertainment are usually continental dishes to cater for international associates. These foods are well prepared by local chefs. However, the foods may be slightly hot for some guests as Nigerians like to spice their foods with chilli and hot curry. In some instances, pepper soup, a locally spiced soup, may be served by the side to cater for the Nigerian guests who may want to get their palate spiced. Drinks are customarily served with food. Drinks that may be displayed on the table include water, soft drinks (such as the various flavored malt drinks), and wine. It is not customary to serve beer at such a function and in the North alcoholic wine may not be served due to the strict sharia law that prevails in that region. At the table, guests may not eat or pass items with their left hand. This practice is frowned upon as the left hand is reserved for engaging in one's private business and, therefore, should not be used to pass items to others, especially at the table. During the entertainment, it is customary to engage in small talk or involve in discussing more serious business deals. It is usually considered rude to leave immediately after eating. It is expected that some form of discussion should follow afterward before finally bidding the host farewell.

See Also: Entertainment and Gift-Giving (Chapter 10).

Further Reading

Commisceo Global Consulting Ltd. (2020). "Nigeria-Language, Culture, Customs, and Etiquette." https://commisceo-global.com/resources/country-guides/nigeria-guide

Expat Arrivals. (2023). "Doing Business in Nigeria." https://www.expatarrivals.com/africa/nigeria/doing-business-nigeria

COURTESY AND RESPECT

Courtesy and respect are two important cultural values that are cherished among Nigerians and such values are inculcated in children at a very young age. Courtesy and respect constitute the hallmark of a culturally grounded person and a demonstration of a well-trained child. Parents are careful to train their children to be respectful because their children are the barometer with which they are assessed and judged by the society. A young man without respect will not only have difficulties getting along with his peers but will bring shame to his family members, especially his biological parents. For this reason, young men and women are under cultural obligation to show a considerable amount of respect to others in the society, especially to those older than themselves. The saying among the Yoruba that the parents are to blame for the child's ill-manners encapsulates the relationship between a disrespectful child and the disapproval of the parents from society. Courtesy and respect are not reserved to those who reside in rural areas, they are expected in the cities as well and in all facets of the society including the workplace, schools, and religious organizations. Courtesy may take different forms, from the expression of appreciation for what has been done to someone to stopping by one's place to greet someone. Among most cultural groups in the country, it is impolite to not invite someone to join in a meal if a visitor walks in while the host is eating. It is also considered uncouth to pass gas in the presence of others. Among the Yorubas, if an elder does pass gas in public due to the weight of age, the younger adults that are present at the gathering are expected to apologize on behalf of the elder. It is regarded as highly disrespectful of children to laugh at elders or make fun of them afterward. Respect is also displayed in a variety of ways. Generally, it is expected for the younger person not to stare directly at the older one when being scolded and the latter is not expected to talk back at an older person when being reprimanded. It is also expected that when a stranger is introduced, they are not to be stared at directly in the eye. In addition to staring at people, it is considered rude for a younger person to call an elder by their first name. When meeting someone for the first time, the average Nigerian prefers to be addressed formally, preferably by their titles such as Chief, Engineer, Doctor, and other honorific titles they have acquired. Meeting a Nigerian for the first time and addressing them by their first name will likely lead to a snub or cautious interaction. It is only after a relationship has been forged that the average Nigerian may be addressed by their first name. The same also applies to those in the rural areas. Characteristically, married couples with children are called by their child's name. For example, the man whose child is called Ngozi will be addressed as Daddy Ngozi, and the mother as Mummy Ngozi. Even among siblings, the younger ones are not expected to call their older ones by name, be they male or female. This is more common in the southwestern part of the country and less so in other parts. Among the Yoruba for example, the younger sibling addresses the older one as *egbon* (elder one) and the older one, in turn calls his younger one *aburo* (younger one).

See Also: Food and Table Manners (Chapter 10); Greetings (Chapter 10).

Further Reading

Deeyor, L. (2022, June 07). "Courtesy, Respect and the Issues of 'Change.'" *Nigeria Info, 92.3 PH*. https://www.nigeriainfo.fm/port-harcourt/news/helloportharcourt/courtesy-respect-and-the-issue-of-change/

Falola, T. (2000). *Culture and Customs of Nigeria*. Westport: Greenwood Press.

ENTERTAINMENT AND GIFT-GIVING

Nigerians are great entertainers and are lavish in their spending especially during functions such as weddings and funerals. When Nigerians invite guests to celebrate with them, they take it as their full responsibility to make their guests comfortable and satisfied. Among the Igbos and other ethnic groups in the South-South, the entertainment of guests is entirely at the expense of the hosts. They do not expect anyone to support them financially or otherwise. Among the Yorubas, on the other hand, entertainment is a collective endeavor that is almost an obligation among family members and, in some instances, among friends. A wedding will typically be the primary responsibility of the groom among the Igbos and those from the South-South, but among the Yorubas, family members are expected to contribute toward the preparation of the wedding as well as toward the entertainment of guests. The culture of *Aso-ebi* is the hallmark of economic and social support among the Yorubas in times of major social events. The *Aso-ebi* concept is designed to support the hosts of an event by making family members and friends to buy (usually at a relatively high cost) a designated cloth pattern for the hosts to raise money toward a successful social event. At the event, it is customary for those who put on the cloth selected for the occasion to be served generously and given special gift items. Gift items may range from mugs to blenders and in some "big" parties the celebrants may give away table fridges to their guests. Among the Hausas in the North, gift-giving is usually between families that are related by marriage. When a bride is being escorted to her husband's house, she is showered with gift items by her family members usually in the form of ornaments such as bracelets, gold trinkets, silver and bronze wares. Across the country, gifts are mostly given during the festive periods such as Christmas, Easter, and the Muslim holidays of Eid. In the southern part of the country where the majority are Christians, gifts are given to friends and loved ones including family members, in-laws, and other well-wishers such as co-workers and neighbors. The gift items range from Christmas cards, wines, tubers of yam, bags of rice, live chickens, and other items that people may use to celebrate Yuletide. Those in the northern part of the country who are Muslims would give out food items including rams, soft drinks, and cooked foods. When invited to celebrate with a family either for a wedding or birthdays, it is customary to take some gifts along as a sign of support and celebration with the celebrants. Failure to do so may breach the friendship and strain the relationship.

See Also: Business Entertainment (Chapter 10); Housewarming (Chapter 10).

Further Reading

Falola, T. (2000). *Culture and Customs of Nigeria*. Westport: Greenwood Press.
Ventures Africa. (2021, December 23). "The Nigerian Tradition of Gift-giving at Christmas."
 https://venturesafrica.com/the-nigerian-tradition-of-gift-giving-at-christmas/

FOOD AND TABLE MANNERS

Generally, Nigerians celebrate food. Food permeates every aspect of their lives from the daily consumption of food for survival to various celebrations including naming ceremonies, weddings, and funerals. Culturally, Nigerians eat with their fingers and customarily eat in groups as members of the family. There are a variety of foods associated with each ethnic group, but a common feature of Nigerian staple food is what they refer to as "swallow"—the processing of food into a pasty form and accompanied with a variety of soup that is consumed by swallowing. Among the Yoruba in the West, they have *amala*, among the Igbo in the East, they are associated with *akpu*, and among the Hausa, *tuwo*. Other ethnic groups such as the Urhobo in the Niger Delta are known for their *eba* as their main staple and among the Tiv of the middle belt they are known for their pounded yam. The final food items, that is eba and pounded yam, are also widely consumed in all parts of the country regardless of ethnic group. Soups and stews of various kinds are associated with different ethnic groups. For example, among the Yoruba, they have *gbegiri*, *efo*, and *ewedu* soups. The Ibibios, Calabars, and Efik, are known for their *edikaikon* soup that is rich in vegetables, assorted meat, and periwinkles. The Igbos are known for their *egusi* and *ogbono* soups, while the Urhobos are known for their *banga* soup and the Ijaws for their pepper soup. Snacks also play an important role in the diet of Nigerians including the consumption of groundnuts, cashew nuts, and roasted plantain referred to as *bole*. In the West and middle belt people there also consume *warra*, the traditional cheese. Among the Hausa in the North, *fura da nono* (fresh milk) is also widely consumed. Today, the most prominent food among Nigerians is rice, grown mostly in the northern part of the country but also imported from other countries due to its high demand in the country. Rice has become the staple food for most households in urban Nigeria and in some rural communities. There are different ways rice is prepared—from plain rice and stew to the popular jollof rice. There is also the more recent fried rice that is ubiquitous in almost all wedding parties. Foods are usually served with meat, fish, or a combination of both with a generous portion of vegetables especially among the Igbos and Calabars. As a rule, children are not permitted to talk while eating, it is regarded as bad manners especially where adults are present. But it is a time of conviviality and discussion among adults especially when hosting visitors. All topics of conversation can be discussed except topics that border on sickness and death, which may not be broached while eating. It is the belief that broaching such topics while eating invites ill-luck and may lead to the untimely death of one of the discussants. Among all ethnic groups it is not allowed for anyone, both children and adults as well as male and females, to eat with the left hand, it is greatly frowned upon.

See Also: Courtesy and Respect (Chapter 10).

Further Reading

Etiquette Scholar. (2019). *Nigeria Dining Etiquette*. Littleton: Yellowstone Publishing. https://www.etiquettescholar.com/dining_etiquette/table-etiquette/africa_west_dinner_etiquette/nigerian.html

Freeman, S. (2019). *The Nigerian Food Experience: Explore Nigeria through 25 Recipes*. Independent Publisher.

GREETINGS

Nigerians greet each other in different ways due to the cultural diversity of the country. While it is common for urbanites to greet by handshakes, this mode of greeting is diverse depending on those involved in the greeting and the context in which the greeting takes place. From the formal shaking of hands among professionals to the somewhat ritualistic three back handshake and one front handshake among the Igbos and every other form in-between. This elaborate handshake involves the parties tapping each other with the back of their hands and at the fourth time they grip their palms in a firm shake. Among the Igbos, titled men, and chiefs, may use their horse whip for this greeting gesture. What is generally unacceptable in all forms of greetings among all ethnic groups is shaking of hands using the left hand. This form of greeting is practiced only among some cult groups and fraternities. When greeting, it is generally considered rude and unfriendly not to ask after one's health and family members. Traditionally, greeting is an elaborate ritual starting first with asking after one's health and family members. As a rule, most ethnic groups consider it rude for a younger person to stretch their hand to the older person for a handshake as a form of greeting. Among the Yoruba, for example, the young man is expected to greet his parents and in-laws by prostrating while the young women kneel to greet the elders. However, this practice is gradually waning especially in urban centers where it is now characteristic for men to greet elders by a slight bow of the head and the women by the bending of the knees. Among the Kabba people of Kogi State, they engage in an elaborate greeting pattern by squatting and exchanging pleasantries for as long as two to five minutes. And this is not restricted only to the home but is also expected along the streets. Biological age is the ultimate definer of greeting patterns among most ethnic groups in Nigeria. Irrespective of gender, social position, or economic fortune, the younger person is expected to give deference to the older person by initiating the greeting. A young man or woman is generally considered uncultured if they ignore to greet an elderly person even if they are not known to them. Greetings, and the elaborate forms of exchanging pleasantries, are regarded as a cultural obligation and a symbol of good manners and friendship. Those who have not cultivated the habit of greeting are highly disregarded and are not spoken well of by the community. Greetings are not a brisk indifferent social obligation but are regarded as a cultural ritual that symbolizes good manners, respect, and consideration for others. When greeting, it is expected to ask after the person's health and general welfare including the health and well-being of the parents and children as the case may be. In addition, part of the greeting will also include inquiring of one's work and any other enterprise of the person that may be of concern. It is also characteristic to appreciate any favor that was rendered by the person even if the favor was rendered the previous day or week. In urban centers and especially among the youth greetings are boisterous, friendly, elaborate, and can be rambunctious in nature with the slapping of back, sketching a dance, and knuckle punching. The "hi-5" sign is also becoming very popular among youth in urban centers.

See Also: Courtesy and Respect (Chapter 10).

Further Reading

Falola, T. (2000). *Culture and Customs of Nigeria*. Greenwood Press.
Omebije, V. (2017, August 08). "Greeting Etiquette." *Local Guides Connect*. https://www.localguidesconnect.com/t5/General-Discussion/GREETING-ETIQUETTE/td-p/407385

HOUSEWARMING

One of the greatest achievements of a Nigerian is the ability to successfully complete the building of their personal house. In a country with limited credit facilities and where the acquisition of land is not easily obtained, citizens depend on their savings and discipline to purchase a piece of land and construct the type of building they need for their family. The gradual process of building and completing a house is a landmark that calls for celebration, otherwise referred to as housewarming. The celebration of completing a building takes different forms: from a simple gathering of family members with some few drinks and food to an elaborate fanfare where the celebrant invites family and church members, and other well-wishers who are treated to live bands and the generous provision of food and drinks. Typically, if the celebrant is a Christian, the pastor and other church members are invited to pray in the house for God to ward off any evil spirit and ill-luck and the ushering in of the Holy Spirit for protection and peace. This service is usually accompanied with singing, prayers, and offerings to be collected by the church for its support. Among some Christian denominations such as the Celestial Church, candles of different colors may be lit throughout the day to ward off bad luck and offensive spirits from the house. Thereafter, the social event will commence with music provided by the church choir or a professional band. The practice of housewarming is not only to show gratitude to God but also a social event to display one's accomplishment. It is a moment of pride and a signifier of the status of the house owner. It is an opportunity to declare loudly to those who attend the housewarming that the owner has "stepped up" from one social level to another. The origin of the practice is not exactly known but it is widespread among the southerners. There is an element of tradition in it as most cultural groups in the South would normally come together to celebrate any major events including the birth of a child, the wedding of couples, or the funeral of an elderly person. However, what seems to differentiate these traditional practices and housewarming is the fusion of religion into the latter and the lavish spending that usually characterizes it. The practice of housewarming is, however, not as common in the northern part of the country as it is in the South. In the North, probably because of their more austere lifestyle, they do not engage in any elaborate celebration of their achievement as do their southern counterparts. Among irreligious Nigerians, the housewarming ceremony is a time of great entertainment as the celebrant provides food, soft drinks, and alcohol. Those with the means also invite secular musicians who entertain the guests. Foods that are normally served are a mixture of both local dishes and a foreign menu with a generous quantity of alcohol.

See Also: Entertainment and Gift-Giving (Chapter 10); Naming Ceremonies (Chapter 10).

Further Reading

Udemagwuna, L. (2016, October 14). "House Warming Ideas for Your Lagos Apartment." *PropertyPro.ng*. https://www.propertypro.ng/blog/house-warming-ideas-for-your-lagos-apartment/

NAMING CEREMONIES

The arrival of a child is a joyous occasion both for the parents of the child and members of the extended family. Thus, the naming of the child is not only the affair of the parents but of other members of the family. Usually, the baby is not named until the seventh day after birth or twenty-one days after birth among the Urhobo of the Niger Delta. It is usually considered safe to wait for some time after the birth of the child to announce the preferred name of the child to the society. This is partly influenced by suspicion that the child may be subjected to evil manipulation if the names are announced too early. The delay in other cultures is borne out of the fear that the child may die in the first few days after birth. But once the child is born the parents begin to prepare for the naming ceremony. On the eighth day after the birth of the child (as is now customary among Christian families), members of the family and invited guests start arriving at the designated venue (usually the parents' house) for the ceremony. In most naming ceremonies, both religious and traditional, it is characteristic to provide some symbolic items such as sugar, honey, the Bible, or Quran as important items for the naming of the child. The items symbolize that the child's life will be devoid of bitterness such as suffering and will be full of joy and happiness. The religious family will invite the priest to say the prayers and will pronounce the names of the child as presented by the parents. Usually, the names are between two and twelve. The parents have the preferred names for the child, but so also are the grandparents, aunts, uncles, and other significant members of the family. Names are not just given; rather they are symbolic not only to the child and the circumstances surrounding its birth but also to the prevailing circumstances of the family or society when the child was conceived or born. Thus, it is not uncommon to name a child Monday, if he was born on that day; or Independence if the child was born on the day the country gained its independence. As a rule, Nigerians, especially among Christians, have both a Christian name or other foreign names and local names. Increasingly though, more Christians in the country tend to favor being called by their Christian names. Among ethnic groups that believe in reincarnation there are names such as Iyatunde (mother has returned) among the Yoruba, and Babarire (father has returned) among the Urhobo. Names are always meaningful. They are given to the child as a prophecy of what the parents wish for the child, for example, Oserakeme (an Urhobo name meaning God is my protector). In modern times, especially among Pentecostal Christians, Nigerians have devised ingenious names for their children to reflect their religious and spiritual conviction. Names such as Praise and Faithfulness have become common in Nigerian homes. Also hyphenated names such Great-Grace, King-David, Marvellous-Crown are starting to become common. Such names hold great promise to the parents of the child, and they believe that symbolic meaning of the names will guide the child through life.

See Also: Holiday Feasts (Chapter 14).

Further Reading

Onyefulu, I. (2003). *Welcome Dede: An African Naming Ceremony*. Frances Lincoln Publisher.
Pulse.ng. (2020, December 24). "Some Nigerian Naming Ceremony Ideas for a Memorable Day." https://www.pulse.ng/lifestyle/food-travel/some-nigerian-naming-ceremony-ideas-for-a-memorable-day/lthdf0h

CHAPTER 11

Literature and Drama

OVERVIEW

The history of Nigerian literary creation goes back to the middle of the eighteenth century in the form of memoirs written by freed slaves. In 1938, Daniel Fagunwa wrote *Ogboju Ode Ninu Igbo Irunmale* (translated into English by Wole Soyinka in 1968 under the title *The Forest of a Thousand Daemons: A Hunter's Saga*) which is today recognized as the first novel to be written in an African indigenous language. The coming of the missionaries with printing press technology, however, was the major milestone in the history of Nigeria's literature. Through the printing press oral folklores were published as pamphlets, novelettes, and novels. The colonial government as well as private commercial publishers produced non-fictional materials to aid governance and education (textbooks in various subjects were produced for pre-university, undergraduate, and postgraduate levels).

In relation to non-fictional literature, the contribution of market literature pamphlets is commendable. In the northern region of Nigeria, the Kano Market Literature series developed in association with the colonial government's aim of educating the Hausa/Fulani people of northern Nigeria about government policies and regulations. This was spurred by the colonial government's realization of the traditional ruler's reluctance to embrace Western education. The pamphlets produced were thus a mass medium of enlightenment and awareness. What made the Kano Market Literature series more unique was the ability of the writers to convert their pamphlets into drama series which some scholars believe was the foundation of what is now known in the northern region of Nigeria as "Kannywood." In the eastern region of Nigeria, the development of the market literature was a bit different. Between 1958 and 1962 (recognized as peak years) the Onitsha Market Literature developed. Within these years, approximately fifty titles were published each year for the reading pleasure of thousands of readers within Nigeria and West African countries such as Ghana and Cameroon. Notable authors at the time include Cyprian Ekwensi. Unfortunately, the Nigerian Civil War brought a dramatic end to this very buoyant phase of history.

A lot of the classical Nigerian literature we have today was written between 1950 and 1970. These include novels like *The Palm-Wine Drinkard* by Amos Tutuola (1952), *People of the City* by Cyprian Ekwensi (1954), and *Things Fall Apart* by Chinua Achebe (1958). These three represent the occurrences in Nigeria's history namely pre-colonial folklore myths, the intrusion of colonial rule, and the conversion of traditional life into urban experiences. This was followed by authors that captured Nigeria as an independent nation. Unlike the first wave of writers, post-independent writers were either undergraduates or postgraduates in Nigerian or foreign universities with formal training in literature. These include novels like *The Interpreters* by Wole Soyinka (1965), *No Longer at Ease* by Chinua Achebe (1960), *The Concubine* by Elechi Amadi (1966), and *Efuru* by Flora Nwapa (1966). Many of these novels were a mixture of traditional folklore and urban life experiences. Between the 1970s and 1990s the horrors of the Nigerian Civil War, the creation of social inequalities through "democratic rule" and the harshness of military rule were major themes. Notable in this category is *The Last Duty* by Okpewho Isidore (1976), *Violence* by Iyayi Festus (1989), and *Abiku* by Kotun Debo (1998).

Within the contemporary Nigerian literary writers are personalities who combined lecturing in the higher institutions with the creative writing of poems, novels, and plays. One of such is Babafemi Adeyemi Osofisan who is known for his critique of societal problems and use of African traditional performances in his plays. Also to be mentioned is Helon Habila Ngalabak who, though based outside Nigeria, has won many prizes and awards for his literary works. Harry Garuba (who passed away in March 2020) a poet and academic is one of the great literary icons to also be remembered.

The history of Nigerian drama can be traced to indigenous *Egungun* masquerade performances that began in the Old Oyo Empire in southwestern Nigeria. These performances were attached to the religious reverence of ancestors but performed for the entertainment of the royal court and masses. The performances included dance dramas, acrobatic displays, and songs. Soon various troupes were formed, and each competed for excellence with the aim of being commissioned by high chiefs to perform outside the palace setting but in association with the *Egungun* festival. It is within this context that the *Alarinjo* or travelling theater was formed. Scholars have noted that this transition meant that these performances were no longer tied to religion/rituals and were more designed for entertainment and material gains. This in turn encouraged professionalism and the proliferation of drama troupes.

Masquerade performances also exist among ethnic groups in southeastern and South-south sections of Nigeria. Like the Yoruba, these performances were linked to ancestral worship and royal court theater. Their transition was initiated first by missionary activities of conversion and later by colonial intervention. In compliance, the festival displays were performed during Christian holidays and the masquerades were modified with some representing priests and colonial officials. The dramas created were more of satires while others were comical displays of Europeans.

In southwestern Nigeria, the coming of the missionaries was initially welcomed until clashes of leadership style and method of worship occurred leading to the establishment of indigenous churches. These indigenous churches developed a fine mix of traditional drama, dance, and music with Christian themes in order to convert traditional worshippers in their communities. Leaders of the indigenous churches used traditional folk songs and drama with Christian themes as a strategy to convert traditional worshippers and to communicate with members of their congregation who spoke limited English. With the rise of indigenous churches, especially in southern Nigeria, more African oriented forms of Christian songs, dance, and worship were practiced. These performances became very popular especially in Lagos but were limited to the church and their property. This was until 1899 when Glover Hall was built to serve as a hall for performances. The building of Glover Hall was very important as performances were no longer limited to church themes and dictates. Now composers were free to create drama themes relating to colonialism, cultural renaissance, and nationalism.

The southwestern section of Nigeria was very active in the development of drama through the foundational efforts of Hubert Ogunde who resuscitated the traditional *Alarinjo* into the Nigerian Popular Theatre of the 1940s. Though mainly made up of Yoruba composers and actors, the Nigerian Popular Theatre was able to attract, connect with, and retain the attention of diverse Nigerian audiences through their use of indigenous symbols, historical experiences, and cultural themes of similarity. Examples of such themes include travel and trade, colonialism, the effect of urbanization on traditional beliefs, and the spirit of nationalism.

The success of the Nigerian Popular Theatre was sustained by theater troupe owners who ensured standard and professionalism in the industry. Ogunde's theater was a trailblazer in the 1950s and 1960s and his dramas and operas became a model for upcoming travelling troupes. One of such was Kola Ogunmola (1925–1973) and his theater troupe which performed plays that drew themes from the Bible and Yoruba folk tales. He worked closely with the University College Ibadan School of Drama and thus, not surprisingly, several of his plays were performed in the English language. Unlike Ogunde's plays which were in Yoruba with a lot of singing, dancing, and musical display; Ogunmola's plays had more drama and was considered by literary critics like Ulli Beier to be of more serious acting. Ogunmola's plays were more of social satires.

Also popular during this time was Duro Ladipo (1931–78) and his troupe. Duro Ladipo was known for his folk operas that incorporated ritual poetry and traditional rhythm. As with previously mentioned artists, his themes were based on Yoruba myths and Biblical stories. His play *Oba Koso* (1963) was so successful that he went on tour of the US and Europe to perform it with his troupe. He was also awarded the national honor of Member of the Order of the Niger (MON). In 1962 he founded the Mbari Mbayo Club with the support of Ulli Beier (a German scholar and researcher) as a performance venue and training center.

The 1960s witnessed several playwrights that graduated from foreign universities. Prominent of course was Wole Soyinka, but another worthy of mention was Ola Rotimi, a graduate of Yale and later Boston University, USA. Rotimi was an academic staff of the University of Ife where he set up the Ori Olokun Theatre Company. Like his predecessors, Rotimi based his plays on traditional Yoruba culture and history. He was especially known for his play, *The Gods are not to Blame* (performed in 1968, published 1971) and *Kurunmi* (performed 1969, published 1971).

Other prominent performers of the time include Moses Olaiya, Oyin Adejobi, and Adunni Oluwole (the first woman to establish a professional theater in Nigeria). The 1970s to the 1990s witnessed the contribution of university educated literary artists like Wole Soyinka, Ola Rotimi, John Pepper Clark, Wale Ogunyemi and Zulu Sofola (the first female dramatist in Nigeria).

Further Reading

Adeoye, J. (2013). "Nigerian Theatre: From 'Masquerade Drama' to Nigerian Video Film (Chapter 1)." In R. Jays and J. Adeoye (eds.), *The Drama of Ahmed Yerima: Studies in Nigerian Theatre*, 21–73. Universiteit Leiden: Leiden University Repository. http://hdl.handle.net/1887/20858
National Open University of Nigeria. (2008). "Eng. 281: The African Novel." https://nou.edu.ng/coursewarecontent/ENG%20281.pdf.

ACHEBE, CHINUA

Albert Chinualumogu (later shortened it to Chinua) Achebe was born on November 16, 1930 at Ogidi in present-day Anambra State; and died on March 21, 2013 at Boston Massachusetts (USA). He was born into a family of the Protestant Church Mission Society who also respected the traditional Igbo ways of life.

Achebe attended missionary Christian schools for his primary and secondary education. In 1948, he gained admission into the University College on a scholarship to read Medicine. He lost the scholarship when he decided to rather study English Literature with supporting courses in History and Theology. His change in academic focus was based on his experiences as a child in terms of the religious and ideological clashes the introduction of Christianity brought as well as the political and social restructuring it resulted into in his community. His course of study also exposed him to European literature about Africa which made him critical of negative Europeans perceptions of Africans. As an undergraduate, these factors inspired him to write his first short story "In a Village Church."

Achebe gained employment in Lagos with the Nigerian Broadcasting Service in 1954 under the Talks Department. The on-the-job skills he acquired of preparing scripts for oral delivery significantly helped him when he started his first novel in 1956. He titled it *Things Fall Apart* in line with the W. B. Yeats's poem *The Second Coming*. In 1957, he sent a handwritten copy of the manuscript to London for typesetting, but it took the intervention of his boss Angela Beattie for this to be accomplished. In June 1958, Heinemann published 2,000 copies of the book and was overwhelmed by the positive reviews. *Things Fall Apart* became one of the most important African literatures selling over twenty million copies and translated into more than fifty-seven languages.

Other successful literary works by Achebe include *No Longer at Ease* (1960), *Arrow of God* (1964), *Man of the People* (1966), and *Anthills of the Savannah* (1987). He was later awarded several fellowships which allowed him to travel around Africa and Europe. At the break of the Nigerian Civil War in May 1967, Achebe strongly defended the Biafran cause

Supporting the Next Generation of Writers

Nigeria has produced world-renowned writers and the vibrancy of the literature and drama space is growing stronger. Various individuals and organizations are contributing significantly to support writing in the country to produce another generation of literary giants. The Purple Hibiscus Creative Writing Workshop is the brainchild of Chimamanda Ngozi Adichie, which organizes an annual writing workshop for budding writers in the country. The purpose of the workshop is to provide a platform for young writers to hone their crafts toward achieving their writing dream. Other writers who are giving back to the society include Lola Shoneyin, and Wole Soyinka through the Wole Soyinka Prize for Literature in Africa. As an apex body of arts and literature, the Nigerian Academy of Letters also provides a platform for the recognition of accomplished scholars within and outside the country. Other similar bodies include the African Theatre Association, Society for the Performing Arts in Nigeria, and the National Troupe of Nigeria among others.

---

and toured the US to raise awareness. At home, he served in the committee that drafted *The Principles of the Biafran Revolution*. 1970 marked the end of the war and the defeat of Biafra. Achebe continued as a lecturer with the University of Nsukka and in 1972 released the novel *Girls at War* which captured his experiences of the war.

University of Massachusetts (Amherst) offered Achebe a professorship in 1972 and he used the platform to critique Western views of Africa and its people. This was especially reflected in his 1975 lecture titled "An Image of Africa: Racism in Conrad's Heart of Darkness." He returned to Nigeria in 1976 and retired in 1982 to take up a more political career with the People Redemption Party. He combined this with public speeches until March 1990 when he was involved in a car accident which left him paralyzed from the waist down. He was flown to the US where he continued as an active academic with several universities with his last appointment being with Brown University.

See Also: Adichie, Chimamanda Ngozi (Chapter 11); Fiction and Nonfiction Literary Works (Chapter 11).

Further Reading

Barksdale-Hall, R. (2007). "Chinua Achebe: A Bio-bibliographic Review." *The Journal of Pan African Studies*, 1(8): 9–11.
Gomba, O. (2013). "Tribute: Things Still Apart: Chinua Achebe's Whetstone." *Tydskrif Vir Letterkunde*, 50(2): 152–7. doi: http://dx.doi.org/10.4314/tvl.v50i2.11
Makinde, A. (n.d.). "Book Review of Chinua Achebe's 'There was a Country': A Personal History of Biafra." http://adeyinkamakinde.homestead.com/index.html

ADICHIE, CHIMAMANDA NGOZI

Chimamanda Ngozi Adichie was born on September 15, 1977, in Enugu State, eastern Nigeria. Her father, James Nwoye Adichie was the first professor of Statistics in Nigeria and later became the Deputy Vice Chancellor of the University of Nigeria, Nsukka. Her mother, Grace Ifeoma Adichie, also worked at the university as a non-academic staff member and later became the first female registrar of the university. Chimamanda was thus born into an academic environment. Growing up she was particularly inspired by the works of the famous Nigerian writer Chinua Achebe and by the fact that she and her family lived in the house he formerly occupied as a professor at the university.

Chimamanda completed her secondary school education in the university's staff school and later gained admission into the same university to study Medicine and Pharmacy. She was at the University of Nigeria for a year-and-a-half during which time she edited *The Campus*, a magazine run by the university's Catholic medical students. She left Nsukka for the USA on a scholarship to study Communication at Drexel University (Philadelphia). On completion, she was admitted into Eastern Connecticut University to read Political Science. As a student at Connecticut, Chimamanda wrote articles for the university journal, *Campus Lantern*. She graduated with a *Summa Cum Laude* in 2001 and went on to do a master's degree in creative writing at Johns Hopkins University, Baltimore. Between 2005 and 2006, she was a Hodder Fellow at Princeton University and, in 2008, successfully completed another master's degree in African Studies at Yale University. She was later awarded honorary doctorate degrees by various universities within the USA and Europe.

Chimamanda's talent for creative writing was recognized in 2002 as a joint winner of the BBC Short Story Competition for her short story titled *That Harmattan Morning*. She started to work on her first novel *Purple Hibiscus* while at Eastern Connecticut University. *Purple Hibiscus* was published in 2003 winning several awards. This was followed by other award-winning novels including *Half of a Yellow Sun* (2006), *The Thing Around Your Neck* (a collection of twelve short stories, 2009), and *Americanah* (2013).

Chimamanda is known for her ability to question and capture her experiences as a Nigerian and a woman in an insightful way. She captures this in her TED Talk (2009) titled "The Danger of a Single Story" which became one of the top ten most viewed. In another TedXEuston presentation (2012) titled "We should all be feminists" she defends the rights of women. Another major passion she holds dearly is the love of her people, especially her ethnic group. The horrors of the Nigerian Civil War as witnessed in Biafra is captured in *Half of a Yellow Sun*.

Chimamanda's international recognition includes her being listed by *Time Magazine* as "The 100 Most Influential People" (2015) and in 2017 her election into the 237th class of the American Academy of Arts and Sciences. She currently conducts annual writing workshops in Nigeria to train upcoming writers.

See Also: Achebe, Chinua (Chapter 11); Fiction and Nonfiction Literary Works (Chapter 11).

Further Reading

The Chimamanda Ngozi Adichie Website. (2022). The Chimamanda Ngozi Adichie Website (ulg.ac.be).

ATTA, SEFI

Sefi Atta was born in January 1964 in Lagos as the third of five siblings. Her father, Abdul-Aziz Atta was, until his death in 1972, the Secretary to the federal government and Head of the Nigerian Civil Service. On his death, Seffi Atta was then raised by her mother, Iyabo Atta.

Atta did part of her secondary school at Queen's College, Lagos but finished at Millfield School, England. She had her first degree in England at Birmingham University and went on to qualify as a chartered accountant. She then went to the United States where she became a Certified Public Accountant. She diverted from her original profession in accountancy to writing in 1997 when she moved to Meridian and found herself in-between jobs. She went on to do an online course to earn a Master of Fine Arts in Creative Writing from Antioch University (Los Angeles, California) in 2001.

In 2002, she began to place her short stories in for competitions and was either shortlisted or recognized as coming in second or third places. It was not until 2003 that she was awarded the first prize for the Red Hen Press Short Story Award. In 2005, she won first place in the PEN International David T. K. Wong Prize; and in 2006 the Wole Soyinka Prize for Literature in Africa. She is the author of novels, short stories, and plays. Her themes concentrate on Nigeria and its social make-up, including her childhood experiences growing up as the daughter of an Igbirra Muslim father and a Yoruba Christian mother. Through her stories, she attempts to bring a new perspective to how Nigeria, and indeed Africa, is defined. Several of her publications are done in Nigeria because she believes the Nigerian population can better identify with it than the American audience. Though publishing in Nigeria has its negative sides such as being criticized for being a feminist it nevertheless got her the 2009 Noma Award for Publishing in Africa.

Some of her books have been translated to other languages while her plays have been broadcasted by the BBC. Her short stories have appeared in literary journals such as *The Los Angeles Review*, *Mississippi Review*, and the *World Literature Today*. She currently runs a Lagos-based production company called Atta Girl which supports reading.

See Also: Fiction and Nonfiction Literary Works (Chapter 11); Hafsat, Abdulwaheed Ahmed (Chapter 11).

Further Reading

Awodipe, T. (2021). "Feminism is not a Glamorous Magazine Cover with a Condescending Headline." *The Guardian*. https://guardian.ng/guardian-woman/feminism-is-not-a-glamorous-magazine-cover-with-a-condescending-headline/

Collins, W. (2007). "Interview with Sefi Atta." *English in Africa*, 34(2): 123–31.

CLARK, JOHN PEPPER

John Pepper Clark-Bekederemo was born on April 6, 1935 at Kiagbodo (Delta State). His early education was at the Native Administration School, Okrika, and later Government College Ughelli (1948–1954).

He gained admission into the University of Ibadan in 1955 to study English. As an undergraduate, he became the editor of the Students' Union magazine, *The Beacon*; and became the first editor of the *Horn* magazine, a poetry journal. On the platform of the

Horn, J. P. Clark published the poem *Ivbie* which questioned imperial power. The *Horn* served as a major launch pad for modern Nigerian poetry and had personalities like Christopher Okigbo and Wole Soyinka as foundational contributors.

He graduated from the University of Ibadan in 1960 and worked as an information officer for the Ministry of Information for a year. He later became the Head of Features and Editorial writer for the *Lagos Daily Express* between 1961 and 1962. He left the journalism industry for a more academic career when he gained employment with the University of Ibadan's Institute of African Studies as a Research Fellow (1964–1966). While in Ibadan, J. P. Clark became a foundational member of a new club of artists and critics called Mbari for which he was made the club's secretary. Mbari grew to be a major platform for performing and visual artists and had branches in Lagos, Enugu, and Zaria. Mbari published his first play, *Song of a Goat*.

J. P. Clark received the Parvin Fellowship to Princeton University (USA) in 1962. There he wrote the plays *The Masquerade*, *The Raft*, and *America, their America*. On his return home, he transcribed and translated the *Ozidi Saga* (1964) which was performed for seven days in Ibadan, Lagos, and Orua. He later transformed the saga into the play *Ozidi* (1966). He left his position in Ibadan for the University of Lagos to become a lecturer and rose to be a Professor of English. In 1980, he retired and returned to his birthplace at Kiagbodo. He later formed the PEC Repertory Theatre with his wife Professor Ebun Clark, a renowned Nigerian actress. The theater became Nigeria's first English speaking performing theater company, producing some of the best plays from Africa including *The Return Home*, *Full Circle*, and the *Wives' Revolt*. J. P. Clark also worked with Abiola Irele as the co-editor of *Black Orpheus*.

J. P. Clark's poems and plays speak of his experiences and incidences as a Nigerian from the Niger Delta region. For example, his first play, *Song of a Goat*, is based on the Ijaw culture and socioeconomic tradition of fishing weaved into a drama of love and tragedy. The poem titled *Casualties* depicts the destruction and violence the three-year-long Nigerian Civil War caused on the country's citizens. In 2007 his documentary, *Oil at the Bottom*, was broadcast by Channels Television.

J. P. Clark has won many national and international awards and titles in recognition of his literary contributions to academics, politics, and the cultural development of Nigeria and indeed Africa.

See Also: Fiction and Nonfiction Literary Works (Chapter 11); Indigenous Drama (Chapter 11).

Further Reading

Amakievi, G. and S. Blackduke. (2019). "John Pepper Clark's Song of a Goat: Hindsight for foresight in Izon Culture of the Western Niger Delta of Nigeria." *Scholarly Journal of Scientific Research and Essay (SJSRE)*, 8(1): 1–6.

Britannica, T. Editors of Encyclopaedia. (2022, April 02). "John Pepper Clark." *Encyclopedia Britannica*. https://www.britannica.com/biography/John-Pepper-Clark

Encyclopedia.com. (July 25, 2023). "Clark, John Pepper (Contemporary Poets)." *Encyclopedia.com*. https://www.encyclopedia.com/arts/culture-magazines/clark-john-pepper

Nnaji, P. O. (2014). "The Role of Literature Education in Curbing Violence: A Focus on John Pepper Clark's 'The Casualties.'" *An International Journal of Arts and Humanities*, 3(2): 18–28. doi: http://dx.doi.org/10.4314/ijah.v3i2.2

HAFSAT, ABDULWAHEED AHMED

Abdulwaheed Hafsat was born on May 5, 1952, in Kofar Mata, Kano City and got married in 1966 at the tender age of fourteen. In her marital home, she completed her primary and secondary school education in Kano State. Hafsat got her initial inspiration from her parents who taught her to explore knowledge, but more especially through her father's Hausa poetry. By 1970, she had completed her first short novel which was written in English. In 1972, when she was in primary five, she translated the manuscript into Hausa and submitted it for a literary competition organized by the Northern Nigerian Publishing Company (NNPC). The novel which she titled *"So Aljannar Duniya"* (Love is Paradise on Earth) came in second place. The novel was published into a book in 1972 but due to a fire incident, was republished in 1980. The novel has been translated into Arabic and even Fulfulde by her father, but neither version has been published yet.

The novel *So Aljannar Duniya* was written at a time in northern Nigerian history when women did not have the liberty of choosing who they would marry. Marriages were arranged and many women only got to meet their husbands on their wedding day. Their marital future was dependent on their parent's judgments regarding their future partners. Unfortunately, some of these marriages were filled with problems and discontentment, especially where the couples were impatient with each other. Hafsat drew her inspiration from personal experiences but more from her elder sister who was married to a Libyan. The cultural differences resulted in frictions in the home and Hafsat felt that these were issues that needed to be discussed in the public space. She wanted to draw public attention to the dangers of forcing girls to marry men they did not love or care about. She also wanted to inspire women to write about these experiences and overcome their fear of discussing sensitive topics like love.

Due to the sensitivity of her novel's theme, Hafsat was sure that it would not be accepted. She was pleasantly surprised that not only was it accepted, but that several institutions such as Bayero University adopted it as a study text. The novel has been classified as foundational for the development of a modern Hausa genre known as *Littattafan Soyayya* (Love Book). The genre was further made popular by the Kano Market Literature which witnessed adaptations of Indian films written in Hausa as short stories.

Since her first publication, Abdulwaheed Hafsat has written up to thirty fiction and nonfiction books, novels, and short stories in Hausa (though only five have been published). She is also a women's rights activist and runs an NGO which assists women (mainly from northern Nigeria) suffering from domestic violence and other issues. She contested for the gubernatorial seat of Zamfara State in 2000 as her way of making a statement; women from the North can also lead if given a chance. Unfortunately, she was denied the party ticket because she was a woman.

See Also: Attah, Sefi (Chapter 11); Fiction and Nonfiction Literary Works (Chapter 11); Gender Relations (Chapter 7).

Further Reading

Adamu, Y. (2008). "Interview with Hafsatu Ahmed Abdulwahid." *African Writer Magazine*. Interview with Hafsatu Ahmed Abdulwahid - AfricanWriter.com

FICTION AND NONFICTION LITERARY WORKS

The Presbyterian Mission introduced the printing press to Nigeria in 1846 in Calabar. Through the press, the church printed nonfiction pamphlets that were a collection of hymns, psalms, and other Bible materials. They also printed pamphlets designed to support the teaching of subjects taught in their mission schools. Later, the British colonial government also established printing presses to aid in their administration. By 1946, they began selling old machines from their printing presses to indigenous traders. With this acquisition, local merchants were able to develop what is now known as market literature. Market literature was based on the mass production of pamphlets sold and distributed in major markets. The most prominent in Nigerian literary history were the Kano and Onitsha Market literature.

The market literature was further inspired by Second World War soldiers who came back with souvenir pulp magazines. These served as sample designs for the market literature printers. Adopting these mixtures of cultures and forms, however, meant that the market literature pamphlets themselves had no standard design, subject matter, or theme. The pages were few and the language structure simple. In the case of the Kano Market Literature, most were written in Hausa with just a few English words included.

The first of the market literature was published in 1947 in Onitsha. Soon the market was flooded with cheap literature pamphlets. The literatures dealt with a variety of issues ranging from politics, religion, social occurrences, cultural values, and philosophy. The authors of the market literature were varied and considered to be the "new literates" comprising Standard Six school leavers. Many of them had steady income and thus their aim of publication was not for financial gains, but rather for their works to be read and appreciated by the society. Their occupations ranged from entry-level career schoolteachers, low-level clerks, and artisans; while others were journalists, printing press owners, or booksellers. There were even authors who were still in high school writing under pseudo names to avoid being identified and punished by their school authorities.

The market literature at Onitsha was popular due to its location which attracted thousands of people from within Nigeria and West Africa to buy and sell their goods. Within the market, the pamphlets were sold in bookshops, the open market, and by hawkers. Travellers and business merchants would purchase not only for their personal entertainment, but also for their loved ones or as souvenirs. During its peak period (1958–62), the popularity of the Onitsha market literature spread to many cities in the eastern region of Nigeria. It also served as a launching pad for the author Cyprian Ekwensi, who after writing several series through this channel published the novel *People of the City* in 1954.

In the case of the Kano market, pamphlets were produced as enlightenment tools of government policies; and to promote Hausa/Fulani cultural norms and values. Some of the writers eventually converted their stories into drama series'. These drama performances were very popular in northern Nigeria.

See Also: Achebe, Chinua (Chapter 11); Adichie, Chimamanda Ngozi (Chapter 11); Atta, Sefi (Chapter 11); Indigenous Drama (Chapter 11); Okri, Ben (Chapter 11); Saro-Wiwa, Ken (Chapter 11); Tutuola, Amos (Chapter 11).

Further Reading

National Open University of Nigeria. (2008). "Eng. 281: The African Novel." https://nou.edu.ng/coursewarecontent/ENG%20281.pdf

INDIGENOUS DRAMA

In 1899, Glover Hall was built in Lagos through the combined efforts of indigenous elites and some European members of the society. Their aim was to meet the entertainment needs of Lagos without the religious restrictions of the church. By 1903 Glover Hall was popular for staging indigenous drama performances. Hubert Ogunde used this platform to resuscitate the Yoruba Travelling Theatre which later became known as the Yoruba Operatic Theatre. By the 1940s and 1950s the Nigerian Popular Theatre was formed. Through the creativity of great Yoruba minds, professionalism was established through theater companies and the Nigerian Popular Theatre became an icon for promoting indigenous entertainment.

By 1955, campus theaters within Nigerian universities also began to spring up. Pioneering this was the Ibadan Arts Theatre, built in 1955 for the purpose of holding concerts and film shows. Student groups such as the University College Theatre Production Group and the Arts Theatre Production Group ran theater workshops to further encourage professionalism. By 1962, the Ibadan School of Drama was established, and this later became the Department of Theatre Arts in 1970.

By 1976, the construction of the National Arts Theatre, Lagos was completed to host the Festival of Arts and Culture (FESTAC) in 1977. The structure is shaped like a military hat and has facilities such as a 5,000-seater main hall and cinema halls. Today, despite the obvious lack of federal government funding and support, the theater ground hosts the Artist Village managed by the Lagos Ministry of Culture, Tourism and National Orientation. The Artist Village serves as a communal center for dancers, writers, sculptors, musicians, animators, and filmmakers to work, create, learn, and perform.

With the introduction of television into Nigeria through the western region in 1959, new opportunities were created. For travelling troupes that made up the Nigerian Popular Theatre the possibility of television drama production drastically reduced the physical strains of mobile live performances. As early as 1960, indigenous playwrights were commissioned to write plays for the television station. This encouraged the promotion of diverse indigenous theater troupes to join the entertainment industry which for so long had been monopolized by Yoruba actors/actresses, composers, and other artists. National television series such as *"The Village Headmaster," "The New Masquerade," "Mirror in the Sun,"* etc. were created and they gained significant national popularity.

By the 1970s the Nigerian film industry had begun to bud with Hubert Ogunde producing the largest body of film on 35mm and 16mm. This was spurred by the low remuneration national television offered artists for their production. By the 1980s improvements in video-film production encouraged practitioners to resort to the cheaper medium of video cassette recording for home viewing. In 1992, the Igbo community in Lagos took advantage of this channel to produce the box office hit, *Living in Bondage*, the first Igbo home video in Nigeria. By 2000, the Nigerian video film industry now known as Nollywood, had become the third largest motion picture industry in the world producing at least 200 indigenous movies a month.

See Also: Fiction and Nonfiction Literary Works (Chapter 11); Ogunde Hubert (Chapter 11); Tales by Moonlight (Chapter 11); Traditional Performances (Chapter 11).

Further Reading

Aduku, A. I. (2018). "Elements of Traditional African Drama in Contemporary Nigerian Video Film." *The Performer: Ilorin Journal of the Performing Arts*. http://eprints.gouni.edu.ng/131/

Britannica, T. Editors of Encyclopaedia. (2018, May 02). "Nigerian Theatre." *Encyclopedia Britannica*. https://www.britannica.com/art/Nigerian-theatre

Igwe, C. (2015). "How Nollywood became the Second Largest Film Industry." *British Council*. British Council Worldwide. https://www.britishcouncil.org/voices-magazine/nollywood-second-largest-film-industry

Lemuel Terlanga. (n.d.). "Chapter 1, Introduction to African Drama." https://www.academia.edu/35396251/CHAPTER_I_INTRODUCTION_TO_AFRICAN_DRAMA

McCain, C. (2013). "Nollywood, Kannywood, and a Decade of Hausa Film Censorship in Nigeria." In D. Biltereyst and R. V. Winkel (eds.), *Silencing Cinema. Global Cinema*. New York: Palgrave Macmillan. https://doi.org/10.1057/9781137061980_14

Okodo, I. (2012). "African Traditional Drama: The Igbo-Nigerian Experience." *Journal of Emerging Trends in Educational Research and Policy Studies (JETERAPS)*, 3(2): 131–6.

Onuzulike, U. (2008). "Nollywood: The Birth of Nollywood: The Nigerian Movie Industry." *Black Camera*, 22(1): 25–6.

OGUNDE, HUBERT

Hubert Adedeji Ogunde was born July 10, 1916, at Ososa Ogun State and died April 4, 1990, in London. As a child he was intrigued by the dancing and drumming of Yoruba masquerade performances and *Ifa* worship (through his maternal grandfather). These experiences shaped his love for Yoruba entertainment.

Ogunde began his employment career first as a schoolteacher (1933–41) and later as a police officer (1941–45). His entertainment career began in 1944 when the Church of the Lord, (*Aladura*) sponsored the staging of his first play (co-produced with Mr. Kuyinu), *The Garden of Eden and The Throne of God* in Lagos. The success of the play encouraged Ogunde to write more plays and form his own theater group, African Music Research Party, in 1945.

Ogunde's theater grew in popularity due to his strategic use of advertisements and posters; and the dramatic realism of his plays using Yoruba dance and folk songs. He soon moved away from religious themes to more sociopolitical ones, which, unfortunately, did not always go well with the government of the day. Between 1946 and 1950 his theater troupe was banned several times by the colonial government from staging plays in sections of the northern region. The sanctions were accompanied with fines and on an occasion Ogunde was arrested. The most controversial of his works, however, was *Yoruba Ronu* based on the political turmoil in the old western region in 1964. After the play's first staging in Ibadan, Ogunde's theater company and the accompanying record were banned in the region. The ban, however, encouraged Ogunde to take his plays to neighboring West African countries until it was lifted in 1966 by Lt.-Col. Adekunle Fajuyi after the January 15 coup.

The management and training of Ogunde's troupe was overseen by Ogunde with support from his senior wives, family members, and close business associates. This unique set-up made mobile touring possible. His first tour was in 1948, when he left Lagos to perform in cities in the western region. His first performance outside Africa was in 1967 at the World Exposition (Canada). His troupe of forty members later conducted a one-year cultural tour of Europe performing the play *Oh-Ogunde* between 1968 and 1969. Ogunde financed this tour having failed to convince the federal government of the viability of such a venture. The tour nevertheless was a success and a great boost to the image of Nigeria.

By 1948, Ogunde had set up his own recording studio which not only made waxing his records easier and faster but also helped other Nigerian musicians to do the same. With the establishment of a television station in the western region in 1959, Ogunde began to produce television programs thus reducing his mobile tours. By 1979, he had co-produced his first celluloid film and in 1982 established a film village in Ososa.

Until his death, Ogunde dominated the Nigerian entertainment industry with his records, plays, broadcast programs, and films. He was awarded national and international recognition for his pioneer and legendary achievements.

See Also: Indigenous Drama (Chapter 11); Traditional Performances (Chapter 11).

Further Reading

Britannica, T. Editors of Encyclopaedia. (2022, March 31). "Hubert Ogunde." *Encyclopedia Britannica*. https://www.britannica.com/biography/Hubert-Ogunde

Nigerian Affairs. (1970). "Hubert Ogunde – A Musical Celebrity." *The People*, 2(2): 8–18.

Oduguwa, A. (2015, May). "Biography of Chief (Dr.) Hubert Adedeji Ogunde – The Doyen of African Theatre." BIOGRAPHY OF CHIEF (DR.) HUBERT ADEDEJI OGUNDE- THE DOYEN OF AFRICAN THEATRE – ebiographer (wordpress.com).

OKRI, BEN

Ben Okri was born on March 15, 1959, in Minna (Niger State). In 1961, Ben's father, moved the family to London to further his education as a lawyer, while Ben attended primary school. When his father completed his law degree in 1968, the family moved back to Nigeria. Soon after, they were caught in the Nigerian Civil War, an experience which later served as a foundation for some of Okri's literature themes.

Ben Okri completed his high school in Urhobo College (Effurun) at the age of fourteen. Okri encountered academic restrictions due to his young age, denying him admission into the university to study Physics. He nevertheless turned this disappointment into inspiration by reading classical literature and exploring oral traditions and folktales of the Urhobo people, his father's ethnic group. These helped to develop his talents as a writer and poet, and he published his short stories in women's magazines and evening papers. Unfortunately, because his writings were laced with strong anti-political undertones, he attracted negative attention from the Nigerian military government of the time.

In 1978, Okri left Nigeria for England and lived with his uncle. During this period, he worked in the daytime with *Afro Scope* as a writer and librarian; and in the evening attended classes at Goldsmiths College reading Afro-Caribbean literature. In 1980, he gained admission to Essex University (London) to study Comparative Literature with support from a grant awarded by the Nigerian Government. Unfortunately, the grant was often insufficient and Okri was frequently forced to live in parks and with friends. He eventually got a job as a poetry editor for *West Africa* (1983–86) and later as a freelance broadcaster for the BBC African Service (1983–85).

Okri published his first novel *Flowers and Shadows* in 1980. He started writing the novel *The Famished Road* in 1988 and in 1991 the novel won the Booker Prize for Fiction making him the youngest winner of the prize. He followed the *Famished Road* with the sequels *Songs of Enchantment* (1993) and *Infinite Riches* (1998). The novels are known as the *abiku* (born to die and live again) trilogy of a spirit-child (Azaro). Azaro, is born and reborn several times and finally stays in the land of the living but with abilities to see into the spirit world. His experiences depict the poverty, pain, and desperation that political and social powers enforce on their masses. The trilogy is a representation of Nigeria, symbolizing the effects of the colonial, independence, and military eras on the country and its transformations.

Okri has been awarded various titles and awards in recognition of his achievements in literature including Officer of the Most Excellent Order of the British Empire (OBE) in 2001 and Fellow of the Royal Society of Literature (FRSL) in 1987. He was awarded honorary doctorates from the universities of Westminster (1997) and Essex (2002). In 2001, he was made the Vice-President of the English Centre of International PEN and a member of the board of the Royal National Theatre.

See Also: Adichie, Chimamanda Ngozi (Chapter 11); Fiction and Nonfiction Literary Works (Chapter 11); Soyinka, Wole (Chapter 11).

Further Reading

McCann, F. (2013). "Ben Okri." *Commonwealth Essays and Studies*, 35(2). https://journals.open-edition.org/ces/5307; doi: https://doi.org/10.4000/ces.5307

O'Connor, M. (2008). *The Writing of Ben Okri: Transcending the Local and the National*. New Delhi: Prestige Books.

SARO-WIWA, KEN

Kenule (Ken) Beeson Saro-Wiwa, born on October 10, 1941, in Bori; and was executed on November 10, 1995, in Port Harcourt. He started his writing career as an undergraduate at the University of Ibadan where he was awarded a scholarship to study English.

During the Nigerian Civil War, Saro-Wiwa joined the Nigerian federal force, and was appointed a Civilian Administrator of Bonny. His experiences during the war were themes for his novels *Sozaboy: A Novel in Rotten English* (1985) and *On a Darkling Plain: An Account of the Nigerian Civil War* (1989). In both books he made known his opposition to the Ibo secession cause.

After the war, Saro-Wiwa was appointed the Regional Commissioner for Education in the Old Rivers State but was dismissed in 1973 due to his support for the Ogoni cause. In 1977, he contested and lost at the national elections to represent the Ogoni people at the Constituent Assembly. After leaving the government service, he established private enterprises including his own publishing outfit. Between 1985 and 1990 he produced the very popular weekly television comical series *Basi & Company* which focused on the streetwise tactics of Basi, a want-to-be millionaire.

In 1990, Saro-Wiwa again became active in politics and co-founded the Movement for the Survival of the Ogoni People (MOSOP). MOSOP's major mandate was to ensure the Ogoni people have a fair share of oil extraction proceeds and the clean-up of environmental damages caused by international oil companies. On this platform, Saro-Wiwa addressed the United Nations Working Group on Indigenous Peoples in July 1992 at Geneva and there presented his new book *Genocide in Nigeria: The Ogoni Tragedy*.

In May 1994 Saro-Wiwa was arrested following the brutal murder of four Ogoni chiefs. He and eight others (later known as the Ogoni nine) were accused by the Nigerian military government of inciting the murders. A trial was conducted and, despite evidence that suggested their innocence, the Ogoni nine were executed by hanging in a Port Harcourt prison.

His last short story titled *Africa Kills Her Sun* (1989) was a premonition of his execution and denial of a decent grave. Two months after his execution, the diary of his experience while in prison, *A Month and a Day: A Detention Diary* (1995) was published. In 2014, *Silence Would Be Treason: Last Writings of Ken Saro-Wiwa (New and Expanded Edition)*, a compilation of letters and poems he wrote to Sister Majella McCarron was also published.

Today, Saro-Wiwa is remembered as a great environmental activist, poet, and writer. While alive, he produced numerous books, plays, children's literature, poems, essays, speeches, and newspaper articles. His bravery and determination won him several awards including: the Right Livelihood Award (also known as the Alternative Nobel Prize) and his nomination for the Nobel Peace Prize in October 1995 (a month to his execution and fifty-third birthday). In 1996 he was posthumously elected to the United Nations Environment Program (UNEP) Global 500 Roll of Honour for advancing the cause of environmental protection.

See Also: Indigenous Drama (Chapter 11); Nigerian Civil War (Chapter 2); Soyinka, Wole (Chapter 11).

Further Reading

Britannica, T. Editors of Encyclopaedia. (2022, November 06). "Ken Saro-Wiwa." *Encyclopedia Britannica*. https://www.britannica.com/biography/Ken-Saro-Wiwa

Corely, Í., H. Fallon, and Laurence Cox, eds. (2018). *Silence Would Be Treason: Last Writings of Ken Saro-Wiwa: Second Edition*. N.p.: Daraja Press.

Doron, R. and T. Falola. (2016). *Ohio Short Histories of Africa - Ken Saro-Wiwa*. Athens: Ohio University Press.

Doron, R., T. Falola, and L. Seay. (2016). "The Complex Life and Death of Ken Saro-Wiwa." *The Washington Post – Democracy Dies in Darkness*.

Kriesch, A. (2015). "Why Nigerian Activist Ken Saro-Wiwa was Executed." *Deutsche Welle (DW) – Made for Minds*. https://www.dw.com/en/why-nigerian-activist-ken-saro-wiwa-was-executed/a-18837442

Project Underground. (n.d.). "The Life and Death of Ken Saro-Wiwa: A History of the Struggle for Justice in the Niger Delta." http://remembersarowiwa.com/wp-content/uploads/life_death_ksw.pdf

Saro-Wiwa, K. (1996). *A Month and a Day in Detention Diary (with an introduction by William Boyd)*. New York: Penguin Books.

SOYINKA, WOLE

Akinwande Oluwole Babatunde Soyinka was born on July 13, 1934, in Abeokuta (Ogun State). He had his primary education at Abeokuta and his secondary education in Ibadan. He gained admission to the University College Ibadan (now the University of Ibadan) to study English Literature, Greek and Western History (1952–54). As an undergraduate, he wrote his first short radio play titled "Keffi's Birthday Treat" and then went to the University of Leeds in England (1954–57) for his Masters. While at Leeds, he wrote the play *The Invention* which was performed at the Royal Court Theatre in 1957. This was followed by *The Swamp Dwellers* (performed 1958) and *The Lion and the Jewel* (performed 1959) both of which were later performed in Ibadan.

Soyinka was an active political critic even as an undergraduate. He co-founded the Pirates Confraternity, an anti-corruption and justice-seeking student organization. He also played an active role during Nigeria's struggle for independence. His play, *My Father's Burden*, was one of the first plays to be featured on Western Nigeria Television and aired in August 1960, a few months after Nigeria's independence. At independence, his play, *A Dance of the Forest*, was selected as the official play to mark the occasion and was performed in Lagos. Soyinka nevertheless was known to be a political rebel who made his displeasure of Nigerian political rule at independence apparent. In 1965, in protest of the political situation of the then western region, he seized the operations of the Western Broadcasting Service studio at gunpoint. He then replaced the recorded speech of the western region's Premier with one that accused the government of election malpractices. He was detained for a few months after which he wrote *Kongi's Harvest* and the BBC Radio play *The Detainee*. He was again arrested in 1967 when his appeal against the civil war was perceived as his loyalty to the Biafran cause. For this, he was placed in solitary confinement for twenty-two months by the military-led government of General Yakubu Gowon. While in prison, he continued to write poems and plays.

After the Nigerian Civil War, Soyinka took up employment at the University of Ife (now known as the Obafemi Awolowo University) and was made a professor of Comparative Literature (1975–99). This was followed by several other appointments with universities in the USA as well as in Europe in fields ranging from creative writing, theater arts, and African culture. He combined this with the writing of poetry, plays, and novels, as well as national and international production and performance of his plays. His themes were very satirical and critical of Nigerian and indeed African governments, and this meant he spent a considerable amount of time in exile. He also uses his writings to criticize social elites and to point out social ills.

His contributions have attracted several awards including the Europe Theatre Prize. He was awarded the 1986 Nobel Prize in Literature which made him the first African to be so honored.

See Also: Indigenous Drama (Chapter 11); Okri, Ben (Chapter 11); Saro-Wiwa, Ken (Chapter 11).

Further Reading

Britannica, T. Editors of Encyclopaedia. (2022, March 16). "Nobel Prize." *Encyclopedia Britannica.* https://www.britannica.com/topic/Nobel-Prize

Britannica, T. Editors of Encyclopaedia. (2022). "Wole Soyinka: Nigerian Author." *Encyclopedia Britannica.* https://www.britannica.com/biography/Wole-Soyinka

Ogunyemi, Y. (2009). *The Literary/Political Philosophy of Wole Soyinka.* Maryland: America Books.

Olayebi, B. (2004). *WS: A Life in Full.* Ibadan: Bookcraft.

TALES BY MOONLIGHT

Traditionally, storytelling for many Nigerian ethnic groups was a method used by members of the older generation to pass morals, history, and cultural norms to the younger members of the society. The narrators were usually symbolic representations of a parent, grandparent, uncle/aunt, who due to their social positions and biological ages were deemed knowledgeable and experienced. The elders told tales in an oral narrative format and their themes would be drawn from current events, history, cultural practices, and personal experiences. The tales were often woven around a mythical or historical character, and through the experiences of this character, morals are drawn and learned. The tale narration would begin after all chores for the day were done. This means most of the stories were told in the late evenings, under the night sky hence the term "tales by moonlight."

In most Nigerian ethnic groups, the narrator in addition to being a good orator, also had to have a good command of proverbs. Proverbs in this sense are short wise sayings which can only be understood within the context of the culture. By using proverbs within a story, the older generation not only taught their audience the art of communicating through proverbs but were also able to ingrain in them cultural knowledge. Among the Yoruba people for instance, a proverb usually has two parts: the introductory (which is given by the narrator), and the end (which is supplied by the audience). The process of chiming the end of a proverb in unison not only makes the story alive but also gives the audience a sense of connection with the story.

The stories told by the narrator did not only apply the use of words but also chorus songs with accompanying gestures or dance. As in the case of using proverbs, the audience is expected to sing along with the narrator. Thus, the narrator may start a tale by teaching the audience the chorus of a song. Once the audience has mastered the chorus, the narrator inserts the song in-between the story signaling to the audience when to come in with the chorus. This technique helps to ensure that the audience not only remembers the story told, but also the moral behind the story. The gestures and/or dance which accompanies the song keeps the audience awake and in tune with the story told.

Scholars who have studied Nigerian tale narration, have identified the transfer of skills like listening, creative thinking, and an ability to obey instructions during the process. Storytelling has also been very useful for academic scholars of history, anthropology, and archaeology who have been able to use the stories to fill gaps in their study of ancient Nigerian societies and peoples. Early Nigerian literary writers such as Chinua Achebe, Wole Soyinka, Amos Tutuola, and J. P. Clark drew inspiration from such oral tales in the composition of their novels and poems. Dramatists like Hubert Ogunde and Duro Ladipo transformed the tales into plays in their drama theaters.

See Also: Indigenous Drama (Chapter 11); Traditional Performances (Chapter 11).

Further Reading

Edosomwan, S. and C. Peterson. (2016). "A History of Oral and Written Storytelling in Nigeria." https://files.eric.ed.gov/fulltext/ED581846.pdf

TUTUOLA, AMOS

Amos Tutuola was born in 1920 at Abeokuta (Ogun State) and died June 1997 at Ibadan. At the age of seven, Tutuola was sent to live with a relative's friend who sponsored his education at the Salvation Army School (1934). Tutuola proved to be a brilliant student and was given special promotion at the end of his first year. After two years, his sponsor was transferred to Lagos and there Tutuola was admitted to the Lagos High School (1936). In Lagos, he again proved to be an outstanding student who topped his class. This prompted the principal to promote him from Standard II to Standard IV and award Tutuola a one-year scholarship. Unfortunately, his sponsor had a wicked staff who made life very difficult for young Tutuola and he decided to go back to his parents at Abeokuta. His father then enrolled him at the Anglican school at Abeokuta; but because his father (who was a cocoa farmer) was not as wealthy as his former sponsor, Tutuola had to do odd jobs to supplement his schooling. Unfortunately, nine months into his Standard VI and final year, his father died. This ended Tutuola's formal education.

Tutuola went on to train as a coppersmith and joined the West African Air Corps in 1944 as a Blacksmith. This career path was cut short after World War II when he was demobilized. After an unsuccessful attempt to start his own business, he eventually went to work with the Lagos Labour Department as a messenger (1948). It was during this time that he began to write his first novel which was inspired by Yoruba folktales told to him as a child. He sent his first handwritten manuscript to Focal Press, an English publisher. The manuscript titled *The Wild Hunter in the Bush of the Ghost* was sent with pencil sketches. The amused publisher paid a small amount to Tutuola in compensation for the work he put into handwriting and sketching the manuscript; believing that no one would possibly publish such a poorly constructed story (it was eventually published in 1982).

Tutuola was luckier with his second manuscript *The Palm-Wine Drinkard* which was published by Faber and Faber (UK) in 1952 and Grove Press (USA) in 1953. By 1978, the book had sold more than 90,000 copies in America and the UK and today has been translated into eleven languages. This made *The Palm-Wine Drinkard* the first African novel to be published outside Africa; written in what scholars called "modified Yoruba English" or "Pidgin English." Though at first labeled "primitive" by Western reviewers and criticized in Nigeria for its "poor English construction," it was eventually accepted for its uniqueness and originality. Tutuola followed this publication with *My Life in The Bush*.

Tutuola's writing style was not the only quality that attracted attention outside Africa; but also, his ability to ingeniously write about the world of the dead, spirits, and magic. Using the first-person narrative, he weaves storylines with Yoruba folklore and scenarios involving rituals and the supernatural.

See Also: Fiction and Nonfiction Literary Works (Chapter 11); Okri, Ben (Chapter 11); Soyinka, Wole (Chapter 11).

Further Reading

Britannica, T. Editors of Encyclopaedia. (2022, June 04). "Amos Tutuola." *Encyclopedia Britannica*. https://www.britannica.com/biography/Amos-Tutuola

Hogan, P. (2000). "Understanding 'The Palm-Wine Drinkard.'" *ARIEL: A Review of International English Literature*, 31(4): 33–58.

Lindfors, B. (1920). "Amos Tutuola." *DLB 125*. https://disa.ukzn.ac.za/sites/default/files/DC%20 Metadata%20Files/Centre%20for%20African%20Literary%20Studies/ALS%204_1_5_55b/ALS%204_1_5_55b.pdf

Tutuola, A. (1954). *The Palm-wine Drinkard and My Life in the Bush of Ghosts*. New York: Grove Press.

TRADITIONAL PERFORMANCES

The foundation of indigenous drama in Nigeria has its origins in two major pre-colonial activities namely: cultural festivals and religious rituals. Cultural festivals celebrated milestones such as harvest, coronations, weddings, births, and burials. Religious or ritual festivals on the other hand involved invoking/reverencing ancestral gods or spirits during occasions such as harvest, religio-political installations, a commemoration of spiritual or historical deeds such as performed by a hero, protagonist, or the gods, or the marking of mythical occurrences. Most Nigerian cultural festivals are usually accompanied with songs, dance, merriment, and feasting. Ritual festivals, however, may start off solemnly with their aim being to worship, make sacrifices, or appeals to the supernatural for protection, direction, or cleansing; but many nevertheless, end with songs and dance. Both occasions are used by traditional leaders to unite their people and reconnect them with their ancestors or the supernatural. Whether cultural or ritual, festivals played an important role in the lives of the people and were recognized as calendar events.

Among many ethnic groups in southern Nigeria, the culture of traditional drama evolved from court theater and the use of masquerades which performed during ritual festivals. The ruling heads of ethnic groups like the Igbo, Kalabari, Ibibio, Opobo, Ijaw, and Efik used this medium to entertain, but more importantly, to sustain their people's knowledge of important themes such as identification and reverence of gods and spirits, the mystical history and foundation of the people, relationships with neighbors, and moral codes of unity. Among the Yoruba people of southwestern Nigeria for example, the introduction of masquerade performance can be traced to *Sango*, the Alaafin of Oyo who reigned in the fourteenth century. The masquerades symbolized the reincarnated spirit of Sango's late father. By the middle of the sixteenth century, this method of ancestral worship had developed into the *Egungun* festival which included entertainment performances like acrobatic displays and dances by masked and covered "spirits." The festival eventually evolved into a competition of skills to entertain the royal court and people, and this improved the quality of performance. Soon the performers were invited by high chiefs to perform outside the palace courts and outside the context of the *Egungun* festival.

The evolution of the *Egungun* masquerade festival from a ritual to one of entertainment was replicated in many ritual festivals observed in Nigeria. Once the traditional drama originally associated with a ritual festival was no longer dependent on the foundational ritual, scholars argue that such events were given new meanings. Factors identified for spurring this evolution in traditional drama include the conversion into Christianity, colonial rule, and the desire for material wealth propelled by "modernization."

Today, some traditional performances are still initiated by calendars of religious/ritual events while others are more as ceremonial or social milestones. The performing members use a fine mixture of contemporary skills and traditional knowledge in their composition of songs and dances. Their themes range from satire, comic, and tragedy to channels of social change, awareness, and education.

See Also: Indigenous Drama (Chapter 11); Tales by Moonlight (Chapter 11).

Further Reading

Morrison, J. (1991). "Forum Theater in West Africa: An Alternative Medium of Information Exchange." *Research in African Literatures*, 22(3): 29–40.

CHAPTER 12

Art and Architecture

OVERVIEW

An understanding of Nigerian art and architecture has helped researchers better understand and appreciate the Nigerian people, their history, and culture. In relation to art, Nigeria is known to be the home of some of the oldest art forms in Africa. Several ancient Nigerian art forms were abstract in nature (meaning that they do not look realistic). Western scholars of Nigerian art often distinguish "art" from "craft" based on the medium used for their production. Within this classification, artworks are believed to be made from expensive materials (such as wood, leather, coral beads, etc.) and valuable metals (such as bronze, brass, gold); while crafts were made with easily obtainable materials (such as raffia, clay, and other plant like materials). Based on this, Nigerian art is referred to as "harder forms" and includes sculptures (this comes in wood and metal), rock art/paintings. The "softer forms" are referred to as craft which include cloth and basket weaving, dyeing, pottery, and calabash carving.

The classification of Nigerian art forms into either art or craft by scholars has resulted in the genderization of Nigeria's traditional art industry. Art forms are given a higher status associating it with men while crafts are considered of lower status being associated with women and domestic use. Items of craft include pottery for storage and cooking (e.g., pots). However, not all traditional art industries could be so classified. Pottery was traditionally produced in almost every part of Nigeria by women, but the gender for specialized crafts such as basket and mat weaving (as were found in southeastern, South-South, and Middle Belt areas of Nigeria), differed based on the ethnic group. Similarly, the ancient craft of glass production (which can still be found being produced among the Nupe people with the use of modern domestic items such as broken bottles and mirrors) are male dominated to produce jewellery and other household decorations. Based on the scholarly classification of art which is seen as a professional skill that produces products to attract monetary gains and spiritual affiliations, the ancient tradition of glass bead making (and in some cases textile production) may need to be reclassified as being similar to other traditional art forms such as palace art and sculpture production.

Nigerian art, whether classified as art or craft, was and still is a symbol and medium through which many ethnic cultures in Nigeria sustained themselves economically, preserved their history, worshipped their gods, transferred knowledge from one generation to the next, and developed family and communal bonds. Thus, unlike European art, which was meant to decorate and beautify, many Nigerian artworks were functional in nature. They were produced as tools for the development of the people in terms of their mind, body, and soul, and in the advancement of their social structures in terms of their technological, cultural, political, and economic development.

A study of art and architecture is an understanding of a people's technological development. They represent the material culture of a people, their ingenuity, creativity, and uniqueness. Several techniques used in the production of Nigerian arts and architecture employed complex methods and an understanding of the delicate balance between nature and science. Each area of Nigeria represents a unique technique with hints of cultural exchange inspired through trade. For example, there is evidence that as early as 500 BCE various parts of Nigeria had people who had advanced knowledge of iron smelting. These include present-day areas such as Argungu, Daura, Katsina, Zaria, Nok, and Gombe in the northern part of Nigeria; Oyo, Igbira, Ogbomosho, and Isie in the western part of Nigeria; and Ukehe, Aku, Abakaliki, Owerre-Elu, and Abiriba in the eastern part of Nigeria. These areas had distinct techniques of iron smelting and used different tools in their production of the iron. In many of these areas, there has been continuity in the skill as iron-smelters can still be found using these ancient methods to produce iron- tools, arts, and crafts.

The history of Nigerian architecture is believed to have been inspired by the need to settle down and trade. For most pre-colonial Nigerian urban settlements, market activities (access to and exit from markets) were a major aspect considered in the settlement plans. It is thus not surprising that markets were often found at the center of their traditional settlements. Individual houses were built in proximity representing the patrilineal leaning of most pre-colonial Nigerian societies. The architectural designs of individual houses were usually rectilinear or circular shapes made from varying materials such as mud, the trunks of trees, grass, palm fronds, and leaves.

In the northern section of Nigeria, Hausa architectural designs were greatly influenced by the Islamic religion which demanded a strict separation of sexes. The spacing of living quarters was thus planned with this in mind. Often the homestead is walled to prevent unwanted visitors from coming in and the women from going out. Within the walls are spaces for children to play, cooking areas, toilet facilities, and meeting rooms for relaxation. The homestead thus comprises several huts designed to meet all the biological, social, and physical needs of the inhabitants. A major characteristic of Hausa traditional buildings are the mural art decorations which can be found on the walls. These mural paintings reflect the wealth and prestige of the male head of the household.

In the southern section of Nigeria, changes in architectural designs were shaped by exposure to Christianity as well as European lifestyle and, later, freed slaves from Brazil. This

The Work of Professor Peju Layiwola
Nigerian art has undergone significant transformation over the years. One such pioneer who combined traditional forms of art with history is Professor Peju Layiwola of the Department of Creative Arts, University of Lagos. Professor Layiwola has used various media such as metal, wood, and textiles to engage diverse themes including the pillaging of Nigerian artworks, especially those of Benin Kingdom, the return of these stolen artifacts from Western countries (including, England, Germany, and France), and cultural history and identities. She has used her exhibitions in Nigeria and abroad to display the beauty of Nigerian art and its symbolism as a text for deeper analysis of indigenous technology, dexterity, and aesthetics. She has also produced DVDs to teach interested persons the art of beadmaking. Her non-profit organization, Women and Youth Art Foundation (Wy Art), is a major source of providing women and youth with a platform for self-empowerment.

---

combination resulted in the firststory building in Nigeria built in 1845 in Badagry. Though this building is still standing, many other historical buildings built during the colonial era in Nigeria have either been pulled down or crumbled due to lack of maintenance. Those still standing are in great disrepair, thus posing a threat to society.

Fortunately, initiatives are under way to preserve some of these buildings. One of such are the efforts of students of the Department of Architecture at the Obafemi Awolowo University. With the support of their department and other non-governmental organizations, they make efforts to restore dilapidated Brazilian-style buildings that hold historical heritage. The intervention exercise included removing plant growth from the walls, repairing cracks and decorative mouldings, repainting, providing reinforcements to weak areas. This intervention has not only helped to make the houses more secure for the residents who still call them their homes, but also makes the ancient town of Ife look more appealing. Such intervention programs should be encouraged all over Nigeria to help preserve the ancient architectural traditions.

Further Reading

Agu, C. S. and V. E. Ali. (2012). "The Role of Art Objects in Technological Development of Nigeria: An Archeological Perspective." *Bassey Andah Journal*, 5: 201–14.

Danja, I., Xue Li, and S. G. Dalini. (2017, March). "Vernacular Architecture of Northern Nigeria: A Review." *International Journal of Scientific & Engineering Research*, 8(3): 1219–26.

Moughtin, J. C. (1964). "The Traditional Settlements of the Hausa People." *Town Planning Review*, 35: 21–34. doi: https://doi.org/10.3828/tpr.35.1.y03303u5115t1711

Osasona, C. O. (2007). "Indigenous Art and Nigerian Contemporary Residential Architecture." *WIT Transactions on the Built Environment*, 109: 59–70. doi: https://doi.org/10.2495/STR070131

Osasona, C. O. and F. O. Ewemade. (2009). "Upgrading Ile-Ife's Vernacular Architecture Heritage." *Structural Studies, Repairs and Maintenance of Heritage XI*, 109. doi: https://doi.org/10.2495/STR090061

Willet, F. (1967). "Ife in Nigerian Art." *African Arts*, 1, no. 1 (Autumn): 30–5.

BEAD ART

Ancient sculptural pieces like Nok, Ife, and Benin, depict male and female figures with beads around their necks, feet, wrists, and on royal crowns. At the Igbo-Ukwu archaeological site more than 100,000 glass beads were found. Among the ancient Yoruba and Benin people, beads were used as a major symbol of authority and power for the monarchy, and a signifier of the spiritual powers of religious priests and priestesses. Beads serve as badges of political offices, economic wealth, and spiritual well-being; if taken away, the person is symbolically stripped of these positive associations. These two kingdoms controlled the production, distribution, and use of valued beads. Beads were sold to neighboring peoples as well as to European explorers and Arab traders. Among the Edo, Ibo, and Niger Delta peoples of Nigeria, coral beads were much valued and thus served as a major source of trade between those peoples.

Among the Yoruba people, bead making goes as far back as the eleventh to the fourteenth century based on archaeological findings from Igbo-Olokun grove, a site close to modern Ile Ife in western Nigeria indicating a beadmaking factory. Materials used to produce beads in Ife were locally sourced though some scholars believe that European and Islamic glass beads obtained through trade were also melted and re-mixed to meet societal needs. Beads produced include *Segi* which were blue or blue-green glass beads, *Akun* which was red, *Segida* was a jasper color and *Ejiba/Edigba* which was a carnelian color, and the red coral beads. There is also the *Akori/Kori* or Aggrey beads which have been found in various colors such as blue, red, yellow, and black whose origin and make have been a mystery (some believe they were made of stone; others believe it grew from a tree, with some claiming it was dug from the ground or a product of the sea). The Kori beads were very prominent in trade within West Africa and outside the region. The *Segi* beads were especially important for their association with healing, protection, and spiritual powers especially during divination.

The Masaga people of Bida, Niger State are also known for their traditional knowledge and production of glass beads. They produced beads from broken glass and sand in beehive shaped furnaces built with red clay. They also make and use other variations of beads including *Akka*, *Erinla* and *Jigida* beads. *Akka* beads come in various colors including white, dark red, blue, yellow, dark brown, and light green, and are also worn by Igbo women. *Jigida* beads are also known as waist beads and are often associated with female sexuality; being a symbol of maturity, fertility, and readiness for marriage; and by married women to accentuate their hips.

Today, the Nigerian bead market consists of traditional glass beads produced in locally made furnaces and imported beads. Contemporary Nigerian bead stringers study and acquire the skill as a strategy to fight poverty and unemployment. They design not only jewelry but also crafts such as flower vases, bags, and phone covers.

See Also: Benin Artworks (Chapter 12); Ife Artwork (Chapter 12); Igbo Artwork (Chapter 12).

Further Reading

Adiji, B. E. (2018). "Use of Beads in Contemporary Fashion Industry of South-Western Nigeria." *International Journal of African Society, Cultures and Traditions*, 6(1): 7–14.

Azuka, N. (2014). "Aesthetics, Typology and Functionality of Beads among the Peoples of Nigeria." *Tropical Built Environment Journal (TBEJ)*, 4(1): 507–11.

Babalola, A. B. (2015). "Archaeological Investigations of Early Glass Production at Igbo-Olokun, Ile-Ife (Nigeria)." A thesis submitted in partial fulfilment of the requirements for the degree of Doctor of Philosophy, Rice University, Houston Texas USA.

Babalola, A. B., S. K. McIntosh, L. Dussubieux, and T. Rehren. (2017). "Ile-Ife and Igbo Olokun in the History of Glass in West Africa." *Antiquity*, 91(357): 732–50. doi: https://doi.org/10.15184/aqy.2017.80

Ibebabuchi, A. O. (2012, June 28). "Bead Making and Ornamentation in Nigeria." *Vanguard*. https://www.vanguardngr.com/2012/06/bead-making-and-ornamentation-in-nigeria/

Mauny, R. (1958, December). "Akori Beads." *Journal of the Historical Society of Nigeria*, 1(3): 210–14. https://www.jstor.org/stable/41856633

Ogundiran, A. (2002). "Of Small Things Remembered: Beads, Cowries, and Cultural Translations of the Atlantic Experience in Yorubaland." *The International Journal of African Historical Studies*, 35(2/3): 427–57. https://www.jstor.org/stable/3097620

BENIN ARTWORK

Benin art culture spans thousands of years and is a creation of the Edo people, the major ethnic group in modern-day Edo State, Nigeria. Its first appreciation outside Africa occurred after the 1897 Punitive Expedition when the British attacked and destroyed Benin City; an act that resulted in thousands of Benin artworks being carted away. These relics include bronze posts and pillars, ivories, and other artworks from the Benin royal altar. These artifacts were taken to London and sold to the British and Berlin museums. Today Benin artworks can still be found in European and American museums as well as in individual private collections all over the world.

Several of the artworks from the ancient Benin Empire were made from cast brass and carved ivory with a few from terracotta. The main aim of the artworks was to glorify the reigning king and past royalties as well as chiefs and title holders who made up the Benin Empire. The ancient artworks served as historical accounts of events that occurred over half a millennium ago, depicting the wealth, power, and greatness of the ancient Benin Kingdom. Through these artworks, contemporary researchers get a glimpse of what the people of the ancient Benin Empire wore, and their philosophy as it relates to the political domination and spiritual greatness of their king. Edo oral tradition has it that the art of brass casting was initiated by Oguola who reigned in the late fourteenth century. He wanted Benin artisans to produce the kind of artworks often sent to him by the Oni of Ife. He thus requested from the Oni a brass smith to teach Benin artisans the sacred skills through which they were required to preserve the royal history of Benin through art. The similarity in the art of Benin culture and that of the Ife can be seen in their naturalistic features and the medium used for their art.

Today, Benin artworks are produced through the efforts of sixty-eight guilds under the control of the reigning king. Within the guilds are artisans who specialize in various skills ranging from blacksmiths, brass casters, ivory and wood carvers, leather workers, bead, and costume makers. Membership within the guild is hereditary passed from one generation to another. They produce many items using media such as brass, certain species of wood and ivory from which they cast brass plaques, portrait heads, standing statues, carved ivory tusks, masks, and jewellery such as ankle and wrist bracelets as well as necklaces made from coral beads. Casted art objects are produced using the ancient lost-wax technique while others are carved out from ivory, terracotta, and wood. Though still obliged to produce court and symbolic items for the Benin king, tourists and other members of society can also commission them.

In 1999, UNESCO listed the Benin Monarch's palace as a cultural heritage site and a museum due to the large collection of ancient court art and ancestral shrines present there.

See Also: Benin Empire (Chapter 2); Bead Art (Chapter 12); Bronze Casting (Chapter 12); Ife Artwork (Chapter 12); Iron Smelting (Chapter 12); Palace Decoration (Chapter 12); Sculpture (Chapter 12); Terracotta (Chapter 12).

Further Reading

Agbontaen, K. A. (1997, September). "An Assessment of Four Centuries (15th–19th) of Benin Art Production in Evaluating the Role of the Craft Guild System in Benin Polity." *African Study Monographs*, 19(1): 45–58.
Crowe, D. (1975). "The Geometry of African Art II: A Catalog of Benin Patterns." *Historia Mathematica*, 2: 253–71.
Ezra, K. (1992). *Royal Art of Benin: The Perls Collection in the Metropolitan Museum of Art*. New York: Metropolitan Museum of Art.
Nevadomsky, J., B. Půtová, and V. Soukup. (2014). "Benin Art and Casting Technologies." *West Bohemian Historical Review*, 4(1): 75–103.

BRAZILIAN ARCHITECTURE

The Brazilian architectural style in Nigeria was initiated by slaves who returned to Africa from Brazil and Cuba. They were warmly welcomed back and offered land in Lagos where many eventually settled. The Lagos area of their settlement was known as Popo Aguda while the migrant slaves themselves were called Aguda or Maro (derived from the Portuguese word for cotton). Some indigenous Africans also referred to them as "Black Whites" due to their adoption of Western clothes and culture.

Many of the Aguda were skilled artisans in bricklaying, carpentry, cabinet making, masonry, and building. With these skills they designed houses which showed a great influence of the Brazilian culture they had been exposed to. They created an architectural style referred to as Afro-Brazilian. The houses they built had a different architectural design from the traditional huts and the colonial styles prevalent in Nigeria at the time. The Brazilian architectural styles were often two to three story buildings with balconies, columns, large corridors, pillars, doors, and shuttered windows which were heavily decorated while some even had attics. Unlike the more traditional forms, Brazilian houses were built with cement. They were designed with a nuclear family structure in mind unlike the more traditional houses that were more like compounds with an extended family structure being the motivating factor.

The Afro-Brazilian architectural design became the major signifier of wealth and prestige. One-story houses were built for middle-class residents while two-story buildings were for more wealthier members of society. The two-story buildings had a ground floor that opened to the street while the rooms on the ground floor were used for storage or accommodation for house helps. The Brazilian returnees were elites in the society and were sometimes referred to as "White Blacks." They became prominent architects who changed the landscape of Lagos.

The Brazilian style was used to build houses, churches, and mansions which can still be found in Lagos today. Prominent among the Afro-Brazilian public buildings was the Holy Cross Cathedral for which construction began in 1878 and was completed in 1880. Though the construction of the building was supervised by French missionaries, it was constructed by Brazilian workers. The *Ilojo Bar* also known as *Olaiya* House was built in 1855 but demolished in 2016. Its demolition caused a national and international outcry as many believed it was a representation of Nigeria's history; depicting the link between Africa and Brazil; depicting the perseverance of the Black slaves to overcome the forced labor on the plantation farms and come out strong.

Another prominent Afro-Brazilian building was in Tinubu Square and was called the Water House. The house was so called because its owner, Joao Esan da Rocha who, through a well dug in his backyard, sold piped water to residents in his area. Through this venture, he became very wealthy.

Today, many Brazilian-style houses in Nigeria have either been demolished or are in a bad state due to neglect and lack of maintenance.

See Also: Indigenous Architecture (Chapter 12).

Further Reading

Alinta, S. (2013). "The Afro-Brazilian Legacy in the Bight Benin." *Pambazuka News*. https://www.pambazuka.org/global-south/afro-brazilian-legacy-bight-benin

Edvige, J.-F. and G. Chris. (2017). "Lagos' Afro-Brazilian Architecture Faces Down the Bulldozers." *CNN – Inside Africa*. https://edition.cnn.com/2017/07/19/architecture/nigeria-afro-brazilian-architecture/index.html

Oludamola, A. (2018). "How Brazilian Architecture Redefined Lagos History and Heritage." *Guardian Newspapers*. https://guardian.ng/life/how-brazilian-architecture-redefined-lagos-history-and-heritage/

The Sun Nigeria. (2018). "Remembering Lagos' Declining Brazilian Architecture." https://www.sunnewsonline.com/remembering-lagos-declining-brazilian-architecture/

BRONZE CASTING

Bronze is an alloy made of copper and tin and sometimes with an addition of aluminium or zinc. Other non-metals such as silicon or arsenic may also be combined with copper or zinc to form a variety of copper textures of hardness, malleability, and ductility. The knowledge of bronze facilitated the production of metal objects that are more durable and stronger than other materials such as stone. Tin bronze which was more common in pre-colonial Nigeria is superior to brass (copper and zinc) and therefore was a perfect metal with which to cast decorative artifacts.

Bronze casting dates to pre-colonial Nigeria. Bronze objects associated with Benin, Ife, Nupe, and the Igbo-Ukwu have been excavated and analyzed by archaeologists and historians. The largest concentration of bronze objects recovered in Nigeria is from the Benin Kingdom. Bronze was used for royal statues and was reserved for the *Oba* (king), his high chiefs, and the Queen Mother. Unfortunately, many of them were confiscated by the British Government after the Benin Expedition in 1897. Some of these bronze objects included the famous mask used by the Nigerian federal government in 1977 as the face of Nigeria's Festival for Arts and Culture (FESTAC 77)—a cultural carnival organized to display Nigeria's cultural heritage. Other bronze objects carted away by the British Government include royal swords, figureheads of former Benin kings, and bronze bracelets. Today, most of the Benin bronze objects are on display at various British and European museums. The Ife and Igbo-Ukwu bronze objects are not as numerous as those of the Benin works, but they are no less intricately produced and complex in their finishing. The bronze objects of Igbo-Ukwu were more ceremonial suggesting the property of a privileged class while Ife, like Benin, were for royalty.

Although details of the sources of procuring the alloys (for example, tin or zinc) to produce these ancient bronze works are still not well known, the works, nevertheless, reflect a rich culture and an advanced stage of economic and political prosperity. The casting of bronze is a complex procedure that requires an advanced knowledge of metals, their composition, and how they behave when subjected to different degrees of temperature. Many ancient sculptural forms were produced through the lost-wax method or the Cire Perdue. This method involves moulding a detailed wax figure covered with clay. The wax inner and clay outer figure is sun-dried to harden. On drying, the figure is furnace heated to enable the melted wax to escape the hardened clay core. The vacuum left from the melted wax is replaced with smelted iron. When the smelted iron is cooled it hardens and takes the form and details of the original wax figure. The hard clay shell when broken off leaves a solid metal figure in the shape and design of the original wax mould.

Today the dying art of bronze casting is still upheld at Igun Street in the Benin Kingdom where the highest concentration of bronze casters in Nigeria can be found.

See Also: Benin Artwork (Chapter 12); Ife Artwork (Chapter 12); Terracotta (Chapter 12).

Further Reading

Agbontaen, K. A. (1997). "An Assessment of Four centuries (15th–19th) of Benin Art Production in Evaluating the Role of the Craft Guild System in Benin Polity." *African Study Monographs*, 18(1): 45–58.

Awogbade, M. O. (2016). "Examination of Ife Bronze Casting Culture and Its Decline in Maintenance Practice in Contemporary Society." *Africa Research Review: An International Multidisciplinary Journal, Ethiopia*, 10(1): 225–33. doi: http://dx.doi.org/10.4314/afrrev.v10i1.17

EMBROIDERY

Embroidery is a decorative art which is employed to improve the aesthetic quality and general finishing of an outfit. Scholars of Nigerian history believe that the art of embroidery was introduced to Nigeria during the reign of Queen Amina of Zaria through trading activities with the Arabs. The art became even more prominent when the people converted to Islam between the twelfth and fourteenth centuries. Today embroidery is still dominantly practiced among the Hausa and Nupe people of northern Nigeria. It is believed that trade between northern and southern groups in Nigeria, especially between the Hausa and Yoruba peoples, was the leading factor that encouraged the Yoruba people to also adopt embroidery as a significant part of their textile decoration. For both ethnic groups, embroidery is a prominent part of the royal attire of their traditional monarchs.

Among the Hausa people of northern Nigeria, embroidery is an acceptable art which does not go contrary to their Islamic belief of representational art which is forbidden. Thus geometric, lineal, and symmetrical motifs are prominent in their embroidery designs. The embroidery designs are done using traditionally spun or imported silk threads and are often very elaborately used on traditional outfits. Among the Yoruba and Nupe peoples, embroidery is used to communicate their culture and worldviews. The embroidery designs are often placed on the neck, chest, arms, and pockets of traditional outfits such as *Babanriga* for Hausa and *Agbada* for Yoruba men. The embroidery designs are also used to decorate men's traditional caps which often accompany the traditional outfits.

There are two types of embroidery techniques: hand stitch (including the chain and buttonhole technique) and machine. The hand-stitched embroidery is more valued than those produced by machine as the hand stitch is more demanding and painstaking, producing designs that are unique and intricate. The skill of hand embroidery was traditionally the preserve of men especially in the northern parts of Nigeria. Today however, women are venturing into the profession with many of them from Zaria. Muslim Zarian married women are obliged because of their religion to stay indoors most of the time. Within this enclosure, they decorate traditional outfits and caps, bed linens, tablecloths, and pillows with embroidery designs which either their husband, other men within the society, or non-Muslim women sell for them. Unfortunately, these women are sometimes at a disadvantage as they are dependent on tailors outside their residence to make outfits for them to put embroidery designs on and there are also cases where they are cheated by their middlemen who do not pay them the correct amount for their work. Notwithstanding, many Zarian women have been able to improve their economic situation through embroidery.

The Yoruba fashion designers and tailors in the southern part of Nigeria are more limited in their knowledge and ability to hand embroidery and thus prefer to use machines to produce their embroidery designs. Many copy the traditional hand embroidery designs of the North, but many also develop their own unique designs and patterns.

See Also: Textiles (Chapter 12).

Further Reading

Adiji, B. E., S. R. Ogunduyile, and E. B. Ojo. (2016, September–October). "The Documentation of Embroidery Type in Southwestern Nigeria." *Global Journal of Interdisciplinary Social Sciences*, 5(5): 7–14.

Renne, E. (2002). "Hausa Hand-Embroidery and Local Development in Northern Nigeria." *Textile Society of America Symposium Proceedings*. Lincoln: University of Nebraska.

IFE ARTWORK

Ife artwork is a naturalistic form produced by the Yoruba people of southwestern Nigeria and dates to 2,000 years ago. Some contemporary scholars of Nigerian art believe that Ife art is a continuation of the Nok art. This is because of certain similarity in the style, namely the use of decorative beadwork. Ife artworks are believed to be an improvement of Nok art mainly because Ife art is a more naturalistic representation of the human body. Ife and Nok art are the only two forms of art in Africa that represent a close to naturalistic form of the whole human body using terracotta. Other forms of terracotta art found in Africa represent only the head and these are on a very small scale.

Ife art was first exposed to cultures outside Africa in 1910 through the German Anthropologist, Frobenius; and later in 1938 when seventeen life-sized brass heads were discovered in Wunmoniie during archaeological excavations. Because these Ife artworks were very unlike other forms of African art which were more abstract in their representation, a few foreign scholars assumed they could not have been a product of Africa but rather imported from Europe through trade. It was believed to have had its origin in Egyptian and Greek art which served as the foundation of European art. Thus, it was concluded that Ife art must have been produced by European explorers or traders who wandered into Africa.

Today a number of these theories have been discarded as not true basically because Ife artworks are very different from Egyptian and Greek art in terms of how it represents the head, eyes, and ears. In some of the full-body depictions, the head would be greatly exaggerated when compared to the rest of the body. This exaggerated head representation is based on the African philosophy south of the Sahara that the head carries in it the soul, fortune, luck, and greatness of an individual and is thus of more importance than the rest of the human body. This is especially so for depictions of royalty indicating a higher status and authority.

Ife artworks were produced in terracotta and brass.

See Also: Benin Artwork (Chapter 12); Ife Kingdom (Chapter 2); Igbo Artwork (Chapter 12); Bronze Casting (Chapter 12); Palace Decoration (Chapter 12); Sculpture (Chapter 12); Terracotta (Chapter 12).

Further Reading

Blier, S. P. (2012). "Art in Ancient Ife, Birthplace of the Yoruba." *African Arts*, 45, no. 4 (Winter): 70–85.
Contemporary African Art. (2020). "African Art History." https://www.contemporary-african-art.com/african-art-history.html

IGBO ARTWORK

The most ancient Igbo artwork is known as Igbo-Ukwu and has been dated to the ninth and eleventh century CE. Archaeological excavation of these sites, unearthed more than 700 artifacts made from copper, bronze, and iron. The ancient sculptural tradition was named after the Igbo village it was founded in namely Igbo-Ukwu in Anambra State, Nigeria. The artworks are the oldest bronze artefacts in West Africa and were made using the lost-wax technique known as Cire Perdue. With this method, complex artworks were produced including the famous Igbo-Ukwu roped bronze pot. Other items found include beaded jewellery, textile remains, ivory, crowns, staff ornaments, swords, pendants, fly whisks, etc. Some of these items have been associated with the male Ozo title association currently practiced among some Igbo people in Nigeria.

Though the producers of the Igbo-Ukwu ancient art are not known, contemporary forms of wood carving culture are still prevalent among the Igbo people suggest some continuity. This association is deduced based on the evidence of wood carvings found in the Igbo-Ukwu sites. Today, Igbo wood carvers produce items such as masks, stools, carved doors, and panels. Carved wooden door panels serve as entrance doorways to the homes of prestigious men with Ozo titles signifying their wealth and importance. Other items such as masks and sculptural figures are associated with ancestors and spirits through which the people remember and relive important events in their history or the gods and spirits in their cosmology.

There is also the promotion of Pyrography as a technique of artistic expression promoted by the Nsukka Art Department.

The Igbo people are the producers of Ulli symbols which some scholars have classified as an indigenous form of writing. Through the symbolic motifs, the producers communicate abstract as well as concrete ideas such as sunbursts, movement patterns of a python, crescent, and hairstyles. Traditionally Igbo women painted their bodies with Ulli patterns using a dye made from the seeds of the Ulli plant which temporarily stained the body black. The Ulli designs served as a means of body decoration or beautification and were painted on girls who had just left the fattening room ready for marriage signifying elegance, history, and lineage identity. Ulli designs were also used to decorate the outside and inside walls of traditional Igbo houses. It was the duty of women to design their houses with Ulli motifs.

Unfortunately, the use of Ulli motifs on the body and house walls is rapidly dying out due to the introduction of Western religious beliefs. Nevertheless, contemporary artists have adopted the Ulli symbols and images into their works known as Ullism. Ullism was encouraged by artists from the Nsukka School in the 1970s. Ullism designs in contemporary art and craft have elicited positive and negative reactions. Some schools of thought believe that the Ulli symbols have lost their meaning; others believe that Ullism has kept the Ulli culture alive as new meanings are given to the symbols incorporating contemporary reflections.

See Also: Benin Artwork (Chapter 12); Ife Artwork (Chapter 12); Igbo (Chapter 6); Nri Civilization (Chapter 2); Painting (Chapter 12); Sculpture (Chapter 12); Wood Carving (Chapter 12).

Further Reading

Nwoye, C. (2011, September). "Igbo Cultural and Religious Worldview: An Insider's Perspective." *International Journal of Sociology and Anthropology*, 3(9): 304–17.

Ohadike, D. (2007). "Igbo Culture and History." https://womrel.sitehost.iu.edu/REL%20300%20 Spirit/REL%20300_Spirit/Igbo%20Culture%20and%20History.pdf

Onuora, C. N. (2012). "Two Decades of Pyrography by Nsukka Artists (1986–2006)." Ph.D. thesis, Department of Fine and Applied Arts, University of Nigeria, Nsukka, Nigeria. Unpublished.

Udeani, N. A. (2014, July). "Synergy of Uli Symbols and Textiles: An Exploration in Textile Sculptural Forms." *Journal of African Studies*, 3: 80–7.

INDIGENOUS ARCHITECTURE

Traditional houses in Nigeria were made of mud, grass, wood, and bamboo. The traditional housing structures were designed to meet the environmental, cultural, and physical comforts of their residents. The walls were made of sun-dried mud and plastered with cow dung to repel insects that disturb at night, while keeping the residential areas cool during the day. The architectural shapes range from squares as could be found among the Yoruba and Igbo people to a more circular shape in the middle belt and northern areas. The shapes of the roofs also differed with dome-shaped mud roofs in the northern part and flat roofs made of thatch in southern Nigeria. In Nigerian traditional compounds, residential houses were built close to each other reflecting the extended family structure based on lineage and ancestral links. Male heads of the households and each wife had their own residential units. Young children lived with their mothers while older male members had their own quarters. Most traditional compounds also had worship areas and shrines.

Contemporary states like Katsina, Kano, Zaria, and Borno in northern Nigeria are dominated by Hausa Fulani; and the major influencer of their architectural designs is the Islamic religious emphasis of female seclusion. To prevent non-Muslim intrusion, high walls were erected, some of which can still be found today in Kano and Zaria dating back to the twelfth century. A traditional Hausa compound is divided into two sections with the first being a reception area for the male head (the *Zaure*) and the women's quarters (where the wives and women of the household are secluded in compliance with Islamic laws). Male visitors are not allowed beyond the male reception area (*Zaure*) and thus do not encounter the resident females. The *Zaure* thus serves not only as a reception area, but also as a physical space of protection, privacy, and security. Only men respected and dignified by the male head is allowed beyond the *Zaure*.

The Yoruba people who represent the largest ethnic group in southwestern Nigeria, refer to their residential compounds as *Abo'le*. The residential buildings were made of thick mud walls of 6–12 inches and bamboo rafters or other termite-resistant wood in the construction of the roofs. Each room was about 10 feet wide and arranged in a linear pattern to form the compound. Each compound has a major front entrance which leads to the residential quarters and a back entrance which leads to the kitchen and convenience areas. The household head usually occupies the residence close to the entrance for surveillance.

The Igbo people who make up the larger ethnic group in southeastern Nigeria consisted of compounds that were made of rectangular-shaped residential houses which had verandas and forked posts to carry the roofs. Apart from the residential houses, the traditional compounds also had massive gates, meeting houses, and shrines. The residential houses included that of the male head, the residential houses of his wives and their children, family house, and reception house for guests.

See Also: Benin Artwork (Chapter 12); Brazilian Architecture (Chapter 12); Ife Artwork (Chapter 12); Igbo Artwork (Chapter 12); Palace Decoration (Chapter 12).

Further Reading

Adedokun, Ade. (2014, February). "Incorporating Traditional Architecture into Modern Architecture: Case Study of Yoruba Traditional Architecture." *British Journal of Humanities and Social Sciences*, 11(1): 39–45.

Adewumi, Jonathan. (2016, September 27). "Nigerian Traditional Architecture: What Are The Building Types?" *Eni-Itan's Blog*. NIGERIAN TRADITIONAL ARCHITECTURE: What Are The Building Types? – Eni-Itan's Blog (wordpress.com).

Agboola, O. P. and M. S. Zango. (2014, June). "Development of Traditional Architecture in Nigeria: A Case Study of Hausa House Form." *International Journal of African Society, Cultures and Traditions*, 1(1): 61–74. European Centre for Research, Training and Development, UK.

Blier, S. P. (2012). "Cosmic References in Ancient Ife." In C. M. Kreamer, *African Cosmology: Stellar Arts*, 204–15. Washington, DC: Smithsonian National Museum of African Art.

Olotuah, A. O. and D. E. Olotuah. (2016, September). "Space and Cultural Development in Hausa Traditional Housing." *International Journal of Engineering Sciences & Research Technology*, 5(9): 654–9. doi: 10.5281/zenodo.155089

Prucnal-Ogunsote, B. (2001). "Classification of Nigerian Architecture." *AARCHES Journal*, 1(6): 48–56. https://desmo.biz/images/Architecture.pdf

Rikko, L. S. and D. Gwatau. (2011). "The Nigerian Architecture: The Trend in Housing Development." *Journal of Geography and Regional Planning*, 4(5): 273–8. http://www.academicjournals.org/JGRP

IRON SMELTING

Iron smelting is an ancient technology prevalent all over Nigeria dating as far back as 500 BCE to 200 CE. The oldest archaeological evidence of iron smelting was recently discovered in Lejji, a small village on the outskirts of Nsukka, Enugu State. The site has been dated to 2000 BCE making it the oldest iron smelting site in the world. The site has mounds of crescent shapes where hundreds of slags were discovered. The Lejji site is just one of the many other sites found all over Nigeria. Through a study of iron smelting remains such as furnace fragments and slags researchers have not only been able to piece together the prevalence of the ancient technology in Nigeria, but also similarities in the methods or techniques employed by the smelters. Due to the archaeological evidence of stone and iron remains found in Nok sites dating between 500 BCE and 200 CE, many scholars believe that the ancient people of Nigeria (and indeed West Africa) skipped the Copper Age and transitioned from Stone Age to Iron Age. This is unlike other ancient societies found in Europe where the Copper Age lasted for nearly a millennium.

Iron smelting was very important in the history of pre-colonial Nigerian societies as they were used in the production of hunting and defense weapons as well as farming tools. Some scholars believe that in the nineteenth century, after the introduction of guns, blacksmiths were able to manufacture guns that used iron shot rather than lead.

Some Nigerian ethnic groups believe that the art of smelting iron was given to them through the gods. For example, among the Awka people of Anambra State southeastern Nigeria, the art was taught to them by Okanube, a supernatural being who came from the sky. The god not only taught them the skill of smelting iron but also the art of making medicine and hunting with iron spears. Similarly, the Yoruba people believe that Ogun was the god who brought the art of iron smelting. Ogun was believed to have been a hunter and a warrior. He is symbolized with the iron sword which the Yoruba people use to take oaths and perform sacrifices. Thus, all traditional Yoruba blacksmiths are worshippers of Ogun. Thus, the process of iron smelting was linked with spirituality.

Today, iron smelting is not very prevalent but blacksmithing is. Nigerian blacksmiths use scrap metal, motor chassis, and other bits of iron tools and scrap to make new items and make repairs to items such as tools, cutlasses, and knives. In states like Bauchi, located in the northeastern part of Nigeria, the government showcases the *Shau Shau* iron smelting works as a form of tourist attraction. The display includes the working of over sixty furnaces by over 100 blacksmiths who forge various iron tools ranging from cutlasses, hoes, arrows, knives, etc.

See Also: Benin Artwork (Chapter 12); Bronze Casting (Chapter 12); Ife Artwork (Chapter 12), Igbo Artwork (Chapter 12); Sculpture (Chapter 12).

Further Reading

Onuoha, C. (2017). "Origin of Iron Technology in Africa: The Abiriba Blacksmithing in Focus." *Pyrex Journal of History and Culture*, 2(1): 1–9.
Things Nigeria. (2018, February). "Lejja, the World's Oldest Iron-Smelting Site in Nigeria." *Places*.

ONOBRAKPEYA, BRUCE

Bruce Obomeyoma Onobrakpeya was born August 30, 1932, in Agbarha-otor, Delta State, Nigeria. His foundation was influenced by his birth as the son of an Urhobo carver and his teacher Edward Ivehivboje who taught him art at the Western Boys High School. He improved his art skills by attending drawing classes at the British Council Art Club and was greatly influenced by the watercolor paintings of Emmanuel Erabor. He attended the Nigerian College of Arts, Science and Technology which today is the Ahmadu Bello University, Zaria. While at Zaria, he joined the Zaria Arts Society which he declared gave him the technical skills that shaped his professional career. He later taught at his Alma Mater the Western Boys High School, Ondo, and St. Gregory's College Lagos.

Bruce Onobrakpeya's works are appreciated both within and outside Nigeria. He is a recipient of various national and international awards some of which include the British Council Award, Pope Paul VI Gold Medal, Honorary Doctor of Letters from the University of Ibadan, and the Delta State Merit Award for Excellence in Art. He also served as an artist-in-residence in various universities in the USA as well as in Nigeria.

The major philosophy behind Bruce Onobrakpeya's works is a fusion of the traditional with the modern. Going back in time for him was a sign of progress and not regression. This was a philosophy developed from his study at Ahmadu Bello University, where he was a founding member of the Zaria Arts Society. He and seven other prominent Nigerian artists including Uche Okeke (the president), Demas Nwoko, Yusuf Grillo, Simon Okeke, Oseioka Osadebe, Okechukwu Odita, and Ogbonaya Nwagbara formed the Zaria Art Society. As artists, their desire was to make Nigeria and the world appreciate the natural substance of traditional Nigerian cultures through art. They called this philosophy Natural

Synthesis and through this method the artists were able to create unique paintings and sculptures that today define Nigerian contemporary art. Their works encouraged Nigerian artists to look inward for inspiration.

The majority of Bruce Onobrakpeya's works have their foundation in Urhobo tradition while he also got inspiration from other major ethnic tribes in Nigeria like the Yoruba, Igbo, Hausa-Fulani, and Benin cultures. His artworks reflect myths, folktales, mythological figures, landscapes, and modern experiences. The major medium used by Bruce Onobrakpeya include paints and prints on woodcuts, engravings, intaglio, and plastography. He uses iconographic as well as psychoanalytic methods in creating his artworks which over the years have given his creations the unique complexity that today serves as his trademark in Nigerian art.

To encourage the development of art in Nigeria, Bruce Onobrakpeya established a studio in Lagos where he teaches and accommodates artists in residence. In his hometown, he also created an art center where he conducts workshops for national and international artists. His artworks have been featured in various international and national exhibitions and can be found in various private and public buildings.

See Also: Benin Artwork (Chapter 12); Igbo Artwork (Chapter 12); Painting (Chapter 12); Sculpture (Chapter 12).

Further Reading

Ezeluomba, N. (2016). "Zaria Art Society." In *The Routledge Encyclopedia of Modernism*. Taylor and Francis. https://www.rem.routledge.com/articles/zaria-art-society-the. doi: https://doi.org/10.4324/0123456789-REM1910-1

Odokuma, E. (2017, May). "Indigenous Tendencies: An Interpretation and Classification of Some of the Works of Bruce Onobrakpeya." *Africology: The Journal of Pan African Studies*, 10(3): 109–31.

PAINTING

The earliest form of paintings done in Nigeria are rock paintings of which the most prominent is the site at Birnin Kudu in the northeastern state of Jigawa. The paintings are of animals such as cows and sheep and even human beings, as well as geometric signs. The paintings were believed to be associated with ritual practices.

Pre-colonial paintings were prominent on the body as was the case with Ulli designs among Igbo women, on residential walls and fences using geometric shapes as was the case in northern Nigeria based on religious beliefs, and on cloth as was the case with the Yoruba people using dye-resistant methods.

The formal study of Fine Arts as a technical skill was introduced to Nigeria by the British colonial government through schools and higher-education institutions. Aina Onabolu, who is known as the father of modern Nigerian art, was the first Nigerian artist to receive formal art education. With his influence he was able to ensure that art was taught in the Nigerian school curriculum. He was also able to encourage Kenneth Murray from Europe to come and teach art in the colonial schools. While Kenneth Murray encouraged his students to use traditional African motifs in their works, Aina Onabolu promoted a more naturalistic form of art depicting landscape as well as live portraits.

The efforts of art at the secondary-school level inspired the establishment of the Zaria Art Society at the Nigeria College of Arts, Science and Technology at Zaria (now the Ahmadu Bello University). The society was the brainchild of Uche Okeke and Demas Nwoko which was formally inaugurated on October 9, 1958. Through the society the ideology of Natural Synthesis was formed which encouraged Nigerian artists to look for inspiration from traditional knowledge and worldviews. It promoted a fusion of the traditional with the modern. Though the Zaria Art Society was not limited to painting, it nevertheless played a significant role in the development of this form of art in Nigeria. It encouraged young Nigerian painters to infuse traditional *Ulli* symbols (prominent among the Igbo) and *Ona* (among the Yoruba) into their works. This was followed with a variety of workshops in art training as well as its inclusion as university-based courses at the University of Nsukka, Obafemi Awolowo and Yaba College of Technology University, and the University of Ibadan.

Nigerian painters and their works are known all over the world. A masterpiece was created by Ben Enwonwu in 1973 titled Tutu which is a painting of the Ife princess Adetutu Ademiluyi. The painting which was tagged the Nigerian Mona Lisa became a symbol of national reconciliation after the Nigerian Civil War. In 2018, during an auction, it was valued for $1.68 million. Currently, Nigerian-born painter Njideka Akunyili Crosby, the daughter of late Prof Dora Nke Akunyili (former NAFDAC Minister) has broken this record with her painting titled *Bush Babies* which was sold for $3.4 million at a New York art auction.

See Also: Igbo Artwork (Chapter 12); Onobrakpeya, Bruce (Chapter 12).

Further Reading

Okeke, U. (1960). "Natural Synthesis." *Recollections from Nigeria*. https://monoskop.org/images/5/5d/Okeke_Uche_1959-60_1995_Natural_Synthesis.pdf

Onyeakagbu, A. (2018, December 13). "4 of the Most Expensive Nigerian Paintings Auctioned in Recent Times." *Pulse.ng*.

PALACE DECORATION

A palace is known as the residential place of the king or rulers. In Nigeria, there were several kingdoms before the coming of the colonial government and these kingdoms had residential palaces for their rulers. Oftentimes, these palaces were not just residential areas for the rulers but also served as administrative quarters, court houses, entertainment areas as well as religious places. The building of the palaces was usually done by members of the society who constructed the palaces voluntarily and out of reverence for their rulers. The building materials used for the palaces were of better quality than the normal residential areas while the palace itself occupied large acres of land. The palace walls were usually thicker than the normal residential areas thus making them more secure against invaders. The space and material used for the construction of the palace were to demonstrate the wealth and power of the ruler. Most Nigerian traditional palaces were also the residential quarters for other members of the ruler's families and servants with spare rooms for visitors. The palace furniture will include items that symbolize the authority and power of the ruler such as the throne and stools, weapons (such as the royal swords, knives), staff of office, animal skins, instruments, etc.

The decorations found in palaces were a direct reflection of the power and authority bestowed on them. For the people they ruled, they were considered the voice of the gods thus symbolic items of worship were usually associated with the palace. For example, among the Yoruba and Edo people, sculptural figures can be found in their palaces. Among the Yoruba, the iron staff of Ogun the god of iron could be found in the courtyard where the king presides over disputes and other matters. This represents the ruler's ability to be upright and stay on the side of justice and truth when presiding over cases in the community.

The size and splendor of the traditional palaces also depends on the status of the traditional ruler. For example, among the Edo people of southeastern Nigeria, there was the major (the Oba of Benin) and other kings such as the Otaru of Auchi who were minor kings. These minor kings had a status like the high chiefs of Benin thus their palaces are smaller with less grandeur.

Part of what makes Nigerian traditional palaces special are the decorations made on them to make them stand out from other residential houses. Among the Hausa of northern Nigeria, the palaces are bright and colorful with intricate engravings of elaborate symbols. These can be found on the façade of the building walls. The engravings are done by professions who first make the outlines on the walls before making the engravings. These engravings serve as symbols of the wealth and status of the ruler. Among the Yoruba, the palaces are decorated with sculptures, decorative pillar posts, and relief panels.

See Also: Benin Artwork (Chapter 12); Ife Artwork (Chapter 12); Indigenous Architecture (Chapter 12).

Further Reading

Umoru-Oke, N. (2010). "Risawe's Palace, Ilesa Nigeria: Traditional Yoruba Architecture as Socio-Cultural and Religious Symbols." *African Research Review: An International Multi-Disciplinary Journal, Ethiopia*, 4(3a): 247–60.

Wilcox, I. S. (2016). "Royals & Regalia: Inside the Palaces of Nigeria's Monarchs: Recent Photographs by George Osodi (review)." *African Arts*, 49(3): 90–2.

SCULPTURE

The earliest Nigerian sculptural art tradition was the product of the Nok civilization originating in Jos, Plateau State. Nok art is dated between 500 and 200 BCE making it the oldest sculptural art culture in Africa. The Nok figures were made from terracotta which means they were moulded in clay and hardened through heat. Other sculptural traditions such as Ife, Benin, Owo, Tsoede, and Igbo-Ukwu were made from metals such as bronze, brass, and copper.

The carving of figures from stone is another sculptural tradition evident in southern Nigeria. One of such are Esie soapstone figures dated to between the twelfth and fifteenth centuries. A total of 1,500 sculptural figures were discovered measuring between 10 centimeters to a meter in height. The soapstone figures were found in Igbomina town, Kwara State and depict men, women, and animals. The human figures are depicted with some seated, others kneeling; some playing musical instruments; others holding machetes; some wearing jewellery such as necklaces, bracelets, and anklets; and many depicting elaborate hairstyles and clothing. There is also the Akwanshi stone tradition in Cross River State among the Ekoi people. Almost 300 of these figures were discovered in about 30 different sites. These stone sculptures depict mainly men portraying their faces with tribal marks and beards, the middle torso ending with the navel.

Sculptural art whether in wood, metal, stone, or terracotta still plays an important role in contemporary Nigerian society and has thus served as a valuable resource in helping researchers better understand the present through the past. For many Nigerian cultural groups especially in southern and middle belt regions of Nigeria, sculptures link the living with their gods by serving as symbols in conducting sacrifices for fertility, protection, and prosperity; or invoking spirits to ask for directions and instructions. Sculptures are also used to instil order when there is chaos, to give judgment, or to signify authority. In some cases, sculptural figures are used in cultural festivals to honor gods or remember the dead. A good example is the burial practice prevalent among the Owo, Benin, and Onitsha people where a second burial ceremony is performed for wealthy and important people. This second burial ceremony involves the production of a life-sized effigy (often made of wood) representing the deceased. Amongst the Owo people of southwestern Nigeria, the effigy looks exactly like the deceased who may have died two or more years before. The effigy which is known as *ako* is first set up in the compound of the deceased to enable the loved ones perform various rituals and rites, after which it is paraded around the town then buried.

Because sculptural figures are significant in the performance of sacrifices to appease or make requests from the gods, they can be found in shrines and groves. In some cases, they are produced for the beautification of the king's palace with expensive materials such as bronze, brass, and gold. Palace sculptures capture the achievements of previous kings and record the activities of reigning kings.

See Also: Benin Artwork (Chapter 12); Bronze Casting (Chapter 12); Ife Artwork (Chapter 12); Onobrakpeya, Bruce (Chapter 12); Terracotta (Chapter 12); Wood Carving (Chapter 12).

Further Reading

Cison. (2010). "Dynasty and Divinity: Ife Art in Ancient Nigeria." *African Masterpieces – The story of the Kingdom of Ife (Art Exhibition)*. The National Museums of World Culture. https://mb.cision.com/Public/1202/9556717/a35c05edf304ca41.pdf

Ezenagu, N. and T. Olatunji. (2014, July). "Nigeria Sculptural Tradition as Viable Option for Tourism Promotion: An Assessment of Esie Mysterious Stone Sculptures." *Global Journal of Arts Humanities and Social Sciences*, 2(5): 57–72.

Oyinloye, M. A. (2017). "Nigerian Wooden Sculptures and Their Preservation in the National Museum Lagos, Nigeria." *Anistoriton Journal*, 15: 1–16. http://www.anistor.gr/index.html

TERRACOTTA

Virtually all ethnic groups in Nigeria are skilled in the production of terracotta which basically involves the baking of moulded clay. Terracotta figures served religious functions while pottery items such as cooking pots, smoking pipes, eating bowls, drinking cups, storage containers, and dye pots were produced for domestic and economic purposes. Clay, which is the major raw material used, was dug out from the edge of water sites, pounded, soaked in water then sifted to remove impurities. The cleaned clay is kneaded and moulded into a desired shape after which it is decorated and fired in furnaces, kilns, ovens, or sun-dried.

Terracotta figures are very important aspects of traditional worship and healing rituals. These figures often have abstract symbols indicating the god or deity worshiped and are supported with religious pottery containers for religious rituals and the bearing of sacrificial offerings. Religious pottery is also used in other ways such as being containers for storing spiritual concoctions for: the empowerment of religious priests/priestesses, warriors, and hunters; medicinal items to prevent spiritual attacks, certain ailments, or to serve as birth control. Some religious pots and figures have taboos attached which must be followed to ensure the potency of their content. For example, pottery containing spiritual concoctions for empowerment must not spill its contents or break as the result could be dire for the person the ritual was made for. For ethnic groups like the Urhobo of Delta State, treatment for healing a newborn baby's umbilical cord is borne in a broken potsherd. In pre-colonial societies, clay pots or containers were used to bury the dead (special clay containers were made to bury hunchbacks, children, or people who died of terrible diseases).

The importance of pottery in the history of Nigeria is evident in the numerous archaeological findings in Afikpo Ebonyi State, Nok, Igbo-Ukwu, and Ife (in Ife, remnants of potsherd pavements used as roads were also discovered). This encouraged the Federal Government of Nigeria to set up the Abuja Pottery Center in 1952 based on the influence of Michael Cardew. The center was later renamed the Ladi Kwali Pottery Center after one of its first trainees.

A revolutionary invention by Mohammed Bah Abba called "Pot-in-Pot Preservation/Cooling System" was developed in 1995. This invention was inspired by Abba's experience as a boy growing up in a family of pot makers and his observation of how water resistant and durable moulded clay storage items could be. This indigenous knowledge was supported with his training in Biology, Geology, and Chemistry. Mr. Abba's invention was motivated by the travails of farmers and vegetable sellers in preserving farm products. Because the invention does not require electricity and is able to preserve fruits, vegetables, and other perishable food items in a humid and hot climate, it has been referred to as the "desert refrigerator." With this invention, the lifespan of vegetables can be preserved for at least twenty-seven days keeping the food items fresh with limited spoilage. Mr. Abba through this was selected a Rolex Laureate.

See Also: Ife Artwork (Chapter 12); Igbo Artwork (Chapter 12); Sculpture (Chapter 12).

Further Reading

Abamwa, O. E. (2018). "The Concept of Beauty in Urhobo Pottery." *Ceramic Art + Perception*. *Mansfield Ceramics*. https://www.mansfieldceramics.com/cap-articles/the-concept-of-beauty-in-urhobo-pottery/

Allen, R. (1983, March). "The Myth of a Redundant Craft: Potters in Northern Nigeria." *The Journal of Modern African Studies*, 21(1): 159–66. https://www.jstor.org/stable/160622

Lamp, F. J. (2011). "Ancient Terracotta Figures from Northern Nigeria." In *Yale University Art Gallery Bulletin*, New Haven: Yale University Art Gallery. https://artgallery.yale.edu/sites/default/files/files/coll_af_bull_2011_terracotta_figures.pdf

O'Hear, A. (1986). "Pottery Making in Ilorin: A Study of the Decorated Water Cooler." *International African Institute*, 56(2): 175–92.

Umuro-Oke, N. (2017). "An Appraisal of Traditional Yoruba Pottery and Potters." *Global Journal of Arts, Humanities and Social Sciences*, 5(6): 17–25. European American Journals.

TEXTILES

Nigerian textiles can be classified into three major categories namely handwoven, traditional patterned or dyed, and imported bales. Traditional handwoven textiles are produced on two types of handlooms (broad and narrow) and both forms can be found all over Nigeria. The cloth forms woven on the broadloom have complex weaves and designs and were mainly operated by Yoruba, Egbira, Edo, and Igbo-speaking women. The Egbira women in Kwara produce *Okene* cloth, the Igbo women of Abia produce *Akwete*, while a generality of Yoruba groups produce *Kijipa*, *Ikale* and *Ala*. Cloth produced on the broadloom served domestic purposes such as baby straps, cover cloth, or shawl; cultural and spiritual functions during occasions such as rituals for burials and funerals; as well as for political identification as with the case of the *Ogboni* cult among the Yoruba people. Though the broadloom is on the decline, narrow weaves are still prominent today in marking milestone events such as weddings, funerals, and birthdays. Traditionally, the cloth produced on the narrow loom was valued for economic purposes as the cloth was used in financial exchange in trade, as bride-price, and as a symbol of prestige. Though the traditional preserve of men, it can be found being operated by both genders especially in Yoruba land. The narrow loom woven cloth can be found in various locations in the northern part of Nigeria but most especially among the Yoruba (known as *Aso Oke*), and the Tiv (known as *Anga*).

Nigerian traditional textiles are also produced using a dye-resistant technique which gives surface designs. This dye-resistant technique varies. In some cases, a plain colored cloth can be painted with free hand using a feather dipped in wax or starch which is then dipped into a dyed solution. The area patterned through the wax prevents the dye from penetrating thus retaining the original color. Other dye-resistant techniques involve: the use of carved-out stamps coated with wax or starch; the use of stitches; or the use of raffia or ropes to prevent the dye from penetrating. Resist dying is popular among the Yoruba (technique locally known as Adire), Igbo of Arochukwu, Gwari of Niger State, Tiv of Benue State, Jukun of Taraba State, and Nupe of Kogi State. Currently, contemporary Nigerian textile dyers use more of imported dyes rather than the traditional ones which they claim is too time consuming while restricting their use of color to mainly indigo blue, brown, yellow, and red.

With the advent of colonialism, industrial cloth production was introduced. The first modern textile factory in Nigeria was established in 1956 in Kaduna. Kaduna was selected as the location for the factory mainly because of the pre-existing textile-producing culture that existed in the northern part of Nigeria. This encouraged the growth of the textile industry in Nigeria and by the 1970s and 1980s the industry had become the third largest in Africa. Unfortunately, this industry has almost totally collapsed with more cloth forms being imported along with threads and dyes.

See Also: Embroidery (Chapter 12).

Further Reading

Makinde, D. O., M. O. Fajuyigbe, and O. J. Ajiboye. (2015). "Nigerian Textile Industry: A Tool for Actualising Economic Stability and National Development." *European Journal of Business and Social Sciences*, 4(8): 331–44. http://www.ejbss.com/recent.aspx-/

WOOD CARVING

Woodcarvers in southern Nigeria carved doors, house posts, chairs, stools, drums, mortars, and pestle to serve domestic and economic purposes while sculptural figures, masks, divination bowls, and staffs or rattles were produced for spiritual worship. These include Yoruba, Benin, Igbo, and Ibibio peoples.

A major item carved from wood are masks worn at masquerades to represent gods, spirits, and ancestors. It is believed that these celestial bodies are very powerful, and their powers can be transferred to the person wearing the mask. Masked masquerades come out during cultural festivals or traditional cleansing. During cultural festivals and events, the presence of a masquerade is seen as fun and entertaining because the masquerades dance and display various forms of acrobatics; but during cleansing, it is a scary event which prohibits women and children with the threat of death. For example, the Olugbobiri people of Bayelsa State believe in water spirits which can be invoked through masks. Some are categorized as spiritual with the power to kill and others as non-spiritual to entertain. Masks worn by masquerades for entertainment are kept and preserved in family homes; while those that represent gods and their powers are kept in shrines built for their worship by chosen priests and priestesses. In the case of the Yoruba Gelede cult which controls the Gelede mask, senior members of the cult are custodians of the masks. Gelede among the Yoruba is based on the belief of Iya Nla, a female supreme being who is believed to have the power over life, death, and fertility. Thus, though the masquerades are men, they dress like women and perform for entertainment. Among the Efik, Ibibio, Benin, and Igbo peoples, the Ekpo belongs to the Ekpo society, and their duty through the mask is to instill order and appease the ancestors. Its masquerade does not come out to entertain.

Among the Igbo people, a wooden carving known as *Ikenga* is made to symbolize the strength of a man's right hand thus representing his success and achievements. *Ikenga* is consulted when he wants to embark on projects or is faced with indecision. For the *Ikenga* to be potent it must be taken to a traditional spiritual priest to invoke the spirit of strength.

A similar cultural practice is prevalent among the Edo who call it *Ikengaobo*, the Igala people of Kogi State call it *Okega* and the Urhobo people of Delta State call it *Oboh*.

Among the Yoruba people, the reverence of twins is represented by carved wooden figures. These figures are carved when one or both twins die. The wooden figure is worshipped because it represents the spirit of the dead twin/s. It is used to appease the dead, not to take the living twin away, to come back and live or protect and prosper the family they left behind.

Traditional masks are painted with indigenous dyes as a way of preserving and protecting them from termites. They often possess abstract qualities; in other words, they do not look realistic.

See Also: Igbo Artwork (Chapter 12); Sculpture (Chapter 12).

Further Reading

Oloidi, J. (2014). "Traditional Wood Carving and the Economic History of Ekiti of Southwestern Nigeria, 1900 to 1960." *Journal of Tourism and Heritage Studies*, 3(2): 31–45.

Sanda, F., O. Ademola, and O. Taiwo. (2017). "Art in the Service of Religion: A Study of Selected Carvers of Ifa Sculptured and Objects in South-Western Nigeria." *International Journal of Architecture, Arts and Applications*, 3(4): 53–62. doi: https://doi.org/10.11648/j.ijaaa.20170304.12

CHAPTER 13

Music and Dance

OVERVIEW

Music and dance in early Nigerian pre-colonial societies played a role in uniting the people with their gods, themselves, their histories, and cultures. During religious, ritual, festival, or ceremonial occasions, music and dance complemented the sacrifices of praise, worship, and offerings the devotees offered to the gods—they were used to unite celebrants during milestone social events such as the birth of a new member, marriages, and social achievements; to honor and remember the dead and ancestors; to make initiations to mark the transition from childhood to adulthood; and to capture essential parts of history, heroes, and events.

Music and the lyrics of songs were important socialization channels used by elders to educate and transfer knowledge from one generation to the next. The lyrics and the rhythm of traditional songs were also important in inspiring people to work in farms, construction projects, war, and physical competitions. The most common format of Nigerian traditional music was the call-and-response style whereby the leader would sing a verse and the choir or listening audience would follow with a response. This way, the leaders teach their audience the song lyrics as well as the meaning behind it. Politically, the lyrics of songs were used by their composers to communicate to their leaders and society their observations, likes and dislikes. Most often, the rhythm and life of the song is sustained with the use of traditional musical instruments like drums, flutes, stringed and wind instruments, rattles, xylophones, clappers, etc.

The rhythm created through the instruments spurred dances of different types. Some dances like the *Nkwa-Umu-Agbogho* (performed among the Afikpo people of Ebonyi) were a dance of maidens used to inspire courage and bravery among male wrestlers during local competitions. The maidens also hoped that through their dance steps, they could attract one of the wrestlers to become their future husbands. Other dances include the *Gelede*,

Ekpo, Ukwata, Ohogho to mention but a few. Today, a lot of these dances are performed outside the context of their creation for entertainment and economic purposes.

With the coming of missionaries and colonial administration, some of the dance and songs were labeled as paganism and thus discouraged. The new colonial economy and the return of ex-slaves encouraged the spread of Christianity especially in the southern parts of Nigeria. To further push this agenda, Christian missionaries and later indigenous church leaders encouraged the use of dance and music as a way of converting "unbelievers" into the Christian fold. Using Christian themes and Biblical passages, songs were composed, and plays written to mark Christian festivals and ceremonies.

In the northern part of Nigeria, Islam was a major determinant of the music and the dances performed. The Caliphate structure of northwestern Nigeria ensured that the music and dance displays not only captured the people's Islamic faith but also represented the Hausa/Fulani heritage and culture.

The Yoruba people of southwestern Nigeria were especially gifted with fusing Christian and colonial knowledge and culture with their own. Traditional folk songs were fused with Christian songs using Biblical passages and themes, while the power and efficacy of some of their gods were transformed based on Christian beliefs. Dances once performed in honor of Yoruba gods and kings, were now performed for Christian worship. Indigenous churches and missionaries sponsored choir performances and trained dancers, and this led to the development of gospel music and theater in Nigeria. The great Hubert Ogunde grew from such platforms.

Nigerian forms of music and dance started to change during the colonial administration when urban centers were created which served as a melting pot for various ethnic groups to come and live together. Not only were urban centers a place for cultural and social interaction, but they were also a space for the colonized and colonizers to interact. Urban centers also created economic development and in turn a need for leisure. It was based on these factors that social clubs and ethnic-based associations were established. With this came new musical sounds and dances which made urban cities like Lagos central in the history of Nigeria's music and dance development.

A major form of music which was developed as a direct influence of urban development in British colonies was "Palm Wine" music which originated in palm wine joints. Palm Wine music was a mixture of Yoruba folk music and other musical forms adopted from Brazil and Cuba. This form of music was promoted and made popular by Tunde King in the 1920s. It is believed that the more contemporary Nigerian musical genre Juju has its origin in Tunde King's Palm Wine music. Tunde King's music included traditional instruments like rattles, tambourines, and drums with a mixture of stringed musical instruments like the guitar and banjo. His music was very popular among Yoruba, Ghana, Sierra Leone, and Liberia migrants in Lagos. Tunde King's musical style influenced other prominent musicians like Tunde Nightingale who perfected the musical genre of *Juju* which was further improved upon by Yoruba musicians like I. K. Dairo and made popular by musicians like King Sunny Ade and Ebenezer Obey.

Another major musical form which developed after the Palm Wine music was Highlife. Highlife has been described as a unique blend of African, African American, and European sounds which originated in Ghana and became very prominent in Nigeria during the

1950s. The earliest Highlife Nigerian musical groups were formed by Bobby Benson and his Cool Cats. Bobby Benson also influenced other musicians like Victor Olaiya who was a trumpeter in Bobby Benson's musical group. Other prominent Highlife singers include Prince Nico Mbarga and his Rocafil Jazz band who sang the famous song *Sweet Mother* (released in 1976).

In the southern part of Nigeria, the development of Highlife music greatly influenced the formation of what would later form other musical genres within southern Nigeria. The influence of freed slaves and migration from neighboring countries such as Sierra Leone helped to create a mixture of various sounds. The musical sounds were a combination of Western musical string instruments and more traditional ones such as drums, rattles, and tambourines. Some of the musicians specialized in composing lyrics in their indigenous language, while others combined Standard English with Pidgin and an indigenous language (e.g., Yoruba, Igbo, or Hausa). The aim of their music was not to spread a religious doctrine, but rather to make known ideologies, attract and entertain fans, and ultimately financially empower themselves. They would thus give live performances during major milestone celebrations such as birthdays, weddings, promotions, or housewarmings. Popular musical genres performed for such occasions include Juju, Fuji, Apala, Highlife to mention but a few.

In the eastern part of Nigeria, several Igbo Highlife musicians rose and became popular in the use of Highlife sounds, one of them was King (Dr.) Oliver De Coque (born Oliver Sunday Akanite in 1947). Oliver De Coque was a Nigerian guitarist who combined Highlife and traditional Igbo music (using traditional Igbo musical instruments like the *ekpili* usually worn around the ankles or wrists; and the *ishaka* or calabash shaker). His music was especially popular in the late 1970s to the 1990s and he released more than seventy music albums before his death in 2008. Similarly, Chief Stephen Osita Osadebe produced a Highlife music genre that combined a series of sounds ranging from calypso, samba, bolero, rumba, and jazz. One of his popular records, "Osondi Owendi" (released 1984) was a major hit. Their performances were often accompanied with traditional Igbo dancers.

Most Hausa singing groups are characterized by a bandleader who is the main singer and thus represents the focus of the music due to the message the lyrics carry. The main singer is supported by a group of either all male or all female depending on the gender of the main singer. The accompanying group supports the main singer with traditional instruments as well as choruses in relation to the call cues given by the main singer. Popular northern Nigerian singers include Alhaji Mamman Shata Katisna and Aliyu Dan Kwairo. Both were solo singers with an all-male group. They sang in Hausa and the music was accompanied with traditional Hausa instruments. Also popular in northern Nigeria were all-female musical bands; the earliest of them being Uwaliya Amada and later Hajiya Sa'adatu Ahmad (AKA Barmani Choge) and her all-female band. They sang using the mature Hausa women genre of music called *Amada* and performed mainly for an all-female audience. The musical instruments used were calabashes turned upside down and struck with sticks or the palms of the hands. The songs deploy a call and response with Barmani Choge being the main singer with supporting dramatic performance. Also popular in the northern part of Nigeria was the soloist, Dan Maraya-Jos (literally meaning the orphan from Jos though his parents were Sakkwato Hausa), one of northern Nigeria's most popular folklorists. While he sang, he played the *Kuntigi* (a small single-stringed lute made from an oval sardine can covered with goat skin) which he made himself.

The Nigerian music and dance scene changed significantly in the 1980s and 1990s due to the influence of Western musical videos and shows, international dance competitions, and American musicians. Solo artists like Felix Liberty (with his most famous release being "Ifeoma"), Dizzy K. Falola (with his most famous release "Baby Kilode"), Jide Obi, Chris Okotie, Mike Okri, Evi Edna Ogholi Christy Essien, Alex Zitto, Majek Fashek, Onyeka Onwenu, Ras Kimono brought a different flavor to the Nigerian music and dance scene. Also becoming popular at the time were R&B groups like Style-Plus who sang about love; and rappers like Ruggedman who sang about the socioeconomic situation of the country.

Unlike the 1980s and 1990s when British and American music was in high demand, the 2000s witnessed more Nigerians seeking out and listening to music from within the country. For example, Rema's official music video "Calm Down" was identified as the most viewed Nigerian music video in 2022 with nearly 300 million views on YouTube. This was followed by Burna Boy's "Last Last" which had 140 million views and Kizz Daniel's "Buga" which had 107 million views. Compared to Yemi Alade's single "Johnny" which was rated the most viewed Nigerian music video in 2017 with over eighty million views on YouTube. Burna Boy was identified as Spotify's 2022 most streamed Nigerian male artist while Ayra Starr was the most streamed Nigerian female artiste. Other prominent Nigerian artistes include Wizkid, Davido, Tiwa Savage, P-Square, Olamide, Simi, Asake, Tems, Fireboy DML to mention just a few. Several Nigerian hits were also played outside the country making Nigerian music popular in Europe and the USA.

Nigerian musicians have also been recognized and awarded within and outside Africa for their creativity. Burna Boy won the 2021 Grammy for the Best Global Music Album for the song "Twice as Tall," won the 2022 MOBO Award for the Best African Music Act and was nominated for the 2023 Best Global Music Performance for the song "Last Last." Wizkid, another much-loved Nigerian artiste has been recognized as an African artist with one of the highest nominations and awards for a Nigerian by prestigious bodies such as the American Music Awards, BET Awards, BreakTudo Awards, Grammy Awards, iHeartRadio Music Awards, Image Awards (NAACP), MOBO Awards, MTV Video (VMA) Music Awards, People's Choice Award (USA), Soul Train Music Awards, Billboard Music Awards, to mention a few. Finally, Davido, an old-time favorite, has more than thirty awards, from awarding bodies like the Headies, BET, the Nigerian Entertainment MTV Africa, MTV Europe to mention a few. He is also the first Nigerian singer to be featured in a FIFA 2022 World Cup single track titled "Hayya Hayya (Better Together)."

Nigerian artists have also collaborated with American singers. Successful collaborations include Omah Lay with Justin Beiber in the song "Attention," Bieber and Wizkid (featuring Tems) in the song "Essence" which won the Bet Award. The American singer and songwriter, Chris Brown has also collaborated with Nigerian musical artists like Rema (in the song "Time N Affection") and Davido in the song "Blow my Mind" which was awarded Best Collaboration at the 2020 Africa Entertainment Awards. Drake is another popular American music artiste who has collaborated with Nigerian artistes such as Tems featured in his song "Wait for You" which ultimately earned Tems the BET Award for Best

International Act 2022. Drake has also collaborated with Wizkid in the Single "One Dance" which debuted at the top of the US Billboard Hot 100. Wizkid has also collaborated with Beyonce, Blue Ivy and Saint Jhn in the song titled "Brown Skin Girl" which debuted at number seventy-six on the US Billboard Hot 100. Other notable collaborations include 2Baba and R Kelly in the song "Flex" (2014), P-Square with Akon in the song "Chop my Money" (2011), D'Banj with Snoop Dogg.

Also trending in Nigeria are Nigerian popular musicians going into contracts with major network providers to sell portions of their hit songs as caller tunes. Others have contracts with Nigerian companies that produce household consumables (such as soft drinks, beer, milk, etc.) and services (such as insurance), as ambassadors or the face of the product.

Further Reading

Adedamola, Q. (2022, November 21). "Some of Davido's Greatest Achievements as He Clocks 30." *Daily Trust*. https://dailytrust.com/some-of-davidos-greatest-achievements-as-he-clocks-30/

Daily Trust. (2022, September 24). "Successes of US-Nigeria Music Collaborations." *Daily Trust*. https://dailytrust.com/successes-of-us-nigeria-music-collaborations/

Daniel, E. (2022, December 01). "Burnaboy Tops Spotify's 2022 Most Streamed Artiste Chat in Nigeria." *Guardian Life*. https://guardian.ng/life/whatsnew-entertainment-celebrity-gist-and-so-on/burnaboy-tops-spotifys-2022-most-streamed-artiste-chat-in-nigeria/

Edeme, V. (2022, December 30). "Rema Tops 2022 'Most Viewed Music Video' List." *Punch Newspaper*. https://punchng.com/rema-tops-2022-most-viewed-music-videos-list/#:~:text=Afrobeats%20star%2C%20Rema%2C%20has%20earned,Dataleum%2C%20and%20released%20on%20Friday

Hafsah, A. M. (2018, October 20). "6 Nigerian Musicians Who have Collaborated with Foreign Stars." *Daily Trust*. https://dailytrust.com/6-nigerian-musicians-who-have-collaborated-with-foreign-stars/

ADE, KING SUNNY

Sunday Adeniyi Adegeye (popularly known as King Sunny Ade) was born on September 22, 1946, at Osogbo, Osun State (though both parents are from Ondo State while his mother's ancestry is linked to the Akure kingship).

On completing his secondary education, Sunny Ade migrated to Lagos to begin his musical career in 1963. There, he became an apprentice, carrying musical equipment until he joined Moses Olaiya's Highlife band (Federal Rhythm Dandies) in 1966 as a guitarist. After a year with the band, he left to form his own band which he called Sunny Ade and His Green Spots in 1967. His band gained popularity during the Nigerian oil boom of the 1970s when elites of Lagos would invite him to spice up their parties and other social events.

Between the 1970s and 1980s, Sunny Ade embarked on international tours of Europe and the United States. In 1982, he released the album *Juju Music* under Island Records (a United States–based record label). Under this record label, he also released the album *Aura* which featured Stevie Wonder and Tony Allen. Sunny Ade however left Island Records after a year because he refused to allow the record label to "Europeanize" and "Americanize" his music. His popularity nevertheless got him nominated for his first Grammy Award (under the Best World Music Album category) in recognition of his album *Synchro System* in 1983. This nomination made him the first Nigerian Grammy Award nominee ever. Again, in 1988 his album, *Odu* (a collection of traditional Yoruba songs) was nominated for the Grammy Award under the World Music Category. This second nomination made Sunny Ade the first African to be nominated twice for the prestigious award. In 2009, Sunny Ade was inducted into the Afropop Hall of Fame at the Brooklyn African Festival (USA), an honor he dedicated to Michael Jackson.

Sunny Ade's music style was influenced by the Juju pioneer, Tunde Nightingale. Unlike the pioneer musical style, Sunny Ade combined Yoruba traditional musical instruments such as the talking drum with more modern musical forms such as the pedal steel guitar. He also introduced synthesizers, clavinet, vibraphone, and the tenor guitar as substitute sounds of traditional instruments used for producing Juju music. Sunny Ade accompanied his musical renditions with energetic dance steps.

Sunny Ade's popularity was also quite prominent at home. Though he had a lot of international record hits, Sunny Ade is loved in Nigeria not only for his music and dance performances but also as a successful businessman with multiple companies. He also established a non-profit organization called King Sunny Ade Foundation. In 2009, he was awarded an honorary doctorate and appointed a visiting professor of music at the Obafemi Awolowo University (Ile Ife). For his contribution to Nigeria, he was recognized with the national honor of Member of the Order of the Federal Republic (MFR) by President Goodluck Jonathan. He is revered by contemporary Nigerian musicians of diverse genres and has even collaborated with some including Alabi Pasuma and Bola Abimbola.

See Also: Fuji Music (Chapter 13); Hip Hop Music (Chapter 13); Music Industry (Chapter 16); Traditional Musical Instruments (Chapter 13).

Further Reading

Gorlinski, V. (2022, September 18). "King Sunny Ade." *Encyclopedia Britannica*. https://www.britannica.com/biography/King-Sunny-Ade .

IndigeDisc. (n.d.). "King Sunny Ade: Biography." https://www.globalartslive.org/sites/default/files/Biography_38.pdf

AFROBEAT

The foundation of Afrobeat can be traced to Fela Anikulapo Kuti's soul searching and strategizing for a new African-based genre. This led him to Ghana in 1967. In Ghana he was exposed to Ghanaian Highlife, a musical genre which employed the use of horns and/or guitars to create a danceable beat. Highlife as a musical genre developed in the 1920s and 1930s first in Ghana then spread to Lagos and other parts of southwestern Nigeria. By 1945, it had become a major musical genre for Anglophone West Africa. Highlife was an integration of both Western and indigenous music created for the enjoyment of elite Africans. Scholars believe that the term was created by people who gathered around dance clubs in Accra to watch couples who belonged to a high social class dance to music. Entrance into these clubs was exorbitant and couples who attended were obliged to dress in corporate Western dinner attires equivalent to their high social status. Fela combined the Ghanaian Highlife music with Nigerian-based *Juju*, and African American jazz, soul, and funk (promoted by James Brown). After a series of experimentation of sound combinations, Fela coined the word "Afro-beat."

Afrobeat must not be confused with Afrobeats. Afrobeats is a more contemporary genre developed in the late 2000s in the UK as a means of accommodating the musical taste of children of African immigrants. DJs then began to play West African pop music to satisfy the growing demand for African-based music during night parties and on radio shows. Many of these songs mixed indigenous languages with English and based the context of their music within their local identities. Initially, most were from West Africa (mainly Nigeria and Ghana) and included names like 2face Idibia, D'banj, and star music producer Don Jazzy; to later include Wizkid, Tiwa Savage, Yemi Alade, Mr. Eazi and Davido from Nigeria; and Sarkodie, Shatta Wale, and Efya from Ghana. Today, the Afrobeats label includes musical stars from all over Africa including Kenya, South Africa, and Congo. The Afrobeats label has gained tremendous respect and recognition outside the continent. This includes Angelique Kidjo (a Beninese-born singer and songwriter) and Grammy Award winner in the Best World Music Album category for her song "Celia" (2020); an award she dedicated to the Nigerian music star and Grammy Award nominee, Burna Boy.

Afrobeat on the other hand is an offshoot of Fela's creation and is characterized by certain features such as the call-and-response pattern of singing, the bell rhythm, the use of chants and traditional musical instruments such as drums (selected from the vast array of Yoruba drums), rattles (*sekere*), and gongs. Fela's music influenced a number of Nigerian musicians including Lagbaja (who performs wearing the Yoruba traditional costume of a masquerade) who replaced Fela's use of the saxophone and piano with varieties of Yoruba talking drums. His music is a combination of about 80 percent Yoruba and the rest is in Nigerian Pidgin English.

See Also: Kuti, Fela (Chapter 13); Hip Hop Music (Chapter 13); Music Industry (Chapter 16).

Further Reading

Claveau, H. (2017, September). "Afro-Beats: From Nigeria to the World." *Trace Studio*. https://trace.company/wp-content/uploads/2017/08/PRESS-RELEASE-AFROBEATS-FROM-NIGERIA-TO-THE-WORLD-US.pdf

CONTEMPORARY NIGERIAN DANCE

Contemporary dance in Nigeria has been accredited to the Yoruba mobile theater groups which presented dance dramas and choreographies derived from a mixture of traditional dance and music fused with versions adopted the dances and music of British culture and former slaves from Brazil and Sierra Leonean immigrants.

The mobile theater troupes encouraged the development of dance theaters and departments within Nigerian universities This created more diversity and professionalism in the creation of choreography and the general performance of dance in Nigeria. In 1997, the Guild of Nigerian Dancers (GOND) was formed under the National Association of Nigerian Theatre Arts Practitioners. The aim of GOND was to standardize professional dance performance and to expose Nigerian dancers to diverse forms of dance, dancers, and competitions both within and outside Nigeria.

Contemporary dance has also been promoted by Nigerian hip-hop singers who create musical videos and live performances to promote their hit songs. Sometimes, the lyrics of their songs include instructions of how to make the moves that make up the dance. Thus, the singers may say move your hands and legs, move your waist, and so on. The dance steps usually involve a lot of waist, buttock, arm, and leg movements.

From the late 1990s, dance videos were created by Nigerian musicians to accompany their hit songs. Some of these dances were created in Lagos by what may be referred as the lower class of the society. *Galala* for example is a dance which originated in Ajegunle, an area in Lagos classified as part of the ghettos. The dance is called Ghetto Dance and was made popular by the Nigerian reggae singer Daddy Showkey in the 1990s. *Shaku Shaku* is another dance believed to have developed in the Agege area of Lagos. The dance steps are likened to the steps of a drunkard or someone who is high on Marijuana. It was made popular by the Nigerian singer Olamide. Olamide is also credited for the dance known as *Shakiti Bobo* which was made popular through his video of the same name. Likewise, the dance known as *Skelewu* was developed by Davido as the dance for the video of his song *Skelewu*. Other dances developed by Nigerian hip-hop artists include *Sekem* by McGalaxy and Atlanta by Artquake. A dance like *Etighi* was adopted from an Efik traditional dance made popular by the Nigerian singer Kukere. In the case of the dance called *Shoki*, the originator is said to be controversial but three major names are associated with the dance namely Dre San, Lil Kesh, and Orezi. Some contemporary dances have other African roots like *Makossa* (originated among the Francophone Congolese) and *Azonto* (originated in Ghana).

In 2006, Kafayat Oluwatoyin Shafau popularly known as Kaffy (a dance entrepreneur and choreographer) broke the Guinness World Record for the longest dance party at the Nokia Danceathon (Africa Music Law, 2020). She has helped to bring professionalism and coordination into the dance culture in Nigeria.

See Also: Hip Hop Music (Chapter 13); Traditional Dance (Chapter 13).

Further Reading

Akinsipe, F. (1999). "Modern Dance and the Nigerian." *Ilorin Journal of the Performing Arts*, 1(2): 85–94.

FOLK SONGS

Nigerian forms of folk songs vary in style and sound based on the region and purpose for the song. For many traditional ethnic groups all over Nigeria, folk music is a living phenomenon which serves a functional role at the communal and individual levels. At the communal level, the rhythm and lyrics inspired physical unification when performing laborious tasks such as farm work, canoe paddling, house building, and even preparations for war. They were also an important component for other less physical communal activities such as communal festivals like harvests, initiation rites, games, dances, and religious ceremonies. At the individual level, folk songs were used to mark important milestones such as birth, initiation, marriage, and burials and promotions.

The rhythm and lyrics of communal folk songs are usually kept simple. Their compositions are often based on a call-and-response format whereby the lead singer calls, and the accompanying choir group responds. This strategy in composition makes it easy for community members to remember because they are an active part of the song. This also meant the songs could be used by the older generation to educate the younger ones in the society. To achieve this, the elders use folk tales and accompany it with folk songs. Through this combination the younger generation is taught the culture, traditions, and norms of their people. This serves as a channel through which the older generation sustains traditional institutional structures as well as their people's heritage.

Other characteristics of Nigerian folk songs are the historical and philosophical meanings behind their lyrics. Some of the themes include accounts of activities of past leaders including their achievements and failures with the aim of inspiring strength and hope in times of difficulty; or teaching the community about the consequences of past errors in a bid to prevent such occurrences in the future. Others are based on myths and folktales of past heroes and gods and an analysis of decisions they took and their consequences. The philosophies behind the folksongs reflect the people's worldview, tradition, and religion. The songs thus serve as a system of mass acculturation and social unification. This makes their functionality very diverse and thus they can manifest in-between the narration of folktales, proverbs, prayers, incantations, rituals, festivals, drama, and praises for royalty. Various ethnic groups in Nigeria likewise used folk music in diverse ways ranging from welcoming visitors to their community, announcing the birth, arrival or death of an important personality or royalty, marking the beginning or end of a communal festival, or religious ritual practice, etc.

There is a strong relationship between many Nigerian peoples' spiritual attachment, ritual re-enactment, and their composition and performance of folk songs. Thus, for many ethnic groups in southern Nigeria, folk songs are used in the ritual performance and worship of gods and ancestors. The northern section is a bit different due to their Islamic beliefs and observance of its doctrines. For them, folk songs are composed and used for entertainment, communal festivals, or royal praises.

See Also: Regional Music (Chapter 13); Traditional Dance (Chapter 13); Traditional Musical Instruments (Chapter 13).

Further Reading

Adamu, A. U. (2019). "Hausa Popular Music (Northern Nigeria)." In H. C. Fieldman, D. Horn, J. Shepherd, and G. Kielich (eds.), *Bloomsbury Encyclopedia of Popular Music of the world: Genres: Sub-Saharan Africa, Volume XII*, 168–78. New York: Bloomsbury Academic.

Akponome, O. A. (2014). "Folk Music in Contemporary Nigeria: Continuity and Change." PhD dissertation submitted to the Department of Theatre and Performing Arts, Ahmadu Bello University, Zaria.

Nnamani, S. (2014). "The Role of Folk Music in Traditional African Society: The Igbo Experience." *Journal of Modern Education Review*, 4(4): 304–10. doi: https://doi.org/10.15341/jmer(2155-7993)/04.04.2014/008

Schuh, R. (n.d.). "The Metrics of Three Hausa Songs on Marriage by 'Dan Maraya Jos.'" UCLA. https://docplayer.net/47269388-The-metrics-of-three-hausa-songs-on-marriage-by-ian-maraya-jos-russell-g-schuh-ucla.html

FUJI MUSIC

Fuji is a popular Nigerian musical genre developed from the traditional Islamic music form known as *Were* or *Ajisari* music. *Were* music was rendered during the annual Islamic Ramadan fast to wake Muslims at dawn for them to prepare the morning meal called *Sari*. *Were* is a Yoruba word which means "quick" while *Ajisari* means "wake up for *Sari*" thus describing the event or action to be taken in relation to the event. The music involves singers who created lively rhythms inspired by the traditional Yoruba *Sakara* music. The origin of the event can be traced back to the 1950s when Yoruba kings would invite performing bands to their palaces for *Were* competitions as a way of celebrating the end of the Ramadan fast. These events attracted large crowds from various towns and judges were appointed to select and award prizes to the best performances. *Were* performances became very popular and grew in size among Yoruba Muslim communities in Lagos metropolis (Lagos Mainland and Lagos Island). One of the prominent performers was Jibowu Barrister and Alhaji Sikiru Ayinde was the lead singer and composer of the group.

Under the tutelage of Jibowu Barrister, Sikiru Ayinde was confident that he could transform the *Were* music genre to one comparable with other popular forms of Yoruba music of the time. He thus decided to retire from the army and after obtaining blessings from his mentors, Sunny Ade, Ebenezer Obey as well as traditional Yoruba rulers, he launched his musical career. Today, Alhaji Sikiru Ayinde Barrister (AKA Barry Wonder) is credited for the creation of Fuji music, which is a combination of Sakara, Apala, Juju, Aro, Afro, and Gudugudu (Yoruba traditional musical forms) and the more modern Highlife. He named his creation *Fuji Music* after being inspired by a poster advert of Mount Fuji at the Nigerian international airport. Soon after, his friend from the army, Kollington Ayinla, adopted the music style and created his own version which included the traditional *Bata* drums. The two friends were to be known as rivals in the music industry and this made the music even more popular throughout Nigeria between the 1970s and 1980s.

Barrister Ayinde was a major ambassador of Fuji music and the first to tour international countries with the music. His first band was a 25-man band which served as a fifteen-year training ground for another popular Fuji musician, Wasiu Ayinde Marshall Barrister (AKA Kwam 1). During the 1990s, Ayinde was able to expand the music of his mentor by adding more modern musical instruments and beats which attracted the youth. Other major Fuji musicians include Adewale Ayuba, Wasiu Alabi Pasuma, Abass Akande Obesere, and Saidi Osupa.

A unique quality of Fuji music is the use of diverse traditional Yoruba drums played with a fast beat. The accompanying dance steps involve rhythmic movements of the hips, waist, and arms. The themes of Fuji musical lyrics range from concerns with quality of political leadership, praise singing, civic duty and issues surrounding socioeconomic life.

See Also: Afrobeat (Chapter 13); Gospel Music (Chapter 13); Regional Music (Chapter 13); Traditional Musical Instruments (Chapter 13).

Further Reading

Klein, D. (2019). "Fuji: Indigenous and Islamic Popular Music Fusions in Nigeria." In H. C. Feldman, D. Horn, J. Shepherd, and G. Kielich (eds.), *Bloomsbury Encyclopedia of Popular Music of the World (Genres: Sub-Saharan Africa) Volume XII*, 145–51. New York: Bloomsbury Academic.

Olaniyan, O. (n.d.). "The Evolution of the Technique of the Creativity of Fuji – A Nigerian Popular Music Genre." Abstract of a paper.

GOSPEL MUSIC

Gospel music in Nigeria can be traced to early mission schools where teachers and students were taught how to sing and play Western musical instruments. The missionaries encouraged choir formations to perform during Christian festivals. This was taken to another level in the 1970s when church-based choral groups began making public performances for social entertainment purposes. Their performances would include the use of traditional as well as Western instruments, but the lyrics would be based on Christian concepts.

Meanwhile, indigenous churches which sprouted between the 1920s and 1950s had choir leaders who would compose songs using the local language. A pioneer of Nigerian coral Christian music was Reverend Josiah Ransome-Kuti who is credited for developing a gospel genre that fused Yoruba language with the melodic structures of missionary-based hymns. As the church organist for St. Peter's Church, he was able to experiment with indigenous and Western music styles in 1922. This was followed by another chorister and composer, Ikoli Harcourt-Whyte who, after a series of experimentations, came up with Christian Choral music in Igbo language in the 1930s. Between the 1930s and late 1960s many of the indigenous Nigerian churches also adopted this form of music in their church worship while evangelical parades were organized with singers and accompanying drums and gongs. Church choirs would also lead performances to mark Christian social functions such as weddings, child naming, and harvest.

The influence of American and European forms of musical worship took a different turn in the 1970s when individual stars and Christian choirs became popular stars. Musical stars like Jim Reeves inspired the rising of Nigerian Christian musicians; some of whom were offshoots of church choirs and Pentecostal movements in universities. International collaborations also became possible when some of the Pentecostal churches would invite foreign choirs as guest performers from their international church branches and encourage their indigenous choirs to also perform during these occasions. By the 1980s individual Nigerian gospel stars began to rise with soloists like Carol Bridi, Bola Are, Sunny Okosun and Panam Percy Paul. They helped to establish what has been referred to as "gos-pop." The "gos-pop" version of gospel music funkified gospel music and it became commercialized and designed for entertainment. By the 2000s, gospel music concerts were being organized and these attracted large crowds. American gospel singers like the Winnans, Ron Kenoly, Don Moen, and Kirk Franklin were invited to share the stage with Nigerian singers and choirs. By 2010, these Christian concerts had become an annual event and were attracting great profit.

Award-Winning, Chart-Topping Nigerian Musicians
Nigeria has continued to dominate the world stage with its music. In the recently concluded Grammy Awards, Nigeria's music sensation, Tems (Temilade Openiyi) won the 2023 Grammy Award for Best Melodic Rap Performance for her contribution to Future's hit single, *Wait For U*. Other notable musicians who have continued with their music feat include Davido (David Adeleke), who released his fourth album, *Timeless*, on March 31, 2023, and within twenty-four hours topped album charts in seventeen countries. The Nigerian music industry, like the film industry, is vibrant and growing rapidly globally. Aside from showcasing the rich culture of the country, the music industry is roughly estimated to generate about $2 billion in revenue annually with over music producers, one thousand record labels, and over fifty radio stations. It is envisioned that with its continuous growth the industry will contribute significantly to the country's GDP by 2030.

Between the 1990s and 2000s, Christian music producers and marketing companies were established. They produced CDs, VCDs, and audio tapes which helped to make the Nigerian Christian industry even more popular. Added to this were radio stations that regularly played the music genre. By the 1990s Christian music schools and recording studios were established and this further boosted the professionalization of the Christian gospel industry.

Today popular Nigerian gospel singers include Sinach, Tope Alabi, Nathaniel Bassey, Lara George to mention a few.

See Also: Folk Songs (Chapter 13); Regional Music (Chapter 13); Traditional Musical Instruments (Chapter 13).

Further Reading

Adedeji, F. (2004). "Classification of Nigerian Gospel Music Styles." *Nigerian Music Review*, 5: 62–80.

HIP HOP MUSIC

Hip hop began in Nigeria in the 1980s with early artists like DJ Ron (AKA Ronnie) Ekundayo with his album "The Way I Feel" during the late 1980s. Later rappers like the duo Junior and Pretty who introduced a unique Nigerian Pidgin style rap through hits like *Bolanle* and *Monica*. Unfortunately, many of the early Nigerian hip-hop artistes had to compete with their more popular foreign counterparts for the limited space the national TV and radio broadcast could accommodate. It was not until the early 1990s with the privatization of the mass media in Nigeria that more hip-hop singers could thrive. Many were influenced by African American rappers like MC Hammer and 2Pac who used hip hop as a channel to make known the harsh political segregation, economic limitations, and social marginalization they faced in the US. The early Nigerian rappers felt a sense of affiliation to these themes due to the poor government style, economic hardships, and general decadence they witnessed especially as Lagos city urban youths.

During the late 1990s many hip-hop groups were formed. Many of them became popular through AIT's TV program titled *AIT Jamz*. Through this platform, hip hop groups like Remedies (with popular hit *Shako mo*), Trybesmen (with popular hit *Shake Bodi*), Plantashun Boiz (with popular hit *Plantashun Boiz*), and Style-Plus (with popular hit *Olufunmilola*) made their versions of Afro hip hop known. Though many of these bands did not last long as a team, they nevertheless became very successful solo artists. For example, Eedris Abdulkareem (from Remedies) became popular through his album *PASS* (Pain and Stress=Success) in 2002. In the same year, he released the album *Mr Lecturer* which considers the degradation of the Nigerian university system which condones the sexual and financial harassment of female students by male lecturers in exchange for marks. However, his third album titled *Jaga Jaga* which criticized the Nigerian government for corruption, was banned by the Nigerian government. Despite its ban, the album was extremely popular among the Nigerian youths who still played it at parties and in night clubs. Likewise, 2Face Idibia after the disbandment of Plantashun Boiz went on to have a very successful career with famous hits like *African Queen*.

It was not until the early 2000s that Afro hip hop rapper Ruggedman brought a new flavor to Nigerian hip hop with his 2002 single "Ehen Part 1" and in 2007, his album *Ruggeddy Baba* which featured 9ice (an upcoming Nigerian hip hop artist at the time). The collaboration made a major difference but more importantly was the quality of the musical video and its sound production which got him awards. Other famous collaborative hip-hop hits include Ice Prince featuring Brymo in *Oleku* (2010).

Today, Afro hip hop has become a major genre in Nigeria with some even collaborating with international hip-hop singers. The musical formation of hip hop in Nigeria is also changing with Fuji musicians collaborating with hip-hop singers to attract more audiences. Prominent hip hop singers include David O, Wizkid, Burna Boy, Olamide, Rema, P-Square, Yemi Alade Flavor, etc.

See Also: Contemporary Nigerian Dance (Chapter 13); Music Industry (Chapter 16); Nigerian Music Producers (Chapter 13).

Further Reading

Adedeji, W. (2016). "The Nigerian Music Industry: Challenges, Prospects and Possibilities." *International Journal of Recent Research in Social Sciences and Humanities (IJRSSH)*, 3(1): 261–71.

Gbogi, M. T. (2016). "Language, Identity, and Urban Youth Subculture: Nigerian Hip Hop Music as an Exemplar." *Pragmatics*, 26(2): 171–95. doi: 10.1075/prag.26.2.01tos

Laidi, O. F. (2012). "Multilingualism and Hip Hop Consumption in Nigeria: Accounting for the Local Acceptance of a Global Phenomenon." *Africa Spectrum*, 47(1): 3–19.

Lamela, M. (2015). "The Contributory Role of Music Artist: An X-ray of Major Satiric Preoccupations in Some Selected Contemporary Nigerian Hip-Hop Music Artists." *Journal of Humanities and Social Science (IOSR-JHSS)*, 20(4): 5–9.

KUTI, FELA

Olufela Olusegun Oludotun Ransome-Kuti (AKA, Fela Anikulapo) was born on October 15, 1938, in Abeokuta, (Ogun State) to Israel Oludotun Ransom-Kuti (a reverend, school principal and first president of the Nigerian Union of Teachers) and Funmilayo Ransom-Kuti (a female activist in the anti-colonial movement).

Fela's father was a composer of hymns and credited for composing the Egba anthem. He was also a strong advocate of Western music being an important component of education, and this moulded Fela into a distinguished musician (at age eight, Fela had mastered the skill of playing the piano from written musical notes). These musical skills were further sharpened when Fela travelled to Lagos after graduation from Abeokuta Grammar School (1957) and joined Victor Olaiya's jazz band (the Cool Cats) as a background vocalist.

In 1958, Fela gained admission into Trinity College of Music (London) where he specialized in various aspects of Western music. In London, he formed the Highlife band, High Rakers with his friend Braimah. The band was very successful and lucrative with the major genre being jazz. Fela came back to Nigeria in 1963 and took up a brief employment with the Nigerian Broadcasting Corporation. He left NBC to form his own band (Koola Lobitos) in 1965, which unfortunately was a disaster. He embarked on a soul-searching trip to Ghana where he experimented with combining the sounds of various musical genres. By 1967, he had perfected what he coined "Afrobeat." Afrobeat was further shaped by Fela's ten-month tour of the USA in 1969 with his band. There he met Sandra Smith, an activist member of the Black Panther Party. Through her, he learned about the Black Power Movement and the philosophies of Malcom X. These encounters significantly shaped Fela's pan-Africanist stance and determination to fight colonial rule, African dictatorship, and corruption through music.

By 1971, Fela's Afrobeat had become a force to be reckoned with. He changed his band's name to "Africa 70" and converted to Pidgin language in composing his songs (thus connecting more people to his music). He established the Afrika Shrine from which he and his band played; and changed his name to Anikulapo (he who carries death in his pocket). In 1975, he established the Kalakuta Republic which he declared independent of Nigeria but open to Africans who wanted freedom from "colonial mentality." Unfortunately, Fela's confrontational lyrics attracted numerous clashes with various Nigerian military governments of the time (the most famous being the 1977 military siege on his residence which led to the murder of his mother and his temporary self-exile to Ghana). By the 1980s Fela and his now Egypt 80 band had bounced back from the 1977 humiliation; and through international tours, he once again became a living legend.

Fela died on August 2, 1997, from HIV/AIDS related infections. Today, Fela's life and the philosophies of Afrobeat have not only inspired the music genre, but also academic research, book publications, documentaries, and even the off-Broadway production *Fela* (2008) which was nominated for eleven Tony Awards.

See Also: Afrobeat (Chapter 13); Hip Hop Music (Chapter 13); Traditional Musical Instruments (Chapter 13).

Further Reading

Botchway, De-V. (2014). "Fela 'The Black President' as Grist to the Mill of the Power Movement in Africa." *Black Diaspora Review*, 4(1): 1–35.

Oikelome, A. (2019). "'From the Koola Lobitos Era to Afrobeat' – A Study of the Artistic Years of Fela Anikulapo Kuti." https://www.researchgate.net/publication/335665769_'FROM_THE_

KOOLA_LOBITOS_ERA_TO_AFROBEAT'-A_STUDY_OF_THE_ARTISTIC_YEARS_OF_F
ELA_ANIKULAPO_KUTI

Sebastine, E. (2017). "The Afrobeat Legacy of Fela Anikulapo Kuti in Nigeria." Being a submission made to Prof John Collins for the Course titled African Music and Dance (SOAN 233) Ashesi University College.

NIGERIAN MUSIC PRODUCERS

Data from Nigeria's National Bureau of Statistics indicates that the Nigerian music industry is growing at a steady rate. Scholars believe that this growth is due to the increase in demand for Nigeria's brand of music within and outside Nigeria. A lot of the progress currently witnessed in the Nigerian music industry can be ascribed to the work and creativity of Nigerian music producers.

Nweze (2020) identifies some of the most influential of music producers in Nigeria and these include: Don Jazzy (who is known not only for his national hits but also for his international collaborations with Jay-Z and Kanye West in 2011; OJB Jezreel who produced *Face2Face* the biggest record by any Nigerian artist with the hit song *African Queen*, he also produced for Ruggedman, Paul IK Dairo, Daddy Showkey, Sir Shina Peters, D'banj, Wizkid, Yemi Alade to mention a few; ID Cabasa was the main producer of 9ice's 2008 album which recorded great hits and in 2019, *Totori* which featured Wizkid and Olamide; Cobhams Asuquo produced Asa's very successful album, *ASA* (he wrote the songs *Fire on the Mountain* and *Jailer*) and also arranges music and performs with bands at national and international music events; Sarz has done great production works for Lord of Ajasa (*See Drama*, 2007), RuggedMan, Ice Prince, Wizkid, Banky W, Wande Coal, etc.; Samklef produced a large portion of Wizkid's album, *Superstar*, and has also worked with Ruggedman, Simisola, D'Prince, Timberland, and Kanye West; Shizzi worked with Wizkid to produce the hit song *Love My Baby* and also with Davido to produce six of the songs on his 2012 album *Omo Baba Olowo* while internationally, he worked with Beyonce on the album, *Lion King: The Gift*; Pheelz produced Olamide's 2012 album *Baddest Guy Ever Liveth* and has also produced for Tiwa Savage, Seyi Shay, and Teni.

Major record labels operating in Nigeria include: Kennis Music founded by the radio DJ Kenny Ogungbe in 1998 was a platform upon which Nigerian R&B music was produced; Empire Mates Entertainment (E.M.E) founded by Banky W and Tunde Demuren in 2002; Chocolate City founded in 2005 by Audu Maikori a Nigerian lawyer and Paul Okeugo an entrepreneur, it became the first Nigerian music company to win a global music award; PentHauze Music established by Chibuzor Azubuike (also known as Phyno) in 2008; Mavin Records founded in 2012 by Michael Collins Ajereh (also known as Don Jazzy); Yahoo Boy No Laptop (YBNL) founded in 2012 by Olamide Adedeji (also known as Olamide); 960 Music Group was co-founded in 2013 by Efe Omoregbe (headed by Mark Redguard) has Hypertek Digital, Aristokrat Records and Ultima Productions as record labels under it; Star Boy Entertainment founded by Ayo Balogun (also known as Wizkid) in 2013; Spaceship Entertainment was established by Burna Boy in 2015; Davido Music Worldwide founded by David Adeleke (also known as Davido) in 2016; Dr. Dolor Entertainment founded by

Osadolor Nate Asemota (also known as Dr. Dolor) in 2016 is the label responsible for singer Teni Apata.

See Also: Afrobeat (Chapter 13); Hip Hop Music (Chapter 13); Music Industry (Chapter 16).

Further Reading

Nzere, S. (2018, January). "The Nigerian Music Industry: Making the Music Pay through Intellectual Property." *Industry Insight*, Infusion Lawyers.

Osinubi, F. (2017). "The Business of Entertainment: Harnessing Growth Opportunities in Entertainment, Media, Arts and Lifestyle." National Branding Conference (PwC).

REGIONAL MUSIC

Regional music in Nigeria varies but has the common characteristic of being band-based and using the call-and-response formation in their performance.

In the northern region, the prevalence of Islam significantly influenced the type of music played. Nevertheless, despite the Islamic influence some traditional musical performances which were within the dictates of Islam are accommodated. Among the traditional Hausa people of northwestern Nigeria, most of the traditional singing bands used limited to no instruments with more attention paid to the band leader and the music's lyrics. When traditional instruments are used, it is limited to one (mainly the traditional drum known as *Kalangu*). The musical bands are more of praise singers who praise clients in return for money or material gratitude. These are different from poet-musicians or *Madhu* singers who promote classical Arabic poetry. Another form of regional music prevalent in the northern part of Nigeria is known as *Koroso* which became popular in Kano in 1972. The music is performed using the traditional Fulani flute known as *Sarewa* and played with other Hausa musical instruments like the drum and feet rattle known as *Koroso* (the dancers have the rattles tied to their ankles thus adding to the musical rhythm while they dance).

In the western region of Nigeria which is dominated by the Yoruba people, musical types include *Apala*, *Sakara*, and *Fuji* all of which have their origin in Islamic practice. This may explain the prevalence of all-male bands led by male vocalists. Scholars have defined them as a mixture of Yoruba praise singing, Yoruba cultural philosophies, Arabic singing, and Quranic recitations. The traditional musical forms are believed to have developed from earlier Islamic-related musical versions known as *Were* and *Waka* used to wake the Muslim faithful during the Ramadan fasting period, and to welcome pilgrims from their hajj to Mecca. Ultimately, these traditional musical versions became forms of entertainment not only for Muslims but also non-Muslims in the celebration of marriage, births, promotions, chieftaincy title awards, burials, etc. While *Apala* is a slower music genre with the main musical instrument being drums, *Sakara* music is faster with more traditional musical instruments involved. *Fuji* music on the other hand has a faster beat, mixes traditional and Western instruments, and has lyrical compositions of Yoruba and Nigerian Pidgin.

Juju, another Yoruba musical genre unlike the previous musical forms, originated in Lagos because of a mixture of peoples and sounds brought by West African ex-slaves, colonial-promoted Western music, and Yoruba traditional music. It was created within clubs and palm-wine drinking joints mainly for entertainment and self-expression. *Juju*, like *Fuji*, is played with a fast beat, involving various Western and traditional musical instruments, and often accompanied with special dance moves created and promoted by the lead singer.

In the eastern and South-south region of Nigeria, beside the traditional folk music used in festivals, Highlife is a prominent form of music genre. A lot of their music was influenced by Western sounds and compositions.

See Also: Folk Songs (Chapter 13); Fuji Music (Chapter 13); Traditional Musical Instruments (Chapter 13).

Further Reading

Idonije, B. (2001). "Old or New: Palm Wine is Truly Enchanting." *Glendora Review: African Quarterly on the Arts*, 13(2): 16–22.

Ogisi, A. A. (2010). "The Origin and Development of Juju Music: 1900–1990." *EJOTMAS: Ekpoma Journal of Theatre and Media Arts*, 3(1&2): 22–33.

TRADITIONAL DANCE

Traditionally, dance functioned as an essential part of rituals for worshiping various deities. They were also prominent in festivals, burials, chieftaincy installations, and other milestone celebrations. Today, traditional dances are also performed by professional dance troupes for entertainment purposes and outside the context of their original function. Some of these traditional dances will be discussed below.

Ekombi is an Efik dance associated with initiates of cults associated with water spirits; and performed at the graduation ceremony of girls who have completed the initiation of *Nkuho* (fattening room). The *Nkuho* is a cultural practice where girls preparing for marriage are taught the skills and values they will need as a mother, wife, and responsible member of the society. On completing this training, they perform the *Ekombi* dance as a symbol of their transition from childhood to womanhood.

Bata is a Yoruba dance traditionally performed in honor of Sango the Yoruba god of thunder. The dance is accompanied by three major drums namely *Iya-Ilu*, *Itotele*, and *Okokonlo*. Traditionally, the dance served as a form of communication between the deity and his worshippers; but today it also serves as a form of social entertainment.

The *Swange* dance started as *Gbanyi* which literally refers to a British imported basin cherished by Tiv women as a domestic utensil for a matrimonial home. Due to its high cost, the women would organize a fundraising feast to acquire it. During the occasion, musical bands and dancers would entertain the guests. It is from these events that professional Tiv musicians standardized the dances and music in the late 1940s. The dances developed into choreographic performances accompanied with drums and the traditional horn called *Al'Gaita*. Both sexes are involved in these dances, especially during traditional festivals to honor warriors, depict love, unity, and culture. It was later renamed *Swange* and adopted by the Benue State Council for Arts and Culture.

Koroso dance is an old dance form performed among the Fulani/Hausa people of northern Nigeria. It was initiated in 1972 when a member of the Kano College community began to experiment with fusing traditional Fulani and Hausa musical instruments and music together. He was supported by a talented dancer who was able to do the same with their dance steps. The result is the present-day *Koroso* dance. The name *Koroso* is derived from the decorative string of rattles tied to the legs of the dancers. The rattling noise it makes compliments the music as the dancers move their feet to the rhythm. Today *Koroso* is recognized as the official symbol of Kano State. The dance is an energetic and fast-paced one performed in a choreographic form by both sexes.

The Atilogwu is an Igbo dance which originated among the Igbo of Anambra state and is performed by youths (male and female). The dance involves a lot of energy and acrobatic displays, and the dancers are adorned with colorful costumes. Atilogwu which means "having magic" in the Igbo language is a dance which fuses about five different Igbo dances together. It was initiated and perfected by the Ezeagu Atilogwu group, established in Lagos (1947). The dance caught on and became the pride of Ndigbo, going on to represent the country and participate in various competitions within and outside Nigeria.

See Also: Folk Songs (Chapter 13); Fuji Music (Chapter 13); Regional Music (Chapter 13); Traditional Musical Instruments (Chapter 13).

Further Reading

Dandaura, E. (2016). "African Dance in Transition: Interview with Arnold Udoka." *Critical Stages/ Scènes Critiques*. https://www.critical-stages.org/13/interview-with-arnold-udoka/
Golikumo, M. and S. Kquofi. (2014). "Masking Art Tradition as a Cultural Manifestation of Olugbobiri People of Nigeria." *International Journal of Humanities and Social Science*, 4(11): 270–80.
Mackay, M. and A. Ene. (1957). "The Atilogwu Dance." *African Music: Journal of the African Music Society*, 1(4): 20–2. doi: https://doi.org/10.21504/amj.v1i4.457
Nwaru, C. (2018). "Ethnic Dance and National Integration: The National Troupe Example." *Hofa: African Journal of Multidisciplinary Research (Special Issue)*, 3(1): 159–70. doi: https://doi.org /10.5281/zenodo.1481858
Okpala, N. (2016). "Traditional Music in Igbo Cultures: A Case Study of Idu Cultural Dance of Akpo in Aguata Local Government Area of Anambra." *African Research Review: An International Multidisciplinary Journal, Ethiopia*, 10(1): 87–103. doi: http://dx.doi.org/10.4314 /afrrev.v10i1.8

TRADITIONAL MUSICAL INSTRUMENTS

Nigerian traditional musical instruments are classified based on their functions and rhythmic sounds. Rattles are a common form of instrument in Nigeria. They are usually strung together and worn on the ankles or waist to add rhythm to the music as the wearers dance. Among the Yoruba people, rattles can also be strung around the *bata* and *dundun* drums. The rattles themselves are made of hollow bells of seeds, pebbles, beads, or metals strung together with strings or a basketry weave.

Shakers are musical instruments made from a hollowed woven basket, wood, or calabash. The material that causes the rattle include pebbles, beads, seeds, etc. placed inside a sealed hollowed container; or woven in a lacy fashion around a calabash. Clappers can either be two flat or rounded pieces of wood that can be struck together; a hollowed piece of wood or a tortoise shell beaten with a stick. In the musical performance they can be used for timekeeping or to fill in gaps in-between musical renditions.

Instruments which are struck hard on the surface with a beater include gongs, xylophones and slit drums. Gongs and large slit drums are not only used in musical renditions but also as a medium of information transmission. Among the Igbo people, large slit drums can "talk" and are used to announce the death of a royalty, the arrival of visitors, a call for war/peace, or an indication of the beginning of an event, while medium-sized ones are used for rituals. In the case of gongs, they are used to get attention and accompanied by a town crier; or used to keep the rhythm during a musical performance. Xylophones on the other hand are regarded as melodic instruments that can be played alone. It is mainly found among the Igbo people.

Drums are traditional musical instruments made of carved wood with a membrane covering. They are mainly rhythm-melodic instruments which serve as the main sound in many traditional Nigerian music compositions. Drums are found all over Nigeria and come in different shapes and sizes. They can be played alone, in company of other drums or other instruments. They can also be used to communicate praises, accompany masquerade performances, drama presentations, festivals, rituals, ceremonies, etc.

Stringed instruments are found in eastern, northern, and some parts of South-south Nigeria. They are made of cane, wood, or calabash and the strings number from one to eighteen. Though not so popularly used among the Ibos today (maybe due to the introduction of the guitar) it is still very prominent in northern Nigeria.

Wind instruments include trumpets, horns, and flutes. The materials they are made of range from animal horns, elephant tusks, wood, cane, reeds, and metal. They can be found all over Nigeria but more especially in the northern and eastern regions. They perform social as well as melodic functions including announcing the entrance of royalty, as a solo instrument in a music composition or played to support other instruments.

See Also: Fuji Music (Chapter 13); Folk Songs (Chapter 13); Regional Music (Chapter 13); Traditional Dance (Chapter 13); Uwaifo, Victor (Chapter 13).

Further Reading

Lo-Bamijoko, J. (1987). "Classification of Igbo Musical Instruments, Nigeria." *African Music: Journal of International Library of African Music*, 6(4): 19–41. doi: https://doi.org/10.21504/amj.v6i4.1259

UWAIFO, VICTOR

Victor Efosa Uwaifo was born in 1941 at Benin City (Edo State) to Pa Wilson Omoruyi Uwaifo and Princess Idusogie Uwaifo (she is from the Benin royal family). Uwaifo had his primary school education in Benin City. While still in Benin, he formed a band with his siblings which they called the Uwaifo Quartet. The band played Benin folksongs on the Nigerian Broadcasting Corporation. Uwaifo left Benin for Lagos where he attended Saint Gregory (1957–61). While in school, Victor joined Victor Olaiya's band then went on to make his first recording for Phillips which he called *Akugbe* (this means strength in unity in Edo Language). In 1961, Victor Uwaifo won a scholarship to Yaba College of Technology to read Graphics (1961–63). While in school Victor joined EC Arinze's Highlife band (1961–64) as a guitarist. While with the band, several Victor's songs were recorded by Phillips and released on the Jofabro Label (run by Joseph Fajimolu). While still with Yaba College, Victor joined the Central Modernairs in 1963 as one of the band's three co-leaders. Through the band, Victor continued to record for Phillips. In 1964, Victor joined the Nigerian Television Station (NTS) as a graphic artist. While with NTS he formed a musical trio for the station's "Minstrel Program" which featured him playing Bini folksongs and Highlife music. He left NTS in 1966 to professionally focus on his band (Melody Maestros) which he formed in 1965. In 1971, Uwaifo opened the Joromo Hotel in Benin through which he was able to establish his own television studio ten years later.

Uwaifo plays many musical instruments. Victor started playing the guitar when he was twelve years old, being influenced by Spanish and Latin American music. He made his first guitar in 1953 on which he practiced until he found out much later that the tunes were all wrong. He was later able to purchase a real guitar and launched out to create unique sounds. Uwaifo was known for his creation of rhythm beats such as the *akwete*, shadow, *mutuba*, and *ekassa* all of which he combined with Edo Highlife.

Today, Uwaifo has twelve golden records. He was appointed as Member of the Order of the Niger being the first musician to receive such an award. He was also appointed as the Commissioner of Arts, Culture and Tourism, a Justice of Peace (JP) Public Notary and Lay Magistrate as well as a Member of the State Executive Council in Edo State between 2001 and 2003. He has also employed as a lecturer at the Department of Fine and Applied Arts at the University of Benin.

Uwaifo passed away on August 22, 2021 at the age of eighty. Before his death he managed an art gallery and the Victor Uwaifo Hall of Fame.

See Also: Folk Songs (Chapter 13); Nigerian Music Producers (Chapter 13); Traditional Musical Instruments (Chapter 13).

Further Reading

Collins, J. (2011). "Victor Uwaifo: Highlife Pioneer, Legend." https://www.academia.edu/32340860/JCollins_VICTOR_UWAIFO_HIGHLIFE_PIONEER_LEGEND_Unpublished_photo_captions_are_included_but_no_photos_provided

CHAPTER 14

Food

OVERVIEW

Nigeria's ethnic diversity is reflected in the diversity of the food and cuisine that are available in the country. In Nigeria, food is not only a means to satisfy human hunger, but it is also an important cultural and symbolic signifier of the various people that make up the country. Food is used as a major means for the entertainment of visitors and guests, to express appreciation, and to mark biological and social landmarks. In most parts of the country, it is commonly regarded as selfish if a host does not invite their visitor to join them while eating or prepare a sumptuous meal to entertain their guests. Food also serves as a way of compensating for work done to someone or a family. For example, food may be served to adolescents who assist with the clearing and preparation of the land for farming to support a family during harvest time. Similarly, portions of food may be given to family members and friends who assist a family to cook a large quantity of food for guests who have been invited to celebrate the birth of a child, for a funeral, and other celebrations. During the preparation of the food, which usually consists of women, information about the household and the community is shared and it is during such interactions that young women are incorporated in the socialization process of becoming adult women. Nowadays, although the practice of inviting relatives and friends to assist with the cooking of food for social occasions persists, the practice is slowly being transformed, especially in urban centers, as families who can afford it contract the cooking to event organizers.

Among many ethnic groups in Nigeria, the preparation of food follows a general pattern. In rural areas, food preparation is a cultural prerogative of women although there is a division of labor in terms of the provisioning of resources and food items. For example, men who are farmers are required to provide certain types of crops such as yam, while hunters and fishermen are expected to provide meat and fish, respectively, for the household. If the men are civil servants or have some form of employment, they are required to provide money for the purchase of groceries and other food items in the home. On the other hand, women are required to harvest vegetables, rear chicken, goats, pigs, and other domestic animals that would be used to supplement the provision of food items, especially during mid-months for salaried homes or during lean months in agrarian homes. Generally, women are responsible for the cooking of meals for the entire household. They are responsible for the menu for the entire household and do the budgeting to ensure that the food items provided or the money for the family is stretched for the week or month depending on storage facilities, or the nature of the husband's occupation. Among rural folks, cooking is done in an open courtyard or in a small kitchen built with mud or palm fronds. Firewood is used for most of the cooking with earthenware pots. Urban dwellers are sometimes nostalgic of foods cooked in this traditional way, and it is not surprising that they still crave for such foods when they travel to the village to visit family members, especially during festive periods. In some large cities, such as Lagos, it is commonplace to see educated, middle-class workers who patronize such traditional food vendors or visit them in their food kiosk (*buka*) for their lunch. However, relatively affluent rural families use paraffin stoves and metal pots for their cooking. In urban households, the majority of women still do the cooking. In homes where the wife is a career woman, a house help may be employed to do the cooking and cleaning of the home.

Food hygiene and etiquette follow a general pattern across ethnic groups. For example, it is expected that both adults and children wash their hands before and after eating. This practice is very important because most local foods are eaten not with cutlery but with the fingers. To avoid ingesting germs and to avoid labeling the cook a witch, should those who eat the food develop any discomfort, it is standard practice for people to wash their hands before eating. Similarly, it is regarded as rude for people to eat with their left hand or to talk while eating. Especially among the Yoruba, to protect children from any food-choking accident that may result while eating and talking, it is almost a taboo for children to talk while eating probably because most of their meals are spicy and peppery. It is also customary for children to thank their parents for preparing and providing the meal. The same is also expected of visitors. It is frowned upon for children to start their meal with the piece of meat or fish that is served. It is regarded as a sign of greed and gluttony, but more importantly, it is to ensure that the child eats a balanced diet of carbohydrate, protein, and vegetables. Food may not be wasted by being thrown away. Mothers get upset when children do not finish their food or when visitors take only a small portion of the food they are served. It is usually interpreted to mean that the food is unsavory. When guests eat heartily and finish the food served, it is commonly regarded as a sign of friendship, acceptance, and satisfaction by the host. However, while it is expected that guests should eat heartily, some portion of the food is sometimes expected to be left for the children in the household. Such food is given to the children who would clean up the table and wash the plates of the guests. It is regarded as a way of the guests saying thank you to the children who would have assisted their mother in the preparation of the meal. Thus, there is a delicate balance between consuming the food served to guests and to show appreciation and reserving a portion not to be judged a glutton. However, this practice of leftovers is becoming less common in urban settings, as households are beginning to loathe the idea of giving leftovers from visitors to their children.

Characteristically, meals are prepared and served three times daily to children and they are also expected to eat some snacks in-between meals. Breakfast is typically served anytime between 7:00 a.m. and 10:00 a.m., and the food may be light or heavy depending on the ethnic group or family. Households with children who attend schools that are far away from their homes or in anticipation of traffic especially in states such as Lagos and Rivers, children are served their breakfast as early as 5:00 a.m. Most states in Nigeria do not have a school meal program, so it is the responsibility of parents to prepare and pack lunch for their children, which they eat during lunch break in school. This practice seems to compromise the nutrition of children as the food is usually not as qualitative as when they eat at home since the logistics of serving children food such as pounded yam and a rich variety of soup and meat, or fish is usually difficult. The typical meal that mothers pack for their children therefore is mainly noodles with boiled eggs or bread and butter, and for families who can afford it, soft drinks with the meal. However, in public schools where children are from relatively poorer homes than children in private schools, most of the students do not take food with them rather they are given lunch money which they use to buy food from food vendors in the school premises. The food sold is expectedly poor in quality and quantity so that the children end up with poor nutritional intake. Children from very poor homes may not have their lunch until they get back from school in the late afternoon. In such homes, which are increasing in the country, children only have two meals daily, which partly explains the poor nutritional status of school children in Nigeria. As inflation continues to climb in the country and households are becoming poorer, food is no longer taken for granted but has become a major challenge among average households. It is therefore not uncommon for families to ask young children to go out to beg for money or food to cater for the household. It is also becoming increasingly popular for families to identify where weddings, funerals, naming ceremonies, and other social functions are taking place with the aim of attending the reception for a meal while children sometimes scramble for leftovers, which they fill in containers and take home for the rest of the family members.

Food production in Nigeria is predominantly generated by rural farmers who rely on the traditional methods of farming with the use of simple gadgets such as hoes and cutlasses. The farmers rely on the natural fertility of the soil though in some parts of the country such as in the North, farmers increasingly rely on fertilizers and an irrigation system to maintain crop production. Genetically modified organisms (GMOs) foods are rare in the country and the federal government is conscious of the health dangers of the consumption of such foods and therefore places restrictions on the importation of GMO products. Because Nigerian foods are mostly organic, Nigerians treat some food items as medicinal. For example, pepper soup and bitter-leaf soup are usually served to members of the family who have malaria or stomach pain, respectively. The combination of a variety of vegetables for cooking and the consumption of fruits are major sources of essential minerals and vitamins.

During social functions such as weddings, naming ceremonies, funerals, and housewarmings, the quality and quantity of food served is a determinant of the success of the event. When guests grumble about the food served at the reception, the host of the event is ridiculed. In urban centers, the food business has evolved to become a major source of income for professional cooks who are contracted to cook at social events, as reception has become a major determinant of the success of the event and to make a statement about the host. It is partly for this reason that when an elderly person dies, they may not be buried in a hurry. It is customary, at least among the Christian population, for the dead person to be in the mortuary for several weeks or months while preparation is being made toward the funeral. Once the family has generated enough resources for the burial, a date is fixed for the ceremony with a substantial amount budgeted for entertainment. Depending on how big the event and the resources of the family, a cow or two will be slaughtered in addition to the purchase of dozens of chickens or turkey. Characteristically, it is not only one type of food that is prepared and served during such occasions. Both traditional food and Western food are usually served to the satisfaction of guests. This assorted food is also accompanied with a variety of drinks including soft drinks, juice, and wine, and among nominal Christians and Muslims alcoholic beverages including beer and spirits. Hot drinks are usually served in gatherings where the majority of the guests consume alcohol, but they are rarely served in strict Muslim or Christian gatherings.

Further Reading

Flanders Investment and Trade. (2020). *Food and Beverage Industry in Nigeria: Market Overview.* Flanders Investment and Trade Market Survey.

Grizzly Publisher. (2020). *Nigerian Cookbook: Traditional Nigerian Recipes Made Easy.*

ALCOHOLIC BEVERAGES

There are varieties of alcoholic beverages in Nigeria, and these are both locally produced and imported. Alcoholic drinks are usually for recreation and social occasions. The legal age for the consumption of alcohol in the country is eighteen, although the sale of liquor to underage children and their consumption of alcohol are usually not strictly enforced. It is not uncommon therefore for high school students and street urchins who are between twelve and eighteen years of age to be regular drinkers. It is also illegal for motorists to drink while driving, but this is not fully enforced. Although Nigerians are very religious people with almost all citizens claiming to be Muslims or Christians, a significant number engage in the consumption of alcohol, making Nigeria the highest alcohol-consuming nation in the West African region. Even though Islam prohibits the consumption of alcohol, and in some northern states, such as Kano and Zamfara, where alcohol is illegal for sale and consumption, alcohol is still surreptitiously sold and consumed in large quantities. Some Nigerians describe themselves as social drinkers, which means they only drink when there is a special need for it, for example, during weddings, or birthday parties. On the other hand, others are regular drinkers who hang out with friends at beer parlors and clubs to catch up with their social lives. Weekends are usually the peak period for alcoholic intake because most social events including burials, naming ceremonies, housewarming, and weddings take place over the weekend. The steady increase in alcohol consumption in Nigeria has been attributed to rapid urbanization, increase in young adults' population, and increase in formal employment. In addition to these factors is the growing sense of anomie among Nigerians due to economic, emotional, and social hardship caused by the country's economic downturn, psychological abuse, and the poor state of social amenities including the paucity of recreation centers. As people navigate these challenges, some find succor in alcohol. The drop in sale and consumption of alcohol after the 2016 economic recession in the country, has witnessed a steady rise again with a strong indicator in 2022 that Nigeria has begun to witness a steady total volume growth in alcohol sale and consumption. In Nigeria, alcoholic beverages are divided into two broad categories: beer and spirits. Some of the major beer companies in the country include Nigeria Breweries Plc. (a subsidiary of *Heineken NV*), which produces *Star Lager Beer*, one of the most popular beers in southern Nigeria. Guinness Nigeria Plc (a subsidiary of Diageo Plc of the United Kingdom) produces the popular *Guinness* brands. Others include *Hero Lager Beer* and *Castle Milk Stout* produced by Intafact Breweries Limited in Onitsha in the East. The International Breweries Limited produces *Trophy Lager* and *Trophy Black*. In the spirit category, the Nigerian Distilleries produces spirits such as *Seaman's Schnapps* and *Lord's Dry Gin*, which are very popular among low-income earners because of their relatively cheap prices and the consumption of less quantity than beer to achieve maximum satisfaction. *Ogogoro*, the most popular locally produced spirit, is consumed by the elderly, commercial drivers, and street touts.

See Also: Local Drinks (Chapter 14); Palm Wine (Chapter 14).

Further Reading

Obot, I. S. (2000). "The Measurement of Drinking Patterning and Alcohol Problem in Nigeria." *Journal of Substance Abuse*, 12(1–2): 169–81.
Statista. (n.d.). "Alcoholic Drinks – Nigeria." https://www.statista.com/outlook/cmo/alcoholic-drinks/nigeria

EASTERN CUISINE

Eastern cousins are very popular among the Igbo people of southeastern Nigeria. Their cuisine includes the dishes and types of vegetables and fruits that have shaped their food culture. Igbo food, as in the case of all cultures, has been affected by their environment and history. There are several dishes common, especially to the Igbos, but one that cuts across Igbos in the Southeast and South is *Abacha* widely known as the African Salad. *Abacha* is a popular Igbo cassava dish served throughout eastern Nigeria. It is made from dried shredded cassava, palm oil, chopped onions, dry pepper, ground crayfish, sliced *utazi*, stock cubes, and *ugba*. *Abacha* can be eaten as a meal served with dry fish or *pomo*. Soups are at the heart of Igbo cuisine. The *oha*, *onugbu*, and *nsala* soups are popular. Also, yam is one of the most popular foods and it can be prepared and eaten in different ways—pounded yam, porridge with or without vegetables, fried yam, yam flour, or as a thickener for soups. Yam may also be fried, boiled, or pounded and eaten with soup. It is also prepared as: pounded yam with *oha* soup, pounded yam with *egusi* soup, pounded yam with *nsala* soup, pounded yam with *onugbu* soup, pounded yam and okro soup or pottage of vegetables and yam. Other delicacies from the East include *nkwobi*. One of the best meals any Igbo person would be grateful to eat is *egusi* soup served with pounded yam. Yam is called "ji" in Igbo language, and it is celebrated annually at the first harvest of the crop. The celebration known as "iri ji" or "new yam festival" shows the importance of yam in Igbo land. The Igbo are optimistic that when a new yam is celebrated, yam farming will be favorable in the following year. So, whether yam is pounded, boiled, fried, porridge, or grounded, it's one of Igbo's best foods.

Ofe Owerri is one of the nutritious soups eaten by the Igbo people. Because of its taste, preparation process, nutritional content, and possible therapeutic or medicinal value of this soup, it stands as a unique dish. The main ingredients used in the preparation of this soup, such as vegetables, meat, snail, periwinkles, and stockfish make a delicious and mouth-watering dish. *Isi ewu* (the head of a goat) is a Nigerian (mainly Igbo) cuisine. It became an African cuisine as its famous edible delicacy spreads—because it is now eaten and celebrated mostly in West Africa as the Igbos' traveling tendency is manifested in the local food they take with them and consume in their sojourns. *Nkwobi* is, thus, among the most popular meals in Nigeria. It is generally called an evening meal and was originally made from bushmeat, which includes rabbits, antelopes, squirrels, and even grass cutters. Other ingredients include *Knorr* cubes, edible potash, palm oil, ointment, salt, pepper, and *utazi* leaves.

See Also: Middle Belt Cuisine (Chapter 14); Northern Cuisine (Chapter 14); Southern Cuisine (Chapter 14); Southwestern Cuisine (Chapter 14).

Further Reading

Banwo, O. (2020). *Igbo Concoction: The Legendary All-Natural Recipes of the Igbo People of Eastern Nigeria, Africa*. US: Amazon Digital Services (Independent Publication).

Nomad Paradise. (2022, May 17). "Nigerian Food: 16 Popular and Traditional Dishes to Try." https://nomadparadise.com/nigerian-food/

HOLIDAY FEASTS

Nigeria is a multicultural society, though it is influenced by two of the most prominent religions in the world, Christianity, and Islam. The religious groups celebrate big holiday feasts in Nigeria. About half the population is Muslim, and about 45 percent of Nigerians are Christians. Religious followers live side by side in Nigeria, and typical Islamic and Christian festivals are celebrated in the country, even though the divisions are very visible at these times. Christmas and Easter festivals are commonly celebrated with unique West African flavor, by Christians who predominantly live in the South and the middle belt of Nigeria. On the other hand, the main Muslim festivals are *Eid al-Fitr, Eid al-Maulud,* and *Eid al-Kabir,* and are celebrated by Muslim faithful in the country. These major Christian and Muslim festivals are officially recognized by the federal government and are usually declared as public holidays to mark the occasions. In a few states, such as Osun, a state holiday is also declared to mark the Osun deity festival. For Muslims, the end of Ramadan is marked by feasting of food and soft drinks from dawn to dusk after a month-long abstinence. Before going to the Eid al-Fitr prayers, Muslims are expected to eat, no matter how little, before the prayers in congregation. Muslims follow the religious event to recall how Ibrahim was prepared to sacrifice his son in compliance with Allah's instructions. Ibrahim had been ordered by Allah according to the Quran to sacrifice his son. As he was almost sacrificing Ishmael, a sudden voice from heaven stopped him. Then Ibrahim offered up a ram instead. Eid, in Arabic, means literally a "festival" or "feast." The Islamic calendar contains two main Eids per year, Eid al-Fitr earlier in the year and Eid al-Adha later. Eid al-Fitr is a three-day festival known as the "Lesser" or "Smaller Eid" compared to Eid al-Adha, a four-day festival known as the "Greater Eid." The two Eids acknowledge, commemorate, and reflect two distinct events that are important to the Islamic narrative.

Likewise, Easter is one of two most significant festivals for Christians in Nigeria. An official public national holiday is usually announced by the federal government to commemorate it. Good Friday is a darker day, when Christians will go to a local church to pay their respects in remembrance of the crucifixion and death of Jesus Christ. Easter Sunday, on the other hand, is a joyful affair, as it celebrates Jesus' resurrection from the dead, and people take to the streets wearing traditional colorful costumes, dancing to African drums' pulsating rhythm. Many Christians consider Easter the cornerstone of Christianity, with the resurrection of Jesus Christ signifying his victory over death, the triumph of good over evil, and the completion of God's redemption of mankind. The festive celebrations are marked with lots of funfair, exchange of gifts with family members, and visits to places of entertainment and recreation. Christmas in Nigeria, celebrated on December 25 each year, is both a religious and cultural festival among the country's millions of adherents. Hospitality, merriment, wining, and dining are essential parts of the yuletide. Prevalent activities during the Nigerian festivity include consuming traditional food, exchanging gifts and cards, and visiting friends, families, and places of interest.

See Also: Food and Table Manners (Chapter 10); Snacks (Chapter 14); Local Drinks (Chapter 14).

Further Reading

Sule, F. (2019). "The Season of Seasonal Feasts and Festivals in Nigeria." https://jd-publishing.com/the-season-of-seasonal-feasts-and-festivals-in-nigeria

LOCAL DRINKS

There are several local drinks in Nigeria, and it is fair to say a huge number of Nigerians enjoy one form of local drink or the other. Although some are limited to certain tribes or ethnic groups, others are popular across the country. Despite the abundance and high consumption of sugar-filled and nutrition-stripped international beverages, Nigerians are still known to enjoy their local beverages, due to the high nutrient levels in most of them. *Zobo* is one of the most popular local drinks in Nigeria—a super drink slightly thick, colorful, fun, and delicious. This is the non-alcoholic "wine" in Nigeria. This natural beverage is made from dried ingredients from the leaves of Roselle (*Hibiscus Sabdariffa*). This drink has many benefits: it is affordable, delicious, refreshing, and has many health benefits. It helps to reduce high blood pressure, improving digestion, and encouraging healthy urinary tracts. *Burukutu* is another popular drink, but common in the North and middle belt of the country. It is a local brew made from fermented grains enriched with sorghum and other proteins. The traditional *burukutu* production process includes malting, mashing, and fermentation. Sorghum fermentation is accomplished using pasteurization usually for forty-eight hours, achieved by boiling and maturation.

Ogogoro is popularly identified by names such as "Kai-kai," "Sapele Water," and many other names on the streets. *Ogogoro* is the premium vodka locally made by the Urhobos and Ijaw of the Niger Delta. Usually, Ogogoro is distilled locally from fermented Raphia palm juice. Although produced in the Niger Delta, the drink is widely distributed in the country reaching as far as Lagos in the Southwest and Kano in the North. The drink is served during social functions and is also consumed by the young and old. Besides its social and recreational function, it also serves as "the drink of the elders" as it is commonly used in the veneration of the ancestors. It is also used to preserve corpses and the elders rely on it for prayers during cultural occasions such as coronation, burial, and marriage ceremonies.

Palm wine is arguably Nigeria's most popular local drink, especially in the southern part of the country where palm trees grow in abundance. In traditional festivities, the palm wine also plays a crucial function, as it is used to conduct many rituals. Palm wine is obtained from various palm tree species such as raphia palms, cotton, palmyra, and coco palms. Palm wine is popularly known as *tombo*, *palmy*, *oguro*, *emu*, etc. Palm wine is popular among young adults, especially among university students. The Kegite Club that is pervasive in most university campuses has as its principal symbol the palm tree and the palm wine is the official drink of its members. Palm wine is a highly nutritious source of nicotinic acid, vitamin C, calcium, thiamin, and riboflavin. It is also medicinal, especially for the cure of measles. *Pito* is another alcoholic drink fermented locally mainly in the northern part of Nigeria. It is derived from guinea corn, including vulgar sorghum, and bicolor sorghum. The drink is also sweetened to improve flavor. Pito is also a Burukutu by-product, as it is mostly filtered off from the tip. As with many local beverages, Pito has a high alcoholic content. On the other hand, *kunu* is a popular fermented non-alcoholic beverage originally produced in the North but has gained acceptance in the southern part of the country. This drink has a milky appearance, and it is sometimes called the "Irish Cream of Nigeria." Kunu is a millet-based food beverage that is best consumed within a few hours of its production. This drink has two varieties; kunu zaki, which has millet as its primary ingredient, and kunu gyada, often coated with rice, which has groundnut as its main ingredient. Kunu is rich in protein, minerals, and vitamins and is high in fiber.

See Also: Alcoholic Beverages (Chapter 14); Palm Wine (Chapter 14).

Further Reading

Dobby's Signature. (n.d.). "Top Nigerian Beverage Drink List." https://dobbyssignature.com/top-nigerian-beverage-drink-list/

Nwokolo, C. (2020). "10 Local Healthy Nigerian Drinks." https://healthguide.ng/healthy-nigerian-drinks/

Disappearing Foods

There is a growing concern that Nigeria may lose some of its traditional cuisines as the northern part of the country continues to experience severe drought and food shortage due to climate change. Some of the crops and vegetables that are used to prepare some traditional foods are becoming either difficult to cultivate or are no longer popular because of the difficulties of accessing them. The same is true in the southern part of the country, though due to a different scenario, where some food items are no longer popular with the indigenous people. To mitigate against this negative development, the Osun state government of Rauf Aregbesola, for example, introduced a project to reintroduce some "lost" vegetables back to popular use in the state. However, apart from the dietary aspect, food loss also has the potential of affecting the health of children as most of the foods that are served are not only nutritious but medicinal.

MIDDLE BELT CUISINE

Nigeria's middle belt is known for its fertile soil which supports both grain and tuber cultivation, and it is commonly referred to as the food basket of the country. The variety of food crops grown in the region also reflects the variety of dishes that are prepared in the region. Some of the basic ingredients used in cooking in this region include sesame seeds, chicken, stockfish, pepper, *dawadawa*, *ugba*, spinach, and bitter leaf among others. *Esa* soup is a cuisine of the middle belt made mostly from sesame seeds. First, the dry seeds are fried and then mashed with onion and then mixed with stockfish, dried meat, *tatashe* pepper, and palm oil to prepare the soup, which also includes bitter leaf and spinach. The cooked soup is like the *egusi* soup common to the Igbo of southeastern Nigeria or the *edikaikong* soup of the Efik and Ibibio people of the Niger Delta. The *esa* soup is typically eaten with pounded yam for lunch. This soup contains lots of vitamins and minerals. The esa soup is also known as "ishwa" soup among the Tiv and in Kogi State it is known as "igogo" soup. It is also popular in areas of northern Nigeria where in Hausa the soup is known as *ridi*. Other names are *ekuku*, *isasa*, and *epigorigo*. The soup contains minerals such as calcium, iron, magnesium, and phosphorus. It is also a good source of fatty acids such as vitamins, protein, natural oils, and omega 3. Dawadawa or locust bean is also a good source of protein, and when fermented is known to boost sight and lower blood pressure. It is commonly eaten with traditional starch staples (commonly called *fufu*) in the middle belt states of Nigeria, including pounded yam and eba. Tuwon shinkafa is another common cuisine mostly prepared and eaten in parts of Nigeria's North and middle belt. It is prepared using the local rice flour. The catfish pepper soup is another food common in the middle belt, although prepared by most ethnic groups in the country. In the middle belt, it is prepared either with fresh or dried catfish with a variety of condiments including pepper, garlic, and different herbs. As the name implies, the soup is very spicy (pepperish), but the quantity may vary to suit different tastebuds. It is sometimes served as an appetizer before the actual meal, or it may be served as social soup that is served with beer or palm wine. As a meal, it may be eaten with eba, pounded yam, fufu, or starch. The soup is regarded as medicinal due to its contents, and it is popular during the harmattan and wet season to keep the body warm as well as increase the immune system.

See Also: Eastern Cuisine (Chapter 14); Northern Cuisine (Chapter 14); Southern Cuisine (Chapter 14); Southwestern Cuisine (Chapter 14).

Further Reading

Freeman, S. (2020). *The Nigerian Food Experience: Explore Nigeria through 25 Recipes*. US: Amazon Digital Services (Independent Publication).

NORTHERN CUISINE

The people of northern Nigeria have a very rich cultural heritage that is exhibited in their language, clothing, music, dance, and particularly in their culinary. There is almost no end to the list of great dishes from this fascinating part of Nigeria, each food being unique, ranging across meals, soups, snacks, and drinks. *Tuwon shinkafa* is northern Nigeria's most popular cuisine, as it is consumed everywhere and the most well-known outside of the North. *Tuwon shinkafa* is rice pudding that is prepared with the local rice and eaten with *miyan kuka*. "Tuwo" is a common term used in Hausa for solid foods (swallow) and there are a variety of tuwo based on what it is made with. For example, *tuwon shinkafa* is made from rice, while *tuwon dawa* is made from guinea corn. Other types include *tuwon masara*, made from maize, and *tuwon acha*, made from the *acha* seed. The soups are also of different varieties. *Miyan kuka* for example, has baobab tree leaves as its main ingredient. The green draw-soup is prepared using the baobab leaves and special spices, ideally "yaji" (a combination of ground pepper, ginger, garlic, and other seasonings/herbs). No tomatoes or ingredients are added to this soup. The *miyan gyeda* is a groundnut soup, while *miyan taushe* is a popular pumpkin soup cooked with dried meat or fish. *Miyan Yakuwa* is a leafy herb with a bitter taste just like the bitter-leaf soup that is common among the Igbo and Urhobo in the South. *Miyan yakuwa* can be prepared with either palm oil or groundnut oil, and beef, grilled salmon, etc. can be garnished. The sour taste is reduced by adding potash to the soup.

Brabusco is another common northern cuisine. This is a local couscous uniquely made, and common in northern Nigeria, particularly in the Northeast. Other snacks include *kulikuli*, a favorite children's snack that is made from groundnut; *alewa*, which is a children's candy that is made with sugar, water, and coloring; and *dankwa*, which is made with dried millet and mixed with spices. It should be noted that some of these snacks such as *dankwa* are very sugary and can be a source of health problems such as obesity and diabetes.

In addition to soups and snacks, people of northern Nigeria also have a variety of drinks. *Fura da nono* is one of the most popular drinks ever produced in the North. *Fura* is prepared by mixing ground millet with ginger, cloves, and pepper, while *nono* is cow milk. This drink is highly nutritious and contains vitamin B3 which helps to lower the cholesterol level and lowers the risk of heart attack. It also helps to maintain strong bones and promotes healthy sleep.

See Also: Eastern Cuisine (Chapter 14); Middle Belt Cuisine (Chapter 14); Southern Cuisine (Chapter 14); Southwestern Cuisine (Chapter 14).

Further Reading

Grizzly Publisher. (2020). *Nigerian Cookbook: Traditional Nigerian Recipes Made Easy*.

PALM WINE

Palm wine is a naturally occurring drink that is obtained by extracting the sap of a palm tree. The palm wine tapper climbs the palm tree and with special tools, he extracts the sap from the tree by using a gourd or a calabash to collect the liquid. The sap may also be extracted when the palm tree is felled, and a hole is made at the base of the crown to extract the sap. The freshly extracted sap is very sweet and non-alcoholic. However, after fermentation, which is achieved by leaving the sap for a couple of days, it becomes alcoholic. There are different types of palm wine depending on the species of palm tree the sap is extracted. For example, the palm kernel and cocoa nut trees produce the sweetest saps with a whitish color and rich froth. On the other hand, the raffia palm produces a bitter sap that is slightly darker in color with less froth, and it is more intoxicating after fermentation than the other types. Palm wine is popular among different ethnic groups and for this reason, it is known by different names. For example, among the Igbo and people of Delta state, it is referred to as *ogoro*, and among the Yoruba as *emu* and among the Efik and Ibibio as *ukot*. The palm wine holds a special place in the social lives of various ethnic groups. Among the Igbo of southeastern Nigeria, for example, it is the symbolic drink to welcome guests, and it is also the main drink required by the bride's family during the traditional marriage ceremony. As a way of accepting the groom and formalizing the relationship, on the day of the marriage ceremony, the bride is given a calabash of palm wine, and through the maze of the crowd, she identifies her groom, gives him the calabash from which he drinks, and offers her to drink also from the calabash, signifying unity. It is also believed that the dreg of the drink that settles at the bottom of the calabash is rich in nutrients and may only be consumed by couples who are ready to have children, as it is believed to enhance fertility. In urban centers, palm wine is becoming a regular drink both for the old and the young. In the universities, the Kegite Club, a socio-cultural, Pan-African club, uses palm wine as its official drink and the picture of the palm tree as its logo. The drink is also popular among rural people and urban dwellers, and it is usually served during social gathering and at drinking "joints." For example, in Akwa Ibom and Delta states, it is a common pastime for adults to convene in drinking bars where palm wine is served with seasoned bush meat, peppered snail, and garnished dog meat. Besides its social function, palm wine is also used for medicinal purposes. For example, it is used for the treatment of measles among children. The wine derived from the raffia palm is especially used for this purpose by sprinkling it over the entire body of the patient.

See Also: Alcoholic Beverages (Chapter 14); Local Drinks (Chapter 14).

Further Reading

Ajakaye, Rafiu. (2015). "Nigeria's Palm Wine. 20 January 2015." *Anadolu Agency*. https://www.aa.com.tr/en/health/nigerias-palm-wine/82526#

Olaigbe, O. (2021). "In Nigeria, Palm Wine Celebrates the Human Experience." https://www.winemag.com/2021/04/29/nigeria-palm-wine-culture-history/

SNACKS

In addition to normal meals, which are prepared and consumed three times daily, Nigerians are also fond of eating snacks and the country has a variety of them, both locally and foreign produced. In some instances, snacks may be consumed as a pastime, and in other cases they may serve as a meal. Snacks are more commonly consumed by children because of their physical activities and for them to meet their nutritional needs. Most snacks are healthy because they are organically produced. Because most of the snacks are fruits or legumes, they are rich in vitamins, protein, zinc, and other vital minerals that are required for growth and good health. Because they are naturally produced and due to lack of storage facilities, most organic snacks are seasonal. One of the popular snacks is groundnut (peanut), which is naturally grown in the northern part of the country. Groundnut may be cooked, roasted, or fried depending on culture and preference and may be eaten alone or as a supplement with other items the most popular being locally produced popped corn locally referred to as *guguru*. *Guguru dey geda* (popcorn and fried groundnut) is quite popular in the North while in the South, groundnut is popularly eaten with roasted plantain called *bole/boli*. Bole is prepared by roasting/baking either a ripe or unripe plantain. Groundnut is rich in potassium and phosphorus while unripe plantain is rich in calories and so ideal as a natural source for protein. In the northern part of the country, groundnut may also be processed by grinding it into a thick paste. It is then manually kneaded to form various shapes and allowed to dry and becomes very hard. This processed groundnut, locally called *kulikuli*, is a children's delight, which keeps them busy as they play together. Organic snacks such as mango, cashew, *agbalumo*, among others, are in abundance during their season and are affordable by most people including those in rural areas where they are mostly produced. However, when not in season, they may be quite expensive and beyond the reach of the average Nigerian. Besides fruits, other snacks are processed by cooking, deep frying, or prepared in other ways. Snacks in this category include *akara* (produced by grinding the processed pasty beans by deep frying); suya, which is spiced barbeque meat eaten alone or with drinks; and dodo (deep fried ripe plantain). In recent times, there has been an increase in imported snacks, especially those that have undergone extensive processing with the addition of preservatives, colorants, and sweeteners. Some of these such as Pringles, NikNaks, and various potato chips are popular in urban centers, but usually beyond the reach of most households. However, the variety of both locally produced snacks and those imported ensures that Nigerians generally are sufficiently served with snacks for their pleasure.

See Also: Holiday Feasts (Chapter 14).

Further Reading

Eatwellabi. (2022). "Popular Nigerian Snacks." https://eatwellabi.com/popular-nigerian-snacks/
Godwin, B. and F. Godwin. (2017). *Nigerian Native Snacks*. Scotts Valley: Createspace Independent Publishing Platform.

SOUTHERN CUISINE

Food and cuisine in the South of the country is as diverse as the people that make up the region. This region, made of people in Edo and Delta states to those in Rivers to Bayelsa States are very creative in their cuisines and have a rich and diverse food.

Banga soup, starch, *edikaikong* are some of the most popular foods that is common among the diverse ethnic groups. *Banga* soup is prepared by extracting oil from the palm kernel and boiled by adding dried fish, dried meat, and other condiments. The finished product is a thick spicy soup that is served with *eba* or starch, especially among the Urhobo of Delta state. Starch is prepared by extracting the starchy sap of cassava, which is then processed and cooked to form a sticky pasty texture that is eaten with the fingers. Edikaikong is the ultimate soup among the Efik and Ibibio in Akwa Ibom and Cross Rivers states, respectively. The soup, which some have referred to as "assorted" because it is made with assorted meat and vegetables with generous palm oil is rich in protein, iron, folate, and potassium. The soup is commonly eaten with *eba*, pounded yam, or *akpu*.

Pepper soup is also a very spicy soup that is prepared and eaten by people of the South. As the name implies, the soup is a specially made food that is prepared with pepper and other spicy condiments with dried fish, fresh fish, or goat meat. Pepper soup may be eaten as a spicy snack with palm wine, soda, or beer. However, pepper soup is sometimes served with eba or starch and eaten as a meal, especially among the Urhobo people. In addition, it is also medicinal as it helps to combat fever by reducing the high temperature of the patient. Most other foods that also serve as medicine include bitter-leaf soup, which is commonly used for stomach ache. People of the South, as in other parts of the country, drink water while eating. The Western habit of taking soda while eating is uncommon among Nigerians. Alcoholic drinks and other beverages may only be consumed after a normal meal, although addicts frequently take alcohol on an empty stomach leading to health complications such as stomach ulcer and emaciation. The commonest alcoholic drinks among people in the South include *ogogoro* and palm wine. While the former is a locally brewed spirit and consumed mostly by adults, the latter is the natural sap extracted from the palm tree and consumed both by the youth and elderly. Other alcoholic drinks common in the South are various lager beers including *Star, Gulder, Stout,* and other drinks that are produced by international breweries located in the country. Popular soft drinks include the ubiquitous *Coca-Cola, Fanta, Pepsi, 7-Up,* and other similar drinks such as *5-Alive, Lacasera,* and *Sprite*.

See Also: Eastern Cuisine (Chapter 14); Ijaw People (Chapter 2); Middle Belt Cuisine (Chapter 14); Northern Cuisine (Chapter 14); Southwestern Cuisine (Chapter 14).

Further Reading

Grizzly Publisher. (2020). *Nigerian Cookbook: Traditional Nigerian Recipes Made Easy*.

SOUTHWESTERN CUISINE

The southwestern part of Nigeria is the home of the Yoruba ethnic group. Like other ethnic groups in Nigeria, the Yoruba have a rich variety of food and cuisine. With tomatoes, palm oil and pepper the Yoruba do wonders. Tomato sauce goes for just about every soup/puree on vegetables, for example, okra and ewedu. This is not to suggest that it is being used all the time. Locust beans (*iru*) are a staple component of almost every soup. The style and way food is cooked and consumed reveals a lot about the Yoruba culture. Most foods are eaten with bare hands (fingers), even though certain foods can be served with cutlery. It is normal for the Yorubas to sit on a mat laid on the floor to eat, mostly in the villages, but due to urbanization, food is eaten on the dining table in cities and towns. Among the Yorubas speaking while eating, especially among young children, is not allowed due to the peppery nature of their food. There is a common saying among the Yoruba that "The soul which does not eat pepper is a weak soul." The explanation for the proverb is that other Nigerian tribes do not even enjoy pepper as much as the Yorubas do, so when a Yoruba person is asked why they want to eat pepper, they only respond with the proverb. Foods popular to the southwestern part of Nigeria include: *eba* (Cassava flour), amala (yam flour), *iyan* (pounded yam), *garri*, *asaro*, brown and white beans, corn, plantain, potato. Soups include: *gbegiri*, *ewedu*, stewed tomatoes, *okra*, *efo riro* (vegetable soup). Chicken, goat meat, beef, and "bushmeat" (animals killed during hunting such as antelope, grass cutter, etc.) are common Yoruba meats. Eba is made by pouring a certain quantity of garri (fine or coarse granular cassava flour) into a small amount of boiling water (depending on the amount of eba being made) and stirring with a wooden spatula until a garri dough is formed. More water may be added to make it smoother or a little lighter. Afterwards the eba can be served in plates and consumed with vegetable soup. Gbegiri is also a popular Yoruba food with significant health benefits. Gbegiri is a special dish belonging to the Yorubas. The soup is prepared with black eyed beans eaten with pounded yam or yam flour. *Efo riro* is a particular kind of Yoruba soup. It can be translated as "greens blended." This dish is like the Efik-derived Afang soup. *Efo riro* is made with local ingredients such as tatashi, spinach and vegetables. There is a variation of smoked fish or beef stock, too. The soup offers a range of health benefits. Efo riro contains various vitamins including vitamins K and E as well as minerals such iron and calcium. Amala is another popular Yoruba dish made from yam or cassava flour. The yam flour is made into a smooth texture, which is served with various soups, such as *ewedu*, *efo*, or *gbegiri*. *Asun* is another Yoruba main culinary dish. It is called "the finger food." The recipe is quick-fried goat meat with a huge amount of pepper. It has a stunning taste.

See Also: Eastern Cuisine (Chapter 14); Middle Belt Cuisine (Chapter 14); Northern Cuisine (Chapter 14); Southern Cuisine (Chapter 14).

Further Reading

Freeman, S. (2020). *The Nigerian Food Experience: Explore Nigeria through 25 Recipes*. US: Amazon Digital Services (Independent Publication).

CHAPTER 15

Leisure and Sports

OVERVIEW

Leisure is an aspect of Nigerian culture which cuts across all ethnic groups. Festivals of milestone celebrations such as political installations, weddings, childbirth, burials, and initiations inspire cooking, social gatherings, outings, and travels on the one hand, and sporting events such as wrestling, boxing, running, and hunting competitions on the other. Outside such celebrations, there are children's games including versions of hide and seek, "catch," and "hopscotch" (known among the Yoruba as *Suwe* and *Obi Chikolobi* among the Igbos). Young girls in twos and threes play games involving rhythmic hand clapping and feet movements in tune with songs they composed or were composed by older girls handed down from one generation to the next. Young boys for their part use small stones and sharpened wood to improve their skills in target shooting, hand-gripping, top-spinning, and running. Older people play games that involve fewer physical activities such as the Yoruba board game "*Ayo*" (the game of the wooden board). These games not only keep the players entertained, but also serve as a communal platform for unity, mental cognition, as well as physical fitness.

Western forms of sports were introduced to Nigeria, and in extension Africa, first through the missionaries and later through various colonial governments. In Nigeria, Western sports as an activity were meant to develop the physical, psychological, and national outlook of the colonies. During the British colonial rule in Nigeria, the British government coordinated and controlled all formal sporting activities/events. These sporting activities/events were linked to various spheres of social development including the military (to build in them discipline and formation of skills needed for combat), school sports (for the physical and psychological development of the students), and among civil servant groups (for their recreation, leisure, and physical development). Through these new sports the British hoped to develop colonies made up of citizens with dexterity, physical, and psychological skills built through competition and teamwork. The British introduced the Empire Day competitions in 1910 to serve as a social function which further encouraged the development of their imported sports as a form of recreation and entertainment on the one hand; but also, to mobilize and unify the very diverse Nigerian colony they ruled.

The British introduced a few sports such as football, badminton and table tennis which gained immense popularity. However, some sports like cricket, despite the efforts of the Nigerian teams did not gain much popularity. Cricket matches have been played as far back as 1904 when Nigeria played against the then Gold Coast. In 1932, the Nigerian Cricket Association which was made up of expatriates was formed while the indigenous version (the Nigerian Cricket Association) was formed in 1933. The two associations became one in 1957 and were known as the Nigeria Cricket Association (NCA). However, the NCA became the Nigeria Cricket Federation in 2006. Through the NCA, Nigerian representatives went on training tours of East Africa in 1973, England in 1975, 1981, and 1990. Currently, Nigeria has qualified for the 2023 final of the just concluded International Cricket Council (ICC) T-20 World Cup Africa Sub Regional B Qualifier in Rwanda.

Some activities which were prominent in Nigeria before colonization such as swimming were reintroduced by the British as a competitive sport. It is believed that the first competitive swimming event was held in 1938 on Lagos Island. Through the efforts of various Nigerian coordinators, swimming as a leisure activity was developed into a sport. In 1958, the National Sports Council established the first swimming association known as the Amateur Swimming Association of Nigeria. In the same year, Nigeria was represented in swimming during the British Commonwealth Empire Games held in Cardiff, Wales. In 1997, this name was changed to the Amateur Nigeria Swimming Federation, and in 2013, the name was again changed to the Nigeria Aquatic Federation. In 2016, during the African Swimming Confederation held in Senegal, Nigeria was placed second after Senegal with thirty-five medals (ten gold, twelve silver, and thirteen bronze); and in 2017 during the second Africa 2 Junior Swimming Championship held in Lagos, Nigeria improved on this achievement by winning eighty-seven medals (twenty-six gold, thirty-five silver, and twenty-six bronze).

Although the British coordination of formal sports in Nigeria created well-developed Nigerian sports men and women, there were considerable accusations of racism in its coordination. This caused some elements of dissatisfaction among Nigerians at the time. A prominent nationalist who spearheaded the indigenous coordination of formal sports was Nnamdi Azikiwe who later became Nigeria's first President. As a young man, Zik was a cross-country runner, swimmer, and boxer. He formed the Zik Athletic Club (ZAC) in 1938 as a form of protest against British domination of Western sports in Nigeria. ZAC ultimately evolved into an alternative platform for Nigerian athletes to develop themselves in formal sports. The club had excellent facilities and equipment for the development of football, boxing, and tennis. At that time, ZAC was the only indigenous sports club in Nigeria and this fact quickly became a symbol of not only Nigerian nationalism but also of African self-determination. Zik was also known for promoting Nigerian sports and sportsmen through his newspaper, the *West African Pilot*. Through this channel, he was especially known for promoting football which later became a sport associated with Nigeria's identity.

It seems the determination of Nigerians to excel in sports paid off as, in 1949, the Nigerian Commonwealth Games Association was admitted by the Commonwealth Games Federation into the British Empire Games; and in 1951 the Nigerian Olympic Committee (NOC) was officially admitted into the International Olympic Committee (IOC) as its sixty-ninth member. Nigeria was represented internationally for the first time during the 1950 British Empire Games held in Auckland, New Zealand. During the games, Mr. Josiah Majekodunmi won a silver medal for the High Jump making him Nigeria's first international medalist. In relation to the Olympic Games, Nigeria was first represented during the 1952 Olympic Games held in Helsinki, Finland, with nine athletes representing the country. Unfortunately, Nigeria's athletes did not come home with any medals until the 1964 Olympics held in Tokyo. Mr. Nojim Maiyegun won a bronze medal for Nigeria under the Men's Lightweight Boxing category making this the first Olympic medal for Nigeria. Today, although the NOC was registered as a non-governmental body as far back as 1993, it nevertheless performs national functions such as: overseeing the process of presenting Nigerians for their participation in international, continental as well as sub-regional multi-sports games; ensuring that participants presented for these occasions are in accordance with the international laws and ethics of the various associations and rules of the games they are registered to compete in; and assisting in the training of coaches and sports administrators. Currently, there are twenty-four national federations of Olympic Sports affiliated with the NOC. Through these bodies Nigeria has been represented in various national and international sporting events.

After Nigeria gained independence, sporting activities were controlled, coordinated, regulated, and promoted at both state and federal levels. Currently, at the state level, sport and its development are administered through State Sports Councils, and at the federal level, through the National Sports Council (NSC) which was established in 1962. NSC was mandated at the federal level to encourage growth, organize the participation of sports in Nigeria, and to encourage the physical well-being of Nigerians. In 1971, NSC was changed from a council to a commission (National Sports Commission) under Decree 34. Other changes made to NSC include its elevation to a ministry in 1975, and its conversion to a parastatal under the Ministry of Youth and Sport in 1991. Over the years, more responsibilities were added to the NSC including serving as the platform through which the federal government develops and maintains government sports facilities, develops programs at the national level to harness talent, monitor and coordinate sporting activities at both national and international levels, bid for and host international sports competitions, and collaborate with the Federal Ministry of Education on matters concerning school sports.

It wasn't until 1989 that the National Sports Policy was formulated making this the first sports policy to be implemented in Nigeria. The policy provided the legislative direction and guidelines for the development and administration of sports and related matters (including the funding for building and maintaining of stadia and other facilities, payment of players and coaches, regulation and monitoring of activities related to sport and its development in Nigeria). The Federal Government of Nigeria implements the objectives of the National Sports Policy through the NSC. Recently, the Federal Executive Council approved the National Sports Industry Policy (NSIP) as proposed by the Ministry of Youth and Sports Development. Through this policy, private sectors can now invest into sports and its development in Nigeria. This includes areas of sports education, science, medicine, health, capacity development, training, provision of facilities and infrastructure, funding, and investment. This decision by the Federal Government of Nigeria reclassifies sport and its development as a business and not merely an activity of leisure and recreation.

However, certain aspects of sports development remain under the responsibility of the Federal Government of Nigeria. One such is the aspect of school sports which the Federal Government of Nigeria has made attempts to encourage and sustain. These efforts began in 1969, when Nigeria held the National Curriculum Conference. Based on the recommendations derived, the National Policy on Education (NPE) was formed. Through the NPE, Physical and Health Education (PHE) was recognized as a compulsory subject at the Junior Secondary level and optional at the Senior Secondary level. To support this, teachers in various aspects of physical education were trained to teach the subject. It was also expected that the federal government through the Ministry of Education would provide the facilities and funding to support this drive.

Sports competitions are also conducted at the university level under the Nigeria University Games Association (NUGA). The NUGA Games as an event was initiated in 1964 when Sir Samuel Manuwa presented two trophies to support the first West African Inter-University games (WUGA) held at the University of Ibadan. This gesture encouraged the Nigeria Sports Council to propose a similar event within Nigerian universities in 1965. The national event was to take place biannually using a rotating system for hosting rights by Nigerian universities. In 1966, the first NUGA games took place with students from the five federal universities competing (Ahmadu Bello University, University of Ibadan, University of Ife, University of Lagos, and University of Nigeria). In 1970, NUGA became a member of the World Federation of University Games (FISU). Through NUGA, several Nigerian youths have participated in competitions within and outside Nigeria. Games recognized under NUGA include team sports such as basketball, handball, hockey, soccer, volleyball, other events include track events, swimming, lawn and table tennis, badminton, chess, judo, and taekwondo.

In 1972, the National Institute for Sports (NIS) was conceptualized but was formally established in 1974 and in 1992 was converted into a parastatal under the Federal Ministry of Youth and Sports. The NIS was set up as an institute for the training of coaches, sports organizers, and other sports functionaries. In 1976, through the collaboration of academics from universities in Germany and Nigeria, curriculum for selected sports were developed to be taught in three Nigerian university centers. These were the University of Ibadan (for tennis and wrestling), Ogbe Stadium in Benin (for swimming), and the then University of Ife (for athletics, football, gymnastics, boxing, volleyball, and weightlifting). Unfortunately, this pilot program was not successful due to the realization that one month was not adequate to cover the curriculum for the coaching program of the lowest grade of coaches. In 1988, the curriculum was expanded to nine months for all courses. In 2001, a bilateral agreement NIS established with the Australian Government led to the Athlete Development Programme. This caused a major restructuring of NIS with one arm in charge of education and research mandated to produce top quality sports manpower and sports research, and the other (Athlete Development Centres) with the aim of discovering, harnessing, and nurturing young talented Nigerians into professional athletes. Currently the NIS runs the National Diploma in Sports Coaching and Training (two years) and the National Diploma in Sports Management (two years).

Today, Nigeria promotes various formal individual and team sports as well as a host of Para-sports for the physically challenged. The more informal and indigenous sports and games are still played within communities and families for leisure and recreation.

Further Reading

Abaga, H. I. (2021). "A Look at Nigeria's Traditional Sports and Its Quagmire." *Transcontinental Times*. https://www.transcontinentaltimes.com/a-look-at-nigerias-wretched-traditional-sports-and-its-quagmire/

Aibueku, S. O. and S. Ogbouma. (2014). "Historical Analysis of Nigeria's Sports Development Policy." *Asia Pacific Journal of Education, Arts and Sciences*, 1(1): 70–2.

Akande, S. (2017). "Before PlayStation and X-Box, We had Suwe, Ten-Ten and Table Soccer." *Pulse .ng*. https://www.pulse.ng/gist/traditional-games-before-playstation-and-x-box-we-had-suwe-ten-ten-and-table-soccer/xs5cq02

Aluko, K. and S. Adodo. (2011). "A Conceptual Analysis of School Sports Development in Nigeria." *African Research Review*, 5(5): 394–403. doi: http://dx.doi.org/10.4314/afrrev.v5i5.31

Commonwealth Games. (n.d.). "History of the Games 1930 to 2010." http://www.cgaj.org/wp-content/uploads/2016/09/History-of-the-Games-1930-to-2010.pdf

ICC. (2022). "Nigeria Cricket Federation." https://www.icc-cricket.com/about/members/africa/associate/126

Mena, O. (2013). "Nnamdi Azikwe at the Olympics." *Zaccheus Onumba Dibiaezue Memorial Libraries*. https://zodml.org/blog/nnamdi-azikiwe-olympics-mena-odu

National Institute for Sports. (2021). https://nis.gov.ng/

National Sports Commission. (1971). "National Sports Commission Decree 1971." *Supplement to Official Gazette*, 58(41). https://gazettes.africa/archive/ng/1971/ng-government-gazette-supplement-dated-1971-08-12-no-41-part-a.pdf

National Sports Policy of Nigeria. (2009). https://www.academia.edu/10705450/NATIONAL_SPORTS_POLICY_OF_NIGERIA

Nigeria Cricket Federation. (2022). "Nigeria Qualifies for the 2023 Finals in Namibia after a Brilliant Outing in Kigali." https://nigeriacricket.com.ng/2022/12/10/nigeria-qualifies-for-the-2023-finals-in-namibia-after-a-brilliant-outing-in-kigali/

Nigeria Olympic Committee. (2022). https://nigeriaolympic.org/

NUGA Games. http://www.nugagames.4mg.com/index.htm

Raji, A. T. (2019). "A Retrospective of Yoruba Indigenous Games and Plays." *Grin*. https://www.grin.com/document/506240

Sports Central. (2022). "How Zik Started Football in Nigeria." https://www.sportscentralngr.com/news/readnews/12403/how-zik-started-football-in-nigeria

Swimming in Nigeria. (2022). https://swimming.sitesng.com/en_History.html#:~:text=History%20of%20Swimming%20in%20Nigeria&text=Traditional%20swimming%20as%20a%20kind,the%20most%20popular%20Olympic%20sports.

Vanguard. (2022). "FEC Approves National Sports Industry Policy." https://www.vanguardngr.com/2022/11/fec-approves-national-sports-industry-policy/

Zikism Tripod. (n.d.). "The Rt. Hon. Dr. Nnamdi Azikiwe, P.C., GCFR. N.D." https://zikism.tripod.com/Owelle.html

ATHLETICS

The British government introduced Athletics into Nigeria and made it into a competitive event known as "Empire Days." This developed into various athletic representations in national and international competitions. To coordinate these events, the Amateur Athletic

Association of Nigeria (AAAN) was established in 1944. In the same year, a group came together to form the Central Committee of the Amateur Athletic Association of Nigeria, and this became the Athletics Federation of Nigeria (AFN). The AFN was registered as an affiliated member of the Confederation of African Athletics (CAA) and World Athletics. Through the AFN, athletes were sponsored to represent the country during track and field athletic events. Today, the AFN is the governing body for athletic events in Nigeria.

In 1948, the AFN sent a team of delegates to the United Kingdom to "observe" the 1948 Olympic Games held in London. In 1950, another team of athletic delegates was sent to New Zealand this time to represent Nigeria during the Commonwealth Games. During these games, Mr. Majekodunmi won a silver medal for the High Jump. In 1952, Nigeria was again represented during the Olympic Games held in Helsinki, Finland, but unfortunately did not win any medals. However, in 1954 during the Commonwealth Games in Canada Emmanuel Ifeanjuna won a gold medal (making him the first Black athlete to do so) in the High Jump category with a height of 2.03 meters; and in 1958 during the British Commonwealth Empire Games held at Cardiff, Wales, Thomas Obi, Jimmy Omagbemi, Victor Odofin and Smart Akrara won silver for the 4 × 110 yards relay. Following these impressive performances, Nigeria has since been represented in various athletic and para-athletic events nationally and internationally.

Recently, during the 2022 Commonwealth Games held in Birmingham, London, Nigeria won twelve gold, nine silver, and fourteen bronze medals (total of thirty-five medals) ranking seventh overall. During the games, Nigerian women proved their talents by winning twelve of the gold, six of the silver, and eight of the bronze medals. Nigerian female athletes not only won gold, but broke African/world records as well. Tobi Amusan broke the world record for the Women's 100 meters Hurdles, Goodness Chiemerie Nwachukwu (broke the world record twice) in Women's Discus Throw F2-44/61-64, Eucharia Njideka Iyiazi in Women's Para-Sport Shot Put F57, Ese Brume in Women's Long Jump, and the quartet of Amusan, Favour Ofili, Rosemary Chukwuma, and Grace Nwokocha in the women's 4 × 100 meters. With these victories, these ladies complemented the feats of previous Nigerian female athletes like Olapade Adeniken (one of the fastest female sprinters in the world) who represented Nigeria at the 1992 Olympic Games held in Barcelona, Spain.

Currently Tobi Amusan holds the World Commonwealth and Africa 100 meters hurdles record. She became the first Nigerian to win a world outdoor title and the first to set a world record of 12.2 seconds. She was nominated by the World Athletics for the Women's World Athlete Award for the year 2022, making her the first Nigerian to be nominated for such an award. She was later named Best Female Athlete in Africa for 2022 by the Confederation of African Athletics (CAA).

See Also: Overview (Chapter 15).

Further Reading

Athletics Federation of Nigeria. (2021). https://www.athleticsnigeria.org/afn/about-afn/
Birmingham. (2022). "2022 Commonwealth Games (detailed records)." https://results.birmingham2022.com/#/athletic-sports-records/broken/ATH/*

Idris, S. (2022, August 8). "Full List: Amusan, Brume…Nigeria's 35 Medalist at 2022 Commonwealth Games." *The Cable*. https://www.thecable.ng/full-list-amusan-brume-nigerias-35-medalists-at-2022-commonwealth-games

Ifeanyi, I. (2022, October 12). "Amusan 'Short of Words' after World Athlete of the Year Nomination." *The Guardian*. https://guardian.ng/sport/amusan-short-of-words-after-world-athlete-of-the-year-nomination

BASKETBALL

Basketball was introduced to Nigeria by the British colonial government in the 1950s through the Armed Forces and establishment of the Royal West African Frontier Force during the Second World War. The game was later encouraged by some missionary bodies as part of their strategy for spreading Christianity to Africa. However, the game was made more prominent in the 1960s through the efforts of Walid Zabadne (a Lebanese/Syrian based in Lagos). Zabadne trained Nigerian youths through a Syrian Club in Lagos on how to play the game. Zabadne was so passionate about basketball that he took his team to watch various professional matches in Africa. His efforts at making the game popular have earned him the title "Father of Basketball in Nigeria."

Male and female basketball in Nigeria is overseen by the Nigeria Basketball Federation (NBBF). The NBBF is recognized as the governing body for Nigerian basketball by the International Basketball Federation (FIBA) and the Nigerian Olympic Committee (NOC). The NBBF was established in 1963 and has the mandate to advance basketball in Nigeria by training Nigerian youths in the game, educating coaches and referees, licensing, and safety, organizing national competitions and registering the national teams for international games. The NBBF also coordinates the Nigerian Male Premier Basketball League (sponsored by DSTV) which consists of sixteen teams categorized into two conferences namely Savannah and Atlantic. Teams under the Savannah Conference include Mark Mentors (Abuja), Bauchi Nets (Bauchi), Kano Pillars (Kano), Civil Defenders (Abuja), Plateau Peaks (Jos), Gombe Bulls (Gombe), Niger Potterss (Minna) and Kada Stars (Kaduna). Teams under the Atlantic Conference include Oluyole Warriors (Ibadan), Delta Force (Asaba), Nigeria Customs (Lagos), NAF Rockets (Lagos), Police Baton (Lagos), CAMAC (Bayelsa), Kwara Falcons (Ilorin) and Rivers Hopers (Port Harcourt). Within the league are Men's Division 1 and 2.

The national female basketball league sponsored by Zenith Bank was inaugurated in 2005 as the Zenith Women Basketball League. It is made up of eighteen teams representing various regions in the country. Prominent teams include First Deepwater (Lagos), Dolphins (Port Harcourt), FCT Angels (Abuja), Nasarawa Amazons (Nasarawa), Delta Force (Asaba), Oluyle Babes (Ibadan), Nigeria Custom (Lagos). Within the Women's League are Women's Group A and B.

At the national level, the NBBF coordinates the NBBF Final eight through which players are selected to represent Nigeria at the international level. The Premier Nigerian male basketball team known as the D'tigers, and Premier Female Basketball team known as D'tigress are ranked high in Africa. D'tigers has featured in the FIBA Africa Championship seventeen times winning one gold, three silver, and three bronze medals and has appeared in the FIBA World Cup twice (1998 and 2006). In 2015, they qualified for the Summer Olympics through the FIBA World Olympic Qualifying Tournament in 2012 making Nigeria the only African nation to achieve this feat. In 2015, they made Nigeria the basketball champions of Africa. D'tigress for their part qualified for the FIBA Women's Basketball World Cup for the second time in 2018, the first time being in 2006. Currently the D'Tigress have successfully achieved their fourth consecutive win for the 2023 FIBA Women's Afrobasket tournament making them the second female basketball team in Africa to do so (after Senegal).

See Also: Football (Soccer) (Chapter 15).

Further Reading

Nigeria Basketball Federation. (2022). https://www.nbbfonline.com/
Omoniyi, O. (2022, November 10). "NBBF Super 8 Finals: Rivers Hoopers, Kwara Falcons Stay Unbeaten." *Premium Times*. https://www.premiumtimesng.com/sports/nigeria-sports-news/564509-nbbf-super-8-finals-rivers-hoopers-kwara-falcons-stay-unbeaten.html
Omoniyi, O. (2022, November 13). "NBBF Final 8: Kwara Falcons Wins First Title as High School Student Emerges MVP." *Premium Times*. https://www.premiumtimesng.com/regional/north-central/565018-nbbf-final-8-kwara-falcons-wins-first-title-as-high-school-student-emereges-mvp.html

BOXING

Boxing as a sport is categorized by the weight of the boxer. Based on this, boxing tournaments are categorized into heavyweights, light heavyweights, cruiserweights, featherweights, and flyweights. During the colonial era, the British encouraged boxing as a sport by patronizing clubs and events related to it, as well as by funding and promoting inter-colonial and inter-empire travel to various boxing events including the Olympics and British Empire Games. This made boxing very popular in Nigeria especially during the post-World War II era. In the late 1940s, boxing served as a professional sport which enabled members of the colonies to travel to America and Europe to fight in various championships including the Empire and World Championships matches. This meant that the earliest Nigerian international and professional sports stars were boxers, and they attracted a lot of press coverage.

In the mid-1950s one of Nigeria's major boxers Hogan "Kid" Bassey (born Okon Bassey Asuquo) won the West African Bantamweight Championship (1951) and later became the first Nigerian to win the British Empire Featherweight Championship (1955) and the World Featherweight Championship (1957). His success was followed with that of Dick Tigger (born Richard Ihetu) who later went on to win the World Middleweight Championship and light heavyweight between 1962 and 1966. After independence, was Nojim Maiygun who won Nigeria's first Olympic medal in the Men's Light Middleweight Category at the 1964 Summer Olympics; and Peter Konyegwahie who won the silver medal at the Men's Featherweight Category during the 1984 Olympic Games. Contemporary Nigerian male boxers include Samuel Okon Peter who briefly held the World Boxing Championship in 2008. Efe Ajagba holds the world's record for the fastest victory in his match against Curtis

Harper in 2018. Efe won the bronze medal at the 2014 Commonwealth Games, at the 2015 African Games, he won the gold medal for the Men's Super-Heavyweight Division, in 2016 he won the gold medal during the African Boxing Olympic Qualification Tournament which qualified him for the Summer Olympics held in Rio. Also to be mentioned is the British boxer of Nigerian descent, Anthony Joshua, a two-time World Heavyweight Boxing Champion.

Nigerian female boxing started in the 1980s. Major female boxers include Edith Agu Ogoke, who won a bronze medal during the Commonwealth Games in 2014 which made her Nigeria's only female Olympic boxer (2012) and a gold medal at the All-Africa Games in 2015 making her Africa's undefeated female boxing champion. Another female junior boxer, Adijat Gbadamosi won a gold medal during the African Championship held in Morocco, another gold in Algiers, and a silver at the Junior Olympics held in Argentina (2018).

Unfortunately, boxing has had very little government support resulting in few professionals, equipment, and coaches. A more recent development, however, is the move by Gotv (an affiliate to MultiChoice), which broadcasts boxing matches weekly. This has given the sport much-needed attention from corporate bodies, some of whom sponsor fights, thus, reviving the sport of boxing once again as a form of Nigerian entertainment.

See Also: Wrestling (Chapter 15).

Further Reading

Gennaro, M. (2012). "Boxing in Colonial and Post-colonial Nigeria, 1920–1970." *Research Report* (Student Sport), 37. Center for African Studies. http://africa.ufl.edu/files/CASRR12-13-Gennaro.pdf

Gennaro, M. (2015). "The History of Boxing in Nigeria." *Center for African Studies: Research Report 2014–2015*, 37–8. University of Florida. http://africa.ufl.edu/files/CASResearch2014Gennaro.pdf

Gennaro, M. (n.d.). "Boxing the Tropics: Boxing, Health, and State Sport Promotion in Nigeria, 1945–1960." file:///C:/Users/Admin/Downloads/Boxing_the_Tropics_Boxing_Health_and_Sta.pdf

Gennaro, M. (n.d.). "Empire Boxers Are the Goods Race, Boxing, and Nigerians in the Black Atlantic." https://www.academia.edu/33023553/_EMPIRE_BOXERS_ARE_THE_GOODS_RACE_BOXING_AND_NIGERIANS_IN_THE_BLACK_ATLANTIC

Green, T. (2015). "Dambe: Traditional Nigerian Boxing." *EJMAS*. file:///C:/Users/Admin/Downloads/Dambe_Traditional_Nigerian_Boxing.pdf

International Journal of African Martial Arts & Combat Traditions (IJAMACT). (2023). "DAMBE: The African Martial Arts of Nigerian Origin." Yaoundé: African Martial Arts. https://ijamact.com/index.php/2023/01/21/dambe-the-african-martial-arts-of-nigerian-origin/

Nomso, O. (2020, March 09). "Nigerian Boxer Who has the Fastest Victory in Boxing History Brutally Knocks Out Opponent." *Legit.ng*. https://www.msn.com/en-xl/sport/other-sports/nigerian-boxer-who-has-the-fastest-victory-in-boxing-history-brutally-knocks-out-opponent/ar-BB10TVau

Ruth, H. (2019, August 14). "Long Read: The Nigerian Rise of Women Boxers in Nigeria." *New Frame*. https://www.newframe.com/long-read-the-rise-of-women-boxers-in-nigeria/

This Day Editorial. (2019, December 19). "Nigeria: Anthony Joshua and Nigerian Boxing." *AllAfrica*. https://allafrica.com/stories/201912190808.html

CINEMAS

Cinema in Nigeria can be traced to the development of the film industry as introduced during the colonial era. The history of film in Nigeria can be categorized into four major eras namely the colonial period (1903–60), the period of the Indigenization Decree (1972–92), and the reign of Nollywood (1992–present). During the colonial era, films in the form of documentaries were shown at the Glover Memorial Hall in Lagos by the British. These documentary films served to entertain as well as educate the colonial audiences on topics related to education, health, and agriculture. Indirectly, however, the British used these documentaries as a channel through which they showcased the superiority of British culture and norms often in contrast to the then labeled "primitive" forms of cultural practices of Nigerian ethnic groups.

After the Second World War, films became a more popular form of entertainment especially in Lagos where cinema houses were being established. By the late 1930s and early 1940s cinema houses had become a major business in Lagos. However, it was not until 1948, when the Cinematographic Law of Nigeria was enacted, that indigenous films were produced. Before this law, the films shown in the cinemas were produced overseas.

In 1972, the Nigerian Enterprises Promotion Decree No. 4, also known as the Indigenization Decree, was enacted. Through this Decree, the then military government reserved entertainment spaces such as cinema houses for Nigerians while the remittance accrued from such entertainment sales were paid to the government. The Nigerian audience were not only entertained by films produced for cinema houses, but also theater performances by local theater troupes. By the 1980s the broadcasting industry began to broadcast locally produced programs, many of which were in the form of comedy and drama. This gave the Nigerian audience another form of entertainment in addition to the already diverse forms available.

The Nollywood era started in 1992 with the production of the film "Living in Bondage." The introduction of Nollywood gave Nigerian film lovers the ability to watch the creation of Nigerians in their homes. The films could be rented and watched at home thus serving as a source of social entertainment. During this period, Nollywood did not only thrive, but its success also encouraged the production of other forms of movie production such as Christian filmmakers (e.g., Zion Faith Ministries) as well as other ethnic oriented film producers under umbrella names like *Kannywood*, *Yoruwood*, and *Urhobowood*.

By 2014, cinema houses had become a thriving source of entertainment once again and couples on dates and family members on outings could watch Nollywood films on the big screen. Going to the cinemas was once again seen as a special outing occasion. However, unlike the colonial and early independence era, Nigerians now have the option of indigenous Nollywood films in addition to Hollywood, Bollywood, and Chinese films.

See Also: Dating (Chapter 15); Movie Industry (Chapter 16).

Further Reading

Anulika, A. (2019). "Cinema-Going in Lagos: Three Locations, One Film, One Weekend." *Journal of African Cultural Studies*. doi: https://doi.org/10.1080/13696815.2019.1615871

Ernest-Samuel, G. and D. Uchenna. (2019). "A Historical Study of the Nigerian Film Industry and Its Challenges." *Ndunode*, 16(1): 170–83.

Iwuh, J. (2015). "Nollywood, Cinema Culture and Tourism Potential of the Movie Business in Nigeria." In K. C. Nwoko and O. M. Osiki (eds.), *Dynamics of Culture and Tourism in Africa: Perspectives on Africa's Development in the 21st Century*, 13–41. Ogun State Nigeria: Babcock University Press.

Onuzulike, U. (2008). "Nollywood: The Birth of Nollywood: The Nigerian Movie Industry." *Black Camera*, 22(1): 25–6.

DATING

Traditionally, each ethnic group in Nigeria has unique methods through which members of their society meet or date. Among some ethnic groups, dating was non-existent because the parents selected the dating partners, monitored the relationship, and saw to the eventual marriage of the couple. This meant that the couple had very limited say on how their relationships developed. The introduction of Western education, norms, and practices has reduced the power of the parents in relationship selection especially in the urban areas where children leave home and go to school.

In urban areas, dating among adolescents is prevalent in high schools and may start between fourteen and nineteen years of age. A number of these dating activities are initiated during after-school interactions with opposite sexes while the formation of what dating entails is shaped by television viewing and social media. For such adolescents, dating involves sharing feelings of care, fun, and intimacy. At this stage, very few of the adolescents discuss their dating activities with their parents but discuss more with their friends. Through such exchanges, they learn about relationships and what is expected during dates.

Many Nigerian youths especially those in tertiary institutions do not consider social media as a good platform for meeting potential partners. Many fear that the virtual personalities of individuals online are not the same as the physical one. The fear of possible violence (including rape, physical/psychological violence, online bullying, or blackmail) is a major deterrent for pursuing online dating platforms. Social media is rather used for contacting and retaining old friends, keeping in touch with family members, or building a social network.

At the tertiary education level, developing campus relationships is considered as a good way to understand the opposite sex and to prepare the individuals for future marriage relationships. Toward the end of the tertiary programs, dates become activities that target seeking a future partner. At this stage, the couples date with the hope that the relationship becomes a courtship which would ultimately lead to marriage. The concept of dating to lead to courtship and eventually marriage becomes even more significant after schooling or as from their early twenties.

Once married however, women who date anyone besides their husbands are frowned upon. Among the Yoruba people, some men who suspect that their wives are dating other men are known to lace their wives with a traditional checkmate known as "magun" or thunderbolt. With Magun, the man with whom the woman is having an affair will go through various painful symptoms and may even die. Among the Igbo and Urhobo people, traditional marriage ceremonies include the potential wives undergoing rituals which may lead to fatal consequences if she engages in any extramarital affairs. A husband who is aware of his wife's infidelity but refuses to report it may end up attracting to himself the punishment meant for his wife. However, most cultures in Nigeria excuse male infidelity if it does not involve someone else's wife.

See Also: Cinemas (Chapter 15); Gender Relations (Chapter 7); Traditional Weddings (Chapter 7).

Further Reading

Agunbiade, O. (2012). "Dating Practices and Patterns of Disclosure among In-School Adolescents in Oyo State, Nigeria." *Africa Development*, 37(3): 19–39.

Agunbiade, O., M. Obiyan, and G. Sogbaike. (2013). "Identity Construction and Gender Involvement in Online Social Networks among Undergraduates in Two Universities in Southwest Nigeria." *Inkanyiso Journal of Humanities and Social Science*, 5(1): 41–52.

Ariyo, A. M., D. I. Osunbayo, J. T. Eni-Olorunda, and W. O. Afolabi. (2018). "Perception on Dating, Courtship and Marriage among Undergraduates in Federal Tertiary Institutions in Ogun State." *Journal of Humanities, Social Sciences and Creative Arts*, 13: 142–52.

DOMESTIC TRAVEL

Within Nigeria are several domestic locations which the people visit for leisure. These sites are symbols of Nigeria's nature and beauty.

Two major outcrops, both of which can be found in Abuja, Nigeria's Federal Capital city, are Aso Rock and Zuma Rock. Both are large outcrops of granite located in the outskirts of Abuja. Though both are very intimidating, Zuma Rock is the largest and highest monolith in the world. Currently, the image of Zuma Rock can be found in Nigeria's currency note. Also of note is Idanre Hill (also known as Oke Idanre) located in Idanre town in Ondo State. The settlement was nominated as a UNESCO heritage site due to its preservation of the traditional settlement patterns, history, and festivals of the Idanre people which field researchers have found useful in their studies of the Yoruba people. Other major rock settlements include Olumo Rock and Oban Hills.

National Parks are another major destination for local travels. Some more popular ones are the Gashaka-Gumti National Park located between Gashaka village in Taraba State and Gumti Village in Adamawa State. The area was made into a game reserve by the Nigerian federal government in 1991 thus making the park the largest in Nigeria. Within the park is Chappal Waddai Mountain, which has the highest mountain peak in Nigeria. Unfortunately, poor funding, transportation, and accommodation to and within the park have been a major discouragement for local and international visitors. Another prominent park is the Cross River National Park which has two sections namely the Okwangwo (established in 1991) and Oban (established in 1988). This is one of the oldest rainforests in Africa and serves as the habitat for diverse primates (including chimpanzees, gorillas, and monkeys). Within the park area are the Kwa Falls and the Agbokim Falls. Although not fully developed, it is hoped the area can be converted into a major tourist attraction with

"Sports as Business"
The Federal Ministry of Youth and Sports Development has continued to support the development of sports in Nigeria with the constitution of a technical committee co-chaired by the Minister of Sports Mr. Sunday Dare and the Minister of Finance, Mrs. Zainab Ahmed. The technical committee has outlined the fiscal incentives that redefines "sports as business" by encouraging more private sector participation. The key incentives include a five-year tax exemption and rebate for sports investors, the provision of land for sports development and the waiver of certain fees associated with land acquisition, and a single-digit loan interest rate for organizations and individuals who are interested in investing in sports in Nigeria. It is hope that this new policy will take sports to a new level in Nigeria in the next decade.

---

a botanical garden, game and bird viewing, hiking, and boat cruising. Other major parks include Yankari, Old Oyo, and Okomu national parks as well as the Obudu Cattle Ranch.

Waterfalls are very popular destinations for domestic travel. Erin-Ijesha Waterfall is a favorite and is situated in Erin-Ijesha, Osun State. The name "Erin-Ijesha" can be directly translated from the Yoruba language to mean "the elephant of Ijesha." The waterfall which is also known as *Olumirin* Waterfall is believed to have historical association with the Yoruba protagonist Oduduwa. Erin-Ijesha is made up of three waterfalls and has seven levels. Ascending the falls has been made easier with steps and bridges. In addition, the water which descends from the falls is regarded as sacred and used for religious rites. Also prominent is the Ikogosi Warm Springs located in Ikogosi in Ekiti State. Ikogosi is made up of warm and cold springs that meet at a confluence. However, some locations like the Gurara Waterfalls (named after the local gods Gura and Rara) located in Gurara local government area of Niger State are not so popular due to poor enlightenment.

See Also: Shopping (Chapter 15).

Further Reading

Vanguard News. (2013, August 15). "Exploring Tourist Attractions in Nigeria's National Parks." https://www.vanguardngr.com/2013/08/exploring-tourist-attractions-in-nigerias-national-parks/

FOOTBALL (SOCCER)

Football as a sport was introduced to Nigeria by the British. The first recorded football match to take place in Nigeria was in 1904 in a match between HMS *Thistle* (a British warship) and students of Hope Waddell Training Institution, Calabar. The Nigerian team won the match (3–2) and this victory opened the door for Nigerian football and football clubs (like the Lagos League in 1931). However, it wasn't until 1932, that Nigeria's first football association (Lagos District Amateur Football Association—LDAFA) was formed.

In 1945, the Nigeria Football Association (NFA) was launched as the national governing body for football. Ten years later (1959) Nigeria joined the CAF and FIFA in 1960. In 1949, through the NFA, Nigeria's first national football team was formed and in the same year the team went on a playing tour of the UK under the name "UK Tourists" Their first official match was played against Marine Cosby which they won 5–2. On their way back they played against a Sierra Leonean team and won 2–0. On getting home, the name of the national team was changed to the Red Devils, but at independence they became the Green Eagles. Today, they are known as the Super Eagles.

The professional league system was introduced in Nigeria in 1990, and, under Decree 101 of 1991, the Federal Government of Nigeria took over the responsibility of regulating football in Nigeria. In 2008, the NFA was renamed The Nigeria Football Federation (NFF). Today, the NFF coordinates Nigeria's league system which is made up of three major leagues namely the Nigerian Premier League, the Amateur League (made up of Divisions One, Two, and Three), and the Women's League.

Since its formation, the national male football team has qualified for six FIFA World Cups. In 1973, Nigeria hosted and won the gold during the All-Africa Games, 1980 hosted and won the Africa Cup of Nations, won the World Cup in 1990, the 1993 Under-seventeens World Cup (Japan), and the 1996 Olympic gold for Football (Atlanta). Famous Nigerian male footballers include Jay-Jay Okocha, Rashidi Yekini, Mikel John Obi, Vincent Enyeama, Nwankwo Kano, Kelechi Iheanacho, Taribo West, Stephen Keshi, Victor Osimhen, Sunday Oliseh, Obafemi Martins, Uche Okechukwu, Ahmed Musa, Segun Odegbami, Alex Iwobi, Wilfred Ndidi, to mention but a few.

The history of Nigerian women's football was not as popular due to the British ideology that football was not a sport for women. It wasn't until the 1980s when the Nigerian Youth Sports Federation organized its first national cup competition for female footballers that female football was given formal recognition. By the time FIFA inaugurated the FIFA Women's World Cup in 1991, Nigeria had established a national female team (Super Falcons) to compete in the games. Today, the Nigeria Women's Football League Premiership (formerly the Nigeria Women Premier League) is the governing body of professional women's association football in Nigeria. The NWFL organizes the three-tier Women's Football League in Nigeria, namely: NWFL Premiership, NWFL Championship, and NWFL Nationwide. The female team has reached the quarter-finals of the FIFA Women's World Cup and the Olympics.

Female Nigerian footballers include Perpertua Nkwocha, Maureen Mmadu, Stella Mbachu, Nikiru Okosieme, Ann Chiejine, Ngozi Ezeocha, Adaku Okoroafor, Omo-Love Branch, Nkechi Mbilitam, Chioma Ajunwa, Rita Nwadike, Florence Omagbemi, to mention but a few. Some of the younger footballers include Michelle Alozie, Asisat Oshoala, Ashleigh Plumtre, and Onome Ibe, the only player who has featured in 6 FIFA World Cup Tournament, and captained the Super Falcons at the 2023 Women's World Cup.

See Also: Basketball (Chapter 15).

Further Reading

Channels Live TV. (2022, October 20). "Things You Need to Know about Nigerian Football."
https://www.channelstv.com/2022/10/20/things-you-need-to-know-about-nigerian-football/
Mail & Guardian. (2021, August). "Women's Football in Nigeria has a Long History of Defiance."
https://mg.co.za/sport/2021-08-11-womens-football-in-nigeria-has-a-long-history-of-defiance/

Nationwide League One. (2021). "History, the National Amateur League." https://nigerianationwideleague.com/history/
NWFL (Nigeria Women Football League). (2021). https://thenwfl.com/
Okolie-Osemene, J. and R. Okoh. (2014). "The Role of Nigeria Football Federation in the Denouement of Premier League Seasonal Disputes: Issues and Prospects." *Recreation and Society in Africa, Asia and Latin America*, 5(1): 1–14.
School Software Pro. (2022, September). "Nigerian Football History." https://www.schoolsoftware.com.ng/nigerian-football-history/#:~:text=Throughout%20history%2C%20the%20team%20has,of%20African%20Football%20 (CAF).
Vanguard. (2022, July). "Women Football Development in Nigeria, Collapsing – Ex-NWFL Boss." *Vanguard*. https://nigerianationwideleague.com/history/

HORSE RIDING

It has been theorized that horses have been a part of northern Nigeria as far back as 2,000 years ago functioning as symbols of royalty, a form of transportation, and as an accessory for warfare.

In northwestern Nigeria, horses play a major part in the 200-year-old annual Durbar festival which occurs in the major Hausa caliphate cities of Kano, Katsina, Sokoto, Zaria, and Bida. The festival has its origin during the wartime era of the Islamization of northern Nigeria. Regiments were formed to defend the emirates and once a year, the regiments would put up a display of their military skills, discipline, and horsemanship. This demonstrated their preparedness for war and their loyalty to the Emirate and the Emir. Today, the festival marks the end of Ramadan, the Eid el-Kabir and Eid el-Fitri Muslim holidays, and the beginning of the Muslim pilgrimage to Mecca.

Horses are the central subject of Polo, a sport introduced to Nigeria in 1904 by British naval officers. The game took up a competitive edge in 1914 when Kaiser Wilhelm II of Germany presented the Kaiser Wilhelm Cup which was competed for by teams representing German Kameroun and British Nigeria (this cup was later renamed Independence Cup after 1960). Polo eventually spread to northern Nigeria being embraced by the then Emir of Katsina, Muhammadu Dikko in the 1920s. He and his four sons promoted the sport to become a dominant elite game in the 1930s. Sir Usman Nagogo, (Muhammadu Dikko successor) eventually established the Nigerian Polo Association which was taken up by his son General Hassan Usman (after whom a polo cup is currently named) at his demise. Within this lineage came some of the most decorated polo players Nigeria ever had.

Today the sport is overseen and regulated by the Nigeria Polo Federation while competitions are organized by the Nigeria Polo Association (NPA). Various polo clubs in Nigeria are members of NPA and these include the Lagos Polo Club, Ibadan Polo Club, Kano Polo Club, and Port Harcourt Polo Club. In addition to the Independence Cup, there are various other cups, many of which are sponsored by banks and major business companies. They include the Majekodunmi Cup, the Silver Cup, Low Cup, Open Cup, Governors Cup. Other polo clubs operating in Nigeria include the Ikoyi Club (Lagos), the Fifth Chukker Polo and Country Club (Kaduna), and the Kaduna International Polo Club, to mention but a few.

Horse riding is not limited to northern Nigeria and polo; but has also been adopted in other parts of the country for pleasure riding, crowd control, and entertainment. More recently, horse riding, especially on Lagos beaches, has become a source of economic income. Horse riders charge visitors a fee for a five- to ten-minute ride with the horse rider who guides the horse through a stretch of the beach. Sometimes, visitors do not want to ride the horse but rather take souvenir photographs on the horse while the horse owner holds it.

See Also: Athletics (Chapter 15).

Further Reading

A24 Media. (2023). https://www.pinterest.com/pin/323625923192779443/
Ehizibolo, D., J. Kamani, P. Ehizibolo, O. Egwu, G. Dogo, and J. Salami-Shinaba. (2012). "Prevalence and Significance of Parasites of Horses in Some States of Northern Nigeria." *Journal of Equine Science*, 23(1): 1–4.
Ekpu, G. (2019, January). "The Horsemen Making a Living on Lagos Beach Nigeria." *BBC News Africa*. https://www.bbc.com/news/world-africa-46890783
Lux, A. (2017). "5 of the Best Nigerian Polo Clubs." http://luxafrique.net/5-of-the-best-nigerian-polo-clubs/
Okoro, E. (2017). "Inside the Durbar Festival in Northern Nigeria. African Voices." *CNN*. https://edition.cnn.com/2017/07/03/africa/gallery/durbar-festival-in-northern-nigeria/index.html
Toledo, M. (2012). "Nigeria Kano Cancels Famous Horse Durbar Festival." https://www.bbc.com/news/world-africa-19274593

SHOPPING

Shopping in Nigeria traditionally served the function of acquiring household goods and as a platform for social interactions. This makes local markets a noisy setting with people bargaining and discussing a variety of issues ranging from politics to social occurrences within and outside their vicinity.

In urban areas the shopping experience has evolved into a new experience with the introduction of shopping malls. In 2004, the Palms Shopping Mall was built in Lekki, Lagos by Persianas a residential and commercial development company. The Palms Shopping Mall became the first shopping mall in the country. With the great success of its Lekki branch, Persianas soon opened other branches in Ilorin (Kwara State), Enugu (Enugu State), and Ibadan (Oyo State). This was soon followed by other shopping mall developers in major cities located in Abuja, Lagos, Ogun, and Port Harcourt. Some prominent shopping malls include the Ado Bayero Shopping Mall in Kano, Ventura Mall in Ibadan, Jabi Lake Mall in Abuja, to mention but a few. Most shopping malls in Nigeria do not only provide a variety of shopping outlets through which buyers can purchase locally and imported goods (the favorite of which are brand fashion items, electronics, computers, phones, etc.), but also other attractions such as cinema houses, food courts, children's play areas, and toilets. Such facilities tend to attract singles who come for dates or girls/boys' outings, while small families use the venues for special get-together celebrations. Though most shoppers do not go to shopping malls to eat major meals but rather to purchase snacks and small edibles, they nevertheless view such outings as a special leisure event. The major attractions of Nigerians to shopping malls are the goods displayed for sale and other extra-curricular activities which encourage social interaction.

Nigerians and their love for foreign imported goods have also encouraged the surge of online shopping and the establishment of local e-commerce shops. Two prominent successful e-commerce malls are Konga and Jumia. Jumia was founded in 2012 as Africa Internet Group (AIG) by Jeremy Hodara and Sacha Poignonnec and has branches all over Africa. Konga on the other hand was established by Sim Shagaya also in 2012 making it the largest indigenously owned online mall in Nigeria. Konga particularly encourages local small and medium-scale business owners the opportunity to sell their products and services online to Nigerians nationwide.

In addition to physical and online shopping malls, there are also large market spaces made up of stalls. These are more common and accessible to the Nigerian population (both within the rural and urban locations) and serve as the major source for Nigerian families to purchase their domestic and professional goods. Shopping in these market spaces is not considered a leisure activity but rather a necessity for everyday life. This makes the human traffic quite high and unfortunately sometimes stressful. This is because the maintenance of these market spaces (often the responsibility of the local governments) is poor with inefficient public amenities like toilets, parking spaces, and road networks.

See Also: Domestic Travel (Chapter 15); Import (Chapter 4).

Further Reading

Iroham, C., O. M. Akinwale, A. Oluwunmi, H. Okagbue, O. Dudla, C. Ayedun, M. Emetere, and J. N. Peter. (2019). "Influence of Facilities on Patronage of the Various Shopping Malls in Ibadan, Nigeria." *Journal of Physics: Conference Series (International Conference on Engineering for Sustainable World).* doi: https://doi.org/10.1088/1742-6596/1378/3/032052

Nkwo, M., R. Orji, J. Nwokeji, and C. Ndulue. (2018). "E-commerce Personalization in Africa: A Comparative Analysis of Jumia and Konga." Conference paper presented during the 3rd International Workshop on Personalization, Persuasive Technology (PPT'18).

TABLE TENNIS

Table tennis also fondly known as "ping pong" is believed to have been introduced into Nigeria in the early 1930s and soon it became a popular sport. Today, the sport is governed and regulated by the Nigeria Table Tennis Federation (NTTF) which is affiliated with the International Table Tennis Federation (ITTF).

Since its establishment, Nigeria has raised several national and international stars of the sport. During the just concluded Commonwealth Games, the Nigerian team brought pride to the country through table tennis with Fatima Atunike Bello, Esther Oribamise, and Offiong Edem. Some notable table tennis players include Quadri Aruna who won his second continental title during the Men's Single 2022 International Table Tennis Federation African Championship held in Algiers, Algeria. Previously, he was named "Star Player" in 2004 and was instrumental in Nigeria's winning of the bronze medal during the 2014 Commonwealth Games. He also featured during the 2012 and 2016 Summer Olympic Games, won two silver and one bronze medal during the Commonwealth Games in Glasgow (2014) and Gold Coast (2018).

Also, notable to mention is Bose Kaffo who featured five times in the Summer Olympics that took place between 1992 and 2008. She also featured during the All-Africa Games between

1987 and 2007. Her career as a professional table tennis player has earned her at least fifteen medals including seven gold medals. Prominent Nigerian female table tennis stars include Olufunke Oshonaike who won the Women's Singles title during the 2016 ITTF Africa Senior Championship held in Morocco. Other prominent table tennis players in Nigeria include Omotayo Olajide (ranked number three in Africa after winning gold at the 2019 African Games in Morocco), Monday Merotohun, Bode, Abiodun, Offiong Edem, Adeyemo Fatai, Atanda Musa, Kazeem Nosiru, Cecelia Out Offiong, Segun Toriola, to mention but a few.

Nigeria also features in Para table tennis. During the recently concluded Commonwealth Games, Isau Ogunkunle won bronze for Nigeria in the men's singles class three to five Para table tennis event, while Faith Obazuaye also won bronze for the female category, and, in 2011, won twelve gold medals out of the nineteen events featured during the Africa Para-Table Tennis Championship held in Egypt. The winners include Oluade Egbinola, Victor Farinloye, Adisa Tunde, and Olabiyi Alabi Olufemi for the men while Chinenye Faith was recognized for the female side. A very prominent player in this category is Tajudeen Agunbiade, a Paralympic table tennis gold medalist who won two gold medals during the Sydney Paralympic Games (2000). Tajudeen Agunbiade won his second gold medal at Sydney in a team event which included other Nigerian Para table tennis players namely Olufemi Alabi Olabiyi and Tunde Adisaas. Tajudeen Agunbiade eventually rose to the finals for men's singles at the World Para Table Tennis Championship which was held in Beijing, China (2018). He qualified after defeating the Chinese player Zhao Oing who ranked the sixth in the world as the best player at that time and Iwabuchi Koyo of Japan who ranked ninth in the world as best player. In 2019, he won the ITTF African Para Table Tennis Championship which qualified him to represent Nigeria during the 2020 Summer Paralympics.

See Also: Athletics (Chapter 15).

Further Reading

Eludini, T. (2022, August 07). "Commonwealth Games: Nigeria Sixth after 14 Medals on Penultimate Day." *Premium Times*. https://www.premiumtimesng.com/news/headlines/547324-commonwealth-games-nigeria-sixth-after-14-medals-on-penultimate-day.html

Gunston, J. (2022, August). "How Nigerian Paddler Quadri Aruna is Reinventing Table Tennis for a Whole Continent." https://olympics.com/en/news/nigerian-table-tennis-quadri-aruna-2022-commonwealth-games

Idris, S. (2022, September). "Aruna Quadri Wins Second ITTF Africa Championship Title." *The Cable*. https://www.thecable.ng/aruna-quadri-wins-second-ittf-africa-championship-title

International Table Tennis Federation. (2019, December 18). "Long Tradition but First for Nigeria." *ITTF.com*. https://www.ittf.com/2019/12/18/long-tradition-first-nigeria/

Paralympic Movement. (2011, November). "Nigeria Dominates African Para-Table Tennis Championships." https://www.paralympic.org/news/nigeria-dominates-african-para-table-tennis-championships

Pulse Sport Team. (2022, July). "Best Nigerian Table Tennis Players of All Time." https://www.pulse.ng/sports/other-sports/best-nigerian-table-tennis-players-of-all-time-featuring-aruna-quadri-segun-toriola/hqwv2pj

Table Tennis in Nigeria. (2022). https://tabletennis.sitesng.com/en_Home.html

The History of Table Tennis in Nigeria. (n.d.). http://tabletennis.sitesng.com/en_History.html#:~:text=It%20was%20believed%20that%20Table,established%20in%20the%20year%201926.

WEIGHTLIFTING

The sport of weightlifting involves an athlete lifting an iron or steel bar (known as barbell) to which sets of cast-iron, or steel disks weights attached to both ends (weights ranging from 1.25 kg to 25 kg). There are three methods for lifting the weights namely, the snatch, the clean and jerk, and the press; all of which aim to measure the strength and power of the athlete. The weight of the athlete is also an important factor. For male athletes, the weight range falls between 56 kg and 105 kg and above; while for the women, weight ranges from 53 kg to 75 kg and above.

In Nigeria, weightlifting became an official event when the Nigeria Weightlifting Federation (NWF) was established in 1963 as the governing body for the sport. Since its establishment, Nigeria has featured in several tournaments including the recently concluded Commonwealth Games held in Birmingham. During the games, the first five medals (two gold, one silver, and two bronze) won for Nigeria came from weightlifting. Adijat Olarinoye set a new Games record with a lift of 203 kg—92 kg in Snatch and 111 kg in Clean and Jerk while Rafiat Lawal won gold with a total lift of 206 kg—110 kg in Snatch and 116 kg in Clean and Jerk—to win the women's 59 kg weightlifting event. Taiwo Liadi competed in the women's 76 kg weightlifting event and lifted a combined total weight 216 kg to get silver. During the 2022 African Open Para-Powerlifting Championship held in Egypt, Nigeria won forty-three gold medals. These include Onyinyechi Mark who broke the world record to win gold for the 61 kg class, Esther Nworgu won eight gold medals and set two world records in the 41 kg weight category, Latifat Tijani (45 kg) who won two gold, one silver, and one bronze plus an African record, Bose Bejide (50 kg) won two gold and two silver, Bose Omolayo (79 kg) won two gold, one silver, and one bronze, Flashade Oluwafemiayo (86 kg) won four gold medals, Loveline Obiji (+86 kg) won four gold medals, Lucy Ejike (67 kg) won eight silver medals, Kure Thomas (65 kg) won four silver medals, and Roland Ezuruike (54 kg) claimed eight gold medals.

Major Nigerian weightlifters include Kalu King (who won gold during the 2019 Africa Games held in Morocco under the 55 kg men's weightlifting). For the female category gold medallists include: Taniamowo Rasaq (2014 Commonwealth Games 56 kg) Chinenye Fidelis (2018 World Championships at Ashgabat, Turkmenistan), Bilikis Otunla (2019 African Championships, Cairo, Egypt).

NWF also organizes local competitions such as the Alhaji Abubakar National Open Weightlifting Championship took place in Jigawa State December 2019. Weightlifting was also a prominent sport that made up the National Sport Festival which took place in December 2022 in Asaba Delta State of Nigeria.

See Also: Athletics (Chapter 15).

Further Reading

Dare, K. (2018). "Para Powerlifting: Oluwafemiayo Breaks World Record in Dubai." *ACLSports, Your Sports Memo.* https://www.aclsports.com/9829-2/

Eludini, T. (2022, August). "Commonwealth Games 2022: Team Nigeria Wins another Medal in Weightlifting." *Premium Times.* https://www.premiumtimesng.com/sports/nigeria-sports-news/546503-commonwealth-games-2022-team-nigeria-wins-another-medal-in-weightlifting.html

Gambari, A. (2022). "Para Powerlifting: Nigeria Wins 12 Medals at African Championship." *The Cable*. https://www.thecable.ng/para-powerlifting-nigeria-wins-12-medals-at-african-championships#:~:text=Roland%20Ezuruike%2C%20Esther%20Nworgu%2C%20Latifat,won%20the%20three%20silver%20medals

This Day. (2022, November). "Nigeria's Para-Powerlifters Return from Egypt with 43 Gold Medals." *This Day*. https://www.thisdaylive.com/index.php/2022/11/02/nigerias-para-powerlifters-return-from-egypt-with-43-gold-medals/#:~:text=The%20all%2Dconquering%20Nigerian%20Para,2024%20Paralympic%20Games%20in%20France

WRESTLING

Wrestling is classified as a martial and combat sport which is used by communities to unite and entertain. Traditionally, the sport serves as a symbol of power and masculinity and is thus accompanied with much singing, drumming, and dancing to encourage and inspire the contestants. To improve their prowess and strength, it is believed that wrestlers make use of spiritual "charms." However, a major factor which prevails with every match, irrespective of the area, losing or winning is ascribed to fortune and contestants embrace the outcome as part of growth and comradeship.

In the eastern part of Nigeria, Igbo people have two types of wrestling namely the *Mgba* and the *Ebenebe*. The wrestling contests are done at the communal level whereby two villages contest against each other. It usually occurs during a time of rest from farm work while the venue is the village arena. Among the Nri people, matches were organized in front of the Eze's palace during the *Aro* festival in honor of the ancestors. Among the Ikwerre people of Rivers State the sport is referred to as *Egelege* where the aim is to ensure that through tackles the opponent falls on his back.

The Yoruba people practice a martial art referred to as *Gidigbo*, *Aki* or *Akin.Gidigbo* which is associated with Ifa and the wrestling matches were traditionally conducted in honor of Ogun, the God of Iron. The Hausa of northern Nigeria refer to their wrestling as *Kokawa* but the form which is most popular is the *Dambe*. *Dambe* resembles boxing and involves two fighters using fists, heads, and feet to defend and strike their opponent. Both fighters have one fist bound in a cloth called *Kara* and knotted with a cord called *zare*. The fighter's dominant hand is bound at the fist and acts as a spear by the fighter to serve dangerous jabs on the opponent while the other hand serves as a shield for defense. Today, Dambe is not limited to northern Nigeria and in fact was included in the 2003 All African Games held in Algiers. Its regulation and standardization are overseen by the Traditional Sports Federation of Nigeria.

Nigeria along with fourteen other countries form The Economic Community of West African States (ECOWAS) and wrestling is a sporting activity which runs through all of them. The importance of wrestling was recognized by the ECOWAS Heads of States which established the annual African Wrestling Tournament of the Community which takes place in Niamey, Niger Republic.

During the just concluded Commonwealth Games, female wrestlers under Team Nigeria made the country proud by winning gold medals. These female wrestlers include Odunayo Adekuoroye (Women's Freestyle 57 kg), Blessing Oborududu (Women's Freestyle 68 kg),

Genesis Miesinnei Mercy (Women's Freestyle 50 kg) while Hannah Reuben won silver in the women's wrestling 76 kg category. Under the male wrestling category, Ebikewenimo Welson, won silver in the men's freestyle 57 kg category, while Ogbonna John won the bronze in the men's freestyle 74 kg.

See Also: Boxing (Chapter 15).

Further Reading

Djibril, B. (2008). "Traditional Wrestling in the ECOWAS Area. Traditional Sport and Games: Perspectives on Cultural Heritage." *TAFISA Magazine*, 17–18. http://www.tafisa.org/sites/default/files/pdf/TAFISAMagazine_1-2008.pdf

Eziwho, A. E. (2017). "Ritual Content in Ikwerre Wrestling Festival: An example of Elimgbu Egelege." *Journal of Humanities and Cultural Studies (JHUCS)*, 2. file:///C:/Users/Admin/Downloads/Ritual_Contents_in_Ikwerre_Wrestling_Festival_An_E.pdf

Folakun, A. (n.d.). "Gidigbo: Yoruba Martial Arts." https://www.blacfoundation.org/pdf/GIDIGBO.pdf

Umoru, A. (2019, September). "The Sport of Wrestling: From then Till Now." *Nigeria Monthly*. https://nigeriamonthly.ng/the-sport-of-wrestling-from-then-till-now/

CHAPTER 16

Media and Popular Culture

OVERVIEW

The Nigerian mass media as we know it today was introduced by Christian missionaries and the British colonial government. For the missionaries, their major aim was to spread the Christian gospel and Western education. Thus, their focus was on print media through which they established printing presses and taught members of their male flock the skills of printing. They also encouraged the growth of the industry by importing printing machines and other equipment. This helped to ensure that printed materials such as Bible supporting educational materials as well as educational aids were available. This was taken a step further when Reverend Henry Townsend began the printing of Nigeria's first newspaper which he called *Iwe Irohin*.

Townsend's *Iwe Irohin* encouraged the establishment of other newspapers, most of which were owned by wealthy businesspeople. Newspapers were seen as a channel through which the voices of the indigenous people could be heard. At first, the voices challenged colonial policies which denied them access to economic opportunities in trade and political decision-making. This tone however changed to a demand for outright freedom and independence from colonial rule. The efforts of nationalists like Herbert Macaulay, Nnamdi Azikiwe, and Obafemi Awolowo paved the way for Nigeria's independence on October 1, 1960.

For the nationalists, the newspaper was a major channel of information dissemination to the indigenous people that made up the colonies. Other print media forms such as magazines and books were also used to educate and entertain both the colonialists as well as the colonized. The British colonial government however dominated the broadcast media and film industry. The British used film as a tool to educate the indigenous members of their colonies about public health issues and sanitation. Most of the films were in the form of documentaries with the earliest dating to 1903 in Lagos.

For the British, the radio was a stronger channel of communication as the receivers did not need to be able to read to understand the information disseminated. Sometimes, the information disseminated by the British was propaganda aimed at justifying colonial rule in Africa. During the First and Second World Wars, the radio was a prominent tool used to convince Nigerian male youths to fight on the British side.

The British also used the radio as a channel to discredit the accusations of racism, social, and political segregation brought against their administration and government by the rising elites and later by the nationalists. Because the colonial government had total monopoly over the radio stations, their views were the most dominant. This domination changed when Obafemi Awolowo the then western region's party head was denied the opportunity to defend his stance through the radio. This prompted him to set up a radio and television station for the western region. Awolowo nevertheless downplayed the power struggle he had encountered with the British Government, but rather emphasized the aim of establishing what became the first television station in Nigeria and indeed Africa, as a desire to improve the quality of education and information dissemination in the region. This feat was quickly embraced by the other two regions and eventually the federal government after independence.

The establishment of the mass media in independent Nigeria however began to lose its value when it was once again used as a tool for political propaganda, but this time by regional political leaders. The military regime of General Yakubu Gowon divided the three regions into twelve states in 1967 and later nineteen states in 1975. Each state fought for a foothold on what was termed "the national cake"—an aftermath of the oil boom wealth Nigeria witnessed. Between 1979 (when the military government handed over power to democratic rule) and 1983 (when the military took over again), there was an increase in the number of television and radio stations established by the states and the federal government. However, rather than the broadcast media being sustained as a channel for educational advancement, cultural unity, entertainment, and information dissemination; it became a means through which propaganda and the ambitions of ruling parties were maintained. This caused a lot of disunity in the country, especially during Nigeria's Second Republic.

The second wave of military takeover of government witnessed an autocratic handling of the Nigerian mass media with a lot of clamping down of opposing voices and views. Many journalists were arrested and some even killed, while media houses that ventured into investigative journalism were shut down and their products seized. The public broadcast media projected only the voices and views of the military government of the day. The Nigerian society was a tense one and it was made worse with the downward turn of the economy. However, the Nigerian entertainment industry came to the Nigerian rescue in the early 1990s when the home video industry was born. It quickly took over from the mobile Yoruba theater, celluloid film production and the now-dying Nigerian Television Network. At the same time, the music industry which was abandoned by large record labels due to the suffocating system that prevailed in Nigeria, began to bud with the efforts of small but independent record producers.

It was not until the privatization of the broadcast media that the government monopoly was broken, and more diversity and numbers were witnessed in the Nigerian mass media. This however did not result in more access to the broadcast media by the Nigerian public.

As of the year 2008, only 40 percent of Nigerians had access to television and radio was the major medium through which Nigerian households were reached. Public television stations are more popular in the northern region of Nigeria and Lagos State. This is even though by September 2007, mobile television networks commenced the digital transmission of television channels through mobile Apps (Akoh and Abiodun, 2012). This was followed by the National Television Authority's partnership with Star Communication Network China to form StarTimes Nigeria launched in July 2010. Nevertheless, major factors such as poor electricity and high cost of digital devices and services limited nationwide access.

Despite these circumstances, the Nigerian entertainment industry is thriving. Today, the Nigeria entertainment industry is made up of hundreds of studios, thousands of performance venues, and countless artists and performing groups. To recognize and award the creativity of the Nigerian film industry and its practitioners, the Nigerian Film Corporation (NFC) established the Zuma Film Festival (ZUFF). ZUFF is a national event set up to encourage the networking of Nigerian film practitioners and provide a platform for co-production opportunities; recognize and reward creativity in the industry, promote productivity and quality audio-visual services and products, while encouraging professionalism and export opportunities. ZUFF gives awards and prizes to nominated winners in the following categories: Best Picture, Best Cinematography, Best Feature Film, Best Actor, Best Actress, Best Foreign Film, and Best Nigerian Language Film. It had its seventh edition in 2014 and was resurrected after three years of silence in 2017.

In relation to the music industry, the Nigerian brand of Afro hip hop is also recognized and awarded by the Headies (originally called the Hip Hop Awards). This has not only taken over the Nigerian taste for music but also the world. The Headies is a music award show established by the *Hip Hop World Magazine* owned by Ayo Animashaun. Its aim is to recognize and award the talents and achievements of members of the Nigerian music industry. The award show was established in 2006 and has since been hosted by various personalities in the entertainment industries. Nominations include Best Rap Single, Song of the Year, Best Collaboration, Album of the Year, Next Rated, Hip Hip World Revelation of the Year, Producer of the Year, African Artiste if the Year, Best Music Video Director, Artiste of the Year, Best R&B/Pop Album, Best Street Hop Artiste, Best R&B Single, Best Pop Single, Rookie of the Year, Viewer's Choice, Best Recording of the Year, Best Rap Album, Best Vocal Performance (Female), Best Vocal Performance (Male), Lyricist on the Roll, Best Performer, Special Recognition Award, Best Performer and Hall of Fame Award.

The creativity of Nigerian music and video producers have been recognized within and outside the country. In 2006, Tade Ogidan won an award for Lagbaja!'s *Skentele-Skontolo*. In 2008, DJ Tee won the Director of the Year during the Hip Hop World Award (HHWA). Other prominent musical video directors include Jude Engees Okoye who was named best Video Director for the P-Squares musical video "*Do me*" at the KORA 2010 Awards. Also, to be mentioned is Emeka Obefe who got the Director's Award for the Best Indigenous Concept at NMVA 2008 for Ruggedman's *Ruggedy Baba*. DJ Tee won the Hip Hop World Awards in 2008 as Director of the Year for DJ Jimmy Jatt's "Stylee." Also, Kemi Adetiba, a female director won Best Director's Award at the NMVA 2014 for Olamide's *Sitting on the Throne* (2013) which also won video of the year (Adedeji, 2015).

The Nigerian government is trying to encourage the industry by providing incentives such as seed funding for young talented Nigerian artists. Those who are investing in motion picture, video, music, and television production can enjoy tax relief for three to five years (Kuwonu, 2018). However, regulating the media products created from the entertainment industry has been a task the Nigerian government is yet to achieve. The menace of pirates and the enforcement of copyright laws to protect the original ideas is yet to become a reality.

The establishment of digitalization of the Telecommunication industry has opened new doors for global connections. Now various entertainment mass media forms in Nigeria have a virtual presence. This includes newspapers, magazines, radio, and television houses. This has also given the Nigerian audience the ability to make their voices heard by sending photographs, videos, and texts to media houses thus contributing toward the production of news. Social media has also become a major source of information dissemination, linking the local to the global.

Further Reading

Ojo, E. (2001). "Broadcasting in Nigeria: Unlocking the Airwaves (Report on the Framework for Broadcasting and Telecommunications in Nigeria.)" *Media Rights Agenda & Article 19.*

DIGITAL SOCIAL MEDIA

The Nigerian telecommunication industry is guided and controlled by the Nigerian Communication Commission (NCC). Nigeria's social media platform is spurred by the rapid internet usage and the expansion of mobile android phones used in the country. It is believed that over a third of the population have access to the internet through their phones. However, this access is concentrated mainly in the urban city centers. Major digital social media platforms used in Nigeria include Facebook, Twitter, Instagram, WhatsApp, websites, and blogs.

The increased use of social media in Nigerian urban spaces among middle-career professionals and youths has made many businesses and corporate brands to rely more on social media networks in reaching their target population than the former traditional channels such as the broadcast and print media. Marketing, advertising, and promoting businesses through the social media space seems to give many Nigerian small and medium businesses the competitive edge they need not only within Nigeria but also globally. For the business environment, social media is a valuable platform through which businesses stay connected with their existing customers and reach out to new ones. Many bigger organizations including public institutions find that social media helps to make services which once depended on physical presence easier. For example, the Joint Admission and Matriculation Board has converted to the use of combining an online portal system and social media to ensure easy registration for the examination and allocation of the centers where the examination will be written. Likewise, the National Youth Service Corp has made allocation and deployment to locations of service easier and faster through a similar method.

Social media is used not only by businesses to promote their goods and services, but also by individuals who use their social media profile platforms to push their ideologies and attract virtual followership. Social media has also become a platform through which friends, families, and co-workers keep in touch. By creating group chats, family members can stay connected no matter where they are in the world. For Nigerians in diaspora, the social media has become an important tool through which they keep abreast of what is going on in the country and among family members at home.

Internet access has increased the number of sources through which Nigerians can access news and information. Today, several Nigerian-based magazines can be found online including soft-sell entertainment magazines as well as hard-core investigative magazines. Likewise, several television and radio stations have downloadable mobile Apps which allows their viewers and listeners to access their programs on the go. Through these channels the media houses not only provide information, but also encourage their audiences to share personal information, photographs, and videos.

In the entertainment industry, many independent music producers have turned to social media to increase their visibility both within and outside Nigeria. Now, many are turning to digital streaming as a channel to make more money and have a more global fan base.

See Also: Media, Privately Owned (Chapter 16).

Further Reading

Akoh, B. and A. Jagun. (2012). *Mapping Digital Media: Nigeria Country Report*. Open Society Foundations. doi: https://doi.org/10.13140/RG.2.2.36248.93443

MAGAZINES

Magazines come out less regularly when compared to newspapers, thus giving more in-depth analysis of events and occurrences. In Nigeria, the first set of magazines published came out during the colonial era and focused on themes like religion, general but national issues and educational matters. After Nigeria's independence, the number of magazines in circulation increased especially between the 1970s and 1980s. The themes during this era were more varied and included social entertainment, women's issues, health, religion, and sports. More prominent titles during this era include *Today's Woman* (1970), *Lagos Life* (1972), *Trust* (1977).

The 1980s witnessed a spike in magazine production. Newspapers also established their own magazines through which they analyzed major news events covered by their daily support of their daily or weekly newspaper production. *Concord* established *African Concord* (1985) which circulated to other African countries as well as Europe and North America; *Guardian* had the *African Guardian*; *This Week* established *Daily Times Magazine*, while *Punch* had *The Super* and *Opheha* and Daily Times Group had *Times International*. Other more independent magazines include *Tell Magazine*, *The News*, and *Tempo Magazine*. These served as the core of Nigeria's news magazines which were characterized by articles that ranged from an analysis of Nigerian politics, business, economics, and other national issues to an analysis of major foreign news and international relations. This era also witnessed the establishment of sports-based magazines such as *Complete Football* (1985).

It was not until the establishment of *Newswatch* magazine (1985) that a new form of investigative journalism was proposed. The magazine was the brainchild of Dele Giwa, Ray Ekpu, and Yakubu Mohammed and its aim was to introduce a bold form of investigative reporting to Nigeria. However, the first few editions praised the then military head of state, General Ibrahim Babangida until its first editor-in-chief, Dele Giwa, was killed by a mail bomb in October 1986. By April of the next year, the military government shut down the media house for six months due to the magazine's publication of an article the government viewed as uncomplimentary. The magazine from then on was more careful in its publication of anything negative about the military head of state and his method of rule.

Other investigative magazines however were not so compliant and thus were often the target of harsh treatment by the military governments of the 1980s and 1990s. There were cases of thousands of magazine copies seized and journalists or editors detained or arrested. An example is the case of *Tell Magazine*, which witnessed a continuous clamping down of its media offices and the violent harassment of its news staff, some of whom had to flee the country in fear of their lives. The targeted attacks on the magazine were so much that the magazine had to go underground to get controversial stories printed and the magazine copies circulated and sold. The bravery and the determination of the magazine's editor-in-chief, editors, and staff in general earned them, and the magazine, international awards between 1993 and 1998.

See Also: Newspapers (Chapter 16).

Further Reading

Edikan, U. (2018). "History of Magazine in Nigeria. Dennie." *Journal of Interdisciplinary Discourse.* https://denniejournal.wordpress.com/2018/07/20/history-of-magazine-in-nigeria/

Olorunsola, R. (1997). "Nigerian News Magazines and their Importance: A Review of Recent Literature." *World Libraries*, 7(2). https://worldlibraries.dom.edu/index.php/worldlib/article/view/202/157

MEDIA, PRIVATELY OWNED

The deregulation of the Nigerian broadcast media was done by the military administration headed by General Babangida in 1992. It was enacted through Decree No. 38, August 1992 put an end to almost forty years of federal and state monopoly of broadcasting in Nigeria. Deregulation was part of the World Bank was part of the requirements for privatization drive economy IMF debtor nations were to comply with. This opened the door to private ownership of radio stations. The deregulation was done through the promulgation of a decree. Fourteen television and thirteen private radio stations were given licenses after the decree. They include Clapperboard TV, Minaj System Television, Channel 38 Kaduna, Africa Independent Television, and Galaxy Television Ibadan.

As of 2011, there were 182 television stations in Nigeria and they included forty-seven federal owned NTA stations, fifty additional NTA stations, thirty-two state-owned stations, fourteen privately owned stations, two direct home, direct satellite stations each, and thirty-five cable stations. The advantages witnessed since the deregulation has been enormous. New and fresh ideas have been introduced to the industry and this in turn has attracted revenue through advertisements and program sponsorships. It has also helped to open employment possibilities in the industry and the improvement of professionalism. To comply with the 60 percent indigenous content by NBC, many of the private broadcast stations have developed programs which analyze national current affairs, talk shows, entertainment competitions, Nigerian movies, and series. Many also have children's hours where they show educational programs aimed to build character and morals while serving as surrogate teachers to support subjects taught in schools. A lot of the private stations invested in technical equipment which have helped to improve the quality of their program signals and transmission.

The diversity of programs brought by private stations meant that the Nigerian public had more access to information both within and outside Nigeria. Many private stations were able to employ more reporters who were able to capture more events than the public stations. Thus, there were cases where even before the public sector got wind of an occurrence, the private stations had already reported the event. Added to this, some of the private stations were able to negotiate licenses to stream live big events like sports and award programs.

The private broadcasting stations had to be innovative in their program production and presentations in order to attract advertisements and program funding. This supported healthy competition and better pay packages when compared to the public sector. This strategy helped many private stations attract experts from the public sector who by now were dissatisfied with the deteriorating state of public broadcasting. More and better staff as well as equipment allowed private broadcasting stations to offer twenty-four hours/seven days a week service to its audience; forcing public broadcasting stations to step up their game to remain relevant.

Thus, though federal radio and television stations still have wider and stronger signals, the Nigerian broadcast audience is no longer obliged to consume their messages.

See Also: Radio Broadcasting, Publicly Owned (Chapter 16); Television Broadcasting, Publicly Owned (Chapter 16).

Further Reading

Ciboh, R. (2004). "Private Broadcasting and the Challenges of Democratization of Electronic Media in Nigeria." *International Journal of Communication*, 1: 1–14.

MOVIE INDUSTRY

In 1992, the first Nollywood film was released. This reality has been traced to Kenneth Nnebue, an electronic dealer and film promoter. He had purchased a large stock of blank video cassettes from Taiwan and believed that he would be able to sell them faster if a film was recorded in them. He thus wrote and produced the first Nigerian home video, titled *Living in Bondage* in 1992. The film which was in Igbo language was shot in one month on a budget of US$12,000 and directed by Chris Obi. The film was recorded to have sold more than a million copies through street vendors. This method soon caught on and Igbo businessmen began to invest in the video industry. They sponsored directors and producers to create films in Igbo and English which they mass-produced. The finished product was transferred into empty audio-visual cassettes that were sold to marketers, many of whom had a nationwide network of smaller distributors. This way, thousands of copies of a mass-produced film in video cassettes were sold. The Nigerian video industry became so profitable that marketers could afford to buy off the rights to a film. To maximize profit, they would become the scriptwriter, producer, and director while friends and members of their families would serve as the cast. They produced these home videos with limited budget, using commercial video cameras to shoot the films. This explains why most of the early films produced were of poor quality. The lighting and audio were bad with poor camera shots and editing.

By the early 2000s, Nollywood was no longer dominated by Igbo businesspeople, marketers, and distributors. The industry had included trained filmmakers, videographers, and cinematographers. This helped to improve the quality of films produced, while the emergence of acting schools improved the quality of actors/actresses. The home video productions were also no longer limited to VHS but were now on Compact Discs (CDs) and later Digital Video Discs (DVDs) and Nollywood had become an industry to be reckoned with.

In southwestern Nigeria, entertainment had always been a part of the Yoruba culture starting with the popular *Alarinjo* masked performance, to the travelling or mobile theater bands, plays staged for television recording, celluloid film production, and finally the film industry. All along, the Yoruba drama artists had dominated the entertainment industry in Nigeria, but in relation to digital film production, Igbo businesspeople had the lead. They were able to capture the English and Igbo-speaking audiences in Nigeria. To appeal to the Yoruba speaking audience, some members of the once vibrant Yoruba mobile theater began to record their plays on VHS for home viewing. By the late 1990s, the Yoruba film industry had taken root with films depicting the Yoruba people's worldview, society, culture, and history.

In the northern state of Kano, film production began to take root, many of which were influenced by Indian films which had become a popular source of entertainment in northwestern Nigeria. The indigenous films created in Kano depicted the Hausa-Fulani cultural context and language. Their themes were inspired by the Hausa language literature market which produced romance or as they were indigenously called *soyayya* (love) novels. *Soyayya* themes were mainly of love, romance, and family politics which the early Hausa film industry also captured. By 1999, the Kano film industry had become so popular that they became known as Kannywood. Kannywood however, met with resistance from the government and religious bodies who feared that the Islamic values used in shaping their youths would be eroded. Unlike the film production industry in southern parts of Nigeria, Kannywood was heavily censored and even banned based on the Shari'a law which the Kano government made official in 2000. To ensure that the Kano film industry adhered to the dictates of the Sharia Laws, the Kano State Censorship Board (KSCB) was established in 2001. The board was especially concerned that the themes depict good Islamic morals and a positive portrayal of the Hausa society. Thus, themes which encouraged alcoholism, sexual immorality, prostitution, and violence were banned and actors/actresses jailed or fined. This led to an exodus of film producers to neighboring states claiming that their films were attacked because they exposed the hypocrisy of the political and religious elites of the North. They claimed their rights as Nigerians of freedom of speech. They also stood on the dictates of NFCB to produce, exhibit, and sell films anywhere in Nigeria if it meets the national and not state approval. It was not until 2011 that some of these restrictions were eased in Kano and film production thrived once again.

Though some scholars differentiate English speaking films from Igbo, Yoruba, and Hausa films many classify any film produced in Nigeria under the generic term Nollywood. Scholars have traced the coining of the term "Nollywood" to a *New York Times* journalist, Norimitsu Onishi who in 2002 was writing about the development of filmmaking in Lagos. It is possible that the resilience of early film producers and directors despite the challenging circumstance may have inspired the thoughts of Onishi when he coined Nollywood. "Nollywood" which has been interpreted to mean "nothing wood" implies that film producers were able to create something great out of nothing. Added to this, Onishi may have also been inspired by the other big stars in the movie production industry, Hollywood in the USA, and Bollywood in India.

By 2009, Nollywood had surpassed Hollywood and by 2013, Nollywood had produced 1,844 movies in that year alone with a net worth of 3.3 billion Dollars (Bright, 2015). Today, Nollywood is rated as the second largest film producer next to Bollywood in terms of film release and the world's leading producer of digital video films (producing about 2,500 films annually). Nollywood film classifications have included animations, horror, musicals, Sci-fi, and drama with themes ranging from love, betrayal, ambition, and religious doctrines. The Nollywood audience include Nigerians, Africans, and African diaspora communities in the USA, Europe, and Canada.

In 2015, Netflix began listing some of Nollywood's films including *October 1* and *Half of a Yellow Sun*. iROKOtv, an online streaming site which was launched in 2011 has the largest number of Nollywood films with over 10,000 hours of movie options. Nollywood films can also be found on YouTube.

See Also: Cinemas (Chapter 15); Piracy (Chapter 16); National Film and Video Censors Board (Chapter 16).

Further Reading

McCain, C. (2013). "Nollywood, Kannywood, and a Decade of Hausa Film Censorship in Nigeria." In D. Biltereyst, R. V. Winkel, and R. Vande Winkel (eds.), *Silencing Cinema: Film Censorship Around the World*, 223–40. New York: Palgrave Macmillan. doi: https://doi.org/10.1057/9781137061980

Obiaya, I. (2011). "A Break with the Past: The Nigerian Video-Film Industry in the Context of Colonial Filmmaking." *Film History an International Journal*, 23(2): 129. doi: https://doi.org/10.2979/filmhistory.23.2.129

MUSIC INDUSTRY

The Nigerian music industry has produced numerous music genres and great musicians and within this context, Lagos has served as the base for the springing up of independent music producers who have been the driving force for these musical artistes and their music.

However, scholars have identified the lack of a proper business structure and government regulation as the major limitation of Nigeria's music industry. This is unlike the early 1970s when the recording industry was dominated by local and international recording companies. But, by the 1990s the system of governance and their policies along with the deteriorating economic conditions in the country forced many record labels to leave the country, while the indigenous ones were left incapacitated. Thus, young Nigerian musicians who entered the music industry in the 1990s were not only left with no big record labels to support them, but also limited finances. To survive, they evolved their own independent local music industry which involves them; developing their own imprints using personal computers and the latest recording software, directing their own videos, recording their music into CDs, and taking their final products to radio and other media houses within Lagos and other major cities in Nigeria for it to be aired and promoted. For these young independent music producers, songwriters, and composers, this process involves a lot of follow-ups, some bribery, and a lot of personal financial commitment. The result is that the Nigerian music industry is made up of resilient youths who have made the industry look like a booming trade due to the high number of music and video releases regularly. Unfortunately, many players of the industry are limited in terms of formal education in aspects of music composition, coordination, and production; and thus, result in merely copying the style and compositions of current artists. This has encouraged mediocre performances and unprofessionalism in the industry.

Unfortunately, some of the policies of the Nigerian federal government adds to the limitations of the music industry. Their unfavorable policies especially as it relates to importation of musical equipment and instruments made it very difficult for musicians to function and produce good quality music. Many were forced to rely on cheap, outdated, and inferior musical instruments, recording, and production equipment.

The lack of structure within the Nigerian music industry has often meant that young talents with limited financial backing sign away their royalties at the detriment of their future growth. It was based on this that the Copyright Society of Nigeria (COSON) was established in 2007. It serves as Nigeria's performing rights organization charged with ensuring artists get paid when their music is played by commercial users. COSON is recognized in Nigeria as the only approved collective management organization for musical works and sound recording; set up to license users of music for commercial purposes, collect and distribute royalties to owners of the used works. The organization operates under the supervision of the Nigerian Copyright Commission (Africa Music Law, 2018).

See Also: Hip Hop Music (Chapter 13); Kuti, Fela (Chapter 13); Media, Privately Owned (Chapter 16); Nigerian Music Producers (Chapter 13); Piracy (Chapter 16); Uwaifo, Victor (Chapter 13).

Further Reading

Forchu, I. (2009). "Nigerian Popular Music: Its Problems and Prospects in Development." *UJAH: Unizik Journal of Arts and Humanities*, 10(2): 103–14.

Censorship of Nigerian Media

The Nigerian media especially private-owned organizations have faced a series of censorship in the past including the Buhari-led administration. After the censorship of some private television and radio stations due to their "infringement" on the Nigerian Broadcasting Commission code of conduct and the suspension of Twitter in 2022, the Nigerian media, even though with some trepidation, have been agog especially with the presidential general elections that were held on February 25, 2023, and the gubernatorial election of March 18, 2023. Despite the precautions that the Nigerian media take to avoid sanctions from the body, advocates of freedom of speech in Nigeria still express concerns that the media is not free in Nigeria. The recent fine of five million Naira imposed on Channels Television on April 2, 2023, following the petition of Bola Tinubu, the President-elect is a case that activists have pointed to as indicating the worst that is to come after Mr. Tinubu is sworn in on May 29, 2023.

NATIONAL BROADCASTING COMMISSION

The National Broadcasting Commission (NBC) was established by the military administration of General Ibrahim Babangida through Decree No. 38 of 1992. The aim of its establishment was to regulate the broadcast industry in the wake of the deregulation of the broadcast industry and put an end to the almost fifty years of monopoly of the broadcast industry by the state and federal government. The functions of NBC as the governing body includes regulating and controlling the broadcast industry and its operations in Nigeria, ensuring a standard is maintained within the industry, promoting the indigenous culture of the Nigerian people through broadcasting, monitoring broadcast content for messages which may be harmful or offensive to viewers, attending to complaints regarding the conduct of broadcast stations, ensuring that technical standards are maintained, applying sanctions or even revoking the licenses of stations that do not comply to the code of conduct laid out by the NBC. Private broadcasting stations are required to have a minimum of 60 percent local and 40 percent foreign content, while cable and satellite stations are required to have 20 percent local content.

The chairman and other members of the NBC are appointed by the president based on the recommendation of the Minister of Information. The Commission's membership consists of the chairman and ten other individuals including representatives of the Ministry of Information and Culture and the State Security Service (SSS). It has been argued that this formulation is an infringement of press freedom as members who make up the NBC are chosen based on the discretion of the ruling party. Other voices such as business owners, opposition party members, and educationists are not represented. NBC is like an extension of the Ministry of Information. There have been many discerning voices which suggest that the regulatory policies of the NBC are neither fair nor just. For example, licensing rights to air big sporting events are denied to private stations to give NTA stations the monopoly to air them. In relation to the licensing fee to operate a private broadcast station, it is noted that as of 2006, the lowest license fee for a private radio station was fifteen million Naira, while for public it is ten million Naira. Likewise, NBC has been accused of enforcing the bidding of the ruling party and clamping down on stations that do not comply. Some of the private stations have been forced to take legal actions on the grounds that some of the actions of NBC are clear violations of their rights. For example, Daar Communication stations, African Independent Television and Ray Power FM were shut down in October 2005 for their coverage of the Bellview air crash. Being the first at the air crash site, they were able to stream the rescue event live and counter some "misleading" information given by NTA. It took the intervention of advocacy group protests for both stations to be reopened.

See Also: Media, Privately Owned (Chapter 16); Radio Broadcasting, Publicly Owned (Chapter 16); Television Broadcasting, Publicly Owned (Chapter 16).

Further Reading

Kugo, U. (2013). "Broadcasting Regulation and Broadcasting in Nigeria: An Overview of the Approaches." *Research on Humanities and Social Sciences*, 3(2): 12–20.
National Broadcasting Commission. (2016). *Nigerian Broadcasting Code (6th edition)*. https://www.nta.ng/wp-content/uploads/2019/09/1494416213-NBC-Code-6TH-EDITION.pdf

NATIONAL FILM AND VIDEO CENSORS BOARD

The National Film and Video Censors Board (NFVCB) was established in 1993 to serve as a regulatory agency to control, monitor and grant licenses for the distribution, exhibition, and marketing of motion pictures in Nigeria. It has its foundation on the Theatre and Public Performance Regulation Ordinance (1912) and the Cinematographic Act (1963).

NFVCB is also empowered to censor, rate, and classify documentary, feature, television, and video films. It is made up of a chairman who is supported by a representative from each state as well as the Federal Capital Territory, Abuja; selected federal ministries namely—Information and National Orientation, Education, Internal Affairs, and Culture and Tourism; the Nigerian Police Force; the Federal Fire Service; Nigerian Copyright Commission; and the Nigerian Customs Service. Representatives of youth, women, religious bodies, and the academia are also members of the board. Appointment of the Executive Director as well as the selection of supporting members is done by the Nigerian President on the recommendation of the Minister. Members of NFVCB may be removed by the Minister if judged as not acting in the interest of the nation and its people. Financially, the NFVCB is sustained through support from federal and state governments, fees it charges for services and penalties, and gifts/donations received from external bodies.

With the establishment of NFVCB, it is illegal for anyone to exhibit a film/video without a license and a censorship certificate from the board; and no premises can be used to exhibit a film or video without approval from the board. Exceptions are given to private or home exhibitions, public exhibitions done by public officials employed for the purpose of cinematography, done within government property, and based on government directives. Films/videos produced by the federal and state governments, selected international, academic, or research bodies such as the UN, ECOWAS, and the Commonwealth do not need such licenses. Also exempt are videos exhibited as part of an educational, training, or business promotion. However, it is an offense to exhibit, store, distribute or sell videos or films as a business venture without proper registration, license, and censorship certificate. This includes imported as well as Nigerian-made films and videos.

To effectively carry out its duties, the NFVCB has zonal film censor offices run by a committee selected by the chairman. Unfortunately, the board is limited in terms of manpower to monitor and censor Nigeria as a country and has presence in only about twenty-five cities throughout Nigeria. This has caused some deviant-minded film makers and distributors to take advantage of this limitation to market and exhibit previewed and censored versions of a film within the areas where the NFVCB zonal office is located, and uncensored versions elsewhere. Though there are cases where officials of the NFVCB have confiscated uncensored and pirated versions of films, these instances are limited to big cities like Lagos and Abuja. Often the NFVCB is powerless to deal with public complaints of scenes of violence and immorality projected through films/videos exhibited within the country.

See Also: Movie Industry (Chapter 16), Piracy (Chapter 16).

Further Reading

Ugor, P. (2007). "Censorship and the Content of Nigerian Home Video Films." *Postcolonial Text*, 3(1): 1–22.

NEWSPAPERS

The first printing press in Nigeria was established through the efforts of Reverend Hope Waddell (of the Presbyterian Church of Scotland Mission) at Calabar in 1946. Through the printing press, religious books and pamphlets were produced. In 1854, another printing press was set up but this time by Reverend Henry Townsend (of the Church Missionary Society) in Abeokuta. By 1859, Townsend had used the printing press to produce the first newspaper in Nigeria which he named, *Iwe Iroyin Fun Awon Ara Egba Ati Yoruba* (Newspaper in Yoruba for the Egba and Yoruba People). *Iwe Iroyin* (the shortened version) was published fortnightly and in the Yoruba language as part of the Reverend's aim of encouraging the Yoruba people to read and seek information. Reverend Townsend's effort of establishing a printing school as well as the newspaper encouraged the production and establishment of other printing presses, printers, and newspapers in Nigeria. Many, for example, *Anglo African*, *Lagos Times/Gold Colony Advertiser*, *Lagos Times*, *Lagos Weekly Record*, etc., were individually owned. Newspapers became a major channel through which the colonized challenged the rules and policies of their colonizers and eventually became a tool which spurred the agitation for economic independence and political self-rule.

Notable newspapers which were very vocal during Nigeria's struggle for independence include Nnamdi Azikiwe's *West African Pilot* (1937), Obafemi Awolowo's *Tribune* (1949) and the then Sardauna of Sokoto established *Gaskiya Tafi Kwabo* (Truth is more than money) in 1939). As the possibility of independence became more certain, the papers began to wear a more partisan look based on regional loyalties. *West African Pilot* and Zik's chain of newspapers supported the eastern region's political party (National Council for

Nigeria and the Cameroun, NCNC), *Tribune* the western region's party, Action Group and *Gaskiya* the northern region's political party Northern People's Congress (NPC).

After independence and the creation of states, publicly owned newspapers were established as the mouthpiece of both federal and state governments. For example, the following papers were owned by their state governments, *The Nigerian Standard Newspaper* by Plateau State, *The Observer* by Edo State, *Daily Star* by Anambra State, *The Chronicle* by Cross River State, etc. The 1980s and 1990s witnessed the emergence of several newspapers aimed to present events with an independent stance and not be influenced by the political views of the ruling parties of the nation. These papers include *The Guardian* (established in 1983 by Alex Ibru), *Vanguard Newspaper* (established by Sam Amukapu in 1990). Likewise, there were newspapers established to serve as a mouthpiece for the propaganda movements of the military regime heads at the time. These include *Third Eye* established by Chief Akanni to promote the activities of General Ibrahim Babangida; and *The Monitor* established by Chief Arisekola Alao to promote Late General Sanni Abacha. Newspapers like the *Concord* established by Chief Moshood Abiola in 1980, were used to promote his presidential campaigns.

See Also: Magazines (Chapter 16).

Further Reading

Odorume, A. (2012). "Historiography of the Print Media: A Global-Cum-Nigerian Perspective." *Journal of African Studies*, 1: 1–9.

PIRACY

In 2004, the Nigerian Copy Commission established the Strategic Action Against Piracy (STRAP) to curb the rate of pirated media goods produced in Nigeria. Piracy here refers to an unauthorized reproduction of a work (including books, videos, song compositions, art, or graphic works) without the permission of the creator; with the aim of claiming ownership or making profit from its reproduction. Scholars agree that such acts are criminal because they do not give the original owners the opportunity to take credit nor financially gain from the investments put into the production of their creativity. For a country like Nigeria which produces thousands of musical and movie videos weekly, this means that the revenues that should go to the original creators are lost to pirates who mass produce, distribute, and market original works illegally.

Stamping out pirate operations in Nigeria is a task the Nigerian government has yet to achieve. Operators in the entertainment industry believe that stiffer laws and penalties should be made if this is going to happen. However, the pirates take the illegal business seriously. They invest in sophisticated software which makes such high-quality mass-produced duplicated copies, that consumers find it difficult to know the difference between the original and the duplicated ones. The duplicated copies are distributed to various destinations through hawkers along busy roads, at open markets, bus stops, gas stations, beside busy public buildings, etc. The price of the duplicated and mass-produced videos is often far cheaper than the original version sold by the copyright owner. In some cases, the duplicated version comes out even before the original version does, thus leaving the owners at a great disadvantage. Currently, pirated versions are not limited to just one movie or musical video but may be a DVD of up to fourteen highly rated productions thus making it almost impossible for copyright owners to keep up with the large distribution networks that the pirates have created and have access to. This distribution network is not limited to Nigeria but extends to Africa and beyond.

Stamping out piracy in Nigeria will take some time, the main reason for this being a weak regulation and formal system for the promotion, marketing, and production of music and movie videos in the country. Unfortunately, this gap has been filled by illegal marketers and distributors located at Alaba International Market (AIM) located in Lagos. AIM is a large electronic market which sells various types of products ranging from original to fake and cheap products. Sometimes the sellers buy original media productions which they mass produce for sale; while in other instances they download them from YouTube, Cable, or national television.

Despite its negative side, piracy in Nigeria has played an important role in meeting the high demand for Nigerian entertainment. Not only does piracy ensure that media goods are produced and circulated farther and faster than the more formal system, but it also helps up-and-coming artists who could never have afforded the large national and even international fan base piracy offers.

See Also: Movie Industry (Chapter 16); Music Industry (Chapter 16); National Film and Video Censors Board.

Further Reading

Ridwan, A., G. Akashoro, and M. Ajaga. (2013). "An Empirical Study of the Trend and Pattern of Video-Film Piracy." *European Scientific Journal*, 9(14): 64–86.
Tade, O. and O. Mmahi. (2018). "Movie Piracy Networks at Alaba International Market, Lagos, Nigeria." *International Journal of Offender Therapy and Comparative Criminology*, 62(1): 274–85. doi: https://doi.org/10.1177/0306624X17692208

RADIO BROADCASTING, PUBLICLY OWNED

Radio was introduced to Nigeria through the British colonial administration as the Radio Distribution Service (1933). The RDS relayed programs of the British Empire Service (as part of the British Broadcasting Corporation external service) to a relay studio in Lagos. Homeowners paid for the installation of the equipment (which included wires connected to loudspeakers for signal reception in their homes) and sustained their access through a monthly fee subscription. This system was known as the Radio Distribution System (RDS). RDS became so popular that other relay stations were set up all over the country and the system was converted into the Radio Diffusion System in 1935. The diffusion system had thirteen reception stations all over Nigeria and was managed by the Post and Telegraphs Department. By 1951, after much research and series of meetings, the British pulled all the re-diffusion stations together to form the Nigerian Broadcasting Service (NBS).

On April 1, 1957, the Nigerian Broadcasting Corporation Ordinance of 1956 converted NBS to NBC. The main aim of NBC was to ensure quality, uniformity, and the smooth running of radio broadcasting in Nigeria. Being a public service, it was fully funded by the Nigerian government.

In May 1960, the Western Nigerian Radio-Vision Service was launched to oversee the television and radio broadcasting stations of the western region located in Ibadan. On October 1, 1960, the eastern region launched both its radio and television stations in Enugu. Both regions went into collaboration with the Overseas Re-diffusion Limited. The northern region did not set up their own broadcasting stations until 1962 with Radio-Kaduna Television under the Broadcasting Company of Northern Nigeria. After the Nigerian Civil War, more states were created, and each state had its own radio station independent of federal control.

In 1979, the NBC ordinance was dissolved and replaced with the Federal Radio Corporation of Nigeria Decree of 1979. The Federal Radio Corporation of Nigeria (FRCN) Act allowed federal government radio stations to broadcast simultaneously to more than one state in the federation at the same time on short and medium wave bands. All other state radio stations had restricted reception to their geographical locations. Though the aim of the FRCN was to provide a public service which was impartial and independent; reflecting the unity and culture of the nation, this was not always the case as most of the time only the voices of the ruling parties were heard.

By 1984 there was a need for expenditure cuts on broadcasting and this included the shutting down of FRCN stations leaving only Lagos, Ibadan, Enugu, Kaduna, and Abuja stations. The Voice of Nigeria (VON) was established in 1990 retrospectively under the Voice of Nigeria Corporation Decree of 1991 to serve as the external radio service of Nigeria.

The federal and state monopoly over radio broadcasting ended in 1992 with the deregulation of the broadcast industry. Privatization led to the issuance of licenses to thirteen private radio stations by NBC, the regulating body.

See Also: Media, Privately Owned (Chapter 16); National Broadcasting Commission (Chapter 16), Television Broadcasting, Publicly Owned (Chapter 16).

Further Reading

Akpede, K. S. (2018). *Introduction to Radio and Television (MAC 142)*. Abuja: National Open University of Nigeria.

TELEVISION BROADCASTING, PUBLICLY OWNED

Television transmission in Nigeria took off on October 31, 1959, and was initiated by the government of the then western region, headed by Obafemi Awolowo. Awolowo and his party members walked out of a Parliamentary Session in protest during a constitutional debate which challenged the 1954 Macpherson Constitution. The British Governor General, James Robertson condemned their action and defended the constitution through the NBS; but denied Awolowo the same opportunity. Rather than set up a radio station to challenge the injustice, Awolowo decided to set up the Western Nigeria Television (WNTV); a television station for the western region commissioned in 1959. Though the station was in Ibadan city, its transmission reached Lagos. This action made the television station not only the first in Nigeria but also the first in Africa. Awolowo outlined the aims of WNTV to include being a channel through which: the quality and pace of education in the region could be increased; the dissemination of information within the region and about activities outside the region could be achieved; and to entertain viewers in the region. A year later, the eastern region established Eastern Nigerian Television (ENTV) in Enugu (1960), the northern region established Radio Television Kaduna (RTVK) under the Broadcasting Company of Northern Nigeria (BCNN) in 1962.

The Nigerian Federal Government did not consider setting up broadcast stations until 1962 with the establishment of The Nigerian Television Service (NTS) in Lagos. In 1977, the Nigerian Military Government took over all the television stations in the country and established the National Television Authority through Decree No. 24 which took effect retrospectively in April 1976. The Decree gave NTA the exclusive right to operate on the more powerful Very High Frequency (VHF), while state-owned television stations operated on the more limited Ultra High Frequency (UHF). The government declared that the reason for doing this was to ensure national unity. However, during the era of the Second Republic NTA became a channel through which information dissemination was hijacked and used purely for political propaganda by the federal ruling party. This forced the ever-increasing number of states created to establish their own television stations when they realized their voices could no longer be heard at the federal level.

By 1984, it became obvious that the federal government could not maintain its nationwide operation of NTA. By 1985, financing over thirty-five stations had become a huge financial expenditure which the government could not afford; despite the TV tax imposed on television owners. Being a public service enterprise, adverts were not allowed which meant that the government was fully responsible and in control of NTA stations. This is unlike the states which accepted regulated adverts to generate revenues and sustain their stations. At the federal level, despite the drastic cuts in staff, training, and equipment acquisition, the strength of NTA as a political propaganda tool for the military governments of the day waxed stronger.

Deregulation of the broadcast industry in 1992 ended the public monopoly of the Nigerian broadcast industry.

See Also: Media, Privately Owned (Chapter 16); National Broadcasting Commission (Chapter 16), Radio Broadcasting, Publicly Owned (Chapter 16).

Further Reading

Onuoha, P. (2012). *History of Nigerian Mass Media (MAC 113)*. School of Arts and Social Science, National Open University.

APPENDIX A

A Day in the Life

A DAY IN THE LIFE OF A FARMER

Farmers are one of the most important people in the society as they are responsible for the provision of one of the necessities of life, food. The farmer works all year round except during the month preceding the harvest of the crops. The daily life of a farmer is tedious, interesting, and rewarding. The farmer wakes up early in the morning when the cock crows, usually by 5:00 a.m., to take care of the house chores including washing their faces, brushing their teeth, and preparing the materials that will be needed in the farm for that day. Most rural farmers do not engage in mechanized farming, instead they rely on their skills and manual labor. For this reason, they must set out to the farm early before the sun rises to ensure that as many tasks as possible are accomplished before the scorching sun climbs overhead by midday. On the farm, work starts immediately, and after a couple of hours a break is taken for breakfast. This is the interesting part of the farming exercise. Foods prepared and served are usually fresh because they are taken directly from the farm such as yam, plantain, maize, cocoyam, etc., depending on their season. A meal is prepared on the farm and consumed by all the workers. After enough rest, work resumes and, intermittently, they take a break to regain their energy to complete the main task of the day. The younger ones are given permission to explore the forest to harvest fruits such as mango, pepper-fruits, *agbalumo*, etc., depending on their season. These fruits are consumed by all during the short breaks to replenish their energy. The tasks for the day vary depending on the season. Typically, farmers prepare the land shortly before the rainy season by clearing the land through the slash and burn technique. Once the rains start in late March or early April, the planting of crops commences, which takes place for about one month depending on the size of the farm. As the crops begin to germinate, the young plants are protected by eliminating the weeds with the use of hoes and cutlasses. This activity continues until it is time for harvesting when the crops are consumed, and the excess is sold in the local market. After the day's work, which usually ends at sunset, the farmer clears the resting area of all waste, keeps it tidy, and returns home to prepare for the evening meal. As the meal is being prepared, the children help in the open kitchen. The very young children are allowed to play outside while waiting for the food to be prepared. Eating is usually communal with the children eating together from the same bowl and the adults eating separately. After the evening meal, the plates are washed by the children while the adults have conversations until they retire for the day to prepare for the next day.

A DAY IN THE LIFE OF A HOUSEWIFE

The Nigerian household is as diverse as the people that make up the country. In the northern part of the country where the majority of the people are Muslims, married women are not permitted to engage in economic activities outside the home according to Islamic injunctions. However, married women may engage in economic activities in the compound such as making beads, stringing of trinkets, cooking for commercial purposes, among other activities. When completed, only women are allowed to make purchases in the compound due to the practice of *kunle* or *ba'shiga* (the practice of prohibiting men who are not relatives of the family from entering the compound). On the other hand, in the southern part of the country where the majority of the population are Christians, women have complete freedom to trade or go to the farm or any other activity they are interested in pursuing. Generally, except in urban centers where Christians are in the majority, the average Nigerian home is polygynous, with the man having an average of three wives. Culturally, Nigerian housewives are the bedrock of the family. They wake up early in the morning, usually by 5:00 a.m. to start the day by praying with the children. In some homes such as those of the Christian Pentecostal faith, the prayer may last for about an hour before the children will have their bath while the mother prepares their breakfast. As the children have their breakfast, the mothers prepare and pack their lunch. Once ready, the fathers take the children to school if they have a car, or the children walk to school by themselves. From 7:00 a.m. when the children leave for school until they arrive home in the late afternoon, the housewife is preoccupied with the house chores, from sweeping and cleaning the house to washing the dirty plates and clothes, to going to the market for groceries in preparation for the evening meal. Once the children arrive home from school, she bathes the youngest ones and commands the older ones to do the same. By the time the children have finished having their bath the evening meal is ready, and after the evening meal, she assists the children with their homework and, after the homework, she tells them to retire for the day. Meanwhile, the mother is still awake to prepare the food of the husband who comes in later. She watches him eat while they discuss the business of the day. After finishing his meal, she clears the table and washes the dishes. When she or the husband has the time, they will both talk about the day's activities until they both retire for the day by going to sleep. Weekend routines are usually different as housewives typically have various functions to attend such as weddings, funerals, naming ceremonies, among others, while on Sunday, Christians spend the most part of the day attending church, visiting family members, and relaxing in preparation for the following week.

A DAY IN THE LIFE OF A STUDENT

Education is an important aspect of life among the average Nigerian and so in every household it is expected that the children must attend school. Although this is not the case in every home especially in the northern part of the country where over fifteen million children are out of school. In that area, which is predominantly occupied by Muslims, the preferred form of education is the Arabic school where the Quran is taught to children between the ages of five and twelve, and by the age of thirteen they are expected to have mastered the recitation of the Holy Book. Typically, the children leave their homes as early as 7:00 a.m. and go to the house of the Mallam (Quranic teacher) who teaches the children the right pronunciation of the Arabic words and the ability to string them together in the recitation of the Quran. Schooling, however, is very different in the southern part of the country, which is predominantly occupied by Christians. The children typically wake up early in the morning by 6:00 a.m. and in some states such as Lagos with a high volume of traffic, children may wake up as early as 5:00 a.m. or 4:00 a.m. depending on the distance of the school from the home. After bathing and breakfast, the children are dropped off at school by their parents, and in households without cars the children either walk to school or go to school by public transport. Most schools in Nigeria start by 7:30 a.m. with a morning devotion where all the students congregate and sing hymns and say a word of prayer. It is also at the devotion ground that important announcements are made by the head teacher or principal. Classes commence by 8:00 a.m. and school closes by 2:00 p.m. However, because most parents are workers or traders, most children stay behind after school for school lessons where they are assisted with their homework by the lesson teachers who are usually the school teachers. The lesson ends by 5:00 p.m. and the students are ready to go back home for the day. Once they arrive, they are required to have their bath and have their supper. After supper they may be allowed to play with their friends in the compound or street or may be asked to run some errands or do some house chores. For students whose mothers are traders they may not go home directly after school but go to where the mother sells her wares where they assist with the commercial activities that go on at the shop. Some may stay with their mothers until they close for the day, which is usually late in the night sometimes by 10:00 p.m. They help their mother with cleaning the shop and assist in carrying any item that will be needed at home. At this time the day is already spent, and the student is tired and retires immediately for the day. This routine is repeated throughout the week but may be altered over the weekend when students may spend half of the day assisting their parents in the shop or engaging with their studies.

A DAY IN THE LIFE OF A BUSINESSMAN

Nigerians engage in diverse business ventures ranging from buying and selling of various products, the production of textiles and food items to the provision of services in the oil and gas sector, the banking industry, or in estate development, or as contractors to the government. Whatever the Nigerian businessperson is involved in, they ensure that they put in their best to see the business succeed. English language is typically the primary language of business although it is not uncommon for businesses to be conducted in Hausa in the northern part of the country. A typical day of a businessperson starts early by 5:00 a.m. As a deeply religious country, the day starts with a devotion in the family to pray for the success of all business ventures of the day. After breakfast by 6:00 a.m., the business owner goes to the office to open shop for the day. In most cases, another round of devotion may be held in the office, and after the prayers the schedule of the day is discussed, and every staff member is expected to meet the day's target. Various meetings may be held in the office with different clients, or the business owner may go out for several hours to discuss business deals with potential partners or attend government functions or other similar events in the state to build a network where business partnership may be established. This aspect of conducting business in Nigeria is very important for the success of most businesses in the country. Once a friendship is struck it is not uncommon to invite the potential client to lunch where discussions on possible business deals can be further explored. As a rule, most Nigerian businesspersons dress smartly, mostly in corporate-tailored suits and a good pair of shoes. While Nigerians may be flashy in their dressing, the business environment is usually not too ostentatious. In the northern part of the country, Hausa businessmen typically dress in traditional attire, usually the *babariga* dress or the smartly cut caftan dress. At lunch, a business deal may be finalized or may require further meeting and discussion. The typical businessperson may have two or three of such meetings per day, and only goes back to the office after meeting all the engagements of the day. In the office, they take briefs from the most senior employee who gives a rundown of the activities of the day while the business owner was away. After taking stock of all transactions and if satisfied with the day's activities, a word of prayer may be said by anyone in the office as a closing session for the day. The owner may stay behind to make some calls to follow up on a business deal before he finally closes for the day. In areas where traffic is heavy, the businessman may get home by 7:00 p.m. or much later. At home, he takes his dinner, watches the news on television, and retires for the day at around 11:00 p.m.

APPENDIX B

Glossary of Key Terms

Abasi The Efik, Ibibio, and Anaang name for the Supreme Being or God.
Acha (A local grain type sometimes referred to as "hungry rice"). The botanical name is *Digitaria exilis.*
Agbada A flowing attire commonly worn by men in southern Nigeria.
Ahmadiyya movement An Islamic sect of the Sunni tradition popular for its missionary activities. The southern Nigeria Muslims belong to this Islamic branch.
Ajami The Arabic alphabet first used to write the Hausa language in the seventeenth century.
Akpu (fufu) A staple mostly among the Igbo of southeastern Nigeria made from fermented cassava to form a dough. It is eaten with a variety of soups.
Aladura movement A Christian religious sect mostly in southwestern Nigeria. The group is known for its fervent prayer and holiness. The Yoruba word "aladura" means those who pray fervently or prayer warriors.
Alkali The royal interpreter of Sha'ria law in the traditional Hausa-Fulani political system.
Almajiri schools An Islamic informal education system that encourages both young boys and girls to learn the Quran from a learned teacher of the Holy Book. The word "Almajiri" also refers to street urchins—these are children who roam the streets to beg for alms on behalf of their Islamic teacher.
Amala A staple food among the Yoruba made from yam or cassava flour.
Ani The Igbo goddess of the Earth.
Aso-ebi Matching attires won during special functions such as weddings or funerals, by a group of people to demonstrate consanguineal ties, unity, or social association.
Babalawo A male Yoruba priest of Ifa. The female counterpart is called Iyanifa.
Babariga A flowing gown typically worn by men in northern Nigeria.
Ba'shiga A practice among Muslims in the northern part of Nigeria where married women are forbidden from engaging in economic activities outside the homestead and men who are non-relatives are forbidden from entering the compound.
Boko The official Hausa orthography based on the Latin alphabet.
Boko Haram An Islamic movement in northern Nigeria that is waging a holy war (Jihad) against the Nigerian federal government to create a true/pure Islamic country. "Boko Haram" is a Hausa phrase which means Western education (culture) is forbidden.
Bole Roasted plantain that is eaten alone or with groundnut (especially in the Southwest) or with peppered fish in the Niger Delta. It is a popular Nigerian street food.

Buka An eating joint by the roadside where indigenous staple foods are usually served.

Chukwu The Igbo name for the Supreme Being who inhabits the sky.

Desertification The process whereby fertile land is turned into barren land due to natural occurrences such as drought or by human action such as overgrazing or deforestation.

Double descent The tracing of one's descent through the paternal and maternal lineage with full rights, privileges, and obligations. This system is practiced in southern Nigeria such as the Yakurr people of Cross River state.

Eba A staple Nigerian food made with garri and boiled water to form a thick paste or dough. It is eaten by swallowing with soup. It is common among the Igbo of southeastern Nigeria and peoples of the Niger Delta.

Eledumare The Yoruba name for God Almighty who is the creator of the universe and everything in it.

Elubo Yam or cassava flour. It is commonly used to prepare *amala* among the Yoruba of southwestern Nigeria.

Emir The head of the Hausa-Fulani political hierarchy in Nigeria.

Eyo festival A ritual performance of masquerades (Eyo) to celebrate and commemorate the death of an Oba (king) and the installation of a new Oba. Also known as Adamu Orisha, the festival is indigenous to the people of Lagos state.

Fulfude The indigenous language of the Fulani ethnic group of northern Nigeria.

Fura da nono A common Hausa beverage in northern Nigeria made from millet (*fura*) and fermented milk (nono). They are served together and are consumed by drinking it with a spoon or directly from a bowl.

Galadima The Head Administrator in the palace of the Emir in the traditional political organization of the Hausa-Fulani ethnic group.

Hakimi The head tax collector in the traditional political organization of the Hausa-Fulani ethnic group.

Harmattan This is the cold dry and dusty wind that blows from northern to southern Nigeria between early December to early February.

Hausa The largest ethnic group in Nigeria.

Holy oil Any type of oil that is believed to have been sanctified by a religious person. It is commonly used by Pentecostal Christians for various purposes including warding off demonic spirits.

Holy water Water that has been blessed and sanctified by a religious person. It is used mostly by Pentecostal or syncretic Christians to wash their feet, face, or other parts of the body to cleanse them from evil.

Ifa The ancient Yoruba religion is characterized by divination.

Igbe movement An indigenous charismatic religious movement among the Urhobo of Delta state characterized by vigorous dancing as its medium of worship.

Igbo The third largest ethnic group in Nigeria.

Imam A Muslim leader who is also learned in the Quran.

In sha'Allah An Arabic word meaning "God's willing." The word is commonly used by Muslims in Nigeria to indicate their commitment to a cause or to acknowledge that humans propose but God disposes.

Maaji The Royal Treasurer in the traditional Hausa-Fulani political system.

Madaki The Commander of the Army in the traditional Hausa-Fulani political system.

Mallam An educated person in Quranic studies or a Quranic teacher.

Maitatsine A Hausa word meaning "one that curses/uses obscenities." It was associated with Muhammed Marwa, the Islamic fundamentalist whose death in 1980 led to the Maitatsine riots and subsequently the Maitatsine movement (Ya Tatsine, those who curse/use obscenities) in Kano, Kaduna, and Katsina states throughout the 1980s.

Minority ethnic group Any ethnic group in Nigeria outside the three largest ethnic groups of Hausa, Yoruba, and Igbo.

Oba Title for a king among the Yoruba and Edo ethnic groups in southern Nigeria.
Ogboni A fraternal society common among the Yoruba people of Nigeria.
Oghene The Urhobo name for God, the creator of the universe.
Ogogoro A locally produced spirit distilled from the sap of raffia palm trees.
Ohanaeze Ndigbo An Igbo sociocultural club that represents the social, political, and cultural interests of all Igbo people both in Nigeria and in the Diaspora.
Olokun movement An indigenous religious group that worships Olokun, the goddess of the marine world. The group is found mostly in the southwest and the Midwest of Nigeria.
Omo Egbe Oduduwa A Yoruba sociocultural society formed in the United Kingdom in 1945 to unite all Yoruba people living in Britain. It was formed in 1945 by Chief Obafemi Awolowo. The meaning of the group is Society of the descendant of Oduduwa. Oduduwa is commonly regarded as the eponymous ancestor of the Yoruba nation.
Osanobua The Edo name for God Almighty.
Palm wine Is a local alcoholic drink that is extracted from the palm tree.
Pentecostalism A Charismatic Christian movement within protestant Christianity that emphasizes the power of the Holy Spirit through its manifestation in the gift of speaking in tongues and performance of miracles.
Quran (Koran) The Holy Book of Muslims.
Rainforest An area with evergreen trees. Nigeria's rainforest is mainly found in the Niger Delta region of the country.
Sango The Yoruba god of thunder and lightning.
Sarkin Fada Head of the palace in the traditional Hausa-Fulani political system.
Sarkin Ruwa Head of water bodies in the traditional Hausa-Fulani political system.
Savannah An area characterized by grass with few trees. In Nigeria, there are three main types of Savannah vegetation namely, the Guinea Savannah, Sudan Savannah, and Sahel Savannah.
Sharia An Islamic canonical law that is derived from the interpretation of the Quran and the teaching of the Prophet. In Nigeria, twelve states, mostly in the North, have adopted Sharia law for both civil and criminal matters.
Syncretism The practice that combines various religious ideas and practices. In Nigeria it mostly refers to the combination of the doctrines and practices of Christianity or Islam and indigenous religions.
Tijaniyyah Brotherhood An Islamic group of the Sufi Order. A sizable number of Muslims identify with this group in northern and southern Nigeria.
Tuwo A staple food common among the Hausa in northern Nigeria. It is prepared from rice, maize, or millet. It is served and eaten with a variety of soups.
Ubangiji The Hausa name for Almighty God.
Umunna Is an Igbo concept that captures the relationship of people who are believed to have descended from a common male eponymous ancestor.
Wara Traditionally processed milk curds prepared by boiling fresh milk and adding coagulant. It is a common source of protein in Kwara and Kogi states.
Waziri The Prime Minister of the Hausa-Fulani political structure in northern Nigeria.
Yoruba The second largest ethnic group in Nigeria.

APPENDIX C

Facts and Figures

TABLE 1 Geography

Location	*Situated on the West coast of Africa, Nigeria is bounded by Niger to the North, Chad to the Northeast, Cameroon to the Southeast, and Benin to the West. The Gulf of Guinea lies to the South*
Time Zone	6 hours ahead of U.S. Eastern Standard
Land Borders	2,515 miles
Coastline	530 miles
Capital	Abuja
Area	356,669 sq. miles
Climate	Nigeria's climate is tropical in the South and semitropical in the North, with high humidity. The average temperature in the South is 90°F. Up to 150 inches of rain may fall in southern Nigeria during the wet season, while rainfall may be as low as 25 inches a year in the North
Land Use	Agricultural land 76.25 percent, Forest land 23.75 percent (estimate) (2020)
Arable Land	76.6 percent (2017)
Arable Land Per Capita	0.37 hectares per person (2017)

Sources: ABC-CLIO World Geography database; CIA World Factbook. http://www.cia.gov; FAO (FAOSTAT database). http://www.fao.org; World Bank. http://www.worldbank.org.

TABLE 2 Population

Population	225,082,083 (estimate) (2022)
World Population Rank	Sixth (2022)
Population Density	247.1 people per square kilometer (2022)
Population Distribution	53.5 percent urban (2022)
Age Distribution	
0–14 years	41.7 percent (estimate, 2020)
15–24 years	20.27 percent (estimate, 2020)
25–54 years	30.6 percent (estimate, 2020)
55–64 years	4.13 percent (estimate, 2020)
65 years and over	3.3 percent (estimate, 2020)
Median Age	18.6 years (2020)
Population Growth Rate	2.5 percent per year (2022)
Net Migration Rate	−0.2 (2022)
Official Language	English

Sources: ABC-CLIO World Geography database; CIA World Factbook. http://www.cia.gov; U.S. Census Bureau (International Data Base). http://www.census.gov.

TABLE 3 Health

Average Life Expectancy	54.2 years (2018)
Average Life Expectancy, Male	53.1 years (2018)
Average Life Expectancy, Female	55.4 years (2018)
Crude Birth Rate	36.5 per 1,000 people (2018)
Crude Death Rate	12.2 per 1,000 people (2018)
Maternal Mortality	917 per 100,000 live births (2017)
Infant Mortality	72 per 1,000 live births (2020)
Doctors	3.8 per 10,000 people (2018)

Sources: ABC-CLIO World Geography Database; U.S. Census Bureau (International Data Base). http://www.census.gov; World Bank. http://www.worldbank.org; World Health Organization. http://www.who.int.

TABLE 4 Environment

Carbon Dioxide Emissions	0.6 metric tons per capita (2019)
Alternative and Nuclear Energy	3.2 percent of total energy use (2019)
Threatened Species	403 (2021)
Total Renewable Water Resources Per Year	1,461 cubic meters, per person, per year (2018)

Sources: ABC-CLIO World Geography database; UN Statistical Database. http://unstats.un.org/unsd/databases.htm; United Nations Statistical Yearbook http://unstats.un.org/unsd/syb/; World Bank. http://www.worldbank.org.

TABLE 5 Energy and Natural Resources

Electric Power Generation	29,830,000,000 kilowatt hours per year (estimate) (2017)
Electric Power Consumption	25,700,460,000 kilowatt hours per year (estimate) (2018)
Nuclear Power Plants	0 (2018)
Crude Oil Production	1,650,392,981 barrels per day (2021)
Crude Oil Consumption	483,074,712 barrels per day (2019)
Natural Gas Production	46,296,922,220 cubic meters per year (estimate) (2019)
Natural Gas Consumption	18,787,630,770 cubic meters per year (estimate) (2019)
Natural Resources	Natural gas, petroleum, tin, iron ore, coal, limestone, niobium, lead, zinc, arable land

Sources: ABC-CLIO World Geography database; CIA World Factbook. http://www.cia.gov; U.S. Energy Information Administration. http://www.cia.gov.

TABLE 6 National Finances

Currency	*Naira*
Total Government Revenue	$13,970,000,000 (estimate) (2017)
Total Government Expenditure	$22,150,000,000 (estimate) (2017)
Budget Deficit	−2.1% of GDP (2017)
GDP Contribution by Sector	Agriculture: 21.6 percent; Industry: 18.3 percent; Services: 60.1 percent (2017)
External Debt	$26,847,000,000 (estimate) (2019)
Economic Aid Extended	$0 (2021)
Economic Aid Received	$1,654,790,000 (2020)

Sources: ABC-CLIO World Geography database; CIA World Factbook. http://www.cia.gov; IMF (World Economic Outlook). http://www.imf.org; OECD (Organization for Economic Cooperation and Development). https://www.oecd.org/development/financing-sustainable-development/development-finance-data/idsonline.htm.

APPENDIX C

TABLE 7 Industry and Labor

Gross Domestic Product (GDP)— official exchange rate	$440,776,970,000 (estimate) (2021)
GDP Per Capita	$2,360 (estimate) (2022)
GDP— Purchasing Power Parity (PPP)	$1,154,069,970,000 (estimate) (2021)
GDP (PPP) per Capita	$5,459 (estimate) (2021)
Industry Products	Lumber and plywood, fuel oils, paper and paper products, hides and skins, textiles, cement, food products, sugar, cigarettes
Agriculture Products	Yams, cassava, corn, sorghum, plantains, millet, rice, taro, peanuts, citrus fruits, rubber, cattle, sheep, goats
Unemployment	9.0 percent (2020)

Sources: ABC-CLIO World Geography database; CIA World Factbook. http://www.cia.gov; ILO (LABORSTA database). http://www.ilo.org; IMF (World Economic Outlook). http://www.imf.org; World Bank. http://worldbank.org.

TABLE 8 Trade

Imported Goods	Consumer goods, foodstuffs, chemicals, machinery and transportation equipment, iron, steel, capital equipment, raw materials
Total Value of Imports	$35,240,000,000 (estimate) (2017)
Exported Goods	Crude petroleum, petroleum products, cocoa beans, coffee, tea, spices, palm products, rubber
Total Value of Exports	$39,940,000,000 (estimate) (2020)
Import Partners	China 30 percent, Netherlands 11 percent, United States 6 percent, Belgium 5 percent (2019)
Export Partners	India 16 percent, Spain 10 percent, United States 7 percent, France 7 percent, Netherlands 6 percent (2019)
Current Account Balance	$10,380,000,000 (estimate) (2017)
Weights and Measures	The metric system is in use

Sources: ABC-CLIO World Geography database; CIA World Factbook. http://www.cia.gov; Europa World Year Book; IMF Direction of Trade Statistics.

TABLE 9 Education

School System	Nigerian students attend primary school for six years, beginning at the age of six. Students then spend either six years in technical school or six years in an academic program, divided into two cycles of three years each.
Mandatory Education	Nine years, from ages six to fifteen
Primary School-age Children Enrolled in Primary School	27,889,387 (2018)
Males	14,393,652 (2018)
Females	13,495,735 (2018)
Secondary School-age Children Enrolled in Secondary School	11,374,084 (2018)
Males	5,932,635 (2018)
Females	5,441,449 (2018)
Literacy	62 percent (2018)

Sources: ABC-CLIO World Geography database; Country government; UNESCO. http://www.unesco.org; World Bank. http://www.worldbank.org.

TABLE 10 Military

Defense Spending (Percent of GDP)	1 percent (2019)
Total Active Armed Forces	223,000 (2019)
Annual Military Expenditures	$1,723,000,000 (2019)
Military Service	Service in the Nigerian military is voluntary

Sources: ABC-CLIO World Geography database; Military Balance.

TABLE 11 Transportation

Airports	54 (2021)
Registered Vehicles	5,791,446 (2015)
Paved Roads	15.0 percent (2016)
Railroads	3,798 miles (2017)
Ports	Major: Six—Calabar, Lagos, Warri, Onne, Port Harcourt, Sapele

Sources: ABC-CLIO World Geography database; CIA World Factbook. http://www.cia.gov; World Bank. http://www.worldbank.org.

TABLE 12 Communications

Facebook Users	31,860,000 (estimate) (2020)
Internet Users	74,210,251 (2020)
Internet Users (Percent of Population)	35.5 percent (2020)
Land-Based Telephones in Use	107,031 (2020)
Mobile Telephone Subscribers	204,228,678 (2020)

Sources: ABC-CLIO World Geography database; CIA World Factbook. http://www.cia.gov; Facebook. http://www.facebook.com.

APPENDIX D

Holidays

Name	Date/Month	Type	Details
New Year's Day	1 January	A national public holiday	If January 1 falls on a weekend, the preceding workday is declared a public holiday. Nigerians celebrate this day by visiting family members in the villages and partaking in various social and cultural activities in the community. Those in the cities go on family picnics, go to the beach, cinema houses, and other places of interest. The day is generally marked as the beginning of a new year as Nigeria uses the Gregorian calendar.
Good Friday /Easter Friday	March or April	A national public holiday	The Friday before Easter, in which Christians observe the crucifixion of Jesus Christ. This day is normally celebrated by Christians who occupy mostly the southwest, southeast, middle belt, and the Niger Delta. Celebration is usually in the church and among family members.
Easter Monday	March or April	A national public holiday	The Monday after Easter Sunday, in which Christians celebrate the resurrection of Jesus Christ after his crucifixion on Easter Friday. Christians celebrate this day by attending church services, organizing picnics, and the exchange of gifts. Other denominations organize visits to orphanage homes to celebrate with the less privileged in the society.

Name	Date/Month	Type	Details
Labor/Workers' Day	1 May	A national public holiday	In celebration of workers in the country. Workers celebrate this day by having time out with their families. Rallies and workshops are also organized by workers' unions.
Eid al-Fitr	May	A national public holiday	A two-day public holiday to mark the end of Muslim fast of Ramadan. The actual dates are determined by the siting of the new moon. This festival is celebrated by Muslims mostly in the North and southwestern parts of the country. Rams are usually slaughtered and shared with family members and friends.
Children's Day	27 May	A national public holiday for school children	Public holiday only for primary and secondary schools. Various activities are organized by schools and several organizations to celebrate children in the country.
Democracy Day	29 May	A national public holiday	This day is set aside to commemorate Nigeria's return to democracy in 1999 when General Abdulsalami Abubakar handed over power to General Olusegun Obasanjo (retired) as the fifth democratically elected president after sixteen years of military dictatorship. Since 1999, the day has become symbolic of Nigeria's transition and every four years after the presidential election, the winner is sworn in on that day.
Democracy Day	12 June	A state public holiday	Only a few states such as Ogun and Lagos celebrate this day to commemorate the June 12 election that was adjudged to be the most peaceful, fair, and credible election conducted in the country. The election was believed to have been won by Chief M. K. O. Abiola, a southwestern businessman, but was annulled by General Ibrahim Babangida, the Head of State. In celebration of the day, various pro-democracy groups organize symposia, conferences, and workshops to reflect on and discuss democracy and governance in the country.

(*Continued*)

Name	Date/Month	Type	Details
Eid al-Kabir	July	A national public holiday	A two-day public holiday to mark the major Muslim festival of sacrifice. The actual dates are determined by the siting of the new moon. As a major festival among Muslims who occupy most parts of the North and Southwest, celebrations take the form of the slaughtering of sheep, which is distributed to family members, and the less privileged in the society. Celebrants put on their best clothes and visit friends, amusement parks, and other places of interest after observing the morning prayers in mosques.
Independence Day	1 October	A national public holiday	This day commemorates the political independence of the country from Great Britain in 1960. Various activities are organized at the local, state, and federal level. At the federal level parades are organized at Eagle Square in Abuja with high dignitaries in attendance including the president. At the individual level, Nigerians organize football competitions, visit parks, zoos, beaches, and other places of interest.
Eid al-Maulud	October	A national public holiday	A two-day public holiday in Nigeria to mark the birth of the Prophet Muhammed (peace be upon him). The actual dates are determined by the siting of the new moon. This is another Muslim holiday celebrated mostly in the North and southwestern parts of the country.
Christmas Day	25 December	A national public holiday	This is a Christian festival to mark the birth of Jesus Christ. The celebration is mostly in the Southwest, Southeast, middle belt, and the Niger Delta where the majority of Christians live. Celebrations usually start with a church service. After church, celebrants visit and host visitors to sumptuous meals and visits to the zoo, parks, cinema, and other places of interest. Children are dressed in their best clothes and are given their gifts by their parents and other well-wishers. Christians generally interpret this day as the symbolic day that Jesus Christ was born into this world to redeem humans from sin and from the wrath of God.

Name	Date/Month	Type	Details
Boxing Day	26 December	A national public holiday	This is a continuation of the Christmas celebration. Although the original activity of this day is to exchange and open gifts that have been given to celebrants, in Nigeria this day is not reserved for that purpose, rather it is regarded as a day for more prayers in the church and celebration of the birth of Jesus Christ. In the average Nigerian Christian home, no special day is reserved for gifts, instead gifts may be exchanged several days before Christmas Day or on that day.

BIBLIOGRAPHY

A24 Media. (2023). https://www.pinterest.com/pin/323625923192779443/
A Brief Overview of the Nigerian Manufacturing Industry. (2019). https://thechrisogunbanjofoundation.org/a-brief-overview-of-the-nigerian-manufacturing-industry/
Abaga, Hamzat Ibrahim. (2021). "A Look at Nigeria's Traditional Sports and its Quagmire." *Transcontinental Times*. https://www.transcontinentaltimes.com/a-look-at-nigerias-wretched-traditional-sports-and-its-quagmire/
Abbass, Isiah. (2010). "The State and Rural Zaria from Affluence to Poverty: Historical Bank." *International Journal of Economic Development Research and Investment*, 1(2&3): 83–100.
Abubakar, Tahir Abubakar and Abdul Hakim Abdullah. (2017). "The Present State of Muslim-Education in Northern Nigeria: Progression or Regression." *The International Journal of Academic Research in Business and Social Sciences*, 7(5): 437–44. doi: 106007/IJARBSS/V7-15/2981
Adamu, Abdalla Uba. (2019). "Hausa Popular Music (Northern Nigeria)." In Heidi Carolyn Fieldman, David Horn, John Shepherd, and Gabrielle Kielich (eds.), *Bloomsbury Encyclopedia of Popular Music of the World: Genres: Sub-Saharan Africa, Volume XII*, 168–78. New York: Bloomsbury Academy.
Adamu, Yusufu. (2008). "Interview with Hafsatu Ahmed Abdulwahid." *African Writer Magazine*. Interview with Hafsatu Ahmed Abdulwahid - AfricanWriter.com
Adedamola, Quasim. (2022, November 21). "Some of Davido's Greatest Achievements as he Clocks 30." *Daily Trust*. https://dailytrust.com/some-of-davidos-greatest-achievements-as-he-clocks-30/
Adedeji, Femi. (2005). "Classification of Nigerian Gospel Music Styles." *África: Revista do Centro de Estudos Africanos*, 24–25(26): 225–46.
Adedeji, Wale. (2016). "The Nigerian Music Industry: Challenges, Prospects and Possibilities." *International Journal of Recent Research in Social Sciences and Humanities (IJRSSH)*, 3(1): 261–71.
Adegboyega, A. (2020, August 12). "Nigerian Trade Office Targets 50% Share in GDP by 2023." https://www.premiumtimesng.com/news/top-news/408411-nigerian-trade-office-targets-50-share-in-gdp-by-2023.html
Adeleke, Ademola. (2005). "Islam and Hausa Culture." *Lagos Historical Review*, 5: 99–110.
Adeoye, Julius. (2013). "Nigerian Theatre: From 'Masquerade Drama' to Nigerian Video Film (Chapter 1)." In *The Drama of Ahmed Yerima: Studies in Nigerian Theatre*. Universiteit Leiden: Leiden University Repository. http://hdl.handle.net/1887/20858
Adeyemi, Kamil Adeleke. (2016). "The Trend of Arabic and Islamic Education in Nigeria: Progress and Prospects." *Open Journal of Modern Linguistics*, 6: 197–201. http://dx.doi.org/10.4236/ojml.2016.63020

Aduku, Armstrong Idachaba. (2018). "Elements of Traditional African Drama in Contemporary Nigerian Video-Film." *The Performer: Ilorin Journal of the Performing Arts.* http://eprints.gouni.edu.ng/131/

Agunbiade, Ojo. (2012). "Dating Practices and Patterns of Disclosure among In-School Adolescents in Oyo State, Nigeria." *Africa Development*, 37 (3): 19–39.

Agunbiade, Ojo, Mary Obiyan, and Gbenga Sogbaike. (2013). "Identity Construction and Gender Involvement in Online Social Networks among Undergraduates in Two Universities in Southwest Nigeria." *Inkanyiso Journal of Humanities and Social Science*, 5(1): 41–52.

Aibueku, Samuel Ovenseri and Solomon Ogbouma. (2014). "Historical Analysis of Nigeria's Sports Development Policy." *Asia Pacific Journal of Education, Arts and Sciences*, 1(1): 70–2.

Ajayi, Ademola. (2010). "The Development of Free Primary Education Scheme in Western Nigeria, 1952–1966: An Analysis." *OGIRISI a New Journal of Africana Studies*, 5(1). doi: 10.4314/og.v5i1.52320

Akande, Segun. (2017). "Before PlayStation and X-Box, we had Suwe, Ten-Ten and Table Soccer." *Pulse.ng*. https://www.pulse.ng/gist/traditional-games-before-playstation-and-x-box-we-had-suwe-ten-ten-and-table-soccer/xs5cq02

Akanle, Olayinka and Olanrewau Olutayo. (2011). "Kinship Construction Variability among Nigerian International Migrants: The Context of Contemporary Diaspora." *Human Affairs*, 21: 470–80. doi: 10.2478/s13374-011-0044-2

Akinsipe, Felix. (1999). "Modern Dance and the Nigerian." *Ilorin Journal of the Performing Arts*, 1(2): 85–94.

Akintola, A. (1992). *The Reformed Ogboni Fraternity: Its Origin and Interpretation of its Doctrines and Symbolism*. Ogbomosho: Ogunniyi Printing Works.

Akinwale, Emmanuel Abiodun. (2014). "A Historical and Comparative Analysis of Colonial and Post-colonial Bureaucracy in Nigeria." *Journal of Public Administration and Governance*, 4(2): 1–11. doi: 10.5296/ jpag.v4i2.5602

Akoh, Ben and Abiodun Jagun. (2012). *Mapping Digital Media: Nigeria Country Report*. Open Society Foundations. doi: 10.13140/RG.2.2.36248.93443

Akpede, Kaior Samuel. *Introduction to Radio and Television (MAC 142)*. Abuja: National Open University of Nigeria

Alapo, Remi. (2014). "Gender and Ethnicity in Nigeria: Post-Colonial Societal Constructs on Culture and Class." Presented at the New York African Studies Association (NYASA) Conference, SUNY Cortland, New York, April 3–5, 2014. Published by CUNY (City University of New York) Academic Works.

All Africa. (2019, March 21). "Nigeria Eclipses Egypt as Africa's Largest Rice Producer." https://allafrica.com/stories/201903210453.html

Alokan, A. (1991). *The Christ Apostolic Church: C.A.C. 1928–1988*. Lagos: Ibukunola Printers Nigeria Limited.

Aloy, Ejiogu and Sheidu Sule. (2012). "Sixty-Five Years of University Education in Nigeria: Some Key Cross Cutting Issues." In *International Perspectives on Education: Volume 10*, edited by Nikolay Popov, Charl Wolhuter, Bruno Leutwyler, Gillian Hilton, James Ogunleye, and Patrcia A. Almeida, 257–64. Sofia, Bulgaria: Bulgarian Comparative Education Society.

Aluko, Kehinde and S. Adodo. (2011). "A Conceptual Analysis of School Sports Development in Nigeria." *African Research Review*, 5(5): 394–403. doi: http://dx.doi.org/10.4314/afrrev.v5i5.31

Amakievi, Gabriel and Sarah Blackduke. (2019). "John Pepper Clark's Song of a Goat: Hindsight for foresight in Izon Culture of the Western Niger Delta of Nigeria." *Scholarly Journal of Scientific Research and Essay (SJSRE)*, 8(1): 1–6.

Amoah, F. E. K. (1992). "Oral Tradition and Ethnicity in the Creation of New States in Nigeria: The Case of Akwa Ibom." *Research Review (NS)*, 8(1&2): 76–89.

Aniche, Alexander. (2017). "Dwindling Impacts of Kinship/Extended Family System among the Ndi Igbo of South Eastern Nigeria." *Online Journal of Arts, Management and Social Sciences (OJAMSS)*, 2(1): 247–52.

Anulika, Agina. (2019). "Cinema-Going in Lagos: Three Locations, One Film, One Weekend." *Journal of African Cultural Studies*. https://doi.org/10.1080/13696815.2019.1615871

Ariye, E. C. (2013). "The Ijo (Ijaw) People of Delta State: Their Early History and Aspects of Social and Cultural Practices." *Historical Research Letter*, 8: 25–31.

Ariyo, A. M., D. I. Osunbayo, Eni-Olorunda, and W. O. Afolabi. (2018). "Perception on Dating, Courtship and Marriage among Undergraduates in Federal Tertiary Institutions in Ogun State." *Journal of Humanities, Social Sciences and Creative Arts*, 13: 142–52.

Arugha, Ogisi Aboyowa. (2010). "The Origin and Development of Juju Music: 1900–1990." *EJOTMAS: Ekpoma Journal of Theatre and Media Arts*, 3(1&2): 27–37.

Athletics Federation of Nigeria. 2021. https://www.athleticsnigeria.org/afn/about-afn/

Auwalu, Musa. (2015). "Federalism and National Integration: The Myth of the Agitations for Confederation of Ethnic Nationalities in Nigeria." *Online Journal of African Affairs*, 4(1): 13.

Ayodeji, H. (2020). "Nigeria: Breaking Diaspora Remittance Players' Monopoly." https://allafrica.com/stories/202006110179.html

Babagana, Abubakar. (2017). *Kanuri Complete*. https://www.researchgate.net/publication/320004428_KANURI_COMPLETE

Babatola, Jadesola and Modupe Babatola. (2020). "Structural Analysis and Policy Framework of Nigeria's Tertiary Education (1947–2020)." https://www.researchgate.net/publication/339593611_

Barbour, Kenneth Michael. (1982). *Nigeria in Maps*. Anambra: Africana Publishing Company.

Barksdale-Hall, Roland. (2007) "Chinua Achebe: A Bio-bibliographic Review." *The Journal of Pan African Studies*, 1(8): 9–11.

BBC News. (2019). "Nigeria Profile – Timeline." https://www.bbc.com/news/world-africa-13951696

Bergstrom, Kari. (2002). "Legacies of Colonialism and Islam for Hausa Women: An Historical Analysis, 1804–1960." *Working Paper #276, Women & International Development*. Michigan State University.

Bible-David, R. (2009). *Enoch Adeboye Father of Nations*. London: Biblos Publisher.

Biobaku, Saburi. (1958). "The Pattern of Yoruba History." *Africa South*, 12(2): 63–7.

Birmingham. (2022). "Commonwealth Games (detailed records)." https://results.birmingham2022.com/#/athletic-sports-records/broken/ATH/*

Blackpast. (2022). "Sir Abubakar Tafawa Balewa (1912–1966)." https://www.blackpast.org/global-african-history/balewa-sir-abubakar-tafawa-1912-1966/

Blogger. (2013). "Ijaw People: Nigeria's Aboriginal Water People of Niger Delta." https://kwekudee-tripdownmemorylane.blogspot.com/2013/02/ijaw-people-nigerias-aboriginal-water.html

Botchway, De-Valera. (2014). "Fela 'The Black President' as Grist to the Mill of the Power Movement in Africa." *Black Diaspora Review*, 4(1): 1–35.

Britannica, T. Editors of Encyclopaedia. (2018, May 2). "Nigerian Theatre." *Encyclopedia Britannica*. https://www.britannica.com/art/Nigerian-theatre

Britannica, T. Editors of Encyclopaedia. (2021, September 19). "Oyo Empire." *Encyclopedia Britannica*. https://www.britannica.com/place/Oyo-empire

Britannica, The Editors of Encyclopaedia. (2022, January 01). "Sir Abubakar Tafawa Balewa." *Encyclopedia Britannica*. https://www.britannica.com/biography/Abubakar-Tafawa-Balewa (accessed December 14, 2022).

Britannica, T. Editors of Encyclopaedia. (2022, March 1). "Olusegun Obasanjo." *Encyclopedia Britannica*. https://www.britannica.com/biography/Olusegun-Obasanjo

Britannica, T. Editors of Encyclopaedia. (2022, March 16). "Nobel Prize." *Encyclopedia Britannica*. https://www.britannica.com/topic/Nobel-Prize

Britannica, T. Editors of Encyclopaedia. (2022, March 31). "Hubert Ogunde." *Encyclopedia Britannica*. https://www.britannica.com/biography/Hubert-Ogunde

Britannica, T. Editors of Encyclopaedia. (2022, April 2). "John Pepper Clark." *Encyclopedia Britannica*. https://www.britannica.com/biography/John-Pepper-Clark

Britannica, T. Editors of Encyclopaedia. (2022, May 5). "Obafemi Awolowo." *Encyclopedia Britannica*. https://www.britannica.com/biography/Obafemi-Awolowo

Britannica, T. Editors of Encyclopaedia. (2022, June 4). "Amos Tutuola." *Encyclopedia Britannica*. https://www.britannica.com/biography/Amos-Tutuola

Britannica, T. Editors of Encyclopaedia. (2022, September 16). "Sani Abacha." *Encyclopedia Britannica*. https://www.britannica.com/biography/Sani-Abacha

Britannica, T. Editors of Encyclopaedia. (2022, November 6). "Ken Saro-Wiwa." *Encyclopedia Britannica*. https://www.britannica.com/biography/Ken-Saro-Wiwa

Britannica, T. Editors of Encyclopaedia. (2022, November 12). "Nnamdi Azikiwe." *Encyclopedia Britannica*. https://www.britannica.com/biography/Nnamdi-Azikiwe

Buchanan, K. M. and J. C. Pugh. (1966). *Land and People in Nigeria*. London: University of London Press.

Canada: Immigration and Refugee Board of Canada. (2007). *Nigeria: Domestic Violence; Recourse and Protection Available to Victims of Domestic Violence (2005–2007)*, August 10, NGA102510.E. https://www.refworld.org/docid/46fa536f17.html (accessed July 20, 2022).

CBN. (n.d.a). *Central Bank of Nigeria | Foreign Exchange Market*. Central Bank of Nigeria. https://www.cbn.gov.ng/IntOps/FXMarket.asp (accessed August 19, 2020).

CBN. (n.d.b). *Central Bank of Nigeria: Reserve Management*. Central Bank of Nigeria. https://www.cbn.gov.ng/IntOps/ReserveMgmt.asp (accessed August 19, 2020).

CBN. (2020, August 18). *Central Bank of Nigeria | Exchange Rate*. Central Bank of Nigeria. https://www.cbn.gov.ng/rates/ExchRateByCurrency.asp

Central Bank of Nigeria (CBN), Real Gross Domestic Product. (2020). https://www.cbn.gov.ng/rates/RealGDP.asp?year=2019

Central Bank of Nigeria | Exchange Rate. (n.d.). https://www.cbn.gov.ng/rates/ExchRateByCurrency.asp (accessed August 19, 2020).

Channels Live TV. (2022, October 20). "Things You Need to Know about Nigerian Football." https://www.channelstv.com/2022/10/20/things-you-need-to-know-about-nigerian-football/

Ciboh, Rodney. (2004). "Private Broadcasting and the Challenges of Democratization of Electronic Media in Nigeria." *International Journal of Communication*, 1: 1–14.

Claveau, Hugo. (2017). "Afro-Beats: From Nigeria to the World." *Trace Studio*. https://trace.company/wp-content/uploads/2017/08/PRESS-RELEASE-AFROBEATS-FROM-NIGERIA-TO-THE-WORLD-US.pdf

CNBC Africa. (2020, July 16). "Nigeria Hopes Gold Mining Reforms can bring in $500 mln a year." https://www.cnbcafrica.com/mining/2020/07/16/nigeria-hopes-gold-mining-reforms-can-bring-in-500-mln-a-year/

CNN. (2020, July 9). "World's Rarest Gorillas Spotted with Babies in Nigeria's Forest." https://edition.cnn.com/2020/07/09/africa/rare-gorillas-nigeria-scn/index.html

Collins, John. (2011). "Victor Uwaifo: Highlife Pioneer, Legend." https://www.academia.edu/32340860/JCollins_VICTOR_UWAIFO_HIGHLIFE_PIONEER_LEGEND_Unpublished_photo_captions_are_included_but_no_photos_provided

Collins, Walter. (2007). "Interview with Sefi Atta." *English in Africa*, 34(2): 123–31.

Commonwealth Games. (n.d.). "History of the Games 1930 to 2010." http://www.cgaj.org/wp-content/uploads/2016/09/History-of-the-Games-1930-to-2010.pdf

Cyffer, Norbert. (n.d.). "Kanuri and its Neighbours: When Saharan and Chadic Languages Meet." A Research on Linguistic Contact and Conceptualization in the Wider Lake Chad Area in the Project *Linguistic Innovation and Conceptual Change in West Africa*, funded by the Australian Science Fund (FWF), Project number P 15764.

Daily Trust. (2022, September 24). "Successes of US-Nigeria Music Collaborations." *Daily Trust*. https://dailytrust.com/successes-of-us-nigeria-music-collaborations/

Dandaura, Emmanuel. (2016). "African Dance in Transition: Interview with Arnold Udoka." *Critical Stages/Scènes Critiques*. Issue No. 13. https://www.critical-stages.org/13/interview-with-arnold-udoka/

Daniel, Eniola. (2022, December 01). "Burnaboy Tops Spotify's 2022 most Streamed Artiste Chat in Nigeria." *Guardian Life*. https://guardian.ng/life/whatsnew-entertainment-celebrity-gist-and-so-on/burnaboy-tops-spotifys-2022-most-streamed-artiste-chat-in-nigeria/

Dare, Kuti. (2018). "Para Powerlifting: Oluwafemiayo Breaks World Record in Dubai." *ACLSPorts: Your Sports Memo*, https://www.aclsports.com/9829-2/

Djibril, Badji. (2008). "Traditional Wrestling in the ECOWAS Area. Traditional Sport and Games: Perspectives on Cultural Heritage." *TAFISA Magazine*, 17–18. http://www.tafisa.org/sites/default/files/pdf/TAFISAMagazine_1-2008.pdf

Doron, Roy and Toyin Falola. (2016). *Ohio Short Histories of Africa - Ken Saro-Wiwa*. Athens: Ohio University Press.

Doron, Roy, Toyin Falola, and Laura Seay. (2016). "The Complex Life and Death of Ken Saro-Wiwa." *The Washington Post – Democracy Dies in Darkness*. The complex life and death of Ken Saro-Wiwa - The Washington Post.

Duke, Joe. (2010). "The Impact of Colonialism on the Development of Management in Nigeria." *International Journal of Business Management*, 5(8): 65–75.

Eboka Tolulope Favour. (2017). "PhD Thesis: Understanding the Practice of Girl Marriage in Northern Nigeria from the Perspective of Key Decision Makers." https://www.academia.edu/43235783/PhD_Thesis_Understanding_the_practice_of_girl_marriage_in_Northern_Nigeria_from_the_perspectives_of_key_decision_makers

ECOWAS. (2016). *Basic Information | Economic Community of West African States (ECOWAS)*. ECOWAS International. https://www.ecowas.int/about-ecowas/basic-information/

Edeme, Victoria. (2022, December 30). "Rema Tops 2022 'Most Viewed Music Video' List." *Punch Newspaper*. https://punchng.com/rema-tops-2022-most-viewed-music-videos-list/#:~:text=Afrobeats%20star%2C%20Rema%2C%20has%20earned,Dataleum%2C%20and%20released%20on%20Friday

Edo, Samson and Augustine Ikelegbe. (2014). "The Nigerian Economy: Reforms, Emerging Trends and Prospects." *Centre for Population and Environmental Development (CPED) Monograph Series* No. 8.

Edikan, Ukpong. (2018). "History of Magazine in Nigeria." *Dennie Journal of Interdisciplinary Discourse*. https://denniejournal.wordpress.com/2018/07/20/history-of-magazine-in-nigeria/

Egwabor, C. (2018). "Human and Trade Union Rights in Nigeria; Experiences, Challenges, Achievements and Campaigns in the Oil and Gas Sector." http://www.industriallunion.org/sites/default/files/uploads/documents/2018/NIGERIA/human_and_trade_union_rights_in_nigeria1.pdf

Ehizibolo, David, Joshua Kamani, Peter Ehizibolo, Okoh Egwu, Goni Dogo, and Josiah Salami-Shinaba. (2012). "Prevalence and Significance of Parasites of Horses in Some States of Northern Nigeria." *Journal of Equine Science*, 23(1): 1–4.

Ekeh, Peter. (2000). "Contesting the History of Benin Kingdom." *Research in African Literature*, 31(3): 147–70. doi: 10.1353/ral.2000.0081

Ekpu, Grace. (2019, January). "The Horsemen Making a Living on Lagos Beach Nigeria." *BBC News Africa*. https://www.bbc.com/news/world-africa-46890783

Eludini, Tunde. (2022, August). "Commonwealth Games: Nigeria Sixth after 14 Medals on Penultimate Day." *Premium Times*. https://www.premiumtimesng.com/news/headlines/547324-commonwealth-games-nigeria-sixth-after-14-medals-on-penultimate-day.html

Eludini, Tunde. (2022, August). "Commonwealth Games 2022: Team Nigeria Wins another Medal in Weightlifting." *Premium Times*. https://www.premiumtimesng.com/sports/nigeria-sports-news/546503-commonwealth-games-2022-team-nigeria-wins-another-medal-in-weightlifting.html

Encyclopedia.com. (2023). "Clark, John Pepper (Contemporary Poets)." *Encyclopedia.com*. https://www.encyclopedia.com/arts/culture-magazines/clark-john-pepper (accessed December 21, 2022).

Encyclopedia.com. (2019). *Ibibio*. https://www.encyclopedia.com/humanities/encyclopedias-almanacs-transcripts-and-maps/ibibio

Ernest-Samuel, Gloria and Divine Uchenna. (2019). "A Historical Study of the Nigerian Film Industry and Its Challenges." *Ndunode*, 16(1): 170–83.
Eyo, E. (1977). *Two Thousand Years, Nigerian Art*. Nigeria: Federal Department of Antiquities.
Ezeibe, Christian. (2009). "Relevance and Limitations of Yar'adua's 7 Point Agenda." *African Renaissance*, 6(3&4): 33–41. https://www.researchgate.net/publication/281625097_Relevance_and_Limitations_of_President_Yar'adua's_7_Point_Agenda
Eziwho, Azunwo Emenike. (2017). "Ritual Content in Ikwerre Wrestling Festival: An Example of Elimgbu Egelege." *Journal of Humanities and Cultural Studies (JHUCS)*, 2. file:///C:/Users/Admin/Downloads/Ritual_Contents_in_Ikwerre_Wrestling_Festival_An_E.pdf
Falola, T. (2000). *Violence in Nigeria: The Crisis of Religious Politics and Secular Ideologies*. Rochester, NY: University of Rochester Press.
Falola, Toyin. (2012). *Power Politics or Welfare Politics? Chief Obafemi Awolowo in the History of African Nationalist Political Thought*. Austin: University of Texas.
Falola, Toyin and Ann Genova. (2009). "Historical Dictionary of Nigeria." *Historical Dictionaries of Africa, No. 111*. Maryland: The Rowman & Littlefield Publishing Group Inc.
Falola, Toyin and Heaton Mathew. (2008). *A History of Nigeria*. New York: Cambridge University Press.
Falola, T. and S. A. Olanrewaju, eds. (1986). *Transport Systems in Nigeria*. New York: Foreign and Comparative Studies Publications.
Falola, T. and T. Pearce, eds. (1994). *Child Health in Nigeria: The Impact of a Depressed Economy*. England: Avebury Press.
Famuyiwa, D. (2019, January 23). "CBN Raises Alarm over Nigeria's Rising Debts Profile." *Nairametrics*. https://nairametrics.com/2019/01/23/cbn-raises-alarm-over-nigerias-rising-debts-profile/
Favioye. (2020). "WAEC, NECO and NABTEB: What you need to know about Nigerian Senior School Certificate Exams (SSCE)." *Opera News*. https://ng.opera.news/ng/en/education/35850a25c17912cfc8743450d4e28ee7
Federal Ministry of Health. (2020, June). *Nigeria National Family Planning Blueprint (2020–2024)*. Abuja, Nigeria. https://www.health.gov.ng/doc/Final-2020-Blueprint.pdf
Federal Ministry of Health, Nigeria. (2005). *National Family Planning/Reproductive Health Policy Guidelines and Standards of Practice*. Abuja: Nigeria National FP/RH Service Policy and Standards.
Fiona, McCann, dir. (2013). "Ben Okri." *Commonwealth Essays and Studies*, 35(2), [Online], Online since April 17, 2021, connection on July 23, 2021. https://journals.openedition.org/ces/5307. doi: https://doi.org/10.4000/ces.5307
Flint, John. (2008). "'Managing Nationalism': The Colonial Office and Nnamdi Azikwe, 1932-43." *The Journal of Imperial and Commonwealth History*, 27(2): 143–58. doi: 10.1080/03086539908583061
Folakun, Awo. (n.d.). "Gidigbo: Yoruba Martial Arts."
Forchu, Ijeoma. (2009). "Nigerian Popular Music: Its Problems and Prospects in Development." *UJAH: Unizik Journal of Arts and Humanities*, 10(2): 103–14.
Gambari, Afolabi. (2022). "Para Powerlifting: Nigeria Wins 12 Medals at African Championship." *The Cable*. https://www.thecable.ng/para-powerlifting-nigeria-wins-12-medals-at-african-championships#:~:text=Roland%20Ezuruike%2C%20Esther%20Nworgu%2C%20Latifat,won%20the%20three%20silver%20medals
Gbogi, Michael Tosin. (2016). "Language, Identity, and Urban Youth Subculture: Nigerian Hip Hop Music as an Exemplar." *Pragmatics*, 26(2): 171–95. doi: 10.1075/prag.26.2.01tos
Gennaro, Michael. (2012). "Boxing in Colonial and Post-colonial Nigeria, 1920–1970." *Research Report* (Student Sport), 37. Center for African Studies. http://africa.ufl.edu/files/CASRR12-13-Gennaro.pdf
Gennaro, Michael. (2014–2015). "The History of Boxing in Nigeria." *Research Report* (Graduate Sports), 27. Center for African Studies. http://africa.ufl.edu/files/CASResearch2014Gennaro.pdf

Gennaro, Michael. (n.d.). "Empire Boxers are the Goods Race, boxing, and Nigerians in the Black Atlantic." https://www.academia.edu/33023553/_EMPIRE_BOXERS_ARE_THE_GOODS_RACE_BOXING_AND_NIGERIANS_IN_THE_BLACK_ATLANTIC

Global Trade Alert. (2016, February 11). "Nigeria: Launch of the National Industrial Revolution Plan (NIRP)." https://www.globaltradealert.org/intervention/12668/state-loan/nigeria-launch-of-the-national-industrial-revolution-plan-nirp

Golikumo, Mangiri and Steve Kquofi. (2014). "Masking Art Tradition as a Cultural Manifestation of Olugbobiri People of Nigeria." *International Journal of Humanities and Social Science*, 4(11): 270–80.

Gold-Idowu, B. (2021). *Research on the Celestial Church of Christ*. Kindle Edition.

Gomba, Obari. (2013). "Tribute: Things Still Apart: Chinua Achebe's Whetstone." *Tydskrif Vir Letterkunde*, 50(2): 152–7. doi: http://dx.doi.org/10.4314/tvl.v50i2.11

Green, Thomas. (2005). "Dambe: Traditional Nigerian Boxing." *EJMAS*. file: https://www.academia.edu/26508537/Dambe_Traditional_Nigerian_Boxing

Gunston, Jo. (2022, August). "How Nigerian Paddler Quadri Aruna is Reinventing Table Tennis for a Whole Continent." https://olympics.com/en/news/nigerian-table-tennis-quadri-aruna-2022-commonwealth-games

Hafsah, Abubakar Matazu. (2018, October 20). "6 Nigerian Musicians Who have Collaborated with Foreign Stars." *Daily Trust*. https://dailytrust.com/6-nigerian-musicians-who-have-collaborated-with-foreign-stars/

Hogan, Patrick. "Understanding 'The Palm-Wine Drinkard.'" *ARIEL: A Review of International English Literature*, 31(4): 33–58.

Ibhawoh, Bonny. (1989). "Nigeria." In Herb Guntram and Kaplan David (eds.), *Nations and Nationalism: A Global Historical Overview*, volume 3, 1945 to 1989. Santa Barbara/Denver/Oxford: ABC CLIO.

ICC. (2022). "Nigeria Cricket Federation." https://www.icc-cricket.com/about/members/africa/associate/126

Idonije, Benson. (2001). "Old or New: Palm Wine is Truly Enchanting." *Glendora Review: African Quarterly on the Arts*, 13(2): 16–22.

Idowu, E. Bolaji. (1994). *Olodumare: God in Yoruba Belief*. New York: Wazobia.

Idris, Shehu. (2022, August 8). "Full List: Amusan, Brume…Nigeria's 35 medallist at 2022 Commonwealth Games." *The Cable*. https://www.thecable.ng/full-list-amusan-brume-nigerias-35-medalists-at-2022-commonwealth-games

Idris, Shehu. (2022, September). "Aruna Quadri Wins Second ITTF Africa Championship Title." *The Cable*. https://www.thecable.ng/aruna-quadri-wins-second-ittf-africa-championship-title

IEA. (2020). "Atlas of Energy." http://energyatlas.iea.org/#!/tellmap/-1920537974/0

Ifeanyi, Ibeh. (2022, October 12). "Amusan 'Short of Words' after World Athlete of the Year Nomination." *The Guardian*. https://guardian.ng/sport/amusan-short-of-words-after-world-athlete-of-the-year-nominationhttps://guardian.ng/sport/amusan-short-of-words-after-world-athlete-of-the-year-nomination/

Ighoroje, J. E. and H. Egedi. (2015). "An Evaluation of the Roles of Financial Institutions in the Development of Nigeria Economy." *G.J.I.S.S.*, 4(4): 1–4. https://www.longdom.org/articles/an-evaluation-of-the-roles-of-financial-institutions-in-the-development-of-nigeria-economy.pdf

Igwe, Charles. (2015). "How Nollywood became the Second Largest Film Industry." *British Council*. British Council Worldwide. How Nollywood became the second largest film industry | British Council.

Ikpe, Ukana. (2000). "Patrimonialism and Military Regimes in Nigeria." *African Journal of Political Science*, 5(1): 146–62.

IMDb. (2023). "Burna Boy Awards." https://www.imdb.com/name/nm9958622/awards

IMDb. (2023). "Wizkid Awards." https://www.imdb.com/name/nm5443614/awards

IMDb. (2022). "Agbani Darego Biography." https://www.imdb.com/name/nm1505341/bio

Increse. (2009). *Report of Survey on Sexual Diversity and Human Rights in Nigeria*. Funding support provided by the Ford Foundation. https://www.sxpolitics.org/wp-content/uploads/2009/10/report-on-sexual-diversity-and-human-rights-in-nigeria-1.pdf

IndigeDisc. (n.d.). "King Sunny Ade: Biography." https://www.globalartslive.org/sites/default/files/Biography_38.pdf

International Journal of African Martial Arts & Combat Traditions (IJAMACT). (2023). "DAMBE: The African Martial Arts of Nigerian Origin." Yaoundé: African Martial Arts. https://ijamact.com/index.php/2023/01/21/dambe-the-african-martial-arts-of-nigerian-origin/

International Labour Organization. (2020). "Regions and Countries." https://www.ilo.org/global/regions/lang--en/index.htm#

International Trade Centre. (n.d.). "Nigeria." *International Trade Centre*. https://www.intracen.org/country/nigeria/ (accessed August 19, 2020).

Iroham, Chukwuemeka, O. M. Akinwale, Adedamola Oluwunmi, Hilary Okagbue, Olufemi Dudla, Ayedun Caleb, Moses Emetere, and J. N. Peter. (2019). "Influence of Facilities on Patronage of the Various Shopping Malls in Ibadan, Nigeria." *Journal of Physics: Conference Series (International Conference on Engineering for Sustainable World)*. doi: 10.1088/1742-6596/1378/3/032052

Iwuh, John. (2015). 'Nollywood, Cinema Culture and Tourism Potential of the Movie Business in Nigeria." In Kenneth C. Nwoko and Omon M. Osiki (eds.), *Dynamics of Culture and Tourism in Africa: Perspectives on Africa's Development in the 21st Century*, 13–41. Ogun State Nigeria: Babcock University Press.

Joint Universities Preliminary Examinations Board. (2022). https://jupeb.edu.ng/

Kirk-Greene, A. H. M. (1975). "The Genesis of the Nigerian Civil War and the Theory of Fear." *Research Report No. 7*. Uppsala: The Scandinavian Institute of African Studies.

Klein, Debra. (2019). "Fuji: Indigenous and Islamic Popular Music Fusions in Nigeria." In Heidi Carolyn Feldman, David Horn, John Shepherd, and Gabrielle Kielich (eds.), *Bloomsbury Encyclopedia of Popular Music of the World (Genres: Sub-Saharan Africa) Volume XII*, 145–51. New York: Bloomsbury Academic.

KMPG. (2017). "Nigerian Mining Sector Brief." https://assets.kpmg/content/dam/kpmg/ng/pdf/advisory/ng-Nigerian-Mining-Sector.pdf

Kriesch, Adrian. (2015). "Why Nigerian Activist Ken Saro-Wiwa was Executed." *Deutsche Welle (DW) – Made for Minds*. https://www.dw.com/en/why-nigerian-activist-ken-saro-wiwa-was-executed/a-18837442

Kugo, Uzoma. (2013). "Broadcasting Regulation and Broadcasting in Nigeria: An Overview of the Approaches." *Research on Humanities and Social Sciences*, 3(2): 12–20.

Laidi, Olusegun Fariudeen. (2012). "Multilingualism and Hip Hop Consumption in Nigeria: Accounting for the Local Acceptance of a Global Phenomenon." *Africa Spectrum*, 47(1): 3–19.

Lamela, Maikano. (2015). "The Contributory Role of Music Artist: An X-ray of Major Satiric Preoccupations in Some Selected Contemporary Nigerian Hip-Hop Music Artists." *Journal of Humanities and Social Science (IOSR-JHSS)*, 20(4): 5–9.

Lasse, Heerten and A. Dirk Moses. (2014). "The Nigeria–Biafra War: Postcolonial Conflict and the Question of Genocide." *Journal of Genocide Research*, 16(2–3): 169–203. doi: 10.1080/14623528.2014.936700

Lemuel, Terlanga. "Chapter 1, Introduction to African Drama." https://www.academia.edu/35396251/CHAPTER_I_INTRODUCTION_TO_AFRICAN_DRAMA

Lindfors, Bernth. "Amos Tutuola." *DLB 125*.

Lo-Bamijoko, J. N. (1987). "Classification of Igbo Musical Instruments, Nigeria." *Journal of International Library of African Music*, 6(4): 19–41.

Lukman, Olaoluwa Olaide. (2018). "Historical Analysis of the Management of Public Universities in Nigeria." *Research & Reviews: Journal of Social Sciences*, 4(2): 264–7.

Lux, Afrique. (2017). "5 of the Best Nigerian Polo Clubs." http://luxafrique.net/5-of-the-best-nigerian-polo-clubs/
Mabogunje, A. L. (1968). *Urbanization in Nigeria*. London: University of London Press.
Mackay, Mercedes and Augustine Ene. (1957). "The Atilogwu Dance." *African Music,* 1(4): 20–2.
Mail & Guardian. (2021, August). "Women's Football in Nigeria has a Long History of Defiance." https://mg.co.za/sport/2021-08-11-womens-football-in-nigeria-has-a-long-history-of-defiance/
Makinde, Adeyinka. (n.d.), "Book Review of Chinua Achebe's there was a Country: A Personal History of Biafra." http://adeyinkamakinde.homestead.com/index.html
Makisaka, Megumi. (2009). *Human Trafficking: A Brief Overview. Social Development Notes*; No. 122. Washington, DC: World Bank. © World Bank. https://openknowledge.worldbank.org/handle/10986/11103
Makozi, A. O and G. J. A. Ojo. (1982). *The History of the Catholic Church in Nigeria*. Macmillan Nigeria.
Marriage Act of Nigeria. (1914). https://citizenshiprightsafrica.org/nigeria-marriage-act-1914/
Marshall, R. (2009). *Spiritualities: The Pentecostal Revolution in Nigeria*. Chicago: The University of Chicago Press.
May, Omogho Esiri. (2021). "Social Change and Marriage Structure in Nigeria." *International Research Journal of Management, IT and Social Sciences*, 8(3): 228–35. https://doi.org/10.21744/irjmis.v8n3.1487
McCain, Carmen (2013). "Nollywood, Kannywood, and a Decade of Hausa Film Censorship in Nigeria." In D. Biltereyst and R. V. Winkel (eds.), *Silencing Cinema. Global Cinema*. 223–40. New York: Palgrave Macmillan. https://doi.org/10.1057/9781137061980_14
McKinnon, A. (2021). "Christians, Muslims and Traditional Worshippers in Nigeria: Estimating the Relative Proportions from Eleven Nationally Representative." *Social Surveys. Review of Religious Research*, 63: 303–15.
Moja, Tebho. (2000). "Nigeria Education Sector Analysis: An Analytical Synthesis of Performance and Main Issues." Report Produced for the World Bank.
Morrison, Joy. (1991). "Forum Theater in West Africa: An Alternative Medium of Information Exchange." *Research in African Literatures*, 22(3): 29–40.
Muhammad, Murtala. (2014). "Military and Politics in Nigeria." In Ahmed Bako, Murtala Muhammad, Yusuf Isma'ila, and Murtala Ahmed Rufai (eds.), *Issues on Nigerian Peoples and Culture*. 139–53. Wudil: Kano University of Science and Technology.
Munir, Arshad and Godwin Odeh. (2014). "The Establishment of the Nigerian Sokoto Caliphate: An Inquest into the Background History of the 1804 Jihad in Hausa Land, 210 Years After." *Al-Qalam*, 61–71. https://www.researchgate.net/publication/282730945_The_Establishment_of_the_Nigerian_Sokoto_Caliphate_An_inquest_into_the_Background_History_of_the_1804_Jihad_in_Hausa_Land_210_years_After
Musa, Abubakar, Deborah Gregory, and Ibrahim Abdulani. (2022). "Higher Education in Nigeria: Private Universities' Challenges and Coping Strategies." *Asian Research Journal of Current Science*, 4(1): 279–86.
Naankiel, Peter. (2015). "A Brief History of the Pre-colonial Economy of the Jukun." *Sokoto Journal of History*, 4: 150–60.
NABTEB. (2021). https://nabteb.gov.ng/
Nairametrics. (2020, January 11). "Nigeria Receives $17.5 Billion Diaspora Remittances in 2019." https://nairametrics.com/2020/01/11/nigeria-receives-17-5-billion-diaspora-remittances-in-2019/
Nairametrics. (2019, September 30). "Non-Performing Loans Hit 4-year Low as Banks Recover N496 Billion." https://nairametrics.com/2019/09/30/non-performing-loans-hit-4-year-low-as-banks-recover-n496-billion/
Nairametrics. (2019, October 1). "Evolution of Nigerian Banks in 59-years." https://nairametrics.com/2019/10/01/evolution-of-nigerian-banks-in-59-years/

Nairametrics. (2020, April 11). "Nigeria's Foreign Debt has Breached a 15-year Trigger." *Nairametrics*. https://nairametrics.com/2020/04/11/nigerias-foreign-debt-has-breached-a-15-year-trigger/

Nairametrics. (2020, May 12). "Economy: Focus on Nigerian Households' Consumption Pattern." https://nairametrics.com/2020/05/12/economy-focus-on-nigerian-households-consumption-pattern/

Nairametrics. (2020, May 26). "Financial Institutions Still the Fastest Growing Sector in Nigeria." https://nairametrics.com/2020/05/26/financial-institutions-still-the-fastest-growing-sector-in-nigeria/

Nairametrics. (2020, July 14). "CBN Gives Banks Approval to Debit Bank Accounts of Chronic Loan Defaulters Starting August 1." https://nairametrics.com/2020/07/14/cbn-gives-banks-approval-to-debit-bank-accounts-of-chronic-loan-defaulters-starting-august-1/

Nairametrics. (2020, July 19). "CBN Reserves 60% of N220 Billion MSMEs Fund for Women." https://nairametrics.com/2020/07/19/cbn-reserves-60-of-n220-billion-msmes-fund-for-women/

Nairametrics. (2020, July 23). "The Top 5 Stock Exchanges in Africa." https://nairametrics.com/2017/07/23/the-top-5-stock-exchanges-in-africa/

Nairametrics. (2020, August 4). "Manufacturing Sector in Nigeria and the Reality of a 'New Normal.'" https://nairametrics.com/2020/08/04/manufacturing-sector-in-nigeria-and-the-reality-of-a-new-normal/

Nairametrics. (2020, August 9). "Exchange Rate Unification: CBN Devalues Official Rate to N380/$1." https://nairametrics.com/2020/08/09/exchange-rate-unification-cbn-devalues-official-rate-to-n380-1/

Nariametrics. (2020, August 12). "How the Newly Amended CAMA Affects Your Business." https://nairametrics.com/2020/08/11/how-the-newly-amended-cama-affects-your-business/

Nairametrics. https://nairametrics.com/2020/05/14/nigerias-external-reserves-increase-by-1-36-billion-in-13-days/

National African Language Resource Center (NALRC). (n.d.). "Language & Culture: Studying Ijaw in the United States." www.nalrc.indiana.edu

National Board for Technical Education. (2022). https://net.nbte.gov.ng/

National Broadcasting Commission. (2016). *Nigerian Broadcasting Code (6th Edition)*. Abuja: National Broadcasting Commission.

National Bureau of Statistics. (2020a). *Foreign Trade in Goods Statistics*. National Bureau of Statistics.

National Bureau of Statistics. (2020b). *Nigerian Domestic and Foreign Debt (Q1 2020)*. National Bureau of Statistics.

National Commission for Colleges of Education. (2021). http://www.ncceonline.edu.ng/colleges.php

National Commission for Nomadic Education. (2017). "NCNE Brochure." https://nbais.com.ng/

National Examinations Council. (2017). http://www.mynecoexams.com/index.html

National Institute for Sports. (2021). https://nis.gov.ng/

National Open University of Nigeria. (2008). "Eng. 218 (African Novel)." Lagos: National Open University.

National Planning Commission. (2020). "National Integrated Infrastructure Master Plan (NIIMP)." https://www.niimp.gov.ng/

National Sports Commission. (1971). "National Sports Commission Decree 1971." *Supplement to Official Gazette*, 58(41). https://gazettes.africa/archive/ng/1971/ng-government-gazette-supplement-dated-1971-08-12-no-41-part-a.pdf

National Universities Commission. (2022). https://www.nuc.edu.ng/

Nationwide League One. (2021). "History, the National Amateur League." https://nigerianationwideleague.com/history/

NBAIS. (2022). https://nbais.com.ng/

Nigerian Affairs. (1970). "Hubert Ogunde – A Musical Celebrity." *The People*, 2(2): 8–18.

Nigeria Basketball Federation. (2022).https://www.nbbfonline.com/

Nigeria Cricket Federation. (2022). "Nigeria Qualifies for the 2023 Finals in Namibia after a Brilliant Outing in Kigali." https://nigeriacricket.com.ng/2022/12/10/nigeria-qualifies-for-the-2023-finals-in-namibia-after-a-brilliant-outing-in-kigali/

Nigeria Marriage Act. (1990). "Chapter 218." *Laws of the Federation of Nigeria*. Nigerian Legislation.

Nigeria Olympic Committee. (2022). https://nigeriaolympic.org/

Nigerian Ports Authority. (n.d.). *Lagos Port*. Nigerian Ports Authority. https://nigerianports.gov.ng/lagos-port/ (accessed August 19, 2020).

Nkwo, Makouchi, Nwokeji Orji Rita, and Ndulue Chinenye. (2018). "E-commerce Personalization in Africa: A Comparative Analysis of Jumia and Konga." Conference paper presented during the 3rd International Workshop on Personalization, Persuasive Technology (PPT'18).

Nnadi, Ine. (2013). "Sex Trafficking and Women – The Nigerian Experience." *Journal of Politics and Law*, 6(3): 179–87. http://dx.doi.org/10.5539/jpl.v6n3p179

Nnaji, Patience Onyinyechi. (2014). "The Role of Literature Education in Curbing Violence: A Focus on John Pepper Clark's 'The Casualties.'" *An International Journal of Arts and Humanities*, 3(2): 18–28. doi: http://dx.doi.org/10.4314/ijah.v3i2.2

Nnamani, Sunday. (2014). "The Role of Folk Music in Traditional African Society: The Igbo Experience." *Journal of Modern Education Review*, 4(4): 304–10. doi: 10.15341/jmer(2155-7993)/04.04.2014/008

Nomso, Obiajuru. (2020, 9 March). "Nigerian Boxer Who has the Fastest Victory in Boxing History Brutally Knocks Out Opponent." *Legit.ng*. https://www.msn.com/en-xl/sport/other-sports/nigerian-boxer-who-has-the-fastest-victory-in-boxing-history-brutally-knocks-out-opponent/ar-BB10TVau

Nordea. (2020, July). *Foreign Direct Investment (FDI) in Nigeria—Investing—Nordea Trade Portal*. Nordea Trade. https://www.nordeatrade.com/en/explore-new-market/nigeria/investment

NS Energy. (2019, April 5). "Top Ten Countries with World's Largest Oil Reserves, from Venezuela to Iraq." https://www.nsenergybusiness.com/features/newstop-ten-countries-with-worlds-largest-oil-reserves-5793487/

NUGA Games. http://www.nugagames.4mg.com/index.htm

Nunn, Nathan. (2008). "The Long-Term Effects of Africa's Slave Trades." *Quarterly Journal of Economics*, 123(1): 139–76.

Nwabara, Samuel. (1963). "The Fulani Conquest and Rule of the Hausa Kingdom of Northern Nigeria (1804–1900)." *Journal de la Société des Africanistes*, 33(2): 231–42. doi: https://doi.org/10.3406/jafr.1963.1370

Nwadilibe, P. Iloeje. (1976). *A New Geography of Nigeria*. Ibadan: Longman.

Nwadiokwu, C. N., E. S. Nwadiokwu, E. N. Favour, and M. E. Okwuazun. (2016). "Rites of Passage African Traditional Religion." *International Journal of Education Research*, 4(9): 41–50.

Nwangwu, Rosemary, Amiel Fagbulu, Flora Aderogba, O. Olapeju, Ramoni Yusufu, and Kalu Kalu. (2005). *Nigeria Education Sector Diagnosis: A Condensed Version, A Framework for Re-engineering the Education Sector*. Education Sector Analysis Unit, Federal Ministry of Education.

Nwaru, Chris. (2018). "Ethnic Dance and National Integration: The National Troupe Example." *Hofa: African Journal of Multidisciplinary Research (Special Issue)*, 3(1): 159–70. doi: https://doi.org/10.5281/zenodo.1481858

NWFL (Nigeria Women Football League). (2021). https://thenwfl.com/

Nzere, Solomon. (2018, January). "The Nigerian Music Industry: Making the Music Pay through Intellectual Property." *Industry Insight*, Infusion Lawyers.

Obiaya, Ikechukwu. (2011). "A Break with the Past: The Nigerian Video-Film Industry in the Context of Colonial Filmmaking." *Film History an International Journal*, 23(2): 129.

Observatory of Economic Complexity. (n.d.). *Nigeria Trade | Data*. OEC. https://oec.world/en/profile/country/nga/#tariffs (accessed August 19, 2020).

O'Connor, Maurice. (2008). *The Writing of Ben Okri: Transcending the Local and the National*. New Delhi: Prestige Books.

Odimegwu, Clifford Obby. (1999). "Family Planning Attitudes and Use in Nigeria: A Factor Analysis." *International Family Planning Perspectives*, 25(2): 86–91.

Odorume, Akpobo. (2012). "Historiography of the Print Media: A Global-Cum-Nigerian Perspective." *Journal of African Studies*, 1: 1–9.

Oduguwa, Adedara. (2015, May). "Biography of Chief (Dr.) Hubert Adedeji Ogunde – The Doyen of African Theatre." BIOGRAPHY OF CHIEF (DR.) HUBERT ADEDEJI OGUNDE- THE DOYEN OF AFRICAN THEATRE – Ebiographer (wordpress.com).

Ogheneovo, Akponome Abel. "Folk Music in Contemporary Nigeria: Continuity and Change." Ph.D dissertation submitted to the Department of Theatre and Performing Arts, Ahmadu Bello University, Zaria.

Ogunbanjo, M. B. (2001). "Political Parties and Federalism in Nigeria: Understanding the Evolution of the Dialectical Relationship." *Journal of Constitutional Development*. 2(2): 12–35.

Ogundele, Samuel. (2010). "Understanding Nigeria within the Context of the Atlantic World." *The African Diaspora Archaeology Network*. http://www.diaspora.uiuc.edu/news0910/news0910.html

Ogundiran, Akinwumi. "The Formation of an Oyo Imperial Colony during the Atlantic Age." In Cameron Monroe and Akinwumi Ogundiran (eds.), *Power and Landscape in Atlantic West Africa: Archaeological Perspectives*, 222–52. doi: http://dx.doi.org/10.1017/CBO9780511921032

Oikelome, Albert. (2019). "From the Koola Lobitos Era to Afrobeat" – A Study of the Artistic Years of Fela Anikulapo Kuti. https://www.researchgate.net/publication/335665769_'FROM_THE_KOOLA_LOBITOS_ERA_TO_AFROBEAT'-A_STUDY_OF_THE_ARTISTIC_YEARS_OF_FELA_ANIKULAPO_KUTI.

Ojo, Edetaen. (2001). "Broadcasting in Nigeria: Unlocking the Airwaves (Report on the Framework for Broadcasting and Telecommunications in Nigeria.)" *Media Rights Agenda & Article 19*.

Ojo, Emmanuel Oladipo. (2010). "Government by Incompatibles: A Case Study of the 1960–1964 Nigerian Federal Government." *African Journal of Political Science and International Relations*, 4(9): 340–9.

Ojo, Jide. (2022, August 03). "Unwise Proliferation of Tertiary Institutions in Nigeria." *Punch Nigeria Limited*. https://punchng.com/unwise-proliferation-of-tertiary-institutions-in-nigeria/

Oke, Afagene. (2022, April). "Traditional Marriage Rites: How its done in Hausa Tradition." *Pulse.ng*. https://www.pulse.ng/lifestyle/relationships-weddings/traditional-marriage-rites-how-its-done-in-hausa-land/1y3xsmy

Okeke, Chidimma. (2022, May). "Private Universities now 111, As FG Issues 12 New Licences." *Daily Trust*. https://dailytrust.com/private-universities-now-111-as-fg-issues-12-new-licences

Okodo, Ikechukwu. (2012). "African Traditional Drama: The Igbo-Nigerian Experience." *Journal of Emerging Trends in Educational Research and Policy Studies (JETERAPS)*, 3(2): 131–6.

Okolie-Osemene, James and Rosemary Okoh. (2014). "The Role of Nigeria Football Federation in the Denouement of Premier League Seasonal Disputes: Issues and Prospects." *Recreation and Society in Africa, Asia and Latin America*, 5(1): 1–14.

Okonkwo, Anthony. (2009). "The Evolution of Gender in Igbo Nation and the Discourse of Cultural Imperialism." BA Thesis submitted to the School of Culture and Society, Department of International Migration and International Relations.

Okoro, Enuma. (2017). "Inside the Durbar Festival in Northern Nigeria. African Voices." *CNN*. https://edition.cnn.com/2017/07/03/africa/gallery/durbar-festival-in-northern-nigeria/index.html

Okpala, Nkechi. (2016). "Traditional Music in Igbo Cultures: A Case Study of Idu Cultural Dance of Akpo in Aguata Local Government Area of Anambra." *African Research Review: An International Multidisciplinary Journal, Ethiopia*, 10(1): 87–103. doi: http://dx.doi.org/10.4314/afrrev.v10i1.8

Olaniyan, Oluyemi. "The Evolution of the Technique of the Creativity of Fuji – A Nigerian Popular Music Genre." Abstract of a paper.

Olawoye, Jaunice, Femi Omololu, Yinka Aderinto, Iyabode Adeyefa, Debo Adeyemo, and C. Olisah. (2020, May 14). "Nigeria's External Reserves Increase by $1.36 Billion in 13 Days." https://nairametrics.com/2020/05/14/nigerias-external-reserves-increase-by-1-36-billion-in-13-days/

Olayebi, Bankole. (2004). *Ws: A life in full*. Bookcraft.

Olomojobi, Yinka. (2016, September 24). "Marriage in Nigeria across Ages: Problems and Prospects." SSRN: https://ssrn.com/abstract=2858618 or http://dx.doi.org/10.2139/ssrn.2858618

Olorunsola, R. "Nigerian News Magazines and their Importance: A Review of Recent Literature." https://worldlibraries.dom.edu/index.php/worldlib/article/view/202/157

Oji, H. (2020). "Repositioning NSE for Contribution to 2020 Growth Plans." *The Guardian*, January 6. https://guardian.ng/business-services/repositioning-nse-for-contribution-to-2020-growth-plans/

Omaka, Arua. (2014). "The Forgotten Victims: Ethnic Minorities in the Nigeria-Biafra War, 1967–1970." *Journal of Retracing Africa*, 1(1): 25–40.

Omede, A. (2012). "The Nigerian Military: Analysing Fifty Years of Defence and Internal Military and Fifty Years of Internal Operations in Nigeria (1960–2010)." *Journal of Social Science*, 33(3): 293–303.

Omoniyi, Oluwaferanmi. (2022, November 10). "NBBF Super 8 Finals: Rivers Hoopers, Kwara Falcons Stay Unbeaten." *Premium Times*. https://www.premiumtimesng.com/sports/nigeria-sports-news/564509-nbbf-super-8-finals-rivers-hoopers-kwara-falcons-stay-unbeaten.html

Omoniyi, Oluwaferanmi. (2022, November 13). "NBBF Final 8: Kwara Falcons Wins First Title as High School Student Emerges MVP." *Premium Times*. https://www.premiumtimesng.com/regional/north-central/565018-nbbf-final-8-kwara-falcons-wins-first-title-as-high-school-student-emereges-mvp.html

Omotosho, Salau. (2011). "ISL 372: Islam in Nigeria." National Open University of Nigeria.

OnlineNigeria.com. (2022). "Bride Price Payment in Nigeria." https://www.onlinenigeria.com/marriages-in-nigeria/Bride-Price/

Onuoha, Philip. (2012). "History of Nigerian Mass Media (MAC 113)." School of Arts and Social Science, National Open University.

Onuzulike, Uchenna. (2008). "Nollywood: The Birth of Nollywood: The Nigerian Movie Industry." *Black Camera*, 22(1): 25–6.

Osadolor, Osarhieme. (2001). "The Military System of the Benin Kingdom c1440-1897." Thesis submitted to the Department of Philosophy and History in partial fulfilment of the requirements for the award of Doctor of Philosophy, University of Hamburg, Germany.

Osasona, Cordelia, Lee Ogunshakin, and David Jiboye. (2009). "Ile-Ife: A Cultural Phenomenon in the Throes of Transformation." In *Proceedings of African Perspectives (The African Inner City)*, 145–56.

Osinubi, Femi. (2017). "The Business of Entertainment: Harnessing Growth Opportunities in Entertainment, Media, Arts and Lifestyle." National Branding Conference (PwC).

Osotimehin, Babatunde. (2004). "Social Construction of Manhood in Nigeria: Implications for Male Responsibility in Reproductive Health." *African Population Studies*, 19(2). https://tspace.library.utoronto.ca/handle/1807/4108

Otache, Innocent. (2019). "The Dilemma of Polytechnic Education in Nigeria: The Way Forward." Paper Presented at the 5th National Conference Organized by the Academic Staff Union of Polytechnics (ASUP), Federal Polytechnic Idah, Kogi State.

Otomiewo, Ufuoma. (2011). "The Provision of Basic Education in Nigeria. Challenges and way Forward (Mini-dissertation submitted in partial compliance with the Degree of LLM)." Faculty of Law, Centre for Human Rights, University of Pretoria, South Africa

Oye, A. (2009). "National Sports Policy of Nigeria." https://www.academia.edu/10705450/NATIONAL_SPORTS_POLICY_OF_NIGERIA

Oyeleye, Anu. (2019). "Expert Seeks Introduction of Accreditation for Specialised Learning Institutions." *The Chronicle of Education*. https://thechronicleofeducation.net/expert-seeks-introduction-of-accreditation-for-specialised-learning-institutions/

Paralympic Movement. (2011, November). "Nigeria Dominates African Para-Table Tennis Championships." https://www.paralympic.org/news/nigeria-dominates-african-para-table-tennis-championships

Peel, J. D. Y. (1997). *Aladura: A Religious Movement among the Yoruba*. Lit Verlag Publisher.

Potokri, Onoriode. (2014). "Evaluation of Availability of Financial Resources and Manpower Development in Selected Monotechnics in Nigeria." *Industry & Higher Education*, 28(5): 361–70. doi: 10.5367/ihe.2014.0219

Premium Times. (2020). "CBN Approves N75billion Loan for Agricultural Lending in States." Abuja. https://www.premiumtimesng.com/business/5486cbn_approves_n75billion_loan_for_agricultural_lending_in_states_.html

Project Underground. (ND). "The Life and Death of Ken Saro-Wiwa: A History of the Struggle for Justice in the Niger Delta." http://remembersarowiwa.com/wp-content/uploads/life_death_ksw.pdf

Pulse Sport Team. (2022, July). "Best Nigerian Table Tennis Players of All Time." https://www.pulse.ng/sports/other-sports/best-nigerian-table-tennis-players-of-all-time-featuring-aruna-quadri-segun-toriola/hqwv2pj

Punch Nigeria. (2020, August 17). "Border Closure should be Reviewed." https://punchng.com/border-closure-should-be-reviewed/

Raji, Afeez Tope. (2019). "A Retrospective of Yoruba Indigenous Games and Plays." *Grin*. https://www.grin.com/document/506240

Reuters. (2020, February 5). "UPDATE 2-Nigeria Sets Ambitious Target for Mining Sector Growth." https://af.reuters.com/article/metalsNews/idAFL8N2A53IU

Ridwan, Adeyemi, Ganiyu Akashoro, and Mukaila Ajaga. (2013). "An Empirical Study of the Trend and Pattern of Video-Film Piracy." *European Scientific Journal*, 9(14): 64–86.

Ruth, Hopkins. (2019, August 14). "Long Read: The Nigerian Rise of Women Boxers in Nigeria." *New Frame*. https://www.newframe.com/long-read-the-rise-of-women-boxers-in-nigeria/

Sagbara, Godwill. (2019). "Awareness of Vocational Innovation Enterprise Institutions among Teachers and Students in Secondary Schools in Rivers State." *Rivers State University of Education (RSUJOE)*, 22(1&2): 124–31.

Santander. (2020). "Foreign Investment in Nigeria—Santandertrade.com." Santander Trade Markets. https://santandertrade.com/en/portal/establish-overseas/nigeria/investing?

Saro-Wiwa, Ken. (1996). *A Month and a Day in Detention Diary (with an introduction by William Boyd)*. New York: Penguin Books.

Saro-Wiwa, Ken. (2017). *Silence would be Treason: Last Writings of Ken Saro-Wiwa (new and expanded edition)*. Daraja Press.

School Software Pro. (2022, September). "Nigerian Football History." https://www.schoolsoftware.com.ng/nigerian-football-history/#:~:text=Throughout%20history%2C%20the%20team%20has,of%20African%20Football%20(CAF).

Schuh, Russell. (n.d.). "The Metrics of Three Hausa Songs on Marriage by 'Dan Maraya Jos." UCLA.

Sciencing. (2019). "Native Plants & Animals in Nigeria." https://sciencing.com/native-plants-animals-nigeria-6569856.html

Sebastine, Ezekiel. (2017). "The Afrobeat legacy of Fela Anikulapo Kuti in Nigeria." Being a made to Prof John Collins for the Course titled African Music and Dance (SOAN 233) Ashesi University College.

Sefi Atta. Official Website. http://www.sefiatta.com/bio.html

Sidi, Tiwugi Sheshi. (2012). "A History of the Nupe, C1068-1810 A.D." PhD Thesis submitted to the school of Postgraduate Studies Ahmadu Bello University, Zaria.

Sports Central. (2022). "How Zik Started Football in Nigeria." https://www.sportscentralngr.com/news/readnews/12403/how-zik-started-football-in-nigeria https://zikism.tripod.com/Owelle.html

Statista. (2020). "Monthly Minimum Wage in Nigeria from 2018 to 2020." https://www.statista.com/statistics/1119133/monthly-minimum-wage-in-nigeria/

Strickland, Melissa. (1999). "The History of Christianity in Nigeria: A Case Study with Special Emphasis on Southern Baptist Mission Work." A senior thesis in General Studies submitted to the General Studies Council in the College of Arts and Sciences at Texas Tech University

Swimming in Nigeria. (2022). https://swimming.sitesng.com/en_History.html#:~:text=History%20of%20Swimming%20in%20Nigeria&text=Traditional%20swimming%20as%20a%20kind,the%20most%20popular%20Olympic%20sports.

Table Tennis for all. For life. (2020). "Long Tradition but First for Nigeria." https://www.ittf.com/2019/12/18/long-tradition-first-nigeria/ (ITTF.com)

Table Tennis in Nigeria. (2022). https://tabletennis.sitesng.com/en_Home.html

Tade, Oludayo and Okoro Mmahi. "Movie Piracy Networks at Alaba International Market, Lagos, Nigeria." *International Journal of Offender Therapy and Comparative Criminology*, 62(1): 274–85. doi: 10.1177/0306624X17692208

Terlumun, Uji. (2015). "Migrant Groups and Inter-group Relations in Tiv Society of Central Nigeria: Pre to Post-colonial Era." *International Journal of Arts and Humanities (IJAH) Bahir Dar-Ethiopia*, 4(1): 88–97. doi: http://dx.doi.org/10.4314/ijah.v4i1.6

The Blueprint Nigeria. (2020, August 12). "Why Buhari should Review Social Schemes." https://www.blueprint.ng/why-buhari-should-review-social-schemes/

The Cable. (2018, April 6). "Private Sector Accounts for 90% of Nigeria's GDP, Says Osinbajo." https://www.thecable.ng/osinbajo-the-private-sector-accounts-for-90-of-nigerias-gdp

The Chimamanda Ngozi Adichie Website. (2022). The Chimamanda Ngozi Adichie Website (ulg.ac.be).

The Guardian. (2022). "2022 UTME: 1.4m Candidates' so Far Sat for Examination, Results Out Soon – JAMB." https://guardian.ng/news/2022-utme-1-4m-candidates-so-far-sat-for-examination-results-out-soon-jamb/

The History of Table Tennis in Nigeria. (n.d.), http://tabletennis.sitesng.com/en_History.html#:~:text=It%20was%20believed%20that%20Table,established%20in%20the%20year%201926.

The Ministry of Mines and Steel Development. (2020). "President Reiterates Commitment to Combat Illegal Mining Activities, Expresses Concern over Loss of $3b to Smuggling of Gold." https://www.minesandsteel.gov.ng/2020/07/16/president-reiterates-commitment-to-combat-illegal-mining-activities-expresses-concern-over-loss-of-3b-to-smuggling-of-gold/

The Nigerian Stock Exchange. (2019). "NSE Launches X-Academy e-learning to Provide Quality and Affordable Learning Experience." http://www.nse.com.ng/mediacenter/pressreleases/Pages/nse-launches-x-academy-e-learning-to-provide-quality-and-affordable-learning-experience.aspx

The Trading Economics. (2020). "Nigeria - Employment in Industry (% Of Total Employment)." https://tradingeconomics.com/nigeria/employment-in-industry-percent-of-total-employment-wb-data.html

This Day Editorial. (2019, December 19). "Nigeria: Anthony Joshua and Nigerian Boxing." *AllAfrica*. https://allafrica.com/stories/201912190808.html

Thurston, A. (2016). *Salafism in Nigeria: Islam, Preaching, and Politics*. Cambridge: Cambridge University Press.

Toledo, Manuel. (2012). "Nigeria Kano Cancels Famous Horse Durbar Festival." https://www.bbc.com/news/world-africa-19274593

Tutuola, Amos. (1954). *The Palm-Wine Drinkard and My Life in the Bush of Ghosts*. New York: Grove Press.

Ubaku, Chika, Anyalewachi Emeh, and Anyikwa Nkiru. (2014). "Impact of Nationalist Movement on the Actualization of Nigerian Independence, 1914–1960." *International Journal of History and Philosophical Research*, 2(1): 54–67.

Udo, R. (1970). *Geographical Regions of Nigeria*. London: Heinemann Educational Books.

Udo, R. Kenrick, Anthony Hamilton Millard Kirk-Greene, J. F. Ade Ajayi, and Toyin O. Falola. (2022, December 4). "Nigeria." *Encyclopedia Britannica*. https://www.britannica.com/place/Nigeria

Ugor, Paul. (2007). "Censorship and the Content of Nigerian Home Video Films." *Postcolonial Text*, 3(1): 1–22.

Umoru, Alex. (2019, September). "The Sport of Wrestling: From then Till Now." *Nigeria Monthly*. https://nigeriamonthly.ng/the-sport-of-wrestling-from-then-till-now/

UNESCO. (2006). "Human Trafficking in Nigeria: Root Causes and Recommendations." (Policy Paper, 14.2 E).

Usman, Suleiman. (2007). "A History of Birnin Zaria from 1350–1902." Master Thesis submitted to Ahmadu Bello University, Zaria.

Utuk, Efiong Isaac. (1975). "Britain's Colonial Administrations and Developments, 1861–1960: An Analysis of Britain's Colonial Administrations and Developments in Nigeria." Dissertations and Theses. Paper 2525.

Vanguard, Nigeria. (2020, August 16). "Interrogating Strategies to Poverty Reduction." https://www.vanguardngr.com/2020/08/interrogating-strategies-to-poverty-reduction/

Vanguard. (2022). "FEC Approves National Sports Industry Policy." https://www.vanguardngr.com/2022/11/fec-approves-national-sports-industry-policy/

Vanguard. (2022, July). "Women Football Development in Nigeria, Collapsing – Ex-NWFL Boss." https://nigerianationwideleague.com/history/

Vaughn, O. (2016). *Religion and the Making of Nigeria*. Durham: Duke University Press.

WAEC Nigeria. (2020). https://www.waecnigeria.org/

Weor, Jonathan. (2005). "The Narratives of Origin and Migration of the Tiv People (of Nigeria) as an Indigenous Interpretation of the Book of Exodus." *Scriptura*, 90: 885–91.

World Bank. (2020). "Country Profile: Nigeria." https://databank.worldbank.org/views/reports/reportwidget.aspx?Report_Name=CountryProfile&Id=b450fd57&tbar=y&dd=y&inf=n&zm=n&country=NGA

World Bank. (2019). "*Overview* [Text/HTML]." World Bank. https://www.worldbank.org/en/country/nigeria/overview

World Bank Group. (2015). "Governance and Finance Analysis of the Basic Education Sector in Nigeria." Report No. ACS14245.

World Bank Group. (2020). "Nigeria in Times of COVID-19: Laying Foundations for a Strong Recovery." http://documents1.worldbank.org/curated/en/695491593024516552/pdf/Nigeria-in-Times-of-COVID-19-Laying-Foundations-for-a-Strong-Recovery.pdf

World Bank Report. (2015). "Governance and Finance Analysis of the Basic Education Sector in Nigeria." World Bank Report No. ACS14245.

World Economic Forum. (2014). "Enabling Trade: Barriers to Imports/Exports in Nigeria." http://reports.weforum.org/enabling-trade-increasing-the-potential-of-trade-reforms/enabling-trade-barriers-to-importsexports-in-nigeria/?doing_wp_cron=1597931033.6356780529022216796875

World Integrated Trade Solution. (2018). "Nigeria (NGA) Exports, Imports, and Trade Partners." WITS. https://wits.worldbank.org/countrysnapshot/en/NGA

Yahya, Mohammed. (2003). "The Nupe People of Nigeria." *Studies of Tribes Tribals*, 1(2): 96–110.

Zaccheus Onumba Dibiaezue Memorial Libraries. (2013). "Nnamdi Azikwe at the Olympics by Mena Odu." https://zodml.org/blog/nnamdi-azikiwe-olympics-mena-odu

Zaccheus Onumba Dibiaezue Memorial Libraries. (2022). "Herbert Macaulay." https://zodml.org/discover-nigeria/people/historicalpeople/herbert-macaulay

INDEX

Aba 16, 27, 51
Abasi 89, 341
Abdulsalami Abubakar 46, 55, 351
Abel Guobadia 91
Abia State 16
Abubakar Imam 52, 186, 202
Abuja 17, 344
Abuja Pottery Center 259
Achebe, Chinua 224
Acheulean period 16
Action Congress of Nigeria 80, 99
Action Group 38, 40, 52–3, 59, 77
Action Party 58–9
Adeboye, Enoch 132
Adichie, Chimamanda Ngozi 225
Administration of Criminal Justice 87
Administrative Division and Structure 79
African Churches 131
African Continental Free Trade Agreement 117–18
African Morning Post 60
Afro-Asiatic language family 202
Agbada 212, 249
Agbakin 73
Agbonmagbe Bank 38
Aggrey beads. *See* Akori
agriculture sector 107
Ahadith 181
Ahmadiyya 139, 182
Aina Onabolu 255–6
ajami 199
Ajayi Crowther 32, 50, 203, 206
Akinniku 73
ako. *See* effigy
Akori 244
Akwanshi stone tradition 258

Alaafin 73, 240
Aladura Church 133
Alantika Mountains 9
Alarinjo 222
Alex Ekwueme 97
Ali Jita 202
Aliko Dangote 151
al-jabr-wal muqabala 185
Alkalis 151
All Nigeria People's Party 81–2
All Progressives Congress 80, 98–9
All Progressives Grand Alliance 81
Almajiri 151
al-mantiq 185
Alpine climate 11–12
amalgamation 33, 36, 50–1
Amino Kano 52
Angas 16, 157
Aniocha war 58
Anioma 34
Ansar-ud-Deen Society 182
Anthony Enahoro 40, 52
Anwarul Islam 182
Anyim Pius Anyim 142
Apapa Port 109
Are Onakakanfo 73
Aro-Anglo war 58
art and architecture 241
Asipa 73
Aso ebi 178
Aso Oke 260
Asset Management Corporation of Nigeria 112
Atiku Abubakar 81, 91, 97–8
Atlantic Ocean 7–8, 11, 21
Atta, Sefi 226
Auchi 257

Augustine Obiora Akubeze   134
Awka   152, 253
Awolowo, Obafemi   59
Awori   206
ayats   185
Azikiwe, Nnamdi   60

Babafemi Adeyemi Osofisan   222
Babanriga   249
Babarire   218
babbaku   185
Babcock University   190
Bachama   10, 157
Bade   157
Balewa, Abubakar Tafawa   61
Bank of British West Africa   111
Banso   158
baobab   15, 292
Barewa College. *See* Katsina Teacher Training College
Basic Education Certificate Examination (BECE)   186
Batta   158
Bauchi Improvement Union   38, 51
Baya   158
Bayajidda   68, 74
Bead Art   244
Ben Enwonwu   256
Benin Artwork   245
Benin City   245
Benin Empire   62, 245
Benin expedition   58, 248
Benson Idahosa   131, 141-2
Berom   157
Bilei   158
Bini   159, 282
Birnin Kudu   255
bitumen   19, 119
Boka   198
boko   199
Boko Haram   47, 56, 93, 138
born again   132, 141
Borno Youth Movement   89
Botlere   158
Brass   157
brass   245
Brazilian Architecture   246
Bronze casting   247-8
Buduma   158
Buhari, Muhammadu   81
Bureaux de Change   114
Burutu   157

bushbabies   13
business entertainment   212
butterflies   14

cacti   14
Calabar Port   109
cash crops   15, 18, 159
Catholic Charismatic   131
the Catholic Church   134
Catholicism   134
Celestial Church of Christ   135
Central Bank of Nigeria (CBN)   39, 48, 52
chandelier trees   14
Chappal Waddi Hills   9
Cherubim and Seraphim Church   131
Chibok   56, 139, 158
Chief Whip   95
Child Rights Act   177
China   114-15
Chinine   158
Chris Anuforo   41
Chris Okotie   99, 266
Christ Apostolic Church   131, 136
Christian Association of Nigeria   141
Christianity   65, 148
Chukkol   158
Church Missionary Society   181, 331
Church of God Mission   131, 142
cire-perdue (lost wax technique)   30
Clark, John Pepper   227
Clifford Constitution   37, 51, 64, 83
cobra   13
colonial rule   37, 39
columbite   16, 105, 119
The Comet   61
Companies and Allied Matters Bill (CAMA)   104
Compulsory Free Universal Basic Education Act   122
Concurrent Legislative List   96
Conditional Cash Transfer (CCT)   123
Congress for Progressive Change   80, 82, 99
Consolidated Revenue Fund   182
Constitutional Conference   64, 83
Constitutional Development   83
Copper   247, 250
Corkscrew Eucalyptus   14
Correctional Institutions   84
corruption   85
Court Marriages   167
Court of Appeal   80, 102
The Court of Equity   32
courtesy and respect   213

Covid-19 pandemic 17, 103
crabs 21
Criminal Code 86, 168
Criminal Law 86
Criminal Procedure Act 87
Criminal Procedure Code 87
Cross River National Park 13, 308
crude oil 17, 19–20, 346
crude oil deposit 19
crude oil exports 109–10
customary (traditional) marriage 177
Cyprian Ekwensi 222, 230
Cyprian Michael Iwene 135

Daka 158
Dan Maraya Jos 202, 265
Dangote group 118
Dangote Refinery 122
Daniel Fagunwa 221
Debt Management Office 106, 125
debt portfolio 106, 125
deciduous trees 14
Demas Nwoko 254, 256
democratic rule 87, 149
Dennis Chukude Osadeba 77
desert encroachment 12
desertification 12
Dghwede 158
Diaspora Bonds 126
Diba 158
Dibia 198
Diepreye Alamieyeseigha 92
Dogo Yaro (Neem tree) 15
Domestic and International Trade 108
domestic violence 168
Donald Cameron 84
double descent 176
Dowry and Bride-Wealth 169
dry season 7, 10, 24
Dufuna canoe 30
Duguwa 154
Duro Ladipo 223, 238
dye 165, 251

Eagle Square 17, 352
Early Political Parties 88
Eastern Guardian 61
Eastern Relief Block 8–9
Ebira 157
Ebola virus 143
Ebrohimi 33
Economic and Financial Crimes Commission (EFCC) 46, 86

Economic Recovery and Growth Plan 104
Edegi. See Tsoede
edikaikon 215, 291
Edionwere 62–3
education 181–94
effigy 258
Effurun 157, 233
Efik 20, 239, 261, 270
Efuru 54, 222
Egba 276, 331
Egbe Omo Oduduwa 38, 51, 59
Egerton Shyngle 51
Egungun 73, 158, 222
egusi 287–8
Ejiba 244
Ekiti Parapo War 34
Ekombi 279
Ekpeye 20
Ekpo 152, 261
Ekumeku Movement 34
Eledumare 129
embroidery 248–9
Emir of Ilorin 35
Emmanuel Ifeajuna 41, 43
English criminal law 86
English language 200
Entertainment and Gift-Giving 214
Ephraim Akpata 91
epiphytes 24
Erediawa II 157
Ernest Shonekan 45, 55
Esan 20
Eso 73
etiquettes 209–10
Etsako 157
Eurobonds 126
European Explorers 65–6, 244
European markets 110
Evangelical Church of West Africa 130–1
evergreen forest 14
ewedu 163, 215
Eweka Dynasty 63
Exclusive Legislative List 95
executive arm of government 78–9
exports 106–7, 109–10
Eyo 145
Eyo Esua 92
Eze-Nri 30

Faith Tabernacle 137
Family Planning Clinics 170
Family Planning Law 170–1
Family Roles 171–2

farfaru 185
Fatihah 179
Fauna 13–14
Federal Capital Territory. *See* Abuja
Federal Government Bonds 125
Federal House of Assembly 79, 98
Federal Ministry of Agricultural and Rural Development (FMARD) 107
Federal Roads Maintenance Agency 25
federal system of government 79
Federal Unity Colleges 186
Fela Anikulapo Kuti 206, 268
fertility rate 22
Festival of Arts and Culture (FESTAC) 44, 85, 157, 231
Festus Okotie-Eboh 41, 78
Fiction and Nonfiction Literary Works 230–1
Financial Information Services Division (FISD) 120
financial institutions 111–12
fiqh 185
First Bank of Nigeria (FBN) 111
First Republic 39–40, 53
Flora 14–15
Flora Nkiru Nwapa 222
Flora Shaw 50
food and table manners 215–16
Foreign Direct Investment (FDI) 106, 113
foreign investment 113
foreign languages 197, 201–2
foreign remittances 114
forest elephants 13
Forex and Currency Exchange 113–14
Fourth Republic 85, 87, 89
France 121, 127
Fredrick Lugard 35
FRESH party 99
fura da nono 215, 292

Ga'anda 158
Galadima 151
Gamergu-Mulgwa 158
Gashaka Gumti National Park 308
Gaskiya Ta fi Kwabo 39, 186
gay and lesbian individuals 172–3
gazelles 14
gbegiri 215, 296
Gelede 261
Gemai 157
gender, marriage, and sexuality 165–79
gender relations 173–4

General Certificate Examination (GCE) 195
Gengle 158
geography 7–26
George Taubman Goldie 33, 50
Germany 121, 127
Gini coefficient 123
Gira 158
giraffes 14
global standing instruction (GSI) 112
Gnetum africanus 14
The Gods are not to Blame 224
gold 19, 31–2
Gombi 158
Gonia 158
Gornun 158
government and politics 79
Government Enterprise and Empowerment Programme (GEEP) 123
Greater Nigerian Peoples Party 89
greetings 210–11
gross domestic product 19, 103, 107
Gude 158
Guinea savannah 24–5
Gulf of Guinea basin 9
Gunguma 68
Gurara Falls 16
Gwa 158
Gwom 158

Hadith 181
Hafsat, Abdulwaheed Ahmed 229
Hakimi 151
harmattan 292
Hausa Constabulary 94
Hausa language 198, 200, 202
Hausa-Bokwoi 74
Hausa/Fulani 150–1
hazy dusty wind. *See* harmattan
Henry Nwosu 92
Henry Townsend 66, 319, 331
Herbert Macaulay 37, 44, 51, 79, 89
hides and skins 10, 18
Holma 158
Holy Ghost Congress 133
Home-Grown School Feeding Programme (HGSF) 123
House of Chiefs 83
House of Representative 78–9, 95
housewarming 163, 217
Hubert Ogunde 223, 231, 264
Humai bn Selemma 155
Human Development Index (HDI) 123

human rights 90–1
human trafficking 174–5
hungry rice (acha) 16

Ibadan School of Drama 223, 231
Ibeno 151
Ibibio people 151–2
Ibrahim Babangida 45, 55, 85, 324
Ichen 158
ICPC 86
Idasha 206
Idomoid 157
Ifa 232
Ife Artwork 250–1
Ife Kingdom 66
Ifewara 132
Igala Union 77
Igarra 157
Igbe 145
Igbinedion University 190
Igbirra Tribal Union 98
Igbo Artwork 250–1
Igbo Federal Union 89
Igbo language 203
Igbomina 206, 258
Igbo people 251–2
Igbo-Ukwu 27, 30, 72, 244
Igun 204, 248
Ijaw people 153
Ijaws (Ijo) 20
Ijebu 34–5, 58
Ijebu Ode 136
Ijebu war 58
Ijesha 204, 206
Ijumu 206
Ikale 260
Ikeji-Arakeji 137
Ikenga 261
Ikengaobo 262
Ikwerre people 17, 316
Ilaje 20
Ile Awon Agbe 41
Ile-Ife 66–7
Ilmul usul 185
imports 115–16
in sha Allah 130
Independent National Electoral Commission (INEC) 46, 55, 91
India 144, 201
Indian Penal Code 87
Indigenous Architecture 252

indigenous drama 231
indigenous education system 184
infant mortality 22, 345
Innoson Motors 118
Innovation Enterprise Institutions (IEIs) 192
Institute of Civil Society 97
Inter-bank Foreign Exchange Market (IFEM) 114
Intermarket Surveillance Group (ISG) 120
International Labor Organization (ILO) 107
International Monetary Fund (IMF) 191
International Trade Policy 116
The Interpreters 222
inter-religious conflicts 138
Investments and Securities Act (ISA) 120
Ipokia 206
Iroko 15, 23
iron smelting 30, 157, 165
Isaac Adaka Boro 42
Ishan 157
Ishiriniyat 185
Isie 242
Islam and trade 67
Islamic education 185
Islamic law 79, 86, 151
Islamic Movement 139
Islamiyya schools 188
Isoama-Ibo: A Primer 203
Isoko 20, 157
Itsekiri 20, 157
Iwe Iroyin 206
Iyatunde 218
Iyayi Festus 222
Iyoba 63

Jacobson Ogunbiyi 142
Jahunawa 158
Jaja of Opobo 33
Jam 'iyyar Jama 'ar Arewa. *See* Northern Nigerian Congress
Jamiat al-Islamiyyah 185
jaundice 15
Jawara 157
Jebba town 21
Jero 158
Jibu 158
Jirai 158
John Beecroft 32, 34, 50
Joint Admissions and Matriculation Board 183
Joint Universities Preliminary Examination Board 187
Jonathan, Goodluck 92

Jonjo 158
Jos Plateau 15, 257
Joseph Ayo Babalola University 137
Joseph Ayodele Babalola 137
Joseph Shanahan 135
Josiah Olufemi Akindayomi 132
Josiah Olunowo Ositelu 133
the Judiciary 80, 113
Jukun 157, 160
Junior Secondary Certificate Examination 186

Kabawa 158
Kaduna Nzeogwu 41
Kaduna refinery 122
Kafanchan 138
Kainji Lake National Park 13
Kaka 158
Kalabari 20, 239
Kambu 158
Kanakuru 158
Kanem-Bornu Empire 27, 30, 181
Kanembu 158
Kano airport 109
Kano city 18, 138
Kano People's Party 98
Kanuri people 154-5
kaolin 16
Karimjo 158
Kasarmu Ce 203
Katsina 242, 252
Katsina Teacher Training College 61
Katsina Training College 51, 185
Khaya Senegalensis 14
Kiagbodo 227
Kijipa 260
King Charles II of England 32
King Kosoko 34
Kingdom of Zaria 68-9
Kinship and in-laws 175
Kola Ogunmola 223
Kolmani River 19
Kolmani River Field 56
Koma 158
Komadugu Gana 29
Kotun Debo 222
Kugama 158
Kulliyat 185
Kunini 158
Kunshi 179
Kurunmi 224
Kutin 158

Kwanchi 158
Kyari Magumeri 52

Labour Party 89
Ladi Kwali 259
Lagos State 16
Lagos Youth Movement 38, 51
Laguna 73
Lake Chad basin 9
Lakka 158
Lama 158
Lamja 158
Land Use Decree 185
language 197
The Last Duty 222
late Precambrian 15
Lateef Jakande 40
Law Enforcement 46, 94
Legislative arm of government 78
Legislature 95-6
Lejji 253
levirate 179
LGBTQI Community 172
life expectancy 22, 345
limestone 119
lions 14
literature and drama 221
Littattafan Soyayya 229
Livelihood Improvement Family Enterprise (LIFE) 107
Local Dialects 204
local government areas (LGAs) 79-80, 188
Lokoja 8
lower class 150
lowland areas 8
Luwo Gbagida 66
Lyttleton Constitution 37, 52

M.A. Majekodunmi 53
Macaulay, Herbert 69-70
Macpherson Constitution 83, 89, 334
Madaki 151
Madonna University 190
Madrasah li ulumul Quran wa tohfiz 185
Mahmood Yakubu 91
Maitatsine 138-9
major cities 16
Majority Leader 95
malaria 15, 65, 285
Mallam. *See* Quranic teacher
Mambilla Plateau 9, 14

Mandara 8, 158
Mangawa 158
mangrove 14, 23
Manufacturers Association of Nigeria (MAN) 118
manufacturing sector 117–18
Mara Murya 203
Margi 158
Marriage Act 176–7
Marriage Certificate 180
Marriage Law 176, 180
Masaga people 244
Mass Mobilisation for Self-Reliance, Social Justice, and Economic Recovery 45
maternal mortality 22, 345
matrilineal system 176
Maurice Iwu 92
Mbari Mbayo Club 223
Mbong Ekpuk 152
Mbula 158
Mbum 158
Mercantile Bank 37
Michael Iheonukara Okpara 77
Michael Imoudu 38, 52
middle class 149–50
Midwest Democratic Front 77
Military Rule 78, 96
Mining Cadastre system 119
mining sector 118–19
minority ethnic groups 156–7
Minority Leader 95
Minority Whip 95
MKO Abiola 45, 141
Mmanwu 153
Mobber 158
modern slavery 177
Modular Trade Certificate 187
Mohammed Bah Abba 259
Mohammed Marwa 138
Movement for the Survival of the Ogoni People (MOSOP) 235
Muchaila 158
Muhammed Murtala airport 109
Mumuye 158
Munga 158
Murtala Ramat Mohammed 42–3
Muslims 138–9

Namenj 202
Namidi Sambo 47
naming ceremonies 215, 218
Nana Olomu of Itsekiri 33
narrow loom 165

National Africa Company. *See* Royal Niger Company
National Agency for Prohibition of Trafficking in Persons and other Related Matters 178
National Assembly 40, 79–81
National Association of Medical Doctors 128
National Board of Arabic and Islamic Studies (NBAIS) 182
National Bureau of Statistics 277
National Business and Technical Examinations Board (NAPTEB) 187
National Business Certificate 187
National Commission for Colleges of Education 193
National Commission for Nomadic Education 183, 188
National Common Entrance Examination 186–7
National Council of Nigeria and the Cameroons 186
National Economic Empowerment and Development Strategy 46
National Entrance Examinations 186–7
National Examinations Council (NECO) 183
National Health Promotion Policy 171
National Innovative Diploma (NID) 193
National Insurance Commission (NAICOM) 111
National Orientation Agency 205
National Party of Nigeria 88
National Population Policy for Development 170
National Technical Certificate 187
National Universities Commission 183
National Vocational Certificate (NVC) 193
Native Authority system 64
Native Court Ordinance 86
natural gas 110, 346
natural resources 18, 346
Ndoki 20
Ndoro 158
net domestic credit 105
Netherlands 110
Niger Coast Constabulary 94
Niger Coast Protectorate 33, 50, 94
Niger Delta 19, 50, 56, 121
Niger Delta Development Commission 46
Niger Delta Militants 56
Niger Delta Volunteer Force 42
The Niger Expedition 49
Niger-Benue basin 9
Niger-Congo family 197
Niger-Congo language family 152, 157, 203
Nigeria Certificate in Education (NCE) 189
Nigeria Civil Service Union (NCSU) 50, 128

INDEX 377

Nigeria Deposit Insurance Corporation (NDIC)   111
Nigeria Family Planning Blueprint   170
Nigeria Incentive-Based Risk Sharing in Agricultural Lending (NIRSAL)   108
Nigeria Labour Congress   99
Nigeria Native Staff Union (NNSU)   128
Nigeria Police Force   94
Nigeria's Contraceptive Prevalent Rate (CPR)   171
Nigerian Civil War   70
Nigerian constitution   95, 97, 101
Nigerian Daily News   70
Nigerian Investment Promotion Commission   112, 116
Nigerian Labour Act   128
Nigerian Law Association   88
Nigerian Mechanics Union   128
Nigerian Minerals and Mining Act   119
Nigerian Naira   54
Nigerian National Democratic Party   37, 58, 70, 89
Nigerian National Petroleum Corporation   82
Nigerian Office for Trade Negotiations (NOTN)   116
Nigerian People's Party   61
Nigerian Pound   113
Nigerian Stock Exchange   120
Nigerian Treasury Bills   125
Nigerian Union of Railwaymen   128
Nigerian Union of Teachers   128
Nigerian Youth Movement   38
nipa palms   14
Njideka Akunyili Crosby   256
Nok art   250, 257
Nok civilization   16, 19, 26, 257
Nomadic Schools   188
Non-Academic Staff Union of Universities   188
non-performing loans (NPL)   112
Northeast Trade Winds   11
Northern Elements Progressive Association   38
Northern Elements Progressive Union, See Northern Elements Progressive Association
Northern Nigeria Police   94
Northern People's Congress   332
Northern Relief Block   8
Nri Civilization   72
Nupe people   157
Nupoid   157
Nursing and Midwifery Council of Nigeria (NMCN)   193
Nyam   158
Nyandang   106

O'kun Yoruba   210
Oba Esigie   31, 63
Oba Koso   223
Oba Ovonramwen   35
obeche   15
Obi, Peter   91
Oboh   262
Obon society   152
Obong Ikpaisong   152
Obudu Cattle Ranch   9, 309
Odionwere   62
Ogboni   131
Ogbonism   142
ogbono   215
Oghene   129
Ogidi   224
ogogoro   287, 290
Ogoja   99
Ogoni   235
Ogoni nine   235
Ogun State University   191
Ogunde, Hubert   232
oguro. See Palm-Wine Drinkard
Ohanaeze Ndigbo   198
oil and gas sector   121
Oil Rivers Protectorate   33
Okega   262
Okpara   53
Okpe   157
Okpewho Isidore   222
Okri, Ben   233
Okrika   17
Ola Rotimi   223
Oladipo Diya   46, 55
Olaiya House   247
Oliver Lyttleton   83
Oloibiri   121
Olokun   131
Olugbobiri   261
Olukayode Ariwoola   102
Olumba Olumba   131
Olumo Rock   9, 308
Olusegun Obasanjo   44, 46, 54–5
Onobrakpeya, Bruce   254
Ooni   66
Oranmiyan   73
Ordovician periods   15
Organization of Islamic Conference   144
Organization of Petroleum Exporting Countries   43
Ori Olokun Theatre Company   223

Orlu 204
Oron 151
Oru 153
Osanobua 129
Oserakeme 218
osu 242
Ota region 14
Oyedepo, David 140
Oyo 206
Oyo Empire 73
Oyomesi 73

painting 255
Palace Decoration 256
Palli 158
Palm-Wine Drinkard 222
Panyam 158
Paris Club 46
Patrick Chukwuma Nzeogwu 96
paw-paw tree 15
Peju Layiwola 243
Pentecostal Fellowship of Nigeria (PFN) 141
Pentecostalism 141
People of the City 222
People's Democratic Party 97
Peter Obi 91
Petroleum Act 122
Petroleum Industry Bill (PIB) 122
Pidgin English 205
Pkanzom 158
Plateau State 15, 100
political parties and their formations 98
poll 39, 47
Popo Aguda 246
population 345
porcupines 14
Port Harcourt 17
Port Harcourt airport 76
Port Harcourt refinery 122
portfolio investments 113
poverty 122
Presbyterian Mission 230
Presidential Artisanal Gold Mining Development Initiative (PAGMI) 105
presidential system 55
pre-tertiary education 189
private sector 124
private universities 190
Privy Council 102
Promissory Notes 125

Proprietary Patent Medicine Vendors (PPMVs) 171
Protectorate of Northern Nigeria 36
Protectorate of Southern Nigeria 36
Public Universities 190
Python 251

Qadiriyyah 139
Quranic schools 181
Quranic teacher 184

raffia palms 14
rainforest 23
rainy season 8, 11
Redeemed Christian Church of God 132
Reformed Ogboni Fraternity 142
Reinhard Bonnke 138
relief regions 8
religion and thought 129
reproductive population 22
Reserves and Foreign Debt 125
Richards Constitution 37, 52
River Benue 8
River Niger 8
Royal Niger Company 34
Royal Niger Company Constabulary 94
rural population 159
Ruwan Bagaja 202
Ruy de Sequeira 31

Sa'adu Zungur 38
Sabon Gari 138
Sahel climate 11
Sakbe 158
saltwater swamp 14
Same Sex Marriage Prohibition Act 172, 173
Samuel Ademulegun 41
Samuel Ajayi Crowther 69
Samuel Akintola 41, 78
Samuel Bilewa Joseph Oshoffa. Oshoffa 135
Sango 159
Sani Abacha 45–6, 55
Sapele 157
saprophytes 24
Sardauna of Sokoto 53
Sarkin Fada 151
Sarkin Pawa 151
Sarkin Ruwa 151
Saro-Wiwa, Ken 234
Sate 158
savannah 24

Sayf bin Yazan 154
sculpture 257
seafood 21
Second Republic 45, 55
Second World War 202, 230
Second-tier Foreign Exchange Market (SFEM) 114
Securities and Exchange Commission (SEC) 120
Sefawa Dynasty 154
Segida 244
Selborne Committee 36
semi-temperate climate 15
the Senate 78–9
Senegal Gum Acacia 14
Senior Secondary School Certificate 183
Sergeant-at-Arms 95
sex trade 118
Shafi Madhhab 139
Sharada 18
shari'a. *See* Islamic law
Sharia law 46
Shau Shau iron smelting 254
Shebshi Mountains 9
Shehu Musa Yar'Adua 46, 55
Shehu Shagari 55
Shendam 157
Sheu 155
Shia 139
Shiroro Hills 15
Shomo 158
shrimps 159
Shuwa 188
The 6–3–3–4 system of education 183
soapstone figures 158
social classes and ethnicity 147
soil types 9, 14
Sokoto Caliphate 35, 49
Sonkwalla hills 160
South Africa 269
South Korea 127
Southern Nigeria Civil Service Union 50
Southern Nigeria Police 94
Southern Nigerian Defender 61
Southwest Trade Winds 11
Soyinka, Wole 236
Spain 302
squirrels 14
state and local governments 99
State creation 99
State House of Assembly 101
Statutory Marriage 176
Structural Adjustment Programme 191

Sudan savannah 24
Sultan of Sokoto 35
Supreme Court 101
Supreme Military Council 44
surahs 185
Sustainable Stock Exchanges (SSE) 120
Synagogue Church of All Nations 143

Tabieorar. *See* Taborar
Taborar 134
Taiwan of Nigeria. *See* Aba
Talakawa 38
tales by moonlight 237
Talimul Islam Ahmadiyya Primary School 182
tantalite 16
Tarak 157
Technical and Vocational Education and Training 187
Teme 158
Temitope Balogun Joshua 143
terracotta 245
tertiary education 189
textiles 260
Things Fall Apart 203
Thurstan Shaw 29
Tigon 158
Tijaniyyah 139
Tikar 158
Timothy Onwuatuewgu 41
Tin Can Island 109
Tiv people 160
Torbiyyah 185
trade partners 126
Trade Union Congress (TUC) 127
Trade unionism 127
Trade Unions and the Labor Movement 127
traditional performances 222
traditional religions 144
traditional weddings 178
Trafficking in Persons (Prohibition) Law Enforcement and Administration Act 175
Trans-Atlantic Slave Trade 31, 49
transformation agenda 93
Translation Bureau of Northern Nigeria 202
transportation 348
Trans-Saharan Trade 49, 68, 155
tropical monsoon climate 11
tropical savannah climate 11
The Truth 139
Tsoede 159

Tutuola, Amos 238
Tuwo 291

Ubbo 158
Uche Okeke 254
Ugep 20
Ughelli 157
Ugwhevwien 157
Ulli Beier 223
Ulli symbols 251
Ullism 251
Umbrella Acacia 14
Umme Jilm. *See* Humai bn Selemma
Umuahia 204
umunna 153
Umunnakwe Aguiyi Ironsi 42
Unified Tertiary Matriculation Examination 183
United Africa Company 33
United Arab Emirates 127
United Kingdom 127
United Middle Belt Congress 40
United States 44
Unity Party of Nigeria 60, 88
Universal Basic Education Commission 183
Universal Primary Education (UPE) 189
University College Ibadan 191, 223, 236
University of Ibadan 236
University of Ife (Obafemi Awolowo University) 236
University of Lagos 243
upland areas 8
upper class 149
uranium 16
urban poor 161
urbanization 26
Urhobo 14
Urhobo College 233
Usman Danfodio 67
Uvwie 157
Uzama n'Ihinron 63

vegetation types 8, 23, 24
Verre 158
Victor Ovie Whiskey 92
Vocational Enterprise Institutes (VEIs) 193
volcanic cones 15
Vommi 158

Waja 158
Wale Ogunyemi 224
Walimah 179
War Against Indiscipline 45, 55
warra 215
Warri Port 109
Warri refinery 122
wasulla 185
waterways 25
Waziri 151
West African Examination Council (WAEC) 183, 194
West African Pilot 61, 298, 331
West African Senior School Certificate Examination (WASSCE) 194
West African Students Union 51
Western Relief Block 8
Western Weddings 179
Westminster system 77
wildebeest 14
Winifred Tete-Ansah 37
The Winners Church 140
woli 136
wood carving 261
World Bank Group 125

X-academy 120
X-Gen 120

Yaba Higher College 182
Yagba 206
Yahaya Gusau 52
Yakubu Gowon 54
Yankari National Park 13
Yar Nono 203
yellow fever 15
Yola 27, 35
Yoruba 162
Yoruba language 206
Yoruba Operatic Theatre 131
Yoruba Travelling Theatre 231
Yott 158

Zakariya Maimalari 41
Zamfara Commoners Party 78
Zaria Art Society 254
Zaure 252
Zulu Sofola 224

www.ingramcontent.com/pod-product-compliance
Lightning Source LLC
Chambersburg PA
CBHW082025300426
44117CB00015B/2358